Darwin's Clever Neighbour

Charles Darwin to his friend J.D. Hooker, 18 April 1860, about a review by Richard Owen of Darwin's *Origin of Species*, of a book by Hooker himself, and of three of Owen's *own* books, in the *Edinburgh Review*:

*My dear Hooker*

*I return Owen's letter: what a base dog he is. Some of my relations say it cannot possibly be Owen's article, because the Reviewer speaks so very highly of Prof. Owen. Poor dear simple folk! My clever neighbour Mr Norman, says the article is so badly written with no definite object that no one will read it.*

– *The Correspondence of Charles Darwin*, ed. by F. Burkhardt, D. Porto, J. Browne, and M. Richmond, Vol. 8, 1860, Cambridge, Cambridge University Press, 1993, p. 162.

# Darwin's Clever Neighbour

## George Warde Norman and his Circle

**D.P. O'Brien**

Emeritus Professor of Economics, University of Durham, UK

**John Creedy**

The Truby Williams Professor of Economics, University of Melbourne, Australia

**Edward Elgar Publishing**
Cheltenham, UK • Northampton, MA, USA

Published by
Edward Elgar Publishing Limited
The Lypiatts
15 Lansdown Road
Cheltenham
Glos GL50 2JA
UK

Edward Elgar Publishing, Inc.
William Pratt House
9 Dewey Court
Northampton
Massachusetts 01060
USA

A catalogue record for this book
is available from the British Library

Library of Congress Control Number: 2009940741

ISBN 978 1 84844 557 4

Printed and bound by MPG Books Group, UK

# Contents



## Norman's Autobiography

# Preface

Norman's Autobiography has literally survived fire and flood. It was lodged in the library of the Norman family home at Bromley Common, the Rookery, the house where Norman was born in 1793, where he lived, and where he died in 1882. About sixty years later the house was requisitioned by the government, and taken over by the Royal Air Force for use as a fighter control centre. Enormous damage was done to the house, in order to create a vast operations room, damage which may well have made the house more vulnerable to fire. The RAF was still in possession of the house when it caught fire, and was burned down. The fire brigade, attempting to control the blaze, and aware that books can go on smouldering for weeks, raked the contents of the library out on to the lawn. When the Rookery was abandoned, and the Norman family moved to East Farleigh, the Autobiography was simply gathered up with other books and moved to the new home. There it remained, apparently unrecognised, until the 1960s.

In the 1960s I was editing the Correspondence of Lord Overstone, the papers of Norman's close friend and counsellor, Samuel Jones Loyd, which I had discovered at Lockinge in Berkshire while working on the Scottish economist J.R. McCulloch. A central thread in the Overstone Correspondence was the exchange of letters with George Warde Norman. I approached General Charles Wake Norman, at that time the head of the family, to enquire about the Norman papers, since these were clearly of considerable relevance to my work on Overstone. He kindly invited me to West Farleigh, and arranged to take me to Maidstone and introduce me to Dr Felix Hull, then the Kent County Archivist. However, before we left West Farleigh for Maidstone, I was shown the library there, and I immediately spotted a book which was not a normal book. I had come across such volumes in the library at Lockinge, though I was certainly not conscious of looking for anything similar at West Farleigh. On examination the 'book' turned out to be the manuscript Autobiography of George Warde Norman.

General Norman very kindly allowed me to take the volume back to Queen's University, Belfast, where I was then working, to use in editing the Overstone Correspondence, for which indeed I found it most helpful. It was, after the fire and the fire brigade, clearly far too fragile to photocopy, and Queen's University generously provided funds to enable a typewritten copy to be made instead. But it would have been quite unreasonable to expect any secretary to cope with Norman's handwriting, deciphering of which required in any case some specialist knowledge. So I settled down with a Dictaphone, put the whole Autobiography on to tape, and a typist then produced a complete transcript of the work.

The transcript was necessarily imperfect, though this did not matter much to me, as I had managed to read all the bits that related to editorial work on Overstone's Correspondence, aided by the inside knowledge provided by the Correspondence itself. However Bromley Public Library subsequently asked for a copy, and in this imperfect form the Autobiography has become a source drawn upon by scholars in more than four decades. It was this typescript which provided our starting point in the preparation of the present edition.

But this was only the starting point. It was clearly not desirable that such an imperfect reproduction of Norman's words should be the last word. The present edition, though it may well still contain inaccuracies, and still contains a few words about which we are uncertain, is certainly vastly different. It is probably as accurate as it is humanly possible to make it, and we have provided it with detailed editorial information, in order to bring Norman's world to life.

To provide the editorial material for Norman's Autobiography has been a very demanding undertaking. We have of course drawn on a huge range of published sources, both printed and electronic, although we have found that such sources need to be used with considerable care. Even the august *Dictionary of National Biography* is not completely reliable, and one example of this is indicated in the notes. In addition, dates of birth and death tend not to be completely consistent between different genealogical sources, and on one occasion a family which appeared to have died out according to one source was found, in another, to be flourishing.

The difficulties in editing a nineteenth century autobiography are extreme, even when compared with editing nineteenth century correspondence, of which one of us has first hand experience. The multiplication of names and places, the extraordinary range of references, the inevitability of elements of faulty recall, and the vagueness of some allusions, all combine to make work on almost every page extremely challenging. Indeed it is noteworthy that the majestic Toronto edition of the works and correspondence of John Stuart Mill began with a version of Mill's famous Autobiography which lacks even the briefest biographical footnotes explaining the allusions and references in the text.[1] Given that Norman's circle of acquaintances, and the spheres in which he moved, were both arguably much wider than those of Mill, and much less accessibly documented, this gives some indication of the magnitude of the task which we faced in editing Norman's Autobiography.

We have however been enormously helped by many individuals, especially perhaps some at local level, who have not only provided reliable information, often from parish records and church memorials, but who have managed to solve what were for us very difficult problems of identification. For Norman's text is littered with references to individuals who do not appear in works of reference, and who can only be identified by those with very specialist, and often highly localised, knowledge. In addition, given both Norman's handwriting and the vicissitudes of the manuscript since he wrote the Autobiography, it has often only been the result of painstaking research that has enabled us to identify a name at all.

Without the help of many individuals, such an enterprise could never have been brought to fruition. First and foremost we must thank Canon W.B. Norman for his help and encouragement at every stage. In particular

[1] The references are confined to identifying literary allusions by Mill, and textual variants, with occasional names supplied for those to whom Mill alludes by description, notably his wife.

Record Office.

The portrait of George Warde Norman is reproduced on the front cover by kind permission of the Bank of England.

Finally, I have to offer heart-felt thanks to my wife Julia and my daughter Juliet, who have put up with an extraordinary degree of domestic disruption during what turned out to be a huge job, one far beyond what even the wildest imaginings could have foreseen, and some hint of which is given by the list of people whose help we have sought in completing the work. I promise never to do it again.

D.P. O'Brien

# Editorial Practice

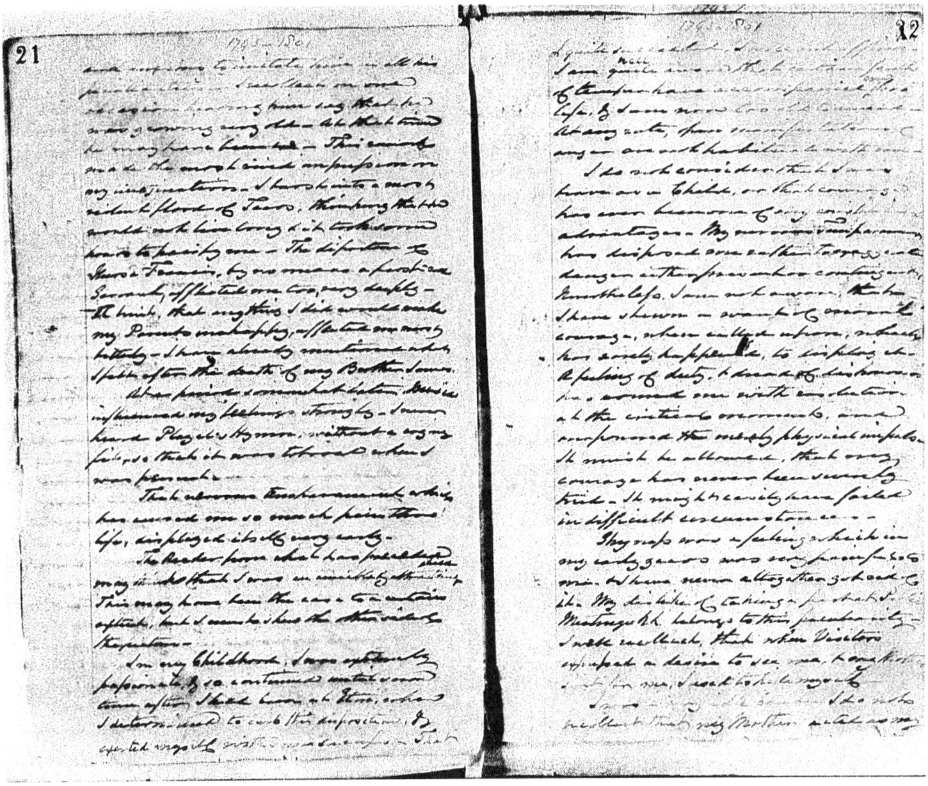

Figure 1: Pages 21 and 22 of the Manuscript

This note describes the process and editorial decisions involved in producing the Camera Ready Copy for the present book. The production of a foolscap typescript of Norman's manuscript has been described in the preface above, and the ageing carbon copy was used as the starting point (the top copy having been given to General C.W. Norman). The carbon, being too frail to be placed in a sheet feeder, was photocopied and this copy was digitally scanned for word processing. Not surprisingly, this initial scan produced a very imperfect document, with missing segments and strange symbols replacing the text in many places. The next step was to go through this word by word to try to produce a reasonably 'clean' version.

Norman's original manuscript contained a number of features necessitating editorial decisions, with a view to making it more readable for modern users. First, it consisted of continuous text without any headings. The division into separate chapters, and the choice of titles, was made by the editors. Second, Norman capitalised initial letters of virtually all nouns, and it was decided to convert these to lower case. Third, virtually the only form of punctuation used was a dash, a not uncommon feature at the time when using a steel nib. As it was often not clear, without repeated reading, to determine the sentence breaks, it was decided to introduce modern punctuation, and this could only be done 'silently'. Fourth, paragraph breaks were not always clear, though often these appeared to consist of single sentences. Thus, not only the structure of sentences but that of paragraphs required many difficult editorial decisions. Fifth, Norman returned to the manscript at various times and added marginal notes, sometimes attaching dates. Most of these notes have simply been incorporated into the text with, where available, an indication of the date. In order to distinguish Norman's notes from our editorial notes, the latter are placed within square brackets.

The sixth and most profound difficulty was raised by the truly dreadful nature of Norman's handwriting, something he himself acknowledged, combined with the state of the manuscript after surviving its exposure to fire and water. Examples are given of a small selection of pages, taken at random, reproduced here (Norman wrote on foolscap paper). This difficulty becomes particularly acute when mention is made of people and place-names, many of which are not English. Norman's autobiography is indeed replete with such names. They resisted attempts both with a magnifying glass applied to the original manuscript and the use of the 'zoom' facility when viewing the

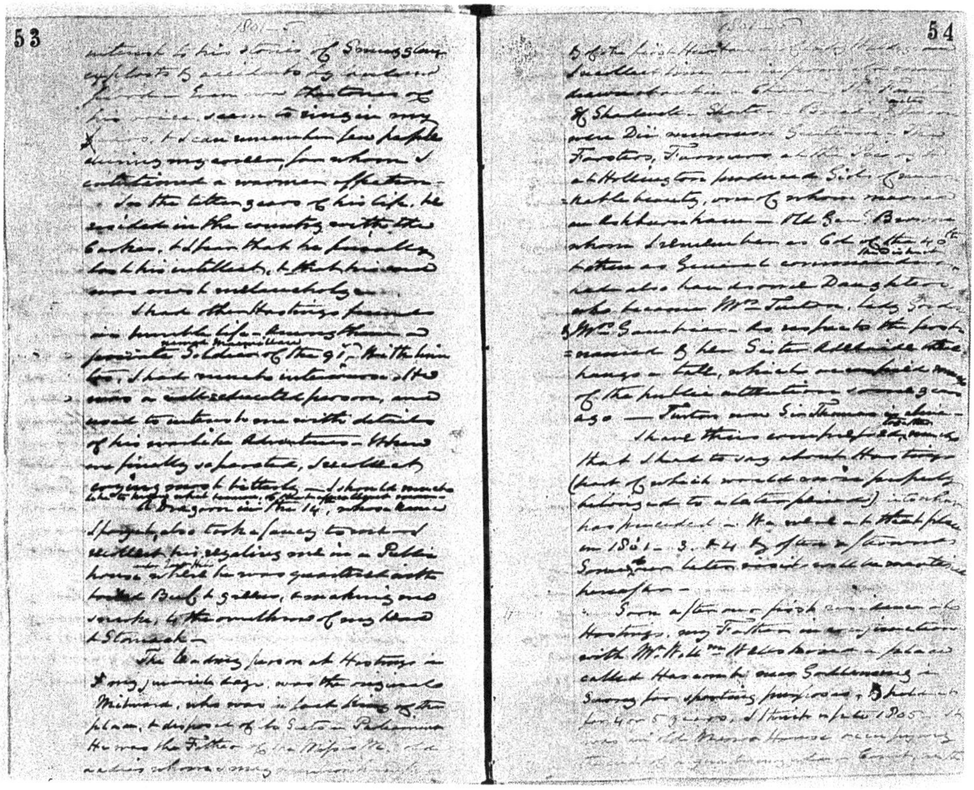

Figure 2: Pages 53 and 54 of the Manuscript

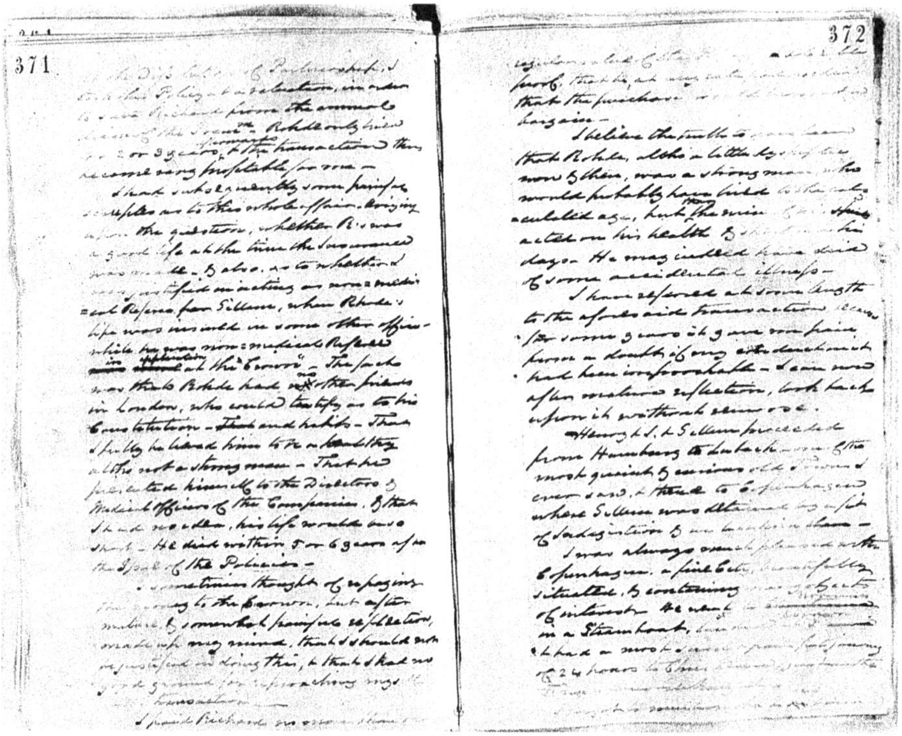

Figure 3: Pages 371 and 372 of the Manuscript

digital copies. It soon became clear that it would be impossible to decipher many of these words without carrying out extensive research based on alternative readings. This process often led us down false paths before a positive identification was found. The idea of first producing an accurate text which could then provide a starting point for further investigations was simply an illusion. As mentioned above, we cannot guarantee that all the readings given are correct, and in some cases mention is made of missing words because of the damaged nature of the manuscript. However, the modern reader should now find that Norman's Autobiography reads fluently and conveys the full range of his interests and the problems he faced.

# Introduction

## D.P. O'Brien

George Warde Norman, 1793-1882, was a central figure in debates concerning the theory of monetary control from the 1820s to the 1860s, and was directly involved in the implementation of measures to place such control on a rigorously argued basis. He was a long-standing Director of the Bank of England and the grandfather of Montagu Collet Norman, perhaps its most famous Governor. It is possible to form some picture of this remarkable individual from his Correspondence with Samuel Jones Loyd, Lord Overstone, who was a constant friend from the time of his introduction to Norman by John Welsford Cowell, about whom Norman has much to say in his Autobiography. The picture of Norman that emerges from the Overstone Correspondence is of a kindly, very honest, intensely neurotic, individual, one who was frequently unhappy and unwell. But now, with the Autobiography, a much fuller picture emerges.

The unhappiness was well known to his friends. There is a moving letter of December 1865 from Overstone to Norman in which the former counsels him to count his blessings and pays a wonderful tribute to Norman's wife Sibella (née Stone)[2] whose name naturally occurs frequently in Norman's account of his life. But on his depression, Norman is for the most part disinclined to spell out the problems in his Autobiography. It is different with the health problems.

Norman clearly suffered from recurrent bouts of poor health and these were sufficiently serious as to threaten his mental stability. Yet there are

[2]Overstone to Norman, 22 December 1865, in O'Brien (1971, vol. III, pp. 1100-1).

strange contrasts. Not only did he become immensely fit at a gymnasium, as he tells us, but he undertook feats of walking, including the length of Wales from south to north, and enormously taxing walks in Switzerland, which are breathtaking.[3] There is no doubt that he sought refuge from his depressions in travel; but once on the road his health often returned, though there is an alarming account of a nervous breakdown which he suffered in Paris.

While there is no doubt that Norman did suffer one major infection, which was probably bacterial in origin, and looks as if it was brucellosis, a complaint which necessarily, in the 19th century without antibiotics, remained in the system and produced recurrent symptoms, it is difficult to escape the suspicion that at least some of Norman's ill health was due to the attentions of the medical profession. As pointed out in the accompanying notes to the Autobiography, the medical stand bys of the 19th century included a remarkable range of dubious products (in an age in which doctors usually charged not for advice but for medicines and other forms of treatment), notably purgatives and even opium. Norman indeed recalls being supplied with the latter, which was, in any case, available over the counter.

As a child, Norman seems to have been, for the most part, healthy. We see Norman attending school, first in Eltham at a school conducted by the local curate, the Reverend John Smith, and then at Eton. To Eton he devotes much space, writing frankly about the inadequacies of its teaching and the incompetence of its medical staff. Most of the account however is devoted to extra curricular activities, especially fighting.

In 1810 Norman joined his father's timber business, in which he was to play an increasing role over the next two decades. It has to be said that, though Norman loved his father deeply, his opinion of his father's business ability does not seem to have been high, and he was concerned to try to collect at least some of his father's Norwegian debts. It was in this role,

[3]As is clear from the accounts of journeys in the Autobiography, Norman travelled extremely fast for the age of horse drawn transport. In September 1860, when Norman had, yet again, become unwell, Overstone wrote to him: 'Have you not been travelling *too fast* and thus knocked yourself up – I fear that you are not discreet on that point.' Overstone to Norman, 26 September 1860, in O'Brien (1971, vol. II, pp. 923-4).

and in particular in trying to regularise the business after the end of the Napoleonic wars, that Norman first developed his taste for travel, in visiting Norway. Norway proved to be a country in which he thrived and in which, as he recounts, he fell deeply in love.

This last is not surprising. Norman was deeply susceptible to female charms, a matter about which he is surprisingly frank in the Autobiography. While there is no suggestion of impropriety, there is no doubt that Norman found a number of women deeply attractive, and the reverse may very well have been the case.

Nonetheless, concerned about the state of his father's finances – and at one stage, it is true, it proved necessary, as Norman relates, to let the Bromley house and move to more modest accommodation – Norman seems to have felt, until his father's death and the discovery that he had been made an eldest son, that marriage would have been financially imprudent. Indeed he seems rather to have resented the speed at which his siblings then also found marital partners.

In the 1820s Norman came under the influence of the Utilitarians, especially the younger ones. He became, with one important exception, a thorough going Utilitarian, as the Autobiography makes clear, and is evident from his *Essay on Taxation* which has now been published. This Utilitarian 'conversion' (it hardly seems too strong a word) was no doubt as a result of his friendship with George Grote, who fell so much under the influence of Jeremy Bentham that he moved from a position of rather public religious belief, of which Norman gives one example, to one of violent opposition to religion, manifesting an aggressive atheism.

But Norman was somehow or other excluded from the inner circle of the young Utilitarians. Although he was a founder member of the Political Economy Club, he was not, it would seem, invited to become a member of J.S. Mill's Utilitarian Society, even though meetings were held in Grote's house.[4] He was, politically at least, as far to the left as the members of that society, if not further, and for long was unthinkingly in favour of revolutions; he recounts in the Autobiography how he wrote a letter to Mrs Grote celebrating

[4]Mill (1886, pp. 81, 119-20).

news of the 1830 revolution in France, even though he knew little about it.

Norman had been a close friend of Mrs Grote, though he denies, perhaps not entirely convincingly, that there was any more to it than that. He was also a close friend of George Grote, of whose intellectual abilities he had such a high opinion, as he recounts, that the modern reader may feel that it parted company with reality. He seems indeed to have accepted Grote's own opinion of his intellectual abilities. Yet when they met on common ground, in the matter of economics, it is quite clear who was the cleverer. As noted in the introduction to Norman's *Essay on Taxation*, Grote's understanding of relative prices was, at best, very primitive, though this did not in any way hinder him in lecturing Norman.[5] It can hardly have been Grote's *History of Greece* which bowled Norman over, since his infatuation with Grote's intellectual powers long predated the appearance of the first volumes of that,[6] even though the aim of that work – to hold up ancient Greece as the archetype of the democratic society, to which Grote, as the leader of the radicals in the House of Commons in the 1830s, aspired – would itself have appealed to Norman.

At the beginning of the 1830s, however, a rupture between Norman and Grote occurred. The occasion for this seems to have been the retailing by Norman's close friend John Welsford Cowell of a conversation between Cowell and Mrs Grote which, as described in the Autobiography, does not require much effort on the part of the modern reader to reconstruct. (There may well have been aspects of Cowell's life of which Norman was unaware; it is known from insurance records that Cowell shared a house with Norman's friend Charles Hay Cameron, and Norman does seem to have been ignorant of the fact that Cameron had fathered two illegitimate children by a German woman who was then sent back to Germany.) Cowell then gossiped about the conversation with Mrs Grote and, when Grote learned of this, he attacked Norman for failing to bring the matter to his attention. Both Grote's

[5] Grote to Norman, 1822, in O'Brien (1971, vol. I, pp. 190-5). See also O'Brien (2009, p. xxii).

[6] Though Grote apparently began work on his *History of Greece* in 1823, the first two volumes did not appear until 1846.

grounds for attacking Norman, and his subsequent refusal to be mollified in any way by Norman's desperate attempts to explain himself, seem so inadequate that one is forced to conclude that Grote seized upon these events as an opportunity to cut Norman, already excluded from the inner circle of the Utilitarians, adrift. Given Norman's exaggerated reverence for Grote, his long friendship with Grote to which he refers in the Autobiography, and his morbid sensitivity, it is not difficult to imagine the extreme distress which he suffered as a result of this episode.

Ultimately there was a limited reconciliation with Mrs Grote, after George Grote's death, but there never seems to have been any reconciliation with George Grote himself. On the matter of the quarrel itself, the Lewin family also seem to have preferred discretion; there is no reference to it in the two large volumes of *Lewin Letters*, published in 1909.

The dealings with George Grote, and possibly other Utilitarians, were also a source of mental turmoil for Norman because, unlike them, he did not become an atheist and an opponent of religious belief. He recounts in the Autobiography his distress at being induced to read the works of Comte and Voltaire, then regarded by opponents of religion as providing a definitive critique of religious belief. For Norman had been brought up as a Unitarian, and he retained religious faith throughout his life, though greatly distressed by positivist scepticism. Overstone, who was not impressed by scepticism, provided some comfort during at least one such episode.[7] It seems likely that, like many Unitarians, Norman drifted into the embrace of the Church of England; he was the key figure responsible for the building of a church on Bromley Common, near to the Norman family home, in his forties, and that church was called Holy Trinity Church.[8] Moreover, Norman became a church warden. He was buried in the grounds of the church in 1882, as was Sibella, his wife, in 1887.

Norman, as already noted, seems to have been excluded from the inner circle of the Utilitarians in the decade before the quarrel. The source of this

[7]Overstone to Norman, 1 January 1866, in O'Brien (1971, vol. III, pp. 1101-3).

[8]Richards and Packe, *The Story of Holy Trinity Church, Bromley Common* (no date).

is not clear. Certainly J.S. Mill, not lacking in confidence, despite a lack of specialist knowledge, trenchantly attacked Norman on matters of monetary theory. But this was later.[9] It seems clear that Norman, in some way, did not fit the social and intellectual requirements of the group, and when, years later, Norman attempted to invite J.S. Mill and Mrs Taylor to Bromley, the reply which he received was a snub.[10]

Yet on policy matters Norman was, and remained, a convinced Utilitarian, with characteristic left-liberal contempt for popular opinion. He was thus a keen supporter of the 1834 Poor Law, based upon the workhouse, and participated enthusiastically in the implementation of the new law in Bromley. He was scornful, as the Autobiography shows, of all opposition to this grand Utilitarian project. Similarly, as he recounts in the Autobiography, the *Essay on Taxation* was 'redolent of Bentham and Mill'. In the *Essay on Taxation*, as in the matter of Poor Law reform, Norman retained his contempt for popular opinion while supporting Parliamentary reform. In writings intended for publication he expressed himself reasonably discreetly; but in a letter to Charles Wood, then Chancellor of the Exchequer, he wrote with a frankness which takes the breath away: 'The public at large is so ignorant and – portions of it so thoroughly selfish that the able and honest financier is met by almost invincible obstacles'.[11]

Despite his radicalism, and his strong political views, Norman never sought to become an MP. Though, as he recorded, he was pressed in 1835 to stand for the City of London, also represented in the House of Commons by George Grote, he knew well that his nervous temperament was not suited to the stress of political life. But his low opinion of popular views, which it would have been necessary for him to conceal, thus occasioning further stress, may also have been a factor. It was not that he lacked the capacity

[9]Mill 1844a, 1844b. Mill also attacked Norman, Overstone and Torrens in his *Principles* – see Mill 1848 Book III, chapter 24. Mill clung to the Ricardian idea, amply disproved in the 1830s, that convertibility was its own safeguard. He also objected strongly to Norman's plan for requiring country banks to give security for their issues, implying that Norman did not understand banking.

[10]J.S. Mill to Norman, 19 August 1852, Norman papers U310 C128/7.

[11]Norman to Charles Wood, 11 March 1851, O'Brien (1971, vol. II, pp. 507-9).

to display great moral courage; it is clear that he displayed this in the Bank, leading on one occasion to a real row with James Pattison – ironically the man whom Norman had suggested to those seeking his own agreement to stand for the City. But he was plagued by insomnia, and writes that he was sometimes unable to sleep at all at times of stress. Though he took enthusiastic, and very strongly partisan, interest in elections in Kent (mainly, after the Reform Bill of 1832, West Kent), that was clearly quite as much as he could cope with in terms of public political activity.

None the less, he remained concerned with public policy, and with a wide range of issues, as his *Papers on Various Subjects* published in 1869 makes very clear.[12] Indeed the range of his interests was wider even than the *Papers* which, in forty five essays, ranged over topics extending from the law of partnership to the doctrine of nationalities. For his interests extended to archaeology, and in old age he published an article on the Saxon invasion.[13] It is thus rather odd to find Norman being referred to in some sources as the local squire. Norman was an intellectual and a businessman. Apart from shooting, then regarded generally as the proper manly outdoor pursuit, anything less like the archetypical English country squire than the hypersensitive, bookish Norman it would be hard to imagine. Though he retired from the timber business in 1830, choosing his time carefully, as he recounts, to sell it to the rival firm of Benjamin Sewell, in the hope of building a career for his brother Richard, business remained Norman's focus. It was business which, as already noted, began Norman's love for travel, with the journeys to Norway.

As a businessman, Norman himself was sharp, as the Donner episode, described in the Autobiography, and others to which he alludes, make clear. Through the man who was to be the father of Cardinal Manning (an irony given that, apart from his support on Utilitarian radical grounds for Catholic Emancipation, Norman considered Catholics as close to heathens), Norman became a Director of the Bank of England in 1821, at the very early age of twenty seven. He managed to occupy that position, with much distinction,

[12] Norman (1869).
[13] Norman (1880).

though 'passing the Chair' (not becoming Governor or Deputy Governor) until 1872. He became not only one of the public faces of the Bank, in appearances before Select Committees of Parliament, but an intellectual driving force in the reform of the monetary system, and the replacement of discretion with rules, culminating in the 1844 Bank Charter Act. He was also, it is clear, a highly effective director of the Sun Fire Office, a position which he occupied from 1830 to 1864. He was also an Exchequer Bill Commissioner 1831-42, and a Public Works Loan Commissioner 1842-75, a position in which he joined his friend Overstone, who was a Public Works Loan Commissioner 1831-75.[14]

Norman's investment in the Sun Fire Office was, as he recounts, a very successful one from a financial point of view. But he was no absentee. As is clear from the Autobiography, he fought hard to make the company more secure financially.

His position at the Sun Fire Office, which came through his friendship with Charles Boulton, was most successful. But by no means all his investment decisions were so satisfactory. He got caught up in the 1825 Mexican silver mining bubble. His losses there were £4,000 or, at today's prices, in excess of £200,000.[15] He also lost substantially on investments in the United States. His faith in democratic governments led him to invest heavily in the stock of some of the American states, and he ruefully regretted his naiveté in being guided in investment decisions by a faith in democracy.

But though he was a businessman Norman was not, as he has sometimes been described, a 'wealthy banker'.[16] The first point to note is that the Directors of the Bank of England were not bankers. They were merchants,

[14]Correspondence concerning the retirement of both Overstone and Norman from the Public Works Loan Commission in 1875 is in O'Brien (1971, vol. III, pp. 1278-81).

[15]To be precise, the price index in Twigger (1999) yields a value for 1998 of £199,022; that in O'Donoghue, Goulding and Allen (2004), which takes indexation up to 2003, yields a value of £236,430.

[16]Norman has even been described as a merchant banker, one in a position to make commercial loans. This confuses Norman's position as a *merchant*, which was a qualification until the 1840s for becoming a Director of the Bank of England with, for instance, the sort of position enjoyed by a member of the Baring family.

and this was, until the 1840s, a qualification for membership of the Bank Court. As Norman relates, it proved necessary for him to become a partner with his father in the timber business when he became a Director of the Bank. Moreover the wealth of Norman's family was modest when compared with a genuinely wealthy banker such as his friend Overstone. When in London, Norman lived initially in Blackfriars, then as now not an especially select area, before renting a property in Half Moon Street; Overstone's house was in Carlton Gardens, one of the grandest addresses in the capital. Although two of Norman's sons eventually joined the bank of Martin and Stone, this was the bank of their mother's family, with which it had been associated since its foundation. But it was not a grand affair, and as partners they do not seem to have enjoyed large incomes.[17] Rather they seem to have been able and sensible, and to have justified their positions.

Coupled with the claims about a rich banking background of a family whose wealth was actually derived from the timber business, one finds charges of nepotism. But the recruitment of family members was essentially a way of screening partners in a world in which unlimited liability partnerships constituted the normal form of business organisation. The bankruptcy of such partnerships was a major problem, as a glance at the issues of the *London Gazette*, especially in the first half of the 19th century, makes very clear. In addition to the screening role of family recruitment, the position of a partner within a family network provided a strong disincentive to recklessness and embezzlement, while such recruits had been brought up in a commercial environment, and had thus acquired some business background.

Away from the pressures of business, Norman had two relaxations: sport and self education. The sport included fishing, which Norman took up at the urging of his uncle and his brother.[18] Indeed this seems in later life to have replaced shooting as an interest. He became a member of the famous

---

[17]Frederick Henry Norman, father of the famous Montagu Collet Norman, became a partner in Martin's Bank in 1879, and Edward Norman became one in 1883. The bank remained a partnership until 1891, when it became a joint stock bank with limited liability for the shareholders.

[18]On fishing as a beneficial relaxation, see Overstone's jocular letter to Norman, 1 May 1836, in O'Brien (1971, vol. I, pp. 208-10).

Houghton Club at Stockbridge on the River Test, in which he had a number of cronies including the great sculptor Chantrey, about whom he writes in the Autobiography, and of whose work Norman himself did not, however, have a particularly high opinion. In addition, in his youth, and partly in an attempt to combat the insomnia, Norman attended a gymnasium on the way to work. This was so successful that, apart from becoming a good fencer, he became an excellent gymnast. Indeed he recounts astonishing the sailors on a ship to Norway by climbing two ropes, upside down and using only his hands.

But his great sporting love, from Eton onwards, was cricket, a love which he passed on to his sons. He was one of the founders of the club which became the West Kent Cricket Club (and is now the Chislehurst and West Kent Cricket Club), and he continued to play at a high standard, as he records, until his retirement in 1847 at the age of 54. But he was careful to keep the cricket subordinate to business; and he records that he did not take part in matches lasting more than one day. This may explain the otherwise puzzling fact that, despite his alliance with William Ward in the Bank, he makes no mention of Ward in a cricketing context. For Ward was a great cricketer, and one who devoted far more time to the game than Norman would have allowed himself.

Self education was even more important to Norman than sport. We learn from the Autobiography that he was hardly ever without a book in his hand, and that it was his custom to read a number of books in parallel. The origins of this clearly lie in Norman's formal educational experiences, combined with his insatiable intellectual curiosity. His comments on the education provided by the Reverend John Smith at Eltham are more or less uniformly negative, though the evidence is that Norman's view was rather ungenerous, to put it no stronger. For Jane Austen's nephews were sent there as a preparation for the academic demands of Winchester, and Lord Chancellor Eldon's son was also a pupil with Norman. With regard to Eton, however, there is no doubt whatever about the justice of his strictures. As is clear from the detailed account of the history of Eton written by Maxwell Lyte, the school was in a deplorable state both when Norman was there and for many years afterwards.[19] Though he acquired (or, more fairly, continued to develop on the basis of what the Rev. John Smith had provided) considerable fluency in Latin, this seems to have been the only academic attainment with which he left Eton. But he set about remedying this with his characteristic energy.

His two main areas of study were initially history and languages. He had indeed been fascinated by history, particularly military history, from an early age. But the study of languages post-dated Eton. As Norman tells the reader, when he left Eton he hardly knew a word of any foreign language. He began lessons in French with the Abbé Chatelain at East Sheen, and records that he made progress. With French as a romance language basis he turned his attention to Italian, and again made considerable progress, for the list of Italian authors whose works he read, which he gives in the Autobiography, is extremely impressive. He also learned Norwegian – no easy matter, given that the official language of the country had been Danish, which he would also have had to learn, and that Norway itself has two different languages.

His venture into Italian led to some strange dealings with a man called Maurizi. Maurizi wrote an account of his activities on the Gulf of Oman. He showed this to Norman, who went to him for lessons in Italian. But he remained a mysterious figure, and Norman acknowledges that he could never find out the truth about him. It is now clear, from material to which we refer in the notes to the Autobiography, that Maurizi was indeed an individual with a past. In the Gulf, Maurizi had been primarily an agent of Napoleon. But, like so many in the intelligence world, he had taken out insurance by becoming a double agent and working, at least spasmodically, for the British. He had left Italy because of family objections to his Napoleonic entanglements; and after 1815 he could return neither to Italy nor to France while, using discretion, and drawing on contacts made in the course of his intelligence work, he could probably count on being safe in England.

Once shown the Maurizi manuscript, Norman volunteered to translate it into English, and it was published.[20] Norman's translation must have been

---

[19]See Lyte (1911) chapters xvi-xix.

[20]Maurizi (1819).

difficult for the printer to read, for there are errata listed at the start of the book, for some of the names as printed in the book are wrong. Maurizi presumably lacked sufficient English to check the proofs. Anyone who has struggled with Norman's handwriting, some samples of which we provide for the reader, can only sympathise with the printer.

Despite travelling in Germany, Norman never learned German. He claims that it was little spoken in England. That was clearly not true. A number of his business and social contacts were German, or of German origin, including his immediate neighbour the sugar refiner Major Rohde. There was a large German business community in London, one which flourished until 1914. There is an interesting contrast here with J.S. Mill. Like Norman, Mill was enthusiastic about the Hamiltonian system of studying a language, using a parallel text. Like Norman, too, he had a strongly developed taste for self improvement. And it was German that Mill studied, using the Hamiltonian system, while Norman, for reasons which are not clear, did not study that language, which would certainly have been useful to him in his business pursuits.

Norman was also keenly interested in geology, in which he also pursued self education. The geological references in the Autobiography, especially in the earlier years, are frequent. On his visits to Norway he took two hammers which he had bought from Knights, the ironmongers in the City, and collected geological specimens. Oddly, though he published on yet another of his interests, archaeology, and provided an article on geology to Caroline Fry, which she seems to have rewritten,[21] he appears to have published nothing on geology under his own name.

Though Norman writes about his historical studies, and his study of languages, as well of geology, he remains silent in the Autobiography, for the most part, about those areas to which he may be regarded as having made a distinct intellectual contribution. These were the areas of public finance, trade theory, and the theory of monetary control. However, in order to provide the background to the Autobiography it seems desirable to sketch Norman's contributions here.

[21] Fry (1823-8).

# Public Finance

## The Essay on Taxation

Norman's contribution to discussions of public finance came in two parts. First there was the *Essay on Taxation*, the Utilitarian exercise which has now been published, but which remained unpublished during Norman's lifetime even though, as the manuscript shows, he returned to it again and again over the years. Second, there was a work published first in 1850 and running through three more editions up to the fourth edition in 1864. This was *An Examination of Some Prevailing Opinions as to the Pressure of Taxation in This and Other Countries.*

In the *Essay on Taxation* Norman developed a scheme which reflected his wholehearted acceptance of the Utilitarian ideology. This is true, even though what he wrote is at some distance from Bentham's own position, which was far less indulgent towards the public sector than Norman's own, even at that time, let alone from 1850. The standard by which taxation was to be judged was the greatest happiness of the greatest number. Unlike Bentham, who considered both sides of the public account, Norman deliberately took the needs of government as given, asserting that taxation was a mark of civilisation, and did not balance, as Bentham did, the burdens of a tax against the benefit of expenditure. Rather, he adopted an ability to pay approach, focusing on the revenue side of the public accounts. His aim then became to frame a tax system in which the sums levied would impose an equal proportional sacrifice of utility on taxpayers, leaving the post-tax relative utility positions of individuals unchanged from the pre-tax position. He believed that this would involve the least aggregate sacrifice of utility, though this is not in fact the case.

In pursuit of this, Norman set out a list of the desirable qualities which a tax should possess. However, as he acknowledges in the Autobiography, Norman found writing difficult, and he struggled to express the desirable qualities.[22] The list of qualities which he eventually adopted was, for all

[22] For a vivid illustration of this see Norman to Grote, 1822, in O'Brien (1971, vol. I, pp. 188-9).

intents and purposes, that supplied to him by Overstone, to whom writing and verbal expression of ideas came much more easily.[23] Overstone had too, as Norman mentions, a remarkable facility for getting to the nub of a question.

The list of desirable qualities was as follows. Taxes should be 'frugal' (or, as Adam Smith had put it, 'economical', that is have low collection costs), 'computable', so that anticipated revenue should be calculable, 'simple', 'constant' (in their yield at given tax rates), and 'divisible' – that is, they should allow the rate levied to be varied with State revenue requirements. Norman also conceded that a tax should be 'popular', a requirement to which he only paid lip service, and 'unvexatious' (that is, it should not cause avoidable welfare losses) and it should not interfere with the allocation of resources. Norman also believed that taxes should be 'uncorruptive', not a trivial requirement in the context of an economy in which smuggling was widespread. Norman's childhood experiences in Hastings, about which he writes in the Autobiography, had made a lasting impression. This was coupled with the idea that a tax should be 'unevasable', though the income tax, to which Norman far more than his contemporaries was partial, had a long history of evasion and was indeed regarded by McCulloch as a tax on honesty.

Finally, and most importantly, a tax should be equal in terms of its impact on individuals with similar abilities to pay. He concluded that equality required proportionality in taxation, and that this would in turn produce an equal proportional sacrifice of utility which, he believed, would result in the least aggregate sacrifice of utility. This last assumption cannot be sustained. Even given identical utility functions for different taxpayers, which are also independent, the loss of utility from paying tax depended on the relative rate of decline of the utility of income at the margin. Since, however, this was not discovered until late in the century,[24] Norman can hardly be blamed for failing to appreciate the point, even though the self confidence with which

[23]For Overstone's suggested scheme see Overstone to Norman, 1822, in O'Brien (1971, vol. I, pp. 198-200).

[24]For references to these later developments see O'Brien (2009, p. xxi).

the Utilitarians delivered their judgments on these matters is remarkable.

Norman initially favoured progression in taxation, rather than a single proportional rate. But he was persuaded by George Grote that this was wrong. According to Grote, the poor benefited more from good government than the rich – an argument later borrowed by J.S. Mill. This implied a regressive tax system. But under such circumstances the rich would get off lightly and the middle classes would be left to bear the main burden. This was hardly conclusive, despite Grote's characteristic Utilitarian self assurance; the far more important argument was surely that of John Ramsey McCulloch that, once proportionality was abandoned, you were at sea without rudder or compass and there was no amount of folly or injustice that might not be committed.[25] However both Norman and McCulloch agreed that a 'subsistence minimum' should be exempted from taxation; this implied a degree of progression, where progression is defined with respect to the average tax rate at different income levels.

The form of tax schedule was of particular importance to Norman because, in contrast to the vast majority of his contemporaries, he favoured direct taxation. Even J.S. Mill had reservations about such taxation. The *Essay on Taxation* worked through an evaluation of all existing taxes in the light of the desirable qualities listed, arriving at the conclusion that it was desirable to base the tax system upon a single tax on property. Balancing the harm done against the revenue which could be raised, Norman believed that this was the taxation ideal, though he never dared to publish this proposal to the world. Failing that, he suggested sweeping reforms of the existing tax system, together with the reintroduction of the income tax which, introduced as an emergency measure in 1802, had been abolished in 1816. Norman viewed the history of its operation during that time in a far more favourable light than the vast majority of his contemporaries who had successfully demanded that the records of the tax should be destroyed in 1816. (The civil service retained a characteristically discreet silence about the existence of a duplicate set of records. When Peel was persuaded to reintroduce the income tax in 1842, supposedly on a temporary basis, the civil service was able to provide

[25] McCulloch (1845, p. 147).

him with immediate assistance.)

Despite concentrating on the revenue side of the account in the *Essay on Taxation*, Norman does concede that government expenditure should be minimised, and indeed plucks a figure from the air for a possible reduction in expenditure. But when we come to his publication of 1850, on *The Pressure of Taxation*, we find a very different outlook indeed.

## The Pressure of Taxation

With Peel's reintroduction of the income tax, the civil service effortlessly illustrated what was to be observed in the next century by C. Northcote Parkinson (1960), that expenditure rises to meet revenue. Though successive Chancellors of the Exchequer battled to abolish the income tax, in accordance with Peel's claim that he had only introduced the tax as a temporary measure, and Gladstone, taking office as Chancellor in 1853, pledged to abolish the tax by 1860, the public sector never looked back. While many of Norman's contemporaries greatly regretted this, and the concomitant shifting of the burden of taxation from indirect to direct taxes, as customs duties were reduced or abolished, Norman became not merely an unrepentant but a positively aggressive exponent of increased public expenditure.

The core of his case was that national income per head had risen, despite British tax levels, which therefore were doing no harm, that these tax levels were in any case low by international standards when measured correctly, and that there was enormous scope for increased public expenditure. The contrast with his enthusiastic involvement in the implementation of the 1834 Poor Law, and his delight in the reduction of expenditure which appeared to have been achieved in the Bromley Poor Law Union, could hardly be stronger.

Norman set out to attack three propositions. These were that public expenditure impeded economic progress; that the ratio of public expenditure to national income was particularly high in Britain; and that the British State was particularly extravagant.

Using population, as recorded in the censuses from 1801 onwards, as a proxy for income, and combining this with the observation that wages had, at the very least, not fallen, Norman felt able to conclude that national income had increased significantly since 1815. He buttressed his conclusion, on the basis of population, that national income had risen, with figures for agricultural exports, tonnage of shipping, the increase of the tax base for the legacy duty, and the increasing estimates of personal property and rental property provided by the statistician G.R. Porter. Norman was also enabled, by his presence in the insurance business, to point to an increase in the value of property insured for fire. In addition, he pointed out that, though the range of taxes had been progressively reduced, tax revenue had continued to increase, in itself a hardly conclusive argument given the reintroduction of the highly productive income tax eight years prior to his first edition. On the basis of his confidence that national income had increased significantly, and given data on public expenditure, Norman felt able to conclude next that the ratio of public expenditure to national income had fallen. He further argued that the tax burden in France was higher than that in Britain, in relation to national income which was itself lower in France. Thus the ratio of public expenditure in Britain was not high when compared with that in France. Finally he concluded that the public sector in Britain was parsimonious, particularly given that defence commitments were funded by taxation, not by conscription as in other countries.

Not surprisingly, Norman's conclusions attracted a good deal of criticism, including some from the Irish economist John Elliot Cairnes, who reviewed the 1864 edition of Norman's work in the *Victoria Magazine*.[26] But Norman remained unswayed by adverse comment, despite his sensitivity.

Indeed his contempt for public opinion on this issue was almost reckless. He wrote to Charles Wood, then Chancellor of the Exchequer:

> our Finances must be ill administered, and the public interest be exposed to peril, while no sufficient effort is made to combat

[26]See Cairnes to Norman, 15 October 1864, in O'Brien (1971, vol. III, pp. 1049-50). Norman's notes in reply to Cairnes are in vol. III pp. 1502-6. Cairnes's critique of Norman is 'Our Financial Burthen', *Victoria Magazine* vol. III, September 1864 pp. 385-95.

> faction and ignorance by a bold, and uncompromising utterance of the truth. The Nation should be told that Taxation is not heavy but light – That England is far less severely taxed than other great European States perhaps even than America, that a good government cannot be had for nothing, and that a private person really spends no money, for which he receives such ample value, as that which he pays to the collector-
>
> That as the whole expences of the State can hardly exceed 15 pr cent of the National Income, petty savings upon Individual items of charges are really felt by nobody, while they produce the most prejudicial effects on the public service –
>
> That the ultimate effect of the mania for reduction and the crusade against Taxation, will probably be, some great misfortune connected with insufficient public establishments, or the non payment of the Dividends –
>
> That as we are wealthy beyond all other Nations, so we ought to indulge in the luxury of a good government to an extent wch they cannot afford.[27]

He pressed for much increased public expenditure, especially on education. Though he did not spell out his preferences for increased expenditure in detail, he apparently believed that there was considerable scope for expenditure in relation to 'public morality' and health. He wanted museums, parks and gardens near all great towns, facilities for athletic sports and other recreations in every parish, and an improvement in sanitary arrangements.[28]

The 1850 work is also remarkable, particularly given Norman's extensive land holdings, and his belief, expressed in the Autobiography, in the wisdom of investing in land, in that it contains a call for modification of the right of property and even the claim that 'the property now belonging by law to all the persons forming the State may be regarded as belonging to the whole

[27]Norman to Charles Wood, then Chancellor of the Exchequer, 11 March 1851, in O'Brien (1971, vol. II, pp. 507-9).

[28]Norman (1864, pp. 220-1).

community', a statement which Norman claimed was 'quite compatible with an utter rejection of Communistic views in general'.[29]

Norman's strong views on these matters are in contrast to the more relaxed, indeed more pragmatic, attitude of Overstone. While Norman argued, in the *Essay on Taxation*, which Overstone had read, for an ideal, Overstone's commonsense view was that there was no point in comparing the existing tax system with an abstract and unattainable ideal; valid comparisons only existed between attainable systems.[30] Moreover Overstone, unlike Norman, would have been perfectly happy if Gladstone had achieved his stated aim of abolishing the income tax by 1860, whereas it is quite clear that Norman would have been outraged.[31] Such differences of opinion cannot be explained by simplistic invocations of personal interest; both men were wealthy, though Overstone much more so, and both men enjoyed significant rental income, while Norman had seven sons and two daughters to provide for.[32]

Norman's writings on taxation, while deeply felt and, in the case of the 1850 work in particular, based upon quite careful consideration of statistical sources, did not explore difficult questions of economic analysis. However in the field of international trade Norman showed himself capable of dealing with difficult theoretical questions.

---

[29] Norman (1864, p. 219).

[30] See Overstone's letter to Granville, 10 January 1853, in O'Brien (1971, vol. II pp. 560-1).

[31] Overstone to Norman, 29 April 1853, in O'Brien (1971, vol. II pp. 570-1). If Norman replied to this, to him provocative, opinion, the letter has not survived.

[32] In May 1865 Overstone sent C.H. Cameron a draft for no less than £1,000. Using the index data in O'Donoghue, Goulding and Allen (2004), extended to 2009, with a figure for 1865 of 9.0 (prices having fallen since the episode of the Mexican silver bubble in 1825) and one of 841.41 for 2009, that would be, in today's prices, about £93,490. Cameron seems to have felt both frequent need of financial assistance, and free to ask for help from his friends. Overstone wrote to Norman, a propos the draft: 'He must not press upon your resources which are sufficiently burdened otherwise'. Overstone to Norman, 5 May 1865, in O'Brien (1971, vol. III, pp. 1078-9). Norman himself had earlier provided financial assistance to Cameron (O'Brien, 1971, vol. III, p. 989, n. 2).

## International Trade – the Cuba Case

The three members of the Currency School, Norman, Overstone and Robert Torrens, were very largely in harmony in matters of monetary theory and policy, despite an episode in which Torrens came close to adopting the view – disastrous for the Currency School, high powered money base, model – that deposits were money. Overstone quickly put a stop to that line of argument. But in trade theory the ever fertile Torrens put forward a case – known as the Cuba Case – which undermined that for unilateral free trade, a case to which virtually every 19th century liberal was signed up. For them, free trade was almost a test of moral character – and Torrens failed this.

The trouble started with a publication by Torrens called *The Budget*, which appeared in a series of parts. It was made up of letters to public figures. In two of these, a *Letter to Lord John Russell*, and a *Letter to Sir Robert Peel*, Torrens put forward an analysis demonstrating the power of tariffs to affect the terms of trade and the distribution of the precious metals. The core of his argument is developed in a two country model – England and Cuba – as follows. We start from a position in which the precious metals, the monetary base for all countries, are distributed internationally according to the productivity of different countries. But a country can then add to its stock of precious metals by imposing a tariff which leads to a balance of payments surplus. It follows from this that a country such as Britain, faced with a tariff imposed by Cuba, could restore the equilibrium distribution of the precious metals by imposing a retaliatory tariff. Conversely, if England acquiesced in the loss of precious metal to Cuba, the result would be monetary deflation, a fall in prices, a fall in profits, a fall in wages, and an increase in the real cost of fixed burdens (rentier income and fixed taxes).

Though the argument was developed in terms of a two country model, in order to show clearly the mechanisms involved, the implications were far more general. The most important single policy conclusion was that unilateral removal of tariffs, while other countries, notably France, retained theirs, turned the terms of trade in favour of France (through enabling France to have a larger metallic base for the money supply, and thus a higher price level) and produced monetary deflation in Britain.

Torrens was not advocating duties on raw materials or food because these would, in the latter case through the effect on wages, raise costs. If this happened, international competitiveness would be reduced, and precious metal outflow would ensue. Rather, Torrens was advocating an imperial customs union, with tariffs imposed on imports from countries like France which would be outside the union.

Overstone, as usual, cut to the core of the argument; setting it out in barter terms, he identified a change in the terms of trade as the essence of what Torrens was describing.[33] But Norman, more sensitive on this occasion to the monetary implications, realised the importance in Torrens's case of the stress upon the deflationary aspects of precious metal loss – a natural thing for Torrens to emphasise, since he had earlier been on the side of those supporting monetary accommodation by the Bank, with the ensuing inflation, during the Bullion debate which will be discussed below.

Norman criticised the Cuba Case in two letters to the *Spectator*,[34] and Torrens replied. But the criticisms themselves did not go very deep. Other contemporary reactions also failed to shake the logic of the case – JS Mill was reduced to appealing to international morality – though Nassau Senior pointed out that if tariffs reduced international specialisation, productivity would fall, and so there would be a consequent loss of the precious metals through the balance of payments.[35]

Norman's considered response, however, was so far superior to these other contributions as to put it into a different league. Unfortunately, and in marked contrast to his robust attitude to critics of his advocacy of increased public expenditure, Norman was so nervous of becoming the target of Torrens's brilliant pen that he suppressed the pamphlet on the Cuba Case for

[33]Overstone to Norman, 13 December 1843, in O'Brien (1971, vol. I, pp. 345-6).

[34]Norman's letters are in the *Spectator* 18 February and 18 March 1843. The reply from Torrens is in the *Spectator* 25 February 1843. Norman's original letter was occasioned by a favourable reception of Torrens's thesis in the *Spectator* 28 January 1843 p. 85. See Overstone to Norman, 22 February 1843 in O'Brien (1971, vol. I, pp. 334-6).

[35]For material on criticism of Torrens by Senior and others see O'Brien (2004, pp. 233-5).

no fewer than seventeen years, only publishing it when, as Overstone pointed out to him, the public had long lost interest in the idea, the issues had been forgotten, and it might be better to let sleeping dogs lie.[36]

Norman nervously (his covering letter is extant) sent a copy to Torrens, at the end of 1859,[37] and in 1860 he finally published *Remarks on the Incidence of Import Duties.* It is extremely rare, though there are copies in both the Overstone and the Norman papers.

The pamphlet provided by far the best critique of the Cuba Case, on theoretical, empirical and practical grounds. The main theoretical point was that Torrens had assumed constant outlay – in terms of modern economic techniques, a unitary elasticity of the offer curve.[38] If this was not the case, however, and there was no a priori reason why it should have been, the terms of trade would not move as far as Torrens, relying on a numerical example, had supposed. In this case part of the tariff would fall on the home consumer. This was an original contribution to the theory of international trade, because it was published before J.S. Mill's analysis of reciprocal demand which itself owed something to the Cambridge polymath William Whewell, of whose work Norman would have had no knowledge.[39] A second theoretical objection was that to a two country model. If one country in a set larger than two were to raise its price level, through engineering a precious metal inflow via a tariff, this would cause it to lose competitive advantage in third markets, and it was even conceivable that the loss of metal might be greater than the initial flow – not only could the flow of metal out be as fast as the flow of metal in, in a multi country case, but the tariff would reduce the efficiency of the dutying country as well, and thus cause it further loss of competitive advantage.

In addition, Norman pointed out that the logic of Torrens's case was not equal duties but higher duties, raising the unavoidable prospect of a tariff war.

On an empirical level, Norman pointed out that there was no histori-

[36]Overstone to Norman, 7 December 1859, in O'Brien (1971, vol. II, pp. 899-900).

[37]Norman to Torrens, 9 December 1859, in O'Brien (1971, vol. II, pp. 900-1).

[38]See O'Brien (2004, pp. 230-8) and O'Brien (1994, vol. II, pp. 53-70).

[39]On Whewell and J.S. Mill see Creedy (1998, pp. 151-66).

cal evidence that wages had been depressed by the pursuit of a policy of unilateral free trade. In addition to that, there were practical problems. A considerable proportion of British imports was made up of raw materials and semi-manufactures, which were necessarily excluded from Torrens's scheme, as already noted; 'luxuries' such as tea and sugar came from the very colonies that Torrens wished to favour in a customs union, and a duty on such luxuries would be regressive (which, apart from other undesirable effects, would tend to raise wages). For Britain, invisibles were an important part of the trade account, and these could not be tariffed; and finally – and here Norman's childhood experiences of Hastings again prove important – smuggling provided a limit to the level of duties that could be imposed.

This was indeed a significant and impressive contribution, and it is only to be regretted that Norman suppressed it for seventeen years. Even then the number of copies printed must have been very small, given the rarity of the work. It is however interesting that Norman does not attempt to confute Torrens's analysis of the economic harm brought about by the deflation consequent upon an artificially induced loss of the precious metals. For on monetary questions, with the exception of deposits mentioned above, the three principal members of the Currency School were very largely at one. Norman's own contribution to the monetary debate was important, and it is important to appreciate this in considering his overall importance.

## Norman's Contributions to the Monetary Debate

Norman's work on trade policy, clever and subtle though it was, was largely unknown to his contemporaries, because of his decision to suppress, for seventeen years, publication of the fully thought out version of his critique of Torrens, leaving only the two anonymous letters to the *Spectator*, albeit that the author of those will have been guessed by a number of people (including, no doubt, Torrens). Half of his work on taxation was also unknown, because the *Essay on Taxation* remained in manuscript, and did not appear for more than a century and a quarter after his death. But Norman's work on money is in a different category. He was famous for it during his lifetime, and all subsequent serious discussions of 19th century monetary controversy have included his name.

## The monetary background

It is important to sketch in the background against which Norman made his contributions. The notes of the Bank of England had, throughout the 18th century, been convertible into gold. But in 1797, in response to pressure from the Bank, and from a City deputation in which Overstone's father Lewis Loyd was an important figure, the government agreed to suspend this requirement. The Bank was thus free to issue inconvertible paper currency.[40] The regime, which lasted without interruption until 1819, produced one of the two great monetary controversies of the 19th century, the Bullion Controversy, during which the theory of an inconvertible paper currency was developed. On the one side there were the Anti-Bullionists, largely representing the Bank itself, which issued notes – albeit quite cautiously – in response to demand for discounts of commercial bills. The conduct was justified by the so-called Real Bills doctrine, under which bills originating in transactions in goods and services, rather than in financial accommodation, could be discounted without causing over-issue of notes, since the transactions involved represented real economic activity, and notes issued in this way would be returned to the Bank when the bills matured. In addition, the fact that interest was charged by the Bank, in the form of discount, would ensure that demand for discount was limited to that arising from transactions in which there was a real profit. As a theoretical model it was fundamentally flawed, because it failed to take account of the price level at which such transactions took place, and if note issues raised the price level of transactions, more currency would remain in circulation, rather than being returned to the Bank, to enable higher priced transactions to take place. In addition, the charging of a rate of discount would not prevent demand for discounting of bills which had no counterpart

[40]On the 18th century currency system see Feavearyear (1963, pp. 150-72). On the suspension of convertibility see Feavearyear (1963, pp. 173-201) and Clapham (1944, vol. I pp. 271-2).

in a real transaction. For if the rate at which discount was charged was lower than the prospective profit from employing the funds made available by the Bank, there would be, as Henry Thornton in particular argued, no limit to the demand for discounts. The Bank's own discount rate was in any case subject to a maximum of 5 per cent under the Usury Laws, a rate easily exceeded in nominal terms in the presence of inflation, an inflation itself generated by excessive issue of Bank notes.

The problems were pointed out by the Bank's critics, above all Henry Thornton, whose *Essay on the Paper Credit of Great Britain* of 1802 is one of the high water marks of the controversy.[41] The Bank became the target for Ricardo's polemical powers which, while not involving any novelty in economic theory, had a powerful impact because of the simplified model employed by Ricardo. As Frank Fetter (1969, p. 74) has written:

> What Ricardo did, in the heat of controversy over the credit policy of the Bank of England, was to strip from existing theory Thornton's refinements on Hume and come up with a simplistic proposition that had a tough cutting edge in the polemics of the day: depreciation of English money on the foreign exchanges was entirely the result of the expansion of the note issues of the Bank of England.

Ricardo charged the Bank with depreciating the currency, and the charge was indisputable, though by modern standards the rate of depreciation was modest.[42] It was against the background to the controversy that Norman came to manhood and joined the family business.

[41] Thornton (1802, especially pp. 252-6).

[42] A major factor in the depreciation was the expansion of the note issues of the country banks. Using figures from Twigger (1999) the depreciation from 1797 to 1816 was 28 per cent. But from 1797 to 1813, the high water mark of the country bank operations, the depreciation was no less than 80 per cent. (The corresponding figures in O'Donoghue, Goulding and Allen (2004) are 29 per cent and 81 per cent.) The country bank failures in 1814-16, and the consequent destruction of their note issue, produced a significant fall in the price level. But the Bank's accommodating attitude had provided the climate in which the country banks felt able to expand, not least because they felt confident of discounting bills in London to augment their reserves.

Norman left Eton in 1810, and started to work for his father's timber business. He was thus aware of the controversy about the conduct of the Bank – indeed the great Bullion Report, reflecting Thornton's honest and incisive analysis, appeared in that year. He was then a witness to the collapse of the country banks over the years 1814-16, and of the demands for the resumption of convertibility of the Bank's notes into gold, especially after the end of the war in 1815.

In 1819 Peel's Act (59 Geo.3 c. 49) laid down the steps for the resumption of convertibility, from 1 February 1820 to full convertibility on 1 May 1823.[43] Norman thus became a Director of the Bank right in the middle of this cautious, and indeed delicate, process of resuming convertibility.

## The monetary debates

At that time the Directorate of the Bank, the Bank Court, was firmly under the control of adherents to the Real Bills doctrine, notably Jeremiah Harman (Deputy Governor 1814-16, Governor 1816-18) whom Norman makes no bones about despising. Norman himself was a founder of the Political Economy Club, and was much impressed by his contact therein with Ricardo whom, as he testifies, he regarded as a great man. It was thus natural that he should have joined a group of younger Directors, led by the great cricketer William Ward, who pressed for a more rational approach to the control of the issue of notes by the Bank. Ward had joined the Bank as a Director in 1817, and had already been embarrassed to find himself at odds with the senior members of the Court.

To be in opposition to the ruling Directors was not an easy matter though, as Norman relates, he was careful not to cause gratuitous offence. Some of the older Directors – such as Samuel Thornton, whose behaviour Norman describes – were not entirely straightforward individuals. Moreover Directors of the Bank had, for practical purposes, to be merchants. They were not bankers. Indeed Norman had to become a merchant on entering the Directorate of the Bank. They thus had an interest in the continuation of the

[43] On the Resumption see Clapham (1944, vol. II, pp. 70-1).

discount policy previously employed by the Bank.

Over the next two decades, following resumption of convertibility in 1823, there developed the second great monetary controversy, now known as the Currency and Banking Controversy. Essentially, as Norman himself explained, in his *Letter to Charles Wood* in 1841, the conflict was between those who believed that banking should be accommodating – the Banking School – and those – the Currency School – who believed that the money supply should be controlled by macroeconomic principles and that, in particular, it should be linked directly to the balance of payments.[44]

An important step in the direction of regulating the money supply in this way was the adoption, under the leadership of John Horsley Palmer, of the so-called Palmer Rule. Palmer had quickly become the dominant force amongst the Directors, from the 1820s, and he was, as Norman testifies in the Autobiography, a man of iron will to whom Norman found it necessary to concede defeat even when he believed Palmer to be wrong. The Palmer Rule, as Norman says in the Autobiography, was a distinct step forward. It was essentially a balance sheet rule. On the asset side of the balance sheet of the Bank were securities – bills of exchange and gilt edged (government debt) – and gold. The aim, as described by both Norman and Palmer, was that when the exchanges were 'full' (just on the point of becoming unfavourable) gold should represent one third of the assets.[45] On the liabilities side, there were notes and deposits. When gold flowed out, due to a balance of payments deficit, the Bank should keep the securities constant (though in practice it exercised considerable discretion) and reduce the liabilities side of the balance sheet to match the loss of gold. The key objection of Norman, forming together with Overstone and Torrens the Currency School, was that such a drain of gold was likely to be reflected simply in a reduction in deposits on the liabilities side. The note issue of the Bank, viewed by them as the high powered money base of the financial system, would be little affected. In that

[44] On this, and the contrast between Currency and Banking principles in controlling the issue of notes, see Norman (1841, p. 97).

[45] Clapham (1944, vol. II, p. 146) says that this was never achieved in the years immediately linked to the renewal of the charter of the Bank, 1831-5.

case aggregate demand would, according to their model, be unaffected, and the balance of payments would not be corrected.

Norman gave evidence, as he recalls in the Autobiography, before the 1832 Committee considering the renewal of the charter of the Bank. He also produced a pamphlet on the issues, though it had only a very limited circulation.[46] There are however copies in existence. The work was based upon the idea, to which Norman was now firmly attached, that the note of issue of the Bank must reflect the constraints of the balance of payments, and that, at bottom, the mixed currency of notes and coins should behave as if it were a purely metallic currency.

The concept of 'metallic fluctuation' of the note issue was not invented by Norman. It is to be found in a number of writers in the 1820s, notably Thomas Joplin. But for Norman the origin may lie in the discussions in the Political Economy Club, though how far Ricardo had any responsibility for the metallic fluctuation concept is doubtful. His own writings seem to imply that convertibility of the note issue would be its own safeguard – resumption would ensure that the demand for gold would be kept within reasonable limits. But Norman and his allies became increasingly convinced that, without making the currency behave as an identically circumstanced metallic one would behave, there was a real danger that the Bank would run out of gold before the balance of payments was corrected, and convertibility would have to be suspended. The reason for this was that, without a direct link between the Bank's gold holdings and its note issues, contraction of the note issue would be delayed in the process of meeting an increased demand for discounts, and remedial action might then be forced upon the Bank too late.

In this 1833 pamphlet Norman produced the first proposal, which followed from the logic of his position, for a separation of the Bank into two separate

[46]Norman (1833) is directly addressed to the matter of the renewal of the charter of the Bank. That the circulation was very limited is shown by the fact that even J.S. Mill, attacking Norman, Overstone and Torrens (Mill 1844a), believed Torrens to have been the first to suggest separation of the issue and banking departments. But the suggestion is in Norman (1833), prior to Torrens (1837), as indicated in the text. For a later suggestion of separation, developed with characteristic clarity, see Overstone (1844).

departments, an Issue Department and a Banking Department as they were later called. Robert Torrens is usually given the credit for this innovation, but in fact it was in Norman's printed, if little known, pamphlet, four years before Torrens's *Letter to Lord Melbourne* of 1837. Though the work was not widely circulated, Torrens would undoubtedly have known of it. The year following Torrens, Norman (1838) published his 1833 pamphlet, slightly reworked, containing the proposal.

Norman was the member of the Currency School actually inside the Bank, pushing for reform from that position. Torrens, a brilliant if sometimes erratic theorist, and Overstone, relentlessly following the logic of the model, were outside it. But both Norman and Overstone gave evidence before the 1840 Committee on Banks of Issue. They faced hostile cross examination, and the hyper-sensitive Norman seems to have stood up to this much better than the normally calm Overstone, who even attempted to withdraw from giving evidence.[47] Subsequently Norman published his *Letter to Charles Wood*, who had been the Chairman of the Committee. In this he insisted upon the monetary base argument, with deposits and bills of exchange categorised as 'economizing expedients' in an inverted credit pyramid, with Bank of England notes acting as the high powered money base of the pyramid, controlling the expansion above it.

There were a number of problems with this approach. A major one was that, as indeed Norman feared, the note issues of the country banks, approaching in amount those of the Bank of England, did not appear to be controlled by this monetary base.[48] Another difficulty was that without fixed reserve ratios it was not clear how bank deposits could be controlled by the monetary base.

The response of Norman and his allies to these problems was two-fold. First, they proposed limiting the issues of the country banks by a fixed ceiling. This provision was incorporated in the Bank Charter Act of 1844, which was the embodiment of the Currency School proposals. Second, they

[47] See the correspondence in O'Brien (1971, vol. I, pp. 280-92).

[48] On the question of how far such monetary base control operated see O'Brien (2007, chapter 6, pp. 107-56).

tried to force upon the financial system caution with regard to the incurring of liabilities, through a clear indication that the Bank should not act as the Lender of Last Resort. In the 1830s Norman had opposed, without much success within the Bank Court, the exercise by the Bank of the Last Resort role under the leadership of Horsley Palmer. But once the prescriptions of the Currency School had been enshrined in the 1844 Act, and the Bank had been separated into a Department of Issue and Department of Banking, the logic of the situation was inescapable – the Bank could not assume an unlimited commitment to acting as Lender of Last Resort.[49] For its capacity to provide assistance was limited by the size of the reserve of notes in the Banking Department. It could not issue extra notes at will to meet requests for assistance. Note issues in excess of a 'Fiduciary Issue' of £14.3 million had to be backed by gold. They were thus limited by the Bank's gold holdings.

In this connection, there is an intriguing problem. For Norman, following the policy of discretion with regard to discussions within the Bank, to which he refers in the Autobiography, throws no light on an apparent contradiction between his public opposition to allowing an increased fiduciary issue at times of liquidity panic – referred to after 1844 as a 'relaxing power' – and his position on this issue within the Bank. According to Clapham, Norman was a member of a committee of the Directors which, prior to 1844, considered separation of the Bank into Departments of Issue and of Banking, and both Norman and William Cotton of the committee favoured a 'relaxing power' – specifically that Norman suggested that the fiduciary issue could be extended in an emergency on the authority of three ministers. This suggestion first appeared in Norman's 1838 re-working of his 1833 pamphlet, and the passage is so remarkable in the light of subsequent events that it is worth quoting. After advocating the separation of the Bank into Departments of Issue and of Banking, Norman goes on:

> yet under the supposition of the country circulation being allowed to remain in its existing state, immense difficulties will occur in maintaining inviolably this separation. Under such cir-

[49] On this issue see O'Brien (2007, chapter 7, pp. 157-76).

> cumstances we may anticipate with almost perfect certainty, and within a few years, a period of over-issue and subsequent discredit of provincial paper, attended perhaps by many failures on the part of the issuers, who ordinarily keep a very trifling reserve, relying upon the resources of the Bank in times of pressure. In such a state of things the Bank of England, as it now exists, would freely extend its issues on all sorts of securities, and thus supply the vacuum. The circulation [Issue] department could not afford aid in this way without a gross violation of the rules. In December 1825 and January 1826 many millions in notes and gold were issued from the Bank, and were all wanted, so enormous was the vacuum, inasmuch as the exchanges rose during that period and long afterwards. Upon the proposed scheme [of separation of Departments] this sum could only be provided by importation of treasure, and notes issued upon it, and would require perhaps a year before it could be put in circulation. The above is doubtless a weighty objection, but not invincible; the difficulty it points out might be met by a temporary deviation from the strict laws of the institution, guarded by the proviso best calculated to prevent their violation in any cases except those of absolute necessity. Thus the Directors of the Bank might be authorized to make advances on securities from the funds of the circulation [Issue] department to a limited extent upon an application to that effect from the First Lord of the Treasury, the Chancellor of the Exchequer, and the President of the Board of Trade for the time being, such application, with the reasons for it, being inserted in the [London] Gazette, and laid before Parliament.

Norman was thus advocating a temporary increase in the fiduciary issue; extra notes not backed by gold.

Clapham, in his great history of the Bank, records that Cotton, Governor of the Bank 1842-5, sent Peel, at the latter's request, a long memorandum on 26 January 1844 which contained the whole skeleton of the 1844 Act[50] – and this memorandum included the suggestion, first made by Norman (1838, pp. 106-7), in the passage above, for emergency expansion of the fiduciary issue. There seems to be no obvious reason why Peel omitted this;[51] and, if it had been included, the crises of 1847 and 1857 would almost certainly never have occurred, since they were undoubtedly liquidity panics. Yet after 1844 Norman never deviated from his opposition to a 'Relaxing Power', as it came to be called, and though he was subject to very hostile examination before the Parliamentary Committee[52] which, in 1857, reviewed the 1844 Act, no one seems to have thought to confront him with this passage from his work of 1838, even when questioning him about possible changes in the Act.[53]

## Defence of the 1844 Bank Act

With the passing of the Act of 1844, discretion, as previously exercised under the leadership of Horsley Palmer, was replaced by rules. The Currency School members believed that in this new situation not only would the monetary base be subject to the balance of payments but that such monetary restraint, and early response on the part of the Bank to an outflow of gold, would act counter-cyclically, to moderate an endogenous trade cycle, a feature of the economy to which Overstone (1837, p. 31) had drawn attention in 1837.

At first things went smoothly. The logic of the Act was impeccable, given the assumptions underlying the model, and for the first three years of its operation it did seem as if the model of monetary control embodied in the Act was working well, though there was a high level of bankruptcies in 1846, including (and it is tempting to think that this may have given Norman some quiet satisfaction) the firm of Jeremiah Harman, though he had died in 1844.

[50] Clapham (1944, vol. II, pp. 178-9).

[51] Even Clapham (1944, vol. II, p. 270), with access to all the documentary evidence, can only speculate about the existence of some political reason.

[52] Norman's interrogation included an input from the Birmingham (or 'Bedlam' as J.S. Mill called it) School, which was opposed not merely to the Act but indeed to convertibility of the note issue into gold.

[53] He told the 1857 Commons Committee that he thoroughly approved of the 1844 Act (q. 2860), and opposed any change (qq. 3538-9, 3610-24).

But in the autumn of 1847 trouble began to loom. First, there was a collapse in the price of corn. This had begun in the second quarter of the year, and accelerated in the third quarter. In addition there was the huge amount of railway investment, involving locking up vast sums of capital, and leaving firms illiquid. It was against this background, and against the sustained advice of Norman that, dropping his normal discretion, he recounts, that the Banking Department had acted aggressively in competing for discount business, offering very low rates of discount. It rapidly became clear that the calls upon the Bank for assistance were likely to exceed its resources, and probably by a substantial margin. Inevitably, given the restriction on the Last Resort role of the Bank in the 1844 Act, a liquidity panic ensued. Eventually the government suspended the Act. Remarkably, this proved sufficient in itself; once the limit on the capacity of the Bank to act as Lender of Last Resort had been removed, it did not prove necessary to breach that limit. The panic subsided.

In the subsequent Parliamentary investigations of the crisis, Norman appeared before the Lords Committee, and maintained the strict logic of the Act.[54] He opposed the introduction of a statutory 'Relaxing Power' which would enable the Chancellor of the Exchequer to intervene and temporarily suspend the limits of the Act, at times of financial crisis and ensuing panic.[55]

It seems fair to conclude that the defence of the Act by Norman, by Overstone, and by Robert Torrens in his *Sir Robert Peel's Act Explained and Defended*, was successful.[56] For the next ten years the Act operated as it was designed to do in the legislation. But in the autumn of 1857 another crisis developed.[57] Unfortunately, unlike events ten years earlier, Norman does

---

[54]See Norman's evidence before the Lords Committee following the 1847 crisis, in *Parliamentary Papers* 1847-8, vol. VIII part iii pp. 298-313, qq. 2679-803.

[55]While Norman agreed, when examined by the House of Lords Committee after the 1847 crisis, that it had been a liquidity panic due to fear of insolvency (qq. 2693-5), and while he reluctantly agreed with the Chancellor's letter temporarily suspending the Act (q. 2723), he maintained that it was not possible to legislate in advance for panics (qq. 2745, 2799), and he did not want the Act altered in any way (q. 2797), for 'any relaxing Power, place it where you would, would be abused' (q. 2798).

[56]Torrens (1848). The work ran to three editions.

[57]For the build up of the crisis see Clapham (1944, vol. II, pp. 226-38).

not provide us in his Autobiography with any information about the events leading up to the crisis, though some can be gained from his correspondence with Overstone at the time.[58] He had begun writing the Autobiography in September 1857, and all that he does to mark the episode is to note that, in December 1857, he resumes writing after the crisis has passed.

Even after this second crisis, when the Act was again suspended, and on this occasion suspension was followed by breaching the limits on issue laid down in the 1844 Act when providing assistance to the City, both Norman and Overstone refused to accept that the Bank was now, de facto, the Lender of Last Resort. They continued to oppose the introduction of a statutory 'Relaxing Power', as Norman had done in evidence to the Select Committee enquiring into the Act before the crisis broke. Their reasoning was simple; if such a power were available to the Chancellor, the City, secure in the knowledge that the Act could if necessary be suspended to permit the Bank to act as Lender of Last Resort, would fail to keep its own reserves, and would behave recklessly. It was however quite clear that, even without incorporation into legislation, such a power now existed to government under the authority of precedent, and that it would be used where necessary.

This proved to be the case. There was one more crisis. It occurred in 1866, and is famous as the Overend and Gurney crisis.[59] The Act was suspended, not as a result of a request from the Bank but following a series of requests from the City. From that time on, the Act worked as its framers had intended, until 1914. Norman's role in this achievement would be a cause for posterity to remember him, even were there no other claim.

## Conclusion

When Norman died in 1882, he had lived a full life. He had made intellectual contributions, he had influenced policy profoundly, he had travelled widely, and he had fathered a large and successful family. Despite his susceptibility to female charms, he had in the end fallen deeply in love, as both the Au-

[58]The correspondence is in O'Brien (1971, vol. III, pp. 754-834).

[59]On this episode see Clapham (1944, vol. II, pp. 261-9).

tobiography and the testimony of Mrs Grote to which we refer show, with Sibella Stone, and enjoyed more than fifty years of happy marriage. His friends no doubt appreciated this. In December 1865, urging Norman, who was experiencing one of his periodic fits of depression, to count his blessings, Overstone wrote of Sibella:[60]

> *Your wife.* what a tender, affectionate, and sensible support do you find in her – You might have lost her, and been confined to the dreadful solitude of widowhood; or she might have proved unkind and unfeeling.

Overstone wrote with particular feeling; Lady Overstone had died on 6 November 1864. But apart from her beauty, Sibella must have had, as Overstone implies, remarkable gifts of personality to cope with the depressions and ills to which Norman was subject.

Though there is no lack of evidence in the Autobiography itself that Norman experienced ill health, depression and insomnia, he managed to overcome these and to make a significant contribution to his era. A businessman, a writer, a linguist, a man with an ever curious intellect which led to him being referred to by Darwin as his 'clever neighbour',[61] Norman is worth remembering, and the reader of the Autobiography will find Norman's account of his life and of his circle throws much light on the environment in which a man with his interests and achievements lived.

[60] See O'Brien (1971, vol. III, p. 1100).

[61] See Darwin's letter to J.D. Hooker of 18 April 1860 (letter number 2763 available at http://www.darwinproject.ac.uk/darwinletters/calendar/entry-2763.html).

# Bibliography

[1] Clapham, Sir J.H. (1944) *The Bank of England.* Cambridge: Cambridge University Press.

[2] Creedy, J. (1998) *The History of Economic Analysis.* Cheltenham: Edward Elgar.

[3] Feavearyear, A. (1963) *The Pound Sterling,* 2nd edition (revised by E.V. Morgan). Oxford: Clarendon.

[4] Fetter, F.W. (1969) The Rise and Decline of Ricardian Economics. *History of Political Economy,* 1, pp. 67-84.

[5] Fry, C. (1823-8) *The Assistant of Education, Religious and Literary,* 10 vols. London: T. Baker.

[6] Lewin, T.H. (ed.) (1909) *The Lewin Letters. A Selection from the Correspondence and Diaries of an English Family 1776-1884,* 2 vols. London: Constable.

[7] Lyte, H.C. Maxwell (1911) *A History of Eton College 1440-1910.* London: Macmillan.

[8] McCulloch, J.R. (1845) *A Treatise on the Principles and Practical Influence of Taxation and the Funding System,* 3rd edition, 1863 (edited by D.P. O'Brien). Edinburgh: Scottish Academic Press for the Scottish Economic Society, 1975.

[9] Maurizi, V. (1819) *History of Seyd Said, Sultan of Muscat; together with an Account of the Countries and People on the Shores of the Persian Gulf, particularly the Wahabees. By Shaik Mansur, a Native of Rome.* London: John Booth.

[10] Mill, J.S. (1844a) The Bank Charter Question. *Morning Chronicle,* 26 April 1844 p. 4 and 27 April 1844 p. 5. Reprinted in *Newspaper Writings by John Stuart Mill February 1835-June 1847* (edited by A.P. and J.M. Robson), pp. 847-52, 852-6. Toronto: University of Toronto Press, 1986.

[11] Mill, J.S. (1844b) The Currency Question. *Westminster Review,* XLI. Reprinted in *Essays on Economics and Society by John Stuart Mill* (edited by J.M. Robson), pp. 343-61. Toronto: University of Toronto Press, 1967.

[12] Mill, J.S. (1848) *Principles of Political Economy with Some of their Applications to Social Philosophy* (edited by J.M. Robson). Toronto: University of Toronto Press, 1965.

[13] Mill, J.S. (1886) *Autobiography*, 8th edition. London: Longman.

[14] Norman, G.W. (1822) *Taxation and the Promotion of Human Happiness. An Essay by George Warde Norman* (edited by D.P. O'Brien with John Creedy). Cheltenham: Edward Elgar, 2009.

[15] Norman, G.W. (1833) *Remarks upon Some Prevalent Errors, with respect to Currency and Banking, and Suggestions to the Legislature as to the Renewal of the Bank Charter.* London: R. Hunter.

[16] Norman, G.W. (1838) *Remarks upon Some Prevalent Errors, with respect to Currency and Banking, and suggestions to the Legislature and the Public as to the Improvement of the Monetary System.* London: Richardson.

[17] Norman, G.W. (1841) *Letter to Charles Wood... on Money and the Means of Economizing the Use of It.* London: Richardson.

[18] Norman, G.W. (1864) *An Examination of Some Prevailing Opinions, as to the Pressure of Taxation in This, and Other Countries*, 4th edition. London: T & W Boone. Reprinted in *The History of Taxation* (edited by D.P. O'Brien), vol. VII, pp. 134-273. London: Pickering and Chatto, 1999.

[19] Norman, G.W. (1869) *Papers on Various Subjects.* London: T & W Boone.

[20] Norman, G.W. (1880) Remarks on the Saxon Invasion. *Archaeologica Cantiana*, XIII, pp. 97-110.

[21] O'Brien, D.P. (ed.) (1971) *The Correspondence of Lord Overstone*, 3 vols. Cambridge: Cambridge University Press for the Royal Economic Society.

[22] O'Brien, D.P. (1994) *Methodology, Money and the Firm*, 2 vols. Aldershot: Edward Elgar.

[23] O'Brien, D.P. (2004) *The Classical Economists Revisited.* Princeton: Princeton University Press.

[24] O'Brien, D.P. (2007) *The Development of Monetary Economics.* Cheltenham: Edward Elgar.

[25] O'Brien, D.P. (2009) Introduction. In *Taxation and the Promotion of Human Happiness. An Essay by George Warde Norman* (edited by D.P. O'Brien with John Creedy), pp. xv-xlii. Cheltenham: Edward Elgar.

[26] O'Donoghue, J., Goulding, L., and Allen, G. (2004) Consumer Price Inflation since 1750. *Economic Trends*, March, pp. 38-46.

[27] Overstone, Lord (1837) *Reflections Suggested by a Perusal of Mr. J. Horsley Palmer's Pamphlet on the Causes and Consequences of the Pressure on the Money Market, reprinted in Tracts and Other Publications on Metallic and Paper Currency.* London: privately printed, 1857, pp. 1-40.

[28] Overstone, Lord (1844) *Thoughts on the Separation of the Departments of the Bank of England, reprinted in Tracts and Other Publications on Metallic and Paper Currency.* London: privately printed, 1857 pp. 237-84.

[29] Packe, J. (no date) The Normans of Bromley Common. In *The Story of Holy Trinity Church, Bromley Common, Bromley.* A. Richards (with M. and R. Holden) and J. Packe. Privately printed.

[30] Parkinson, C. Northcote (1960) *The Law and the Profits.* London: John Murray.

[31] Parliamentary Papers (1832) *Report from the Secret Committee appointed to inquire into the expediency of renewing the Charter of the Bank of England, and into the System on which Banks of Issue in England and Wales are conducted*, 1831-2 (722) VI, 1.

[32] Parliamentary Papers (1840) *Report from the Select Committee appointed to inquire into the effects produced on the Circulation of the Country by the Various Banking Establishments issuing Notes payable on demand*, 1840 (602) IV, 1.

[33] Parliamentary Papers (1847-8) *Report from the Lords' Secret Committee appointed to inquire into the Cause of the Distress among the Commercial Classes*, 1847-8 (565) (565-II) VIII Part III, 1, 537.

[34] Parliamentary Papers (1857) *Report from the Select Committee appointed to inquire into the Operation of the Bank Act of 1844 and of the Bank Acts of Scotland and Ireland 1845*, 1857 (220 Session 2) X Part I, 1 (220-I Session 2) X Part II, 1.

[35] Richards, A. (with M. and R. Holden), and Packe, J. (no date) *The Story of Holy Trinity Church, Bromley Common, Bromley.* Privately printed.

[36] Thornton, H. (1802) *An Enquiry into the Nature and Effects of the Paper Credit of Great Britain* (edited by F.A. Hayek). London: Allen and Unwin, 1939.

[37] Torrens, R. (1837) *A Letter to the Right Honourable Lord Viscount Melbourne on the Causes of the Recent Derangements in the Money Market and on Bank Reform.* London: Longman.

[38] Torrens, R. (1841) *A Letter to the Lord John Russell on the Proposed Alteration in the Import Duties upon Corn and Sugar*. London: Smith Elder.

[39] Torrens, R. (1842) *A Letter to the Right Hon. Sir R. Peel ... on the Condition of England and on the Means of Removing the Causes of the Distress*. London: Smith Elder.

[40] Torrens, R. (1848) *The Principles and Practical Operation of Sir Robert Peel's Act of 1844 Explained and Defended Against the Objections of Tooke, Fullarton and Wilson*. London: Longman.

[41] Twigger, R. (1999) *Inflation: the Value of the Pound 1750-1998*. House of Commons Research Paper, 99/20.

# Norman's Autobiography

# Preface

I have often thought of writing a sketch of my life, recollecting how much pleasure and instruction I should have derived from similar documents had my father or grandfather left such behind them.[1]

As my career has been uneventful, few exciting passages will be found in the following pages, nor will they be written with any view to artistic effect. A plain unvarnished narration, interspersed with a few remarks will be all I shall attempt, and the reader must not be surprized, if he meet with occasional repetitions and chronological irregularities, as I shall write during my few intervals of leisure, and with little opportunity for reflection and arrangement.

I anticipate some, perhaps often, painful interest to myself from a review of the varied incidents of my past life, at a moment when the decay in my bodily powers informs me that the day is all but past, and the evening at hand, and that if I have anything to do, I must hasten to do it.[2] I am not too without hope that my children, long after I shall be gathered to my fathers, may peruse these pages not without pleasure. At any rate they will find in them nothing but the truth.

---

[1] [Norman's paternal grandfather was James Norman 1713-87, a timber merchant. Norman's father was George Norman 1756-1830, who succeeded his father in the timber business.]

[2] [George Warde Norman was born 20 September 1793 and lived until 4 September 1882. He was thus not quite 64 when he commenced the Autobiography 10 September 1857, and he still had another quarter of a century to live.]

# Chapter 1

# Early Years

I was born on the 20th day of September 1793 in the house where I now reside,[1] and I believe in the room occupied till her death by my dear mother,[2] the eldest of ten children. My father was George Norman of Bromley. My mother Charlotte his wife, second daughter of the Reverend Edwards Beadon Rector of North Stoneham-Hants.[3] I say nothing more about my parents, here, having in another book, drawn up a slight memoir of each.[4]

The accoucheur who attended my mother was, I believe, Mr Waring of St Mary Cray, father of Dr Waring and grandfather of Mr Waring of Chelsfield.[5]

---

[1] [According to a memorandum by Norman, now in Bromley Public Library (cited henceforth as Bromley Memoir), James Norman settled at Bromley in 1755 and at first rented what was to become the family home on Bromley Common, the Rookery. It seems that he bought it within three or four years.]

[2] [Norman's mother died in 1853. In the Norman papers at Maidstone, at U310 C47, there are letters about her death.]

[3] [The Beadon family originated in Devon. Norman's maternal grandfather, Edwards Beadon, whose mother was the niece of the Bishop of St David's, was the Rector of North Stoneham, Hants. Norman's mother was not the eldest of the children of Edwards Beadon, but his second daughter, as Norman correctly recalls. Norman's parents were married in 1792.]

[4] [This has not been traced. It is not in the Norman papers at Maidstone.]

[5] [According to the Bromley Memoir, the elder Waring, Walter was 'an old and respected Medical Practitioner at St Mary Cray, who brought me and many of my generation into the World'. (St Mary Cray was, at that time, four and a half miles south east of Bromley.) In legal documents concerning property, he is described as a surgeon, and there is a record of his lancing an abscess in the axilla (armpit). He left many children. The eldest son, Thomas, became a farmer, married a rich heiress and, through her, inherited property at Chelsfield. He also inherited money

My mother nursed me herself.

I have no doubt but that my arrival in the world was hailed with enthusiastic delight by my parents, for both were of tender and affectionate dispositions. At any rate, their love for me, from the earliest moment to which my memory extends, was intense, and continued so to be, until we were separated by death.

I was a healthy, but not a very robust, child and often was attended by Mr Read, the Surgeon of Bromley, and doubtless swallowed more of his medicines than did me good, for such was the fashion of the day.[6] I can recollect about four in the afternoon, a dram glass of port wine used to be brought to me, which I drank with considerable disgust.

My first nurse was named Frances. She has not been dead a great many years, and in her old age, she used now and then to apply to me for assistance. At one part of her life she was a matron in a hospital.

Of my appearance in my early years, some idea may I apprehend be formed from a very bad drawing of my sister Charlotte[7] and self made at Ramsgate, when I was about two years old, and now in our bedroom. I present rather a beadony face. I do not recollect this visit to Ramsgate, but I have a very faint recollection of a subsequent visit to Bognor, when I could not have been three years old.

I recollect however perfectly well an important event which took place on my third birthday. The change from the costume of infancy to that of boyhood. I was brought into my parents' room before they were up, in a

---

from a widowed sister, and purchased Chelsfield Hall. Richard Waring 1780-1868, who became a doctor, married another heiress, called Miss Mary Cecilia Morgan (1800-72), who had herself acquired money through her father marrying a rich old lady. He bought the house Marlings near Chislehurst, which he insured with the Sun Fire Office of which Norman was an active director.]

[6] [According to the Bromley Memoir, the practice was Read, Tagnton and Scott. Though Norman had a very low opinion of Read's medical skills, he remembered him as attending to the family.]

[7] [Charlotte Norman was born 30 June 1795, and died in February 1855.]

complete suit of Nankeen,[8] a good deal braided in front. The trousers came over the lower part of a jacket or waistcoat with sleeves. The two latter garments were not separate. This was the usual dress of boys in my early days, until they reached the age of twelve and thirteen years. The waistcoat then lost its sleeves, and covered the upper part of the trousers, or more commonly breeches, instead of being covered by them. A swallow tailed coat was worn over the waistcoat. In short as respected dress, the boy became a man.

I have no very distinct recollections of events during the two or three years which followed my change of dress, probably because they presented no very salient event. I will mention however two or three matters without an attempt to arrange them in chronological order.

My sister Charlotte and self had the whooping cough and to aid our recovery were taken to my uncle R[ichard] Norman's at Leatherhead.[9] This must have been about 1797 or 1798. I have a general idea of the house, which I have never entered since, as he left it after his second marriage. We used to walk on Box Hill, and my mother brought from it in a comfit box the beech tree, which now stands at the bottom of the gravel walk, close to the hand gate which opens upon the drift way.

The birth of my eldest brother, James, has vanished from my memory, but I perfectly remember that of my sister Henrietta in 1799, and the cradle, which was made in consequence, and which I thought very good.[10] She had a wet-nurse, named Dolby, the first in the family.[11]

About this time my parents were in the habit of going to the seaside

[8] [A kind of cotton cloth, originally unbleached, named after Nanking in China.]

[9] [Richard Norman (baptised January 1758, died February 1847) was the brother of Norman's father George. His first wife was Emilia (or Emelia) Grigg or Gregg. The marriage settlement of Richard Norman of Blackfriars, London and Emelia Gregg is in the Norman papers at Maidstone, at U310 T62. It is dated 1783. After her death he married Lady Elizabeth Manners 1769-1853, daughter of the Duke of Rutland, and left Leatherhead.]

[10] [Henrietta, the second sister, was born 21 July 1799 and died July 1866.]

[11] [The name of the wet-nurse may be Dalby: MS is not clear.]

almost yearly. I can just remember being at Broadstairs, I should think in 1797, and can remember well two subsequent visits to Eastbourne, the last of which cannot have been later than 1800. One I know to have been in 1799 from the following circumstance. The Denbigh Militia were quartered in the neighbourhood. Among the officers was a Captain Jones with whom we got acquainted, and who paid great attention, and I believe proposed, to Nellie Hunter, my mother's companion, and subsequently Mrs Cumming.[12] An order came from the Horse Guards that volunteers for the line should be called for, in order to strengthen the Army which was going to Holland under the D[uke] of York.[13] I recollect seeing the Regiment paraded in obedience to this order, and that they wore cocked hats, powder and pigtails.

I was very ill at Eastbourne from a singular circumstance. I had caught a number of small crabs among the rocks, and persuaded the cook to dress them for me. After eating them, I became violently feverish and delirious, and was, I fancy, in some danger. However I soon recovered. The crabs were poisonous.

After the two visits to Eastbourne I never went there again till my marriage tour, when I stopped there for a day between St. Leonards and

[12] [Eleanor Hunter, c.1769-1828, also known as Nellie, daughter of Henry Lannoy Hunter 1739-89, a barrister of Beech Hill, Berks. She was the sister of Sir Claudius Stephen Hunter (see p. 8), and of Mary Manning, wife of the Bank of England Director, William Manning (see pp. 11, 104), and mother of the future Cardinal Manning. She married the Russia merchant John Cumming (see pp. 146, 158, 249). A search of the marriage index for Hampshire parishes, including Stratfield Saye in which the Hunter estate of Beech Hill was in part located, compiled by the Hampshire Genealogical Society, and a search of the index to Stratfield Saye marriages and of the Phillimore Marriage transcripts for Hampshire have not revealed any record of the marriage of Eleanor Hunter with John Cumming. In addition, a search of the Berkshire marriage index, since Beech Hill was also partly in Berkshire, has failed to find a record of the marriage. We are indebted to staff of Hampshire and Berkshire Record Offices for this information.]

[13] [Frederick Augustus, 1763-1827, second son of George III. He was created Duke of York in 1784, and commanded British forces in Flanders in 1793-5, and again on the occasion of the Helder expedition in 1799. An ineffective General, who was the subject of the nursery rhyme about 'The Grand Old Duke of York', he was made Field Marshall in 1795, and Commander in Chief in 1798, but resigned in 1809 following financial scandals.]

Brighton. This was in 1830. I at once pointed out to my wife the houses in which I had previously resided.

My sister Charlotte and I were both inoculated for the smallpox and must have been among the last children so treated, excepting in a few exceptional cases.[14] I suppose that we had the disease mildly, as I recollect nothing about it. Vaccination became general soon after the year 1800.

It was, I think to aid our recovering from the smallpox, that we were sent down with the nurse to Stoneham, and took up our abode in the old mansion of the Flemings, which stood close to the church, looking into the park.[15] Sally Kirby, afterwards Hallet, and still alive at present (1857) was nursery maid at that time, and I mention her with a feeling of regard and gratitude, thinking that I owe her a great deal for encouraging in me a taste for literature, but more on this subject hereafter.

Now for an anecdote or two of my infancy, which I cannot fix to any particular time. We had an old horse named Peacock who, having become unserviceable was killed and given to the dogs. I saw his limbs hung up near the stack yard, and was much disgusted by the sight. For long afterwards

[14][Following the spread of knowledge of the Turkish practice of infecting people with a mild dose of smallpox, to develop resistance to the disease, promoted in England by Lady Mary Wortley Montagu 1689-1762, inoculation became widespread, particularly after Robert Sutton (1707-88) and his son Daniel (1735-1819) developed a simple and cheap way of performing inoculation. One of those who performed inoculations was a country doctor called Edward Jenner (1749-1823), who developed a method of vaccination using cow-pox rather than smallpox pustule. The advantage was that it proved a great deal less risky than the smallpox inoculation, and this explains Norman's comment that he and his sister were amongst the last to be inoculated with smallpox, for Jenner swiftly brought about a revolution in immunisation, with the publication of an account of his discovery in 1798.]

[15][The Willis Fleming family of Stoneham and Bletchley was a great family of landed proprietors – the Willis family in 1766 adopted the additional name and arms of the extinct Fleming family of Stoneham. In the heyday of the family, Stoneham Park was at the heart of a great estate with land in Hampshire and the Isle of Wight, extending in 1844 to some 15,000 acres and reaching to Buckinghamshire and Cambridge. The houses at Stoneham included North Stoneham House and (from 1818) South Stoneham House. The ancestral mansion at Stoneham Park was demolished in 1939. At the time of Norman's account, John Willis Fleming 1781-1844 was the leading member of the family.]

nothing could induce me to eat any underdone meat or red meat, as I always assumed that these were portions of poor Peacock.

My father was fond of ships and boats, bought models, and gave me child's boats to sail on the pond. Two or three of these, a cutter and a peter boat, still remain in rigged in my room; one of them sunk in the pond and remained at the bottom of the water for some time. Now it so happened that my parents went on a visit to Mr Joshua Smith of East Stoke Park near Devises[16] and left me on their way with Mrs Hunter,[17] mother of Sir Claudius,[18] of Mrs Manning[19] and of Nellie, afterwards, Cumming, who then lived at Wargrave a few miles on this side of Reading. I recollect her house well. It was small, stood in the street and had a garden, which reached the river where I used to catch small fish. Mrs Hunter, hearing of my naval tastes, thought I should like a row in a boat and kindly persuaded a neighbour to take me in his. I embarked gaily but, why I know not, soon got frightened, screamed violently and could not be pacified until I was replaced on terra firma.

From Wargrave I was taken to Park Place,[20] now I believe Mr Henley's,[21]

---

[16] [Joshua Smith, 1735-1819 of East Stoke, or Erlestoke, Park Wiltshire; see p. 70.]

[17] [Mrs Hunter was the wife of Henry Lannoy Hunter (see p. 6) and the mother of Sir Claudius Stephen Hunter. She was Mary, third daughter of William Sloane, the great nephew of Sir Hans Sloane. The family seat was at Beech Hill, near Reading, though Mrs Hunter had clearly moved to lesser accommodation.]

[18] [Sir Claudius Hunter, 1st Bt (1812), 1775-1851, Sheriff of London 1808-9, Lord Mayor 1811-12.]

[19] [The sister of Sir Claudius Hunter, Mary (1771-1847), was the second wife of William Manning MP. He had married in 1786 Elizabeth, the daughter of Abel Smith the banker. After her death he married in 1792 Mary Hunter (see p. 6). One of their sons was the future Cardinal Manning.]

[20] [Norman was mistaken in believing that this estate belonged to a Mr Henley. It is possible that he was confusing the ownership with the location, as Park Place is in Remenham, near Henley on Thames. The owners, during the majority of Norman's lifetime, were (with periods of ownership), 1752-95 the Hon. Henry Seymour Conway, 1795-1816 James, 1st Lord Malmesbury, 1816-24 Mr H.P. Spurling, 1824-58 Mr E. Fuller-Maitland, 1858-67 Mr William Fuller Maitland, 1867-70 Mr Charles Easton.]

[21] [Joseph Henley, ship owner and collier. His son was Joseph Warner Henley,

where a druidical monument, removed from Jersey by Marshal Conway[22] and re-erected in his grounds, still remains there, and to other objects of interest in the neighbourhood. The Earl of Barrymore had a theatre, if I recollect right, at Wargrave.[23] He was the last of a very old Anglo-Hibernian family, and had two brothers; all three were roués and unworthy of their noble progenitors. He and his two brothers, one of them a clergyman, were nicknamed Newgate, Hellgate and Cripplegate; one of the brothers was lame.

I have mentioned my journey to Wargrave and Stoneham, I will now allude to one or two other journeys during my infancy. The first was to Avisford in Sussex on a visit to Admiral, afterwards Sir G. Montagu, my father's first cousin.[24] Of this I have only the faintest recollection, it must

---

1793-1884, MP Oxfordshire 1841-78, President of the Board of Trade 1852 and 1858-9.]

[22] [Henry Seymour Conway, 1719-95, army officer and politician. Appointed Field Marshall in 1793.]

[23] [Richard Barry, 7th Earl of Barrymore, 1769-93, rake and actor, the eldest son of Richard Barry, 6th Earl of Barrymore, 1745-73, and Lady Emily Stanhope, 1749-80. On his father's death, he succeeded to substantial wealth, 14,000 acres in County Cork. He entered Eton in 1784 where he spent lavishly and left in 1786. The following year he began gambling heavily on horses and cards. He was one of the Brighton cronies of the Prince of Wales, later Prince Regent, who named him Hellgate. His brother Henry, with a club foot, was known as Cripplegate. His sister Caroline, whose language was notoriously coarse, was apparently known as Billingsgate. At Wargrave the 7th Earl set about creating an imitation of Louis XIV's Fontainebleau, and in 1788 he built a private theatre which is reputed to have cost £60,000. In 1790 he spent further, in extending the theatre. Barrymore himself appeared in a number of productions. In order to evade his creditors, he attempted to obtain a seat in Parliament, and in 1791 purchased the rotten borough of Heytesbury, Wiltshire. But his belongings were seized on behalf of his creditors, and the private theatre was demolished. He sold the family estates, though reserving £4,000 per year for himself. He was shot accidentally while escorting French prisoners, as an Ensign in the Berkshire Militia, in 1793. His brother Henry succeeded to the earldom, but on his death in 1823 it became extinct.]

[24] [Sir George Montagu, 1750-1829, was the son of Admiral John Montagu, 1719-95 (a man said to be remarkably foul mouthed) who married Sophia Wroughton of Wilcot, Wilts in 1748. John Montagu had one daughter and four sons, and the three younger sons all followed their father into the services. George's father ensured his promotions, and from 1777 to 1779 he commanded the Romney as Flag Captain to his father at Newfoundland. He was prominent in activity on the North American station. In 1794 he was promoted to the rank of Rear Admiral.

have taken place when I was very young. The next was to Rendlesham, when I was six or seven years old, and which I remember perfectly.[25] We travelled in a coach and slept, I think, at Witham in Essex. Among the party at Rendlesham were Colonel Stopford,[26] afterwards Sir Edward, and a distinguished officer in the Peninsular War, and Captain Capel,[27] who also rose to be a General, but was less distinguished. I met him subsequently at Rendlesham in 1810. The twins William and Frederick Thellesson,[28] both subsequently Barons Rendlesham, were infants at this time. They were born in 1799 and this circumstance marks the time of our visit. On this occasion, my father one evening took me out of bed, and exhibited me in night clothes from the open gallery in the Great Hall to the assembled company below. I never could make out the reason of this.

I was once at Gloucester while Dr Beadon was Bishop, but have only the faintest recollection of the fact, and also at Stanford Rivers where he was Rector.[29] I remember enough of the parsonage to have recognised it during

---

In 1801 he was made Admiral, and in 1803 Commander in Chief of Portsmouth. He married his first cousin, Charlotte daughter of George Wroughton of Wilcot, Wiltshire. His mother was also a Wroughton, as was Henrietta, the mother of George Norman, and the wife of James Norman, whom Norman's grandfather married in 1751. On James Norman, see pp. 1, 123.]

[25][Rendlesham is in Suffolk, three miles from Wickham Market. Rendlesham Hall was rebuilt about 1780 though destroyed by fire for the second time in 1855 and rebuilt in 1869.]

[26][Colonel, later Lieutenant General, Sir Edward Stopford, second son of James Stopford, 2nd Earl of Courtown, Ireland, 1766-1837.]

[27][Thomas Edward Capel, 1770-1855, brother of Admiral Sir Thomas Bladen Capel, Ensign, 1st Foot Guards 1793, Captain 1803, served in Flanders and the Peninsula, General 1846.]

[28][Frederick, 4th Baron Rendlesham, 1798-1852, succeeded his twin brother William, 3rd Baron, on the latter's death in 1839. MP East Suffolk 1843-52. He lived for many years in Italy.]

[29][Bishop Richard Beadon, 1737-1824, Bishop of Gloucester 1789, of Bath and Wells 1802. Nominated to the living of Stanford Rivers, Essex by Lord Hyde in 1775. The living yielded no less than £1031 (1831). He did not resign it until his translation to Bath and Wells in 1802. He was the brother of Norman's maternal grandfather Edwards Beadon. He married Rachel Gooch, daughter and co-heir of John Gooch, Prebendary of Ely and son of Sir Thomas Gooch the Bishop of Ely.]

a ride with Raikes Currie when we were staying with him at Albyns.[30] We probably took in Stamford Rivers on our way from Rendlesham.

My riding education commenced early. My first mount was a very small donkey. It was always said in the family that Coates the gardener lifted this animal with me on its back over a little stream, which according to the fashion of his kind he was unwilling to cross. My second mount was a grey New Forest pony given me by my friend Mr Manning, the first of several kindnesses, extending over many years, which I owe him.[31] He was in truth a most amiable person, although not able, or well-informed, and of rather a feeble character, as his subsequent career, and its unhappy termination in bankruptcy, sufficiently evinced.

I mentioned some pages back that my sister Charlotte and self were inoculated for the small pox, not so unfortunately, my eldest brother James, born in 1797.[32] He had the complaint naturally when three years old and died. His death chamber was the further half of the sleeping nursery which was then divided. He was a pretty fair boy, like Richard my brother and the darling of his parents, whose hearts were almost broken at his loss.[33] He was buried in Bromley church yard on the Southern side of the church on a spot, which a book kept by Dunn the Sexton distinctly marks, and where my youngest sister Elizabeth,[34] was subsequently buried. I have often thought of

[30] [Raikes Currie, 1801-81, banker, member of Glyn & Co, bankers, MP for Northampton 1837-57. St Albyns was a manor house at Stapleford Abbots.]

[31] [William Manning, 1763-1835, West India merchant, MP for Plymouth Earl 1794-1796, for Lymington 1796-1806, for Evesham 1806-1818, for Penrhyn 1826-1830, Director of the Bank of England, 1790-1831, Deputy Governor 1810-1812, Governor 1812-1814, father as noted on p. 6, of Cardinal Manning. In 1813 he had purchased the Coombe Bank estate at Sundridge near Sevenoaks for £40,000. In 1831 he became bankrupt, and was thus forced to relinquish his Directorship of the Bank.]

[32] [James Norman, Norman's younger brother, was born 24 October 1797, and died in 1800.]

[33] [Richard Norman born 20 October 1800, Norman's business partner in the 1820s. Died 7 March 1860.]

[34] [Elizabeth Hemming Norman, the tenth and youngest child of George and Charlotte Norman, was born in 1809 and died in 1810.]

placing our first born there.[35] James's death was my first great misfortune. I felt it most acutely and, for I believe years afterwards, used occasionally to cry over him at night in bed when there was no distraction to keep off gloomy thoughts. I well recollect this happening at school.

Having now gone over the principal events of my infancy, so far as they now present themselves to my memory, I will proceed to make a few remarks upon my temper, disposition, education &c, before I arrive at my school life.

I presume that it was impossible for any child to be more spoilt than I was, by my parents, who regarded me with unfathomable, and illimitable love. My will and wishes were laws to them, and I recollect my utter astonishment, when a violent outbreak of tears and entreaties failed to produce the effect of preventing my being sent to school, when that step had been finally resolved upon. It was the first time that these means had failed of success.

I do not believe that I ever received a blow in anger from either father or mother, and the only punishment, which I recollect as having been inflicted by either occurred under the following circumstance. As mentioned some pages back, I was recommended a small glass of port wine in the afternoon. I disliked it, and one day being in the carpenter's shop with Quint[36] when the obnoxious beverage was brought to me by Mary Hodge, the nursery maid, resisted violently and scratched her arm, which bled. My father came along at the moment and was very angry. The duty of treating kindly servants, labourers and dependants of all kinds was one on which he most strongly insisted, and as a punishment he led me to the shoe and knife-house, put me in and locked the door upon me. In about half an hour, I became very

---

[35] [On George Hermann Norman, see p. 405.]

[36] [Norman wrote in the Bromley Memoir that Quint, the estate carpenter, was 'one of my earliest friends. Many an hour have I passed in the [carpenter's] shop talking to him. He was a thoroughly good tempered fellow with plenty of gab. He kept the Crown, and acquired in his vocation a habit of tippling which shortened his days. He was a cricketer, could bowl and bat a little and blocked in his crease. The consequence was that he used to get his fingers rapped and I have seen the blood spurt from them over the bat, without causing him to leave the wicket. Gloves were unknown in those days.']

penitent and was released.

I have no doubt that the extreme indulgence shown me in infancy produced some bad effect upon my character, yet I believe that the effect of a system of severity would have been far more pernicious to a disposition such as mine. My father had been treated with severity by his father, who followed in that respect the precepts of the old school and was very sensible of the evils in the filial and parental relations arising from that system. He often used to say that the time must come, when paternal power necessarily ceased in a great degree, and that he did not like to draw too tight a chain which would, as a matter of course, break at last. I believe he was right, and that although no one theory of the management of children can be laid down which will suit all cases, yet that, on the whole, indulgence answers far better in most cases than severity.

There is another form of mismanagement as respects children, which I have always studied to avoid as productive of very injurious consequences on one of the most important of social relations. It is not exactly severity but what is nearly allied to it. I mean a practice of constant fault-finding and nagging and interference. If the child finds that nothing he can do is right, that he is always scolded, and almost in the same tone, he gradually becomes unaware of the difference between large and small offences and almost of the difference between right and wrong. He finds that do what he can, he never gives satisfaction, and at length becomes hopeless of pleasing and careless as to the giving offence.

I have studiously endeavoured to avoid this fault; it has been my endeavour to interfere with the free agency of my children as little as possible, to pass over small errors without remark, or if I mentioned them, to do so without the appearance of scolding. It has ever been my intention however to hit hard, if I found it necessary to hit at all, and in the case of a great offence to shew that I felt deeply, even if I might not think it wise or necessary to punish severely.

I thank God that I have never yet had occasion to punish severely, indeed I may almost say at all. I do not recollect having ever struck a child even in infancy, unless when the child struck first, and thus in the way of retaliation, and since the advancing age of my children has put corporal punishment out of the question, I recollect hardly any occasion when I have thought it right to speak to any of them with great severity.

In short, among the many blessings which God has bestowed upon me, I place my affectionate and dutiful children in the very first rank. I am persuaded, that a desire to give their parents pleasure, and an unwillingness to give them pain, are sentiments by which they are all constantly actuated. They have been to me a source of the purest pleasure, unless when as in the case of Gerard now,[37] I feel anxious about their safety, or as in that of dear Herman,[38] when after twelve months of the most acute solicitude, I finally lost a son, the glory of whose death did not prevent his disappearance from the earthly scene from filling me with the deepest and most enduring grief. That grief at the end of more than two years is still fresh. May we meet hereafter.

One more remark, and then I quit this subject and return to myself and my doings. I think that no parent is justified in ruining himself, and still less in ruining his other children, in order to minister to the extravagance of one. In making this observation I have specially in mind the case of my old and excellent friend Mr Hodges,[39] who dissipated the far greater part of a splendid estate and fortune in paying the debts of his son, and thus brought

[37] [Gerard Norman, Norman's third son, was born 19 July 1835 and died 31 May 1901. He was employed in the Bengal Civil Service. The Indian Mutiny had broken out on 10 May 1857. Norman began his Autobiography four months later.]

[38] [George Herman Norman, eldest son of George Warde Norman, Captain in the 57th Middlesex Regiment, born 26 July 1831, died of wounds received in action in the Crimea, 30 June 1855. There are accounts and papers (2 volumes and 6 documents) relating to Herman Norman in the Norman papers at Maidstone, at U310 F30/2.]

[39] [Thomas Law Hodges, 1776-1857, MP for Kent 1830-2, and for West Kent 1832-41 and 1847-52.]

a cloud of sorrow over the evening of his days.

A child, however worthless and prodigal, should not be allowed to starve, but he should be left to feel the consequences of his vice or folly, and thus the best means will have been taken to produce a permanent improvement in his character. T. Hodges must lament that this course was not adopted with him.

The idea of founding or maintaining a family may appear to many an antiquated idea, little consonant with the spirit of the age or with the teaching of a sound philosophy. I am not of this opinion. It seems to me that the habit of looking beyond the actual reality, in the affairs not only of the future life but of the present, is most beneficial. And that England owes much of her wealth and of her intellectual and moral superiority to that sentiment, so ingrained in the minds of the Nation, which makes us regard the honour, the fortune, and the social standing of our name and race much or more important than the insulated advantage of the individual.

I will now say a little as to the moral and intellectual character, which was the result of my natural disposition and of the training through which I had gone at the moment of passing from infancy to boyhood.

My health had not been very strong but I had had no serious illness and possessed a robust and active body, as speedily appeared when I went to school. This however was not my father's opinion of me. He had somehow imbibed the notion that I was weak and puny and was fond of comparing me with the sons of Admiral Wells,[40] then living during the absence of their

---

[40] [Vice Admiral (1808) Thomas Wells, 1759-1811, son of William Wells 1729-1805, shipbuilder. He joined the navy in 1774. He was in the three squadrons of Red, White and Blue, in ascending order of seniority. His promotions apparently owed something to his father's political connections. In 1805 he was one of the pall-bearers at Nelson's funeral. His sons were Thomas John Wells, born in 1787, admitted to Cambridge in 1805, died of 'consumption' in 1810; William Wells, 1788-1826; Henry born 1789; John Neave 1790-1854, who was present at Waterloo, later Colonel in the Royal Engineers; James, 1793-1816; St Vincent born 1797; Richard born 1800; Frederick Octavius, 1793-1847; and Charles 1807-19. Of the sons of Admiral Wells, James, born in 1793, was at Eton with Norman and died

father at sea, in a house at Bickley, now pulled down. These boys were very chubby and high-coloured, but they were, as my Eton and other experience subsequently shewed, very inferior to me in physical power, and none of them reached old age.

I may here remark with thankfulness that I have never been confined to my bed by serious illness for many days at a time more than three times in my life *viz.* when attacked at Eltham by inflammation in the stomach, in 1816 with malignant sore throat, and about 1836 with an affection of the mucous membrane. Of this illness the two first were dangerous. The other complaints which have obliged me to keep my bed, have all been Influenza, or forms of feverish cold and have never lasted more than three or four days, occurring at intervals of three or four years.

I have however had much illness of a chronic character, as will appear in subsequent pages.

I was of a very impressionable, and affectionate disposition, passionately fond of my parents, nurses &c, thinking my father the greatest man in the world and anxious to imitate him in all his peculiarities. I recollect on one occasion hearing him say that he was growing very old. At that time he may have been forty-two. This remark made the most vivid impression on my imagination. I burst into a most violent flood of tears, thinking that he would not live long, and it took some hours to pacify me. The departure of nurse Frances, by no means a first rate servant, afflicted me too, very deeply. A hint, that anything I did would make my parents unhappy affected me most bitterly. I have already mentioned what I felt after the death of my brother James.

At a period somewhat later, this influenced my feelings strongly. I never heard Pleyel's hymn,[41] without a crying fit, so that it was tabooed when I

in 1816, after going to King's College, Cambridge in 1813.]

[41][Ignaz Pleyel, 1757-1831, prolific Austrian composer, pupil of Hayden, and founder of a piano manufacturing firm. He was a member of an Austro-Hungarian Masonic Order, and his composition for the Anglican hymn 'Children of the Heav-

was present. That nervous temperament which has caused me so much pain through life, displayed itself very early.

The reader from what has preceded may think that I was an amiable and attractive child. This may have been the case to a certain extent, but I must shew the other side of the picture.

In my childhood, I was extremely passionate, and so continued until sometime after I had been at Eton, when I was determined to curb this disposition, and exerted myself with some success. That I quite succeeded, I will not affirm. I am well aware that certain faults of temper have accompanied me through life, and I am now too old to amend. At any rate, open manifestations of anger are not habitual with me.

I do not consider that I was brave as a child, or that courage has ever been one of my constitutional advantages. My nervous temperament has disposed me rather to exaggerate the danger either present or contingent. Nevertheless, I am not aware that I have shewn a want of moral courage when called upon, which has rarely happened, to display it. A feeling of duty and dread of dishonour has armed me with resolution at the critical moment, and overpowered merely physical impulses. It must be allowed, that my courage has never been severely tried. It might easily have failed in difficult circumstances.

Shyness was a feeling which in my early years was very painful to me and I have never altogether got rid of it. My dislike of taking a part at public meetings &c &c. belongs to this peculiarity. I well recollect that when visitors expressed a desire to see me, my mother sent for me, I used to

enly King' is also used by the Masons as a funeral dirge. Thus the second verse reads 'Brothers, now indulge a tear, /for mortality is here! /See how wide her trophies wave, /o'er the slumbers of the grave'. The author of these words is now believed to be an American Mason, known as Brother David Vinton, in 1816. He was active in Masonic circles, but expelled from the Grand Lodge of North Carolina in 1821, for 'un-Masonic conduct'. The second verse is not used in some Masonic jurisdictions. It is unlikely that most Anglican and Methodist congregations are aware of the origin of the hymn, and this would have been true of Norman as well.]

hide myself.

I was a very idle child. I do not recollect that my mother acted as my teacher, but doubt not that she did so. At any rate her efforts failed. I was sadly spoiled. She would never have thought of recourse to coercive means, and at the age of seven and a half I was quite unable to read, knowing little more than my letters.

There was a man named Bentley, a drunken schoolmaster at Bromley, who was employed to teach my sister Charlotte and myself, writing and arithmetic, with little success however. I can recollect the man and a few lessons, but I also recollect that we used to run away and hide ourselves when he was expected. On one occasion we took refuge in the carthorse stable, then a place of deposit for hay, and hid ourselves among the trusses.

Although so idle and unwilling to learn, I was very sensible to the pleasure to be derived from books, and listened with great avidity to any body who would read them to me.

Aesop was the first I recollect to have heard.[42] My edition was an old-fashioned affair, bearing little resemblance to the spruce productions of the children's press in modern days. It was carefully preserved by my mother till her dying day, and will be found even now, with letters and other relics of the past, in one of the tea boxes in my room. I heard the fables so often that I learned a large part of them by heart, and used to repeat them before my parents and their guests. The first of whom thought, and the latter doubtless said, that I was a prodigy. I could not have been then more than three or four years old.

Subsequently works of a heavier calibre than Aesop engaged my attentions

[42][Although Aesop (fl. c.570 BC) had prose fables attached to his name which were popular at Athens, the modern view is that the fables now known to us, which have been translated into many languages, and of which numerous versions have been available in English, are certainly spurious. A second century Greek poet called Babrius apparently versified the fables which circulated in Athens; those are not the same thing as the modern fables, and were published in English in 1883.]

and I listened to them with delight, and it is somewhat singular that from a very early age history was what pleased me most, as it has ever continued to do. Sally Kirby (Mrs Hallett)[43] read to me, before I went to school, Stanyan's History of Greece,[44] a very poor and now forgotten book, and Leland's Philip of Macedon.[45] I have already mentioned that she also read

[43] [In the Bromley Memoir, Norman wrote 'Sarah Kirby was Nursery Maid and a person educated above her station. I owe her an obligation for helping to cultivate literary tastes in me. I recollect her reading to me Leland's Philip of Macedon, before I could read myself and also portions of Pope's Homer. We used to act together the duel between Hector and Ajax, using hazel wands for spears, in the Avenue at Stoneham. S[arah] K[irby] married an Exciseman named Hallett, and kept for many years a school at Wokingham. She writes to me now and then, and I lost some money by one of her Sons, and put another in the Bank, who died.']

[44] [Temple Stanyan, 1676/7-1752, author of *Grecian History*, was the younger brother of Abraham Stanyan, c.1669-1732, a diplomat. He matriculated at Christ Church College, Oxford, aged 18, in 1695, but does not appear to have graduated, and he entered the civil service. In 1719 he was appointed Clerk in Ordinary to the Privy Council; in 1724 he became an Under Secretary of State for the Southern Department, and served until 1735. His book is *Grecian History from the Origin of Greece, to the Death of Philip of Macedon*, 1707, second, enlarged, edition 1739. This was an important work for its time, though it was replaced by William Mitford's *History of Greece*, published between 1784 and 1810, a multi volume work. Norman's comment on Stanyan simply reflects the extraordinarily hostile – indeed blinkered – attitude of those associated with George Grote towards earlier writings on Greece, especially the work of Mitford himself. Stanyan's work was sufficiently important to be translated into French by Diderot, the chief editor of the famous *Encyclopédie*, one of the great literary products of the Enlightenment. The date of his translation (Paris: Briasson) is 1743. William Mitford 1744-1827 was savagely attacked by Grote and his entourage for ideological reasons. Not only was Mitford a Tory, and intermittently a member of the House of Commons between 1785 and 1818, but his interpretation of the political structure of ancient Greece was completely unacceptable to the Utilitarian radicals. Grote attacked Mitford in 1826 in the *Westminster Review*, the Benthamite organ. Amongst those who published attacks upon Mitford was Thomas Babbington Macaulay, and his extravagant assault leaves a particularly bad taste, for Mitford was a dying man and, in the small world of intellectual London, Macaulay is unlikely to have been unaware of this. The Utilitarian radicals, including Edward Bulwer Lytton, and J.S. Mill, wished to establish the idea of Athens as the ideal of democracy, whereas writers like Mitford looked to Sparta as a model with associations contrary to egalitarianism, and appeared to favour oligarchy rather than democracy.]

[45] [Thomas Leland, 1722-85, historian and Church of Ireland clergyman. In 1758 he published *The History of Philip, King of Macedon.* Leland was a considerable scholar, who was appointed Professor of History at Trinity College, Dublin in 1761 and Professor of Oratory in 1762. He is perhaps most famous for his translation of the *Orations of Demosthenes Against Philip*, which appeared in parts from 1754

to me at Stoneham, Pope's Homer's Iliad,[46] and that we acted together some of its fighting scenes. We used hazel shoots for spears. Robinson Crusoe was also a special favourite of mine.[47]

to 1761.]

[46][Alexander Pope, 1688-1744. He learned Latin and Greek at a Catholic school at Twyford, Hampshire. As a child he had read John Ogilby's translation of Homer's Illiad and in March 1714 he undertook to begin work on his own version of the Illiad. The huge project took him about six years.]

[47][A novel by Daniel Defoe first published in 1719 in the form of a fictional autobiography of a castaway who spends 28 years on a remote tropical island. The story appears to have been based on the real life experience of Alexander Selkirk, a Scottish sailor who lived for more than four years on the Pacific island then called Mas a Tierra. The book subsequently appeared in many editions and many languages. Selkirk himself had been rescued in 1709 and an account of his ordeal had already been published by his rescuer, Woodes Rogers, in 1712.]

# Chapter 2

# Eltham School

On the whole, although an idle, I was not a stupid child, but it was of course necessary that I should learn to read and as I would not learn at home, it became necessary to find a school for me.

Upon this important question my father seems to have been greatly influenced by his friend, Dr Smith of Bromley, for the school selected was kept by the Curate of Eltham. The Reverend John Smith,[1] a Cousin of the Doctor. Both these gentlemen were Natives of Cumberland, both had been brought up at St Bees School,[2] and subsequently at Queen's College, Oxford, and

[1] [John Smith was Curate of Eltham 1798-1820, when he was succeeded by W.T. Myers. For this information obtained from parish records, and for other information relating to Eltham noted below, we are indebted to Miss Margaret Taylor, Hon. Archivist of the Church of St John the Baptist, Eltham. Unlike his cousin Henry (see p. 22), John Smith is not listed in Alumni Oxoniensis, and Norman appears to have been mistaken in the belief that he attended Queen's College, Oxford. Eltham Church, to which John Smith was attached as Curate, is in the centre of Eltham, on Eltham High Street, so that, given Norman's location of his house in relation to the church, Mr Smith himself lived in the centre of the town, and Norman himself was schooled there.]

[2] [St Bees is a village in the Copeland district of what is now Cumbria, about five miles south of Whitehaven. St Bees School was founded by Edmund Grindal, Archbishop of Canterbury, who died in 1583. It received further endowments from Dr Lamplugh, Archbishop of York, a Dr Smith, Bishop of Carlisle, and Sir John Lowther of Whitehaven. The right of presenting a master to the school lay with the Provost and Fellows of Queen's College, Oxford. Grindal had assigned revenues to Queen's College for the maintenance of one Fellow and two scholars, to be chosen from St Bees School. Queen's College graduates in turn provided the headmasters of St Bees at least from 1630 to 1916, with only two exceptions.]

both I conceive were of humble origin, and not necessarily the worse for that. Of Dr Smith,[3] I have said enough in another place and I must now describe my Master. He was a high colored and, on the whole, good looking man, rather tall than short, rather thin than stout. He spoke a broad Northern dialect, was not distinguished for general acquirements, and knew very little of the business of education, so that he was not likely to turn out very well-crammed pupils. He was however kind, honourable, and eager to do his best, rather hot in temper, and thus likely to make a mistake as he did on the only occasion when I recollect him punishing me and when I was really innocent. The infliction however was not very severe, only a blow or two on the hand with a flat ruler.

As a moral teacher, I have reason to be obliged to Mr Smith. He had a scorn for anything like falsehood and dishonesty, and when offences of that kind appeared under his observation he reproved them with a contemptuous severity, which manifestly came from his heart.

Before he settled at Eltham, Mr Smith had been Curate to Lord George

[3][Henry Smith of St Bees, Cumberland, and Queen's College, Oxford, matriculated 1769 aged 19. BA 1773, MA 1776, BD 1788, DD 1793. Chaplain to the Duke of Devonshire, 1794, Rector of Headley, Hants, 1801, Perpetual Curate of Bromley. He died 23 July 1818. According to Norman's Bromley Memoir, Dr Smith was 'a square, burly person of great strength and a constitution which ought to have lasted for 100 years, but which was destroyed by intemperance. He would drink 3 bottles of port at a sitting and was habitually a great consumer of grog, eating little, and that of such things as ham or bacon. He and his Clerk, Dunn, were supposed to absorb more alcohol than any other two men in the Parish. Yet I never saw the Dr drunk. He was very fond of hare hunting ... For the greater part of his life, he was a very poor man, but he finally was presented by his College [Queen's College, Oxford] to the Rectory of Headley in Hampshire. When over sixty he married the daughter of James Wilson who kept the Bell at Bromley, and had by her two daughters ... He died about 1818 aged I think sixty nine ... It was his habit to drive in the middle of the day and he used frequently to walk up to this house at about 6 o'clock ... and drank a good deal of wine with my Father, to whom these visits became at length very distasteful. Dr. Smith had an important influence on my destiny, for he induced my Father to send me to a small School kept by his cousin, the Rev. John Smith, curate of Eltham, where I remained 4 years from Easter 1801 to Easter 1805. I learnt little there for Mr Smith was a bad instructor, but at any rate, I learnt nothing bad, for he was a good man and kind to me.']

Murray,[4] father of the Bishop of Rochester at Hunton in Kent. He there married Miss Ballard,[5] daughter of a respectable farmer, who lived, I believe at Wateringbury. Mrs S was a large fat woman, with but few accomplishments, but kind and motherly. They had several children,[6] and I recollect that when we had sometimes a glass of homemade wine, which by the way was very good, given us after dinner, used to drink the healths of the whole party, thus, Mr Smith your good health, Mrs S[mith] Ditto Mr Ballard Ditto Mrs B[allard] Ditto Elizabeth Ditto Catherine Ditto Henry Ditto boys Ditto repeating the formula after each name. This was a long job.

The Ballards were excellent people and passed much time at Eltham, having, I fancy, given up their Farm. After his tea at breakfast, Mr B always drank a glass of Ale. Mrs B was always ready to interfere in favor of a boy who had got into a scrape.

If I have been in any way free from these faults, I must be grateful in the first place to my parents for the admirable example set me by them, but

[4][Lord George Murray, 1761-1803, Bishop of St David's. He was the second surviving son of John Murray, 3rd Duke of Athol, the inventor of a shutter telegraph system. George Murray, 1784-1860, was Dean of Worcester 1828-54, Bishop of Sodor and Man 1814-27, and Bishop of Rochester 1827 to death. Eltham was in the diocese of Rochester until 1924 so that John Smith's progress from the Murray household to Eltham may not have been coincidental.]

[5][According to the church records (see p. 21) John Smith married Elizabeth Ballard (born 10 January 1777) at Eltham Church, 30 April, 1798. Oddly, the marriage entry gives no hint of his being a clergyman. One daughter, Catherine (1801-85), married George Miles Cooper (1797-1875) who became Vicar of Wilmington, Sussex. One of the witnesses to the marriage of John Smith and Elizabeth Ballard was John Smith's cousin Henry Smith (see p. 22). James Ballard of Wateringbury, father of the bride, is described in his will, dated March 1808, which was proved 3 December 1816, as 'gentleman'. James Ballard died aged 83 and was buried in Eltham by the Vicar, J.K. Shaw Brooke, 10 June 1816. He was a tenant of the estate of Sir Charles Booth. He held two leasehold farms in the parishes of Nettlestead and Mereworth, In his will, John Smith is correctly described as the Reverend John Smith of Eltham. John Smith and his wife were the executors of the will.]

[6][The Curate's children were baptised in Eltham Church, and their birth dates recorded in the Register. They were Elizabeth, 7 March 1795, Catherine, 25 January 1801, and Henry, 1 April 1802. Information from church records has been supplied by Margaret Taylor, the Honorary Archivist of St John the Baptist Church, Eltham.]

I feel that I owe a great obligation to Mr Smith for the excellent precepts which he never failed to inculcate.

There was another matter to which he paid great attention, the reading well. We had to read a good deal out loud, and also to learn by heart and repeat select pieces of poetry and speeches in prose. These were taken out of Enfield's Speaker[7] or the Elegant Extracts[8] and we were required to pay great attention to clearness of enunciation, and a correct and expressive emphasis. I derived great advantage from this. At present, such matters seem much neglected at schools. Some things which I learned to recite at Mr Smith's I have not altogether forgotten even now. I may mention among them.

> 'My name is Norval'[9] and from Douglas,[10]
>
> 'tis done dread Winter spreads his latest gloom' &c from Thomson's Seasons[11]

[7] [William Enfield, 1741-97, Unitarian minister. He published a best selling book on elocution entitled *The Speaker* in 1774. Despite his Unitarian connections, he was in favour of friendly relations with the Church of England, and attacked Joseph Priestley for his abrasive attitude towards it. This presumably helps to explain why Mr Smith at Eltham was sympathetic to use of the book.]

[8] [This was a work in two volumes by the headmaster of Tonbridge School, Vicesimus Knox, 1752-1821. The prose extracts appeared in 1783 and the verse extracts in 1790. The work was famous in its day.]

[9] ['My name is Norval; on the Grampian Hills my father feeds his flocks, a frugal swain whose constant cares were to increase his store.' Douglas, II, i. The play attracted much popular comment, not all of it favourable, but the philosopher David Hume was enthusiastic about it.]

[10] [This is a blank verse tragedy by John Home, first performed in Edinburgh in 1756. The play was very successful, in both England and Scotland.]

[11] [It is not clear how much of this poem Norman learned; it is an extremely long work. The passage to which Norman refers is the start of verse 25. 'Tis done! – Dread Winter has subdu'd the Year, and reigns, tremendous, o'er the desart [sic] Plains! How dead the Vegetable Kingdom lies! How dumb the Tuneful Horror wide extends his solitary Empire.' James Thomson, 1700-48, was a Scottish poet. His *The Seasons* is regarded as a masterpiece. He entered Edinburgh University in 1715, destined for the Presbyterian ministry. In 1719 he entered Divinity Hall to train as a minister. He moved to London in 1725. *Winter*, the first poem of *The Seasons*, was published in 1726 by John Millian. *Summer* appeared in 1727, *Spring* in 1728, and *Autumn* in 1730. The set of four poems was then published together as The Seasons. The set was translated into German and, through the subsequent

'Farewell, a long farewell to all my greatness' Henry VIII[12]

'Thy wish was father Harry to that thought' Henry IV.[13]

The Speech of Brutus and Antony, Julius Caesar.[14]

A Poem called 'Death' by Porteus.[15]

'Gray's Elegy'.[16]

The Speech of Hannibal and of Galgacus to their Soldiers &c.[17]

---

work of Gottfried van Swieten, became the libretto for Haydn's famous oratorio *The Seasons.* Thomson also wrote the words of *Rule Britannia*, which were part of a masque *Alfred* in which Thomson collaborated with his friend David Mallet. It was first performed at Cliveden, then the country home of Frederick, Prince of Wales, and the Prince bestowed on Thomson a pension of £100 per annum.]

[12] ['Farewell! a long farewell to all my greatness! This is the state of man today he puts forth the tender leaves of hope, tomorrow blossoms, and bears his blushing honours thick upon him; the third day comes a frost, a killing frost and when he thinks, good easy man, full surely his greatness is a-ripening, nips his root, and then he falls, as I do.' William Shakespeare, 1564-1616, *Henry VIII* Act 3 Scene 2.]

[13] ['Thy wish was father, Harry, to that thought: I stay too long by thee, I weary thee. Didst thou so hunger for mine empty chair that thou wilt needs invest thee with my honors before thy hour be ripe? O foolish youth!' Shakespeare, *Henry IV* Part 2 Act 2 Scene 1.]

[14] [The speeches by Brutus and Anthony are from Shakespeare's *Julius Caesar* Act 3 Scene 2. That by Brutus begins 'Be patient till the last. Romans, countrymen, and lovers! Hear me for my cause, and be silent, that you may hear; believe me for mine honour, and have respect to mine honour, that you may believe: censor me in your wisdom, and awake your senses, that you may the better judge.' That by Anthony is even more famous. It begins 'Friends, Romans, Countrymen, lend me your ears; I come to bury Caesar, not to praise him. The evil that men do lives after them; the good is oft interred with their bones.']

[15] [Beilby Porteus, 1731-1809, successively Bishop of Chester and Bishop of London, Anglican reformer, and leading opponent of slavery. He was educated at York and Rippon, became a classics scholar at Christ's College, Cambridge, and in 1759 won the Seatonian Prize for his poem *Death: a Poetical Essay.*]

[16] [Gray's *Elegy Written in a Country Churchyard* begins with the lines which once every schoolboy knew: 'The curfew tolls the knell of parting day, /the lowing herd winds slowly o'er the lea, /the ploughman homeward plods his weary way, /and leaves the world to darkness and to me'. Thomas Gray, 1716-71, English poet, classical scholar at Cambridge (see p. 94). Like Norman, he was educated at Eton. He spent most of his life in Cambridge. His *Elegy* is regarded as a masterpiece. It was published in 1751.]

[17] [Hannibal Barca was a Carthaginean military commander 247-183 BC. He is famous for marching an army, which included elephants, from Spain over the

As I have observed already, Mr Smith was not a good general instructor. He did not get us over the ground fast enough. We were in school from seven till nine, ten till one, three till five and had besides something to do in the evening. This was far too much, and yet we learnt little, owing to a fault in the system. We had to puzzle out by ourselves, a few lines of Phaedrus,[18] or of the Selecta Profonis,[19] which occupied hours, or to do a little of the Exempla Minora.[20] In short we were always at work and never got on.

---

Pyrenees and the Alps into Northern Italy, defeating the Romans in a series of battles including Trebia, Trasimene and Cannae. But a Roman counter invasion of North Africa forced him to return to Carthage, and he was defeated in the battle of Zama. Hannibal's speech is recorded as having been delivered to the Carthaginean army in crossing the Alps, and is reported by Titus Livius, 59 BC-17 AD, known to history as Livy. He was the author of a history of Rome *Ab Urbe Condita* (*From the Founding of the City*) of which only 35 of 142 books survive. Books 21-30 recounted the war with Hannibal. Galcacus was the leader of the 'Caledonian Confederacy' who fought the Roman army of Gnaeus Julius Agricola at the battle of Mons Graupius in Northern Scotland in AD 83 or 84. Publius or Gaius Cornelius Tacitus, 56-117 AD, who was a Roman Senator and historian, wrote a speech he attributed to Galcacus, delivered in advance of the battle, in which he describes the exploitation of Britain by Rome, to raise the fighting spirit of his followers. 'Whenever I consider the origin of this war and the necessities of our position, I have a sure confidence that this day, and this union of yours, will be the beginning of freedom to the whole of Britain' (paragraph 30). He features in Tacitus's *De Vita et Moribus Julii Agricolae* (29-38), which is the only source. It is not clear whether Norman had learned the speech in Latin or in English; given the rigours of education by the Reverend John Smith, it was possibly the former. However Tacitus was freely available in English translation. One such translation was *The Works of Tacitus*, translated by Thomas Gordon (London: T. Woodward and J. Peele, 1737). There were also earlier translations, including one by several hands published by Gillyflower (London, 1698). The quotation above comes from a later translation by Alfred John Church and William Jackson Brodribb (1864-76). To children like Norman, conscious of the wars with France, this speech could well have had a special appeal.]

[18][Written by Plato, this is a dialogue between Plato's main protagonist, Socrates, and Phaedrus. It is thought to have been composed around 370 BC. Although ostensibly about the topic of love, and a somewhat surprising choice for children of that age, the focus of the dialogue is on rhetoric. But the pederastic relationships common in ancient Greece are prominent in the dialogue.]

[19][A Latin text by Jean Huezet. It is a Latin primer first published in 1727, and was popular in both Europe and the United States, well into the early 19th century.]

[20][This was a Greek grammar printed and published by E.P. Williams at Eton College and at No. 5 Bridge Street, Blackfriars, London. It also contained some Latin work, and it seems likely that this is what it was used for at Eltham.]

I may here give a very strong opinion, that all languages ought in the first instance to be learnt by rote, leaving grammar to be learnt afterwards, if at all.

Mr Smith's plan was the opposite of this. We learnt the Latin grammar till I hated its very name, and were sometimes required to repeat as much as we could of it without making a mistake, as a matter of competition. He who got on farthest in the book received a sixpence as a reward.

Spelling was a matter to which Mr Smith paid considerable attention. The boys used to spell in rivalry with each other, as in the case of repeating the Latin grammar, but I do not recollect that any reward was given to the victor.

Mr Smith was no good penman and we made little progress in writing or arithmetic under his care. He was perhaps conscious of his deficiencies in these matters and therefore, for some time, hired a Master from Bromley, named Jones, who was perhaps the most beautiful penman that could be imagined. He came twice a week, not often enough to make his pupils great proficients. This as respects myself I have always lamented.[21] The act of writing is disagreeable to him who is conscious of his want of skill and facility, and becomes an uphill toil which is avoided as much as possible. Thus come the disagreements to correspondents, and illegible letters, which hide or distort the writer's meaning, instead of conveying it. In short, among the accomplishments, which an educated man ought to possess, I know of few more important than penmanship. Now by good penmanship, I do not mean, the power of making flourishes or ornamented characters, but that of writing easily, quickly and legibly a plain hand.

The shortcomings of Mr Smith in arithmetic teaching were still more important to me. Followed as they were by the deficiencies of Eton, they were the origin of my ignorance in every branch of mathematical science,

[21] [The reader will see from the plates of Norman's handwriting in this volume that his complaints were well founded.]

which has so far placed me behind all well-educated men.

Mr Jones, mentioned above, was a man of some mark. He always said, I suppose with truth, that he had been an Officer in the American War. He served as Sergeant, in my father's company of Bromley volunteers, and just before the Corps was disbanded at the creation of the Local Militia, he became Ensign.[22] He lived in the last house in the town, opposite the college, with a wife, two sons and a daughter, and my brother Henry[23] was placed with him for a time, as a boarder.[24] He was a fair, pursey man, I have him now before me. I know not what has become of the family.

The boys at Eltham were regularly drilled. We had each a musket and bayonet and cross belts. Our military instructors came from Woolwich. I recollect one among them very well. He was Sergt-Major Carlile, a good-looking man in a long blue coat, with a cocked-hat, white breeches and long black gaiters, powder in his hair, I suppose.[25] The practice of drilling in schools, common in the Great War, is now generally abandoned, and ought to be restored. Even now, I have not forgotten the manual and platoon exercise.

Our games at Eltham were cricket, prison bars, peg tops, eggs in the hat &c. I was rather a proficient in all, having great physical strength, some aptitude and a strong desire to excel in such matters. This I have preserved

---

[22] [Militia dated from Anglo Saxon times, but Militia Acts of 1761, 1768, and 1802, including powers of conscription, regulated the operation of Militia during the Napoleonic wars. The Militia were organised by counties and cities. Mr Jones has not been identified.]

[23] [Norman's brother Henry 1801-1867, 4th son and 6th child of George and Charlotte Norman.]

[24] [It is not clear how this came about; the context would suggest that Henry was a pupil at the Eltham school at the time. However even now, as Margaret Taylor has pointed out to us, the journey from the end of Bromley to the school in Eltham would take about 20 minutes by bus. A journey on horseback would take longer. It was however a good deal closer than Bromley Common was to the school. The college in 'the last house in town opposite the College' is a reference to Bromley College (see p. 383).]

[25] [The Royal Artillery garrison was at Woolwich 1746-2007, and Sergeant Major Carlile's uniform sounds like a Royal Artillery uniform of the period.]

through life, and have desired that my children should also excel in all games and exercises.

I well recollect that on one occasion, when we boys were struggling together, Mr Smith called out to me, 'well done, young Hercules'.

We used sometimes to take long walks and I then strove to act Robin Hood. My bow being pea-shooter and the sheriff and his associate, one of my companions. The Ballads relating to the brave outlaw greatly excited my imagination.

I first went to Eltham[26] after Easter, say in April 1801, when I was seven years and seven months old and remained there exactly four years, that is until Easter 1805. The first separation from home and family was exquisitely painful to me and no less so to my mother. I begged and entreated her not to send me and cried for hours. By these means I obtained a respite for a single day, but the day following I was sent to school, much to my astonishment, for this was the first occasion in my life when I found that tears and entreaties failed in their object with my parents. I may here observe that during the whole nine years, which I passed at Eltham and Eton, my parents never to the best of my knowledge, paid me a single visit.[27] This course was adopted advisably, not from any want of affection, but rather from an excess of it. The moment of separation and the looking forward to it, were so exquisitely painful to all of us, that it was thought a wise course, to render these trials as rare as possible.

I recollect an instance which proved the wisdom of this. Mr Wells[28] was

[26] [At that time Eltham was a rural parish, 13 miles round, with only the High Street built up. The London-Maidstone turnpike road passed through it.]

[27] [The Norman papers at Maidstone (C20/U310) contain letters written by Norman to his mother from the school at Eltham, and also from Eton as well as later letters from Germany, Norway, and Ireland and while travelling on the Continent, covering the years 1805-53 until his mother died.]

[28] [William Wells, 1729-1805, shipbuilder. He was the eldest son of Abraham Wells, who was also a shipbuilder. The Wells family had been shipbuilders since the 17th century. The building of ships for the East India trade proved highly profitable, and the Rotherhithe yard became one of the largest yards on the Thames.

living at Lee in a curious old house, then the property of the Boone family,[29] but since pulled down.[30] My father was there on a visit, and I was invited to pass[31] Sunday there to meet him, I did so, and passed the night sleepless and in tears thinking of the parting and return to school, which was to take place the next day. The room in which I was placed was hung with old tapestry, and the uncouth figures which surrounded me, appeared to my sad imagination to fix their eyes upon me and rather to gloat upon my woe. This did not tend to raise my spirits.

On only one occasion did I ever visit home from school, unless in case of illness. This was for the Whitsuntide Holy days, reckoned at two days, E.

---

William Wells traded in business with his brother John, who died in 1794. William Wells succeeded in extracting from a reluctant Navy Board a higher price for naval ships than that previously paid. Following this the firm built a series of warships. The firm was joined in 1788 by William's son John (1761-1848). After the death of the elder John Wells, William and his son John then controlled the firm with William inheriting his brother's estate at Bickley which had been purchased in 1759 and on which the elder John Wells built Bickley Hall in 1780. The Wells family had lived in the Bromley area before the Norman family. Norman records in the Bromley Memoir that the title deeds of Chelsfield Hall Farm showed that it was owned by the Wells family as early as 1735. After the death of William Wells the elder in 1805, his son John very largely withdrew from the business and became involved in Kent politics, dying in 1848. Another son was Thomas Wells the Admiral (see p. 15). A third son, William Wells junior, 1768-1847, was involved in the shipbuilding business, supervising the building of battleships at Blackwall during the French wars, but retired to Penshurst in 1811 and became famous as an art collector, building on a substantial inheritance of paintings (see p. 99). After the Napoleonic wars, the shipbuilding industry suffered a severe recession, intensified by the number of prize ships which became available on the market.]

[29] [According to Norman's Bromley Memoir, the Boone family 'pretended to be de Bohuns [and] lived in the old house at Lee, now pulled down, and which was occupied by Mr John Wells.']

[30] [The tithe apportionment map of 1839 for Eltham shows 'Site of Boone's House'. It was called Lee Place. Parts were 16th and 17th century. Lee Manor House, on the other side of Old Road, Eltham, was the property of Sir Francis Baring. The Boone family was a long established one in the neighbourhood, and the Boone tombs in Lee Old Church Yard cover the years 1683-1819. Lee Place had three gables to the front of it, and 21 chimneys. It was demolished in about 1825, when the road was straightened. There was a lake that had been the moat of the medieval Lee Manor House. We owe this information to Margaret Taylor.]

[31] [Norman later changed this to 'remain'.]

Knight then Austen[32] and Patton[33] accompanied me.

While at Mr Smith's, Cordery the Groom used to ride over to enquire about me every week or fortnight.[34] I went to the gate to speak to him and he carried back intelligence as to my health. Dr Smith, who dined occasionally with his Cousin, used also to make report as to my condition.

I took very little money to Eltham, indeed I required very little. There was no shop where sweets were sold, and to which the boys had access. So that excepting for the purchase of a bat or some other plaything and perhaps a book, I know not how we spent the little we had.

I may here remark that I never while at school asked for money until a good deal was required for my leaving expenses at Eton, nor was any ever sent to me. I was not very abundantly, yet still sufficiently supplied, and I cut my coat according to my cloth. Three pounds and a few shillings,[35]

---

32 [The brother of Jane Austen, Edward Austen, 1767-1852, assumed the surname of Knight in 1812. He had succeeded his cousin Thomas Knight who died childless in 1794. His wife was Elizabeth Bridges, 1773-1808. Edward Knight their son, still named Austen when he was at Eltham with Norman, was a little younger than the latter, having been born in 1794.]

33 [Possibly Robert Patton, 1791-1883, son of Charles Patton, Captain, Royal Navy. He entered the navy in 1804, served at the battle of Trafalgar in 1805, and retired as Admiral in 1864.]

34 [Cordery had been an indoor servant, and had then gone into business, running a coach. He failed, losing both his own money and £100 belonging to George Norman, Norman's father. He returned as a gardener and then became a groom. He stayed until the Rookery was rented by Sir Henry Meux (see p. 241) in 1821. He subsequently kept the Rose and Crown in Bromley. According to Norman's Bromley Memoir, Cordery was 'rather shatter-brained owing to a fall'. He subsequently married a lady of means.]

35 [Maxwell Lyte, *History of Eton College, 1440-1910*, London: Macmillan, 1911 pp. 369-70, provides some information about Eton costs. For a half year, from Christmas 1800 to the 25 June following, the dames would charge something like £15 for 'board', £2.12s.6d for 'bed', £2.2s for 'fire and candle', 14s for study, and £2.2s for 'washing and mending'. The total was thus £22.10s.6d, or £22, 52.5 pence, in the decimal currency equivalent. In addition a further two guineas (£2.2s.) were payable to the Headmaster, four guineas to the boy's tutor, and one guinea to a servant. Thus a further £7.7s was added to the account. A further 6s.8d (one third of a pound) was payable to the Headmaster for 'candles, post, chaple [sic], fields, boats'. Further additions to the minute itemisation included 1s for music on 4 July, and 1s.6d for music on 'Election Saturday'. The boy himself received a further £1.7s by way of 'allowance', and 2s.6d on promotion to

was what I took to Eton, and things were dearer then than now, and our allowance was only two small rolls at breakfast and nothing to eat at tea, so that something necessarily went for simple food.

At Eton latterly, I always paid my bills before I went home, reserving a certain portion of what I brought with me for that purpose. I was never without money.

I must here remark that peculiarity in my money arrangements was in no wise connected with any want of liberality on the part of my father. On the contrary, although simple in his own habits and tastes, he was generous, and even careless as to money, and disposed as respects myself to be rather lavish than otherwise. This will be sufficiently proved by facts which I shall have hereafter to relate.

Mr Smith's house at Eltham was situated to the North West of the Church,[36] and opposite the Chequers Public House.[37] It presents at present very nearly the appearance which it did in my day. The room in which I slept, was on the first floor to the left of the doorway. It contained three or four beds. An addition was made to the house at the back while I was at school.[38]

---

the Remove. In addition there were other small sums – in the case discussed by Maxwell Lyte, these included 2s.6d for mending windows, and a further 8s.2d for washing waistcoats and breeches. Thus £35 would comfortably have covered a half year at Eton.]

[36][The church of St John the Baptist was in the centre of Eltham, on Eltham High Street. ]

[37][Though Norman does not make this clear, this was the vicarage. It was indeed opposite the Chequers public house, and a later vicar, complaining in 1870 of the state of the vicarage, included in his list of complaints the location of the vicarage opposite the Chequers. (Rev. W.J. Sowerby to the Bishop of Rochester, Greater London archives DR/OP/146. We are indebted to Margaret Taylor for this reference.) It is clear from available plans of the vicarage that it was, however, spacious, and capable of providing boarding accommodation, though Norman also records that his brother Henry was boarded out.]

[38]I saw the house and the windows of my sleeping room yesterday. [Note added by Norman dated 11 July 1864. This 'addition' was apparently a canvas lined wooden erection, of which a later vicar, the Reverend W.J. Sowerby, complained bitterly to the Bishop of Rochester in 1870. Sowerby's complaint, in the letter cited in footnote 36 above, was that the vicarage was in a most dilapidated state

The normal number of pupils was twelve. I will name a few of them. Colonel John Wells[39] R.E. son of the Admiral who left just after my arrival, and has now been dead for two or three years. Doctor Thomas Mayo P.C.P.,[40] John Mayo and H. Mayo his brothers, the latter a very distinguished surgeon, Edw[ar]d Knight (when at school Austen) now of Godmersham and Chawton, with G. Knight and Henry [Knight] his brothers.[41] G. K[night] was the introducer of throwing bowling into cricket although a poor player himself.[42] He married Lady Nelson. G. Knight became a Major in the Army and married Miss Portal.

---

and should, he argued, be demolished. Apart from his complaint that many of the rooms were unfit for habitation, and that the proximity of the vicarage to a tavern called the Chequer's Inn, confirmed by Norman, caused problems, he told the Bishop that the large room added at the back was a 'weatherboarded erection canvassed inside with slated roof and exposed to both extremes of temperature'.]

39 [See the reference on p. 15 to the sons of Admiral Wells.]

40 [Dr Thomas Mayo, 1790-1871, son of John Mayo, physician 1761-1818, FRCP 1819, doctor at Tunbridge Wells, 1818-35, Wimpole Street 1835-62. His brother was Herbert Mayo, 1796-1852, surgeon, FRS 1828, FRCS 1843, founder of Middlesex Hospital Medical School in 1836. John Mayo took Holy Orders.]

41 [Edward Knight, Norman's contemporary at Eltham, and then called Austen (see p. 31) 1794-1879. He succeeded to the estates at Godmersham and Chawton in 1852. He married Mary Dorothea Knatchbull, daughter of his brother in law Sir Edward Knatchbull, who opposed the marriage. Knatchbull relented after ten years, but the next year his daughter died in childbirth. Edward Knight then married Adela Portal, and had another family. His brother George Thomas, born in 1795, married in 1837 Hilaire, the widow of Lord Nelson. He died in 1867. Another brother, Henry Knight, 1797-1843, of Milgate, Kent, became a Major in the army. William Knight, 1798-1873, who succeeded to the family occupation as Rector of Steventon, Hampshire, married Caroline, the eldest daughter of Sir John Portal, of Laverstoke, Hants, an old friend and neighbour of the Austens. Finally, there was Brook John, 1808-78.]

42 [John Major, in his important history of cricket, *More than a Game: The Story of Cricket's Early Years*, London: Harper Collins (2007, p.134), does not agree with Norman's assessment of George Knight: 'George Knight was a round-arm bowler of some skill. More importantly, he had intellect, cool judgment, and a gift for words that must have been genetic. For Knight was not the name with which his father had been born. That name was altogether more famous.' The reference is of course to George Knight's aunt, Jane Austen. The Knights were a famous cricketing family who succeeded in forcing MCC to permit round arm bowling. It is worth noting that the Austen boys were at Eltham preparing for Winchester, which certainly suggests that the school was a good deal better than Norman indicates.]

I proceed with my enumeration. Mann a son of Mr Mann of Linton,[43] R.W. Sibthorp[44] who became a clergyman, and after oscillating between high and low Church, became a Papist, and then once more a Protestant. W[illiam] H[enr]y Scott, a son of Chancellor Eldon and who, although apparently dull at school, afterwards evinced considerable talent and died of intemperance at about the age of forty.[45] I was also at Eton with him. Miller, the son I believe of a farmer in Mid Kent, and his brother Giles Miller, afterwards an Attorney at Goodhurst and a man of great ability.[46] Patton, whose father, a naval man, lived on Blackheath, and Brummell, son of a Treasury official who resides in Berners Street, F. Pigou of gunpowder fame.[47]

---

43[Robert Mann, at one time a London merchant, acquired Linton Place, near East Farleigh, in the 18th century and built a modest country house, in which he lived until his death in 1751/2. The estate passed to his eldest son and then to Sir Horatio Mann, c.1701-86, Bt, a diplomat who was Envoy to Tuscany 1740-86, and the second son of Robert Mann. He was created a Baronet in 1755, and succeeded to the Linton estate on the death of his elder brother. He died at Florence, unmarried, in 1786 and was succeeded by Sir Horace Mann, his nephew, to whom he bequeathed the estate. Horatio Mann, who was at Eton with Norman, was the eldest son of another member of the same family, James Mann of Linton. Horatio Mann was born in April 1790, proceeded from Eton to Trinity College, Cambridge in 1808, BA 1813. He was Rector of Mawgan and St Martin in Meneage, Cornwall 1816-46. He died in a fall from his carriage in 1846. His father James Mann had married in 1786 Lucy Mann, the daughter of Sir Horace Mann who had succeeded his uncle in the Linton estates in Kent, and as 2nd Bt in 1786. James Mann was a notable athlete and cricketer.]

44[The Reverend Richard Waldo Sibthorp, 1792-1879, brother of the famous reactionary Charles de Laet Waldo Sibthorp, 1783-1855. Dean of Divinity at Oxford 1818-27, became a Catholic in 1841, ordained priest 1842, returned to the Church of England in 1843, re-admitted as a Catholic priest 1865.]

45[Chancellor Eldon was John Scott, 1751-1838, first Earl of Eldon, Lord Chancellor 1801-6, 1807-27. William Henry Scott was his second and only surviving son. He died in 1832. It is possible that Norman is mistaken about the presence of William Henry Scott at Eton. The lists for Eton include a James Edward Scott in the Remove in 1805. (At that time Norman was in the 4th form.) Eldon's other son, John, died in 1805; see p. 38. Eldon had eloped in his youth with Bessie Surtees, whose family, Newcastle bankers, opposed the match.]

46[John Miller is named in the will of James Ballard (see p. 23). He appears to have been a trustee, and was described as a farmer of Bowhill in the parish of Yalding. He could well have been the farmer to whom Norman refers.]

47[Frederick Pigou, in partnership with Miles Andrews and Richard Wilks, had bought a former paper mill at Wilmington, near Dartford, Kent, in 1778, after the previous owners, who had already converted it to a powder mill, had become

I formed no particular friendship with any of these boys. Edw[ar]d Knight was my classmate and sat next to me. With him I often quarrelled, he was not good-tempered, nor perhaps was I. It was not the custom of the school to fight in form, but I can recollect our pulling out each other's hair out by handfuls during schooltime, and that the subsequent pain and swelling was a great annoyance.

Our house at Eltham then had, as it has now, a good garden and field, planted with elms and walnuts attached to it. The walnut season furnished us with much amusement, as we took part in the threshing. We had little gardens allotted to each boy, in which we cultivated flowers.

Besides the amusement derived from games played in the grounds, we used occasionally to take walks with Mr Smith, visiting Shooters Hill, Pope St, Mottingham &c. No usher was ever kept. Mr S undertook the whole work of instruction, excepting writing and arithmetic. Discipline was by no means very severe. I have known boys flogged now and then, but blows on the hand with a flat ruler were the usual corporal punishment, and these were not severe.

The chief residents at Eltham, when I was there, were as follows.[48] Mr

---

bankrupt. The Pigou who was at school with Norman was a member of this family. By 1841 a member of the family called Clarence Pigou, son of Frederick Pigou of Putney, was reputed to be the richest man in Dartford. He may well have been the one at Eltham with Norman; he was born in 1798 (matriculated at Christ Church College, Oxford, 2 December 1815 aged 17), and though five years younger than Norman could have joined the school before Norman left for Eton in 1805. He was a Fellow of Merton College 1821-58, but the wealth referred to may have been inherited rather than a direct result of his own involvement in business. Members of the Pigou family were also merchants involved in the trade with China, and one member of the family, Frederick Pigou, 1711-92, was a Director of the East India Company.]

[48] [One notable figure whom Norman does not mention was the banker Sir Francis Baring, who lived in the adjoining parish of Lee in the years 1797-1810. He was one of the early customers of the bank of Martin and Stone, and thus was connected to Norman through the latter's marriage to Sibella Stone. Richard Stone II married in 1766 Mary Herring, and her sister married the then Francis Baring. In 1764 John and Francis Baring had opened an account at The Grasshopper as the bank was styled. See G. Chandler, *Four Centuries of Banking* (London: Batsford, 1964) vol. I pp. 148-51.]

Shaw Brook, the Rector[49] during more than 50 years, and the brother of Sir Shaw of Kenward[50] near Wateringbury to whom for the next baronet, he left a considerable fortune, now dissipated.[51]

The Shaw family, received after the restoration a beneficial lease of the crown property at Eltham, which they continued to enjoy until a few years ago.[52] It was given as a reward for services rendered to the royalist cause. At

[49] [The Vicar (not Rector, Norman was mistaken) of Eltham was the Reverend John Kenward Shaw, later Shaw Brooke, 1758-1840. On this remarkable individual see R.R.C. Gregory and others, *The Story of Royal Eltham* (Eltham: Kentish District Times Co Ltd, 1910). He was Vicar of Eltham, and Rector of Hurstpierpoint, Sussex. He died 16 December 1840 at Eltham. Such was his standing that a memorial booklet of 22 pages, *An Humble Tribute of Regard and Respect to the Memory of the Rev. J.K. Shaw Brooke, MA by the Reverend W.T. Myers MA* (London: Roake and Varty, 1841) was published. Shaw Brooke was born in London 22 December 1758, but grew up at Eltham Lodge, the family seat built by the Shaw family. BA Oxford 1778, MA 1782, Fellow of All Souls 1783. In 1783 he took Holy Orders and, in the same year, became Vicar of Eltham. (He succeeded as Vicar a Dr Pinnell who had himself been Vicar since 1749 and in 1775 became a Prebendary of Rochester Cathedral.) In 1796, on the death of Mrs Brooke, he succeeded to the property of the late Joseph Brooke of West Malling in Kent, and assumed the additional name of Brooke. He also resigned his Fellowship of All Souls. His funeral on 23 December 1840 seems to have been a grand occasion.]

[50] [Sir John Gregory Shaw, 5th Bt, 1756-1831, of Kenward Park, Yalding, Kent. He was succeeded by Sir John Kenward Shaw, 6th Bt, 1783-1857, Colonel of West Kent Militia 1832-53. The family was descended from Sir John Shaw, 1st Bt, c.1615-80, a 'customs farmer' who supported the royal cause during the Commonwealth and was rewarded with a multiplicity of public offices after the Restoration; see the following note.]

[51] [Sir John Shaw, 1st Bt, c.1615-80, was a customs farmer (one who collected customs revenue on commission). During the Commonwealth he supported the royal cause, providing money for the king, and acting as a channel of communication between the exiled court and the English royalists, an extremely risky activity under the Cromwellian regime. After the Restoration in 1660 he was rewarded for his loyalty and bravery with a variety of lucrative official positions, and in 1662 became part of a syndicate to farm customs revenue. He obtained a lease of the Crown manor of Eltham in Kent in 1663, and built a new house (see next fn). When the customs farm syndicate was deprived of its franchise in 1671, Shaw lost his main source of revenue, but still held minor government offices. He was knighted in 1660, and created a baronet in 1665. His heirs retained the lease of Eltham until 1839.]

[52] [Eltham Palace was a medieval building which was in royal use from the early 14th century until 1526. Much of it has been demolished, and only the Great Hall now survives. The Great Hall itself came close to demolition, but a campaign to save it was successful and it was restored in 1828, though it continued to be

length the time came, when it was thought right to make the most of national estates. The lease was not renewed and the Shaws have since gone to decay. One of them was drowned[53] at Eton off the Brocas[54] when I was there. Captain Richard Lewin,[55] brother of Mr T. Lewin[56] of the Hollies, Bexley and father of the present T. Lewin was another of the Eltham aristocracy. First Sir W. Fawcett, Adj[utan]t General,[57] and then Mr Farrer, a master in

---

used as a barn. Henry VIII was the last monarch to spend substantial amounts of money or time at Eltham. After the 16th century the palace fell into disrepair, and Sir John Shaw seems to have played his part in reducing it to a ruin. It is quite possible that the palace was used as a quarry for the building of his house, Eltham Lodge, for Shaw did not occupy the palace, but rebuilt Eltham Lodge in the great park to the south east of the palace. The new house was designed by the architect Hugh May, 1621-84. Sir John Shaw also rebuilt, in 1667, the north aisle of Eltham Church. The palace was occupied in the 1930s by a wealthy member of the Courtauld family who built a new house adjoining the Great Hall.]

[53][Lewis James Shaw died 15 May 1807. See *Times* 18 May 1807, 2d. The paper reported that he was in the boat with some other boys and drowned when 'owing to some mismanagement, the boat filled' and he stepped into deep water by accident in attempting to reach the bank. He was the son of Sir John Gregory Shaw (see p. 36).]

[54][A large riverside meadow, just across the river Thames from Windsor Castle. The name comes from the Brocas family, who were local nobility in the 13th century.]

[55][In the mid 18th century one Richard Lewin became commander of an East India Company ship. He married in 1752 Mary Brown who died in 1760 or 1772. He died in 1810. He started a connection with the Company which was to continue through his sons Thomas and Richard Lewin, as well as his grandson Thomas Herbert Lewin. He was the father of Thomas Lewin, 1753-1837/43, of the Hollies. Another son of the sea captain was a second Richard Lewin who also became captain of an East India ship. He was born about 1757, married H. Vanderpoel, and died 7 June 1832 aged 75, as recorded on a memorial tablet in Eltham Church. He was thus the brother of the father of Harriet Grote, as indicated by Norman.]

[56][Thomas Lewin, 1753-1837/43 (sources differ), retired employee of the East India Company, father of Harriet Lewin, later Mrs Grote. Mr Lewin had twelve children of whom Harriet was the fifth. Seven of them were boys, and they included another Thomas Lewin, and Frederick Mortimer Lewin born in 1798; it was presumably to him that Norman was referring. Though the manuscript is unclear, it is clear from the 1860 edition of Burke's *Landed Gentry* that the master of the Hollies at that date was Frederick Mortimer Lewin. There is a portrait of the younger Thomas Lewin (1797-1872) in R.R.C. Gregory, *Royal Eltham* (see p. 36 above) opposite p. 273.]

[57][Sir William Fawcett, 1727-1804, professional soldier, Deputy Adjutant General 1766, Adjutant General 1781, Lieutenant General 1782, full General 1796. He was a prolific translator of military works, including *Regulations for the Prussian*

chancery and a relative of Lord Eldon lived at Eltham Place.[58] He and Mr S. Brook once invited us boys to an evening entertainment.

Mr Boldero the banker,[59] and uncle to C[h]ar[le]s Boulton[60] lived first at Avery Hill, and afterwards in the last house on the right, in the road leading to the palace.[61]

---

*Infantry* (1754), the first English translation of Saxe's *Reveries* (see pp. 55, 58) (1757), *Regulations for the Prussian Cavalry* (1759), *Regulations for the Exercise of Riflemen and Light Infantry* by Francis de Rottenburg (1798). He also updated Bland's *Treatise of Military Discipline* (1759).]

[58] [The eldest son of Lord Eldon, John Scott, born 8 March 1774, died 24 December 1805, married in 1804 Henrietta Elizabeth White Ridley (died 1853). She married secondly, in 1811, James William Farrer, Master in Chancery, who died in 1863.]

[59] [A banking business, established in the 1730s by Thomas Minors, was joined by a member of the Boldero family in 1742, and the firm became Minors and Boldero. It was later (1760) Boldero, Carter and Co., though members of the Boldero family were later involved in another bank, after some kind of rupture took place in 1770. One of the firms ceased to exist in 1812; this was Boldero, Lushington, Boldero and Lushington, of 30, Cornhill. It is listed in the Post Office London Directory for 1812, but not in that for 1817. The other stopped payment in the crisis of 1825. However the latter seems to have severed its Boldero connections in 1790, so that the one to which Norman refers is the one that disappeared in 1812. In R.R.C. Gregory's *Story of Royal Eltham* p. 327 (see p. 36) a map of 1790 is reproduced, showing part of the coach road from New Cross to Maidstone, and Mr Boldero's house, Avery Hill, is shown, with his name, to the north of the coach road and west of what is now the crossroads with New Eltham. The house, rebuilt in the late 19th century, is now part of the Avery Hill Campus of Greenwich University. Despite the Italian sound of the name Boldero, the family seems to have been resident in Suffolk for many generations. The Boldero referred to here was probably Henry Boldero. His father was Edward Gale Boldero, the only surviving son of Daniel Boldero of Humbertoft, Norfolk and his mother was Mary Lewyns. Edward Gale Boldero died in 1753 aged 53, or 1761. Henry Boldero of Avery Hill, Eltham, who married a Miss Randal, had only one surviving child, Edward Gale Boldero, a Governor of Christ's Hospital. He seems to have inherited Avery Hill, which he is said to have sold to a Mr Thomas Hale. He married Sophia, the daughter of John Cornwall. In a legal document dated 1819 both Henry Boldero and Edward Gale Boldero are named as being former bankers, now bankrupts.]

[60] [Charles Boulton was later associated with Norman in the Sun Fire Office; see pp. 323-4.]

[61] [Mr Boldero may have moved there from force of financial circumstances connected with his bankruptcy (see fn. 59). A number of small banks had failed in the years towards the end of the Napoleonic wars. The last house on the right has been identified for us by Miss Margaret Taylor. It is what is now known as '38 Courtyard'. 36-38 are medieval and Tudor buildings, now known together as The Lord Chancellor's Lodgings. The road leading to Eltham Palace was a spur

Lord Rancliffe had just left the large place opposite F. Lewin's before my time.[62] Warburton's father had also left Eltham,[63] but his brother Chas Warburton was a schoolfellow of mine, whom I omitted to mention a page or two back. He was a strange being, and as we thought rather cracky. He did not possess the ability of his brother Henry. He became, I have been told a dissenting minister, and died early. John W. Warburton, the father, was a timber merchant, and great customer of my father.[64] His yard was next to Lett's at Lambeth.

The parish clerk was named Whomes,[65] and was uncle to him of Chisle-

leading south from Eltham High Street.]

[62][George Augustus Henry Anne Parkyns, 2nd Baron Rancliffe, 1785-1850, MP Minehead 1806-7, Nottingham 1812-20, 1826-30, Provincial Grand Master of Freemasons, Leicestershire, 1812-50. He lived at Park Farm Place, Eltham, having married the daughter of its owner, Sir William James, who died just before the wedding, which took place in December 1793. The property was extremely extensive. Severndroog Castle, a triangular folly, was built the following year, 1784, on Shooters Hill, in his memory. The property thus extended all the way from Park Farm Place, which was north of Eltham High Street up to Shooters Hill, a distance of about one mile. It was thus indeed, as Norman writes, a 'large place'. We are indebted to Margaret Taylor for this information.]

[63][Henry Warburton, 1784-1858, politician, ran his father's timber business 1808-31, FRS 1809, member of the Political Economy Club, MP Bridport 1826-41, Kendal 1843-47, friend of both Norman and Overstone.]

[64][John Warburton was a timber merchant. He is listed in a 1794 directory as a merchant at Cuper's Bridge, Lambeth. The firm was still at that address in 1812, according to the Post Office London Directory, though by that time it was in the name of John Warburton's son Henry. Cuper's Gardens was the name of an 18th century pleasure garden on the south side of the Thames in Lambeth. There was a continuous line of timber yards from Stangate (site of the present Westminster Bridge) downstream to Cuper's Bridge (Waterloo Bridge site). The wood yards imported timber, cut it into planks, and seasoned it in large stacks. Norman says that 'Warburton's father', by whom he means John Warburton, had left Eltham. It seems possible that he had moved to Chevening, as a servant recorded as being employed by him in 1791 is believed to have moved there. However we are indebted to Elizabeth Finn for the information that he does not appear on the land tax returns for Chevening for 1796 or 1800.]

[65][Richard Whomes was parish clerk of Eltham, and first appeared in parish registers in 1785 in connection with the death of a child, but is first recorded as parish clerk in 1795. His occupation was 'breechesmaker' – essentially tailoring. His wife Ann (or Anna) worked in the same occupation. We are indebted to Margaret Taylor for this information.]

hurst. The surgeon named Laurence[66] was brother to Dr L. of *Rolliad* notoriety.[67] Todman a Nurseryman[68] has left descendants, and so has John Green,[69] a farmer, who resided at South end on the road to Chislehurst, as his son does now. Rob[er]t Green, a brother died early.

While at Eltham I had one most severe and dangerous illness. It occurred I think in the Summer of 1804. It was a case of internal inflammation, and I

[66][The brother of French Laurence (see next fn.) was a medical practitioner called John Laurence, whose name was spelt in the same way as that of the contributor to *The Rolliad.* John Laurence had two children baptised at Eltham, one of whom, baptised 31 July 1794, was christened Richard French Laurence.]

[67][French Laurence 1757-1809 was born at Bath, the eldest of the four children of a watchmaker. He was educated at Winchester and Oxford, and became an associate of Charles James Fox. He published political pamphlets, and was one of the authors of a satirical poem called *The Rolliad.* He succeeded Edmund Burke as the editor of the *Annual Register.* He was also much involved in the impeachment of Warren Hastings. *The Rolliad* itself, published in 1791, is regarded as a pioneering work of British satire. It was directed principally at the government of the younger Pitt. It was originally published in serial form in the *Morning Herald* in 1784-5. Laurence was not the principal author; that was Joseph Richardson. Laurence was one of the members of the Esto Perpetua club, and it is not known for certain who amongst the members were the authors of the *Rolliad*, apart from Laurence and Richardson. The names of the members included Lord John Townshend, later Lord Sydney of Frognal, with whom the Norman family had connections. *The Rolliad* itself took its name from one of Pitt's supporters, John Rolle, MP, and was a collection of Whig political satires directed against Pitt himself. Laurence became Regius Professor of Civil Law at Oxford in 1796, and was an absentee. In the same year he was elected MP for Peterborough.]

[68][Todman's nursery was where Eltham Hill Technology School for Girls is now located. It is to the south side of Eltham Hill. In earlier parish records, dating from 1785, two members of the Todman family are described as gardeners.]

[69][John Green's South End House survived, though decaying, until about 1980 when it was revived as apartments. It was to the east of the Foots Cray road out of Eltham.]

was removed home before the crisis. Mr Scott[70] and Dr Fraser,[71] the latter of whom resided in the house at Widmore, since burnt down, attended me. I became delirious and so continued for some days. After the return of my reason, I found myself so much reduced, that I could not stand. I recollect the ravenous appetite I then felt and which I was not at first allowed to gratify. After some time I was allowed to eat my fill and a whole boiled chicken was not too much to satiate me.

When quite free from disease, my parents took me to Hastings for change of air, and we lived at the Swan Inn, then the only one in the place.[72] My sick bed was that in my mother's room usually occupied by my father and mother. My usual bed when at home was a small one, by the side of the

[70][James Scott, MRCS, 1770-1849, a general practitioner living at Clay Hill, Beckenham. He was particularly successful in the treatment of chronic ulcers and diseased joints, and the father of John Scott, a distinguished surgeon who predeceased him. Of Dr Scott, Norman wrote in his Bromley Memoir: 'He was most kind, honourable and generous, inspiring respect and love among all who knew him. His professional education had not probably been pushed very far, but he possessed mental qualities almost amounting to genius. His patients had the greatest confidence in him, often with reason, for his application of adhesive plaster and bandages was a most useful advance in the art which has spread his fame even to Paris. He told me, that he made in one year over £11000, yet he was most liberal, both in his charges and mode of living. He left a fortune of over £100,000, a large sum to have made from nothing. I gave him a Silver Claret jug, which cost £80, as a token of friendship and respect.']

[71][Oddly Norman makes no mention of Dr Fraser in the Bromley Memoir, even though he devotes some space to local members of the medical profession. They were Drs Read, Tagnton, Scott, Child, Roberts, and Ilott (both father and son). Norman's opinion of them was not high. Of Read and Child he wrote: 'Their medical skill, I apprehend, hardly could have extended with safety to their patients beyond the giving a dose of salts, a black dose or James's powder. In short I apprehend that in Anatomy and the treatment of disease they must have been more ignorant than Skinner or Bath, the Horse Doctors now, yet the length of life in those days among the easy classes was hardly shorter than it is now.' Widmore is now part of Bromley. Widmore Lodge was originally owned by the Tweedy family which, like the Fraser family, was of Scottish origin. The Tweedy coat of arms contains a reference to the Fraser connection.]

[72][Hastings enjoyed a number of hotels in the early 19th century. Pigot's Directory of Kent for 1823 lists the Albion, the Emory, the Castle, the Marine, the Royal Oak 'commercial', the Seaside, and the Swan, at which the Norman family stayed. The proprietor of the Swan at the date of the directory was George Robinson. It was in the High Street.]

larger, and this I retained till I was 14 or 15.

The first introduction of Mr Scott, as medical attendant in our household, took place at this time. Dr Fraser, who was the father of Jack F[raser], the rough Colleger[73] predicted his future fame. When I was recovering from this illness, my father made me kneel down in the library and thank God for the mercy shewn me in preserving my life.

In December 1801 commenced our visits to Hastings which were continued at intervals for many years. The first house we inhabited belonged to Slatterley the surgeon and was near to the battery on the West.[74]

Hastings had then not extended beyond the original town, and merely occupied the valley between the Castle Hill and East Hill, while to the North its limits were All Saints Church and the Milwards house. The population did not I think reach 3000, and comprehended the finest men and handsomest women one could see anywhere. Its chief industrial occupations were fishing, smuggling and gambling. The smuggling was carried on in the most open manner by large cutters, over 100 tons, with crews 30 to 40 strong.[75] They might always be recognised by their fixed boatsprits,[76] being exposed to extra

[73] [This was presumably Sir John Fraser, a King's Scholar at Eton (and thus a 'Colleger') in 1805, Captain 8th Light Dragoons, on staff in India, afterwards secretary to the Chief Commissioner of the Ionian Islands.]

[74] [John Slatterley of Hastings St Clement, surgeon. The battery to which Norman refers was sited on the sea front at the eastern end of East Parade, near the fish market in St Clement Hastings.]

[75] [Norman's estimate of the size of the vessels and crews is, surprisingly, an underestimate. The cutters had crews of up to 100, and vessels of 250 and even, in the case of one vessel called the Liberty, 300 tons. Moreover they were heavily armed and must have been formidable fighting vessels. They carried up to 20 'carriage guns' and 16 'swivel guns', and each member of the crew was armed with a cutlass and small arm. A number of vessels would share the same name, which no doubt helped to confuse the authorities. Details of a number of vessels are to be found in the remarkable *Part 2* (1955) of the book *Hastings Saga* by M.A.N. Marshall referred to on p. 44 below.]

[76] [Norman's manuscript is clear but the correct word is 'bowsprit', believed to be not an English compound but coming from the Dutch word 'boegspriet'. There is an alternative 'boltsprit' but this is extremely rare (it is not in Fowler) and Norman did not write that.]

penalties if captured with running boatsprits.[77] You saw them anchored in the road before their departure for Flushing or after they had run their tubs of spirits without let or molestation from the authorities. They resisted the custom house officers when strong enough, and loss of life occasionally occurred in consequence. They were I think employed by the government to obtain intelligence, and in 1809 some of them piloted the expedition to the Scheld.[78] Much capital was employed in their trade which possessed the full sympathy of the Hastingites. A person named Wenham was the leading adventurer.[79]

[77][In 1786, in an attempt to combat smuggling, a law (24 GEO 3 c.47) was passed which required cutters to be licensed. A sloop was not required to be licensed. When the bowsprit was fixed, the vessel was classified as a sloop, and when it was a 'running bowsprit', that is it could be extended or retracted, it was classified as a cutter and thus required a licence. Cutters had a larger sail area, which gave them more speed, and were the vessels normally used for smuggling. However simply bolting the bowsprit in place would not, legally, convert a cutter into a sloop, so that the Hastings cutters were probably made with fixed bowsprits. Cutters could be stopped to check if they were licensed, which might result in the detection of contraband.]

[78][This is a reference to the Walcheren expedition commanded by the Duke of York in 1809. The Scheldt is a long river in northern France and the Low Countries, with Antwerp on its banks. It was thus of considerable strategic importance, but unfortunately the campaign was an unmitigated disaster, due largely to military and logistical incompetence. 40,000 soldiers, with 15,000 horse and artillery, were landed at Walcheren on 30 July 1809. 4,000 troops died, but only 106 of those perished in combat. The British seized the swampy island of Walcheren at the mouth of the Scheldt, but the troops were overcome with disease, primarily malaria. The troops were finally withdrawn on 9 December 1809. According to M.R. Howard (*British Medical Journal*, 18 December 1999) it was a medical catastrophe involving not only malaria but typhoid, typhus and dysentery. The senior medical staff in the army seem to have displayed astonishing indifference to the fate of the rank and file. The role of the Hastings smugglers in providing pilotage may have been connected with the fact that they sailed, as armed privateers, under 'Letters of Marque' issued by the Admiralty which gave them freedom to engage enemy ships, which they did to considerable effect and private profit.]

[79][The Wenhams were a large family, with extensive interests in smuggling, and were intermarried with other smuggling families. The identity of the 'leading adventurer' can be established from a later reference in Norman's Autobiography when Norman's father, to save money, let the house at Bromley to the brewer Meux, and rented a house 'belonging to old Wenham the Smuggler on the East Hill'. This house belonged to James Wenham, certainly the leading member of the family at the time, and thus the 'leading adventurer' was James Wenham 1749-1826. The information about this extraordinary family, and about James Wenham

The gambling above alluded to took place usually on the Strand and when the weather was so bad, as to keep the fishermen on shore. I have frequently seen them tossing for guinea and pound notes and many were reduced to poverty by this pernicious practice, which invariably lends to prodigality in ordinary expenditure.[80] A man who is constantly winning or losing pounds will naturally neglect shillings or pence.

Hastings and the neighbourhood were full of troops in the Great War rather to the detriment of female chastity. There was a range of barracks above the town, others at Battle and Bexhill, the German legion being stationed at the latter place.[81] In the summer, camps were formed in various

---

in particular, is to be found in M.A.N. Marshall, *Hastings Saga* (London: St Catherine Press, 1953), an extremely rare book. (We are indebted to Christopher Whittick for the discovery of this work.) The frontispiece of the book is actually a picture of East Hill House, which belonged to James Wenham. Remarkably, since Marshall's book was published in 1953, some time before the discovery of Norman's Autobiography, the tenancy of Norman's father, referred to above, is mentioned in the book. Marshall's book, which incorporates earlier work by other researchers, contains information about the commercial activities of the Wenham family, and about the smuggling industry of Hastings. The government had been hoist with its own petard. In a situation in which smuggling was a major activity on the south coast, it had encouraged the building and arming of privateers at Hastings, particularly following the outbreak of war with France. However, as Norman relates, the smugglers came to rule the town. The most openly active smuggler in the family was William Wenham (1742-98), some of whose ships were owned jointly with James Wenham. William was a great deal less discreet than James, and eventually he found it necessary to flee to exile in France. However, though the government did make spasmodic attempts to control the smuggling, and to reinstate its authority through the employment of troops, the smugglers were, for the most part, able to pursue their activities without interference.

The smuggling was big business, especially for the Wenhams. Of the 38 cutters listed in *Hastings Saga Part 2* (1955), no fewer than 16 were wholly or partly owned by James and William Wenham, and they owned virtually all of the big vessels. The capital investment must have been very substantial indeed, and though some of this will have been financed by prize money, through raids on French shipping, there can be no doubt that some of the profits of smuggling were ploughed back into the fleet of armed privateers.]

[80] [One guinea was 21 shillings, or £1.05 in decimal currency. The 2009 equivalent of that would be £58.51.]

[81] [The King's German Legion was a German military unit 1803-16. It had the distinction of being the only German force to fight without interruption against the French during the Napoleonic occupation of the German states. It was formed in Hanover but became an integral part of the British army in 1803. When Napoleon

spots, where target practice reviews and sham fights frequently happened.

There was one person at Hastings for whom I entertained a warm and long-continued regard. His name was Phillips (John I think), his nick-name Rugged P.[82] He had made a little money, I fancy by smuggling, and owned

dissolved the electorate of Hanover, many Hanoverian officers and other ranks fled to Britain where the King, George III, was also Elector of Hanover. In the same year warrants were issued for a corps of light infantry to be named The King's German Regiment. It was stationed at Bexhill on Sea. The number of officers and men grew over time to around 14,000, and during the thirteen years of its existence about 28,000 men served in the Legion, which came to include both light and heavy cavalry, and foot and horse artillery batteries, by 1805, as well as its own corps of engineers. It served with distinction in the Peninsula and throughout the Napoleonic wars, up to and including Waterloo. The Legion's headquarters was at Bexhill from 1804 to 1814. At its zenith in 1805 the barracks in Bexhill was occupied by 3,570 soldiers. It is reported that many of these married locally.]

[82] [John Phillips (1752-1818) was baptised at Hastings All Saints on 6 December 1752, the son of Thomas Phillips and his wife Ann. By his will of 17 January 1818, Phillips, describing himself as a mariner, confirmed a contract to sell three houses in George Street, Hastings, to Richard Harman of Hastings, tailor, for £2,800. He died on 28 February 1818 and was buried at Ashburnham, being described as 'of Hastings', on 5 March 1818. A tombstone survives in the churchyard. His will was proved at Lewes by his son-in-law Joseph Cooke on 6 April 1818, his personal estate amounting to under £450, and the residuary legatees were Joseph Cooke, his wife Rebecca and their issue. Sarah, daughter of John Phillips and his wife Sarah, was baptised at Hastings St Clements on 9 February 1777. Rebecca Frood, the daughter of James Frood of the Warwickshire Militia and 'his wife' Sarah (actually Sarah Phillips, spinster), was baptised at Hastings St Clements on 24 June 1796. Sarah Phillips was buried at Hastings St Clements on 2 March 1801. Rebecca Frood of Hastings St Clements, spinster, married Joseph Cooke of Ashburnham, bachelor, at Hastings St Clements with the consent of her guardian John Phillips on 2 November 1815. Their first child, Sarah Phillips Cooke, daughter of Joseph Cooke, farmer, and Rebecca, was baptised at Ashburnham on 2 February 1817. Their son Tilden Cooke was baptised at Battle on 16 April 1819. On 11 June 1819 Joseph Cooke of Ashburnham, farmer, was ordered to pay £2 towards the lying-in and 4s 0d [per week] maintenance for his child born to Sarah Barber of Ashburnham, single woman. Joseph and Rebecca's daughter Charlotte was baptised at Ashburnham on 9 December 1821. By 1826 the Cookes had moved to Crowhurst, where three more children were baptised in 1826, 1827 and 1833. They occupied Hye House Farm by 1841. Joseph Cooke was buried at Crowhurst, aged 64, on 10 January 1849, and his will of 29 December 1848 was proved at Lewes on 20 November 1849, his personal estate amounting to under £1,500. In the census of 1851 Rebecca was enumerated at Hye House Farm, described as a farmer of 211 acres, employing nine labourers. In the first quarter of 1854 Rebecca's son Tilden Cooke married Selina Clarke in the Hackney registration district. Selina was born in Birmingham, and may have been related to Rebecca's father James Frood of the Warwickshire Militia. In 1861 and 1871 Rebecca lived in a neighbouring house;

a large house in George street which he let in the season, sometimes to us. He had also a wooden cottage on the ascent of the hill behind. He was a tall, thin, handsome old man, whom I can now see with a long blue coat, breeches and worsted stockings. He had a wife and granddaughter. The latter named Rebecca being the offspring of an illicit connection of a deceased daughter with an officer named Froude, whose name she bore. She was a pretty, delicate looking girl, became heiress to the old man, and subsequently married a farmer named Cook, who resided near Battle.[83]

Old Phillips took a great fancy to me, and during my first and many subsequent visits to Hastings, I was his constant companion. I was with him every day, and almost all day, accompanied him to church, and in numerous walks to every remarkable spot in the neighbourhood, and listened with never failing interest to his stories of smuggling exploits and accidents by land and flood. Even now the tones of his voice seem to ring in my ears and I can remember few people during my career for whom I entertained a warmer affection. In the latter years of his life, he resided in the country with the Cookes and I fear that he finally lost his intellect and that his end was most melancholy.

I had other Hastings friends in humble life. Among them a private soldier named Macmillan of the 9lst.[84] With him too I had much intercourse. He

---

the farmhouse was occupied by her son Tilden Cooke and his family. In 1881 Rebecca Cooke, aged 85, was lodging at 35 Albion Road, Tunbridge Wells; the landlady was Mary Beeching, 35, a charwoman, with her illegitimate son William Beeching and Emma Blagburn, 26, an invalid nurse. Rebecca can thus probably be identified as the Rebecca Cooke, aged 90, whose death was registered in the East Ashford Registration District in the second quarter of 1886. We are very grateful to Christopher Whittick whose remarkable researches provided this otherwise obscure historical information.]

[83] She applied to me in a destitute state about 2 years ago, and I sent her some money. [Note added by Norman dated 1861.]

[84] [The 91st Regiment of Foot was a line regiment of the British army, first formed in 1759. The 1759 formation was disbanded in 1763, and the regiment was raised again in 1779, and disbanded in 1784. In 1793 Campbell's Regiment was raised in Scotland, and in 1794 it was re-designated as the 91st Foot. It served in the Peninsula, in the 1809 Walcheren campaign, and in the South of France. In 1881

was a well-educated person and used to interest me with details of his warlike adventures. When we finally separated, I recollect crying most bitterly. I should much like to know what became of that excellent man.

A Dragoon in the 14th,[85] whose name I forget, also took a fancy to me. I recollect his regaling me in a Public house under East Hill, where he was quartered, with boiled beef and greens, and making me smoke, to the overthrow of my head and stomach.

The leading person at Hastings in my juvenile days, was the original Milward, who was in fact King of the place, and disposed of its Seat in Parliament.[86] He was the father of the Misses M, old ladies whom I may mention hereafter and of the first husband[87] of Lady Waldegrave,[88] and I recollect him an infirm old man drawn about in a chair. The families of Shadwell, Shorter, Breads, Thwaites and Amoore were die minorum Gentium. The

it was to become the 1st Battalion of the Argyll and Sutherland Highlanders.]

[85] [The 14th Foot was an infantry regiment (dragoons being originally mounted infantry, intended to fight on foot), raised by Sir Edward Hales in 1685, on the orders of King James II, to meet the Monmouth rebellion. It subsequently fought against the 1715 Jacobite rebellion, and defended Gibraltar against Spain. In the 18th century it was employed in the United States and in the colonies. The regiment served in the early battles of the wars against Revolutionary France, and even adopted the French revolutionary song *Ça Ira* as its regimental march. During the Napoleonic wars, the second and third battalions of the regiment were formed.]

[86] [Edward Milward 1723-1811. Married Mary Collier 1725-83, daughter of John Collier of Hastings 1685-1760 and his second wife Mary Cranston 1696-1768.]

[87] [Edward Milward junior, 1765-1833, married Sarah (1787-1873), daughter of Rev. William Wheater of Hastings. Edward Milward served several terms as Mayor of Hastings.]

[88] [After Edward Milward's death his widow married, in 1846 aged 59, the widowed William Waldegrave, 8th Earl Waldegrave, 1788-1859, who had previously been married to Elizabeth Whitbread. The son of 4th Earl Waldegrave, he was a midshipman in the navy in 1802, commander by 1809, and fought during the war of 1812 against the United States. He took over the Parliamentary seat of his father in law Samuel Whitbread. He retired from the navy in 1842 as a Rear Admiral. He was promoted to Vice Admiral in 1858 and died a year later. The former Mrs Edward Milward became Sarah Waldegrave, Countess of Waldegrave. She was very active as a philanthropist in Hastings, inheriting considerable wealth on the death of her first husband. She used her wealth to endow churches, schools, wash and bath houses.]

Forsters, farmers at the priory and at Hollington, produced girls of remarkable beauty, one of whom married an Ashburnham.[89] Old General Browne whom I remember as Colonel of the 40th[90] and then as General commanded the district, [and] had also handsome daughters, who became Mrs Turton, Lady Gordon[91] and Mrs Gambier.[92] As respects the first-named and her sister Adeline, there hangs a tale which occupied much of the public attention some years ago. Turton, now Sir Thomas, is alive.[93]

---

[89] [The Rev. Sir John Ashburnham, 7th Bt, born 1770, married in 1804 Fanny (died 1838), 4th daughter of William Foster of Hollington, Sussex, then about two and a half miles from Hastings. The Ashburnham estates, centred on Ashburnham Place, East Sussex, with elaborate grounds designed by 'Capability' Brown, occupied some 22,000 acres.]

[90] [The 40th Regiment of Foot was an infantry regiment of the British army, formed in 1717. It was raised by General Richard Philipps. It was a Somerset regiment, known as the 2nd Somersetshire.]

[91] [Sir Orford Gordon, 9th Bt, of Embo, Sutherland, Capt 78th Highlanders, died 1857. He married Julia the eldest daughter of General Gore Browne and they had four children.]

[92] [Caroline Gore, 4th daughter of Major General Gore Browne, married in 1815 Captain Robert Gambier RN, born 1791, son of Samuel Gambier 1752-1813 and Jane Matthews. They had four children.]

[93] [Thomas Edward Michell Turton, 1790-1854, son of Sir Thomas Turton 1764-1844, married at Hastings 2 November 1812 Louisa Browne, born in 1794/5, daughter of Major General Gore Browne (born 1764). Louisa's younger sister Adeline eloped to India in company with the then Mr and Mrs Turton in 1822, and she became Mr Turton's mistress. Mrs Turton returned from India in 1824. Adeline Browne bore Thomas Turton several children, one of whom was born at sea off Ushant and two of whom were born in India. After a spectacular case, in which Mrs Turton obtained a divorce, in 1831, only the second divorce action brought by a woman, Turton married Adeline as his second wife. (The divorce was noteworthy not only for the behaviour of some of the parties in mid-Victorian England but also because, prior to the establishment of the divorce court in 1858, only four divorce actions, of which Mrs Turton's was only the second, had been brought by women, each of which required a separate Act of Parliament. The only grounds for divorce were incest, which was held to be involved in the Turton case, or bigamy. Since they were adjudged guilty parties, it is likely that the marriage between Thomas Turton and his former sister-in-law would not have been recognised in England.) She died in 1841. In 1842 Turton married Maria Hume, the daughter of Captain Edward Denman RN. In 1844 Turton succeeded his father as 2nd Bt. Turton filed for bankruptcy in 1848. His estates were mostly sold, though a part of them at Felcourt in Surrey was in trust for the benefit of his ten children. He was also involved in political scandal when the Earl of Durham, in defiance of the rest of the Cabinet in which he was Colonial Secretary, appointed Turton to various posts in Canada.]

I have thus compressed together much that I had to say about Hastings, part of which would more properly belong[94] to a later period into what has preceded. We were at that place in 1801, 3 and 4 and often afterwards. Some of our later visits will be mentioned hereafter.

Soon after our first residence at Hastings, my father in conjunction with Mr William Wells hired a place called Hascomb, near Godalming in Surrey,[95] for sporting purposes, and held it for four or five years, I think up to 1805. It was an old Manor house occupying the end of a quadrangular Court, with Offices and farm buildings and high walls to right and left and a sort of garden in front. It had belonged to the Frederick family[96] and subsequently to the Morsheads, who sold it some 30 years ago.[97] Attached to it were large ponds and stews,[98] which supplied our table in the winter. In front of the house rose a lofty hill on which a Telegraph was placed. This hill belonged to the Green Sand Range, was covered with wood and furze traversed by paths, and furnished a magnificent view over the Weald and to the South Downs. The scenery is very like that of Selbourne, as described by White.[99]

---

94 [Norman wrote 'belonged' here.]

95 [Hascombe is 4 miles south east of Godalming. The high ridge to the south of the village is known as Telegraph Hill.]

96 [Sir John Frederick, 1749/50-1825, 5th Bt, MP Newport, Cornwall, 1774-80, Christ Church 1781-90, Surrey 1794-1807. Succeeded to baronetcy in 1783. Lieutenant Colonel of 2nd Surrey Militia. His main seat was at Burwood Park, Walton on Thames, Surrey. He married in 1778 Mary (died 18 November 1794 aged 35), third daughter of Richard Garth of Morden.]

97 [The Morshead family was a south west family, Morshead of Lamerton, Tavistock, Devon. The sixth son of William Morshead of Cartuther, Cornwall, 1722-84, was the Reverend Edward Morshead, 1764-1852, Rector of Hascombe, Surrey, 1791, Rector of Calstock, Cornwall, 1796, Rector of St Dominic, Cornwall, 1800-1803. The living of Hascombe was in the diocese of Winchester, with an annual income of £204 with residence.]

98 [A 'stew' is a fishpond.]

99 [Gilbert White, 1720-93, naturalist, born at the vicarage of Selborne, Hants. His grandfather, the Reverend Gilbert White, 1650-1728, was Vicar of Selborne, 1681 to death. White's father, John White, 1688-1738, a lawyer, had retired from practice in 1719, and soon established himself with his wife and family in Selborne. Gilbert White was brought up with a detailed schooling in the countryside around him. He became a Church of England curate at a small country parish, Swarraton in Hampshire. However he acted for much of his life as the curate in charge at

When looking from the steep southern face of the telegraph hill. I have often repeated the lines from Collins's Ode to Evening,[100]

['Or if chill blustering wind, or driving rain,
Prevent my willing feet,] Be mine the hut
That from the mountain's side
Views wilds and swelling floods,
And hamlets brown, and drive discover'd Spires
And hears their simple bell, and marks o'er all
Thy dewy fingers draw
The gradual dusky veil'.

There was indeed a hut on the top of the hill in which dwelt the telegraph men. On our arrival we found that one of these was our old coachman Thackerey, who had driven my mother when she was robbed on Chislehurst Hill about 1793.[101]

---

Selborne, and kept a daily record of his activities in the garden, and of natural phenomena, for more than forty years until shortly before his death. He published a number of papers on his observations. His famous *Natural History and Antiquities of Selborne* was finally published in 1788 (though dated 1789); it had been in preparation since 1771. The style, simple and informal, has helped to ensure its continued popularity.]

[100] [William Collins, 1727-59; *Ode to Evening*, lines 33-9.]

[101] [According to Norman's Bromley Memoir, the district was so lawless that, when Norman's grandfather rode to London on business, he carried pistols in his holsters and travelled with an armed servant. In illustration of this, Norman writes: 'About 1793, my Mother who had gone to dine at Chislehurst was stopped at the bottom of Chislehurst hill by some Footpads, who took her purse, but missed the watch which she had taken out of her girdle and placed on the seat beside her. They also missed a handsome diamond ring which she wore, although it hurt her so much when they insisted upon shaking hands with her that she could hardly refrain from crying out. This shaking of hands was intended as a sort of reconciliation, it being supposed, that after it, the aggrieved party would not appear as witness on a trial. The coachman on this occasion was named Thackeray. I recollect him well at Hascomb where he was employed at the Telegraph. He imagined that the voice of a Footpad who spoke was that of a resident at Bromley, and after depositing my Mother at home, he rode off to call on this man, whom he found in bed and who was therefore pronounced innocent.']

My father used to go to Hascomb, about one week in each month during the season and also occasionally in the summer. It was a most primitive place, quite out of this world, the road from Godalming almost, impassable. A good day was employed in reaching it from Bromley. The shooting was rough but good. Pigeons, pheasants, hares, rabbits and woodcocks. The Manors or farms belonging to the estates were Hascomb Lodkim, Tuesley, Munsted and Sydney. The latter was situated in the Weald, a very low and wet district, and is now the property of Mr Nicholson of Waverley,[102] father to Mrs B. Carter. The Keeper at Hascomb was named Taylor. His wife was cook. His daughters housemaids, son under keeper. Under the regime of Sir C. Scott, who was a subsequent tenant, both father and son were placed in the excise.[103] After a long and wet day shooting, Taylor used to change his dress and wait at table. The standard bill of fare was a joint carp or tench, and apple dumplins.

Round the hall and morning room were ranged portraits of Sir J. Frederick's horses. The names I recollect, Nero, Neptune, Flora, Phoenix, Chanter, Bucephalus[104] and Syphax.[105] My memory is not yet gone. Hascomb fifty

[102] [Samuel Nicholson, of Waverley Abbey, Surrey, son of George Thomas Nicholson, 1787-1853, who purchased the Waverley Abbey estate some time between 1832 and 1840. There were three sons and two daughters, the younger of whom, Laura Maria, married John Bonham Carter, 1817-84, MP for Winchester 1847-74, a Lord of the Treasury 1866-8. Since two of Norman's daughters married Bonham Carters, there was thus a family connection with the Nicholsons.]

[103] [The Scott family were neighbours of the Normans. They bought the estate of Sundridge about 1800. Sir Claude Scott, according to Norman's Bromley Memoir, built the house which stood in Norman's time, and Sir Samuel Scott greatly added to it. According to a directory of London bankers, Sir Claude Scott, starting from humble beginnings, became a wealthy merchant, was created a baronet, and in his later years became a banker. He started the banking business in 1824/5 (and was thus lucky to survive the crisis of 1825). The firm was styled 'Sir Claude Scott and Company' until 1847. The partners were by that time Sir Samuel Scott, Bt, Claude Edward Scott, and Samuel Scott. After that time it was styled 'Sir Samuel Scott and Company' in which form it appears in the Post Office London Directory for 1857. It was at 1, Cavendish Square.]

[104] [Bucephalus was, according to legend, the horse of Alexander the Great. Norman wrote 'Bucaphalus'.]

[105] [Syphax was a king of the ancient Libyan tribe Masaesyles during the last

years ago was a most primitive place. Gentry none, clergy all but boors, farmers &c in a high degree rough and illiterate. I visited it twice on visits to Sir S. Scott, I should say about 1812 and 1815, and the site during a ride from Sutton Place[106] in company with Sir Jo[hn] Lefevre in 1854.[107] One of these visits was at the time of the Chennel Patricide at Godalming or near it.[108] I found the old mansion pulled down and replaced by a farmhouse, the garden overgrown with weeds, the upper ponds a foul swamp.

I have thus spent a good deal of space upon Hascomb, which my father gave up when I was twelve years old and which hardly merits so much of my autobiography, but it constitutes a bright spot in my past life. It is connected only with pleasurable recollections and I place all I have to say about it together, in order to avoid renvois.

I now revert to Eltham. When I first went there, I could not read but

quarter of the third century BC. In the wars in North Africa he allied himself with the Romans.]

[106][Sutton Place is a 16th century mansion and estate, four and a quarter miles NNE of Guildford. It was for long owned by the Salvin family, and was associated with Catholic recusancy. In the 20th century it became famous as the home of the oil millionaire John Paul Getty. Kelley's Post Office Directory of Surrey for 1859 shows that the house was then occupied by one Charles Lefevre. This was Charles Shaw Lefevre, later Viscount Eversley, a famous Speaker of the House of Commons, and brother of Sir John Shaw Lefevre. We are grateful to Duncan Mirylees of Surrey History Centre for this information.]

[107][Sir John George Shaw Lefevre, 1797-1879, the second of the four sons of Charles Shaw, 1758-1823, and his wife Helena 1767-1834, daughter and heiress of John Lefevre of Heckfield Place, Hampshire. Charles Shaw assumed the extra name Lefevre on marrying into the Huguenot family. His son was originally a mathematician. He was elected Fellow of Trinity College, Cambridge, in 1819. FRS 1820. He married Rachel Emily Wright, 1801-85, the sister of Lady Overstone. In 1821 he was, with Norman, one of the founder members of the Political Economy Club, and remained a member until 1831. He later made a successful career as a lawyer and civil servant. Like Norman he was educated at Eton. He was knighted in 1857.]

[108][The murder by George Chennell, and William and George Chalcroft his associates, of Chennell's father and his housekeeper. They were also responsible for the murder of two other elderly men, one near Petersfield and one near Farnham. Though robbery was the motive, the degree of violence was exceptionally horrible. The murder of George Chennell senior took place on 10 November 1817. For a report of the case see the *Times* 8 December 1817, 3f, and for a report of the trial of Chennell and his associates see the *Times* 13 August 1818, 3b.]

I soon mastered this grand step in knowledge and can remember the delight I derived from Mrs Barbauld's pretty tale, Robin, Dicksey Flapsy, and Pecksy.[109] I then began to read a little on my own account out of school and one of my first books, was a translation of Finelon's Telemachus.[110]

I had little spare time for reading at school but at home I read a great deal desultorily. History was my favourite study, as it has always been since, and this I found of all kinds and qualities in the Universal History.[111] I destroyed the binding of one volume containing the barbarians who overthrew the Roman Empire, by constant perusal. The book was rebound and may even now be remarked as differing in appearance from its brethren.

When reading, I used to place myself in all sorts of odd postures. Head down and heels up, prostrate on floor &c. Why I did this I cannot explain. At any rate the habit seems to be hereditary, for my son Philip is noted for the same thing.[112]

---

[109] [Anna Letitia Barbauld, 1743-1825, née Aikin. She was the daughter of a Presbyterian clergyman and associate of the Unitarian Joseph Priestley. Around the mid 1760s she began to write poetry, often on the subject of animals. In 1774 she married the Reverend Rochemont Barbauld, 1749-1808, who was of French descent. A Dissenter, he became a Unitarian. The couple ran a school for boys at Palgrave in Suffolk. It is from this time that Mrs Barbauld's most influential book, *Lessons for Children*, dates. She and her husband became admirers of the French Revolution, and defended it against its critics, notably Edmund Burke. After her death Mrs Barbauld was chiefly remembered as a writer for children.]

[110] [François de Salignac de la Mothe-Fénelon, more commonly known as François Fénelon, 1651-1715. He was a French Catholic theologian, poet and writer. His *Adventures of Telemachus* is an attack on the French monarchy, first published in 1699. It is a novel about Ulysses's son Telemachus, and was actually a biting attack upon the idea of absolute monarchy. Born into a noble French family, he was ordained priest in 1675. Much of his early career was spent attempting to convert the French Huguenots to Catholicism. He became Archbishop of Cambrai and, incurring the displeasure of the King, he was, in later years, confined to his diocese. He left behind a large body of theological and other works, of which *Telemachus* is much the most famous.]

[111] [The universal history was a popular form from the Middle Ages onwards. However the one to which Norman is referring was probably *An Universal History, from the Earliest Account of Time to the Present*, London: printed for J. Batley, 1726-44 and later editions (see p. 120).]

[112] [Philip Norman was born 9 July 1842, and died 17 May 1931. An outstanding sportsman at Eton, where at the age of 17 he won the 120 yards hurdles in a

From the moment when I could read, up to the present time, I have always been a reader, although never a severe student, for amusement not instruction has been my main object, and in this way I have got through a great number of books as any one will perceive who looks only at those I have read since 1814, a list of which I have preserved. As I have rarely read during the day, having been always a busy man as respects business, and besides an ardent sportsman, cricket player &c. I could never have attained this result had it not been my invariable custom for 55 years, never when in the house, to sit down idly. If not writing or talking or eating, or sleeping, I have invariably had a book before me, and by constant practice I read very fast. Even when dressing, so long as the state of my eyes permitted, I always contrived to read, and to recollect a great deal of what I read.

It has almost always been my custom to have in hand three or four books at the same time, and usually in different languages, the object being to keep up my acquaintance with foreign tongues which I find quickly to diminish if not maintained by constant practice.

I consider the power which I have so long enjoyed of deriving pleasure from books to be among the first of the many blessings for which I have to thank a kind providence. It has served me at all times, and under all circumstances. In youth and age, in sickness and in health, abroad and at home, its advantage in the way of procuring innocent pleasure is of inestimable value taken alone. I regret to say that with the exception of Sibella,[113] my children are deprived

---

record time, he played first class cricket for Kent, and rose to become a widely respected artist, author and antiquary. He was trained as a draughtsman and painter at the Slade School, and often exhibited at the Royal Academy. This is rather ironic, given his father's expressed disdain for the Royal Academy. He did much to establish the historical and pictorial record of the buildings of London, and was elected a Fellow of the Society of Antiquaries in 1886, being Vice President 1913-17. His drawings and water colour paintings of London are in the Victoria and Albert Museum.]

[113] [Born 27 March 1837. In 1862 she married Henry Bonham Carter, and died in 1916.]

of it.[114]

I have said that history was always my favorite study. I early followed this into two of its main branches, war and politics. As respects the first, I consider my knowledge greater than[115] what is usually found among civilians and I can give some curious instances of the extent, in which it gained my attention. While at Eltham, and long afterwards, I used to carry on in my head imaginary wars. The Belligerents were French and Spaniards, Pisans and Florentines, Danes and Swedes &c. I took up a war from its commencement. Supposed armies of a certain force and, with recognised commanders, making regular movements, fighting battles and undertaking sieges, all of which, and often in detail, I went over in my mind until a peace under certain conditions was concluded. The times employed on these singular mental exercises were when I was in bed or walking, chiefly the former. I never forgot the point I had reached one night, on recommencing my musings on the following. Thus the result was a complete whole. I had always a favorite side, which after many changes of fortune was successful at last, and I may here observe that this was never that of France.

The scene of operations, whatever it might be, was usually constructed with due attention to geography, but while at Eltham, I connected the various belligerents and their operations with certain defined portions of the garden. It is with some difficulty that I can give to the reader anything like a correct idea of these imaginary wars, which if written down would have occupied numerous volumes, and the more so because I never heard of any other person possessed by so singular a fancy.

It sometimes happened that the perusal of a single book greatly affected my warlike notions. It was thus with a translation of 'Saxe's Reveries',[116]

[114]Some of them are now readers. [Note added by Norman in 1866.]

[115][Norman wrote 'that' here.]

[116][Maurice de Saxe *My Reveries upon the Art of War.* This work was written in 1732, but not published until 1757, seven years after the death of the author. It is regarded as a major classic, and received in the 20th century the endorsement of

from which I derived legions and amusettes, which, strange to say, I supposed to be employed by the Pisans.

But besides my imaginary armies, I had numerous soldiers cut out of card, and distinguished into cavalry and infantry. The generals were also marked and had their aides de camp. Each card soldier reckoned for 500 men in my head, and when drawn up in battle array, a piece of cork was placed before him, the overthrow of which implied his capture. The armies were divided into brigades. The weapons employed were shot and peas thrown from my hand with closed eyes. In a pitched battle, the quantity of the former, supposed to be cannon balls, was equal to one half the number of combatants. That of the shot was equal to the whole number. A charge of cavalry implied that the whole of the shot, and the whole of the peas belonging to them should be discharged at once. In the infantry fire the shot were discharged two at once, the peas singly.

I had fortresses which were besieged and taken. These were constructed of pieces of wood of various shapes and sizes. There were also ships with their crews, the former smooth lathes cut into lengths, the latter bits of card placed upon them, which resembled the soldiers being perhaps one third of an inch high.

The scene of combat for my pasteboard warriors was any vacant room, in the house, usually the drawing room. My operations covered the whole floor and were carried on upon a regular plan. Thus any displacement of the

Bernard Law Montgomery, the British Field Marshall. Maurice, Comte de Saxe, or in German Moritz, Graf von Sachsen, 1696-1750, French General and later Marshall of France, an illegitimate son of Augustus the Strong, King of Poland and Elector of Saxony, and of Countess Maria Aurora of Königsmarck. As early as the age of twelve, he was with the army of Prince Eugene of Savoy. He next served under Peter the Great against the Swedes. Like his father, he was a man of immense physical strength, but of a dissipated youth. He served in the war of the Polish Succession, in which he rose to the rank of Lieutenant General. In 1743 he became Marshall of France, and from that time enjoyed a brilliant military career. He was naturalised as a French subject in 1746. Like his father, he had several illegitimate children.]

pieces of card was most highly inconvenient and distasteful to me and exerted violent anger on my part towards the housemaids, who on this point were my great enemies. The number of my soldiers was very great. I should say full 1000, and with them and their accompaniments the floor of the drawing room was fully occupied.

I will here relate an anecdote of some interest. During the volunteering times, General Fox,[117] who commanded the district, had come to inspect and review the various corps in this neighbourhood, becoming the guest of his friend Governor Cameron at Southborough.[118] There was no room for his aide de camp, who accepted a bed here. In the morning the young man, of whom I have a faint recollection, found his way into the drawing room, and when he saw my warlike preparations, he remarked to my father, 'Captain Norman you have a son of a military turn' or something to that effect. The truth of this remark has been hardly borne out, by subsequent history, yet it was made by a person of no small mark. No less than Captain Napier,[119] he, I believe who became in after life Lieutenant General Sir C. Napier G.C.B. the Conqueror of Scinde, alike distinguished for the sharpness of his sword, his tongue, and his pen. I have a faint recollection of his physiognomy.

[117] [Henry Edward Fox, 1755-1811, army officer. He was the son of Henry Fox, 1st Baron Holland, 1705-74, and his second wife Georgiana née Lennox, Baroness Holland of Holland in her own right, 1723-74. She was the eldest daughter of Charles Lennox, 2nd Duke of Richmond. General Fox was the younger brother of the politician Charles James Fox, 1749-1806. He entered the army in 1770, was promoted Captain in 1774, and participated in the early battles of the American War of Independence. He was promoted Brigadier in 1782. In 1793 he was appointed Quartermaster General on the Duke of York's staff in Flanders, and was soon promoted Major General. In 1803 he was appointed Commander in Chief of the forces in Ireland, but was caught unawares by Robert Emmet's uprising, and was soon replaced by Lieutenant General Cathcart, whose place as commander of the London district he then took. It was presumably during this time that he visited Bromley. However in December 1804 he was sent to Gibraltar as Lieutenant Governor.]

[118] [The father of Norman's friend Charles Hay Cameron was Charles Cameron, 1766-1828, who served at various times as Governor of the Bahamian Islands (1804-20) and as Civil Commissioner of Malta (1801-2). He was also a partner in Harley, Cameron and Company, bankers.]

[119] [See p. 59.]

My interest in war considered as science, and also as having influenced in so remarkable a degree the destinies of man, has continued up to a recent period, and I have been an attentive reader of most of the great authorities in such matters, such as Machiavelli,[120] Montecuc[c]uli,[121] Saxe, L[l]oyd,[122]

[120][Niccolo Machiavelli, 1469-1527, Italian statesman and author. Though Machiavelli is chiefly famous for his book *The Prince*, which was published in 1532, five years after his death, he was also a writer on warfare. In 1521 he published *Dell' Arte Della Guerra.* The book is in the form of a Socratic dialogue, in which one of the participants is a thinly disguised Machiavelli who, under the name Fabrizzio, details how an army should be raised, trained, organised, deployed, and employed. Though basing himself on extensive study of existing writings on warfare, Machiavelli seems to have failed to appreciate fully the potential of firearms.]

[121][Raimondo, Count of Montecuccoli or Montecucculi, 1608/9-80, Austrian general, and Prince of the Holy Roman Empire. His family was of Burgundian origin. He began his military career at the age of sixteen under his uncle Count Ernest Montecucculi, a distinguished Austrian General, and displayed considerable bravery in the course of which he suffered severe wounds. He rose to the rank of Major in 1632, and of Colonel in 1635. In 1643 he went to Italy and was promoted Lieutenant Field Marshall. He was promoted to the rank of Field Marshall during the war of 1657-60 against Prince Rákóczy of Transylvania, who was in alliance with the Swedes. His *Memorie della Guerra* was published at Venice in 1703 and, within a few years, editions appeared in Latin, French and German.]

[122][Norman's misspelling of this name no doubt reflected his close connections with Samuel Jones Loyd, Lord Overstone, and his father Lewis Loyd. Henry Humphrey Evans Lloyd, c.1718-83, was a military writer and mercenary soldier, born in Merionethshire. Failing to obtain a commission in the British army, he was commissioned in the French army during the War of the Austrian Succession, 1740-48, and accompanied Charles Stuart, the Young Pretender, on the ill-fated Jacobite expedition to Scotland, 1745-6. He reconnoitred the south coast in preparation for a French invasion, but was arrested. A friend, John Drummond, obtained his release and he returned to France where he enjoyed a successful career as an engineer officer in the French army. He was subsequently in the Austrian army, rising to the rank of Major General. After that he changed sides and joined the Prussian army. He subsequently commanded a Russian division at the siege of Silistria in 1773. As a result of his extensive military experience, he became a recognised military writer. The best known of his works are *The History of the Late War in Germany Between the King of Prussia and the Empress of Germany and her Allies* (1766), and *Reflections on the Principles of the Art of War* (1781). The 1766 work was translated into five German and three French editions.]

Frederick of Prussia,[123] Dumas,[124] Napier,[125] Napoleon[126] &c.

---

[123][Frederick II of Prussia, 1712-86, King of Prussia 1740-86, known to history as Frederick the Great, who engineered the first partition of Poland. In the court at Potsdam he cultivated intellectuals such as Voltaire, and promoted the arts. He formed the Bayard order to discuss warfare with his friends. He is regarded as one of the greatest tactical geniuses in the history of warfare, and he was admired by Napoleon. The military writings to which Norman refers were probably *Military Instructions, Written by the King of Prussia for the Generals of his Army: being his Majesty's Own Commentaries on his Former Campaigns. Together with Short Instructions for the Use of his Light Troops. Translated by an Officer.* London, 1762.]

[124][Guillaume Mathieu, Comte Dumas, 1753-1837, French General born at Montpelier. He joined the army in 1773, and entered upon active service in 1780, in the American war. He returned to France in 1783, with the rank of Major. At the Revolution he acted with Lafayette and the Constitutional Liberal Party, but after the extremists gained control of the Assembly he escaped to England. His extensive writings include *Précis des événements militaire, ou essays historiques sur les campagnes de 1799-1814, avec cartes et plans; par M. le comte Mathieu Dumas.* Paris, Strasbourg and London: Treuttel and Würtz, 1816-23. The first part of this work was written in exile in Holstein. He was recalled to France by Napoleon, and fought at Austerlitz. He was subsequently Minister of War to Joseph Bonaparte, Napoleon's brother, in Naples. In 1808 he fought in the Peninsula, after Joseph had been transferred by Napoleon to the throne of Spain, and in Germany in 1809. He was employed in negotiating the armistice after the Battle of Wagram, to which Norman refers, and in 1810 Napoleon made him a Count of the Empire. In 1812 he was involved in the retreat from Moscow. With the restoration of the Bourbons in 1814 Dumas at first served them, but after Napoleon's escape from Elba he presented himself to the Emperor. This made it necessary for him to retire in 1815 and continue with his Précis. He was eventually restored to favour by the Bourbons in 1818, took part in the Revolution of 1830, and died in 1837.]

[125][Sir Charles James Napier, 1782-1853, army officer, brought up in Ireland. His mother was a daughter of the 2nd Duke of Richmond, and a cousin of Charles James Fox, after whom he was named. He was Aide de Camp to his cousin General Edward Fox, and at that time a Captain in the Staff Corps, a new body organised to assist the Royal Engineers. He had entered the army at the age of 12. Growing up in Ireland, he was deeply sympathetic to the Irish, though he served in 1799 as the Aide de Camp to Sir James Duff, the Commander of the Limerick District. He moved to England, but in 1803 he was back in Ireland as Aide de Camp to General Fox, returning to London with Fox after the latter's transfer following Emmet's Rebellion. He served in the Peninsula under Sir John Moore, and in 1812 he served in the Anglo-American war. He was little impressed by his superiors, and was free in his expression of criticism. In 1842 he was appointed commander of the British army in Sind in India. In 1843 he defeated the princely Rulers of Sind, culminating in a famous victory near Hyderabad. He was appointed Governor of Sind. He was the author of many books, including one on the Ionian Islands (where he had held office), on military law, on the poor law, and on the militia. As Norman implies above, his writings lacked generosity.]

[126][Napoléon Bonaparte, 1769-1821, Emperor of the French, military cadet 1784,

I have said above that politics have deeply occupied my thoughts and feelings from an early age. The first public event, which I well recollect, was the Battle of Alexandria,[127] but from that time to this, no event of importance to this nation or to Europe has escaped my attention, and I have read newspapers from the time I could read any thing. My taste in such matters was well known to Mr Smith and I recollect his coming into my room late at night and waking me up in order to tell me that the preliminaries of the peace at Amiens had been signed.[128]

My views as a politician partly no doubt inherited from my father and partly the result of reflection have always been liberal, and for very many

General 1793, suppressed the Paris mob September 1795, conducted brilliant military campaign in Italy 1796, became First Consul and effective ruler of France in 1799, declared himself Emperor 1804, defeated Austria at Ulm in 1805, Russia at Austerlitz in 1805, and Prussia at Jena and Auerstadt in 1806. In 1808 he placed his brother Joseph on the Spanish throne leading to the Peninsula war and ultimately to the victory of Wellington. Invaded Russia in 1812, a disastrous decision which cost him five-sixths of his army. Defeated by an alliance of Russia, Prussia, Austria and Britain and banished to Elba in 1814, he escaped and led his forces against the combined forces of Britain and Prussia, under the overall command of Wellington, at Waterloo, where he was defeated. Regarded by history as one of the greatest generals, and a man who had turned Continental Europe into a war zone for almost two decades, it was inevitable that Norman should study his writings though, in truth, they are quite limited. See *Maximes de Guerre de Napoléon*, Paris: Annelin, 1830.]

[127][French troops had stormed the city on 2 July 1798, and it remained in French hands until the arrival of the British in 1801. On 21 March 1801 the British, under General Sir Ralph Abercrombie, defeated the French under General Menou. The British forces numbered about 14,000 and the French about 20,000. The British suffered 1,468 killed, wounded and missing, including General Abercrombie who died on 28 March. The French suffered 1,160 killed and up to 3,000 wounded. The disproportionate French losses were due in part to the employment of British naval artillery. The actual battle took place on a narrow spit of land between the sea and Lake Abukir. The British subsequently advanced on Alexandria itself, which finally surrendered on 2 September 1801.]

[128][The Peace of Amiens was signed on 27 March, 1802. Under it, British conquests from France were to be restored. It was greeted with great rejoicing, and was of considerable advantage to France, giving Napoleon a breathing space. The preliminaries had been signed in London on 1 October 1801, and ratified on 10 October. But on 18 May 1803 war was resumed. Britain's undertaking to restore French territories was not implemented. The treaty provided nothing more than an interlude in the wars with France.]

years my feelings, connected with them were most ardent. They are no longer so to the same extent. The change has many sources. The revulsion connected with advancing years. The attainment of all the great internal measures, which I most ardently desired during youth and middle age, such as Catholic emancipation, reform in Parliament, free trade, altered Poor Laws, doubts as to the value of certain things, which I once considered essential such as the Ballot. Disappointment at the conduct both as respects wisdom and morality of popular bodies of all kinds and in all countries, more especially in that archetypal democracy, the United States of America,

Upon all the above subjects, I shall have many occasions hereafter of explaining my views, should these memoranda be ever carried down to the present time. I will now take leave of them for the present with a declaration that whatever changes my feelings may have undergone, I continue a warm advocate of progress and improvement, and of freedom and good government as their most efficient promoters. My objects are what they have ever been. I only think myself rather wiser than formerly, as to the best means of attaining these objects.

The oldest and most intimate friendships I have ever had were commenced during that period of my life, which now employs my pen, *viz* those with Charles Hay Cameron and George Grote.[129] I ought perhaps to add al-

[129] [Charles Hay Cameron, 1795-1880, was the eldest son of Charles Cameron, 1766-1828 (see p. 57). His mother was Lady Margaret Hay, 1769-1832, daughter of James, 15th Earl of Errol. His grandfather, Donald Cameron, was the younger son of Dr Archibald Cameron, 1707-53, physician and Jacobite. After Eton he qualified as a lawyer and became a legal writer and deeply convinced Benthamite. He is said to have been able to recite from memory much of Homer and Virgil. In 1826 and 1828 he had illegitimate children, a matter of which Norman appears to have been ignorant. In 1829 he went to Ceylon, to advise upon legal reform, basing his advice upon Benthamite principles. The result was a re-organisation of the courts in Ceylon. He later purchased coffee estates on the island. In 1833 he became one of the Assistant Commissioners on the Poor Law, another great Benthamite project. After this he worked with Thomas Babbington Macaulay to reform the Indian legal system on Benthamite lines. In 1836 he went on sick leave to the Cape of Good Hope, where he met Julia Margaret Pattle, 1815-79, whom he married. She became famous as a great photographic pioneer, under her married

though falling into a lower category, those with George Robert[130] and Oswald Smith.[131]

Charles Cameron was the only son of Mr Charles Cameron, who commenced life as a Banker in London, and upon the failure of his house, bought the small house at Southborough, once Thomson Hankey's.[132] His mother was Lady Margaret Hay, daughter of an Earl of Errol. He is thus of high descent, and counts among his ancestors the Earl of Kilmarnock[133] beheaded

name; see J. Cox and C. Ford (eds.) *Julia Margaret Cameron: The Complete Photographs*, Los Angeles: The J. Paul Getty Museum, 2003. Her first camera, a sliding box camera using glass plates of approximately twelve by ten inches, was a Christmas present in 1863 from her daughter Julia and son-in-law Charles Norman. Her portrait of George Warde Norman is one of only two surviving negatives; see Cox and Ford, pp. 48-9. This book (p. 307) has a picture of Charlie Hay Cameron (son of Julia and Charles Norman), with the inscription, 'For George W. Norman from his old friend C.H. Cameron'. See pp. 377, 412-17 for pictures of Cameron's Norman grandchildren, and pp. 335-8 for pictures of Charles Lloyd Norman, George Warde Norman and Lord Overstone. C.H. Cameron resumed work in India, paying particular attention to the educational system. He spent his last years in Ceylon, where he and his wife both died. On Grote see p. 64.]

130 [George Robert Smith, 1793-1869, son of the London banker George Smith, 1765-1836. He was educated at Eton, where he was a contemporary of Norman. He was MP for Midhurst, 1830-2, and for Chipping Wycombe, Bucks, 1838-41. He joined the family banking firm.]

131 [George Smith, banker, of Selsdon, 1765-1836, had nine sons and six daughters. The second son, Oswald, 1794-1863, of Blendon Hall, Kent, married in 1824 Henrietta Mildred, daughter of the Very Reverend Robert Hodgson, DD, Rector of St George, Hanover Square, and Dean of Carlisle.]

132 [Thomson Hankey, 1805-93, was the son of Thomson Hankey, a merchant who died in 1857. He was a partner in Thomson Hankey and Company, West India merchants, a Director of the Bank of England 1835-93, Deputy Governor 1849-51, Governor 1851-3, contested Boston, Lincs, 1852, and Peterborough 1853. Following an inquiry, the election of George Whalley for Peterborough was disallowed and Hankey was declared elected in his place. MP for Peterborough 1853-68, 1874-80. Like Norman, he was a member of the Political Economy Club.]

133 [William Boyd, 4th Earl of Kilmarnock, 1705-46, Jacobite army officer. Succeeded to earldom in 1717. Originally a supporter of Walpole, he was drawn to the Stuart cause for financial reasons, and married Lady Ann Livingston, heiress presumptive of the Countess of Errol. He took no part in planning the rising of 1745, but joined it in October. He distinguished himself at the battle of Falkirk, was captured at Culloden, 16 April 1746, and was beheaded on 18 August 1746 on Tower Hill. His title and estates were forfeited at death. He was the highest ranking peer to be executed for participation in the '45.]

in 1745, and Dr Cameron,[134] hung some years afterwards, and I believe the last victim of the Stuart and Hanover strife.

Mr Cameron came to Southborough, I think in 1799, and I at once formed an acquaintance with his son. Our intercourse has been kept up ever since, personal when we could meet, epistolary when we were separated. Our separations indeed have been frequent. Charles Hay Cameron went with his father to Malta where the latter was Governor in 1800, to the Bahamas under similar circumstances more than once, and subsequently to Mexico and Ceylon. Finally in 1835 or 1836 to India, where he remained filling the highest offices until 1848. He was at Eton with me.[135]

I shall often have occasion to mention him hereafter. I will now only say of him that in intellectual power he has few superiors, in a high sense of honor, and duty fewer still. In knowledge he is also highly distinguished. His main defect, and that only as respects his own interest, is that he has not the art of making his way with official men, so as to obtain and to keep place and salary.

While Cameron was in India, we kept up a monthly correspondence and when he returned we interchanged letters.[136] Mine to him, which will be found in one of my boxes, ought to be about 120 in number, but some I think are lost. They may be interesting hereafter, containing as they do, not merely domestic intelligence, but also my views upon all the most important matters of foreign policy, which occurred during a period of twelve or thirteen

---

[134] [A medical practitioner at Lochaber. It is clear that Dr Cameron, while opposed to the 1745 rising, made himself technically liable to be treated as guilty of participation in it by attending to the wounded. Having escaped to France after the battle of Culloden, he went to England in 1750 and 1752 in search of funds for the relief of himself and others who had fled. He was captured, summarily tried, and executed at Tyburn in June 1753 despite the complete insignificance of his part in the rising.]

[135] [Like Cowell and Overstone (see pp. 230,251), Cameron is recorded by H.E.C. Stapylton as being in the Upper School, Fifth Form, Lower Division, in 1811.]

[136] [Notes for Norman's letters to Cameron in India are in the Norman papers at U310/C122/1*.]

years. The Afghan expedition was one of these. I hope to read them over, one of these days.

Another friend of my infancy was George Grote the Historian of Greece.[137] Our knowledge of each other must go back further than our respective memories. Our fathers were great friends. Mr Grote lived at Shortlands[138] now Mr Wilkinson's, and I can remember as a child attending a twelvth night ball there, I drawing King, and having for my Queen a Miss Hoggarts, daughter of the auctioneer, who was a woman of remarkably high stature. The contrast between us excited much mirth.

My friendship with G. Grote continued without any interruption until about 1832 when it was put an end to, by my being involved in a violent quarrel, which took place between Grote and Cowell,[139] and with which di-

[137][George Grote, 1794-1871, was born 17 November 1794 at Clay Hill, Beckenham. He was the eldest of the eleven children of the banker George Grote, 1762-1830. From Sevenoaks Grammar School he went to Charterhouse which, after a thorough education in Latin and Greek, he left at the age of 15, to join the family bank of Prescott and Grote, of which he became a partner at the age of 21. While working in the bank, he engaged in an extensive scheme of self education. About the time that he became a partner, he met Harriet Lewin, 1792-1878; Grote's father opposed their marriage, and in 1820 the couple eloped. Coming under the influence of James Mill, Grote embraced both Utilitarianism and atheism, and supported the radical programme of Parliamentary reform espoused by the Benthamites. Under the influence of Bentham himself Grote, previously religious, became an aggressive secularist. After 1832 he became a Member of Parliament for the City of London in the first reformed Parliament. He assumed leadership of the Radical faction, but was cautious compared with his followers. He decided, in 1841, to withdraw from Parliament rather than fight another election. He had begun work on a *History of Greece* in 1823; the first two volumes appeared in 1846, and the last volume appeared in 1856. Grote's interpretation of Greek history was inevitably influenced by the Benthamite view of ideal democracy. In 1865 he published a 3 volume work on Plato and other Greek philosophers, and he was still at work on Aristotle when he died. As a Benthamite radical, Grote was involved in the foundation of London University, and was a member of its Council 1849-71. Despite Norman's admiration for Grote, there is little surviving correspondence, some from 1818-19, and some, surprisingly, from 1834-5, which presumably postdates the rupture between Norman and Grote which is discussed on p. 356 below, at U310 C38 in the Norman papers at Maidstone.]

[138][Norman's Bromley Memoir confirms that the house was subsequently known as Shortlands, and that this gave its name to the district when, subsequently, the estate was built over.]

[139][On Cowell and the quarrel, see p. 356.]

rectly I had nothing whatever to do. If I ever live to complete these memoranda as far as the year 1833 when this quarrel occurred, I shall be obliged to say something as to its nature and causes. At present I will merely allude to it.

On the whole G. Grote was certainly for more than 30 years my most intimate friend. We walked and shot and played at cricket together and when in London there were few days when I did not pay him a visit at the banking house. He used often to dine here and I with him. I have paid him a visit at his father's place Badgemore near Henley,[140] and in 1817 we went abroad together, that being my first visit to the continent.

My intercourse with Grote had the most important effect on my intellectual character, and aided by the intercourse with C.H. Cameron acted as a stimulant on my mental energies. I lost in some degree through the example and influence of my companions the habit of desultory reading for the purpose of mere amusement, in which I was tempted by disposition to indulge and was induced to engage in something like a regular course of study, with a view not only to increase, but to methodize my knowledge, and thus render myself more conversant with the loftier objects of thought. Upon this matter I shall however have more to say hereafter, and only allude to it at present, concluding with the remark, that I should have been a very inferior person, had I not acquired these two friends in early life.

It is of course hardly necessary to remark that Grote could have learnt little from me. Yet after all he owes me one of the greatest blessings that have

140 [H. Grote, *The Personal Life of George Grote* (London: John Murray, 1873) relates that Andreas or Andrew Grote, founder of the family firm, who came from Bremen in 1710 (died 1788), married in 1745 Ann Adams. Her brother, having no issue, left to Joseph Grote, her son by Andreas, a residence called Badgemore near Henley on Thames as well as the remainder of his landed property in Oxfordshire. She died in 1757 and in 1760 Andreas married Mary Anne Culverden (died 1787). They had three sons and six daughters. The eldest son of the second marriage was George Grote senior, the father of Norman's friend. In 1793 he married Selina Peckwell. When his half brother Joseph died in 1814, George Grote senior inherited Badgemore.]

fallen to his lot, I mean his wife. How this happened will appear hereafter in these pages.

Of all those, with whom I have been acquainted, Grote is decidedly the first man. First I mean in intellectual power and energy, while in industry, power of application and of acquisition he yields to none. This was my opinion from the earliest time when I attempted to form a judgment on such matters. Nature designed him for Poet but under the influence of Jeremy Bentham[141] and James Mill,[142] which commenced about 1820, he strove to curb his imagination, which he found a difficult task. At length however he succeeded to an extent which has I think been disadvantageous to the quality of his mind, and his judgments of men and things. After all, man is not purely a reasoning animal. His feelings and affections enter into his being, and form an essential part of it and he who ignores this important fact is apt to form one-sided judgments and to come to erroneous conclusions upon some of the most important subjects in politics, morals and religion.

I have said that G. Grote was by nature a poet. He often indeed wrote poetry, of which I have had specimens in English, French, Latin and spoken Greek. Many years ago, Mrs Grote collected from his various friends all that they possessed or could find of his poetical offspring and I gave her what a cursory examination of my papers disclosed. I fancy however that a few lines written in his inimitable manuscript are still in my possession. When his life comes to be written hereafter, fragments of his poetical effusions will appear

[141][Jeremy Bentham, 1748-1832, British writer on law, government and economics. He is regarded as the fount of English Utilitarianism, though the ideas which he attempted to embody in legislative proposals long predated him. His proposals for reform of the legal system, of Parliament, of the criminal law, the jury system, the Poor Laws, and education, attracted the support of many disciples.]

[142][James Mill, 1773-1836, leading Utilitarian and author of a history of *The History of British India* (London: Baldwin, Cradock and Jay, 1817) viewed from a secularist and Benthamite perspective. He wrote on economics, and on political and philosophical subjects. He was born near Montrose in Scotland, and was educated at Edinburgh University. He went to London in 1802, and supported himself by journalism. He is famous as a close friend of Bentham and Ricardo. He was the father of John Stuart Mill.]

in it.

I should not wonder if enlarged experience of men, and events, and deeper reflection on the phenomena, they exhibit, had by this time to a considerable extent 'unbenthamized' him, and convinced him that aesthetics have played, and ought to play, a considerable part even in the lucubrations of the philosopher and the historian. His great work would have gained in point of style and I believe too in truthful delineation, had he given a little more rein to his imagination.

I must now return to my school days. After I had been four years at Eltham it was determined that I should go somewhere else. I know not who my parents consulted as to my future but suppose that Mr Barnard, my uncle, must have given his advice on the object.[143] At any rate neither my own opinion or wishes were ever asked for, so far as I recollect, when I was informed that I was to go to Eton.

When I was to take leave of Mr Smith, he addressed me in very affectionate terms. Told me that I was to be exposed to evil temptations of many kinds, which I should find it most difficult to resist. Urged me to recollect that it was my bounded duty to strive with all my energies against their influence and concluded by expressing a strong opinion that I should not succumb, as he had the utmost confidence in my good disposition and in the soundness of my principles. I was certainly a favorite pupil, why I can hardly say, and I can add with truth that I always regarded him with respect,

[143] [Mary Anne Beadon, daughter of the Reverend Edwards Beadon, Rector of North Stoneham, Hants, sister of Charlotte Beadon, Norman's mother, married the Reverend Edward Barnard, the only son of Edward Barnard, 1717-81, who was himself educated at Eton, 1732-5. The elder Barnard was appointed Headmaster in 1754. He oversaw a significant expansion of the school from 350 to 550 boys. He became Provost of Eton in 1765 and remained in the post until his death. In 1760 he married Susanna Hagatt of Richmond. His son Edward, Norman's uncle, was baptised in 1763. The elder Edward Beadon held other appointments, being a Canon of Windsor, Vicar of Ospringe, Kent and Rector of St Paul's Cray, not far from Bromley, to which he was appointed in 1752. The Barnards were thus part of the Bromley social circle.]

and with something like affection. He was a very indifferent instructor so far as the imparting [of] positive learning went but he was a kind, honest and conscientious man, and if I have always retained an unfeigned respect for virtue and honour, however little I may have practised them, and a sincere attachment to truth, I so far owe a great deal to him.

I saw but little of Mr Smith in after life. After some time he left Eltham and fixed himself at Newhaven in Sussex,[144] the living of which had been given him by Lord Chancellor Eldon; he had another living in some central county. After a time he gave up the School.

I recollect riding over from Brighton where we were staying with Mr Stone[145] to visit him at Newhaven sometime after my marriage and he subsequently paid me a visit here. He must have died at no very advanced age soon after 1840.

---

[144][John Smith, see p. 21. On the dissolution of Lewes Priory by Thomas Cromwell in 1537, the advowson of Newhaven passed to the Crown, which held it, apart from a brief period in the hands of Thomas Cromwell himself, until 1863. The Rector of Newhaven in this time was presented by the Lord Chancellor, which explains the role of Lord Eldon, to which Norman refers. The Institution of John Smith as Rector of Newhaven was 21 May 1805, and the living was served by curates until June 1821 when Smith took up residence. In the 1832 election he voted for Cavendish and Derby, and is described in the annotated poll book as a Tory, which is noteworthy, given that Norman was a fierce Whig. Smith retired to Brighton in September 1838, and ceased to perform his religious duties at Newhaven. He was brought to Newhaven for burial on 22 May 1846, aged 77. He was thus technically Rector of Newhaven for 41 years, as noted in the Newhaven Register, even though he did not himself take up residence until 1821. (We are indebted to Christopher Whittick for this information.) The connection with Lord Eldon which Norman mentions would have come about directly through John Smith's school; one of Norman's contemporaries was a son of Lord Eldon (see p. 34). In addition Lord Eldon could well have had his attention drawn to the school by his relative, Mr Farrer, the Master in Chancery whom Norman mentions as one of the Eltham notables (see p. 37).]

[145][Henry Stone, Norman's father in law; see pp. 289, 411-12.]

# Chapter 3

# Eton

I went to Eton for the first time at the end of April or beginning of May 1805. The family were at that time staying in Conduit Street, in a house hired from Mr North, afterwards Lord Guilford,[1] which has since been burnt down.[2] I may here remark that it was in attempting to save the books from this conflagration, that Mr Windham received the injury which ultimately caused his death. My father had hired this house, in order that my mother might be attended by a London accoucheur in the confinement which produced my brother Robert.[3]

I was removed from Conduit Street in a two wheel carriage, then called Gig by my uncle, Mr Wilder,[4] who drove me in the first instance to a house at Harefield near Rickmansworth, then owned and inhabited by Mr Barnard, and I was thence, after one night's rest, taken to Eton and placed there.

---

[1] [The title of Earl of Guilford is associated with one branch of the North family, descended from the lawyer and politician Sir Francis North, second son of Dudley North, 4th Baron North and economic writer. The peerage of Baron Guilford of Guilford was bestowed on Dudley North in 1683. The Lord Guilford to whom Norman refers was the 5th Earl, MP for Banbury 1792-4, and Governor of Ceylon 1798-1805.]

[2] [The *Times* 31 January, 1809, 3b. The fire was on Sunday 29 January. At the time of the *Times* report it was believed that no lives had been lost.]

[3] [Robert Cumming Norman, born 30 April 1805, died 13 June 1875.]

[4] [John Wilder, of Purley Hall and Sulham, Berks, baptised 1769, married 1797 Harriet, daughter of the Reverend Edwards Beadon of North Stoneham, Hants, the sister of Norman's mother. She died in 1825 aged 52, he died in 1834 aged 65.]

The dame selected for me was Mrs Slingsby, who had a house behind the Chapel burial ground, and close to Simons's Yard.[5] All the Barnards were there,[6] a sufficient ground for the choice, even had not Mrs Slingsby and her handsome sisters, been as they were, kind and respectable women. In the summer holidays after I went to Eton, I paid a visit to Earl Stoke Park near Devises, then the property and residence of Mr Joshua Smith,[7] father inter alia of a Lady Northampton,[8] and of Emma Smith who is still alive in 1858.[9] I was extremely delighted with this beautiful place with its wood and lake and ornamental village.[10] From it, Miss Smith was kind enough to drive me over Salisbury Plain to Stonehenge, of which I retain a tolerable recollection. My taste for archaeology, inherited from my Father, was even then known. Stoke Park is now the property of the late Mr Watson Taylor's heirs[11] and

[5] [In 1805 Elizabeth Slingsby started to run one of Eton's boarding houses. Her sisters were Mary and Susan, and they took over the job after her death in 1839.]

[6] [Charles Townsend Barnard, born 1790 at Chislehurst, admitted pensioner at St John's College, Cambridge, 1808 (see p. 85). Henry Watson Barnard, born 1792 at Chislehurst, admitted pensioner at St John's, Cambridge, 1811. John Barnard, King's Scholar at Eton, born 1794, died 1878. Fellow of King's College, Cambridge, 1817-78. Died in college. George William Barnard, also a King's Scholar at Eton, was too young to have been there with Norman. He was born in 1804, at Harefield, Middx, and died at Cambridge in 1857.]

[7] [Joshua Smith, 1735-1819, of Erlestoke (or Earl Stoke) Park, Devizes.]

[8] [Charles Compton, 1st Marquess of Northampton, 1760-1828, succeeded his father the 8th Earl of Northampton in 1796. On 18 August 1787 he married Maria (died 24 March 1843), the eldest daughter of Joshua Smith.]

[9] [Joshua Smith married in 1766 Sarah Gilbert, daughter of Nathaniel Gilbert of Antigua, and they had four daughters, Maria, who became Lady Northampton, Augusta, who married Charles Smith of Suttons, Essex (see p. 387), Eliza, who married William Chute of The Vine, and Emma, whom Norman mentions above, who did not marry.]

[10] [Joshua Smith was responsible for the form of Erlestoke. Between 1780 and 1810, he replaced the original Elizabethan house, landscaped the park, and moved the village cottages. He also re-modelled the High Street.]

[11] [After the death of Joshua Smith, the estate was sold to a wealthy and extravagant Jamaican slave owner called George Watson Taylor, 1770-1841. He was originally George Watson. The Jamaican estates of Simon Taylor, 1740-1813, were inherited ultimately by his great niece Anna Susannah Watson-Taylor, 1781-1853. In 1810 she married George Watson, and he assumed the additional name of Taylor by Royal Licence in 1815. As a result of this match he came to own between 2,000 and 3,000 slaves on sugar estates and cattle ranches. The access of substan-

was long rented by L[or]d Broughton.[12] After quitting Stoke Park, we went for some time to the Palace at Wells then inhabited by Bishop Beadon.[13]

My tutor was a son of Dr Drury of Harrow, to whom I must devote a few lines as the Reverend Benjamin Drury was no ordinary parson.[14] To commence with his personal qualities. He was, I think the handsomest young man, when I first knew him, that I ever recollect. He had lustrous dark eyes and dark hair, the most complete Greek nose I ever saw, a noble forehead, well formed mouth and chin, and a clear brown complexion. He could have sat as a study for Diomede or Sarpedon. He was, I should think, six feet high with limbs denoting strength and activity and of a noble Carriage. He excelled in all bodily exercises, which required strength and activity, was an excellent cricketer, fives player and he knew music and sung and played well

tial riches in mid-life seems to have turned Mr Watson Taylor's head. He became MP for Newport, Isle of Wight, then Seaford, East Looe and Devizes, and spent money lavishly in trying to prevent the abolition of slavery, cultivating influential contacts. In 1816 he purchased a town house in Cavendish Square in London, and he later bought Erlestoke Park on which he spent further. He became a collector of fine furniture. But the combination of extravagance and a fall in the price of sugar caused him financial difficulties and he became bankrupt in 1832. The artistic contents of Erlestoke Park were then auctioned. (The subject of West Indian estate owners and their conduct is touched upon by Jane Austen in *Mansfield Park* although in that case she deals with Antigua, from which Mrs Joshua Smith came, rather than Jamaica.) The house was later let to Cam Hobhouse (see next fn). In about 1860 the Watson Taylor family returned to Earlstoke. In the 1890s it was still the seat of the Watson Taylor family.]

[12] [John Cam Hobhouse, 1786-1869, partner in Whitbread brewers, FRS 1814, MP Westminster 1820-33, Nottingham 1834-47, Harwich 1848-51, Secretary at War 1832-3, President of the Board of Control 1835-41, created Baron Broughton 1851, died in 1869 without heirs, when the peerage became extinct.]

[13] [Richard Beadon, 1737-1824, Bishop of Bath and Wells (see p. 10).]

[14] [Benjamin Heath Drury, born in 1783. He was educated at Harrow and Eton, Browne Medallist at Cambridge, 1804, Fellow of Eton 1804-7, Assistant Master at Eton, 1804-23. He was forced to resign on the grounds of an addiction to boxing. Ordained Deacon of Ely 1809, Vicar of Tugby, Leics, 1810-35, married twice and died in 1835 in Guernsey. It appears that Drury was indeed a scandalous figure who, with his crony Henry Hartopp Knapp, would disappear from the school on a Saturday afternoon, disport themselves in theatrical circles over the weekend, and return to the school on Monday morning, doing their marking on the way back. His addiction to fighting was legendary. See Maxwell Lyte, *History of Eton College*, pp. 400-2. Lyte (p. 402) refers to another master, one whom Norman does not mention, William Heath, 'who was believed to be an opium eater'.]

on some instruments.

His mental were not inferior to his physical qualities. He was an excellent scholar, on the Eton model. That is to say he was a first-rate Latin and I believe Greek versifier, and, as a corrector of a boy's exercise, I never saw or heard of his equal. He used to read and alter as he went on with an ease and quickness quite marvellous, and the changes he made were usually most ingenious, always of course for the better, and yet not affecting too much the character of the composition.

He had a wonderful influence over the boys and I recollect on one or two occasions, when there existed some approach to insubordination, the most mutinous quailed before him. In this respect, he was unrivalled.

It is greatly to be deplored that a man of such remarkable accomplishments, should not have pursued a line of conduct somewhat in harmony with them. This however was far from being the case. Drury was extravagant and dissipated. He was very intimate with Kean the actor,[15] used to go to London in a tandem, after school duties were over, sup with his profligate friend at some coffee house near the theatre, pass great part of the night in revelry and return to Eton in time for eight o'clock school. Such habits produced their natural results. Drury although with a large income derived from pupils, was compelled to abscond from Eton in order to avoid his creditors. He afterwards resided in Brussels and I think in Jersey and died in middle age, having ruined a noble constitution by excess.

As a tutor, I cannot say that I derived any special advantage from Drury's superintendence. I was not a private pupil and all I could fairly ask was that he should admit me to his pupil room for construing and look over my exercises. This he did.

The Headmaster of Eton, excepting for my last half year was Dr Goodall

[15][Edmund Kean, 1787/9-1833, English actor. He appeared on the stage as a child, and played Prince Arthur in 'King John' in 1799. His greatest success was from 1814 when he appeared at Drury Lane as Shylock, but it is said that drunkenness and extravagance characterised his later years.]

afterwards Provost.[16] He was a man of good temper and sufficient learning and discharged his duties respectably, but he was the sworn foe of any improvement, and carefully eschewed all important innovations. He was also a tufthunter.[17] I well recollect the favor he used to show to the D[uke] of Leinster.[18] He wore a cauliflower wig and a green cocked hat with the sides sewed to the centre part.

The Undermaster was Keate, who became Headmaster at the beginning of 1810, one half year before I left.[19] The assistant Masters in the upper School were Thackeray, afterwards Provost of Kings,[20] Bethel[21] just dead as

16 [Joseph Goodall, 1760-1840, King's Scholar at Eton, BA King's College, Cambridge 1783, DD 1798, Headmaster of Eton 1802-9, Provost 1809-40. He restored the reputation of the school after George Heath, Headmaster 1792-1802, and was well regarded. He was particularly good at Latin verses, and this accorded well with the emphasis on Latin in the school.]

17 [One who seeks the society of titled persons.]

18 [Augustus Frederick Fitzgerald, 4th Duke of Leinster, second but first surviving son of William Robert Fitzgerald, 3rd Duke, 1748/9-1804. He succeeded in 1804, Grand Master of Freemasons, 1813 to death. Died 10 October 1874 aged 83. He had very large Irish estates with an income of £20,000 per annum in 1799.]

19 [Goodall was succeeded by John Keate, 1773-1852, classical scholar, educated at Eton and King's College, Cambridge, BA 1796, DD 1810, Headmaster 1809-34. He was an extensive flogger, apparently in a vain attempt to secure order in a riotous school with inadequate staff. However he rose to the occasion, and spoke with authority after the death of Anthony Ashley Cooper (see p. 81). He retired in 1834 but did not wish to succeed Goodall as Provost when the latter died in 1840. On Goodall as Headmaster see Maxwell Lyte pp. 431-3. On Keate as a flogger see Maxwell Lyte, *History of Eton College*, pp. 392-5.]

20 [George Thackeray, 1777-1850, King's Scholar at Eton 1792, King's College, Cambridge 1796, BA 1802, Fellow of King's Cambridge 1800-3. In 1803 he married, thus sacrificing his Fellowship. Assistant Master at Eton from 1801, Lower Master 1809. In 1814 he was elected Provost of King's College, and obtained a DD by Royal Mandate. He was a book collector and an efficient Provost, though obstructive of reform.]

21 [George Bethell, baptised 1 August 1779, 4th son of Roberth Bethell, Rector of St Peter's, Wallingford, Berks, admitted to King's College, Cambridge as a scholar from Eton, 30 June 1798, Fellow of King's 1801-7, Assistant Master at Eton 1802-17, Fellow of Eton 1818-57, Rector of Worplesdon, Surrey, 1833-57, Vice Provost 1851-7, died at Eton 16 March 1857.]

Fellow of Eton, Carter[22] and Plumptre[23] still Fellows, Sumner, now Archbishop,[24] Drury, Yonge[25] and Abbot,[26] who was replaced by Hodgson afterwards Provost,[27] and he again by Knapp.[28] I do not think that any of these persons require any special remark, although most of them were respectable Gentlemen who did their duty to the best of their power.

The system of instruction in the school was as bad as it could well be. Not a line of mathematics,[29] a fact which has placed me in a condition of inferiority during the whole of my subsequent life, and very little Greek, greatly to my disadvantage. In truth I knew so little of it, that having a great deal to learn, when I reached manhood, I allowed by degrees my little

[22] [Thomas Carter, 1774-1868, educated at Eton and King's College, Cambridge, BA 1798, Fellow of Eton 1829, Vice Provost 1857-68. Vicar of Burnham, Bucks, 1833-68.]

[23] [John Francis Plumtre, 1782-1864, an extreme Protestant who is said to have regarded Catholic Emancipation as the greatest sin since the Crucifixion. Assistant Master 1803, Fellow of Eton 1822. He was the son of John Francis Plumtre, 1754-1825, entered Eton 1770, King's College, Cambridge 1773, BA 1777, Fellow of King's 1776, resigned 1778.]

[24] [John Bird Sumner, 1780-1862, at Eton 1791-8, Archbishop of Canterbury 1848-62, he was the brother of Charles Richard Sumner, 1790-1874, at Eton 1802-9, Bishop of Llandaff 1826-7, Bishop of Winchester 1827-69.]

[25] [Charles Yonge, 1781-1830, a descendant of James Yonge, 1647-1721, FRS, celebrated naval surgeon. Charles Yonge was admitted at King's College, Cambridge, a scholar from Eton, 1799. Assistant Master at Eton 1803-29, Lower Master 1829-30.]

[26] [William Abbot, baptised 1770, admitted aged 19 at King's College, Cambridge, as scholar from Eton, 1789, BA 1793, ordained 1796, Fellow of King's 1792-1815, Assistant Master 1797-1806, Rector of Horstead and Coltishall, Norfolk, 1814-46, died 4 February 1847 aged 76.]

[27] [Francis Hodgson, 1781-1852, educated at Eton 1794-9, admitted to King's College, Cambridge, 1799, BA 1804, Fellow and Tutor at King's 1808-14. Friend of Byron, Vicar of Bakewell, Derbyshire 1816-40, Archdeacon of Derby 1836-40, Provost of Eton 1840-52.]

[28] [Henry Hartop Knapp, baptised 1782, admitted at King's College, Cambridge, as a scholar from Eton, 1801, Browne Medal 1803, BA 1806, Fellow of King's 1804-21, Assistant Master 1808-30, Lower Master 1830-4. Rector of Ampthill, Beds, 1820-46. Died of malaria at Rome, 1846, aged 64.]

[29] [Writing of the period around 1830, though there is no reason to believe that things had been any better 20 years earlier, under the same Headmaster, Keate, Maxwell Lyte wrote: 'Mathematics fared little better than divinity, eighty years ago, the study of Euclid, of algebra, and even of arithmetic being practically optional.' *History of Eton College* p. 390. ]

modicum of Greek to escape from me. No modern languages formed part of the curriculum, and of this I do not complain, thinking that they may be more readily and perfectly attained by rote at home or on the continent. To work away at them by grammar and dictionary I know by experience to be a futile work and, as I think, a great waste of time and energy.

Latin alone was tolerably taught at Eton, and that chiefly through the medium of versification, for dexterity in which all honours were bestowed. Those who could not skilfully get through their verses and lyrics every week were thought stupid and obtained at least no credit for ability, and such was my case.

The facility in versifying attained by some boys was truly wonderful. They could almost extemporise longs and shorts. The greatest proficient among my acquaintances was the present Sir H. Oxenden,[30] who used to do excellent exercises for himself, and also give perhaps ten exercises a week for other boys. He was really a walking poet. His after life unfortunately did not fulfil the promise of his youth.

I may have something more to say as to my contemporaries at Eton, and as to the mode of instruction prevailing there in my time 1805-10 and will now return to my personal history.

A boy could hardly arrive in the school less prepared for the Eton scheme than myself. I had hardly done a sensa versa[31] at Eltham and my progress in Greek had been very slight. Nevertheless, at eleven and a half I was placed in the middle remove fourth form and had the greatest difficulty for some time in making my way there. In the roll call the names of boys in my part of

[30] [Sir Henry Chudleigh Oxenden, 8th Bt, of Broome House, Barham, Kent, born 1795, educated at Eton and St John's College, Cambridge, succeeded 1838, died 14 August 1889.]

[31] [A Latin mnemonic verse, a device for teaching and remembering Latin grammar. One of the earliest was by Alexander of Villedieu, written in 1189 and comprising 2,000 lines of doggerel verse. It was used as a standard Latin grammar book across Europe for three centuries.]

the Remove[32] ran thus. Mr Percy (C. Percy now of Guy's Cliffe, married to Miss Greatheed),[33] Douglas,[34] Duckinfield (Egerton an Indian civil servant, afterwards a clergyman, and dead within a few years[35]), Norman, Antrobus (Gibbs Crawford, brother of Sir Edmund and a diplomatist[36]). The Captain of our house was Hoare, now I believe Sir Charles,[37] and in my room were Nembhard[38] and Lambie,[39], 2 Wyvills.[40] The other boys at Slingsby's

32 [This is puzzling. Norman is listed in the *Eton School Lists* as being in the 4th Form, not the Remove.]

33 [The Hon. Charles Bertie-Percy of Guy's Cliffe, Warwickshire, 1794-1870, a member of the Percy family of Northumberland, youngest son of 1st Earl of Beverley. In 1822 he married Anne Caroline Greatheed, heiress of Greatheed, and became Charles Greatheed-Bertie-Percy. Guy's Cliffe House, on the banks of the river Avon, just outside Warwick, is now a ruin. Samuel Greatheed was the son of a West Indies sugar planter. He died in 1765. He was succeeded by his infant son Bertie, 1761-1832, an artist and friend of Napoleon. The house passed to his daughter Anne, who married Norman's Eton contemporary Charles Percy.]

34 [John James Douglas, possibly the Douglas admitted as 'pensioner' at Trinity College, Cambridge, May 1810, MA 1813. May have been Curate of Wrawby, Cumberland, Brigg, Lincs, 1846, and later Rector of Kerriemuir, Scotland.]

35 [Charles Egerton Dukinfield (Norman mis-spelt the name as Duckinfield both here and below) Vicar of Edenhall, Cumberland. He had previously been in the Madras Cavalry rather than an Indian civil servant. He died at Salcombe, Devon, in 1840.]

36 [There were two pupils of this surname, Sir Edmond Antrobus 2nd Bt, 1792-1870 (son of Sir Edmond Antrobus, 1st Bt (1815), FRS, FSA, died 6 February 1826) and Gibbs Crawford Antrobus of Eaton Hall, Congleton, Cheshire, died 1861.]

37 [Sir Hugh Richard Hoare, 4th Bt, 1787-1857, of Stourhead, Wilts.]

38 [Ballard Jaques Nembhard. According to Eton records he was the son of a Jamaican gentleman, and was for some time in the 98th Regiment.]

39 [John Lambie was apparently in the 14th Regiment. There was also a William Lambie who became the proprietor and manager of estates in Jamaica.]

40 [Norman's manuscript is extremely unclear at this point. There were the twins William and Armytage Gaussen in the Remove, but the nearest name in H.E.C. Staplyton's *The Eton School Lists* (2nd edition, London: Williams, 1864) to the name which Norman appears to have attempted, 52 years later, to write is Wyvill. There were two brothers of this name in the 4th Form, rather than the Remove, in which Norman was also to be found. They were Marmaduke Wyvill of Constable Burton, Yorks, MP for York 1820-30, and Christopher Wyvill, later Rear Admiral Wyvill, at one time Superintendent of Chatham Dockyard. He died at Bedale Grange, Yorks, in 1863. This would be consistent with Norman referring to '2 Wyvills' as there were other Wyvills in the school. They were Edward Wyvill, later Rector of Fingal and Spennithorne, Bedale, Yorks, and, in the 2nd Form, William Wyvill, later Rector of Black Notley, Essex, who died in 1834.]

with whom I had any particular connection, either on my arrival or subsequently, were Jo[hn] Barnard,[41] my cousin Sir Ch[ristopher] Willoughby, afterwards Dean of Asaph,[42] C.T.C. Luxmoore now a clergyman,[43] Chapman,[44] H. Wilder,[45] my Cousin, Fendal Colonel in the Dragoons[46] &c and – [left blank by Norman].

Very soon after my arrival at Eton I got into a dispute with Lambie, in my room, the result of which was a fight. Other boys encouraged us. I knew nothing of the rules of Eton pugilism but I was strong and active and in a few minutes gave my antagonist, a bigger boy than myself, more than he liked. The combat ceased after black eyes and bloody noses had been exchanged by a sort of tacit consent on both sides, but its ultimate result was that Lambie

---

41 [King's Scholar – see p. 70.]

42 [Sir Christopher Willoughby, 1793-1813, who died at Oxford from a blow from a cricket ball (see p. 91). His brother was Sir Henry Pollard Willoughby, Bt, 1795-1865. MP for Yarmouth, Isle of Wight, 1831-2, Newcastle under Lyme 1832-4, Evesham 1847-65. The younger Willoughby, who succeeded to the title on his brother's death, pioneered the simplification of national accounts.]

43 [Charles Thomas Coryndon Luxmoore, 1793-1863, son of Charles Luxmoore of Okehampton and Joanna, daughter of Walter Murrayfield of Okehampton, Devon. Admitted to St John's College, Cambridge 1811, BA 1815, MA 1818, Fellow of St John's. Married 1822 Frances, daughter of Thomas Brooke of Minshull, Cheshire. Marriage required him to give up his Fellowship. Rector of Marchiviel, Denbigh, 1817-23, Vicar of Guilsfield, Montgomeryshire, 1819-63 where he died. There was also at Eton at that time Charles Scott Luxmoore (died 1854), Dean of St Asaph and eldest son of the late Bishop of St Asaph.]

44 [Probably Thomas Chapman, son of a London merchant. Admitted to Trinity College Cambridge, 1809, BA 1813, Curate of Meopham, Kent, 1814, Rector of Measdon, Buntingord, died 1859. James Chapman, born 1799, died 1879, who attended Eton, was almost certainly too young to be the one whom Norman mentions, despite a later Eton connection. He was admitted to Trinity College Cambridge in 1819 but moved to King's. BA 1823, DD 1845, Fellow of King's 1822-35, Assistant Master at Eton 1822-34, Fellow of Eton 1862, Rector of Dunton Waylett, Essex 1834-45, first Bishop of Colombo, 1845-61.]

45 [Henry Wilson Wilder, of Purley. He matriculated in 1816 at Cambridge, aged 17, BA 1820, Rector of Sulham, Berks from 1823. Drowned with his wife, by upsetting of boat, off Yarmouth, Isle of Wight in 1836. He is listed in the Upper School, 4th Form in 1808.]

46 [John Fendal served in the Bengal Civil Service, and was drowned. William Fendal served in the 4th Dragoons through the Peninsula War and retired as Lieutenant Colonel. There was also Henry Fendal, of Emmanuel College, Cambridge, Vicar of Crambe, Yorks, who later moved to New Zealand.]

felt his inferiority, and as was the practice, would have taken a licking from me afterwards. However I believe we were always subsequently good friends, so that I never tried him. Perhaps the above supposition is wrong.

I never fought but one battle in the playing fields and that was a very short affair lasting only one round. My opponent was my next neighbour in school Dukinfield Minor,[47] brother of the present Sir Henry; he was a year or two older and much stronger than myself and was always attempting to bully me. To this I never would submit and the consequence, besides the regular fight above alluded to in which neither party received much damage, was a constant series of boils in school, very detrimental to my comfort. Having made up my mind that I would fight him if necessary, I was compelled according to the laws of Eton honour, to resist by force any attempt on his part to bully me. His conduct materially interfered with my comfort during several half years and I could not help recollecting this when I met him a man of broken health at Stansted about 20 years ago.

I had no other regular battle at Eton than that with Duckinfield but I recollect two skirmishes in the School Yard, one with Craufurd Major,[48] and another with Marsham,[49] which to my great delight were made up on

[47][Dukinfield major was Sir Henry Robert Dukinfield, Bt, Rector of St Martin's in the Fields 1834-48, Prebendary of Salisbury. He died without heir in 1858. Dukinfield minor was Charles Egerton Dukinfield (see p. 76).]

[48][Craufurd major was Thomas Gage Craufurd, born 1792, Captain of 3rd Guards, killed at Hougoumont, Waterloo, 18 June 1815. His younger brother was Alexander Charles Craufurd, born in 1794, Lieutenant Colonel, died 1838. They were the sons of Sir James Craufurd of Kilbirnie, 2nd Bt, 1761-1839. There was another of the same surname, Sir George William Craufurd, Bt, King's College Cambridge 1815, Rector of Burgh, Lincs, and previously a chaplain in India.]

[49][The list of Eton pupils in H.E.C. Staplyton, *The Eton School Lists from 1791 to 1850* (London: EP Williams, 1863) contains a reference to Henry Shovel Marsham, later Rear Admiral, son of a Canon of Windsor, who at that time was in the 2nd Form. Marsham was of the family of Baron Romney. Robert Marsham, 1st Baron Romney, born in 1685, married Elizabeth, daughter of Sir Cloudesley Shovel, Rear Admiral of Great Britain, who was famously wrecked on the Isles of Scilly. Robert Marsham, 1712-93 was the 2nd Baron Romney. His eldest son, born in 1744, was Charles Marsham, 3rd Baron and 1st Earl of Romney. Jacob Marsham, son of 2nd Baron Romney, 1759-1840, married in 1784 Amelia Frances Bullock. He became a Canon of Windsor, Prebendary of Rochester, a Prebend

the spot. And here I must confess that I was never a hero, I felt painfully the prospect of a conflict, and always strove to avoid it by any means not involving disgrace. My fear of being regarded as a coward being in fact greater than the pain of a few fistycuffs.

I had always a strong desire to obtain the renown of being a good pugilist, used frequently to spar, both with and without the gloves, and being known to possess strength activity and readiness of limb, was regarded as likely to prove a formidable opponent. My rule of action was that I would not 'take a licking from' any boy not both bigger and older than myself, using my discretion with my superiors under both categories.

At a later period of my Eton life I was very near getting into a battle with Cornwall,[50] a glutton, who was known to love fighting and who had proved his prowess in many a ring. We were playing at football on opposite sides and he kicked me when the ball was gone. The fact was patent. Had he been less of a fire eater, I should have allowed the thing to pass by as an accident. As it was, I thought myself bound to turn round and kick him again at the risque of receiving a blow in return, which must have led to a battle. But for reasons which I never could divine, but among which, I am sure that fear had

---

in Wells Cathedral, and held two vicarages, one in Yorkshire and one in Kent. Jacob Marsham was the father of Rear Admiral Henry Shovel Marsham. Henry Shovel Marsham entered the navy 17 May 1807 as a 1st Class Volunteer on board *Superb*. Midshipman 1810, on *Defiance*. Saw service in the Bay of Biscay against the French. Commissioned 1813, Commander 1825, Captain 1833, half pay 1834. He married in 1838 Maria, daughter of W. Jones of Ballinmore, Co. Leitrim, and of Hayle Place, Kent, but Norman does not record any social contact with him. See W.R. O'Byrne, *A Naval Biographical Dictionary Comprising the Life and Services of Every Living Officer in Her Majesty's Navy, from the Rank of Admiral of the Fleet to that of Lieutenant, Inclusive*, London: Murray, 1849, p. 731.]

[50] [Frederick Hamilton Cornwall of Delbury, Salop. Baptised 1791, admitted St John's College, Cambridge 1809, MP Bishop's Castle, Salop, 1830-1, died 30 December 1845. He was the son of Folliot Herbert Walker Cornewall, baptised 1754, died 1831, MP Montgomeryshire 1771-4, educated at Eton and St John's College, Cambridge, accumulated ecclesiastical preferments, and became Bishop of Bristol in 1797, Bishop of Hereford in 1803, Bishop of Worcester in 1808. The mother of the schoolboy was Anne, daughter of George Hamilton, Canon of Windsor. She married in 1787 and died in 1795, having borne two sons and two daughters.]

no place, he did not adopt this course and the affair ended by an attempt to spin each other when ever we met, a course which from my superior skill and activity could only lead to victory on my part.

I may say a few words on the subject of Eton pugilism in my days, as it may interest those who have only known the school in later days, when, as I am told, the habit has altogether passed away. Fights seldom grew out of a direct quarrel but usually in the following way. One boy took offence at something another had said or done and threatened to lick him for it. The threatened, if he felt strong or brave enough, said that he would not submit to be beaten, and the threatener was then obliged in honour to propose a meeting in the playing fields. It happened sometimes that a scuffle took place, which was also adjourned to the regular place of combat.

The battle was fought in a ring formed by the spectators linked together by the arms. The two principals and two seconds alone entered the ring. The rounds, which terminated by mutual consent or at the demand of the seconds or because one of the parties had been knocked down or slipt or fell voluntarily, were separated by intervals of a minutes rest during which time each combatant reposed on his seconds's knee. Water was at hand for the purpose of refreshments and also to wash off blood and mud.

It seldom happened that a battle was decisive, that is that either party yielded. In a great majority of cases after a longer or shorter time, the spectators interfered and recommended peace. In that case, the combatants were too happy to agree. I have known the Headmaster to interfere and stop a fight after it had gone on an unreasonable time, but usually the practice of pugilism was winked at by the authorities, being regarded as a part of the Eton system.

It will be seen above that quite little personal animosity was involved in these conflicts, but usually more a point of honour. There were of course exceptions. After a little the boys involved usually became good friends. The same pair seldom if ever engaged twice.

I never knew anybody permanently injured in a battle, although the apparent injury in cut faces, bloody noses and black eyes was often formidable to see. Some years after I left school a brother of Lord Shaftsbury was accidentally killed.[51] This circumstance and the growing unpopularity of the pugilistic ring, helped to discourage fighting at Eton and I believe that at present, it is hardly known.

It was certainly attended with some advantages, in keeping up a manly spirit and checking one form of bullying and, with my old recollections of the important part it played in our social economy, I can hardly imagine how things can go on well without it.

A lower boy could not fight a fifth or sixth form without having obtained leave from the captains of the Oppidans or Collegers as the case might be. A formal application was made for the permission.

A good fighter was a great man and received high respect and admiration from his companions, the more so if, as often happened, he was a good fellow. A battle between Colleger and Oppidan was always attended by extra excitement, and demanded the display of special courage on the part of the combatants. Of this kind was the fight between Mann[52] and Coleridge,[53] the most celebrated event of the kind in my day. This battle lasted the whole

---

[51] ['The Hon Francis Ashley Cooper, aged 15, 5th son of the Earl of Shaftesbury, having quarrelled with the son of Colonel Wood, they fought on Monday evening when Master Cooper was killed.' *John Bull* 6 March 1825. Wood was the son of Thomas Wood of Littleton, Colonel of East Middlesex Militia, born 1777. He married in 1801 Lady Caroline Stewart, second daughter of Robert, 1st Marquis of Londonderry. His son was thus the nephew of the Marquis of Londonderry. Wood was the younger combatant, having only just reached the age of 14. This information indicates that the son engaged in the fight was the second son of the marriage, William Henry Wood, Captain 10th Hussars, who died in 1834. The Earl of Shaftesbury was Cropley Ashley Cooper, 6th Earl of Shaftesbury, 1768-1851. His son, Anthony Francis Ashley Cooper, was born in 1810, and was thus indeed the older of the two combatants.]

[52] [Horatio Mann, Rector of Mawgan, Cornwall, died falling from his carriage, 1846 (see p. 34).]

[53] [Rt Hon. Sir John Taylor Coleridge, a King's Scholar and later a judge of the Court of Queen's Bench.]

of after twelve and was attended by a large portion of the school. Both were in the upper division fifth form. Mann, a son of Mr Mann of Linton,[54] was the Oppidan and fifteen to sixteen. Coleridge, now I believe the Judge a Colleger, was perhaps a year older and much bigger. Mann was beyond comparison the most skilful. He guarded himself well, put in a blow now and then, and when driven back fell voluntarily, and without a blow. The falling without a blow was allowable in the Eton code of pugilism, although not in that of the prize ring. At two o'clock, Coleridge, who had shown much courage, though no skill, was a fearful spectacle. One eye quite shut. The other all but closed. His lips cut and of double their proper dimensions and his shirt soaked in blood. Mann too was covered with blood, but it had come from Coleridge's veins and his only mark was a slight cut on one cheek. The battle was indecisive and was to have renewed after four, but this could not be from the state of the combatants, both of whom required surgical advice. Mann, who boarded at my Dame's, had leeches applied to his arms, which had greatly suffered in warding off blows.

Just before my day, had been fought a celebrated battle between Duberley[55] (now of Ganies's Hall Hunts) and Campbell,[56] again Colleger and

[54][Robert Mann, at one time a London merchant, acquired Linton Place, near East Farleigh, in the 18th century and built a modest country house, in which he lived until his death in 1751/2. The estate passed to his eldest son and then to Sir Horatio Mann, c.1701-86, Bt, a diplomat who was Envoy to Tuscany 1740-86, and the second son of Robert Mann. He was created a Baronet in 1755, and succeeded to the Linton estate on the death of his elder brother. He died at Florence, unmarried, in 1786 and was succeeded by Sir Horace Mann, his nephew, to whom he bequeathed the estate. Horatio Mann, who was at Eton with Norman, was the eldest son of another member of the same family, James Mann of Linton. Horatio Mann was born in April 1790, proceeded from Eton to Trinity College, Cambridge in 1808, BA 1813. He was Rector of Mawgan and St Martin in Meneage, Cornwall 1816-46. His father James Mann had married in 1786 Lucy Mann, the daughter of Sir Horace Mann who had succeeded his uncle in the Linton estates in Kent, and as 2nd Bt in 1786. James Mann was a notable athlete and cricketer.]

[55][James Duberley of Gaines Hall, St Neot's, later Captain in 11th Hussars.]

[56][Charles Campbell, son of Charles Campbell. He was a King's Scholar at Eton, admitted to Caius College, Cambridge, 1809, Scholar of Caius 1810-12, later at King's College. He was in the army for three years. He was Curate of Weasenham,

Oppidan, and also a series of battles between the crews of the ten Bar and Dreadnought, which involved the biggest boys in the school. I recollect some of the pairs, but I will not occupy space by mentioning them – Clive[57] and Arkwright[58] – Downshire[59] and Bathhurst[60] – Dawson[61] and Bidwell.[62]

The most celebrated fighters of my day were Mann, Duberley, Campbell, Arkwright (now the Revd Joseph of Marks Hall), Byam,[63] Cornwall, above-

Norfolk to 1822, Vicar 1822-78, Rector of Beechamwell and Shingham, Norfolk, 1822-78. Died 20 May 1878.]

57[Richard Clive, Indian Civil Service, Chief Secretary, Madras, 1831, died in India.]

58[Rev. Joseph Arkwright of Mark Hall, Essex and Normanton Turville, Leics (Arkwright minor). There was also Charles Arkwright of Dunstall, Staffs (Arkwright major).]

59[Arthur Blundell Sandys Trumbull, 3rd Marquess of Downshire, 1788-1845, Earl of Hillsborough 1793-1801, at Eton 1800-5, MA Oxford 1809, Lord Lieutenant of County Down, 1831-45, died suddenly of apoplexy at Blessington, Co. Wicklow 12 April 1845, a Whig until 1834, then a Tory.]

60[There were two pupils of that name: William Lennox Bathurst, Clerk of the Privy Council, and Thomas Seymour Bathurst, Lieutenant Colonel in the Guards, died 1834.]

61[There were several pupils with this name. There was a King's Scholar, Charles Dawson, son of Pudsey Dawson of Lang Cliffe Hall and Bolton Hall, 1752-1816. Charles Dawson did not, despite being a King's Scholar, proceed to Cambridge as would have been the norm but instead became a Lieutenant in the 52nd Light Infantry. His elder brother in the same regiment, Henry Dawson, was killed in Spain in November 1812. Charles Dawson also served in the Peninsula and died in 1815 aged 22. Others with that surname were William Mackenzie Dawson (died 1859), brother of the Earl of Portarlington, and Frederick Dawson, a barrister of Oriel College, Oxford; the Rt Hon. George Lionel Dawson-Damer Dawson, 1st Dragoon Guards and later MP for Portarlington; and Francis Dawson, admitted to Trinity College, Cambridge in 1807, BA 1812, later Rector of Chislehurst 1815-46 and Canon of Canterbury from 1833. He died 24 October 1852, aged 64. This last is probably the one to whom Norman is referring. According to Staplyton's Eton list, Francis Dawson was in 1805 in the Upper School 5th Form, which means he could have been involved in the fighting to which Norman refers. He was in the same form as Duckinfield major. He was described by Staplyton as the nephew of Archbishop M. Sutton's wife. Charles Manners Sutton, 1755-1828 was Archbishop of Canterbury 1805-28. He married in 1778 Mary (died 1832) daughter of Thomas Thoroton of Screveton, Notts.]

62[George Bidwell, son of Shelford Bidwell of Thetford, Norfolk, born 1787, educated at Eton, admitted to Clare College Cambridge, 1804, BA 1809, MA 1814, Fellow of Clare Hall, Cambridge 1810-12, ordained priest of diocese of Ely 1811, Rector of Stanton All Saints with St John the Baptist, Suffolk 1811-65.]

63[Probably Sir William Byam, of Cedar Hill, later President of the Council

mentioned. John Barnard too was brave and skilful, but wanted power. I have seen him fight with great 'kudos' several times. Scarlett, now I believe Lord Abinger,[64] obtained great credit by resisting all after twelve, and part of after four, the redoubtable Cornwall, who by the way was a glutton but not a punisher. I recollect seeing Milman, now Dean of St Pauls, fight.[65] I forget with whom.[66]

I have said that no boy could have been worse prepared for Eton than myself. Either owing to this circumstance or to my having no turn for Latin versification, or to my idleness, perhaps in some respects owing to all these things, I made no distinguished figure in the school. For my own sake however, and in order to avoid trouble, I took care to avoid getting into scrapes. I always did my own exercises, never but once, so far as I recollect, having ever used an old copy. Was usually able to say by heart, according to the farcical plan adopted at Eton in my day, when each boy repeated six or eight lines, which he learned while those above him were repeating their portions, having probably never looked at his lesson, until he got into the school room.

---

in the island of Antigua, and Lieutenant Colonel of the local Dragoons, though it could be his younger brother Edward Byam, later a Lieutenant General and Colonel of the 18th Light Dragoons. The Byam family originated in Pembrokeshire. However there were members of the family in Surinam until, in 1667, this was handed by the British to the Dutch. The Byams then removed to Antigua.]

[64][Robert Campbell Scarlett, Baron Abinger, 1794-1861, BA Trinity College, Cambridge, 1815, MP Norwich 1835-8, Horsham 1841-4. Died at Abinger Hall, Surrey. He was the eldest son of a judge, James Scarlett, 1769-1844, KC 1816, MP Peterborough 1819-30, Malton 1830-1, Cockermouth 1831-2, Norwich 1832-4, created Baron Abinger 1835. Made Lord Chief Baron of the Exchequer by Peel in 1835.]

[65][Henry Hart Milman, son of Francis Milman Bt, of St James's, Westminster. King's Scholar, at Eton. Admitted to Brasenose College, Oxford 1810, aged 19, 1st Class honours 1813. Fellow of Brasenose 1814-19, DD 1849, Professor of Poetry at Oxford 1821-31, Vicar of St Mary's, Reading, 1817-35, Canon of Westminster 1835-49, Dean of St Paul's 1849-68. Died September 1868.]

[66]P. Purnell. [Note added by Norman. Purnell Bransby Cooper Purnell of Stancombe Park, Glos, chairman of quarter sessions. The name was originally Purnell Bransby Cooper. He was born in 1791 and he assumed the additional name Purnell on the death of his mother in 1804, when he succeeded to the Gloucester estates.]

I could always also construe.

I had certainly far more general knowledge than most of my peers and when I was in the lower division Thackeray, when he failed to get an answer on any particular point of geography, history &c. would often appeal to me, by the title of 'The Well-Read Man'.

I was never flogged but twice, and on neither occasion recollect that I felt a blow. The offences I forget, but they were trifling, I think not saying.

When I was at Eton, a flogging was the general, I may almost say the universal punishment. At eleven o'clock on monday there would be 30 to 40 boys flogged and there were some who exhibited their posteriors on the block, almost every day, at any rate three or four times a week. The punishment was little dreaded, and in general gave little pain. About four cuts was the usual allowance for an ordinary offence, these being administered with little severity. For a great offence such as shooting or tandem driving, I have known ten or twelve blows administered, and with sufficious force to wheal the skin and to draw blood.

It is difficult to say anything in favor of the employment of the rod as a means of punishment in schools, especially in the first school in England. Yet it exists even now in spite of the argument and ridicule, of the philosophers of the newspapers. This at any rate proves that it does no flagrant mischief and that it is very difficult to find a substitute. This is all at least, that I can say for it. It did little in the way of affrighting offenders but it was convenient, summary, and easily graduated. Confinement, which might be substituted for it would be very inconvenient and demand places of seclusion, which would be very difficult of management. I have known boys of seventeen flogged.

On the whole, I think we must be contented to retain flogging under proper restrictions until something better can be found.

One of the offences which occasioned the greatest noise when I was at Eton, was committed by a cousin of mine, Charles T. Barnard, now resident at Coburg.[67] He was caught coursing in the park by the keepers, a companion, named Rawnsley I think,[68] having the luck to escape. He was taken to the keeper's lodge and there remained for two or three days. He was finally released, brought back and flogged. It was said that George Villiers the ranger who knew his family, interested himself in his favor. C.T.B[arnard], soon afterwards snared a four pound trout in the river, opposite Poet's Walk, and sent it to Mr Villiers, who shortly afterwards proved a public defaulter, in token of gratitude.

Goodall made a long speech in School, Etoniae in prose, about this event, and expressed great fears least the culprit should be sent to Reading Jail. It would have been well, had nothing worse been done than this boyish escapade in the school under his Mastership.

I may here make a few remarks on another peculiarity. I mean the system of fagging.

According to the rules existing in my time, all the fifth and sixth forms had the right of fagging all below them. If there was any exception at all, it was, I think that an Oppidan could not fag a Colleger, nor I think a Colleger an Oppidan, unless the former was in the sixth form. There was no intermediate class who could neither fag nor be fagged.

Lower boys, all below the fifth form, were exposed to fagging in two shapes. Each had a master in his own house, whom he attended chiefly at breakfast and tea. He went to the shop for 'socks', alias eatables, toasted bread, muffins, such things &c. These duties occupied little time and were but slightly onerous. Service to a fixed master was fagging in one shape. The other shape consisted in the service which every lower boy was bound to yield to every boy in the fifth or sixth forms. This was a matter of chance, and a little management, but seldom involved much severe duty. 'You sir, go to

[67] [Charles Townsend Barnard, one of Norman's Barnard cousins (see p. 70). He was Chargé d'Affaires at Coburg, 1842, married Emily Unges, and died in 1878.]

[68] [Thomas Hardwicke Rawnsley, a King's Scholar, Rector of Falkingham, Lincs.]

my dame's and say that so and so will mess with me', or 'go to Jack Smith's and buy me a five's ball'. The worst form of the casual fagging was what was called 'fagging at cricket'. In this case the fags, there was usually more than one, had to stop the balls behind wicket at practice in the shooting fields and to run after the balls when hit, and were thus employed perhaps a whole after four or six[69] in a work to them the most uninteresting, while they were deprived of their own amusement.[70]

I always thought this a great abuse of the fagging power and great shame and tyranny. I never fagged a boy at cricket in my life, thus giving up what was certainly a great convenience. I may add that the grievance extended to but few. I do not think that I was fagged at cricket more than twice, while a lower boy, in two whole seasons.

It was common for some lower boys to escape the burthen of external fagging by what was called 'having the name of an upper boy'. This meant a permission, when ordered to do anything 'by Smith or Jones', to say that you were fagging for Thomson, although in reality you were not so employed. This may [be] considered by some as a blamable part of that system of white-lying, which prevailed at Eton, but hardly amounted even to this, for it was thoroughly understood that an upper might properly give his name to a lower boy.

I have said on the whole, fagging is but a trifling burthen, so I found it, and I am sure that a majority of lower boys would have said the same

[69][The Eton timetable was somewhat unusual by modern standards. According to Maxell Lyte, 'In a regular week, Tuesday was a whole holiday, Thursday generally a half-holiday, and Saturday a "play-at-four". On the three stricter working days, the normal school-hours lasted from eight to nine, from eleven to twelve, from three to four, and from five to six, except that on Friday the first lesson in the afternoon lasted from two to half-past three.' This régime had apparently been introduced in 1766 and lasted until about 1840. See Maxwell Lyte, *History of Eton College*, p. 308. 'After four' would thus be the period between 4pm and 5pm, and 'After six' would be the period between 6pm and the assembly of the boys in the Hall at 7pm 'apparently' for the purposes of study (Lyte, pp. 309-10).]

[70][See Maxwell Lyte, *A History of Eton College 1440-1910*, London: Macmillan 1911, p. 411.]

thing. There were however exceptions, for instance I imagine that the lowest collegers who in all respects had much rough work to go through, found their fagging very severe, and were to use the Eton phrase much bullied. Among oppidans and collegers too, bad masters were to be found who abused their power and tormented those beneath them.

The punishment inflicted on a fag was either extra duty or a licking, usually the latter, which consisted in blows on the twisted arms, ears, behind &c according to the nature of the offence or the disposition of the master. On the whole however I think that few Etonians of my day, will look back on their lower boy days with any painful reminiscences as respects fagging.

If I am asked if on the whole I thought the practice of fagging to have been salutary or injurious, I must say, and that without much hesitation, that I regard it as having been salutary with a very large majority of boys. Instances of real hardship and tyranny I believe to have been very rare, and on the whole it seems to me that the institution formed an useful part of that complicated set of influences, which rendered the Etonian system, with its numerous and glaring faults, so admirable a preparation for the active business of life. It taught the boy how to command and how to obey, how to exercise power without abusing it, and how to submit to authority without degradation.

Having said so much to the school in general, I must now return to my self. I have said that I was a bad versifier, but always did my own exercises. That I could usually say by heart, and always construe fairly when called up. After having been at Eton a short time all these things became extremely easy to me, and really occupied very little of my attention. In truth my inmost heart and mind were devoted to play. That was my real business. I have said, that I was strong and active of body, and possessed much manual dexterity. I have ever had great pleasure in bodily exercise. I was also very ambitious, and play opened a wide field, productive of great pleasure, and also of forwarding the full gratification to my ambition for, be it observed, a first-rate cricketer occupied, in the public opinion of the school, a position quite as elevated as a first-rate versemaker.

Of cricket I certainly thought more in summer at least, than of anything whatever. I played at it every day and almost after every twelve, four and six.[71]

When I could play at wicket, I did so. When no wicket game was attainable I played at single wicket,[72] always trying to play as well as I could and to improve myself, for which purpose I studied carefully the performances of all the good players I met with. And when I grew a big boy, I joined a companion, usually Sir Christopher Willoughby, a good con of mine in hiring a professional, Goodman, Wakeman or Powell to bowl to us. I thus speedily became a good bat, and was generally in the eleven of every club I belonged to. Of these I recollect a club of little boys, among whom the late Lord Darnley was distinguished.[73] The lower college, which was kept by John. Barnard and myself for both oppidans and collegers, the lower shooting fields, where I recollect in both the eleven and twenty-two games in after twelve meant knocking down my wicket voluntarily at five with more than 80 runs to my name, and the upper club.

I was only once in the upper club *viz.* in 1809, and was then placed in the eleven of the school under the age of sixteen, an almost unheard of event

[71] [Two of Norman's Barnard cousins are mentioned by Maxwell Lyte as outstanding cricketers at Eton, John Barnard, Captain of Montem in 1814, and a younger Barnard, G.W. Barnard, Captain of Montem in 1823. See Maxwell Lyte, *History of Eton College*, p. 410.]

[72] [On single wicket cricket see John Major, *More Than a Game. The Story of Cricket's Early Years*, London: Harper Collins, 2007, pp. 45, 49, 121, 150, 170, and especially 155-67 and 403-10.]

[73] [Edward Bligh, 5th Earl of Darnley, 1795-1835, second but first surviving son of 4th Earl, born 25 February 1795, died of tetanus after a wound from an axe while felling timber at Cobham Hall. Thus he was 'the late' when Norman was writing in 1857. Educated at Eton and Christ Church, Oxford, 1st Class Classics BA 1816, MP (Whig) Canterbury, 1818-30, FRS 1833. Succeeded to the title in 1831. He married in 1825 Emma Jane (died 1884), the third daughter of Henry Brooke Parnell, Baron Congleton, to whose work Norman refers in his *Essay on Taxation.*]

in my time. The eleven being almost all big fellows.

We played two or three matches in 1809, against the Rickmansworth,[74] and Berkeley clubs, and Garrison of Windsor, and I remember that in one match, I was sent in first to take wicket, and that when I came out, having got fifteen runs, or notches as we called them, my tutor said to me, 'you hit like Beldham'.[75]

It must be remembered that my forte was batting, and that I was a good field. I never could bowl, nor could any Norman excel in that part of the game. I apprehended that our arms were too short. All good bowlers have long arms.

The general style of play, when I went to Eton, was very rough. Runs were got by swipes into the field chiefly to the leg, and an occasional leg hit. The bowling was all fast and underhand. About 1809, some of the elevens opposed to the school brought slow bowlers, among whom an old man, named Timber was most conspicuous.[76] The slow bowlers at first, mere lobbers, did great execution. The boys of course imitated them, as they also did the offhitting, slicing and cutting, practised by their opponents. The best Etonian cricketer in my day was Kaye, son of the Bank solicitor who died in India.[77] My friend

[74] [Norman wrote 'Ricksmanworth' here.]

[75] [William Beldham, 1766-1862, the most famous cricketer of his day, especially as a batsman. He was particularly noted as a powerful attacking batsman, but was an all-rounder who took many wickets as well. A stylish stroke maker, known as 'Silver Billy', his first class career yielded 7,064 runs at an average of 21.40, with three centuries in an age when these were rare. The average should be related to the fact that, in that era, 110 was regarded as a good team score. When playing for Surrey against England in 1794 at Lords he scored 72 and 104, took 2 wickets and 3 catches. Though he had a reputation as a prolific father, his children were only nine in number, a not unusual figure for the time, by two wives. The book by John Major, cited on p. 89, contains many details of Beldham's career.]

[76] [Timber, dates unknown, was an English professional cricketer who made ten known appearances in major cricket matches from 1792 to 1795 and was a Berkshire player.]

[77] [John Hilbert Kaye, son of the solicitor to the Bank of England. He was in the Madras Cavalry, and died in India. His brother was Sir John William Kaye, 1814-76, who was also educated at Eton, Bengal Artillery 1836-41, entered the Home Civil Service of the East India Company 1856, succeeded J.S. Mill as Secretary in

Sir C. Willoughby was the stiffest bat I ever saw. It was almost impossible to get him out, and this rendered him a great nuisance in a club game. He was the elder brother of the present Sir H. Willoughby and died at Oxford of the effects of a fall on his head in hunting.[78] He was a tall, lanky person, with a very long reach, which gave him a great advantage in playing forward.

Cricket although my chief, was not my sole amusement in the summer. I pulled twice in the boats once in the *Defiance*, once I think in the *Mars*.[79] I threw my self with my usual impetuosity into this new pastime and became an expert rower, although not very fond of the oar and lamenting sorely when, on Saturday, I was compelled to go up to Surley Hall. On a Sunday morning I have rowed up to Water Oakley and breakfasted. I never sculled.

The present Lord Exeter steered the *Defiance*.[80] Our dress was an orange silk tunic, laced with silver. A belt of silver lace, tight net pantaloons with red bottines and an oriental looking cap. Expense of hire dress and boat: £8 each boy.

In my day, all the boats, but the *Dreadnought* pulled in fancy dresses. The steerers as fine as velvet and lace, and silk and feathers could make them. The general effect was I think better than now. The boats heavy clumsy affairs. There was no lock between Eton and Maidenhead.

---

the India Office 1858-74, FRS 1866, KCSI 1871. Their parents were Charles Kaye of Acton, Middlesex, and his wife Eliza, daughter of Hugh Atkins. James William Freshfield, 1774-1864, was an English lawyer and founder of the international law firm of Freshfields (he was also Overstone's solicitor). He qualified as a solicitor in 1795 and, after initially setting up in practice on his own in Smithfield, joined the firm of Winter and Kaye. By 1811 this was Kaye and Freshfield, but by 1819 Freshfield was involved in litigation relating to the misappropriation of Bank of England funds by Charles Kaye, who was forced to resign from the partnership. Earlier the firm had been active in bringing counterfeiters to the gallows.]

78 [This was a slip on Norman's part. Sir Christopher Willoughby died at Oxford from a blow from a cricket ball.]

79 [On the rowing at Eton, see Maxwell Lyte, *History of Eton College*, p. 415.]

80 [Brownlow Cecil, 3rd Marquess of Exeter, first surviving son of the 2nd Marquess, born 1795, styled Lord Burleigh to 1804, educated at Eton and St John's College, Cambridge, MA 1814, died Burghley House, January 1867, Lord Lieutenant of Rutland 1826-67, and Northants 1842-67.]

I also bathed a good deal, having learnt to swim of Charles Hester[81] in Cotton's hole. But my favorite bathing places were the Weir, and Dow's Mill in the Back Fields. I was not a first rate swimmer and never went into the water, excepting in the morning. Allowed bathing places were Cotton's Hole, Bargeman's Bridge, Upper and Lower Hopes and Cuckoo Weir; Deadman's Hole was not allowed, but much resorted to.

Between August and the winter holiday I played at football with little less enthusiasm than at cricket in the summer and with equal success. I was always in the eleven of my class, and finally, I think in the eleven of the school. I was a very good player speaking generally, firm on my legs, active, an excellent bullier, and knowing all the tricks of the game.

Football in my day was different from what it is at present, comprehending the play both at and away from the wall. My shin bones bear at the present day some marks of wounds inflicted by the foeman's kicks, but I never received a serious injury. I have witnessed a broken or dislocated arm more than once.

Between Christmas and Easter, I employed many of my play-hours in leaping, either with or without a pole, chiefly without. The usual scene of operations was the common ditch, where the exploits of celebrated leapers was commemorated, appellation's legg leap, Codrington's leap &c. When a little boy I was fond of hoops and marbles and have won greatly at the latter, which I played scientifically. I once paid 700 marbles, for one, for a blood ally – a sort of precious marble. The school yard near Goodall's Chambers was the usual scene of action. The projecting flints gave much room for skill and finesse.

At all times I was fond of fives, which I played generally at odd times, and became an adept; during the latter part of my Eton life I was one of the four of the school.

---

[81] [Charles Hester was not a pupil at Eton, but a waterman. His duties included patrolling the bathing places, and teaching the boys to swim.]

I was equally one of the four at billiards. My tables were at Gray's on the left over Windsor Bridge. I was then, and long continued, distractedly fond of this game and devoted a great deal of time to it. This was chiefly deducted from leaping.

I also played at quoits and with success. In the evenings we occasionally had a whist table at my dames.

This long account of my amusements and of my devotion to them will bear out my assertion that school business was the very last and least thing about which I thought.

I must not however forget that I shot a good deal at Eton and with some success. I used to go out in the five fields near the park and in other places with various companions, and have killed partridges, snipes, moorhens and small birds of course. I was once caught by Lord Montagu's keeper at Beaulieu or Ditton Park and kindly released.[82]

Shooting was reckoned a great crime and would have entailed a heavy punishment if detected. But upon the point I had no apprehension. I used to select times and seasons, as almost to secure myself from the risque of being caught by a master. I had always a companion and an attendant, the latter belonging to the class of dependants attached to the school, Joe Cannon, Jim Miller, Jack Hall &c.

I recollect on one occasion going early in the morning with a great friend of mine, H.P. Powys, whose nickname was Jupiter and who is now Mr Powys of Hardwick, Oxon to ferret rabbits in the Bank outside of Stoke Park.[83]

[82][Ditton Park was an ancient square mansion surrounded by a moat and in a park of about 260 acres. The mansion was burnt down in 1812, and a new house was built by Elizabeth, Duchess of Buccleuch in 1813. Lord Montagu was Henry James Montagu-Scott, Baron Montagu of Boughton, third son of Henry Scott, 3rd Duke of Buccleuch, by Elizabeth, daughter and heir of George, Duke of Montagu. Henry James Montagu Scott was educated at Eton, 1785-93. The Buccleuch family did own Beaulieu when Norman was at Eton, even though the title Montagu of Beaulieu dates from 1885.]

[83][Henry Philip Powys, born 24 November 1791, died 1859. Hardwick is 5 miles north of Bicester.]

We caught two or three but were driven into the lodge by the rain, nobody molested us and on our way home we breakfasted at Botham's Hall.

On Sunday I used to be very fond of taking long walks to Gray's Monument,[84] where my poetical sympathies were excited, or to the ruins at Burnham Abbey,[85] for I was even then a bit of an archaeologist, or to Old Windsor. Upton Church too, I was very fond of with its ivy clad tower.[86] I used to take it in my way to Langley[87] or to Beaulieu Park, where I explored the Ditches in search of Jack.

Between Christmas and Easter, hare and hounds was a common amusement, which I much liked. The scent consisted of small bits of paper strewn at intervals by the hares, who were ordinarily two, and as the likely country after a few hunts was crossed by many lines of scent, it became necessary to distinguish between Virgil or Homer or Gradus or Greek grammar scent.

When a little boy, I was rather celebrated as a wrestler, having brought some knowledge of this art with me from Eltham. I recollect gaining great kudos in it on one occasion. Joe Arkwright,[88] as mentioned some pages back, was a noted fighter, much bigger, stronger and older than myself. One day before absence in the school yard, he challenged me to a trial of skill. I

---

[84] [Thomas Gray, 1716-71, English poet, classical scholar, and Professor at Cambridge University. Educated at Eton (an uncle was one of the masters). Lacking in self-confidence, published only 13 poems in his lifetime. The 'Elegy Written in a Country Churchyard' is believed to have been written at the church at Stoke Poges, Bucks in 1750. The poem's famous depiction of an ivory-mantled tower is believed to be a reference to the early medieval St Laurence's Church in Upton, Slough to which Norman refers. Gray himself was buried in the Stoke Poges churchyard beside his mother. The Gray monument stands in Stoke Poges opposite the church.]

[85] [Burnham is 3 miles north east of Maidenhead. It was an Augustinian house, founded in 1265. It was given at the Dissolution of the Monasteries to William Tyldesley.]

[86] [Norman is referring to the old parish church of St Lawrence Upton, which is now within Slough. It has a small but ancient Norman building with a chancel, nave, a south aisle, a north porch and a central tower.]

[87] [Langley Marish was three and a half miles north east of Windsor, with a mansion built in 1755 for the 3rd Duke of Marlborough, set in about 380 acres.]

[88] [Arkwright minor – see p. 83.]

accepted, although with little hope of success. However after a long tussle I succeeded in throwing him upon his back and obtained no little renown by the exploit. C. Barnard in after years used to describe me, when I was first at Eton, as a sturdy little fellow, in corderoy trousers much inked, who was in the habit of going about and proposing to other boys a match in wrestling.

Hockey was a popular game at Eton when I was there and I might have easily made myself like it but I rarely tried it, as it would have interfered with cricket and football which I liked much better. It may be asked how I could play so much, and yet be able to get through the school business? I replied that I never looked at a lesson, excepting in school or at my tutors when construed. My theme was always finished on Sunday, while verses and lyrics were invariably finished between tea and supper or after supper in the summer.

During the two or three last half years I paid considerable attention to my exercises, having been a little ashamed of my idleness and a considerable improvement in them was the result. At any rate, they became much longer than previously, thirty-six verses long and short or ten stanzas of alcaics became my usual allowance. My most labored copy of verses was my vale. I wish that I had a copy of it but I gave away all my old copies to Wigsell before I left.[89] However I recollect the beginning:

'Qualis ubi implumis nidi de tegmine coelum
Turbatum boreae flatibus horret avies'

*Sic ego.* The train of thought may easily be imagined.[90]

There was no public library accessible to the boys or any easy means of

---

[89] [Attwood Wigsell, of Sanderstead, Croydon. He apparently died young of 'consumption', the Victorian term for tuberculosis.]

[90] [Norman's Latin, modelled on a two line 'Alcaic' as in Horace, is very difficult to read. However a literal translation of the above, rather than the poetic equivalent that Norman would have had in mind, might be: 'Where such unfledged [birds] from the cover of the nest/ [while] the stormy sky, with snorts of the North wind, disturbs the birds'. More poetically, it would be, 'Just like when the stormy sky/ Shivers the unfledged birds/ Torn from the cover of the nest'.]

obtaining useful books for private reading at Eton in my time. However I used to borrow such from friends when I could, and thus to a certain extent kept up the habit of reading. At home in the evening I read with as much pleasure as previously.

The usual private reading of the school consisted of what were called pamphlets. These were meagre romances, ghost and bandit stories bought of Ingalton, the bookseller up town, sometimes worse.

I was an ardent politician at Eton and of very liberal views and used to read a newspaper whenever I could get hold of one. At the confectioner's in conjunction with Powys, I took the Reading Mercury. I can well remember now the enthusiasm I felt for the Spaniards and my grief at the news of the Battle of Wagram[91] after the elevation of my hopes produced by the check of Napoleon at Aspern.

I was at Eton when the Battle of Trafalgar took place, and with my father witnessed a portion of Nelson's Funeral. We had a view of the river procession from the window of a house belonging to Greenaway[92] at Blackfriars. I cannot say that my recollection of what I saw is very vivid. However I must finish with Eton, and then go back to a few events which occurred to me in the holydays.

I was at two Montems. In the first as polebearer, I walked with a slender pole five or six feet long in my hand, dressed in a blue coat, white waistcoat, nankeen[93] trousers and silk stockings, cocked hat and sword. It was the fashion to have the red coat dyed afterwards. Mine was so treated.

As Montem will soon be forgotten I think it advisable shortly to describe it.[94] The object was to raise a sum of money for the captain who was going

[91] [Napoleon's 1809 campaign against the Austrians ended with the pitched battle of Wagram, followed by an Austrian retreat and armistice on 12 July. Napoleon had earlier been defeated at Aspern (Essling) on 22-25 May while advancing on Vienna.]

[92] [Probably, as MS is not clear here.]

[93] [A kind of cotton cloth, originally unbleached, named after Nanking in China.]

[94] [Norman's account of Montem is supported by that to be found in *Reminis-*

to King's. The fifth form and lower boys were corporals and polebearers, as delineated above. The sixth form furnished the Captain, Marshal, Colonel, Ensign and Saltbearers. The Saltbearers in fancy dresses scoured the country and stopped passengers to collect money, Etoniae Salt. A Procession was formed which went to Salt Hill, where on a little eminence the Ensign waved his flag and the boys dined. The sight was rather pretty but the whole thing was absurd and useless in a great degree as to its object. The Captain was pillaged right and left and retained but little of the money.[95] I consider the abolition of Montem to have been a very proper measure.[96]

The ordinary dress of boys at Eton in my time was a long swallow-tailed coat, tight breeches and shoes. Trousers came as an innovation. No boots or black or coloured neck-cloths were permitted. Straitcut coats were admitted at last with some difficulty. Nothing could be more absurd than a little boy in the established dress, his white stockings as a matter of course being excessively dirty.

The Collegers having no means of getting a tolerable breakfast or tea in college used to hire rooms up town, where they took their morning and evening meals. This was of course against law but was tacitly allowed.

There were other matters connected with the school, in which the law was universally violated. The observance of bounds was one of these. The

*cences of an Etonian*, London: Hackman, 1831, the author of which was one J. Boynor, pp. 137-42. A number of Norman's Eton contemporaries subscribed in advance, to ensure the publication of the book, but Norman's name does not appear amongst the list of subscribers.]

95 [Despite Norman's view that the Captain of Montem was left with little money, it seems that the net proceeds could have been the not inconsiderable sum of £200. Maxwell Lyte, pp. 514-17. However he was certainly right that the sum collected was much greater than the net figure. J. Boynor in the *Reminiscences*, p. 142, puts the gross figure at £800 to £1,000, and agrees with Norman that the majority of it disappeared in various ways.]

96 [Montem was finally abolished in 1847. Norman's view is supported by the author of the *Reminiscences*, p. 141, who considered Montem to be a form of 'genteel begging'. Norman's cousin John Barnard achieved the Etonian distinction of being Captain of Montem in 1814. He was later a Fellow of King's College, Cambridge.]

bounds only extended from Barn's pool to just beyond the school yard on the Slough road and from the end of the shooting fields to Angels's and Keale's. It was of course impossible to keep 550 boys within such narrow bounds. There was no object in doing so either. The practice was when a boy met a master out of bounds to get behind a hedge or tree or door. This was intended as a mark of respect for his authority, and was called shirking. A boy who did not shirk got a punishment, but the simple act of being out of bounds was never punished.

In the same way a lower boy was obliged to shirk a sixth form. The sixth form might go where they pleased.

I have sometimes thought that one's ideas of right and wrong were confounded, and bad moral effects produced, by the Eton habit of enacting laws, which were never obeyed or meant to be obeyed, but I doubt if it were really so to any considerable extent, I could mention other instances of what I mean, besides the shirking. There was the evening dresses.

I now[97] resume my labours which had been interrupted for some time by more pressing demands on my time arising chiefly out of the money crisis.[98]

During my residence at Eton the habits of the boys were very expensive. Some of them brought very large sums of money with them. I have heard as much as £50 a half. Lisle of Acton, since called Delisle[99] a minor and heir

[97] December 16th [1857].

[98] [The great financial crisis of 1857 had begun with failures in the United States, notably bank failures. These began in September; in October alone, 1415 banks stopped and business came to a standstill along the Eastern seaboard. Inevitably the crisis spread to Britain, but it was petering out by the end of November though not officially over until Christmas Eve, with the reduction in Bank Rate from 10 to 8 per cent.]

[99] [Robert Lisle, afterwards de Lisle of Acton House, Felton, Northumberland, married Mary Orde, who died in 1825. His 'natural son', Robert, who was at Eton with Norman, proceeded from Eton to Magdalen College, Oxford. He appears to have inherited the family estates. Acton and Old Felton was an area of 1,244 acres, of which the Lisle family owned a significant part. It was a rich agricultural area with coal seams. The Lisle family also owned property in Scotland. Robert Lisle, the 'natural son' died at Edinburgh. On Lisle of Acton, Northumberland see p. 137. The Lisle family were descended from the 12th century figure of Robert

to a large estate, was especially favored or rather disfavored in this respect. In his case the consequence was extravagance and early ruin. Boys with full pockets used to drive tandems, give breakfasts and dinners and sock morning, noon and night.

I have always endeavoured to steer clear of this folly with my boys, taking care however that they should not be stinted in the attainment of any proper project by want of the needful.

The greater part of the school was always in debt. The money brought to school was employed in discharging old scores, and the pocket was subsequently empty, unless replenished by an accidental pouch.

As mentioned I think already, my financial arrangements were better managed. I usually laid by enough of the money brought with me after the holidays, to pay my trifling bills at the end of the half, so that I began next half without any calls upon my purse. I had no expensive habits. My money went in paying bowlers, billiard tables and hire of guns. Hardly any for sock, excepting that once or twice in the half I used to dine with Powys at Slough, when we had a roast chicken, potatoes, cheese and some ale. The whole costing five to six shillings for the two.

I have mentioned before that I never received money from home during the half, nor did father or mother ever come to see me. Indeed I doubt if either of them ever saw Eton. The latter fact aroze from their extreme affection. They could not bear to part with me.

Digression: In 1808 or 1809, I first went to Redleaf which had just been purchased by Mr. W. Wells.[100] He was not there, my father and I put up at

---

de Lisle of Gosforth. John Hodgson, *A History of Northumberland* Part 2 vol. 1 (London and Newcastle: Baldwin and Cradock, 1827) p. 174.]

[100] [William Wells the younger, 1768-1847, shipbuilder, investor in Meux brewery, and art collector, son of William Wells the shipbuilder 1729-1805. In 1811 he sold his shipbuilding interests and retired to Redleaf, Penshurst, six miles north west of Tunbridge Wells. He was a noted collector of paintings and a patron of Landseer. He left his estate to his grandnephew William Wells, 1818-89, who dissipated most of the fortune, through agricultural experiments. He was one of those who financed the draining of Whittlesey Mere, once England's largest lake,

the Leicester Arms, stayed two or three days and visited Penshurst Castle, Chidingstone and Hever. In returning, my father got out at Barnet and left me to drive the gig home. I continued, to run against a wagon, the carriage was smashed but no further mischief done. At that time I imbibed a great love for that charming close, which I ever retained.

About the same time, I accompanied my father and Uncle F. Beadon from Stoneham to Lyndhurst.[101] They shot for three days. I was a looker on. They had fair sport with cocks and snipe. Black game was tabooed. Toomer, the Keeper who trained a son to hunt and point, went out with us one day, taking out about ten pointers, a measure, which of course did not make the snipes lay the better. I enjoyed this trip vastly, it was the first wild scenery I had ever seen. End of digression.

Thomas Gaze,[102] my father's servant in Crescent Place, usually, at least when I was a little boy, conveyed me to Eton by this coach. We supped at the Christopher and I then proceeded to my dame's.

There was a good deal of drinking and drunkenness at Eton in my time. The favorite liquor was bishop, mulled port wine.[103] In college, when a boy was put into the sixth form or liberty, an entertainment took place, which was called drinking in. I never had any fancy for drinking. I recollect being once made drunk by a teacup of port given at Surley Hall and again by a portion of sherry bought by my friend Powys, the produce of an accidental pouch. In both cases I was very sick, ill, and wretched. In my subsequent life I recollect having been drunk twice. Once in 1812 at the city of Dublin Militia Mess and once after a dinner which in the early days of the Prince's

---

south of Windermere.]

[101] [Frederick Beadon, 1777-1879, was the brother of Norman's mother Charlotte Beadon and became Rector of North Stoneham, Hants (1811-79), in succession to his father. He married Mary-Anne, the eldest daughter of the Reverend Henry Wilder of Purley Hall, Berks. He died aged 101 years and 6 months. He was Canon of Wells Cathedral 1812-75, and Chancellor 1823-79.]

[102] [This is the most likely reading, though Norman also appears to write 'Gage'. Both surnames exist.]

[103] [Bishop is mulled port spiced with oranges, sugar, and cloves.]

Plain Club used to terminate the season.[104] I resisted all temptations to excess in Ireland and Norway, no easy matter. In fact I doubt if I ever drank a bottle of wine in a day three times in my life. The exceptions, if any must be sought in Norway, when one drank light wine at dinner and supper.

I take no merit to myself for abstinence from excess of drink, the truth being that I had no taste for it. Had I been tempted I should probably have succumbed, for I have ever found it difficult to resist my inclinations to evil.

Boys at Eton often pretended to be ill in order to escape school. This was called 'staying out for a shuffle'. I had no taste for this form of malingering. To me the loss of play was a far greater evil than the doing my lessons. I never therefore stayed out unless from strong necessity.

My longest stay out aroze from a swelling of the glands in the neck, which finally caused me exquisite pain, and absolutely deprived me of the power of mastication. Old Macqueen, the surgeon,[105] tried in vain, inter alia, wool warm from the sheep, with the simple effect that a tick stuck to my face. On hearing of this, and also that Mrs. Slingsby proposed to send me into school, Mr Scott recommended my parents to send for me home. Tommy Gaze in consequence came for me, and found me engaged in deciding a bet with another boy, as to which of us could stand longest on one leg. On his

[104] [Norman was personally involved in the establishment of this ground on Bromley Common, and was its first treasurer. However, after the enclosure of the Common in 1821, the Club moved to Chislehurst and became the West Kent Cricket Club. See also Major op. cit. p. 51 for cricket on Bromley Common. Bromley had long been associated with cricket. The earliest recorded match on Bromley Common was in 1735, between a Kent side and a London Cricket Club. The Common was used for major cricket matches on a number of occasions.]

[105] [John Donald Macqueen, a surgeon of Eton, with two apprentices, is listed in P.J. and R.V. Wallis, with J.G.L. Burnby and T.D. Whittet, *Eighteenth Century Medics (Subscriptions, Licenses, Apprenticeships)* Newcastle upon Tyne, Project for Historical Bibliography, 1988, p. 387. We are indebted to Geraldine O'Driscoll of the Royal College of Surgeons for this information. That he employed two apprentices indicates that he enjoyed a reasonably lucrative practice. Like many surgeons, he was also employed as a gynaecologist, and actually delivered Boynor, the author of the *Reminiscences*, as the author recounts. He was one of the trustees of the original charity school in Windsor, set up around 1800, which was designed to teach 60 boys and 40 girls.]

arriving I had remained in that position for one and a half hours.

On reaching Bromley, Scott strove to disperse the swelling by mercurial applications. These failed and the gathering at length burst with an immense discharge. I was very ill for some days. I presume that the whole affair was connected with the age of puberty.

I may here remark that the Etonian medical staff was disgraceful. Battiscombe[106] and Macqueen, the Podaleirius and Machaon[107] of college were more ignorant than a clever farmer of these days. I would bet Dr Bath against the pair.[108]

When I was at Eton, the terrace used to be open to the boys and I have often seen George III walking there on a summer evening with one or two of his daughters and some Court people.[109] When my uncle Mr Barnard[110] has been there, I have known the King address him, while I was standing bye. Mr Barnard was a most loyal subject and had reason to be so, as he received a Pension of £400 per annum from the royal bounty. This was a tribute of respect and esteem for Provost Barnard, his father.

In 1809 took place the jubilee in celebration of the King's having reached the 50th year of his reign. There were immense rejoicings all over the kingdom. At Windsor fireworks, oxen roasted whole in Batchelor's acre and a great fete at Frogmore to which a large portion of the school was invited.[111]

---

[106] [Robert Battiscombe, an apothecary at Windsor. He died aged 85, 13 February 1839. He was Royal Apothecary to the Person, 1805-20.]

[107] [Two figures from Greek mythology. Machaeon was a son of Asclepius and one of the two surgeons of the Greek army in the Trojan War. His brother Podaleirius was the other. Both were legendary healers.]

[108] [Dr Bath was one of the Bromley veterinary surgeons. He is mentioned in Norman's Bromley Memoir.]

[109] [George III and Queen Charlotte had six daughters in a family of 15 children. They were Charlotte Augusta Matilda, 1766-1828, Queen of Württemburg, Augusta Sophia, 1768-1840, Elizabeth, 1770-1840, Landgravine of Hesse-Homburg, Mary, 1776-1857, Sophia, 1777-1848, and Amelia, 1783-1810. The reluctance of their parents to let them marry kept them at Court, and George III was much more fond of his daughters than of his sons.]

[110] [See p. 67.]

[111] [A mansion and grounds within the Royal demesne of Windsor, half a mile east

I went there with Charles Percy[112] and can well remember the rockets, music &c. not to mention the sock. The boys were allowed to remain till long after the usual hour for locking up.

George III at that time was a most popular sovereign.[113] His ignorance, bigotry, and obstinacy are the qualities in his character best known to a later generation which has thus formed a very unfavourable opinion of him.[114] But his contemporaries, themselves ignorant and bigoted, judged him by a different scale. They admired his courage and domestic virtues, and before his mental illness,[115] while I recollect him, he was a fairly popular sovereign. I was certainly one of the minority.

I will now say a few words upon the Eton slang of my day and that by giving some examples.

Pest or Nuisance – a disagreeable thing
Levy – An Assemblage of several persons
Con – a friend
Brozier – make bankrupt
Shuffle – deceit - as staying out for a shuffle
Sharp – steal
Swiped – flogged
Sock – eatables

of the town of Windsor. It was the residence of Queen Charlotte and of Princess Augusta, and of some of George III's sons.]

[112][See p. 76.]

[113][Indeed the boys at Eton showed their appreciation of the King with great enthusiasm, as J. Boynor (see p. 97) in the *Reminiscences*, p. 139, recalled.]

[114][George Frederick William, 1738-1820, King of Great Britain and Ireland 1760-1820, son of Frederick, Prince of Wales, and grandson of George II. In 1810 the death of his youngest daughter Amelia is said to have brought on his final attack of insanity, leaving his son, the future George IV, as Regent.]

[115][The King had experienced his first attack in the autumn of 1788, and was treated by robust methods by a clergyman-doctor called the Reverend Dr Francis Willis, 1717-1807 who ran a 'madhouse' in Lincolnshire. By February 1789 George had largely recovered, though this may have been a spontaneous recovery from a bout of porphyria, as this can occur with one form of porphyria.]

Pouch – Gift

Very few people got the leave from Eton.[116] Miss Townshend,[117] who lived in the castle occasionally; Colonel Wells,[118] once; Mr Wells,[119] also once, dinner at Slough; Lord Rendlesham[120] the first peer once; old Mrs Gosling[121] at Langley once or twice; Mrs Hunter[122] who had a house in Sheet Street[123] opposite the Barracks frequently – she was mother to Sir C. Hunter, Mrs Cumming and Mrs Manning,[124] a kind and amusing old lady and a great friend of my mother's family. I recollect an odd dialogue between her and her footman, Bird. Mrs Manning 'You are always out to drink at night. Why cannot you go out to drink in the morning, I want you at night'. 'Can't drink in the morning, Marm, must drink at night' and so he always did, and was generally muddled.

[116] [This is difficult to make sense of, despite help from Eton College. It might refer to parents allowed to take their children out from the school, but that would hardly apply to Miss Townshend. 'Leave' is an Eton term for permission, such as permission for absence. Half terms at Eton are called 'Long Leave'.]

[117] [Georgiana Townshend, 1761-1835, the sister of Viscount Sydney. She was State House-Keeper and was appointed by George III, holding the post for 35 years. Her father, the politician Thomas Townshend, 1733-1800, was created Viscount Sydney in 1783. His son, brother of Miss Townshend, was John Thomas Townshend, 2nd Viscount Sydney, 1764-1831.]

[118] [John Wells, Royal Engineers, son of Admiral Wells (see p. 15), died 1855.]

[119] [William Wells the younger; see p. 30.]

[120] [Peter Thellusson, born Paris 1737, naturalised Great Britain 1762, died 21 July 1797 had two sons. One was Peter Isaac Thellusson, 1761-1808, created 1st Baron Rendlesham 1806, a Director of the Bank of England 1787-1806, MP Midhurst 1795-6, Malmesbury 1796-1802, Castle Rising 1802-6, Bossiney 1807-8. His brother was George Woodford Thellusson, Director of the East India Company 1799-1807, who died in 1811.]

[121] [Possibly the wife of William Gosling, a London banker, 1765-1831. He married, firstly, Margaret Elizabeth (died 1803) daughter and heir of Sir Ellis Cunliffe, 1st Bt, and secondly, in 1806, Charlotte (died 1839) eldest daughter of the second Baron Walsingham.]

[122] [See p. 8.]

[123] [Sheet Street still exists in Windsor, and is a continuation of the High Street.]

[124] [William Manning of the Bank of England married in 1786 Elizabeth, daughter of Abel Smith. After her death he married, in 1792, Mary (1771-1847), the daughter of Henry Lannoy Hunter (see p. 8), by whom he had four sons, including the future Cardinal Manning.]

There was an abominable custom at Eton when I was there, which wonderful to say, still exists. That a boy on leaving pouched the Head Master and his tutor.[125] I who was not very high in the school gave the former £15, the latter £10. I also gave a dinner at the Christopher to about a dozen friends at which Matt Bell a great ally of mine and ex MP for Northumberland, got drunk and made a row.[126]

I have employed a disproportionate portion of these pages on my Eton days thinking that my anecdotes of the school may interest those who may read these pages and compare what they know of Eton with my experiences. Eton when I knew it was at a very low ebb, both as a place of tuition and of moral education.[127] It taught but little and that badly. All I learnt there was a little Latin and less Greek, and I ran great risk of losing my taste for the acquisition of knowledge. Skill in a variety of games, and a strong taste for them, I certainly attained, and this I consider no small advantage. My character and habits however suffered in no slight degree, and the effect of this deterioration has extended throughout my whole subsequent life. Even now I feel its evil results.

While at Eton however I learned one good habit, that of punctuality. This I have retained to my great comfort and advantage up to the present time. Eton however did not cure me of that passionate disposition which had perhaps been born with me, and which had been fostered by over-indulgence during childhood. I used to get into most violent fits of anger, almost involving inability of self-control. I made however great effort to get rid of these dominant impulses and with some success. At any rate, I do not recollect

[125] [On the business of 'pouching' see Maxwell Lyte, *History of Eton College*, p. 394.]

[126] [Matthew Bell, 1793-1871, educated at Eton, and Christ Church, Oxford, of Woolsington, Northumberland. Sheriff of Northumberland 1816, Lieutenant Colonel of Northumberland and Newcastle Yeomanry Cavalry 1826-63, MP for Northumberland, 1826-31, South Northumberland 1832-52.]

[127] [On the state of Eton at that time and subsequently see H.C. Maxwell Lyte, *A History of Eton College*.]

having often given way to them in my subsequent life, although I am quite aware that I am irritable, to my frequent and great discomfort, and that I am not what is called a good-humored man.

I left Eton at the close of the winters half 1810, in other words at the end of March being sixteen and a half years old, having made no intimate and permanent friends there who would not have been my friends under any circumstances.[128] The exceptions, if any, were Sir C. Willoughby,[129] H.B. Powys, and C.T.C. Luxmoore.[130] The first was taken from me by death, residence at a distance and accidental circumstances have separated me from the other two. Still we always treat each as old cons. With Willoughby and Luxmoore at different periods, I used constantly to mess.

I might here say a few words as to my physique on reaching adolescence. At sixteen or seventeen I was I believe as tall and big as I am now, strong and active, dark in complexion and much tanned by exposure so as to be called by some brown George. I had abundance of dark hair, dark hazle eyes, which one of my schoolfellows used to compare to those of Sophy Blagrave a

[128]I was in the Upper Division, and should have been in the 6th Form before Election. I have been in Play. [This refers to a period at the end of July at Eton, when the Provost of King's College, Cambridge, and two of the Fellows, visited Eton to assist in the examination of boys to be placed on the roll for places at Eton or King's the following year, an examination known as 'Election'. 'Play' means that Norman had done a piece of work good enough to be 'sent up for Play' which meant that the Provost of Eton granted the school a half holiday. Only members of the 6th form, that is the top ten King's Scholars and top ten Oppidans, could be sent up for Play, so Norman had a rather better academic record than his account would suggest, and was, according to the school, certainly entitled to expect that he should be promoted. We are grateful to Mrs P. Hatfield, College Archivist at Eton, for this and other information concerning Norman's time at Eton. According to Maxwell Lyte, 'Before 1829 [when the Newcastle scholarships were introduced] the talent and industry of boys in the "Upper Division" and in the Sixth Form could be measured only by a reference to the number of their "sent up" exercises, or, in other words by the proficiency they had shown in the composition of Latin and Greek verses'. *History of Eton College*, p. 387.]

[129][Sir Christopher William Willoughby, 2nd Bt, born 2 September 1793 and thus almost an exact contemporary of Norman, educated at Eton, succeeded to baronetcy 5 April 1808, matriculated Corpus Christi College, Oxford, 29 April 1811, died there 24 June 1813 from the effects of a blow at cricket.]

[130][See p. 77.]

Berkshire beauty, and altogether, I was, I am told, a good looking boy.

I heartily wish that I had been sent to Cambridge, especially in order that I might have got up a little more Greek and learned somewhat of mathematics, of which I am almost wholly ignorant today. My want of knowledge on these two points has, as I conceive, been of the greatest disservice to me in my subsequent career. I have indeed suffered both directly and indirectly. There has been the want of knowledge which would have been useful in itself and the injurious effect upon my powers of thought and mental condition in general.

It must not however be supposed that I at all blame my father for the course he adopted. He was 54 years old, had no partner, and his business owing to the restoration of intercourse with the North, through the medium of licenses, had greatly increased. It was quite natural then that with as little delay as possible he should make me useful in the counting-house, both with a view to lessen his own labours and to place me in a condition to succeed him in the event of death or illness.

Having now finished my course of education I must say in looking back, that as respects the portion of it which was carried on under the paternal roof, I was treated too softly and indulgently. My wishes and feelings were always consulted and followed out with too much minuteness. My will was almost the law, as to what I was to do, or not to do. It seems to me that the fancies and caprices of a child ought not, for his future happiness, to be carried out too promptly and completely, that occasional disappointment and rebuffs are useful in preparing him for what will certainly occur to him in his subsequent career. God forbid that I should make any charge, even of mismanagement, against my dear and honoured parents, for what was at any rate the result of excessive love. If they erred at all, their error proceeded from their tender affection. I may add that I do not think my character suffered from the peculiarity of my treatment in this respect. If harm aroze from it, this harm must be sought for in an excess of sensibility to the crosses and troubles of life.

No parent could be more ready to sacrifice himself, his comforts and feelings, for the benefit of his children. Of this he gave me many instances.

# Chapter 4

# Early Working Life

I do not recollect that I was consulted as to the time of my leaving Eton, or as to my subsequent destination. At any rate, I neither intimated or indeed felt any objection to the course chalked out for me, and soon after leaving Eton I was duely installed in my father's counting-house.

His business had just been transferred from Crescent Place Blackfriars to Earl Street Blackfriars No 21.

The going to London and returning the same day, obtaining time for a day's work was, in 1810 and indeed for many years afterwards, quite out of the question owing to the state of the roads and of the means of communication. My father always kept his house in London, where he had two servants, Tommy Gaze and his wife.

We used to drive to London in a gig, always through Beckenham over Norwood and through Dulwich and Camberwell every Tuesday and returned to Bromley on Wednesday, went again on Friday and returned on Saturday. It may have happened occasionally that we were in London on Thursday, but this rarely occurred.

It may be thought that my father's business was neglected or that it was of a very peculiar kind. The latter supposition was correct. The foreign connections of the house were chiefly in Norway, only a few in Sweden or at Memel.[1] Before the bombardment of Copenhagen in 1807,[2] it had chiefly been carried on, on my father's account, but from the time I knew it, it was almost exclusively on commission. We used to receive consignments chiefly of wood, which we sold ourselves to yard-keepers, brokers being hardly employed. We shipped goods occasionally and had a good deal of banking and insurance business.

Our capital was greatly employed both by our foreign correspondents and by the buyers here. We made large advances abroad and gave long credits at home. These circumstances, and the heavy duties paid in cash,[3] rendered a very large capital requisite, and the more so, as my father did not anticipate his means to any extent by discounting. I recollect that about 1812, when the calls upon his capital were universally large, he borrowed a small amount

[1] [Memel was a commercial town of the then East Prussia, the principal entrepôt of the country traversed by the Niemen river. The principal export was timber which, though of poorer quality than that obtainable at Danzig, was cheaper and available in larger quantities. It was floated down river on rafts. According to figures given by McCulloch, the vast majority of the ships leaving Memel were carrying timber. In 1824, 866 of 876 ships were carrying timber. McCulloch quotes evidence from a Commons Committee on Foreign Trade of 1821 on the decline of imports of wood received from that port. McCulloch also provides an account of shipping from Memel, 1814-24. Up to 1816, timber exports through Memel declined, reaching a low of 348 vessels in 1816, but from 1817 timber carrying ships leaving Memel increased almost without interruption from 475 in 1817 to 866 in 1824. J.R. McCulloch, *A Dictionary of Commerce and Commercial Navigation*, London: Longman, 1832, pp. 742-3, 1040.]

[2] [From 1800 in the Napoleonic wars, the armed neutrality of Prussia, Sweden, Russia and Denmark threatened the power of Britain. Parker and Nelson destroyed the Danish fleet in 1801 under the guns of Copenhagen. In 1807 a British fleet was sent to Copenhagen to take possession of the reconstituted Danish fleet. When the Danes resisted this, the British bombarded the city and commandeered the fleet.]

[3] ['Any individual acquainted with the purposes to which timber is applied, but ignorant of our peculiar policy with respect to it, would never, certainly, imagine that such an article could be made the subject of oppressive duties, and of still more oppressive preferences ... It is against all principle to impose duties on materials intended to be subsequently manufactured; but timber is the raw material of the most important of all manufactures – that of the instruments of production.' McCulloch was scathing about the preferential duties enjoyed by Canadian timber, while we had a natural advantage in trade with the Baltic. In addition, the Baltic timber was not only cheaper but of superior quality to that from Canada. McCulloch op cit pp. 1038-45. Clearly Norman's complaints were well founded.]

of stock from his friend Mr William Wells which was speedily repaid.

I commenced my counting house career by copying letters. At that time copying machines, manifold writers &c being unknown. This was a very good plan for obtaining a knowledge of the mechanism of business. I used to accompany my father to change and on his visits to the great bars on the other side [of] the river, Quincey, Lett, Browning,[4] Warburton &c.[5]

I never kept a book. My bad handwriting and imperfect knowledge of arithmetic rendered me unfit for that sort of work. Subsequently I became a somewhat better accountant but I never was an adept at the mysteries of double entry.

During the summer after leaving Eton I had no opportunity of keeping up my skill at cricket. There was no club in the neighbourhood and all the practice I got was at an occasional match. Soon after 1810 it became a custom in our neighbourhood to give cricket matches, which were followed by a ball. There was usually one a year at Frognall,[6] and I recollect several

[4] [Quincey and Co., timber merchants, were at Albion Wharf, Blackfriars. Thomas Lett and Son, were timber merchants in Commercial Road. John Browning, timber merchant, was at 66 Bankside, Southwark.]

[5] [The timber yards were in an area known as Prince's Meadows on the south side of the Thames. Thomas Lett and John Lett of Narrow Wall, timber merchants, obtained a 99 year lease on the land in 1810, for £55,100. Most of the land appears to have been for development, however. John Warburton, who lived in Eltham, was a timber merchant at Cuper's Bridge, Lambeth and father of Henry Warburton the politician who ran his father's business 1808-31. Cuper's Gardens was formerly an 18th century pleasure garden opposite Somerset House on the north bank of the river, though closed in 1753 on moral grounds. There was a continuous line of timber yards from what is now the site of Westminster Bridge to Cuper's Bridge, the site of Waterloo Bridge.]

[6] [Frognall was the seat of John Thomas Townshend, 2nd Viscount Sydney, 1764-1831.]

at Footscray Place, Mr Horne's, and one or more at Kevington,[7] Bickley[8] and the Hollies.[9]

In the Autumn of 1810 took place what was then a most important event to me, my father gave me a shooting licence. I had for some time previously used a gun at home in pursuit of fieldfares, blackbirds, rabbits, snipes &c and at Eton had done a good deal in this way, but the 1st September 1810 was the commencement of my lawful career as a sportsman. The season was productive, and the ground we took was over the way in the neighbourhood of the Scrubbs. There was a plenty of birds and we brought home six or seven brace. My gun, which still exists was a small single barrel, given to my father by Mr W. Wells.[10]

Subsequently during that season I went to Rendlesham and had thus an opportunity of seeing sport on a great scale.[11]

I was however at that time and long afterwards a very poor performer. Indeed I never became a tolerable shot until about 1821, when percussion guns were carried to great perfection by the invention of the copper cap. The locks had previously been very awkward and complicated affairs, which seldom acted satisfactorily.

---

[7] [Kevington at St Mary Cray was the seat of Mr Joseph Berens (died 11 January 1853). He had married in 1799 Charlotte (died July 1854) daughter of Richard Benyon of Englefield, House, Berks. The Berens family, whom Norman believed to be originally from Holland, were merchants who settled in England and bought Kevington at St Mary Cray, soon after 1760. According to Norman, the marriage of Mr Berens greatly added to the wealth of the family. The head of the family in Norman's childhood was Herman Berens, and he was succeeded by Joseph Berens whom Norman says he knew well.]

[8] [Bickley was the home of William Wells the elder (see p. 29). He sold Bickley Hall to his son John Wells, 1761-1848, a partner in the Blackwall shipyard and in the banking firm of Whitmore-Wells, MP for Maidstone 1820-30.]

[9] [The Hollies at Lamorbey, Bexley was the residence of Thomas Lewin, 1753-1843 (see p. 37).]

[10] [William Wells the younger; see pp. 30, 99.]

[11] [Rendlesham is in Suffolk, 3 miles from Wickham Market. Rendlesham Hall was rebuilt about 1780, though the house was destroyed by fire in 1855 and rebuilt in 1869.]

I have said that 1810 was a very good season. Cope,[12] a Stockbroker who lived at Crofton Pound and had all the Crofton shooting, had a great deal of game.[13] There was also much at Langley (Lord Gwydir[14]) and I suppose at Kevington and Frognal.

My father had a good many pheasants. My best day with him was seven brace $2\frac{1}{2}$ ditto pigeons and one hare. The keeper was old Wolfe, whose face and person are admirably portrayed in the chalk drawing in my room.[15] He lived in a cottage now pulled down at the top of Barnet, close to the sheep wash, was honest and zealous but would have shown badly against modern poachers.

My father used to keep a setter or pointer and half a dozen wild, noisy spaniels, which he had used in cockshooting before I became his companion. How he ever got a shot with them I never could understand, as they never kept together or hunted close.

---

[12] [This was Thomas Cope, a broker of Fenchurch Street, according to the Post Office London Directory for 1812.]

[13] [Norman later acquired the shooting at Crofton Pound. There is related material in the Norman papers at U310/T45, 1843-5. However he relates in his Bromley Memoir that he had an ally in a keeper at Crofton named Hall, who was employed by Cope. Norman wrote: 'To show the lawlessness of those days, I may mention that I recollect one day meeting Major Rhode, who like me was after Snipes, on Bromley Common. We agreed to join our forces, and make an expedition into the Scrub Woods. This we did, found much game, and killed some and finally found ourselves at Crofton Pound, without leave or license. Cope hearing our guns came to us, invited us most civilly to luncheon, and gave us eggs and bacon. We merited nothing so good.']

[14] [According to Norman's Bromley Memoir, Lord Gwydir at Langley was the first person in the neighbourhood to keep pheasants for shooting. The family name was Burrell. Norman relates how the family had settled in Beckenham after a marriage with an heiress. All the daughters, whom Norman describes as 'very handsome', made good marriages. One of the family married the sister of the Duke of Ancaster. The Duke died and his sister inherited the estates. Peter Burrell, husband of the Duke's sister, was first created Sir Peter, and then Lord Gwydir. According to Norman, 'This is a somewhat curious history and shows that personal beauty even if unattended with any loftier qualities may suffice to elevate a Family in the world. It ought to be added that so far as I know the Burrells have always been respectable persons'.]

[15] [Norman makes the same observations in the Bromley Memoir, adding that it was he who pulled down the cottage.]

During my first visit to Rendlesham I had the misfortune when shooting at a hare to put a shot into the thigh of one of the keepers, named Michael Mayhew. He jumped about a little, but five shillings soon cured his pain. Admiral Sir Bladen Capel was close to me at the time.[16] The head keeper was old Lennings, father of the now living John Lennings.[17] Jorgen Knudtzon[18] and Alexander Baillie were amongst the guests invited to meet us on that occasion. Both are now dead, but G.P. Berkeley, whom we always met at Rendlesham, is still alive, and I hope well.

For the sake of convenience I think it well now to say a few words as to the mode of life at Rendlesham, which will apply to all my visits to the place. John Lord Rendlesham was married to a Miss Dickens, a most amiable person with bad health.[19] He was most kind to us and I always felt great gratitude towards him on that account, but some of his habits were remarkable. I suppose that he never kept an engagement exactly in his life or ever breakfasted or dined at the appointed hour. When he could do exactly as he liked, he would lie in bed half the day and stay up half the night. He was a very free liver in all ways and owed probably his early death to his want of prudence. One of his eyes had been shot out by a friend. The other was defective and he always used glasses stuck in his hat when out of doors, yet notwithstanding his defective vision he was an excellent shot.

My father became his trustee along with his uncle Sergeant Heywood[20]

---

[16] [Sir Thomas Bladen Capel, 1776-1853, youngest son of the 4th Earl of Essex, 1732-99. He served with great distinction during the French wars, and was Signal Lieutenant to Nelson at the Battle of the Nile, Captain 1798, Rear Admiral 1825, KCB 1832, Admiral 1848.]

[17] [Possibly Leamings.]

[18] [See p. 153.]

[19] [John Thellusson, 2nd Baron Rendlesham, 1785-1832, died without surviving male issue, married 30 November 1809 Mary Andalusia (died without issue, 15 August 1814). She was the second daughter of Lieutenant General Samuel Trevor Dickens, RE. After her death, the 2nd Baron married, in 1816, Ann Sophia (died 1856), the second daughter and co-heir of William Tatnall of Leiston Old Abbey, Suffolk.]

[20] [Samuel Heywood, 1753-1828, Serjeant at Law, Chief Justice of Wales.]

and Mr Manning,[21] and as Lord Rendlesham was customarily cut, and as his minority lasted till he was 21, some differences arose regarding money matters, which a little interrupted the intercourse between the families. Everything however was going on smoothly in 1810 and for several years afterwards.

Perhaps a more potent cause of estrangement was the little warmth with which the attentions paid by Lord Rendlesham to my sister Charlotte[22] during his day of widowhood were received by our family. These however were delicate matters of which I knew little. To me Lord Rendlesham was uniformly kind and friendly.

His next brother George, who had been at Eton with me, was killed at Vitoria[23] as an Officer of Dragoons.[24]

Before I leave Rendlesham now, (and I shall have occasion to return to it) I may mention that the first Lord Rendlesham[25] Peter Isaac and his brother George Thellesson[26] both dropped down dead in apoplectic fits within a few yards of the same spot in a wood near Butley Abbey[27] and within five or six

---

21 [William Manning, 1763-1835, merchant, a Director of the Bank of England 1792-1831, Deputy Governor 1810-12, Governor 1812-14, father of Cardinal Manning.]

22 [Charlotte Norman was born 30 June 1795. In 1830 she married William Whitmore, to Norman's disapproval, and died in 1855.]

23 [Norman clearly wrote Victoria here.]

24 [He was in the Remove at Eton with Norman. He was a Lieutenant in the 11th Dragoons, and was a son of the 1st Lord Rendlesham (see p. 104). He was killed at the Battle of Vitoria in 1813. The allied casualties at Vitoria were just over 5,000. Vitoria is the capital of the Province of Alava in Spain. Wellington's victory here was a decisive step in the defeat of the French, after Wellington had moved out of Portugal.]

25 [Peter Thellusson born Paris 1737, naturalised Great Britain 1762, died 21 July 1797 had two sons. One was Peter Isaac Thellusson, 1761-1808, created 1st Baron Rendlesham 1806, a Director of the Bank of England 1787-1806, MP Midhurst 1795-6, Malmesbury 1796-1802, Castle Rising 1802-6, Bossiney 1807-8. The other was George Woodford Thellusson (see next fn).]

26 [The brother of the first Lord Rendlesham was George Woodford Thellusson, Director of the East India Company 1799-1807, who died in 1811. He created what has been described as a magnificent Gothic revival mansion, Wall Hall, at Aldenham, Herts, the manor of which he had purchased in 1799. He features in Charles Dickens's *A Tale of Two Cities.*]

27 [Butley was an Augustinian house on a sea creek 3 miles west of Orford.

years.

The small double Manton, a Kent gun,[28] belonged to Peter Isaac and was bought by my father after its previous owner had missed twenty cock pheasants running with it. I retain it as a specimen of the first class weapon of a previous generation. Its original cost was £70 guineas.[29]

In December 1810, I went to Stoneham with my mother. I used to go out shooting on Hursley Common beyond Chandler's Ford, then unenclosed, where were a great many snipes.[30] I recollect one day getting three couple, which, considering my bad shooting, implies many shots. I missed on that day a double snipe, the only one I ever saw on the wing. There were a great many snipes also on the Stoneham Commons and quantities of birds along the valley behind the rectory.

After passing a few days at Stoneham, I was suddenly sent away leaving my mother at the rectory on account of the sudden illness of my grandfather, Mr Beadon. The malady led to his death shortly afterwards. He was a thorough gentleman and most amiable in all his domestic relations, but extravagant in expenditure so as to have reduced his fortune considerably. That angel, my mother, mourned over him with intense grief. I have heard

Though it was founded in 1171 by Ranulph de Glanville, it was largely constructed more than a century later. The priory grounds were about 20 acres, and the priory is reported to have been an important destination for medieval pilgrims. There were a number of royal visitors to the priory, including Henry III and Edward I. It was seized at the Dissolution of the Monasteries in 1537. At the time of the Dissolution the annual income of Butley, which had a very substantial church, was estimated at £3,182.17s.1d. The site was then granted to Thomas, Duke of Norfolk. A later owner, George Wright, turned the gatehouse of the priory into a shooting lodge. The walls and ruins still occupy nearly 12 acres. Butley is 2 miles from Rendlesham forest and it may have been in the forest that the deaths, to which Norman refers, took place. The living was in the gift of the Lords Rendlesham.]

[28] [Joseph Manton, 1760-1835, celebrated British gunsmith who revolutionised sports shooting, and greatly improved the quality of guns. So successful was he that he earned a fortune which he then lost in a dispute over payment by the British army.]

[29] [Assuming the purchase was circa 1800, the 2009 equivalent would be £4,361.]

[30] [This is beyond Chandler's Ford, proceeding north from the Rev. Beadon's Rectory at North Stoneham.]

my father say that he considered her accidental presence at Stoneham during the fatal malady as a reward to her, for her filial devotion.

I recollect that in going to Stoneham on this occasion I set out at five o'clock in the morning from the Belle Savage Ludgate Hill, by Coach, and was twelve or fourteen hours on the road. The coachman drank something every three or four miles. This a singular fact, that at this moment I recollect well a doleful ditty which the ostler at the Belle Savage whistled as he was putting to. What a capricious instrument is the memory to preserve such a trifle and forget so many more important things.

On leaving Stoneham, I stopped at Mrs James's at Southampton. Her daughter Gertrude was a very large, fine woman and her beauty greatly excited my youthful admiration.[31]

When I left Eton, as was natural enough, I thought the composition of good Latin verses, the ne plus ultra of education, and feeling within a strong desire for improvement and a wish to excel, I devoted for several years a good deal of time and attention to them. I wrote upon various subjects, including epistles to C.H. Cameron and to G.R. Smith. Several of my Latin compositions, along with a good many English, are preserved in one of my MS books. They are not very bad, at any rate far better than any of my Eton productions. I continued to versify until about 1818 or 1819 when I finally abandoned poetry for severer studies, retaining however great love for it and delighting in the compositions of the mighty masters of the art,

[31] [Not positively identified. Cunningham's directories of Southampton, for 1803 and 1811, list tradesmen and tradeswomen but not residents. A search through parish registers yielded details of the family of a Southampton hatter Giles James, but this is unlikely to be the family that Norman knew. However the 1841 census does include a Gertrude and Mary James, aged 50 and 80 respectively, then living in the parish of Stoke Demerel, Devonport, Devon, both being of independent means, and it is possible that these are the two to whom Norman refers. We are indebted for this information to Penny Rudkin of Southampton Library Local Studies.]

Shakespeare,[32] Milton,[33] Virgil[34] Juvenal,[35] Dante,[36] Tasso,[37] and Tegrimi.[38]

At this period of my life I contracted the habit of desultory reading, making history alone a matter of serious study.

In reading history I used to form a series of chronological memoranda containing all the remarkable events, the times of death of eminent personages &c. Labours in this way were continued during many years; the results are still preserved. The plan is a good one for impressing facts deeply on the memory, and my knowledge of history at the present day, which in point of extent of surface is not exceeded by that of any of my acquaintances, has mainly arisen from this habit of my youthful days.

I abandoned the above mode of proceeding about 1820, and from that

[32] [As Norman recounts earlier, he had been introduced to the works of William Shakespeare, 1564-1616, the English poet and dramatist, at Eltham.]

[33] [John Milton, 1608-74, English poet, who held office under the Commonwealth but whose main achievements date from the years of the Restoration of the monarchy after 1660, though he lost his sight. The most famous works are *Paradise Lost*, published in 1667, *Paradise Regained* and *Sampson Agonistes*, published in 1671.]

[34] [Publius Vergilius Maro 70-19 BC, Latin poet traditionally referred to as Virgil. His most famous works are the *Eclogues*, finished in about 37 BC, the *Georgics*, published in 30 BC, and the *Aeneid*, which tells the story of Aeneas's arrival in Italy after the fall of Troy.]

[35] [Decimus Junius Juvenalis, c.AD 50-c.130, Roman satirist of whose life very little is known. He was the author of 16 *Satires*, which paint a deeply unattractive picture of contemporary Roman society.]

[36] [Dante Alighieri, 1265-1321, author of *La Divina Commedia* with *The Inferno*, regarded as Italy's greatest poet.]

[37] [Torquato Tasso, 1544-95, Italian poet who produced in 1562 *Rinaldo*. However he suffered a mental breakdown from 1576, and was imprisoned by Duke Alfonso at Ferrara from 1578 to 1586. During this period he continued to write. His major work, *La Gerusalemme Liberata*, which had been completed in 1574, before his breakdown, and which, after his release, he re-wrote as *La Gerusalemme Conquistata*, appeared in 1592. The *Gerusalemme* is an idealisation of the First Crusade.]

[38] [The Luccan humanist Niccolo Tegrimi, 1448-1527, was a lawyer. He wrote a life of Castruccio Castracani Degli Antelminelli, 1281-1328, the ruler of Lucca, Pisa and Pistoia, who was a tyrant but whom Tegrimi praised because of his valour in war. His work is the *Vita Castruccii Antelminelli Lucencis Ducis*. It appeared in 1496. Norman probably came across the name because Tegrimi's work was known to Mary Shelley, who wrote an historical novel *Valperga, or the Life and Adventures of Castruccio, Prince of Lucca* (1823). Machiavelli wrote a life of Castrucio Castracani, based upon Tegrimi's work, published in 1520.]

time adopted the plan of again going over history with a more philosophical view, looking at not merely the simple facts but their connection in the way of cause and effect. In short that mode of regarding history, of which the Neapolitan Vico is said to have been the originator,[39] but which Guizot has popularized and which is now met with in the works of very inferior writers.[40] In some cases I have studied the history of a given country three or four times over, on each occasion taking out old bricks and putting in new until I had formed to myself something like an entire system destined to hold together, until new facts or more mature reflection discovered defects in the fabric.

The general result of my historical studies is a conviction that all history requires to be rewritten in order to convey to the present time a vivid and correct impression of the past, and that England in this respect has fared perhaps worse than any other great and civilised country, especially considering that the materials she possesses are unrivalled in extent and completeness. I here allude especially to the Charters, Acts of Parliament, Law Records and other public documents.

I may here remark, as a sort of measure of my historical knowledge, that at this moment I feel quite capable of giving from memory, and viva voce, a sketch of the history of Greece and Rome and of any of the Western nations, as well as of the Eastern people of Asia, including the successors of Mohamed and of the different dynasties which aroze upon the disruption of the Kali-

---

[39] [Gianbattista Vico, 1668-1744, Italian philosopher, rhetorician, historian and jurist. He is famous for having developed a theory of history based upon the idea that civilisation develops in a recurring cycle. His philosophical work, in which probability and circumstance are central, was strongly opposed to the dominant Cartesian influences of his time.]

[40] [François Pierre Guillaume Guizot, 1787-1874, French historian, orator and statesman. Foreign Minister of France, 1840-47, and Prime Minister 1847-8. In 1794 his father was executed at Nîmes, during the Reign of Terror, and Guizot was brought up by his mother. In 1812 he was appointed to a chair of modern history at the Sorbonne. He did important work in reviving historical studies in France, translating Gibbon, writing on the history of representative government, of England, and of civilisation, and publishing extensively on historical sources.]

fate. I owe the latter chiefly to the New History,[41] and to d'Herbelot.[42] Of course, the precise extent of my knowledge differs greatly as respects different countries. Spain and Portugal are my weakest points.

As I am now mentioning my studies, if that can be called a study which has been little more than an amusement, I may say a little about my habits of reading.

I have never really been a student. That is to say, I have never devoted days or nights to study. As a merchant or director of the Bank scene, serving as magistrate, or as a cricketer or sportsman or traveller, my time between breakfast and dinner has always been occupied by business or pleasure, unless in the event of illness which, I thank God, has seldom confined me to the house. My opportunity of reading has thus been almost confined to the evening and to odd moments at other times. Thus I always read when dressing as long as the state of my eyes permitted, and have thus got through hundreds of volumes. I am never or have been wholly idle, even for five minutes together. If neither eating or talking or listening while in [blank], I have always had a book before me. A catalogue of books read each year since 1814 will be found in a drawer and with a correct notion of the number of pages I have turned over.

It has always been my habit to have several works in hand at once. As my knowledge of languages increased, usually a work in each tongue with which I am acquainted, and I never found that these works, often on very different

[41] [*An Universal History, from the Earliest Account of Time to the Present*, London: J. Batley, 1736-44, and later editions. See also *A New History of England from the Invasion of Julius Caesar to the Beginning of the Year MDCCXCIV* [1794], London: Darton and Harvey, 1797.]

[42] [Barthélemy d'Herbelot de Molainville, 1625-95, French scholar of Eastern languages and history whose great work, essentially a translation of an earlier Arabic work, buttressed by other Arab and Turkish sources, was *Biblioteque Orientale ou Dictionnaire Universelle Contenant Tous Que Se Regarde La Connoissance des Peuples de l'Orient.* The work occupied him nearly all his life, and was completed in 1697 by Antoine Galland. It was reprinted on a number of occasions, and a popularising version was issued in 6 volumes (Paris, 1781-3).]

subjects, jostled or interfered with each other in my mind. On the contrary I find that their variety prevents fatigue and that the knowledge they each convey finds its way into the several pigeon holes of my memory and that a great portion of it is preserved for subsequent use.

Having a continuous application to any one subject always tired me and produced exhaustion of my bodily and mental powers, sleepless nights &c.

I must now pass on to another subject before I resume the thread of my biography. When I left Eton and for some time I knew hardly a word of any foreign language. The exception was a very little French picked up from a Swiss footman named Samuel Pitcet,[43] and the fruits of a few lessons taken in the Holidays. At any rate, in 1810 I could hardly have translated a line in [?] the existing [?] work [?],[44] about 1812 or 1813 I began to take lessons in East Sheen from the Abbé Chatelain and made a certain progress.[45] These lessons however were but few. As soon as I could well distinguish the parts of speech from each, after getting through the inevitable Voltaire[46] Charles Douze, I began to read with a dictionary by my side, the most interesting prose works in the language (for French poetry I never had any taste). My

[43] [Possibly Pittat.]

[44] [The manuscript is damaged here.]

[45] [It is likely that the Abbé Chatelain had moved to England to escape the dangers of the Revolution in France, and returned there after 1815. There were very large numbers of refugee Catholic clergy, fleeing from the clerical massacres of the French Revolution. According to some later accounts, there were as many as 8,000 of these. With remarkable generosity, especially given that Catholic Emancipation was several decades away, the Anglican community, from George III downwards, rallied to relieve their distress, both through the grant of public funds and through subscriptions. Penniless as they were, teaching was one of the few ways in which the refugees could obtain some income, and the Abbé Chatelain whom Norman mentions was doubtless pursuing this path. However the individual concerned cannot be identified, as he does not appear in the rate books for Mortlake either for 1810 or 1812. Later on an Abbé Chatelain was Vicar General of the Diocese of Mans, and there was a connection with England – his name occurs in connection with the French Catholic Mission in London. It is possible that this was the same man.]

[46] [Norman wrote Volterre here. Jean François Marie Arouet, 1694-1778, French historian, dramatist and critic of religious belief. A prolific author, his *Histoire de Charles Douze* dates from 1731.]

first or one of the first attempts was on Pascal's 'Lettres Provenciales'.[47] In a short time I could read with facility. Some years afterwards I was placed under the necessity of speaking French and after a little practice, having a plentiful stock of words at command, was able to converse fairly well. My pronunciation however was always bad.

The mode of acquiring a modern language described above, I afterwards employed with Italian, Danish and Swedish and always with success. I shall mention hereafter under the proper year when these several acquisitions were made. It has always been to me a matter of bitter regret that I am altogether ignorant of German. In my youth it was little studied in England.

I have always been opposed to the ordinary mode of learning foreign language. The method by rote, that by which the child learns from its mother and nurse, is the natural plan, and the nearest approach to it is the Hamiltonian system as respects foreign languages.[48] The object to be attained is the most rapid and exact knowledge of the meaning of the largest number of foreign words. When this object has been obtained it is very well to look into the grammar, but to learn a language by grammar and a dictionary is disagreeable, slow and imperfect work.

I believe that the Hamiltonian system might be applied with great success to the antient languages, but I allow that a well-educated man ought to learn some grammar in order that he may be able to take a philosophical view of

[47] [Pascal Blaise, 1623-62, French mathematician. In France he was associated with the Jansenists, and it was in defending the Jansenist Antoine Arnauld that Pascal produced his *Lettres Provenciales* in 1656-7.]

[48] [This was essentially a method of language teaching through the use of bilingual texts. It depended crucially upon the translations being literal and not free. The system was a matter of intense controversy, especially in the 1820s. James Hamilton, 1769-1829, was born in London. He went to New York where he at first encountered resistance to his method, and from 1823 he taught in Britain. John Stuart Mill was also a disciple of the system. According to his *Autobiography*, 'While thus engaged [in 1825] in writing for the public, I did not neglect other modes of self-cultivation. It was at this time that I learnt German; beginning it with the Hamiltonian method, for which purpose I and several of my companions formed a class.' J.S. Mill, *Autobiography*, 8th edition, London: Longman, 1886, p. 119.]

the structure of language in general. Perhaps the Greek grammar is the best for this purpose. I never read an English grammar.

But now once more for my biography. I recollect nothing important as having occurred in the early part of 1811, but towards the end of the summer my grandmother, Mrs Norman,[49] proposed to take me with her into Leicestershire, that I might become better acquainted with my relatives who seldom came to us in the South.

At this time I was painfully shy. It was distressing to me to go into strange company, and I fancy the good old lady thought me half a fool. It may seem odd to those who know me now if I tell them that this feeling of shyness has always belonged to me and that I suffer from it even to the present day. It is this circumstance that has made me an inefficient public speaker, although practice would doubtless have improved me, and I owe to it also, the painful nervousness, which with me always precedes the necessity of exhibiting myself to the gaze of a large audience.

However to return to my narrative, my grandmother and I went first to the residence of my uncle Richard Norman at Melton Mowbray.[50] There we stayed some little time and we paid subsequent visits to Belvoir for two or three days,[51] and to Normanton, a place near Hinckley belonging to one of

[49][James Norman, Norman's grandfather (see p. 1), married in 1751 Henrietta Wroughton, the mother of George Norman, Norman's father. After her death, James Norman married secondly Eleanora Innocent. The marriage settlement of James Norman of Blackfriars, London and Eleanora Innocent of Bromley, dated 1760, is in the Norman papers at Maidstone at U310 T61.]

[50][Richard Norman was Norman's paternal uncle. Baptised 1758, died 1847. He was twice married. By his first wife, Emilia Grigg (see p. 5), he had eight children, of which six died young. Their daughter married in 1811 George Pochin (died December 1829). They had five sons and two daughters. Richard Norman's second wife was Lady Elizabeth Isabella Manners, 1769-1853, daughter of Charles Manners, 4th Duke of Rutland. She married Richard Norman 21 August 1798. They had eight sons and five daughters. As Norman recounts, this meeting with Richard Norman took place in 1811. Subsequently there was correspondence between Norman and his uncle, and U310 C30 in the Norman papers at Maidstone contains letters dated 1825-30 from Richard Norman to his nephew.]

[51][Belvoir Castle, seat of the Dukes of Rutland, near Bottesford, Leics. The property had been rebuilt several times and around 1800 the 5th Duke employed

the Arkwrights,[52] and then hired by George Pochin[53] afterwards of Barkby,[54] who had married my cousin Elizabeth Norman. From Barkby I went with the Dowager Duchess of Rutland[55] and one or two other people to attend the races at Leicester. We staid at the Bell inn there for two or three days, the Duke[56] joined us and there was a public dinner and a ball. I, being one of the Ducal party, was considered I suppose an important personage. I recollect however that my shyness prevented my enjoying myself. Among the persons I saw at Leicester were Lord Alvanley,[57] who looked very like a fair butcher,

the notorious architect James Wyatt to re-convert it to a castle – it had been rebuilt in 1654-8 as a mansion. A fire in 1816 necessitated rebuilding by Wyatt's sons Benjamin and Matthew, supervised by the Duchess and a relative, the Reverend John Thoroton (see p. 125).]

[52][Richard Arkwright, 1755-1843, cotton entrepreneur, son of Sir Richard Arkwright, 1732-92, British inventor, originally a barber but who, with the assistance of John Kay a watchmaker of Warrington, invented cotton spinning machinery and became an entrepreneur on a large scale. He was knighted in 1786. The younger Arkwright lived at Willersley Castle, Derbyshire, which his father had built but never occupied. Richard Arkwright the younger owned Basset House in Normanton Turville, a hamlet six miles north east of Hinckley. Norman's Eton contemporary Joseph Arkwright was at Normanton Turville, though this may have been later.]

[53][See p. 182.]

[54][Then four and a half miles north east of Leicester.]

[55][Lady Isabella Somerset, 1756-1831, the youngest daughter of the 4th Duke of Beaufort. Her husband, the 4th Duke, had died in 1787.]

[56][John Henry Manners, 5th Duke of Rutland, 1778-1857, son of Charles Manners, 4th Duke. He married Elizabeth Howard, daughter of Frederick Howard, 5th Earl of Carlisle, in 1799. They had ten children.]

[57][William Arden, 2nd Baron Alvanley, 1789-1849. He was the son of Sir Richard Pepper Arden, 1st Baron Alvanley, 1744-1844, lawyer and MP, who in 1801 was appointed Chief Justice of the Court of Common Pleas and created Baron Alvanley. William Arden, the second Baron, was an army officer and, for a time, a Captain in the Coldstream Guards. He later transferred to the 50th and then the 100th Regiment of Foot, and was placed on half pay in 1812. He was a 'regency buck' and member of the Prince Regent's circle, and a friend of Beau Brummell. When the Prince Regent snubbed Brummell in 1813, it was Alvanley to whom the famous question 'who's your fat friend?' was addressed by Brummell. Because of his extravagance, the family estates had to be sold to pay his debts over the years 1823-33. He was extremely critical of the support provided in Parliament by the faction led by Daniel O'Connell for the Melbourne Whigs, and fought a duel with O'Connell's son Morgan.]

but set up for a wit and was rather amusing, and Thomas Assheton Smith[58] who kept the Quorn hounds and was the hardest rider in the county. I often saw him also at Lord's. He was a very good bat for the time.

G. Pochin[59] gave me a double gun, which I had changed into a copper cap and which I still retain but never use.

The visits to Belvoir did not at all delight me. The Duke was very kind but the society was too stiff and stately. The Dutchess was a beautiful woman, then under thirty. She never joined the company in the drawing room until dinner was ready when a door opened and she made her appearance, preceded by the house steward or groom of the chamber, with two candles in his hand, and was conducted by the leading guest into the dining room without sitting down. Among these guests was the Reverend Mr Peters the painter,[60] the father of Mr Edward Turton sometime of Brasted,[61] W. Whitmore's friend.[62]

Before I left Leicestershire I again visited Belvoir with my uncle and found only Sir John Thoroton, the Chaplain and architect.[63] At that time

[58][Thomas Assheton Smith, 1776-1858, of Tidworth, Hants, and Vaynol, Carnarvon, who died without issue September 1858, leaving everything to his widow Matilda née Webber who died in May 1859. Educated at Eton and Oxford, MP Andover 1821-31, and for Carnarvonshire 1832-41. Devoted his life almost entirely to sport. An all round sportsman he was a keen huntsman, Master of the Quorn (Leics) hounds 1806-16, and Master of the Burton hounds in Lincolnshire 1816-24. He was also a keen sailor and member of the Royal Yacht Squadron, and a cricketer, being an outstanding amateur batsman. The family fortune derived from the Welsh slate industry.]

[59][For George Pochin, see p. 182.]

[60][Reverend Matthew William Peters MA, FLS, 1742-1814, Chaplain to HRH Prince of Wales, afterwards George IV, Rector of Knipton-Woolsthorpe, Leics, Prebendary of Lincoln Cathedral, celebrated painter of often erotic pictures. He was an active Freemason. Charles Manners, 4th Duke of Rutland, presented Peters to the living of Scalford, Leics, in 1784. He was employed as curator of pictures at Belvoir. He married Margaret Knowsley. Edmund Peters, later Turton (see next fn) was his third son.]

[61][Edmund Peters, 1796-1857, of Brasted Park, Kent, assumed the name and arms of Turton, MP Headon, Yorks, 1818-20.]

[62][William Whitmore was later Norman's brother in law; see p. 333.]

[63][Sir John Thoroton was the Vicar of Bottesford, a living in the gift of the Duke of Rutland. The living was valued at £800 per annum in 1894. Bottesford is in the Vale of Belvoir. Charles Manners Sutton, grandson of the 3rd Duke of

the celebrated comet was in its greatest splendour, and was seen admirably from the Terrace. I recollect that Sir John informed us that the last comet he had previously seen fell at Redmile, a village about two miles from the Castle.[64] A year or two after my visit, the greater part of the buildings were burnt and the restoration cost I believe £200,000.[65]

I may here remark that my uncle was chief manager of the Duke's finances and in that capacity, I firmly believe, saved him from ruin. There was a regular counting house in the Castle, of which my father's old clerk Drew Townsend was Chief.[66]

My uncle gained nothing in the way of money owing to his marriage to the Duke's sister. On the contrary, he lent his brother in law £40,000, which he sold out of the consols when they were about 47 and was paid off when they were 93, thirty or forty years afterwards. The loss was more than half the capital. I have often wondered how the Duke, a very respectful man, could have so acted. I believe that John Irving was his adviser and overcame his scruples if any.[67]

---

Rutland, 1755-1828, Archbishop of Canterbury 1805-28, married Mary (died 10 March 1832) daughter of Thomas Thoroton of Screveton. John Thoroton, son of Thomas Thoroton, was admitted to Trinity College, Cambridge in 1777 aged 17, BA 1781, ordained priest in the diocese of Peterborough 1782. He died in 1821. He was knighted at the time of the Prince Regent's visit to Belvoir in 1813. The Thoroton family changed the name to Hildyard in 1815 when Colonel Thomas Blackborne Thoroton married a Hildyard heiress, the niece of Sir Robert d'Arcy Hildyard, 4th and last Bt, who died without issue, leaving his estate to his niece. The family subsequently acquired Flintham Hall near Newark.]

[64] [Village in Leicestershire, nine and a half miles west of Grantham, and near to Bottesford. It was part of the estates owned by the Duke of Rutland. The living was however much less valuable than that of Bottesford, being valued in 1894 at £230 per annum.]

[65] [See p. 124.]

[66] Drew Townsend, altho' a very honest man, left, I believe more than £10,000 behind him. In the latter part of his service, he was allowed to sign for my Father, and had a salary of £800 per annum.

[67] [Norman's memory may have been slightly at fault here. The yield on Consols, which carried a coupon of 3 per cent, reached a maximum of 5.9 per cent in 1797 and 1798, and Richard Norman married Lady Elizabeth Manners in 1798, a time at which he may have felt under some pressure to help the Duke. This however implies a price of 3 per cent Consols of 51. From the late 1830s the yield fell to

Before I returned home from this survey I went with my [grand]mother to Castle Ashby, the Seat of Lord Northampton.[68] Emily Carr was of the Party.[69] There is a fine old house built round a Court of the time, I suppose of James I. The grounds are not very handsome. The peer of those days was grandfather to the present and had married the eldest daughter of a very old friend of my family, Mr Joshua Smith of Earl Stoke Park,[70] near Devizes, brother of Sir Drummond Smith.[71] Hence sprung up a great intimacy with my grandmother, who used to pass two or three months of every year at Ashby. In the church were monuments of cross-legged Knights.

The old Earl was very kind to me and used to take me out shooting. I used also to hunt with a rough pack of harriers, which included I recollect a newfoundland dog. On these occasions the field was very small, the most prominent members being Lady Elizabeth Compton, now Dickens,[72] and myself. I was rather smitten with her, although she could hardly be considered pretty unless by a youth of nineteen to whom a young woman can hardly be

little over 3 per cent, giving a price of Consols approaching par. A yield of 3.2 per cent, first reached in 1838 and again in 1843, would imply a price of 93.73, which may have been what Norman had in mind. His general point is however unaffected by any slight imprecision in the figures he quotes; had Norman's uncle retained his Consols, instead of selling them in order to assist the Duke, he would have had twice the capital when interest rates returned to peace time levels. For the yield on Consols see B.R. Mitchell with Phyllis Deane, *Abstract of British Historical Statistics*, Cambridge: Cambridge University Press, 1962 p. 455.]

[68] [Charles Compton, 1st Marquess of Northampton, 1760-1828, MP (Tory) Northampton 1784-96, President of the Geological Society 1820-2.]

[69] [Emily Carr was a daughter of Richard Norman. She became Emily de Clarville, and married Ralph Carr in 1831. The identification is from the Norman papers, U310/C32, F62.]

[70] [Charles Compton, 1st Marquess of Northampton, 1760-1828, succeeded his father the 8th Earl of Northampton in 1796. On 18 August 1787 he married Maria (died 24 March 1843), the eldest daughter of Joshua Smith, 1735-1819, of Erlestoke (or Earl Stoke) Park, Devizes; see p. 70.]

[71] [Sir Drummond Smith, 1740-1816, created 1st Bt 1804, who bought Tring Park, Herts, in 1786. He landscaped the park, removing extensive formal gardens to the east of the house.]

[72] [Lady Frances Elizabeth Compton, daughter of Charles Compton, 1st Marquess of Northampton (see fn 70 above), married 18 February 1829 Charles Scrase Dickins DL, JP, of Coolhurst, 1794-1875, and died 2 March 1883.]

otherwise. On one occasion I recollect getting a severe fall.

Lord and Lady Northampton used to come to Bromley and I kept up an acquaintance with the family for many years. The late Lord Northampton was very kind to me at Rome in 1823. The last time I recollect seeing him was at St Leonards, about 1840, when we exchanged visits. The whole family was remarkable for being short-sighted. It had been almost ruined by a Northampton election, the opponent being Lord Spencer,[73] but had been relieved by a long course of economy, aided by Lady Northampton's fortune, which had been employed in buying up Post Offices.[74]

In the winter of 1811 I went to Rendlesham. The following year 1812 was remarkable in my history on many accounts. In it was established the Princes Plain, since 1821 West Kent, Cricket Club.[75] It originated at a dinner held at the Plough, which was attended by Mr Wells, Cator,[76] Horne,[77] Berens,[78]

[73] [As the career of Lord Althorp demonstrated (see pp. 372-3), the Spencer family had a powerful influence over elections to Northampton seats.]

[74] [Probably, as MS is not clear here.]

[75] [The Princes Plain Club took some time to get established. Their first playing season was 1814. Neither Mr Horne nor Mr James seems to have played. What is now the Chislehurst and West Kent Cricket Club has the complete score book for the Princes Plain Club, before it became West Kent Cricket Club, but there are unfortunately no minutes of the Club predating the move to Chislehurst.]

[76] [John Cator, of Beckingham Place, Kent (died 1858). His brother was Rear Admiral Bertie Cornelius Cator, 1787-1864. He entered the Royal Navy in 1800, Captain 1814, retired 1846, Rear Admiral 1862. Both were the sons of Joseph Cator, a merchant, and John succeeded to the estates of Joseph's brother John Cator. Joseph Cator died in 1818.]

[77] [Not identified. The name Horne was associated with cricket in Bromley from an early date, and a Mr Horne is recorded as having played in a local match in 1773. There was also a Reverend George Horne, 1730-92, born near Maidstone, and Fellow of Magdalen College, Oxford, who may have been part of the same Kentish family, and William Horne, 1783-1828, originally a painter, who became the proprietor of a large scale transport firm with, by 1827, between 700 and 800 horses. He was succeeded by his son Benjamin Worthy Horne, 1804-70, who drove the business to great heights and had an estate at Highlands, near Mereworth, Kent, which was within easy travelling distance of Bromley. Horne is not mentioned in Norman's Bromley Memoir.]

[78] [Probably Joseph Berens of Kevington, St Mary Cray (died 11 January 1853). Norman says in his Bromley Memoir that he knew him well. Berens married Charlotte daughter of Richard Benyon, of Englefield House, Reading, Berks. His second son was Henry Hulse Berens 1804-83, Deputy Chairman of Public Works

James[79] &c. I was appointed Treasurer and held the office for several years. The ground was on the common and formed the farther portion of my field called Princes Plain. Much money was spent to improve it, and a most excellent ground it was. Having now practiced, my cricketing skill soon revived, and as a bat and field I was a shining light, and used to get very long hands. The chief opponents of the Princes Plain were the Vine and Epsom;[80] of both of which I became subsequently a member. The chief obstacle to my ranking extremely high as a cricketer was my great nervousness, which has acted so much to my prejudice in more important matters. I was strong and active, had an excellent eye and had studied and well-understood the game. My hitting and stopping was performed in a style little practised in those days where scientific play was confined to a few, but when I went to wicket I used to turn pale and felt my heart sink within me, and for a few balls altogether lost my self-possession.

During 1812 I made the acquaintance of my excellent friends the Ords. Mrs Ord had been known to my mother from infancy.[81] They then lived at Richmond and I was introduced to them by Hobbes Scott, who had recently quitted an active position in a wine business and fixed himself in the neighbourhood of Southampton at a place which he called Thon Hill. I vis-

---

Loan Office, 1849-52, a Director of the Bank of England 1849-80. He married in 1841 Ellinor, daughter of George Stone, of Coopers, Chislehurst. He was thus related to Norman by marriage. According to Norman's Bromley Memoir, the Berens family was originally from Holland. They bought Kevington at St Mary Cray, soon after 1760.]

[79] [Not identified. Commodore Sir William James, c. 1721-83, 1st Bt, FRS, a distinguished naval commander of Welsh origin, acquired Park Farm Place at Eltham (see p. 39). However his son died unmarried in 1792. James is not mentioned in Norman's Bromley Memoir.]

[80] [The Vine was, and is, the Sevenoaks Cricket Club to the north of the town.]

[81] [William Ord, 1781-1855, MP for Morpeth 1802-32, Newcastle 1835-52, married in 1803 Mary, daughter of the Reverend James Scott of Itchen Ferry, Hants, Rector of St Lawrence, Southampton, and neighbour to the Beadons at North Stoneham. She was the sister of Norman's friend Hobbes Scott, of Jane Harley, Countess of Oxford, and of Charlotte Scott who married Thomas Hanway Bigge, a Newcastle banker, who died in 1824 leaving four sons and two daughters.]

ited him there in the Spring of 1812 and accompanied him and his brother James Scott on a journey to Weston super Mare in Somersetshire, the living of which had passed to the latter from uncle Frederick. Before our return we had visited Portsmouth and Salisbury, Wells where we paid our respects to the Bishop and Bath; when I called on Sir William Watson, my mother's uncle, I thought Weston the most lonely and desolate place I had ever seen with extensive banks of mud at low water to the South west. It is now a fashionable watering place.

I used to visit the Ords at Richmond where they kept a gay house, gave balls &c, and with them have gone to balls at Hampton Court and at old Lady Howe's. She inherited Pope's villa at Twickenham[82] and I recollect meeting there The Duke of Clarence and his children.[83] The beauty of Miss Fitzclarence,[84] afterwards Lady Delisle struck me much.

---

[82][Alexander Pope, 1688-1744, poet (see p. 20). In 1715 Pope had come to live in Chiswick near to Lord Burlington, who was able to protect Catholics. In 1718 he leased several pieces of land and cottages at Cross Deep, Twickenham; the following year he built himself a riverside villa in the Palladian style. The building incorporated a tunnel which led from the riverside, under the house and the road behind it, to a garden. Adjoining the tunnel was a grotto. Sophia Charlotte, Baroness Howe, 1762-1835, was the widow of the son of Admiral Richard (Blackjack) Howe, 1st and last Earl Howe, created Baron Howe of Langar, Notts in 1788, brother of General William Howe, 5th Viscount Howe, 1729-1814. When Lady Howe acquired the property, which she may have bought, she found the visitors such a nuisance that in 1807 she decided to demolish the villa. The villa was painted by Turner, a near neighbour, who was outraged at this act of vandalism, and Lady Howe became known as Queen of the Goths, apparently an allusion to Tamora, the Queen of the Goths, in Shakespeare's *Titus Andronicus*.]

[83][William, 1765-1837, Duke of Clarence, who became King William IV, 1830-7. He had two elder brothers, Prince George, Prince of Wales, later George IV, and Frederick, Duke of York, and he was not expected to be King. His father, George III, was reluctant to make him a duke, but William pressed for this, and threatened to seek election as an MP, if a dukedom were refused him. He was created Duke of Clarence in 1789. He had ten illegitimate children, five sons and five daughters, by the Irish actress Dorothea Bland, better known as 'Mrs Jordan', with whom he lived for twenty years. In view of the size of the family, in which all the children were given the surname of Fitzclarence, William and Mrs Jordan were allocated Bushey House as a residence. Frederick, Duke of York, died in 1827, George IV died in 1830, and William then ascended the throne as William IV.]

[84][The eldest daughter of William and Mrs Jordan, Sophia, Lady De L'Isle. She married, 13 August 1825, Sir Philip Charles Shelley Sidney, 1800-51, 2nd Bt, 1st

In August 1812, I went with Hobbes Scott[85] to Whitfield. We travelled by coach and slept the first night at Stamford. A night coach from London picked us up the next morning early and we proceeded on by Tuxford, Bawtry, Doncaster &c to York, which we reached about eleven o'clock in the evening. We only stopped to sup, and arrived at Newcastle about twelve o'clock the following day. I was outside behind the coachman and recollect that I felt very cold just before sunrise and so sleepy that I was often on the point of falling off. From Newcastle we posted and employed four hours in going from Hexham to Whitfield, although the distance was only twelve miles. The road was detestable, especially about the Cupola Hill.

I was of course greatly struck with the beauty of the scenery, so unlike any thing I had previously seen. My reception at the hall was as kind as possible. Among the visitors were Charles Ord,[86] Charlotte Scott (Mrs Bigge),[87] Mr and Mrs H. Ogle and Mr H. Streatfield,[88] father to Oswald Smith's son in law, Mr Merry Deputy Secretary at War and J.W. Lukin.[89] Every one of

---

Baron De L'Isle and Dudley of Penshurst 1835, KCH 1830, GCH 1831, MP (Tory) Eye, 1829-31, equerry to his father in law William IV, 1830-5. She died in childbirth in April 1837, causing William great distress. (Her husband died at Penshurst 4 March 1851.) William IV died of heart failure 20 June 1837. Though William had eventually ended his association with 'Mrs Jordan', and married in 1818 Adelaide Louisa Theresa Caroline Amelia 1792-1849, daughter of Georg Friedrich Karl, Duke of Saxe Meiningen, he was a fond father of the children that he had fathered with her.]

[85][Thomas Hobbes Scott was the youngest of the eight children of James Scott, Vicar of Itchen, Hampshire and Chaplain in Ordinary to George III. His mother was Jane Elizabeth Harmood. At 30 he matriculated and entered St Alban Hall, BA 1817, MA 1818. Norman's statement on p. 144 that Hobbes Scott did not graduate is incorrect.]

[86][Charles Ord, 1787-1816, was the brother of William Henry Ord (see p. 133), Norman's friend. He attended Eton, and graduated BA from Cambridge in 1808, MA 1811. He died, unmarried, at Pisa.]

[87][See p. 137.]

[88][Not identified. Oswald Smith (see p. 62) married in 1824 Henrietta Mildred, daughter of Robert Hodgson, Dean of Carlisle. Their daughters were Isabella Mary, Laura Charlotte, and Frances Dora who, in 1853, married Captain the Hon. Claude Bowes Lyon.]

[89][William Merry, many years Deputy Secretary at War, died 23 November 1855 aged 93. He married in 1785 Elizabeth Walker of Huntingdon. He had two sisters,

these people is[90] dead excepting Mrs Bigge.

We used to ride and walk and shoot and practice waltzing, then a recent introduction, in which Charlotte Scott specially excelled. I recollect an expedition to Steward Peak[91], and another to Featherston Castle. On the 12th Aug I went out shooting with Hobbs on Parmentley[92] Beat and killed only one grouse. I was rather more successful on other occasions, but on the whole was a wretched shot in those days.

Nothing could exceed the kindness with which the Ords treated me and my time passed most agreeably.[93]

At that time the Valley of Whitfield was an oasis in a desert of moors. A short time previously there had not been a wheeled vehicle in the parish, only sledges. The load was carried on the backs of ponies, which were seen winding along in strings of thirty or forty. The place was undergoing a great change under the civilising influence of its kind and intelligent landlord who made roads and introduced carts to go upon them, established a school and replaced the miserable huts with a dungheap before the door with neat stone houses. The new houses were utterly disliked by the people and considered for some time as a great grievance.

---

one of whom, Mary-Amelia, married James William Lukin of Sandhill Lodge, Dorset.]

[90] [Norman wrote 'are' here.]

[91] [Probably, as manuscript is unclear.]

[92] [Norman clearly but incorrectly wrote 'Palmently' here.]

[93] In the spring of 1812 (I think) an accident happened to my Father and me, which might have [been] very serious. We were returning in a gig, when just beyond the grounds now occupied by Mr Wathen at Beckenham on the road to Penge, the Strap connecting the splinter bar to the body of the carriage broke, and the splinter fell on the heels of the grey mare. My father was driving. She set off full gallop. The ends of the shafts first struck the ground, then mounted into the air, and to make a long matter short, we were thrown out, and the carriage smashed. My Father's knee was injured, and my head cut. The horse who had galloped off was brought back, and I led her home. My Father becoming lame, stopped at Mr Latter and procured a conveyance. Neither of us suffered permanently from the accident. The grey mare had been brought from old Taylor at Norheads, was a vicious ill tempered beast, who was always getting into scrapes. [Mr Wathen lived at Beckenham Lodge. Norheads was a farm. There is material relating to it in the Norman papers at U310/E25, 1844 and 1862.]

Mr Ord also consolidated farms.[94] In his father's or grandfather's time there were seventy-six cultivating tenants.[95] There are not now more than ten or twelve. This change would be considered by some people a great evil.

The estate had been bought by Ord, who had made a fortune as a merchant at Newcastle, about 1750 for £28,000[96] of a Whitfield. The Whitfields having held it since about the year 1200 under a grant from the Queen of Malcolm of Scotland to her Chaplain. Their house, which was pulled down by Mr Ord's father, stood in the valley near the present gardener's house and was replaced by the present dwelling.

I have always considered the inhabitants of Whitfields among the best-conditioned and happiest of Englishmen. The climate is very healthy and the rate of mortality low. Nobody can build houses and the young people have acquired the habit, if they do not get employment at home, of migrating into the mining or manufacturing districts. The population once consisting

[94] [William Henry Ord, 1781-1855, English Whig politician and landowner. He was the son of William Ord and Eleanor Brandling. His father had estates and coal and lead mining interests at Whitfield near Hexham, and these his son inherited; his mother was part of a powerful Newcastle family. The Ords themselves were a long established political family in the North East. Robert Ord, 1700-78, was MP for Morpeth, representing the interests of Henry Howard, 4th Earl of Carlisle. William Henry Ord was a left-wing Whig, a follower of Samuel Whitbread who married the sister of Earl Grey. As noted on p. 129 Mr Ord married Mary Scott. His son was William Henry Ord, 1803-39, a barrister and MP for Newport, Isle of Wight. The elder William Ord, whom he had predeceased, left his estates to his son's widow Frances Vere Lorraine, whom his son had married in 1829. She subsequently (1851) married Sir Edward Blackett, 6th Bart. Her niece married the Reverend John Alexander Blackett, Rector of Wolsingham, on condition that he changed his name to Blackett-Ord.]

[95] [William Ord of Fenham, 1715-68, the grandfather of William Henry Ord, was a land and mine owner, the second son of Thomas Ord of Fenham and Anne Bacon. In 1745/6 he married Anne Dillingham, heiress to estates at East and West Langton, Leics. He became High Sheriff of Northumberland in 1747. He purchased the estate at Whitfield near Hexham in 1750, from the financially embarrassed Whitfield family, developing lead and silver mining there, and coal mining at Fenham and at Benwell, an estate he bought in 1756. His eldest son, William Ord 1752-89, the father of William Henry Ord, married Eleanor Brandling of Gosforth, while his second son, the Reverend James Ord, 1761-1836, who inherited the Langton estates, married Barbara Brandling.]

[96] [This would be £4,619,440 in 2009 prices.]

of miserable cottears, consists at present of wealthy farmers and well paid labourers, with the necessary proportion of artizans. The inhabitants on the whole have[97] somewhat diminished during the last half century.

The result of all this is that the Whitfields are a healthy and robust race and nobody among them knows what it is to want employment or to be without plenty of food, comfortable clothing, and lodging. The only drawback to their well-being I could ever discern is that they have little taste for amusement. There is no cricket or football, or in short any game and I fear that they have a strong taste for and drink spirits. The women are not all virtuous. I always urged upon Mr Ord the propriety of introducing games and he agreed with one in opinion upon this point. The difficulty was how to begin.

The above is a digression from my narration but a recollection of the many happy days I have passed at Whitfield and of the affection I felt for its kind and estimable owner, have forced it upon me.

Before I return to my narrative I must dwell for a moment on the character and biography of Mr Ord. He became early the possessor of a large estate property at Morpeth, wrested a seat in that borough from Lord Carlisle and sat in Parliament for it from about 1801 till the passing of the Reform Bill and subsequently for Newcastle for two or three Parliaments. He was out of the house for one Parliament having failed in a contest for the county. He was a staunch Whig, connected in blood or friendship or both to the

[97] [Norman wrote 'has' here.]

Greys,[98] Ridleys[99] and Brandlings,[100] and Sheridans,[101] Lords Holland[102] and Lansdowne,[103] and in short was well acquainted with all the notabilities of

[98] [The family of Grey of Howick. Charles Grey, 1764-1845, 2nd Earl Grey, Whig MP for Northumberland 1786-1807, First Lord of the Admiralty in Greville administration 1806-7, MP Appleby 1807, Prime Minister 1830-4. The great aim of his life was Parliamentary reform, and he sponsored the Reform Bill of 1832. He also supported Catholic Emancipation.]

[99] [Those associated with Sir Matthew White Ridley, 2nd Bt, 1745-1813 and with Sir Matthew White Ridley, 3rd Bt, 1778-1836, MP for Newcastle upon Tyne. The 2nd Bt was a land and coal owner and politician, and the second of 12 children of Matthew Ridley, 1711-78. He succeeded at the age of 17 to the baronetcy of his maternal uncle Sir Matthew White 1727-63. He was elected MP for Morpeth in 1768, became a Newcastle Alderman in 1774, and was subsequently MP for Newcastle, a seat which his father had held unopposed since 1747. He in turn handed on the seat to his eldest son in 1812. This son was the 3rd Bt, Matthew White Ridley, 1778-1846. The Ridley family was probably the most important in Newcastle, its fortune founded on coal, in partnership with the White family. Control of the city was effectively in the hands of a merchant oligarchy in which the Ridleys were important. They were also quite prepared to mobilise their workforce to deal with opposition.]

[100] [The Brandlings of Newcastle were a wealthy family of merchants and coal owners. They had been an established power in Newcastle since the beginning of the 16th century. They possessed estates at Gosforth and Alnwick and the family seat was at Felling, ultimately undermined by their own coaling activities. Charles Brandling, 1733-1802, was MP for Newcastle 1784-98, Charles John Brandling, 1797-1856, was MP for Newcastle 1798-1812, and for Northumberland 1820-6. He was active as a coal owner though ultimately he over-reached himself, and was forced to sell land. As noted, p. 133, William Ord's mother was Eleanor Brandling.]

[101] [Richard Brinsley Sheridan, 1809/10-88, MP for Shaftesbury 1845-52, Dorchester 1852-68, and Helen Selina née Sheridan 1807-67, successively Mrs Blackwood, Lady Dufferin and Countess of Gifford. She was the daughter of Caroline Henrietta Sheridan née Callander, who married in November 1807 Thomas Sheridan, 1775-1817, the only son of Richard Brinsley Sheridan 1751-1816, politician and playwright. The Whigs were extremely close knit, and amongst Grey's numerous lovers was the second wife of Richard Brinsley Sheridan.]

[102] [Henry Richard Vassal Fox, 3rd Baron Holland, 1773-1840, Lord Privy Seal in the Ministry of All the Talents, 1806-7, Chancellor of the Duchy of Lancaster 1830-4 and 1835-40, FRS 1811.]

[103] [Henry Petty Fitzmaurice, 3rd Marquess of Lansdowne, 1780-1863, MP for Calne 1802-6, Cambridge University 1806-7, Camelford 1807-9, succeeded 1809, Chancellor of the Exchequer 1806-7, admirer of Charles James Fox, Home Secretary 1827-8, Lord President of the Council 1835-41, 1846-52, Leader of the Opposition in the Lords, 1841-6, FRS 1811. He refused the Premiership in 1852, and was in the Cabinet without office 1852-8. His father was a friend of Bentham, and he was sent on a Continental tour with Bentham's protégé Etienne Dumont.]

the party. He was an assiduous member of the House of Commons, useful in committees but seldom spoke. I only recollect his appearing prominently on two occasions *vizt* in an attack upon certain commissioners appointed to dispose of the Dutch prizes who, although men of great pretensions to loyalty and extra-sanctity, had unduly feathered their nests. And once in some strictures on the Duke of Clarence for cutting down or disfiguring the ornamental trees in Bushy Park.

Mr Ord had respectable abilities and a mind cultivated by reading and by constant intercourse with the best society of his day. He was a man of a most kind and gentle disposition, with the highest sense of honour and probity. In short, in every sense of the word he, was a gentleman.

I must not dwell so long on Mrs Ord who however was an estimable person, always most kind to me. She had a great deal of drollery in her disposition. The only child was a little boy in 1812, I shall have more to say about him hereafter.

After I had been at Whitfield for two or three weeks, I agreed, with my father's permission, to accept an invitation from the Ords to accompany them into Scotland. The party consisted of Mr and Mrs Ord, Charlotte and Hobbes Scott. We stopped first at Morpeth, where there was a public ball attended by all the nobility[104] of the neighbourhood. I recollect particularly Sir M. W. Ridley, Mr and Mrs Ridley[105] the latter then a very handsome woman (mother to Mr Martin Smith),[106] Mr C. W. Bigge and his family.[107]

[104] [Probably, MS unclear here.]

[105] [Laura (died 1864) daughter of George Hawkins, married Sir M.W. Ridley in 1803.]

[106] [Louisa, the daughter of Sir Matthew White Ridley, 3rd Bt, married in 1831 Martin Tucker Smith, 1803-80, MP for Midhurst 1831-2, Wickham 1847-65, banker in London.]

[107] [William Bigge of Benton, 1707-58, High Sheriff of Northumberland 1750, married in 1736 Mary, daughter and heir of Charles Clarke of Ovingham. Their son was Thomas Charles Bigge, 1739-94, landowner, banker, and Sheriff of Northumberland 1771. He married in 1772 Jemima Ord, 1748-1806, daughter of William Ord of Fenham. They had three sons: Charles William, to whom Norman refers here, John Thomas, 1780-1843, later Chief Justice of Trinidad and colonial com-

I danced with two Miss DeLisles of Acton, fine girls.[108] From Morpeth we drove one day to Bothal Castle, a fine ruin charmingly situated. After leaving Morpeth, our first sleeping place was Berwick. We found at the inn the coffin of Miss Brand[109] whom I had known at Rendlesham as a visitor to the Shepherds of Campsey Ashe.[110] She was engaged to be married to Alderman, afterwards Sir W. Heygate[111] the Possessor of Holwood,[112] and died of consumption. We proceeded to Edinburgh by Dunbar and Haddington and

missioner (see p. 145), and Thomas Hanway, who became a Newcastle banker, married Charlotte Scott, and died in 1824 leaving four sons and two daughters. Charles William Bigge born 28 October 1773, married 27 January 1802 Alicia, only daughter of Christopher Wilkinson of Newcastle. He died 8 December 1849. She died 19 February 1848.]

[108][Acton and Old Felton, a joint township in the Felton parish, are two and a half miles from Acklington. Robert Lisle had married Mary Orde and lived at Acton House. His daughters were Isabella, Susannah, Anna Maria, and Eliza Lisle. There was an illegitimate son called Robert Lisle by a woman called Ann Bell. It was the 'natural son' who was at Eton with Norman and who later became De Lisle.]

[109][Miss Brand was possibly one of the children of Thomas Brand, 1745-94 and his wife Gertrude née Trevor Roper, 1750-1819. There was a daughter Gertrude Brand born in 1772, about whom no further information is available. The second child and first son of the marriage, Thomas Brand, 1774-1851, inherited, through his mother, the title of Baron Dacre. Though the family is chiefly associated with the Hoo estate in Hertfordshire, Miss Brand seems to have come from Great Bradley Hall in Suffolk, which came into the hands of Thomas Brand in the middle of the 18th century.]

[110][Campsey or Campsea Ashe was an estate of 2,350 acres, near Aldburgh in Suffolk. It was acquired about 1600 (or 1652 according to another account) by the Shepherd family, in whose possession it remained until 1882-3. St John the Baptist Church there contains a grand memorial to Frederik Shepherd who died at the battle of Badajoz in 1812, when he was just 22 years old.]

[111][Sir William Sudbury Heygate, 1782-1844, Bt 1831, Alderman of City of London 1812, banker in London and Leicester, Sheriff of London and Middlesex 1811-12, Treasurer of the London Orphan Asylum, Lord Mayor of London 1822-3, MP for Sudbury 1818-26. He had houses at Chatham Place, Blackfriars, and Holwood House, Kent. Though possessor of the Holwood estate, he appears to have lived in Southend, and to have been instrumental in the building of its pier, with the passing of the Southend Pier Bill in 1829. His estate at Southend was called Porters. His fortune seems to have derived from the Leicester banking house Pares's Leicestershire Banking Company Ltd, a private bank established in Leicester in 1800 as Pares, Heygate and Company. William Heygate himself joined the bank in 1813.]

[112][Holwood House is a country house in Keston near Hayes, now in the London borough of Bromley. It was designed by Decimus Burton, and built between 1823 and 1826, on the site of an earlier building owned by William Pitt the Younger.]

put up at Dumbrick's where we remained for a few days and drove over to see Roslyn Abbey, one of the most beautiful of Ruins.

At Edinburgh, Hobbes received the news that his house was in difficulties, which soon after ended in bankruptcy, and set off at once for London. I remained with the Ords and accompanied them in a tour through a portion of the highlands. Our sleeping places, if I recollect rightly, were Callender, Lough Erne Head, Tyndrum, Dalmally, Invarary, Arrocher, Glasgow, Lanark and again Edinburgh.

From Callender we went to Loch Catherine, then rendered popular by Scott's poem, the 'Lady of the Lake'.[113] I was greatly struck with the beauty of the Trosacks, broken and wooded hills which guard the approach to the lake, and of the mountain Benlede[114] which overhangs it. The Castle of Inverary greatly disappointed me being neither a palace, or a fine baronial castle. Dalmally seemed almost out of the world. There was no inn and we slept at the Manse. From Lanarkshire we visited the Falls of the Clyde[115] called Corra Linn,[116] and also the factory of Mr Robert Owen who had already rendered himself celebrated by the schools he had established for the children of his work people.[117] Wonderful to say he is still alive and I believe

[113][Sir Walter Scott, 1771-1832, Scottish novelist, historian and poet. His poem 'The Lady of the Lake' dates from 1809. This, with other long narrative poems, 'The Lay of the Last Minstrel' (1805) and 'Marmion' (1808), were very successful, and made Scott wealthy.]

[114][Possibly, Ben Venue or Ben Bhreac.]

[115][This is blank in the MS.]

[116][This is blank in the MS.]

[117][1771-1858, born at Newtown, Montgomeryshire. He progressed through selling cotton, manufacturing it, and mill management, to paternal concern for working conditions. He married Caroline Anne Dale, whose father had a weaving mill at New Lanark, south of Glasgow which, with other partners, Owen acquired. He showed energy and skill, both managerially and in improving working conditions. New Lanark became famous throughout Europe and between 1815 and 1825 it attracted thousands of visitors. He became an advocate of largely self-sufficient model industrial townships, and campaigned, with the elder Peel, to limit child labour in factories. His self-publicising activities however brought his ideas under the critical gaze of economists like Torrens and McCulloch, who discerned the fragile intellectual basis, even before he started to advocate a bizarre scheme of mone-

hearty (in January 1858).[118] I have frequently met him since at the late Mr John Smith's[119] and Political Economy Club. He is a man of one idea, pushed to an extent, which has kincked upon his sanity. I have known him to listen with patience and courtesy to arguments which blew his opinions out of the water, and when he replied, you perceived that they had not produced the slightest effect upon him.

From Edinburgh we returned to Whitfield.

It must be observed that at this time the continent was closed to the English, who were thus compelled to exercise their touring propensities at home.

I derived great pleasure from the expedition, but with some danger to my heart from the close association to Charlotte Scott, then an attractive young woman of twenty-four with fine hair and eyes and a lovely brunette complexion. She was never, I dare say, aware of the impression she had made. Nothing could exceed the kindness of the Ords to me and my gratitude to them in consequence was unbounded.

I kept a detailed journal of my Highland Tour, which I have lost. My dear mother, who thought that any thing of mine must be excellent, took the trouble of copying it out and sending the copy to the Camerons at the Bahamas.[120] On its way it fell into the hands of an American privateersman and doubtless served to light pipes.

I have always followed up the habit, thus begun, of keeping a journal during my various travels, and with great benefit firstly in impressing objects on my memory, secondly in affording pleasure from their subsequent perusal.[121]

---

tary reform based on 'labour notes'. This is the background to Norman's comment about Owen's imperviousness to criticism at the Political Economy Club.]

[118]He died in 1858.

[119][The most likely candidate is John Smith the banker, of Smith Payne and Smith, 1767-1842, father of the banker John Abel Smith, 1802-71.]

[120]It still exists among my papers. [Note added by Norman in 1866.]

[121][In thc Norman papers at Maidstone U310 F12 contains notes and journals of Norman's travels abroad.]

I returned home by coach from Newcastle, having passed two or three days at Whitfield, after leaving Scotland. It took me one day to go to Newcastle. There I slept and started next morning, (it was a Sunday) at eight o'clock. I travelled without stopping, unless for meals, and did not reach London until tuesday between two and three in the afternoon. The vehicle held six insides and I had an inside place, but my companions being pilots or fat and odiferous drovers, I could only bear the squeeze and stench for a few hours in the middle of the night.

I have since gone from Bromley to Whitfield in one day and without inconvenience.

It was through Hobbes Scott and the Ords that I became acquainted with the Lewin family.[122] Mr Lewin was a retired East India civil servant, a quiet and amiable man who had taken part however in the treasonable arrest[123]

[122] [The Lewins were a Kentish family from Bexley and Eltham, with a long connection with the East India Company. Richard Lewin was commander of an East India Company ship, and his son Thomas, 1753-1843, to whom Norman refers here, worked for the Company 1770-1800, spending 20 years in India itself, and realised a modest fortune in Madras. The family were thus comfortably off. The grandson of Thomas Lewin, Thomas Herbert Lewin, 1839-1916, enjoyed a distinguished career in India, rising to the rank of Lieutenant Colonel. He became Deputy Commissioner of Cooch Behar, and later Deputy Commissioner of Darjeeling.]

[123] [This is not referred to in *The Lewin Letters* (see Thomas Herbert Lewin (ed.), *The Lewin Letters. A Selection from the Correspondence & Diaries of an English Family, 1756-1884*, 2 vols., London: Constable, 1909). There is some material (p. 3) about Mr John Whitehill, temporary Governor of Madras during 1777, 1778 and 1780, who was suspended by Warren Hastings and the Council at the end of October 1780. When the House of Commons came to enquire into the war in the Carnatic in May 1782, Thomas Lewin, a protégé of Whitehill, declined to attend the hearings, was held to be in contempt of the House, brought to the Bar of the House, in custody, by the Sergeant at Arms, reprimanded and fined. But there is no reference in the two volumes to Lord MacLeod.]

of Lord Macleod.[124] Mrs Lewin was a Hales of Yorkshire,[125] a warmhearted woman but rather eccentric, a quality which has been inherited by some of her descendants. They had become intimate with the Scotts from having lived near Southampton, then in little Bengal, but when I knew them they resided in Bedford Square and subsequently at the Hollies, Half Way Street Bexley.[126]

---

124 [MacLeod, Norman of MacLeod, 1754-1801, army officer and politician. He was born at Brodie Castle, Morray, and in 1772 he succeeded his grandfather Norman MacLeod as chief of the Clan MacLeod. In 1775 he was commissioned as a Captain in the 71st Regiment. In 1779 he became Lieutenant Colonel of the 2nd Battalion of the 42nd Regiment. In 1782 he went to India and in 1783 was raised to the brevet rank of Brigadier General though in 1788 all brevet ranks of British officers in India were cancelled. In 1785 he transferred to Bengal and was appointed Second in Command of the army there, at a salary of £6,000 per annum. However following the abolition of brevet ranks MacLeod returned in disgust to England in 1789, and immersed himself in radical politics in England and Scotland.]

125 [There is a good deal on the Hale marriage in vol. 1 of *The Lewin Letters*; see p. 140. Richard Lewin, the father of Thomas Lewin and the grandfather of Harriet Lewin, obtained for his son Thomas Lewin a 'writership' in the East India Company's service. He went to Madras at the age of 18 in 1771. He served in the military department of Fort St George and at a later point was apparently private secretary to the Governor. In 1780 he was sent to England to report on the war in the Carnatic. He did not return to India for two more years. On his journey home from India he sailed on the same ship as Madame Grand, who had become the mistress in India of Sir Philip Francis, a member of the Governor General's Council, and found it politic to leave India. It seems that the young Mr Lewin became the lover of Mme Grand. They went to Paris together but then separated and she subsequently became Princess Talleyrand. Mr Lewin went to Yorkshire to visit some relatives, and then, according to the family account, fell in love jointly with the sisters Miss Mary and Miss Anne Hale, the twin daughters of Major General John Hale of The Plantation, Guisborough, Yorks. The sisters were identical twins. When pressed by the General to choose, Mr Lewin seems to have chosen Mary Hale (1768-1837) more or less at random. She was barely 16, and consented meekly to the arrangement. They were married 2 February 1784. Twelve children, seven sons and five daughters, are listed as having been born of the marriage, between 1785 and 1811. The eldest son of the marriage was Thomas Lewin, 'the present Thomas Lewin' to whom Norman refers, though the occupant of the Hollies later on was Frederick Mortimer Lewin, born in 1798. See *The Lewin Letters*, vol. 1 pp. 1-5, 134-5.]

126 [The house seems to have had about 80 acres of garden and woodland, with a further 200 acres leased to farmers, with more than 20 houses and cottages. It was originally called Marowbone Hall, and it was bought by Richard Lewin. The name was probably changed to the Hollies soon after his death in 1810. The mansion was pulled down in 1853, and a new house built.]

The cynosure[127] among them who attracted me, in common with many other young gentlemen, was the second daughter Harriet, one of the most remarkable persons, of her sex, whom it has been my fortune to know.[128] As respected her physical qualifications. She was tall and well-proportioned and possessed a beautiful complexion and hair, good eyes and a general cast of features, which may be considered handsome although not strikingly beautiful. She walked and danced well and was eminently cheerful, amusing and kindhearted. Her mental powers were of a very high order. She was somewhat masculine in her habits[129] and possessed in full measure the quaintness and oddity of her race.[130]

I fell much in love with her if a passion, which did not engross me, and which was quite objectless as I had not the least idea of marriage could be called love.[131] At any rate, for years I admired her more than any other female, and now, looking back to what she was, I am persuaded that I have never known altogether so brilliant a woman.

If however we never stood to each other in the relation of lovers,[132] at

[127] [Pole star, thus centre of attention.]

[128] [Harriet Lewin was courted by George Grote, 1794-1871, whose radical opinions on a wide variety of subjects she eagerly adopted. After a five year acquaintance, and a two year engagement, the pair eloped, and married on 5 March 1820, because Grote's father refused to agree a date for the marriage. She became a prominent figure in radical circles, during the years 1832-41, when Grote was MP for the City of London and leader of the radical faction in the House of Commons.]

[129] [On Mrs Grote's masculinity, see the observations of contemporaries referred to in M.L. Clarke, *George Grote. A Biography*, London: Athlone Press, University of London, 1962 pp. 24-5. Sydney Smith found George Grote 'ladylike' and Mrs Grote 'a perfect gentleman'.]

[130] [This rather oblique comment may be illuminated by the fact that *The Lewin Letters* (see p. 140) is headed by a quotation from The Talmud: 'There are three Crowns. The Crown of the Law; the Crown of the Priesthood; and the Crown of Royalty: but the Crown of a good Name is superior to them all'.]

[131] [Norman remained in touch with Harriet Grote, as she had become, after her marriage, and until the breach between Norman and her husband; see p. 356. The Norman papers at Maidstone contain letters from Mrs Grote to Norman, 1822-9, at U310 C39.]

[132] [However they were more than just good friends. Harriet Grote wrote to her brothers Thomas and Edward Lewin and her sister Francis Lewin, 5 November 1830, 'G. Norman is marrying Sibella at last. I felt his marrying very deeply. He

any rate we were great friends for many years and if I could not marry her myself, I introduced her to a husband far more worthy of her,[133] in my friend George Grote,[134] as will be mentioned hereafter. As will also my final quarrel and separation from the Grotes about 1832, of which she was the occasion, and which at the time, was a source to me of bitter sorrow.

It may be remarked that the influence of her husband, and his philosophic friends have greatly changed Mrs Grote from what she was in her youthful days. It is much to be lamented that she has no children. One was born and the mother narrowly escaped. Had she been surrounded by a youthful family, I cannot doubt that her intellectual and moral character, would have been essentially modified, I think for the better.

I will now say a few words upon the life of my poor friend Hobbes Scott, which has been, for a private gentleman, very singular and eventful. The youngest son of a Hampshire clergyman of small means, the marriage of his beautiful sister to Lord Oxford[135] threw him into distinguished society. He well knew Horne Tooke,[136] Burdett[137] and Dr Parr,[138] and was frequent guest

came and doled all out to me a few days before the event: very rational but pretty deeply in, I promise ye'. *The Lewin Letters*, vol. 1 p. 274.]

[133] [Mrs Grote does not refer to this in her biography of her husband, though she reproduces (p.26) a quite extraordinarily star-struck letter written by her husband to an unnamed correspondent, probably Norman, about the effect produced upon him by accidentally meeting her subsequently.]

[134] [George Grote 1794-1871; see p. 64. He was the eldest of the eleven children of George Grote the banker, 1762-1830, and Selina Mary Peckwell, 1774-1845.]

[135] [Edward Harley, 5th Earl of Oxford, 1773-1848, married in 1794 Jane Elizabeth daughter of the Reverend James Scott of Itchen Ferry, Hants, Rector of St Lawrence, Southampton, and sister of Hobbes Scott. She died in 1824 aged 51. According to the *Complete Peerage*, vol. 10 p. 269, 'She, who was a very beautiful woman, had so indifferent a reputation that her children were referred to as "the Harleian Miscellany", and her name was freely coupled with Lord Byron's and the Duke of Cumberland among others'.]

[136] [John Horne, later Tooke, 1736-1812, radical agitator, and close friend of Norman's great uncle Richard Beadon, Bishop of Bath and Wells.]

[137] [Sir Francis Burdett, 5th Bt, 1770-1844, radical politician and associate of Horne Tooke. ]

[138] [Samuel Parr, 1747-1825, LL. D 1781, son of a surgeon to whom he became apprenticed. An associate of Burdett and Horne Tooke.]

of Mr Bosville, who kept an open table for a certain class of Liberals, some of them men of mark, others mere toadies.[139]

The Scott family[140] clubbed the means of putting Hobbes into business.[141] This proved a bad move as I have already related and in 1812, being then about twenty-nine, Hobbes was once more thrown upon the world.

He found means to go to Oxford where I visited him at Alban Hall[142] but

[139] [William Bosville, 1745-1813, society host and radical. On each weekday he received no more than twelve guests to dine with him at 5pm precisely. He was a supporter of Horne Tooke (see fn 136 above). He held dinner parties up to the day of his death but died before 5pm.]

[140] [The Scott family was far from wealthy. The father of Hobbes Scott, Rector of St Lawrence Southampton, had died in 1794 leaving his son no inheritance. But the marriage of Mary Scott to William Ord in 1803, and the earlier marriage of Elizabeth Scott to the Earl of Oxford in 1794, may have made some financial support available. Since Hobbes Scott was born in 1783, he would not have been liable for his debts, and thus able to enter into trade, until 1804, thus after both marriages mentioned.]

[141] [Thomas Hobbes Scott, 1783-1860, son of the Reverend James Scott. His father died in 1794. He had no inheritance, but the family raised a small capital which enabled him to set up as a wine merchant. The business failed. Bankrupt, he entered St Alban's Hall, Oxford (BA 1817). After a spell in Australia as secretary to John Thomas Bigge (see p. 136), to whom Scott was related by marriage, and who had been appointed Commissioner to investigate New South Wales, he was ordained in 1821, and in 1822 was appointed Rector of Whitfield, the living in the gift of William Ord his brother in law. He subsequently returned to Australia in 1824, after being appointed, through the efforts of William Ord, Archdeacon of New South Wales. This was an important position, and Scott set about his task with enormous energy, dealing with teachers, churches and schools, and showing great concern for the welfare of the congregations. Ultimately he became responsible for the entire educational system in New South Wales. But he became the target for abusive journalism and, after an unsuccessful and difficult time to which Norman refers later in the Autobiography, he set out in 1829 to return to England. After a delay caused by shipwreck, he returned to Whitfield in 1830. There he remained, becoming an honorary Canon of Durham Cathedral in 1845. He died unmarried in 1860, leaving an estate valued at less than £800. The Norman papers at Maidstone contain letters from the years 1827-30 to Norman from Hobbes Scott, written when he was in Australia, about life in the colony, at U310 C36, and a copy of his will, of which Norman was an executor, at U310 F32/4.]

[142] [St Alban Hall, which originally belonged to the Convent of Littlemore, was purchased by Merton College, Oxford in 1548, following the Dissolution of the Monasteries. Throughout much of the 19th century it remained a notionally independent academic institution, although it was finally incorporated into Merton in 1881. The later Cardinal Newman was Vice Principal in 1825.]

did not then take a degree, and soon after the peace became the guest of the younger Hoppner, who was consul at Venice. There he remained some time and was acquainted with Byron. About 1817 or 1818, Mr T. Bigge[143] being appointed Commissioner of Enquiry in New South Wales, took Hobbes with him as secretary. On his return he continued to take orders and was presented by Mr Ord to the Rectory of Whitfield. After a short interval he was named Archdeacon of Australia, and had he remained there would have become Bishop instead of his successor Broughton,[144] but the unmerited abuse hurled upon him and various tracasseries[145] drove him to a premature resignation and he returned once more to Whitfield never again to quit it, unless on an occasional visit to a friend. A more varied life can hardly be conceived, nor can many private gentlemen be named low in fortune and of no great mark in talent or accomplishment, who have been brought into contact with more distinguished men and more striking events than Hobbes, among whose adventures not before alluded to, I may mention a voyage round the world and a shipwreck at the Swan River. He was generally a poor, sometimes a very poor man,[146] but his honour and probity are unimpeachable, and his vein of kind and benevolent feeling, were above all praise.

[143] [John Thomas Bigge, 1780-1843, third son of Thomas Charles Bigge (see p. 137), educated at Newcastle Grammar School, Westminster School, and Oxford. Called to the Bar in 1806, Chief Justice of Trinidad 1813-18, 1819 Commissioner of Enquiry into the colony of New South Wales. He returned to England in 1821 and was sent on similar missions to Cape Colony, Mauritius and Ceylon. Worn out by his travels he returned to England in 1829, and died unmarried in December 1843.]

[144] [Scott had resigned in November 1828, and in September 1829 he was replaced by Archdeacon William Grant Broughton, 1788-1853, who, like Scott, was English. A legacy had enabled him to go to Cambridge, BA 1818, MA 1823. He was ordained Deacon in 1818 by Bishop Burgess of Salisbury. As a parish clergyman he was scholarly and successful. He went to Australia in succession to Hobbes Scott without optimism, but spent the rest of his life there, proving much more adroit than Scott in avoiding colonial quarrels, though in this he was not completely successful. Consecrated Bishop of Australia, in London, 14 February 1836.]

[145] [Entanglements, quarrels, harassment.]

[146] [As noted above, when Scott died he left an estate valued at less than £800 including his bible, his gun, and some works of art.]

About four or five years ago, I granted him an annuity of £90 per annum for a payment of £600.[147] This was a good deal more than the Government would have given and I am happy in the thought that I shall probably lose money by the transaction and have contributed to his comfort.

I may here mention another family with whom I passed a good deal of time, both anterior to 1812 and subsequently. I mean the Cummings. Mr J. Cumming had been a Merchant at Riga, where my father became personally acquainted with him. He came to England with a large fortune after the rupture with the Emperor Paul,[148] and married my mother's friend Nelly Hunter, sister of Alderman Sir C.S. Hunter[149] and of Mrs Manning.

The Cummings lived for some years [in] an old house called Ruscombe, situated near Twyford in Berkshire, subsequently inhabited by the Blakes and now demolished. I have often staid there. There was a good Jack fishery in a muddy stream on a common near by.

In 1811 I shot at Reescombe early in September with Sir Claudius [Hunter] and he observing that I had need of a razor, presented me with the first shaving apparatus I ever possessed.

Mr Cumming bought about 1813 or 1814, a place called Trent Park near Barnet, where I have often been, and laid out much money upon it.[150] The

147 [This was written in 1857 or 1858, and so the annuity was probably granted no earlier than 1852 or 1853. Thus Norman's intended generosity probably redounded to his financial benefit, since Scott died in 1860, though it is difficult to know what sort of life expectancy Norman had in mind, when setting the terms of the annuity, given that Scott was born in 1783. The two values in 2009 prices would be £9,349 and £62,328.]

148 [Russian Emperor, 1754-1801, son of Peter III and Catherine II, succeeded his mother in 1796. Strangled during a palace revolution in favour of his son Alexander I.]

149 [Sir Claudius Stephen Hunter, 1775-1851, 1st Bt 1812, younger son of Henry Lannoy Hunter 1739-89. Sheriff of London 1808-9, Lord Mayor 1811-12.]

150 [Trent Park or Cockfosters, Middlesex, later one of the homes of the Sassoon family. See Patrick Campbell, *Trent Park: A History*, London: Middlesex University, 1997. John Cumming, a merchant who had been in business at Riga, bought Trent Park from Sir Henry Lushington, who was bankrupt, in 1813. He very soon set about 'improvements' and spent lavishly on the property. When Cumming died in 1832, aged 75, the *Times* reported that he had spent £35,000 on extension

grounds were very pretty, having been part of Enfield Chase. I have had good sport there with rabbits, hares and cocks.

The later years of Mr Cumming's[151] life were clouded by a remarkable circumstance. Although not avowedly in business, he was a deep speculator and chiefly [in] a sort of partnership with a Mr Samuel Schneider.[152] For some years judging from his communications to me, he must have been very successful, but at length fortune turned and after his death it was discovered that the whole of his original fortune, perhaps £200,000 had been dissipated,[153] and that only the sum settled on his wife remained; she had died previously.

All books of accounts and papers which could have thrown any light on the transactions which had produced this catastrophe, had been carefully destroyed. I have known one parallel case to the above, that of Mr W. Entwistle, uncle to Sir John Lubbock.[154] He was a batchelor of ample means, and no lavish expenditure, but died rather suddenly leaving behind little more than the money in his pocket.

---

and improvement of the house. After Cumming's death the house was bought by the banker David Bevan.]

[151] [Norman actually wrote 'Mr C-'s' here.]

[152] [There was a John Schneider, a Russia merchant, like John Cumming, at 16 Broad Street Buildings. Samuel Schneider has not been traced in any edition of the Post Office London Directory. He may well have been in business in a commercial centre other than London.]

[153] [In 2009 prices this is the equivalent of £16,662,000.]

[154] [Sir John William Lubbock, 2nd Bt, 1774-1840, married in 1799 Mary, the daughter of James Entwistle of Rusholme, Manchester. The nephew was Sir John William Lubbock, 3rd Bt, 1803-65, London banker, partner (and sole working partner 1840-60), in Lubbock and Company, FRS 1829, astronomer and author of a book on probability erroneously attributed to Augustus de Morgan.]

# Chapter 5

# France and Napoleon

The year 1812 was a time to me of intense political interest. My boyish days had been passed under the apprehensions of invasion. I had witnessed the rapid growth of French power and the matchless conquests and victories of Napoleon. I formed the fixed opinion that the extension and permanence of the French empire would be fatal to the freedom and prosperity not of this country alone, but of Europe. The insurrection in Spain had excited my most enthusiasm.[1] My hopes had occasionally been elevated by the successes of the British Arms in that country, but it was plain that the Colossus could not be overthrown by blows which however well-dealt, touched no vital part nor met him in the fullness of his power. The Invasion of Russia involved a struggle of a very different kind from that in the Peninsula.[2] There such a disciplined army, as in point of number had never before obeyed a single leader, under the greatest captain of modern times, was hurled against the last independent realm of the continent. The interests involved were momentous. The changes of fortune on the largest scale. At first one hardly dared to hope, as one had done after Aspern.[3] At length the star of Napoleon grew pale, and when the

[1] [In May 1808 the Spanish King had been deposed by Napoleon and replaced by Napoleon's brother Joseph, and the Spanish rose in revolt.]

[2] [After fruitless negotiations between Napoleon and the Czar in April and May 1812, the French crossed the river Niemen without any formal declaration of war.]

[3] [Napoleon had been defeated at Aspern (Essling) on 22-25 May while advancing on Vienna in the campaign of 1809.]

news arrived of the retreat from Moscow,[4] the return of the invading host and the evacuation of Russia, my delight and enthusiasm were raised to the highest point. I can never forget those stirring times, or the interest which continued to attach to foreign politics up to the conclusion of the general peace after the second capture of Paris.[5]

Early in 1813, the Russian Armies following the remains of the French, after occupying the Dutchy of Warsaw,[6] entered Germany. Then followed the resurrection of Prussia, which out of a population of five millions sent into the field within a few months 200,000 men. The Battle of Lutzen and Bautsen[7]

[4] [The French retreat from Moscow began on the night of 19 October 1812.]

[5] [After defeat at Waterloo, Napoleon barely escaped capture. He travelled through the night and reached Paris in the early morning of 21 June 1815. Astonishingly, he then proposed to defend Paris against the allies. The news of Waterloo had reached Paris on the evening of the day following the battle, and the political forces in the capital, organised by Fouché, demanded the abdication of the Emperor. A provisional government was set up on 22 June and, after an initial refusal, Blücher, the Prussian General, who was advancing on Paris, granted an armistice. On 4 July the City of Paris surrendered, and on 8 July Louis XVIII re-entered the capital.]

[6] [After victories over Russia, Prussia and Austria, in 1805-7, Napoleon created the independent Duchy of Warsaw, thus giving the partitioned Poland a measure of independence. It was created from Prussian territory which had been part of Poland and was still inhabited by a Polish population. In 1809, under Josef Poniatowski, the Duchy managed to reclaim some of the territories seized by Austria in the third partition of Poland. From 1813, however, it was under Russian control and from 1815 the third partition of Poland was very largely reinstated.]

[7] [1 May 1813, Marshall Ney fought an indecisive battle at Lutzen (Grossgorschen) 10 miles south west of Leipzig against the Prussians and the Russians commanded by Wittgenstein, though the French claimed victory. The allies retired without difficulty to Dresden. Napoleon attacked them again at Bautsen (Warschen) 30 miles east of Dresden on 20 May 1813. Again though the French claimed victory, the battle, costly like Lutzen, was indecisive. An armistice was concluded at Plasnitz on 4th June 1813. Napoleon refused to accede to Austrian demands in an interview in the Marcolini Palace at Dresden on 26 June, but agreed to a conference at Prague which sat from 12 July to 12 August without result. Napoleon was intransigent. He established his position at Dresden, though suffering a series of defeats at Grossbeeren and Hagelberg in the north, Katzbach in the east, and Kulm in the south. With Blücher approaching from the north, and Schwartzenberg approaching from the south, the French were forced to retreat to Leipzig. It was there that the 'Battle of the Nations' took place, 16-19 October 1813. On the 18th the Saxons joined the allies, and Bernadotte's Swedish army came into action. A rout of the French followed. A fifth of the French army was

exhibited Napoleon once more as a Conqueror, and his star appeared again in the ascendant. The Armistice of Plasnitz[8] was signed, Austria joined the coalition, whose first operations after the rupture of negotiations at Prague, were mocked by the repulse at Dresden and the Defeat of Moreau.[9] But this reverse was speedily revenged by the victories of Culin and of the Katzbach, of Gross Beeren and of Dennewitz[10] and all was crowned by the 'Battle of Nations', the three days conflict at Leipzig,[11] which ruined the French host, raised with so much difficulty after the Russian campaign and obliged its scattered remains to seek for shelter behind the Rhine, leaving 150,000 of its veterans shut up in the several fortresses of the Vistula, the Oder and the Elbe, without a hope of succour and all destined successfully to succumb to the troops left to blockade them, unless where their garrisons contrived to hold out till the peace.

---

unable to make its escape. By 9 November Napoleon was back at the palace of St Cloud, having lost an army of nearly half a million men. The quality of his forces had been much reduced by conscription of youngsters and foreigners. Over 200,000 men were stranded in garrisons. According to J.M. Thompson, *Napoleon Bonaparte. His Rise and Fall* (Oxford: Blackwell, 1952, p. 350), the garrisons which surrendered were as follows: Dresden 11 November, Zamosk 22 November, Stettin 30 November, Modlin 1 December, Danzig 2 December, Torgau 26 December, Magdeburg 6 May 1814. Hamburg held out until after Waterloo and surrendered to the Bourbons.]

[8] [The MS is actually blank here.]

[9] [Jean Victor Moreau, 1761-1813, was a French General who enjoyed a successful military career and in 1800 won the key battle of Hohenlinden. But he was jailed after implication in a royalist plot, and exiled. He spent almost ten years in America. In response to a request from Czar Alexander I, he returned to Europe and became a military advisor during the 1813 campaign in Germany, accompanying the Russians and the Prussians in the march on Dresden. But his leg was broken by a cannonball at Dresden, and he died five days later.]

[10] [Battle of 6 September 1813, between the French, and the Prussians and the Russians, following the breakdown of the talks at Prague (see p. 150). After the attempt by Marshall Oudinot to march on Berlin, with the aim of forcing Prussia out of the war, he was replaced by Marshall Ney, who was opposed by Prussian and Russian forces under the overall command of Bernadotte at Dennewitz. The battle seems to have been confined within a single road and, after a mistake by Ney, who ordered Oudinot to fall back and form a reserve, Bernadotte attacked the French left flank and the French were routed, with casualties of 10,000. The allied casualties were 7,000.]

[11] [Norman wrote 'Leipsic' here.]

Never can I forget what I felt and thought during that eventful year. My enthusiasm for the Prussians, my earnest longing for the overthrow of Napoleon and the intense interest with which I followed the changing scenery of that bloody drama, and my delight at its close.

I ever felt gratitude to Russia for the noble stand made by her against the modern Alexander and for the part she subsequently took in the liberation of Europe. This sentiment has continued to animate me up to the present time. I never considered that the West had any thing to fear from her ambition, however great, and I regarded her conquests to the South and East as gains for humanity, only to be paralleled in that respect by those of England in India.

The war of 1854 was always rather opposed to my feelings, however I might rejoice in the French alliance and however desirable I might think it right that no one power should be allowed to cut and carve states and provinces at her will and pleasure. The notion that we should be the allies of the Turks, and help to uphold their corrupt, effete, and barbarous despotism, filled me with disgust. Yet it was for this Alas! that dear Herman's blood was shed.[12]

It has always appeared to me that France after all is the great continental power, by whom the independence of Europe is most seriously threatened. I must allow the war of 1854 had one admirable effect in putting an end to the pernicious gabble of the peace society, which unless checked, might have left us without Army or fleet and perhaps led to a foreign conquest of England.[13]

[12][See p. 405. Herman Norman was wounded in the head in the assault on the Redan, 18 June 1855, and died of his wound on 30 June.]

[13][Crimean War 1853-6, between Russia, on the one hand, and Turkey, Britain, France and later Sardinia on the other. The ostensible cause was Russia's claim to the guardianship of the Holy Places and protection of Orthodox Christians in the Turkish Empire. Underlying this was the usual concern of diplomats for the 'balance of power', and the fear that Russia would exploit the weakness of Turkey to expand into the Balkans and Mediterranean. Turkey declared war on 4 October 1853, Britain in March 1854. The British gained important victories over the Russians, bearing the brunt of the fighting in the battles of Alma (September

During the summer of 1812, we passed some time at Hastings when I recollect being made tipsy at the mess of the City of Dublin Militia, one of the few times in my life. One of the officers named de Hautenville afterwards became a clerk in the London docks and used to apply to me to procure him promotion. He is now alive, January 1858, as I read of his wife's death in 'Times' the other day.[14]

The year 1813 produced little remarkable in my personal history. I passed it in my usual way, playing at cricket and shooting as amusements and attending to business as much as my father or the necessity of the case required. Early in the year I was at Rendlesham, and later probably at other places, but I do not now recollect any other excursion from home. About this time I became intimately acquainted with the two Norwegians, Jorgen and Broder Knudtzon, the sons of a respectable merchant at Trondhjem.[15] They were

---

1854) and Balaklava and Inkermann. But under winter conditions, for which the army was not equipped, they settled down to a siege of Sevastapol. In August 1855 the French and Sardinians defeated the Russians at the Battle of Chernaya, and the French captured the Malakove redoubt, though the British were driven back from the Redan. In September 1855 the Russians surrendered Sevastapol, and in March 1856 the war ended with the peace of Paris. Britain and France committed 405,000 men to the Crimea of whom 25,600 were killed and a further 38,800 died of disease.]

[14] [See *Times* 13 January 1858, 1a. Mary Maria Hautenville, wife of Mr D. Hautenville, died 1 January 1858 at 12 Portland Street, Stepney. Although Daniel is a name which occurs in the Hautenville family records, this particular member of the family has not been traced. An obvious ancestry, given the dates, would have been descent from the paternity of Rawdon Hautenville, born 1743, who died in 1815. However there is no Daniel or other initial D amongst the children of Rawdon Hautenville, a Captain in the 14th Foot Regiment (later West Yorkshire Regiment) listed in R.R. Bertrand, 'The Huguenot Family of Hautenville in Ireland and Some of Its Connections', *Proceedings of the Huguenot Society of London*, vol. 17, 1944, pp. 262-6.]

[15] [Information about these brothers is scarce. Broder is recorded as being instrumental in obtaining admission to the Storthing (Norwegian Parliament) in the early 1830s for visitors from England to Norway. His full name was Broder Lysholm Knudtzon. He was born in 1788. He was a merchant at Throndhjem. A later member of the family, Jorgen Alexander Knudtzon was a Norwegian linguist and expert on the Hittite language. The Norman papers at Maidstone contain a number of letters from the two brothers, written in French, over the years 1814 to 1827, at U310 C34.]

very amiable and accomplished persons. Broder [was] one of the best English scholars for a foreigner whom I have ever known. At the request of Lady Charlotte Campbell[16] afterwards Bury he translated Ingeman's tragedy of Blanca into the appropriate English verse.[17] I looked over the manuscript for him and could detect hardly any errors or solecisms.

Jorgen Knudtzon was for fifty years the companion of Alexander Baillie, both at home and abroad. He died in Paris four or five years ago. Broder is still alive, but I fear very infirm.[18]

I kept up an intercourse personal and epistolary with these gentlemen for very many years, and had a sincere respect and regard for them both; one of their sisters married Mr A.M. Labouchere of Nantes, an uncle of the present Minister.[19]

The following year 1814 brought with it some important events for me. I went to Rendlesham at the end of the shooting season and owing perhaps to irregular living while there, got a liver affection, which ended in jaundice, a nasty complaint it is. I was of the colour of an orange and felt constant

---

[16] [Charlotte Susan Maria, 1775-1861, daughter of the 5th Duke of Argyll, 1723-1806, Lady in Waiting to the Princess of Wales, later Queen Caroline. Published anonymously *Poems on Several Occasions by a Lady* (1797), *Love* (3 vols.) 1837, 2nd ed. 1860, *Diary Illustrations of the Times of George IV* (4 vols.) 1838-9, and under her own name, *The Divorced* (2 vols.) 1837, 2nd ed 1858. She married (1) 1796, John Campbell, MP for Ayr Burghs, died 1809. Married (2) 1818, Reverend Edward John Bury, Rector of Lichfield, Hants, who died May 1832 aged 42.]

[17] [Bernhard Severin Ingemann, 1789-1862, Danish novelist and poet. He published his first collection of poems in 1811-12, and a long allegorical poem *De Sorte Riddere* (*The Black Knights*) in 1814. *Blanca* is the most popular of his six plays, and it appeared in 1815. He subsequently produced historical novels modelled on the work of Sir Walter Scott's Waverley novels. He was also a very successful writer of hymns.]

[18] Broder died in 1864.

[19] [Pierre César Labouchère, French financier, 1772-1839, sent to his uncle at Nantes, 1785, worked in his office for five years, then moved to Amsterdam. Married the sister of Sir Francis Baring, 1st Bt, in 1796. Emissary of Napoleon to Britain in 1810, seeking peace terms. In 1821 moved to England, and died near Chelmsford. Henry Labouchère, 1798-1869, politician, was his elder son. He held various government offices and, at the time that Norman wrote, was Colonial Secretary (1855-8). A.M. Labouchere, presumably the brother of P.C. Labouchere, has not been traced.]

sickness and nausea, but was not confined to my bed, excepting just about the crisis of the complaint when I suffered for some time exquisite pain and was said to have passed a gallstone through the liver. I afterwards slowly recovered.

It was I think during this visit to Rendlesham that I perceived in our kind friend Lady Rendlesham a great change for the worse.[20] She was consumptive. I told my mother that if she wished to see her alive, she had no time to lose. In a few weeks my mother went to Rendlesham and during the summer I think, poor Lady Rendlesham died. She had no idea of her danger until a few hours before she expired. She was a most amiable person and I felt her loss deeply.

After my jaundice had in some degree passed away, it was suggested that a course of Cheltenham Waters would do me good and Mr and Mrs Cumming, being about to pass some time there, were kind enough to invite me to be their guest. I remained with them several weeks, drinking regularly at the Salt Springs, and on the whole passing my time very agreeably. Miss Fenton, a niece of Mr Cummings and a very pretty woman, who was engaged to be married to Mr Bailey, brother I think to Sir D. Bailey and afterwards mother to the Miss B, now Bob Ricketts's[21] tenants at Wood Lodge, was also a guest of the Cummings and I found her a very lively and agreeable person and flirted with her as much as was proper under the circumstances.[22]

At Cheltenham we found Mr Henry Bosanquet[23] and a cousin of his Diana

[20][Mary Andalusia, died without issue 15 August 1814. She was the second daughter of Lieutenant General Samuel Trevor Dickens.]

[21][Not identified. The Six Home Counties Directory for 1845 records a Mrs Ricketts among the 'Gentry' at Knockholt, Sevenoaks, nine miles from Bromley.]

[22][Miss Fenton, Mr Bailey, Sir D. Bailey, Miss Bailey and Bob Ricketts have not been identified.]

[23][Jacob Bosanquet married in 1748 Elizabeth, daughter of John Hanbury. Their third son, Henry of Clanville, Hants, High Sheriff in 1815, married in 1790, Caroline, daughter of Christopher Anstey the poet. His son, who was also Henry Bosanquet, and thus the cousin of Diana Anstey, married however Mary, the daughter of William Richards. Christopher Anstey, 1724-1805, was the author of the highly successful *New Bath Guide* (1766), a series of letters in verse. He was the father

Ansty, upon whom I wrote some Latin Alcaics subsequently which still exist among my 'Opuscula'.

I also met Mr and Mrs Cator of Beckenham.[24] She was then young and beautiful. I used to breakfast and dine with them and no bad job this was, for his kitchen was thoroughly well organised. I greatly admired Cheltenham. The rich Vale of Gloucester, the Oolite Hills to the North East,[25] and the many objects of interest in the neighbourhood, well suited my taste. I recollect a very ancient mansion hard by, the name of which I forget, but which [was] inhabited by an old gentleman with the Norman name of de la Bere.[26]

Cheltenham life in those days was an odd affair. All the world met in the morning on the walks where the water was drunk. During the day people walked and rode and drove and a good many met again at the rooms in

by Anne, 1732-1812, third daughter of Felix Calvert of Albury Hall, Herts, of 13 children.]

[24][John Cator of Beckenham Place, Kent, died 1858, married 25th September 1806 Elizabeth Louisa, daughter of Sir Ross Mahon Bt, of Castlegar, Galway. She died in February 1847. An earlier John Cator had been in the timber trade and, Norman supposes in his Bromley Memoir, had been a customer of James Norman, Norman's grandfather. He bequeathed Beckenham Place to John Cator his nephew, the son of John Cator's brother Joseph, a former employee of the East India Company.]

[25]['Inferior Oolite' is what is recognised as typical Cotswold limestone. It is thickest in the north of the Cotswolds, and caps the highest point of the Cotswolds at Cleeve Common, to the north east of Cheltenham.]

[26][Near Cheltenham there is a fine 15th century mansion of Southam de La Bere. Members of the De La Bere family are buried in the church at Cleeve. The mansion contains a tiled floor from Hailes Abbey. There is a tomb at Cleeve of Richard De La Bere, Lord of the Manor of Southam, who died in 1636, and of his wife Margaret. One of the De La Bere family was a crusader, and there is a monument in the church. However the De La Bere name seems to have fallen into disuse, until William Baghot assumed the additional name of De La Bere. He died in 1764. His son was Thomas Baghot De La Bere. He was the owner of Southam at the time of Norman's visit, as is confirmed by the land tax return. He died in 1821. He was succeeded by his two sisters, Grace Webb and Sarah Baghot De La Bere. They in turn were succeeded in 1829 by their cousin Thomas Edwards, who sold the estate in 1833 to Edward Law, Earl of Ellenborough. See the *Victoria History of the County of Gloucester*, ed. C.R. Erlington, London: Oxford University Press for the University of London Institute of Historical Research, 1968, vol. 8 p. 10. The mansion is now an hotel. Bishop's Cleeve is three miles north of Cheltenham. The De La Bere family also owned Lypiatt Park, which was later acquired by the famous Richard Whittington, Lord Mayor of London, in satisfaction of a debt.]

the evening. There was dancing, I think twice a week. The Master of the Ceremonies, Mr King, regulated all the amusements. He used to call on every fresh visitor and had a book at the libraries in which one was called upon to enter a subscription for his benefit. He attended all the amusements. Now and then there was a ball unlimited in duration, but on ordinary dancing nights the company assembled about eight o'clock and at eleven precisely, the Master of the Ceremonies, having looked at his watch, held it up and the music instantly stopped, even in the middle of a figure.

Mr King was a singular person really seventy or more, but looked forty-five. He was made up to perfection. A wig, rouge, high coat, false calves and plumpers in his cheeks.[27] I will not indeed vouch for all these particulars,

[27] [The first Cheltenham MC, Simeon Moreau, died in December 1801. James King, who had been appointed MC at the Lower Rooms in Bath in 1785, and who features in Jane Austen's *Northanger Abbey* as introducing the heroine Catherine Morland to the hero Henry Tilney, was subsequently MC at the Upper Rooms in Bath. He succeeded to the position vacated by the death of Moreau. King was able to hold both Cheltenham and Bath appointments, as Bath had a winter season and Cheltenham a summer season. He continued to do so until his death in 1816. He was the son of Thomas and Mary King of Dublin, and had fought with distinction in the British army in the American war. He had married Margaret Bulkeley of Anglesea in 1794; they had no children, but he fathered an illegitimate son, also James King, whom his wife adopted, and who himself followed a military career. It seems that the situation inherited by James King as MC, after the death of Simeon Moreau, was chaotic, and that in order to restore order he introduced strict rules. This would explain Norman's reference to the prompt ending of dances. The rules of the Lower Assembly Rooms, Cheltenham, came into effect in 1803. There were balls on Mondays and Fridays. One and a half guineas admitted a family to the season's balls. The subscription for a single person was 15 shillings. As Norman reports, balls began as soon after 8pm as possible, and ended precisely at 11pm. Ladies of rank were to be given priority of place in the dances, and were entitled to keep those places for the remainder of the evening. There were firm rules governing how a dancer joined a dance, and how many times a lady could change partners during the evening. King also insisted, and this is again consistent with Norman's account, that, in order to prevent improper company being admitted to the Assembly Rooms, strangers must be introduced to him beforehand. He called on visitors, and was conscientious in taking around his subscription books at the end of the season. As the number of visitors increased so did his income, and he built himself a fine house. This in turn provoked jealous gossip – the name of Cheltenham's Postmistress, Mrs Entwistle is mentioned in this context – and this no doubt explains the gossip which Norman reported about Mr King's employment of artificial aids to disguise the ravages of time on his

but they were universally believed to exist and I have no reason to doubt that they were really employed to mitigate the ravages of father time. I apprehend that Masters of the Ceremonies belong to a class of things which have altogether passed away.

Besides the persons whom I have already named, I used to see at Cheltenham some mercantile friends of Mr Cumming. These were Mr E. Parsons a thorough Bon Vivant,[28] Mr Hubbard,[29] I fancy father of my colleague at the Bank, and a Mr Byron or Byrom of Liverpool.[30]

On leaving Cheltenham my kind friends the Cummings took me with them by Tewkesbury to Worcester where I saw the porcelain manufactory, which I well recollect, to Malvern. At the last-named place we staid several days and I enjoyed myself very much. The views on one side over the rich Vale of Evesham, which spread out beneath the syenitic hills[31] from which

appearance. He died in Cheltenham 16 October 1816, and had been aged 70 when appointed to the position of MC in 1801. He was thus in his early 80s when Norman was there in 1814. It seems that he continued to perform his functions as MC with efficiency right up to his death. A wall tablet in St Mary's parish church, Cheltenham, commemorates him. We are indebted to Fr Brian Torode of Leckhampton, Cheltenham for making available to us the results of his remarkable research into the history of Mr King.]

[28] [The Post Office London Directory for 1812 lists Edward Parson and Co., Russia merchants, 6 Billiter Lane. Since John Cumming was also a Russia merchant, this seems to be his associate.]

[29] [John Hubbard, died 1847, a Russia merchant of Stratford Grove, father of Norman's colleague at the Bank, John Gellibrand Hubbard. His wife was Marian (died 1851), daughter of John Morgan of Bramfield Place, Herts. The Hubbard business was J. Hubbard and Company in London and W.E. Hubbard and Company of St Petersburgh. J.G. Hubbard's brother, William Egerton Hubbard, 1812-83, was the senior partner in Russia until he settled in Sussex in 1843. The main interests in Russia were in cotton spinning and weaving; the London house also accepted bills on Russian houses.]

[30] [There are several Liverpool businessmen of the name Byrom (though not of Byron) in Gore's *Street Directory of Liverpool* of 1813. The mostly likely ones to be the friends of John Cumming are Ashton and Henry Byrom, both of whom are listed as merchants and sugar refiners. There was also a William Byrom, described simply as a merchant.]

[31] [Syenite is a coarse grained igneous (once molten) rock composed of alkali feldspar and up to 20 per cent ferro magnesium minerals. It is the coarse grained equivalent of the lava trachyte. Together they constitute the commonest form of igneous rock. It is no longer believed that the Evesham side of the Malverns is

I regarded them and on the other over the wooded and broken country, which characterizes Herefordshire, were charming. I used to pass my days in wandering over the elastic and aromatic turf and admiring the prospect and the elevation which gave a coolness to the air, after the hot and dusty Cheltenham, increased my pleasure. All these things put together added in my memory to the brightness of Die [Diana] Ansty's eyes, and the final result, were the few stanzas alluded to some pages back. I have never seen the lady since, and have Alas! forgotten her subsequent destiny.

It was so far as I recollect, while at Cheltenham in 1814, that I began to keep a list of all books, read by me which I have continued to the present time.

The winter of 1813-14 was the most severe within my memory, perhaps the most severe known for a century past, although there was a very hard winter in or about 1797. The frost began just after Christmas and lasted for three months. The snow was deep and laid long. Game birds and a large portion of small birds perished by starvation and cold. The Thames was frozen over and an ox [was] roasted whole upon it between London and Blackfriars Bridge. There was a sort of fair held on the river with booths and whirligigs and the usual accompaniments of a fair. Crowds of people were to

---

syenite. According to an authoritative source: 'The most ancient rocks of Malvern are those which form the main ridge, and consist of hornblendic gneiss with numerous dykes of diorite ... These "Malvernian" rocks form the nucleus of the Malvern ... range and they are overlain by Cambrian, and again by Silurian rocks.' *The Victoria History of the County of Worcestershire*, edited by J.W. Willis-Bund and H.A. Doubleday, London: Constable 1901, vol. 1 p. 4. However it seems that during most of Norman's lifetime the Malvern Hills were believed to be syenite, though by the last quarter of the 19th century, following the work of a geologist called Harvey Holl, it was accepted that the rocks which had been described as syenite were of metamorphic origin and belonged to the pre-Cambrian age. Yet the old ridge of the hills is referred to as 'syenite granite'. For a detailed discussion of the geology of the parts of the Malvern Hills on which Norman was sitting, see W. Dreghorn, *Geology Explained in the Severn Vale and the Cotswolds*, Ross on Wye: Fineleaf Editions, 2005, pp. 140-65. As the quotation above indicates, the geology of the Malvern Hills is complex. When looking towards Hereford, Norman was probably sitting on Herefordshire Beacon, which Dreghorn describes as 'a tough crystalline rock – hornblende gneiss'.]

be seen on the ice.

It was just as the severe frost began that the allied armies, after the negotiations at Frankfort had been broken off, crossed the Rhine and invaded France.[32] They were greatly superior in number, and speaking generally in composition but being composed of troops of different Nations, and accompanied by the Emperors of Russia[33] and Austria,[34] the King of Prussia,[35] and the Crown Prince of Sweden,[36] who left among them but a nominal command to the P[rince] of Schwarzenberg,[37] the titular Generalissimo, their movements were ill-combined, and the general direction of the Invasion fee-

[32][Metternich, the Austrian Foreign Minister, offered, as at Prague (see p. 150), to recognise the natural frontiers of France up to the Rhine, and including Belgium. But then Britain and Russia both disowned Metternich's terms, as Britain could not allow French control of the Belgium ports and the Czar Alexander was bent upon dictating peace terms from Paris.]

[33][Alexander I, 1777-1825, Emperor of Russia, succeeded his murdered father Paul I in 1801. He allied himself alternately with Britain and Napoleon. However, in alliance with Britain, Prussia, Sweden and Austria, he ultimately helped crush Napoleon.]

[34][Francis II, 1768-1835, was the last Holy Roman Emperor, 1792-1806, and the first Emperor of Austria 1806-35. He succeeded his father Leopold II in 1792. With Metternich as his Foreign Minister he helped to defeat Napoleon.]

[35][Frederick William III, 1770-1840, son of Frederick William II, acceded to the Prussian throne in 1797. In 1806 he was defeated by Napoleon at Jena and Auerstädt, after which the French overran Prussia, and the Russians, coming to their aid, were defeated by Napoleon at Friedland. But, at the beginning of 1813, Frederick William entered into an alliance with Russia and Austria, and Napoleon was defeated at the Battle of the Nations at Leipzig.]

[36][Jean Baptiste Jules Bernadotte, 1763-1844, Charles XIV of Sweden and Norway. French General under Napoleon. Son of a lawyer at Pau, he entered the French army in 1780. He was the brother in law of Joseph Bonaparte, Napoleon's brother. He was made Marshall of France in 1804, took a significant part in the French victories of Austerlitz and Jena, was appointed by Napoleon to command in the Netherlands, and was elected Crown Prince of Sweden 1810. Subsequently he led the Swedish forces against Napoleon, forming an alliance with Russia in April 1813. He was adopted by Charles XIII of Sweden, and succeeded him as King in 1818.]

[37][Charles Phillip, Prince of Schwarzenberg, 1771-1820, Austrian Field Marshall. At Ulm he commanded the right wing of the Austrian forces against Napoleon, and had advised against fighting the battle of Austerlitz, which proved a significant French victory. In 1809 he commanded the rearguard after the battle of Wagram, in 1813 he was given command of the army in Bohemia and, after Austria's full entry into the war, he was made overall commander of the allied forces.]

ble.

Blood flowed in torrents. Napoleon with his central position, struck right and left, throwing his whole force successively on the heads of columns advancing against him from the East and South. He thus gained repeated advantages and at times it seemed that the foe would be driven back to the Rhine. But Napoleon was too weak to fight pitched battles. When he attempted such, as at Brienne and Laon he was beaten. At length a bolder spirit began to actuate the allied counsels. The Emperor of Russia with the main Army determined to advance on Paris giving up in great measure his communications. This movement was successful. The French Corps d'Armée left to cover the Capital, was overwhelmed, forced back, and along with the garrison finally defeated in a battle fought outside the barriers which left Paris at the mercy of the allies. A capitulation was then agreed upon as the only means of preventing a successful assault and the probable pillage and destruction of that rich metropolis and on 1st March, I think the Allied Armies entered triumphing twenty-two months after the passage of the Niemen.

I can hardly describe how great was the interest I felt in the mighty contest carried on in France, or in the intense anxiety with which I followed the variable fortunes of the Campaign. At first there was the unopposed advance of the Allied Armies and the successful combat of Brienne[38] and La Rothière,[39] which went far to shew that the existing armies of France were

[38] [Brienne, 29 January 1814, was the first battle of the campaign for France. On this occasion Napoleon was indeed almost taken by Russian Cossacks, as reported by Tom Jordan; see p. 163. Napoleon had 30,000 raw troops against 25,000 Prussians under Blücher. Marshall Grouchy led cavalry and artillery attacks against the Prussians, while Marshalls Ney and Victor secured the town of Brienne. Blücher was forced to withdraw, leaving 4,000 casualties. French casualties were 3,000.]

[39] [La Rothière, battle of 1 February 1814. Blücher quickly reorganised, following the defeat at Brienne. Napoleon had 40,000 troops, but Blücher had now 53,000 and there were another 63,000 allied troops within striking distance. Napoleon sought to withdraw, but the Prussians would not let him. Both sides suffered 6,000 casualties.]

no longer capable of fighting a pitched battle with success. The allies continued their advance, but with divided forces acting on two lines, either from choice or from the difficulty of otherwise obtaining supplies. The reverses of Etages,[40] Champaubert,[41] Montmirail[42] and Montereau[43] followed and it appeared for a moment that the star of Napoleon was once more about to blaze supreme in the firmament. But there were partial successes obtained over detached bodies. The result of the Battle of Laon[44] shewed that the allies were still superior in a general conflict. The flank movement of the French to act upon the rear of the combined armies[45] and the battle and capture of Paris soon followed and was the closing scene of the mighty drama.[46] The delight and exaltation I felt at the downfall of him whom I regarded as the great enemy of my country, and indeed of the human race, can hardly be imagined, much less described.

---

[40] [Blucher was at Etages before the planned advance towards Montmirail.]

[41] [Champaubert, battle of 10 February 1814, when Napoleon caught General Olussiev's 5,000 Russians with a 6:1 advantage. The Russians suffered 4,000 killed, wounded or captured, to French losses of about 200, and the Russian General was captured.]

[42] [Battle of 11 February 1814. This time Napoleon attacked the Russians under Sacken and Prussians under Yorck. Through the speed of his actions, Napoleon managed to defeat the Russians before the Prussians were ready for battle. The Prussians were then forced to retreat by Marshall Mortier. Allied casualties were 4,000 against 2,000 French casualties.]

[43] [Battle of 18 February 1814. A second allied army, in addition to that under Blücher, commanded by Prince Schwarzenberg, moved against Paris with the army of Bohemia. A heavy artillery bombardment, and a ferocious assault, enabled the French to take the town of Montereau, and Schwarzenberg lost 6,000 men, while Napoleon lost 2,500.]

[44] [Battle of 9-10 March 1814. After success at Craonne, Napoleon again attempted to outflank Blücher's 85,000 men, sending Marmont with almost 10,000 against the left flank, but the allies were prepared and the French suffered 6,000 casualties. The allies suffered 4,000.]

[45] [Napoleon planned to cut allied communications north of the Marne, but a letter telling the Empress of this fell into allied hands, and Czar Alexander seized the opportunity to urge an immediate march on Paris on 19 March.]

[46] [At 2am on 31 March 1814 Marmont, as commander of the defences of Paris, signed a capitulation. At midday the allied troops, led by Czar Alexander of Russia, Frederick William of Prussia, and Count Schwarzenberg made their formal entry into Paris.]

I well recollect the effect produced by the fraud of Cochrane Johnstone, and M. Besanger, in which Lord Dundonald[47] was supposed to be implicated. The news of the fabulous capture of Napoleon by the Cossacks was brought to this house by Tom Jordan[48] and believed by us all. The disappointment which followed was bitter.

The slowness and uncertainty of intelligence in those days can hardly be understood by those who have only lived in the present. The roads were everywhere detestable, The means of communication ill-organised. There were no steam boats, railroads or electric telegraphs.

However I must return to the autobiography, I do not remember any point of my personal history during 1814 worth recording, excepting that on my way per coach from Cheltenham, I met many distinguished foreigners on their way to the grand doings at Oxford and recognized Marshal Blucher[49] in a carriage with Sir C. Stewart, the late Lord Londonderry.[50] Whenever the carriage stopped, the people insisted upon shaking the old veteran by the

---

[47] [Thomas Cochrane, 10th Earl of Dundonald, 1775-1860. Famous naval commander, Rear Admiral 1832, found guilty of rigging the Stock Exchange in 1814, stripped of KCB though later reinstated. The real culprit seems to have been his uncle Andrew Cochrane-Johnstone. Lord Dundonald was unseated as an MP (he sat for Westminster), and he was fined £1,000. He was however pardoned in 1832.]

[48] [According to Norman's Bromley Memoir, Tom Jordan was 'a remarkable person in our District'. His father had been a large London brewer, with a country house, then called Pheasant Lodge, in St Paul's Cray. But he subsequently went bankrupt. Tom Jordan dined almost entirely at the expense of his friends, 'dining out uninvited almost every day, and probably fasting when he was compelled to remain at home'. Norman mentions that one of Jordan's 'chief patrons in the dining line' was Norman's father. He apparently dined at the Norman home for about 25 years, three times a fortnight, and became a considerable nuisance. 'He also pretended to knowledge which he did not possess.' However he subsequently paid addresses to Norman's sister Charlotte, and Norman's father put an end to Jordan's association with the family.]

[49] [Gebhard Leberecht von Blücher, 1742-1819, Prussian Field Marshall, led the army of Silesia and stormed Leipzig on the last day of the 'Battle of the Nations'. Led the decisive attack on the French at Waterloo. Was prevented by Wellington from sacking Paris as an act of revenge for what the French had done in Germany.]

[50] [Charles William Stewart, 3rd Marquess of Londonderry, 1778-1864, Adjutant General 1809-12, served in the Peninsula war, Major General 1810, Minister Plenipotentiary, Berlin, Military Commissioner of Allied Armies 1813-14, Lieutenant General 1814.]

hand. He was then the popular idol.

I may mention however that I was present in the parks at the grand Fête given in commemoration of the peace. Morton Eden,[51] Lord Auckland's older brother[52] who died a few years afterwards, was with me on this occasion. I was very well acquainted with the Eden family who then resided at Eden Farm[53] and I often dined with them. Emily Eden, who is still unmarried, was a person whom I greatly admired. She was tall, fair, had pretty blue eyes and was very accomplished and agreeable and I also knew her older and younger sisters Mary (Mrs Drummond) and Fanny now dead very well. Emily and Fanny accompanied their brother Lord Auckland to India.

The old Lord Auckland[54] who must have died about this time or earlier

[51][This is puzzling. It may be a reference to Morton Frederick Eden, 1752-1830, eighth but fifth surviving and youngest son of Sir Robert Eden, 3rd Bt, of West Auckland, younger (not elder as Norman wrote) brother of the 1st Lord Auckland. After Eton and Oxford he entered the diplomatic service. He was Minister to Bavaria and to the Diet of Ratisbon 1776-9, to Copenhagen 1779-82, to Dresden 1782-91, Berlin 1791-3, to Vienna 1793-4, 1795-9, to Madrid 1794-5. He was created Baron Henley in 1799, GCB 1815. However, it may be a reference to the brother (again a younger brother) of the second Lord Auckland. This was Morton Eden who died in 1821 aged 27.]

[52][George Eden, 1784-1849, 2nd Baron Auckland, succeeded his father, the 1st Baron, in 1814. He succeeded to the barony because his elder brother Frederick had drowned in the Thames in 1810. He was created 1st Earl of Auckland in 1839. Like his father, he qualified as a barrister, and was admitted to the Bar in 1809. In 1830 he became President of the Board of Trade, and Master of the Mint. In 1834-5 he was First Lord of the Admiralty. He was Governor General of India 1835-9, returning to England after the disastrous first Afghan war, which he launched in 1838. He handed over the Governor Generalship to Lord Ellenborough, and returned to England. In 1846-9 he was again First Lord of the Admiralty. His sister was the traveller and author Emily Eden, who visited and wrote about India. George Eden never married, and the earldom became extinct on his death, while the barony passed to his younger brother, the 3rd Baron Auckland, 1799-1870, who was Bishop of Sodor and Man, and of Bath and Wells.]

[53][This was part of Langley in Kent. There were three farms close together. Eden Farm was the name given to the land leased by the Eden family. The owner of the freehold was Peter Burrell, who died in 1820. It covered 300 acres. After Burrell's death, the freehold was sold. Both Overstone and, later, his cousin Lewis Loyd owned properties in the same area.]

[54][William Eden, 1744-1814, 1st Baron Auckland 1789. He was educated at Eton, and read law at Oxford. He qualified as a barrister, and in 1771 published *Principles of Penal Law* (London: White and Cadell, 1771, third edition 1775).

was a distinguished statesman. I recollect him well, a tall, thin man, with an expression of countenance denoting knowledge and ability. He had filled high offices, among them the Chief Secretaryship of Ireland, and had negociated the treaty of commerce with France in 1785, the most decided step on the path of free trade until quite a recent period.

At Eden Farm I used to meet men of mark, among them I remember Mr Vansittart, then Chancellor of the Exchequer afterwards Lord Bexley. He had married a daughter of Lord Auckland but was a widower.[55] He presented but little the appearance of a man of ability. He lisped. His manners were gauche and his conversation uninstructive and uninteresting. It was the fashion to laugh at and quiz him, and this I have known his eleven sisters in law do without mercy.[56] Yet I hold it to be impossible for any body to be finance,

He was Chief Secretary for Ireland 1780-2, envoy to France 1785-7, Ambassador to Spain 1787-9, to Netherlands 1789-93, President of the Board of Trade 1806-7. He was the third son of Sir Robert Eden, 3rd Bt, of West Auckland. His brother was Morton Eden, 1st Baron Henley.]

[55][Nicholas Vansittart, 1766-1851, 1st Baron Bexley, married Catherine Isabella, 1778-1810, the second daughter of the first Lord Auckland. He withdrew from public life in the spring of 1809 because of his wife's poor health and was with her when she died at Torquay in August 1810 aged only 32.]

[56][William Eden married Eleanor Elliott (died 1818) in 1776. There were six boys and eight girls born of the marriage. The daughters of Lord Auckland were Mary Dulcibella, 1794/5-1862, Caroline born 1793, Elizabeth Charlotte, 1780-1847, Catherine Isabella, 1778-1810, Eleanor Agnes, 1777-1851, Emily, and Mary Louisa. The sons were Frederick William Elliott (born in 1782, drowned in the Thames in 1810), George (born 1784, see p. 164), Henry born in 1786 who died in 1794, Charles died 1798 aged 7, and Morton who died in 1821 aged 27. Another son Robert John, 1799-1870, became Bishop of Bath and Wells (see p. 164). He had at least seven children with Mary Hurt. Eleanor in 1799 married the widower Lord Hobart. William Pitt, who was in debt and nearly 20 years older was an unsuccessful suitor. Charlotte married Lord Godolphin in 1800, Caroline married in 1806 Arthur Vansittart, and in the same year Catherine married Nicholas Vansittart, and Mary Louisa married Andrew Wedderburn (who became Colville by Royal Licence 22 June 1814). They had 17 children. Mary Dulcibella married Charles Drummond in 1819, and the remaining daughters, Emily (whom Norman admired) and Frances (Fanny), set up house with their unmarried brother George. At this time they left Eden Farm and set up home in Grosvenor Street. Emily was a keen Whig politician, which would have appealed to Norman. She wrote, in addition to witty and critical correspondence, two novels, *The Semi-Detached Couple* and *The Semi-Detached House*. She also wrote books based on her time in India with her brother George; *Up the Country* and *People and Princes of In-*

or indeed Minister of England, sitting in the Commons, and that for a long period like Lord Bexley without the possession of a very considerable ability. In short Van was the reverse of a fool, although often called so. To be sure he was no shining light of Oratory. He did not make the best of himself. He always kept upon the beaten track and attempted no brilliant innovation. His lowest descent into the bathos was when he moved the resolution affirming the equality of value between Bank notes and gold, when he was purchasing specie for the foreign service of the Government at a high premium.

Before I leave the Edens, I may mention what I forgot in its proper place, that in 1813 I accompanied the younger portion of the family and the Wedderburns, who then resided at Langley (they were afterwards Colvilles),[57] to the Victoria Fete at Vauxhall. It was a brilliant affair, and I enjoyed it greatly.

I recollect nothing particular as having happened to me during the last half of 1814, excepting that the restoration brought with it a vast and I may add a calamitous increase in my father's business, which however was not fully developed until 1815, as the renewal of intercourse with Norway only took place after its Union with Sweden late in the autumn in pursuance of the capitulation of Moss.

The badness of my father's business aroze in various ways. A great fall in the price of goods (timber and deal) and of freights ruined the people to whom we had made advances, which consequently were never recovered. Then great building speculations exploded and produced insolvency among our debtors the yardkeepers. Finally my father had to put a very large capital into his business and with that object sold, if I recollect aright above 100,000

*dia.* She was also a gifted artist. She had the chance to marry the widower Lord Melbourne, but declined. She outlived all the family except her brother Robert and died in 1869. Charlotte, Caroline, Mary Dulcibella and Mary Louisa all had a large number of children.]

[57] [The 5th daughter of the 1st Lord Auckland, Marie Louise (died 1858), married Andrew Wedderburn (Colville), 1779-1856. The name was changed to Colville by royal licence in 1814.]

consols under 60. At that time the duty was enormous,[58] credit losing, and there was no bonding in the docks.

In the Winter of 1814, I went as usual to Rendlesham and was very nearly getting a second attack of jaundice.

Little of interest occurred in our domestic circle in 1815. The most important event, that I recollect was a grand ball given by my parents which cost £200. The supper provided, I think by Gunter, was served in the library. The guests danced in the dining room and the whole affair went off with great eclat. It was supposed that the ball was intended to be in celebration of my majority, but this I fancy was a mistake. It was the fashion in the neighbourhood to give balls. Several of our friends gave them and ours was sort of requital for their hospitality.

Of the balls and cricket matches on the same day I have already spoken and I may here mention, that Bertie, now Admiral Cator[59] and I were at this time perpetual stewards or managers of the Bromley Balls, which were held in a tolerable room in the old White Hart, which has since been pulled down. The shining lights among the ladies were Sophy Newnham,[60] the Misses Fosters, both alive, one I fear under unhappy circumstance, Miss

[58] [On the discriminatory timber duties see the table in J.R. McCulloch, *A Dictionary of Commerce and Commercial Navigation*, London: Longman, 1832, p. 1041. The duties on Baltic timber were typically around ten times the duties on timber from Canada. Thus for instance the duty on battens up to 16 feet in length was £10 per 120 on Baltic timber, and £1 per 120 on Canadian timber.]

[59] [Admiral Bertie-Cornelius Cator, 1787-1864. He entered the navy 1800, retired as Admiral 1862. Both he and John Cator were the sons of Joseph Cator (see p. 128). He married at Calcutta in 1780 Diana (died 1829), sister of Admiral Sir Albermarle Bertie of the Ducal family of Ancaster.]

[60] Afterwards Cust. [According to Norman's Bromley Memoir, the family lived at Southborough, and Mr Newnham belonged to a timber firm in Sussex and had been a brewer and underwriter. 'He was a gruff man. His wife, once very handsome, was a Johnson from Newcastle.' One of his daughters, 'Sophia, an old flame of mine, married Mr Cust, Captain of the Oppidans when I went to Eton'. Mr Cust was William Cust, barrister and Commissioner of Customs, born 23 January 1787, died 3 March 1845. He married 8 July 1819 Sophia Newnham, 1789/90-1884, daughter of Thomas Newnham of Southborough.]

Merry afterwards Mrs Lukin,[61] Miss Rohde[62] and I must not omit my kind and joyous friend Penelope Farnaby,[63] sister of Sir Charles and mother of Colonel Cator,[64] Mrs Marland &c. The Edens went to these balls occasionally.

About this time, and a little before and afterwards I used to go often to Redleaf,[65] which I always greatly admired, and I also took pleasure in examining the old house at Penshurst with all its associations of Sir Philip Sydney, Algernon Sidney and sacrifice.[66]

---

[61] [Mary Amelia Merry, married James William Lukin of Sandhill Lodge, Dorset. She was the niece of William Merry, for many years Deputy Secretary at War; see p. 132.]

[62] [Rohde, a sugar refiner of German descent, was the neighbour of the Norman family, at Oakley, a house that George Norman later bought. He had a large family and according to Norman's Bromley Memoir his daughters 'all most amiable persons' married well. The Norman papers at U310 A168A contain material relating to George Norman's purchase of Oakley.]

[63] [According to Norman, the Farnabys were descended from a famous schoolmaster, who had a school at Sevenoaks in the reign of James I. He bought much property in the neighbourhood, and Kippington was the seat of his family for several generations. Penelope Anne, 1789-1833, was the only daughter of Col. Sir John Farnaby of the Horse Guards, who married an heiress called Lennard. Penelope Farnaby married General Cator. She was the sister of Sir Charles Farnaby who, according to Norman's Bromley Memoir, dissipated the property. General William Cator 1785-1866 was the second son of Joseph Cator and Diana Bertie; see p. 167. He entered the Royal Artillery in 1803, and served in the campaigns of Walcheren and Flushing, and also in the Peninsula (including the lines of Torres Vedras, and the battle of Vitoria) and in the South of France 1809-14. Major General 1854, Lieutenant General 1859, KCB 1865.]

[64] [The elder son of General Sir William Cator was John Farnaby Cator, Royal Artillery. He inherited the Wickham property of the family, on the death of Sir Charles Farnaby and took the additional name of Lennard. Created Bt 1880. Chairman of Kent County Council 1889-99. Sir Charles Francis Farnaby, 5th Bt, was the eldest son of Sir John Farnaby, 4th Bt, 1743-1802, of Wickham Court, West Wickham, near Bromley. He was born in 1787 and died at Wickham August 1861. He was educated at Eton, like Norman, and was Rector of West Wickham 1815-48.]

[65] [William Wells, 1768-1847 (see p. 99), shipbuilder and art collector, son of the shipbuilder William Wells, 1729-1805, sold his shipbuilding interests in 1811 and retired with his wife Mary to Redleaf, Penshurst. He was a noted collector of paintings, and patron of Landseer.]

[66] [Norman wrote 'Sydney' here. Algernon Sidney, 1623-83, brother of Philip Sidney, 1619-98, Viscount Lisle, and later 3rd Earl of Leicester, the Cromwellian politician. Algernon grew up at the family seat of Penshurst Place, Kent. He was

There was another matter, which added to my interest in Penshurst. At a Seat called South Park on a hill a little beyond the village, lived a Mr Robert Allnutt who had married a Woodgate and at this time had three daughters, of these the second Susan, was nearly the most beautiful girl I ever saw. I can see before me now, her laughing face and blue eyes and her hair in ringlets clustering round the fair forehead. She had also a beautiful figure and was good-tempered and simple, apparently quite unconscious of the admiration she excited.

I was only one of her many admirers and by no means a favored one, nor did I ever make the least effort to gain her affections. I nevertheless enjoyed her society greatly and felt much for her sad end.

I and my sisters, who knew her well, had met her and her sister Fanny at a New Year's ball at Sevenoaks. The Allnutts in returning home, found River Hill so much frozen, that they were obliged to get out of the carriage in their dancing dresses and walk down. Fanny caught cold and soon shewd symptoms of consumption. Susan, although previously the picture of health and strength caught the complaint from her.

Within a twelve month both had left this world.[67] They were buried under a rather pretty tomb in Penshurst church yard, with an Epitaph composed by their father and little worthy of the subject, although bearing the impress of intense grief.[68]

---

executed for treason in 1683 and became celebrated as a Whig hero and martyr.]

[67][A mural in the north aisle commemorates Frances Anne Allnut who died 3 July 1820, aged 23 years and Susanna Allnut who died 4 May 1821 aged 21 years. They were daughters of Richard Allnutt and Frances his wife. Richard Allnutt died 19 November 1827 aged 55. He was a descendant of another Richard Allnutt who was born in 1713 and founded a wine business which was very successful. He built the house at Penshurst. The younger Richard Allnutt was his grandson, educated at Gervaise Whitehead School at Sevenoaks and Christ's College, Cambridge. He married Frances Woodgate in 1794. His sister Anna married William Woodgate in 1795.]

[68][Near this place\ (But without these walls)\ Repose the remains of two sisters\ The beloved daughters of\ Richard Allnutt Esqr and Frances his wife\ Of South Park, in this parish.\ FRANCES ANN died July 3rd 1820 aged 23.\ SUSANNAH died May 4th 1821 aged 21.\ They were lovely and pleasant in their lives,\ And

The mother, Mrs Allnutt, is yet alive (in 1858). Many have been her sorrows: the ruin of her own family; the loss of her children; cruelty and infidelity on the part of her husband during the latter years of his life. She was a great friend of my mother and used to call here on her way to London. I have not seen her since railroads commenced. I can never think of the death of the Allnutt girls without emotion. They were cousins to the Potts.[69]

The Blockade of Norway by English ships and the forced union of that country with Sweden affected my liberal feelings very deeply, nor under the circumstances of the case were my regrets unreasonable. The event however has shown that these regrets were unfounded. The Norwegian Revolution has been to that country a source of almost unmixed advantage. I doubt if history can shew another instance in which the sudden change from a despotic to a very free Government has produced so much good and so little evil. This arose in some degree from the nature of the Danish rule, which had never excited disgust or hatred, or exhibited great and patent evils, calculated to create a demand for rash and immediate change. The laws in existence at the time were mild, on the whole just and honestly administered, while strenuous efforts had been made to educate the people. No aristocratic Class the depositories of power existed in Norway, and the only powerful Class was a well-educated and paternal bureaucracy.[70]

in death they were not divided.\ If tender pity ever touch'd your breast,\ Mourn for these much lov'd sisters now at rest,\ And with their sorrowing parents drop a tear,\ O'er every virtue which could life endear;\ There is no balm to heal parental grief,\ For wordly pleasures fail to yeild [sic] relief;\ Sweet filial love can never be forgot,\ And Rachel weeps her children who 'are not'.\ But deepest grief by Christian hope is cheer'd,\ And faith's the rock on which that hope is rear'd.\ Hope points triumphantly to joys more sweet,\ Where faith has promis'd kindred souls all meet\ Maternal love records their early doom\ O! could her prayers and tears recal [sic] them from the tomb.]

69[Arthur Pott of Bentham Hall, Kent, purchased Bentham Hall in 1831. Susanna, 1751-92, the daughter of John Pott married Richard Allnutt, 1752-87, of South Park, Penshurst, 1 June 1771.]

70[At the start of 1814, Norway was still part of the kingdom of Denmark, which it had been since 1536. Frederick VI of Denmark-Norway had backed the wrong side in the Napoleonic wars, and the British had bombarded Copenhagen and

But allowing for all this, the success of the Ejdsvold Constitution is still a matter of wonder and must in a great degree be attributed to the Constitution itself, admirably adapted as it was, to the requirements of the country.[71] Yet

seized the Danish fleet. By January 1814 Denmark was in danger of being overrun by the combined forces of Sweden, Russia and Prussia, under the command of Bernadotte (see p. 160). To avoid invasion, Frederick ceded Norway to the King of Sweden, a measure approved by the British. However, Christian Frederik, the Danish ruler of Norway itself, resisted the surrender of Norway to Sweden. He claimed the throne of Norway, as an independent ruler, an idea which initially enjoyed popular support. Bernadotte, though occupied with the allied offensive against Napoleon, refused to accept this. Christian Frederik held a meeting at the estate of Carsten Anker, in Eidsvoll, where he met some opposition to anything less than full independence for Norway and, in accordance with this, he proclaimed himself on 19 February 1814 Regent of Norway. The Swedish government refused to accept this, but Christian Frederik attempted to organise support around Europe, on the basis that he was reflecting the Norwegian desire for self-determination. Carsten Anker was sent to London, in an attempt to obtain support from Britain. But in Norway opposition to the Regency crystallised around Count Johan Caspar Herman Wedel-Jarlsberg, and the British responded to the overtures of Carsten Anker by re-imposing the naval blockade of Norway, and re-affirming support for Bernadotte. Christian Frederik then sent Carsten Anker's brother Peder to London, but he was no more successful, and Carsten Anker himself was imprisoned in London for debt, as Norman relates (p. 173). On 10 April a Norwegian constitutional convention, to which Wedel-Jarlsberg had been elected, convened and eventually voted for Norwegian independence. Over the next month a constitution, written in Danish and inspired by the United States Declaration of Independence, was constructed, and on 17 May Christian Frederik was elected King. A further attempt was then made to secure support from Britain and, at the end of May, Major General Johannes Klingenberg Sejersted proposed to organise defence against the likely Swedish invasion. In June Carsten Anker told Christian Frederik that Prussia and Austria were weakening in support of Sweden's claims, but at the end of June emissaries from Russia, Prussia, Austria and Britain arrived in Norway and delivered an ultimatum. At the end of July Sweden moved to invade Norway, and met with little effective military resistance. Peace negotiations with Swedish envoys began in the town of Moss in early August, and on 14 August, by the Convention of Moss, a ceasefire was agreed. Bernadotte offered a compromise in which he recognised the Norwegian constitution, amended to allow for a union of Norway and Sweden, and at the end of August he proclaimed himself the ruler of both countries. Britain then lifted the naval blockade of Norway. By October it was clear that Bernadotte had won, and on 10 October Christian Frederik abdicated. On 20 October the Storthing, the Norwegian Parliament, voted to accept union with Sweden, and on 4 November unanimously elected Bernadotte as King of Norway. According to the constitution, executive power then rested with the King, but it became increasingly to be exercised by Norway's Statsrad, the Council of State.]

[71] [The Norman papers at Maidstone contain a translation by Norman of the constitution of Norway at U310/F8.]

it was not the production of philosophers, painfully weighing for months and years the nature of man, the lessons of history and the special circumstances of Norway. It appears to have been drawn up in a few days by a few plain men. However it has now satisfied the country for forty years and is still its boast and pride.

In my view the system of double election under which the Storthing is chosen, is the enactment, which on the whole has most contributed to the success of the Norwegian Constitution and more especially in the first few years of its existence.[72] This has filled the ranks of the Storthing with the very elite of the community, many of whom would never have been chosen by the general constituency. I do not believe that there exists so favorable a specimen of the materials which a given country can furnish to a legislative assembly, as that which meets every three years at Christiania,[73] I mean other things being equal.

I do not of course pretend that the Norwegian Constitution is perfect, far from this. The exclusion of the ministers of the Crown from the Storthing is a great blot, the maintenance of the absurd and injurious Odelsthing another.[74] The general course of legislation since 1814 has been affected by the

[72] [In Norway the first election involved 'Election Men', who then met to elect members of the Storthing from amongst their number. Until the election of 1906 the members of the Storthing were chosen by these electors, themselves chosen by the voters. The Storthing was elected every three years, and sat for three months. It set taxes for the ensuing three years, and dealt with the division of expenditure. The franchise was males of at least 25 years of age and a taxpayer. Those elected had to be of at least 30 years of age, and to have lived in Norway for 10 years, and not be employees of the State. Every third year the electors would choose their Election Men in proportion to the number of voters, though this varied between town and country districts. The Election Men, within a month at the latest, had to assemble to make their choice from amongst their number of the Storthing members, again in proportion, this time to the number of Election Men already chosen.]

[73] [Oslo was the original name of the city, though it was spelt Aslo. Much of the medieval city was destroyed by fire in 1624 and, when it was rebuilt nearer to the Akershus fortress, it was renamed Christiania by King Christian IV of Denmark and Norway. This name became the legal name of the city, though both names were used. In 1924-5 the original name of Oslo was restored.]

[74] [The Storthing, when chosen by double election, then chose from among its

bureaucratic tendencies of a body, in which placeholders are very numerous and comprehend the most intelligent and instructed members.

Prince Christian Frederick of Denmark, afterwards Christian the VIII, the ephemeral King of Norway, for a few months before the Convention of Moss, sent to England an Envoy named Carsten Anker,[75] who had been an old correspondent of my father's and already owed him money. This person, by the way a great rogue, not being recognized by the English Government was arrested by a person named Atkinson for a still larger debt. My father bailed him at the solicitation of the Knudtzons, and of other Norwegians then in London and afterwards advanced a large sum to satisfy Atkinson's claim.[76] This led to further transactions and an ultimate loss to my father, self and brother Richard of not less than £20,000. Ejdsvold with its estate and the Hovedegaard where the constituent Storthing sat passed into our hands and the latter was finally sold to a patriotic association by my brother after 1832.

But I must return to my personal history. After what I have said as to my feelings respecting Napoleon and his rule, it may be supposed with what sorrow and alarm I regarded the return from Elba. My aspirations for peace and freedom were for the moment crushed and I feared a renewal of the past scenes of bloodshed and tyranny. Enthusiastically then did I rejoice at the Battle of Waterloo and its consequences. I was at Trent Park when the news

---

members one fourth to constitute the Lagthing, or upper house. The remainder constituted the Odelsthing or lower house.]

[75] [Carsten and Peder Anker (see p. 171) were the sons of the wealthy merchant Christian Anker who had acquired extensive forests around Christiania for timber export. The founders of the family fortune were Christian Anker, 1711-65 and Bernt Anker, 1746-1805.]

[76] [The Norman papers contain (U310/B29) documents relating to the bail for Carsten Anker. There is a bond from George Knudtzon to Alexander Anderson and George Norman, to indemnify them for standing bail for Carsten Anker. There is a bond of Carsten Anker (U310/B31/5) and there is an assignment of a bond securing £3,788 owed by Carsten Anker to Thomas Atkinson, and bonds from Carsten Anker and George Norman to Messrs Kensington, Levy and Mobray, securing £3,788 and £3,211 both dated 1815. George Norman appears to have mortgaged property to secure the latter debt (U310/B31/6).]

arrived, and well do I recollect the delight I felt.

Looking backwards after an interval of forty-three years, I am of opinion that my views respecting Napoleon were neither exaggerated nor misplaced, although it was the fashion among the liberals of those days to admire him and to lament his downfall.

The ungrateful conduct of the continental sovereigns to the people who had overthrown the oppressor and reestablished their thrones, their efforts to maintain despotism and to repress every aspiration after free institutions, gave some slight colour of justification to this reaction of feeling against the conquerors of Napoleon. Still their conduct, however bad, did not make that of Napoleon good, and I cannot doubt, but that half-dozen despotic states with varying tendencies and at any-rate for the most part, national, and peacefully disposed, constituted a state of things in Europe, far less prejudicial to the interest of humanity, than one vast tyranny ruled by one man of surpassing genius, who delighted in war and who earnestly strove, by an elaborate machinery most skilfully applied, to crush every attempt to oppose his sovereign will, and to silence every whisper in favor of freedom of action or even of thought. The Cinq Codes appear to me the only real blessing which Napoleon conferred on humanity.[77] He had no sufficient motive to deprive the people of a good system of laws. He had a tabula rasa before him, profound lawyers at his dispositions and unlimited authority, unfettered by adverse interests and prejudices, and honestly availed himself of his admirable good sense to make the most of all these advantages.

I have little of personal anecdote to relate before I finish with the year 1815. I recollect however that in the autumn of that year, I passed a day or

[77][The *Cinq Codes* were a set of legal codes established under Napoleon between 1804 and 1810. The *Code Napoléon*, as printed in 1810, contained fewer than 120,000 words in 2,281 articles. The first and best known is the *Code Civil* (1804). Book 1 deals with persons, Book 2 with property, Book 3 with contracts and other legal commitments. Then came the *Code de Procédure Civile* (1806), *Code de Commerce* (1807), *Code d'Instruction Criminelle* (1808), and finally *Code Pénal* (1810).]

two at Trent Park with the celebrated Russian General Wittgenstein,[78] the conqueror of Kliatisty.[79] He had come to England with an Aid du Camp or

[78][Prince Peter Khristianovich Wittgenstein, 1769-1843, Russian Field Marshall of German descent. He was born Count Ludwig Adolf Peter of Sayn-Wittgenstein-Ludwigsburg. In 1805 he fought against Napoleon at Austerlitz, in 1806 against the Turks, and in 1807 again against Napoleon, this time at Friedland. In the war of 1812 he commanded one of the Russian armies at the first and second battles of Polotsk, and in 1813 he took command of the Russian army after the death of Kutuzov, commanding it at Lutzen, and Bautzen. He ceased to command the Russian army after the early defeats in 1813, but as a corps commander at Dresden and Leipzig he was active. He was severely wounded in France at Bar-sur-Aube in 1814. Field Marshall 1823, Commander of the Russian army against Turkey 1828.]

[79][See *Times* 24 August 1812, page 2 col. e. Oudinot, the French Marshall, was defeated by Wittgenstein at a place initially reported to be between Schebesch and Polotsk (or Polosgh). It was reported that Oudinot had crossed the Duma (Dwina) river and was marching upon Riga, with a view to cutting communications with St Petersburg, but was forced back across the river by Wittgenstein. The battle, it was reported, took place on 30 and 31 July 1812, and 3,000 French prisoners were taken. See also *Times* 31 August 2c, 7 September 1e, 15 September 2d. But in *Times* 14 September 3b the victory is reported to have been at Klastisa which is presumably the source of Norman's 'Kliatisty'. Wittgenstein was rewarded by Czar Alexander with the Order of St George and a pension of 24,000 roubles. It was regarded as an important victory because, had Oudinot succeeded in breaking communications between Riga and St Petersburg, he would have been able to place Riga under siege. The battle at Klastisa had come about following a combined operation by Oudinot and Macdonald. The Russians had destroyed a bridge over the Dwina, near Pokhaewze, cutting off a large number of French troops. Oudinot crossed the river at Disna while Macdonald crossed it at Jacobsdadt. Oudinot was heading for Sebesch and Macdonald was moving in the direction of Luzyn. They intended to cut off Wittgenstein from the road to St Petersburg but Wittgenstein forestalled this by attacking the advancing French under Oudinot at Klastisa. According to Wittgenstein's own account, the battle lasted three days. It ended in a significant victory for the Russians. Another victory of Wittgenstein over the French was reported in *Times* 28 September 1812, 2d. It is not clear where Norman got the name Kliatisty, as the *Times* can have been his only source of information. However, in a Soviet military encyclopaedia published in 1976 the battle is described as being at Kliastitsy, which is nearer to Norman's spelling. Despite some attempts to minimise the importance of Oudinot's defeat, notably in French writings, there is no doubt, as the Soviet article by O.K. Parkhaef and O. Papkov (*Soviet Military Encyclopaedia*, vol. 4, 1976) makes clear, that the battle was important, as Oudinot was supposed to protect Napoleon's left flank in the advance on Riga and St Petersburg. The need to send reinforcements to Oudinot following the defeat weakened Napoleon's main thrust. The victory was also psychologically important, as it was one of the first Russian victories in the 1812 campaign. Though Norman only mentions this one particular battle, Wittgenstein's name was prominent to readers of the *Times* as the French retreated

two to see the country and to purchase agricultural implements to be used on his estates. He was a fine looking old soldier, in 1828 he commanded as Field Marshal, an Army which invaded Turkey and failed at the Siege of Silistria.[80]

It was I think in 1815, that I took Grote to the Hollies at Bexley, then inhabited by old Mr Lewin, to dine and sleep, telling him that he would be charmed by Miss Lewin. He was so, I shall never forget the transport with which he spoke of her the following morning.

From this period he became intimate with the family, and at length the young people eloped, why I could never quite understand, and were married. I believe that some opposition was anticipated on the part of old Mr Grote.

One child was born of the marriage but the mother suffered so much in her confinement, as to be assured, that a future pregnancy would cause her death.[81] No child has since been born, a circumstance greatly to be lamented.

---

from Moscow. By a combination of good intelligence work and deployment of cavalry, of which he was in command, he inflicted further defeats on the French. He took 2,000 prisoners at Polotsk, and in the subsequent retreat the French suffered further losses, and 100 officers and 6,000 other ranks were reported to have been taken prisoner. See *Times* 12 November 1812, 2d, 5 December 1812, 3d. Wittgenstein was active in the pursuit of the retreating French, recovering loot abandoned by the French. See *Times* 29 December 1812, 2e, 18 January 1813, 3d, 25 February, 2e. Wittgenstein was thus much more than just the victor of 'Kliatisty', and to readers of the *Times* he must have, to some extent, symbolised the disastrous reverses inflicted upon Napoleon by the Russians.]

[80] [The Russo-Turkish war of 1828-9 was occasioned by the Greek war of independence, when the Russians participated at the Battle of Navarino (see p. 312), and the Sultan retaliated by closing the Dardanelles to Russian ships. The Russian forces were commanded by Wittgenstein, and they laid siege to three key citadels of Bulgaria, Shumla, Varna, and Silistria. In February 1829 Wittgenstein was replaced by a less cautious General, Hans Karl von Diebitsch, and Silistria fell to the Russians in June. Wittgenstein owned huge estates on the banks of the Dniester river at Kamenka which, at various times, was part of Poland, Russia and the Ukraine.]

[81] [This episode is described in Mrs Grote's biography of her husband, which is also in some sense her autobiography, *The Personal Life of George Grote*, London: Murray, 1873, p. 40. A child was born prematurely but lived for only one week. 'This premature delivery was followed by puerperal fever, of so virulent a character that, after three days, Dr. Batty indicated to George Grote his conviction that there could be but one termination to the disorder. At the end of the sixth day ... Dr. Batty discerned, not without astonishment as he confessed, a slight diminution in the pulse. A crisis had supervened; her naturally fine constitution had enabled

A houseful of sons and daughters would have greatly improved the mother certainly, perhaps both parents.

In the Winter 1815-16, I went to Rendlesham for the last time during the reign of Lord John. He was then a batchelor, although engaged to his second wife Miss J. Tatnall.[82] There was a large party of men, among whom were G.P. Berkeley, Barnard Hankey,[83] Charles Thellesson,[84] Mr Rous the present Earl of Stradbrook[85] and Admiral Rous, his brother.[86] We had a week of hard-going, the hardest indeed I ever went through, shooting all day. A late and long dinner with much wine and then billiards and grog for half the night. The night previous to my departure, I never went to bed at all, but merely washed, shaved and dressed and then lay on a sopha till the carriage came to the door. This dissipation by no means suited me and I was much knocked up by it.

The old house at Rendlesham in which these roysterings doings took place

her to resist the brain fever which apparently had burnt itself out, and she was saved.' Mrs Grote then refers to 'the miserable circumstances which accompanied her slow convalescence'.]

[82][The first wife of the 2nd Lord Rendlesham, Mary Andalusia, died 15 August 1814, as noted on p. 155. He married secondly, in 1816, Anne Sophia (died 1856), the second daughter and co-heir of William Tatnall of Leiston Old Abbey, Suffolk.]

[83][Thomson Hankey, 1805-93, one of Norman's colleagues at the Bank of England, was the son of Thomson Hankey, a merchant who died in 1857. The family was related to Norman's cousins, the Barnards. There was also a banking firm with three generations of Hankey, William Alers Hankey 1771-1859, head of the firm of Hankey and Company, bankers of Fenchurch Street, London, and his son Thomas Alers Hankey 1805-72, and his grandson Frederick Alers Hankey 1833-92. John Barnard Hankey, of Fetcham Park, Surrey, born 31 March 1784, married 9 June 1807 Elizabeth, second daughter of John, 1st Lord De Blaquiere.]

[84][Charles Thellusson was the third son of Peter Thellusson, 1737-97, and the brother of the 1st Baron Rendlesham. He was MP for Evesham and died in 1815.]

[85][Sir John Rous, 6th Bt and 1st Earl of Stradbroke, 1750-1827. His eldest son, John Edward Cornwallis Rous, 2nd Earl of Stradbroke, 1794-1886, rose to the rank of Captain in the Coldstream Guards during the Peninsula war, Vice Admiral, Suffolk, 1844-86. His brother was Henry John Rous, see next fn.]

[86][Henry John Rous, 1795-1877, second son of 1st Earl of Stradbroke, naval captain 1823-36, luminary of the horse racing world, MP Westminster 1841-6, made First Lord of the Admiralty by Peel in 1846, Rear Admiral 1852, Admiral of the Blue 1862, Admiral of the White 1864.]

was burnt a few years afterwards.[87] The present mansion is the stewards house added to.

[87] [Norman refers to this in 1816. The fire occurred 2 February 1830. The house was entirely destroyed, and the damage estimated at £100,000. The fire was reported to have originated in the conservatory, which was warmed by flues. When a new house, itself to be the victim of a fire in 1855, was built, it was at a site about a quarter of a mile from that of the house destroyed in 1830. The house which Norman visited had been rebuilt about 1780.]

# Chapter 6

# Serious Illness

The year 1816 was one of the most important in my career. It brought with it events of the gravest character in their immediate effects, and which in their consequences, have influenced my whole subsequent life and will continue to be felt till my dying day.

Up to this time I had had no important illness since the internal inflammatory attack in childhood, unless the jaundice in 1814 may be considered such.[1] Slight attacks of feverish cold were the chief exceptions to a fair state of general health, but in May of this year the scene changed. A Norwegian named Heyerdahl from Christiansand had been visiting us at Bromley. I drove into town in a gig, a heavy shower of rain came on, I had a great coat with which I endeavoured to protect both of us, and failed. I got wet and remained all day without changing my dress. Why I know not. The next day I became very ill and sore throat of a most malignant type speedily developed itself. In a very short time I was so reduced that I could not stand. Scott of Bromley attended me. My room was that on the right at the end of the passage up stairs, which has since been occupied by a governess. It had been fitted up for me when I was thought too old to sleep on a small bed near the window in my parent's room, where I had reposed for many years.

[1]In 1811 I had a sort of what the French call unc Maladic de Longeur, but it soon yielded to munatic acid.

The symptoms of my malady were most severe. The ulceration was awful. It appeared to me that all the interior of my mouth and throat slaughed off and I lost all my hair. The pain was dreadful, I was treated with stimulants of the most energetic character and recollect, on one occasion that Scott administered with his own hands two successive tumblers of port wine, which hardly seemed to elevate me. I took bark, was blistered and used astringent gargle. Either these remedies or the strength of my constitution carried me through the malady, and in about a fortnight, I began to recover. It was thought that change of air would do me good, and as Henry and John Barnard, one of whom had also been ill, were going to Ramsgate, it was settled that I should accompany them.

We set out about a month after the beginning of my illness and took up our abode at a lodging house kept by a Mrs Witherden. I liked the mode of life there very much and for some little time appeared to regain strength but, presuming too much upon this, I overexerted myself and speedily fell into a state of languor which continued more or less for several years. I can hardly describe or account for it. I ate, drank and slept well, was not emaciated but rather the contrary, yet I was utterly unable to bear exercise even of the slightest kind. Indeed for some time I grew worse and worse and at length could not walk a quarter of a mile, indeed hardly one hundred yards. If at any time, I in the least exceeded in this respect, I was punished by increased languor. Even when I began to grow better I used to count my steps, about 300 was my usual allowance at one time and this promenade was repeated three or four times during the day. I recollect thinking it a great effort to go from our house to the Shady Walk and back.[2]

My days were usually passed in an armed chair in my room. In summer, I often sat or reclined in the open air or drove out in the carriage. I rode

[2]While at Mrs Witherden's I bought from a fellow, whose person I well recollect, although I forget his name, the 9 or 10 volumes of the *Histoire des Républiques Italiennes du Moyen Age* by Sismondi now in the library. I completed the work afterwards. [See p. 282 for details of this work.]

almost incessantly. My spirits were greatly depressed. For a long time, I despaired of recovery and thought that a lingering and not distant death was my inevitable destiny.

I particularly lamented my inability to help my father in his business, especially at a time when I well knew how that tender and loving parent was almost overwhelmed by the pressure of his affairs, then most impropitious, and was in earnest want of all the aid that I could give him. The uniform patience and kindness with which he bore my infirmity and its consequences without uttering a word of complaint or impatience, endeared him twofold to me, while it perhaps increased the poignancy of my grief. That my mother thoroughly devoted herself to me, all who knew her, will well imagine. To all these matters I shall have to return, and will now therefore resume my narrative.

I forget whether it was before or after my long illness, but I think before, that I belonged to a spouting club, managed by Dr King,[3] now of Brighton, and of which. G.R. Smith and others of my friends were members, and held in Queen Ann's Street near Cavendish Square. The greatest orator among us was Mr Shore, afterwards Lord Teignmouth, who possessed a wonderful flow of words, but with little matter to correspond.[4] I spoke two or three times, but never well, being unable to overcome my nervousness and retain a fair amount of self-possession.

I subsequently belonged, I should say in 1821, to a far more ambitious society, held in Lincoln's Inn Fields. Of this Roebuck,[5] and I think Grote,

[3][Possibly David King, 1787-1865, MRCS 1816, President of West Kent Medico-Chirurgical Society, author of a history of Eltham.]

[4][Charles John Shore, of Heathcote, Derbyshire, 2nd Baron Teignmouth, born Calcutta 1796, died 1885, FRS 1834, DCL Oxford 1834, LL D Cambridge 1835, MP (Conservative). Marylebone 1835-41. He was the eldest son of Tom Shore of Melton, Romford, Essex, born 1751, member of Provincial Council of Calcutta 1775-80, of the Calcutta Board of Revenue 1780-5, of the Supreme Council of Bengal 1786-9, Governor General of India 1792-7, created Baronet 1792, created Baron Teignmouth in 1798, died 1834 aged 82.]

[5][This was probably John Arthur Roebuck, 1802-79, political radical, although

were members. The former spoke often and well, I recollect something of a speech he made on the Catilinarian Conspiracy,[6] and the character of its Chief. I suppose that I spoke, but have no recollection of doing so. He disliked Catiline as being a mere political adventurer. I suppose that he was right.

After having remained some weeks at Ramsgate, the Barnards left me. Just at that time George Pochin[7] and his wife, my cousin Elizabeth came to the place and most kindly offered to receive me as a guest in their house. I passed several weeks with them and was treated with a degree of attention and sympathy which I can never forget.

I almost forgot to mention that George Robert Smith came from London to pay me a visit while at Mrs Witherden, one of the many acts of kindness received from him during an intercourse, which has now lasted for nearly sixty years. George Grote did the same thing.

After I had been about three months at Ramsgate, as no symptoms of returning strength appeared, it was determined that I should return home and my mother came down to take me away. She brought the carriage with her and so great was my weakness, that I was obliged to sleep on my journey at Canterbury and I think also at Sittingbourne, certainly at Rochester. Even

---

he would only have been about 19 at the time. It may however have been another member of the family as he was the fifth of six sons born to Ebenezer Roebuck of the East India Company. But the family did not return to Britain from Canada until 1824 in any case. It is of course possible that Norman has not remembered the date correctly. He makes clear that he is not sure about the date 1821.]

[6][Lucius Sergius Catilina, c.108-62 BC, Roman conspirator. Disqualified from Consulship on charge of maladministration, he conspired with other Roman nobles. In 63 BC he planned the assassination of Cicero, and hostile Senators. He escaped from Rome after the plot was discovered, but the next year he was killed by republican forces at Pistoria (Pistoia).]

[7][George Pochin, 1786-1829 or 1831, High Sheriff of Leics 1828. He lived at Basset House, Normanton. He married 6 March 1811 Elizabeth Norman, the second daughter of Norman's paternal uncle Richard Norman 1757-1847, of Melton Mobray, and his first wife Emilia Grigg, with whom he had eight children of which, however, six died young. George Pochin and his wife had five sons and two daughters. He succeeded to the Barkby estates in 1817. The Pochin family had a long association with Barkby, with records dating back to the 13th century.]

with these short journeys, I was quite exhausted when evening came. In truth my whole condition at that time and long afterwards was very remarkable and anomalous. The great functions necessary to life appeared to be healthily performed, nor did I want muscular power for a short effort, but continued exercise of the slightest kind completely exhausted me and produced most distressing symptoms.

This extraordinary condition of my bodily health was accompanied by severe mental despondency. I quite made up my mind that I should never recover and considered that I was in a state of gradual decay. So strongly was my mind made up on this point that I penned an elaborate letter to my father, still in my possession, which I meant to reach his hands after my death. It contained, if I recollect aright, an expression of heartfelt gratitude for all his kindness to me and of regret that I had been able to show so imperfectly my sense of it. I ventured to add some hint as to the management of his many affairs. He seldom talked to me about his commercial affairs, but I well knew how great had been his losses and how much he required assistance.

I passed the winter of 1816-17 at home. My mother used to take me out driving in the open carriage when the weather permitted and on one occasion, recollect that we stopped at Bromley before a[8] van containing wild beasts, and that the showman put a lion cub into my arms. In appearance and habits it much resembled a gigantic cat.

My many hours within doors were chiefly passed in reading, and I could not be sufficiently thankful for being enabled to derive pleasure from books, wrote too occasionally, verses. English and Latin, Chronological Memoranda &c.

My usual medical attendant during my long illness was old Scott, but I

[8] [Norman wrote 'an' here.]

also consulted Pemberton,[9] and I think Baillie,[10] but the latter it may be on some previous occasion.

In the Spring of 1817, no improvement having taken place, we all went to Dover and remained there many weeks. I was a great deal in the open air, lying down on the beach or sitting in the chatting box, a sort of look out place much frequented by people, who like myself had nothing to do. Philpot Elsted, the surgeon,[11] used to drive me out in his gig to see objects of interest;

[9] [Christopher Robert Pemberton, 1765-1822, MB Cantab 1789, MD 1794, FRS 1796, Physician to the Prince of Wales and later the King, expert on abdominal diseases.]

[10] [Matthew Baillie, 1761-1823, Scots anatomist and physician. His maternal uncles were the famous anatomists William and John Hunter. FRCP 1790, FRS 1790, international authority on morbid (diseased) anatomy. Appointed physician to St George's Hospital, 1787, from which he built up a practice. In 1799 he gave up teaching and his St George's appointment, and devoted all his time to private practice. By 1810 his annual fee income had risen to £10,000. In that year he was appointed Physician Extraordinary to George III. He had many famous patients.]

[11] [In July 1804 Kent, in the front line of any French invasion, was divided into three volunteer brigades, and the Cinque Ports Volunteers were incorporated into the Cinque Ports Infantry Brigade, along with the Deal Infantry and the Ramsgate and Margate Marksmen, under the overall command of Brigadier General Charles Hope. Philpot Elsted was appointed Surgeon to the Dover (7th Company) of the Kent Volunteers. Indeed Elsted's appointment as Surgeon predated 1804, as he is listed as the Surgeon of the Dover Company in 1803. Elsted appears in the list of the Canterbury marriage licences as marrying, 30 January 1802, at the age of 26, Fran Whitfield of Canterbury. His parish is given as St Mary, Dover. The parents of Philpot Elsted were Edward Elsted, c.1736-87, and Affra née Rouse, c.1735-1812. They married at St Mary's, Dover, 27 September 1763. Edward Elsted is described in New Romney churchyard as a 'Riding Officer'. Philpot Elsted was the youngest of their children. Philpot's brother Edward was also a surgeon. Pigot's Directory of Kent for 1823 shows that Dover boasted no fewer than nine surgeons at that date, though the list does not include Edward Elsted. Edward Elsted married Rebecca Whitfield, 18 August 1798, at St Mary Magdalen, Canterbury. It is possible that his bride was related to Frances Whitfield, the wife of Edward's brother Philpot. There were at least two surviving children of Philpot Elsted and Fran Whitfield: William Philpot and Frances. William Philpot Elsted enjoyed a number of official positions in Dover. He was a member of the Dover Paving Board, a tax commissioner for Dover, and a magistrate. He is listed under 'Gentry' in the *Post Office Directory of the Six Home Counties* for 1845 at 13, Snargate Street, Dover. Philpot Elsted himself was clearly a leading figure in Dover; he was one of those involved in the pioneering provision of gas in Dover, as early as 1823, following the passing of a private Act of Parliament in 1822. A company with an authorised share capital of £9,000 was set up, and Elsted was one of the 34 Dover dignitaries listed as involved in the enterprise. Elsted was also involved

among others, I remember visiting with him the ruins of St Radegund's Abbey.[12]

In the summer of 1817, G. Grote proposed to me to accompany him and his brother Andrew for a few weeks tour on the continent.[13] I thought the effort would kill me but determined to risque it, well-knowing how thoroughly I could depend on the kindness of my friends.

We embarked at Calais and then proceeded by St Omers, Bethune, Lillers,[14] Verdun, Metz, Saarbrücken, Mainz[15] and Frankfurt. There we made a halt of a few days and I was obliged to consult a German physician having been knocked up by some hard days work in intense heat. From Frankfurt we went along the Berg Strasse, staid a day at Manheim, descended the Rhine in a sort of floating Barge, which nearly dropped down the stream to Cologne, whence we returned to England by the way of Aix la Chapelle, Brussels Lille &c. From Brussels we visited the field of Waterloo, which then retained many marks of the mighty conflict, which had taken place only years before.

I was absent from home four or five weeks and derived great benefit from the change of air and scene. I have always thought that a tour of six months

---

in local politics. He is mentioned in a report of the 1818 election as one of those in a committee seeking the election for Dover of the banker John Minet Fector. Mr Fector declined the honour. Philpot Elsted himself was still active in 1834 as he was reported in the *Dover Telegraph* 11 January 1834 as attending a suicide of a ship's captain. Philpot Elsted died 3 April 1837, and was buried at St Mary's Dover on 10 April. His death was reported in the *Dover Telegraph* 8 April 1837, 'in the 63rd year of his age'. According to the paper, 'The loss of this gentleman will be seriously experienced by the poor of Dover and the neighbourhood, to whose wants his private fortune was often applied in common, with his professional assistance gratuitously in their afflictions.']

[12] [This is two and a half miles west of Dover, a Premonstratension abbey founded in 1193 by Hugh, the first abbot. It was a daughter house of Prémontré. It was dissolved in 1536 and granted to Archbishop Cranmer.]

[13] [According to Mrs Grote's account (see p. 65) George Grote's life 'passed unmarked by adventure or accident down to the spring of 1818' (p. 26), though in a footnote she remarks that 'It was diversified by a few weeks' tour among the Rhenish provinces, in the summer of 1817, in company with G.W. Norman, then in weak health'.]

[14] [The MS seems clear here but Lille is on the route followed.]

[15] [Norman wrote Mentz.]

would have quite set me up.

I do not recollect keeping any journal during the above tour, as has been my constant custom on subsequent occasions of a similar kind, but I well recollect how much I was interested and delighted.

I may mention as a curious circumstance to the friends of G. Grote that at this time he was remarkable for the depth of his religious fervour. I well recollect on one occasion, he offered up aloud an extempore prayer for himself and his companions, and that I subsequently followed his example. He had not then imbibed the doctrines of the elder Mill.

It may here be worthwhile to remark, that we were greatly struck with the effect which Revolution and War had produced on France. I never, during this tour, recollect seeing a new house or indeed a house under repair. Every thing wore the appearance of ruin and desolation, nor indeed could it well be otherwise considering what the country had gone through since 1789. The harvest had failed, corn was at an extravagant price and the population starving. This added to the mournful impression produced on our minds. We used at every relais[16] to buy a loaf or two of rye bread and give it away in slices.

During the course of this tour we went through the cantonments of a large portion of the Allied Army of occupation. We saw English, Prussian, Russian, Danish and Bavarian troops. This was very interesting to me, the Cossacks, with whom I often conversed, excited my special attention. They did not appear unpopular.

The benefit derived from my foreign trip was not permanent, and in a short time after my former condition returned, somewhat improved however beyond what it had been a year before. In the spring of 1818, some of my sisters having been recommended to use the Leamington Waters and it being surmized that the action of my liver was at fault, it was determined that I

[16][This is short for relais de post, that is, coaching inn.]

should join them there (I forget if we travelled down together). We took up our residence at the Bedford hotel, then kept by a couple named [Williams],[17] who had been servants to the Greatheed family[18] at Guy's Cliffe[19] and who subsequently built and kept the great Regent hotel on the other side of the way.[20] My medical attendant was Dr Wake,[21] no very distinguished follower of Aesclepius,[22] by whose direction, I swallowed an immense quantity of hot salt water of drastic power with, as may be imagined, no perceptible benefit.

After a time my sisters left me, and I felt very lonely. It so happened however, that among the persons at the Bedford, was a portion of a family named Galton consisting of an old gentleman and his eldest daughter, three sons, Samuel Tertius,[23] Hubert[24] and Howard,[25] used to come to Leamington now and then on a visit to their Relatives.

Old Mr Galton had originally been a Quaker and had married a daughter

---

[17] [Name left blank in original manuscript.]

[18] [Norman's Eton contemporary the Hon. Charles Bertie Percy (see p. 76), born in 1794, married in 1822 Anne Caroline Greatheed, granddaughter and heir of Bertie Greatheed, son of Samuel Greatheed by Lady Mary Bertie, daughter of Peregrine, Duke of Ancaster. The seat was Guy's Cliffe, Warwickshire, then about a mile and a half north east of Warwick.]

[19] [Norman clearly wrote Guyscliff. For Guy's Cliffe see p. 76.]

[20] [The proprietor was John Williams. It was the first of the new hotels built in Leamington. It stood at the centre of Union Parade, now called The Parade, and opened under the direction of John and Sarah Williams in 1811. They had been butler and housekeeper to the Greatheed family. It had fifty rooms, and was said to be extremely popular. Seven years later they expanded their business. They obtained a mortgage of £10,000 for a second and larger hotel on the other side of Union Parade. This was known as Williams Hotel. In September 1819 the Prince Regent stayed at Warwick Castle and visited Leamington. He gave his permission to use his coat of arms on the new hotel and it was re-named the Regent Hotel.]

[21] [Probably Charles Wake of Church Street, Warwick.]

[22] [A Greek God who became a cult figure and the patron of physicians.]

[23] [Samuel Tertis Galton, 1783-1844, married in 1807 Frances Anne Violetta Darwin, 1783-1874, one of the many daughters of Erasmus Darwin, 1731-1802. They had three sons and four daughters. Though the family were Quakers, by 1822 Samuel Tertis had joined the Church of England.]

[24] [Hubert John Barclay Galton, of Warley Tor, Salop, 1789-1864. He married in 1815 Mary (died 1859), daughter of Robert Barclay of Clapham Common.]

[25] [John Howard Galton, 1794-1862, married Isabella Strutt in 1819. They had four sons.]

of old David Barclay.[26] He had acquired a very large fortune as a manufacturer at Birmingham and having retired from that business became a Banker, and established the concerns subsequently transformed to a joint stock company. He was I believe expelled by the Quakers for making guns, but retained something of the peculiar manner of his sect. His sons were smart young men, the eldest already married to a Darwin. His eldest daughter still a plain female.[27] He was a member of the Royal Society and a man of considerable scientific acquirements, so as to render his society very interesting.

My sisters and I gradually became acquainted with the Galtons. The marriage of Sir W. Watson with a Barclay[28] was a bond of union, and on

---

[26][Samuel John Galton, FRS, 1753-1832, of Dudson House, Warwickshire, married Lucy Barclay 1757-1817 in 1777. She was the daughter not of David Barclay, as Norman believed, but of Robert Barclay, 1731/2-97, and the granddaughter of a David Barclay of an earlier generation. They had five sons and three daughters. The sons were Samuel Tertis (see fn 23), Theodore 1784-1810, Hubert John (see fn 24), Ewen Cameron 1791-1800, and John Howard (see fn 25). Their daughter Mary Anne, 1778-1856, their eldest child, married Lambert Schimmelpenninck in 1806. Another daughter, Sophia, 1782-1863, married in 1833 Charles Brewin . A third daughter, Adele, 1784-1869, married John Kaye Booth (died 1827). Despite the fact that they were Quakers, the father of Samuel John Galton, Samuel Galton 1720-99, together with Samuel John himself, had a large gun making factory in Birmingham. When Samuel died in 1799, Samuel John and Samuel Tertis wound up the gun business, and set up a bank.]

[27]His eldest daughter was Mrs Schimmelpenninck the authoress. [Norman wrote Schimmeltennink. Mary Anne Galton – see fn 26 – was educated by her mother, who gave her Voltaire, Molière and Swift to read. She suffered spinal problems and chronic pain, and wore a spinal brace. Possibly under the influence of Dr Erasmus Darwin, who attended her mother, she seems to have lost, at least in part, her religious faith. She was encouraged in her literary aspirations by visitors to the family home, including James Watt, Maria Edgeworth, and Mrs Barbauld with whom she stayed in London. She married and devoted time to teaching and to various charities, but financial difficulties, and a rift with her family, caused her to turn to writing to earn her living. She was not only an authoress, but also active in the anti-slavery movement. She gained a reputation in her family for engineering discord. Her works included *Select Memoirs of Port Royal* (London: J. Stephen, 1858). She also wrote an autobiography, *Life of Mary Anne Schimmelpenninck* which was edited by a relation, Christiana C. Hankin (3rd edition, London: Longmans, 1859).]

[28][Sir William Watson was the uncle of Norman's mother. Edwards Beadon, Norman's grandfather, had married Mary, the daughter of Sir William Watson, MD, 1715-87, FRS 1741, physician and botanist, and one of the founding trustees of the British Museum in 1756. He also conducted early electrical experiments, and

the departure of my sisters, they took compassion on me and shewed me the highest degree of kindness and sympathy. I always dined with them and they took me a daily drive in their carriage – in short had I been a near relative, they could hardly have treated me more tenderly.

At length they returned to their residence Dudson, which has now been absorbed in the station of the London & North Western Company, and took me with them. I remained their guest for a fortnight and had a severe feverish cold under their roof during which I was nursed as if I had been at home. At Dudson I had the pleasure of seeing Mr Watt[29] whom I also visited at his own house and was greatly struck with the variety and richness of his general conversation, as I have been subsequently by the striking resemblance of his statue by Chantrey to the original.[30] It is the very man. I also visited Mr

published a number of medical works including one on smallpox inoculation. He was knighted in 1786. His son, also Sir William Watson, 1744-1824, married about 1772 Christiana Freame (c.1739-96), formerly Barclay, thus giving the Normans a connection with the Barclay family. He was also a physician and naturalist. FRS 1767, MD 1771. He practised medicine in Bath, and was a close friend of Herschel who, under his influence, became a scientist, having been previously a Bath musician. He worked with Herschel on astronomical problems. He was linked by marriage with members of the Lunar Society of Birmingham, including Samuel Galton. He was knighted in 1796.]

[29] [James Watt, 1769-1848, Scottish engineer, partner with Matthew Boulton in the firm of Boulton and Watt.]

[30] [Sir Francis Legatt Chantrey, 1781-1841, friend of Norman and a crony in the Houghton fishing club. Chantrey rose from humble beginnings (his father was a tenant farmer and carpenter in Derbyshire) to be one of the most famous sculptors of his era. He enjoyed universal recognition, and was knighted by William IV in 1835. He declined a baronetcy because he had no heirs. He left about £150,000. He had a wide circle of friends and, in particular, his cronies in the Houghton fishing club. He was indeed charitable and benevolent; about one third of the £150,000 went as legacies, leaving Lady Chantrey with £100,000. His fees were substantial; for a large monument the figure could be £6,000. For his statue of the Duke of Wellington he charged £9,000. He began work as a portrait painter, but from 1808 concentrated on sculpture. His work was widely praised for its naturalistic achievement, and he had little time for the artistic flights of fantasy of Italian sculpture which so appealed to Norman. Though Norman here praises the realism of the Watt sculpture, he indicates elsewhere in the Autobiography that he found Chantrey's outlook very restricted. Chantrey's bust of James Watt, exhibited at the Royal Academy in 1815, and a version of which, dated 1818, is in the Soho House Museum, Birmingham, is regarded as an outstanding work which helped to consolidate Chantrey's already high reputation as a sculptor, one who was able

Boulton at Soho.

Among the many, who at different periods of my life have shown me kindness, I can hardly name any persons to whom I felt a warmer gratitude than to Mr and Miss Galton. Their kindness was so unlooked for and uncalled for and was so valuable to me in my days of bodily feebleness and mental depression. Had the lady been a little younger and personally more attractive I should of course have fallen in love with her. She subsequently married a plain friend named, I think Brewin who had acted as a sort of secretary to her father.[31] The other daughter married a Swiss physician, Hubert [married] a Barclay and Howard Miss Strutt, Sister of Lord Belper;[32] of him I shall have more to say hereafter. Our acquaintance with the Galtons has always been kept up, although we have seen but little of each other, owing to our several orbits having so seldom intersected. In the second generation of the Galtons are to be remarked the African traveller,[33] and the engineer,[34] if these are

in a remarkable way to convey the personality of the sitter. His statue of James Watt, commissioned in 1820 for a fee of £2,000, exhibited at the Royal Academy in 1824, and to be found in Handsworth Church, Birmingham, is regarded as a masterpiece.]

31 [See p. 188.]

32 [Edward Strutt, 1801-80, first Baron Belper, the grandson of Jedediah Strutt, 1726-97, inventor and cotton manufacturer.]

33 [Sir Francis Galton, 1822-1911, was the youngest of the seven children of Samuel Tertis Galton, 1783-1844. After the death of his father, Francis Galton set out on a year long tour of the Middle East, during which time he learned to speak Arabic. In 1850 he undertook a journey of exploration, under the auspices of the Royal Geographical Society, to south west Africa which was at that time almost unknown to Europeans. There were two books as a result; *Tropical South Africa* (1852) and *The Art of Travel* (1855). The first of them received the Gold Medal of the Royal Geographical Society, and Galton was elected FRS. After his marriage in 1853, Galton settled upon an academic career, becoming a famous pioneer statistician and the leading authority on heredity, especially human heredity, and was one of the most active promoters of eugenics, a word he invented in 1883.]

34 [Sir Douglas Strutt Galton, 1822-99, born at Spring Hill, Worcs, the son of John Howard Galton of Hadzor House, Droitwich, and his wife Isabella, the elder daughter of Joseph Strutt of Derby. He was a military engineer, trained at the Royal Military Academy, Woolwich, and at Chatham. He spent his early army life overseas. He was active in the affairs of the Red Cross. In 1851 he married Mary Anne, daughter of George Thomas Nicholson of Waverley Abbey, Farnham, Surrey, to whom Norman refers elsewhere. His engineering work covered a huge

not the same person.

Dudson was Rus in Urbe[35] as pretty and retired as a villa could be made, situated quite close to Birmingham. The house was good and contained a library in which I revelled. The fortune of the old gentleman must have been immense, for his three sons have always lived like men of large fortune.

On my return home, or in going I forget which, I passed a day at Alban Hall with Hobbes Scott, then a student there, or it might have been with Richard Barnes at All Souls.[36] Perhaps I have got into a jumble as to two visits to Oxford in 1814 and 1818.

The Summer of 1818 was the dryest in my recollection. No rain fell from May till September. The large trees lost their leaves. The meadows were so parched that my father burnt portions of his. The fire ran along the ground as if the grass had been so much hay and Lord's Wood was saved with difficulty from a conflagration. The farmers on the hills could only procure water from the spring at Keston,[37] and sent stock there from a distance of many miles. At that time tanks were unknown.

Towards the end of the year my health improved and I was able to go to London and afford my father some aid in his business. This was to me a matter of extreme delight. About this time too I think, Richard returned from Norway where he had been sent to learn the language under the protection of the Knudtzons at Trondhjem.

My leisure in the country was devoted mainly to the acquisition of Italian.

range of problems, from railway structures, London drainage, and sanitation in military barracks and hospitals, to underwater telegraph cables. He was elected FRS in 1859. He was knighted in 1887. He was awarded honorary degrees by Oxford, Durham, and Montreal.]

35 [Country in the city.]

36 [*Alumni Oxoniensis* has no Richard Barnes at All Souls. There are only two people of that surname listed at All Souls, and neither has dates that fit the narrative.]

37 [Keston was the neighbouring parish to Bromley Common. There were two huge ponds on Keston Common, which still exist today, which in Norman's time supplied water to the great house at Holwood; see p. 137.]

My master was named Maurizi, an adventurer whose whole history I never could exactly make out. He had been however a patient of Mr Scott, by whom he was introduced to us.

The plan I adopted in learning Italian was the same which I had found to succeed tolerably well with French. I took but a few lessons, perhaps thirty or forty in all, and went over the grammar, did a few exercises and as soon as I could distinguish nouns from verbs, began to read the best works in the language, my first attempt however being on Goldoni's comedies,[38] which are hardly to [be] reckoned in this class.

In the course of two or three months, Maurizi showed me a manuscript of his own, describing his adventures when in the service of the Imam of Muscat. I told him that I would translate it for him, which I did, putting it however in somewhat a more popular shape than that of the original.[39] This

[38][Carlo Osvaldo Goldoni, 1707-93, famous Venetian playwright. Though Norman writes disdainfully of his work, it is now ranked very high indeed. Though educated as a lawyer, and initially engaged in legal work, he pursued a career as a playwright, though his early attempts were tragedies and not successful. However he discovered a talent for comedy, beginning in 1738 with L'uomo di mondo (The Man of the World). He also wrote librettos for musical comedies, including Il filosofo di campagna (The Country Philosopher) with music by Galuppi (1752) and La buona figliuola (The Good Girl) with music by Piccinni (1760).]

[39][Vincenzo Maurizi, adventurer and spy. The book to which Norman refers was *History of Seyd Said, Sultan of Muscat; together with an Account of the Countries and People on the Shores of the Persian Gulf, particularly of the Wahabees. By Shaik Mansur, a Native of Rome, who after having practised as a Physician in many Parts of the East, became Commander of the Forces of the Sultan of Muscat against the Geovasseom and Wahabees Pirates. Translated from the Original Italian M.S. Hitherto not published.* London: John Booth, 1819. Maurizi's preface (pp. xxxiii-xxxiv) contains the following rather strange allusion to the translator, without naming Norman: 'And now to conclude, I return my sincerest thanks to the translator of ... my work, for the assistance he has rendered me; I cannot help stating as a mitigation of the censure which its numerous imperfections may provoke, that he is a gentleman unknown in the paths of literature, and unpractised in the art of composition; while the greater proportion of his time is fully occupied by the urgent calls of a laborious profession. He has no claim, therefore, to any praise except that of having adhered as faithfully to the original text as the idiomatic differences of the Italian and the English languages would allow; and he hopes that this frank avowal will dispose his readers to regard the result of his labors [sic] with a disposition inclined rather to praise than to censure.' In 1984 a new edition with an introduction by Robin Bidwell was published by the

work was published and a copy of it is to be found in the drawing room. I do not suppose that I have looked into it for thirty-five years and I almost forget it. It was my first attempt in print.

I was greatly charmed with Italian literature, both in prose and verse, and the list of books read by me, to which I have before referred, will shew how much attention I had devoted to it. Ariosto,[40] Tasso and Petrarch[41] have often occupied a place in my pocket during foreign expeditions. On the banks of the [river] Test, in coaches and on railroads and as respects the two first, I may say with a pleasure, greater after every perusal.

I may here remark that after Shakespeare, the World's poet, and Homer, I know of no poets superior to the three great Italians, of whom, of course I reckon Dante as the first, but then his extreme difficulty renders it a matter of study to read him effectually. I consider Milton as perhaps equal to the other two, but he is less amusing. The Gerusalemme[42] is I think, much superior

Oleander Press (Cambridge and New York). On Maurizi's strange career see also B. Nicolini, *Makran, Oman and Zanzibar. Three-Terminal Cultural Corridor in the Western Indian Ocean (1799-1856)*, translated by P.J. Watson, Leiden: Brill, 2004, pp. 101-10. It is not perhaps surprising that Norman found Maurizi evasive about his past. Of Italian origin, he was a strong supporter of Napoleon. It was thus hardly surprising that, after 1815, and having severed his connection with Muscat, he found it prudent to be in England rather than Bourbon France or Italy. However, like many involved in espionage over the centuries, he had hedged his bets and provided some information for the British, as well as for Napoleonic France, on several occasions.]

40 [Ludovico Ariosto, 1474-1533, whose great work is the *Orlando Furioso*, published in 1516, and in a final revision in 1532. It contains characters taken from the Charlemagne legends.]

41 [Francesco Petrarca, 1304-74, known in English as Petrarch, Italian poet and one of the earliest Renaissance humanists. His sonnets were much admired and imitated. He was also a scholar and collector of Latin manuscripts. He revived the works of Cicero, but he is best known for his Italian poetry, especially the *Canzoniere* and the *Triomfi* (*Triumphs*). A prolific author, he wrote works on religion, biographies, and two major sets of books called *Epistolae Familiares* and *Seniles*. He was also a prime mover in the Greek Renaissance. In addition, he was one of the first to climb Mont Ventoux.]

42 [This work, by Tasso (see p. 118), first appeared as *Gerusalemme Liberata* (*Jerusalem Liberated*) in a pirated edition in 1579. It was regarded as a patriotic description of Christian Europe's heroic past. He is credited with influencing both Spenser and Milton. Tasso later re-wrote the piece, removing elements which he

to the Aeneid.[43] Almost equal in style and more interesting and imajinative. As for the Orlanda, it is written with a pen dipped in the morning light. How gay, and easy, and fanciful. What charming episodes, such as the Angilica e Medoro.[44] You may open the book and read where you please, certain of being delighted. To be sure, it is impossible to take much interest in the general story, or in the heroes and heroines, who singly defeat armies and cut a Knight down to his saddle, as if he were a carrot, but even among them one finds an occasional trait of humanity and then what a fertile invention are their adventures.

The Italian poets have given me more pleasure than any others I have subsequently read, with the single exception perhaps of the Swedish Tegnèr.[45]

I am a great admirer too of the Italian prose writers. Think of Gio Villani.[46] How much had he seen and knew, traveller, merchant, politician, man

---

regarded as morally objectionable.]

[43][Publius Vergilius Maro, 70-19 BC, known in English as Virgil. He was a classical Roman poet, author of the *Bucolics* (or *Eclogues*), the *Georgics* and the *Aeneid*, an epic poem inspired by Homer, which became the epic of the Roman Empire. He worked on this during the last ten years of his life. The first six books, held to be modelled on Homer's *Odyssey*, relate the escape of the Trojan hero Aeneas from Troy to Italy, by way of Carthage and a dalliance with the Queen of Carthage, Dido. It became the central Latin literary text of the Middle Ages.]

[44][Ludovico Ariosto, 1474-1533, Italian poet, best known as the author of an epic poem called *Orlando Furioso*, (*Orlando Enraged*). Angelica and Medoro are the characters who fall in love in Ariosto's poem. Although *Orlando Furioso* was first published in 1516, its complete form dates from 1532. Ariosto's work, at nearly 39,000 lines, is one of the longest poems in European literature. The character Orlando is a translation of Roland from the 12th century Song of Roland. In the poem Medoro is a wounded Saracen knight and Angelica a pagan princess. The work is regarded as one of the most influential in European literature. Amongst those influenced was Edmund Spenser in his *The Faerie Queene.*]

[45][Elaias Tegnèr, 1782-1846, Swedish poet and churchman, professor of Greek at Lund, 1812-26, Bishop of Växjö 1824.]

[46][Giovanni Villani, 1276/80-1348, Italian banker, official diplomat and historian. He was the author of the *Nuova Cronica* about the history of Florence. He began work on the book about 1300, but was unable to finish it because of his death. It was later finished by his brother and his nephew. He was one of the first writers to introduce statistics into history; this no doubt reflected his commercial career, which at one stage resulted in imprisonment. Though some of the history is undoubtedly loosely based on legend, he provided considerable details on matters with which he was familiar, such as floods and famine, and plague of which he

of the world. There is not, I think a chronicler of the Middle Ages to be compared with him. Then descending[47] to the sixteenth century, we have the great prose writers Machiavelli, philosopher historian, statesman. Guicciardini, soldier and statesman,[48] whose great work never appeared tedious to me, although it excites, in narrating the ruin of Italy at the hands of the Barbarians, one of the most mournful episodes in the history of humanity. How thorough was Guiciardini's knowledge of man and of men. How profound are his political reflections. Then we descend to Davila and Bentivoglio.[49] The Guerre Civili di Francia[50] is perfect as a work of art, hardly indeed inferior in that respect to Tacitus, but then how thoroughly immoral in its judgements on the characters of individuals and their actions. Witness what he says of Caterina de 'Medici.

Indeed it must be allowed that his greater predecessors, Machiavelli and Guicciardini seem hardly ever disposed to blame villainy, provided only that it is successful.

himself died. He was active in the politics of Florence, and in its business life, though some of his business practices, in particular his accounting, seem to have been highly questionable.]

[47] [Norman wrote 'discending' here.]

[48] [Francesco Guicciardini, 1483-1540, Italian historian and statesman, and friend of Machiavelli. He is regarded as one of the major political writers of the Italian Renaissance. He is credited with extraordinary powers of observation and analysis, which he applied both to the Italy of his time and to Spain, to which he had been sent as a diplomat. He subsequently spent a long career in Papal administration under Leo X, and Clement VII, as Governor of Modena and Regio. As a soldier he defended Parma against the French in 1521, and Pope Clement gave him the rank of Lieutenant General of the Papal Army. Nonetheless he was much opposed to the territorial ambitions of the Papacy. His support for the dissolute Alessandro de Medici severely damaged his posthumous reputation. His most famous work is his *Storia d'Italia* regarded as an historical masterpiece. Another famous work, which rivals that of Machiavelli, is his *Ricordi Politici*. His memoirs were published in 1857, long after his death.]

[49] [Guido Cardinale Bentivoglio d'Aragona, 1579-1644, Italian Cardinal, statesman and historian. Under the patronage of Pope Clement VIII, and Pope Paul V, he rose rapidly in the Church as a diplomat. He was also a patron of the arts. Amongst those he supported were the composer Frescobaldi and the painter Van Dyck. He came from a family of princely rank long powerful in Bologna.]

[50] [This work, published in 1630, is by Enrico Caterina Davila, 1576-1631.]

The Dei Minorum Gentium,[51] such as Nardi[52] and Varchi,[53] with their interminable periods, are I confess, at times rather tiresome, but I must tear myself from il bel paese, 'che l'Apennin parte, e l'Alpe e dil Mare circonda'[54] and proceed with my narration.

---

[51][A favourite expression used by Norman to indicate moving on to the minor figures. The Roman Senate had consisted of 100 members originally. These were called Patres (Fathers). A subsequent addition of a further 100 members was called Patres Minorum Gentium, those of the first creation being thus Patres Majorum Gentium.]

[52][Jacobo Nardi, 1476-1563, Italian historian. He was a member of a Florentine family, and a follower of Savonarola. Banished from Florence in 1530, he died in poverty in Venice. His *Istorie della Città di Firenze* (*History of the City of Florence*) was written in the last years of his life.]

[53][Benedetto Varchi, 1502/3-65, Italian historian and poet who fought in the defence of Florence, and was exiled in 1530 after the surrender of the city, to which, however, he returned in 1543 with a commission to write a history of the city. His work covers the years 1527-38. He also wrote a number of plays and poems, and made translations of the classics.]

[54]['The beautiful country "which the Appenines divide and the Alps and the sea surround".' This is from the *Canzoniere* by Petrarch. This phrase is often attributed to Dante.]

# Chapter 7

# Travels

Early in 1819, Mr Lyons,[1] a solicitor of Dublin who had done business for my father and acquired his regard, invited me to accompany him to Dublin and pass some weeks there. I did so, thinking it might be the means of thoroughly reestablishing my health. We travelled by Chester and Holyhead and took up our residence in his house on Arran Quay. We saw much society, chiefly but not exclusively among Lawyers, Lessing, Maturin the poet,[2] Dr Griffin now

[1][John Charles Lyons, c. 1780-c.1870. He was the third son of John Lyons of Williamstown, County Dublin. He was apprenticed in January 1800 aged 16, as a lawyer, to Armstrong Fitzgerald, an Attorney at the Court of Exchequer in Ireland. In 1807 he is recorded as an Attorney at the Court of Exchequer. *Wilson's Dublin Directory* for 1819 gives his address as 21 Arran Quay. A Dublin lawyer he was at various addresses in Dublin. He was a member of the Reform Club from 1839 though, oddly, Norman was never a member. At the time of his election to the Reform Club, for which he was proposed by Daniel O'Connell, seconded by William Curry, MP, he was at Birkbeck Street, Dublin. There is some correspondence from him amongst the Norman papers (U310/C127). His address on that correspondence is Roebuck Cottage, Dublin. A Dublin directory for 1850 lists him as being at 23 Kildare Street. He married Lucinda Boyle, and three of his sons were lawyers.]

[2][Charles Robert Maturin, 1780-1824, writer and Anglican clergyman of Huguenot descent. He graduated from Trinity College, Dublin, BA, 1800. He was ordained and appointed to the curacy of Loughrea, County Galway, in 1803. In 1804 he returned to Dublin as the curate of the church of St Peter. He wrote a number of romantic novels, including *The Fatal Revenge* (1807), *The Wild Irish Boy* (1808), and *The Milesian Chief* (1812). He enjoyed the patronage and support of Sir Walter Scott. In 1814 he wrote the play Bertram which was successfully performed at Drury Lane. Subsequent plays however failed. His book *Melmoth the Wanderer* of 1820 is generally regarded as his masterpiece. His final novel *The Albigenses* of 1824 was modelled on the work of his patron Scott. Oscar Wilde

Bishop of Limerick,[3] who with his wife and sisters used to sing charmingly Moore's Ballads, then in the zenith of reputation.[4] Franks afterwards Judge in Bengal.[5] Holwell Walshe, famed for his imitations of Curran. By the way Holwell Walshe had married a daughter of Sir W. Burrows,[6] who had owned Hayes Place,[7] and from whom my father bought Hayes Farm and Brook

---

was a descendant.]

3 [The Right Reverend Henry Griffin, 1786-1866, Bishop of Limerick, Ardfelt and Aghadoe 1854, Fellow of Trinity College, Dublin 1811-29.]

4 [Thomas Moore, 1779-1852, now best remembered for the words of *The Minstrel Boy* and of *The Last Rose of Summer*. He was educated at Trinity College, which had recently allowed entry by Catholics, and studied law in London. But it was as a poet and composer of the words to songs that he became famous. His ballads were published as *Moore's Irish Melodies* in 1846 and 1852. He obtained official appointment, as Registrar to the Admiralty in Bermuda, travelled in North America, and published poems on his return. Despite the large sums which he earned from his writings, he got into debt, and found it necessary to leave the country, living in Paris until 1852. He became literary executor for Lord Byron. His work is as highly regarded in Ireland as that of Robert Burns in Scotland, and a number of composers, including Robert Schumann, have set the poems to music.]

5 [Sir John Franks, QC, 1769-1852, Judge of the Supreme Court of Bengal. He was born at Loher Cannon near Tralee, Kerry. He was educated at Trinity College, BA 1788, Ll.B 1791. He was called to the Irish Bar in 1792, practised successfully as a barrister, and in 1822 took Silk. In 1825 the Board of Control, on the recommendation of William Conyngham Plunket, the Irish Attorney General, appointed him Judge of the Supreme Court at Calcutta. For this he received the customary knighthood. He remained in this post until health problems forced his resignation in 1834, when he returned to Dublin. The ever susceptible Norman mentions a Miss Franks. Franks married three times. He married first his cousin Catherine, daughter of Thomas Franks of Carrig, County Cork. She died in 1812. They had two sons and three daughters. It was presumably one of those daughters to whom Norman was referring. Franks married secondly his cousin Jane, daughter of John Marshall of Gurteen, County Cork. In 1849 he married Sarah Wollaston, daughter of William O'Regan.]

6 [Holwell Walshe, 1782-1844, a practising barrister in Dublin, of 9 Merrion Row, Dublin, married 1813 Louisa (1778-1835) widow of John Miller, and daughter of Sir James Bond, 1744-1820, MP Naas, Ireland, 1790-7, 1st Bt 1794, of Coolamber, Co. Longford, and Anne Hornby. Louisa had two daughters by John Miller and three daughters by Holwell Walshe. Norman wrote Sir W. Burrows, rather than Sir J. Bond, but no one of that name who could possibly fit the circumstances has been traced.]

7 [Hays Place, a house at Hays, Kent, two miles south of Bromley, was bought in 1757 by William Pitt the Elder, later Earl of Chatham, who rebuilt it. His son William Pitt the Younger was born there in 1759. It was sold to Sir James Bond in 1785 and sold again in 1789 to Viscount Lewisham. Documents concerning Hays

Wood, last but not least Shiel[8] and O'Connell.[9]

Lyons was, I am happy to add, still is, a Catholic. Of course I was an Enthusiast for Emancipation and an Abhorrer of the old Orange system then in baleful luxuriance. I once told O'Connell, for whom I then felt unbounded admiration as the first combatant in a noble cause that I should see him in St Stephens Chapel. He heartily laughed at the idea of this. Subsequently, and

Farm and some parcels of land are in the Norman papers at U310/T35, T36, T37, E32/3.]

[8][Richard Lalor Sheil or Shiel, 1791-1851, playwright and politician, educated by the Jesuits at Stonyhurst College in Lancashire, and then at Trinity College, Dublin. BA 1811. Called to the Irish Bar in 1814. On the foundation given him by Stonyhurst and Trinity, he became a fine orator, and quickly began to devote himself to the cause of Catholic Emancipation. He was initially critical of O'Connell, but joined with him in organising extra-Parliamentary popular pressure. He became an MP in 1831, initially for the rotten borough of Milbourne Port, and subsequently for Louth. He was active in Parliament during the 1830s and 1840s, and in 1850 Lord John Russell nominated him as Minister to Tuscany, where he died the following year. He differed fundamentally from O'Connell in that, educated at Stonyhurst, he had no desire for the repeal of the Union.]

[9][Daniel O'Connell, 1775-1847, Irish politician and leader of the movement for Home Rule, known as 'The Liberator'. He was born near Cahirciveen, County Kerry. Qualifying as a lawyer he was called in 1798 to the Irish Bar though, as a Catholic, he was barred from higher legal posts. In 1823 he formed the Catholic Association to campaign for two things. Firstly he sought Catholic Emancipation from the disabilities imposed on Catholics by the Test and Corporation Acts, which prevented non-Anglicans from holding office though in practice these only disadvantaged Catholics. In Ireland this had the effect of excluding 80 per cent of the population from holding public office. Secondly O'Connell, in contrast to his ally Shiel, also campaigned for the repeal of the Act of Union between Britain and Ireland. O'Connell believed that by concentrating on a single issue – Catholic Emancipation – it would be possible to secure the election of Catholics to the House of Commons, and then to move on to Home Rule for Ireland. In 1828 the Parliamentary seat in County Clare fell vacant, and O'Connell, barred from the House of Commons as a Catholic, decided to stand. He was elected with a huge majority and, rather than trigger civil disturbance on a large scale in Ireland, the government, led by the Duke of Wellington who in any case favoured Catholic Emancipation (though including Peel who had long opposed it), passed the Catholic Emancipation Act in April 1829. O'Connell became an important force in Parliament in the 1830s, and leader of the radical faction. For a while this hindered his freedom to agitate for repeal of the Act of Union but, once it became clear that the Whig administration of Lord Melbourne was doomed, O'Connell set about organising mass meetings all over Ireland. The government retaliated by imprisoning him for sedition in 1843. He was released after a few months but his influence was fading, and the Irish famine pushed the issue of Home Rule to one side.]

for many years, I used to exchange messages with him, through Lyons, and when he was returned for Clare I called upon him at his lodgings close to St James's Street and was very well received. A Gentleman was with him, whom he introduced to me as Mr Nicholas Purcell O'Gorman.[10] After a good deal of conversation, I took my leave, and had never any subsequent intercourse with the great agitator. He became too great a man, for so humble a person as myself and soon commenced a course of action, which deprived him of my respect. For his genius and industry it was impossible however not to entertain feelings of profound admiration.

It is a great misfortune, for a man's morality and permanent fame, to become a leader in a popular agitation, carried on mainly at public meetings and by the means of platform oratory.

To such a man, popular applause becomes almost a necessary of life. To obtain or keep it, he must often advocate doctrines, which he knows to be erroneous by arguments which he knows to be fallacious. He must suppress the most firm convictions of his mind. He must distort or invent facts. He must say, not what he considers true, but what he thinks will be agreeable to his hearers and finally he must be prepared to steer and change his course, to suit the popular gale. It was thus with O'Connell, at first he had a noble cause, when this was gained, it became necessary to find out or imagine fresh grievances with which to excite the popular mind. In doing this his perception of truth, never perhaps very lively, was wholly lost and he became in the highest degree false and unscrupulous.

The best that can be said for him is that he probably never altogether lost a vague desire to benefit Ireland. His own selfish glorification however was long his leading principle.

But to return to my Dublin life and acquaintances. Among the latter

---

[10][Nicholas Purcell O'Gorman, 1778-1857, the only child of James O'Gorman of Ennis 1717-87, called to the Irish Bar 1803, KC 1835. He worked with O'Connell for Catholic Emancipation in Ireland, as Secretary of the Catholic Association. His brother Richard O'Gorman was prominent in the Young Ireland movement.]

was Mr Lyndon Bolton, who having been deeply compromised in the affair of 1798,[11] had been obliged to seek safety in France and had striven in vain to obtain employment in the French Army.[12] It seems that Napoleon never fancied the Irish Exiles and gave them little encouragement. I presume at the peace of Amiens, Bolton was allowed to return to his country. He set up in business at Dublin, soon acquired a large fortune and became a faithful subject of the British Crown. His wife was a very handsome and amiable woman. Both were very kind to me and many a rubber at whist have I played with them. They were Protestants.

I was much struck with the beauty and amiability of the Dublin ladies, and ran some danger of being captured by the second Miss Franks.[13] But the handsomest woman, whom I saw at Dublin indeed one of the handsomest women I ever saw in my life, was Mrs Moore the daughter of Sir John Stevenson the musical composer.[14] I think I heard her say, (perhaps the story was told me) that she once knew a gentleman who rode seventy miles without stopping to dance at a ball with her. I said I supposed that the gentleman was

[11] [The Irish rebellion of 1798, which had been building up for at least a decade, finally broke out on 23 May 1798. According to a leading historian, 'The 1798 rising was probably the most concentrated episode of violence in Irish history. Mass atrocities were perpetrated in circumstances of chaos and confusion ... By the end of the summer, the death-roll of both sides, from various causes, has been estimated at 30,000.' R.F. Foster, *Modern Ireland, 1600-1972*, London: Penguin, 1989, pp. 279-80.]

[12] [Lyndon Bolton of Monkstown Castle, Dublin. The Boltons were part of the Protestant Ascendancy, and were thus targeted in the rising of 1798. William 'Black Billy' Bolton married secondly in 1754 Mary Lyndon, and their son Lyndon Bolton was born in 1760. He married Jane Carpenter in 1793. She was the daughter of a Dublin apothecary Richard Carpenter. They had 13 children, of whom 4 died young. Lyndon Bolton actually joined the rebels in 1798, and was disowned by his father 'Black Billy'. However he seems to have recovered from this misfortune, and became a successful woollen draper in Dublin and also took over the apothecary business of his father in law. Jane Bolton died 3 September 1834 and Lyndon Bolton died 29 January 1852.]

[13] [Presumably the daughter of Sir John Franks; see p. 198.]

[14] [Sir John Andrew Stevenson, 1761-1833, composer, born in Dublin and died at Kells, Co. Meath. He married Anne Singleton née Morton. They had two sons and two daughters.]

Mr Moore and that he wanted to dance with you. She nodded assent. Alas alas! O frailty, frailty thy name is, the ungrateful hussy subsequently ran away with Lord Bective,[15] and died of cholera as Marchioness of Headfort.

The Dandy of Dublin was Lord Allen,[16] a sort of exquisite, something of the Alvanley cast.[17]

I knew an Irish exile in Norway who had settled and married at Christiansand, and was called Robert Major.[18] It was supposed that his real name was different. I liked him much. He had toned down into a very quiet every day person and had quite forgotten Irish politics. He was from the North.

Lyons used to lend me his horse and when the weather was fine I used to ride in the Phoenix Park, a beautiful appendage to a large City.

Part of most days, I passed in the four Courts, going into each separate Court, when any thing interesting was going on, such as a speech of O'Connell

---

[15] [Thomas Taylour, 2nd Marquess of Headfort, married Olivia (died 1834), the second daughter of Sir John Stevenson. At the time of the marriage he was Lord Bective but succeeded his father Thomas Taylour, 1757-1829, 2nd Earl of Bective, who had been created Marquess of Headfort in 1800, as 2nd Marquess of Headfort in 1829. According to *Burke's Peerage*, Sir John Stevenson's daughter was the widow of Edward Tuite Dalton of Feunar, Co. Meath.]

[16] [Joshua William Allen (c.1782-1845), 6th Viscount Allen and Baron Allen of Stillorgan, succeeded to the titles in 1816, MA Oxford 1804, served under Wellington in the Peninsula as an officer in the Guards, and distinguished himself at the Battle of Talavera. He died unmarried in 1845 at Gibraltar, aged 64, when the title became extinct. He was described by Creevey (*The Creevey Papers*, edited by Sir H. Maxwell, London: Murray, 1903, p. 288) as 'a penniless Lord and Irish pensioner, well behaved and not encumbered with too much principle'.]

[17] [See p. 124.]

[18] [On the rebellion of 1798, see p. 201. Oddly, given that Norman believed Major to come from the North, Ulster and the South West of Ireland were hardly affected by the rebellion, though there was limited action in Antrim and Down, which was associated not with the Catholics but with radical Presbyterianism. There was a Robert Major in Norway at the time, and he was married there as Norman relates, but he was born in Norway (at Odderness, Vest-Agder) and there does not seem to be any obvious connection with Ireland, even though the surname Major is one that occurs in Ireland. He was Robert Major, 1806-54, whose mother is recorded as Sophie Benedicta Weidermann and whose father was called Robert Gonsale Major. The younger Robert Major married, in 1836, Emilie Kristiane Matthiesen, and the marriage is too late for the reference that Norman makes to a marriage prior to 1819. In the circumstances it seems likely that the Robert Major to whom Norman refers was Robert Gonsale Major.]

to Lord Manners the Chancellor[19] or of Bushe[20] before the Chief Justice (Downes I think[21]). Or I might just look in to the Common Pleas and laugh at the eccentricities of Lord Norbury, who with some wit, more impudence and a great display of apparent bonhomie, scandalised all my notions of justice.[22] I recollect his asking of a witness what was his occupation, on being told a racket count, he observed so do I, and a very good business it is.

I have already remarked that Dublin society was very witty and amusing. It wanted however something like seriousness. Everything seemed to be considered a fit matter for a joke.

A great deal of wine and punch were drunk and I found it very difficult

---

[19] [Thomas Manners-Sutton, 1756-1842, 5th son of Lord George Manners-Sutton, himself third son of the third Duke of Rutland. He was educated at Cambridge, 5th Wrangler 1777. Commissioner of Bankrupts 1783, MP (Tory) Newark, 1796-1805, KC 1802, Solicitor General 1802-5, created 1st Baron Manners of Foston 1807 and appointed Lord Chancellor of Ireland, in which position he remained until 1827.]

[20] [Charles Kendal Bushe, 1767-1843, opponent of the Act of Union, and advocate of Catholic Emancipation. Solicitor General for Ireland 1805-22. On the retirement of Lord Downes he was appointed Lord Chief Justice of the King's Bench. He resigned in 1841.]

[21] [William Downes, 1751-1826, 1st Baron Downes. He was the third and youngest son of the six children of Robert Downes, 1708-54, MP for Kildare 1735-54. William Downes was aged only 2 or 3 when his father was found dying in the parlour of their home in Dawson Street, Dublin, with a sword run through his body. The circumstances remain a mystery. William Downes graduated from Trinity College, Dublin in 1773, and was called to the Irish Bar in 1776. The government arranged his election for Donegal in 1790, and two years later he was made a Puisne Judge in the Irish court of King's Bench. In 1803 he was promoted to Chief Justice of the King's Bench, to fill the vacancy caused by the murder of Viscount Kilwarden. In 1806 he also became Vice Chancellor of the University of Dublin. He remained Chief Justice for nearly 19 years. His position was difficult. On the one hand he abominated the use of military trials and executions in dealing with civil unrest; at the same time he was given no credit by O'Connell for an indulgent attitude towards Catholic defendants, while his handling of such cases outraged the government. He resigned the office of Chief Justice in February 1822, and died in March 1826.]

[22] [John Toler, 1745-1831, 1st Earl of Norbury 1800, MP Tralee 1766, KC 1781, Solicitor General for Ireland 1789, Chief Justice of the Court of Common Pleas 1800. While sometimes described as a jovial figure, the truth is that Norman's view is accurate; Norbury was a scandalous figure with a ribald and often irresponsible sense of humour.]

to maintain my habits of sobriety without the risque of giving offence. My father had some correspondents, whose firm was T.W. & H. Sneyd[23] by whom (it was almost a matter of course with him) he finally lost money. I recollect being invited to sup with one of them. We had a splendid banquet of so substantial a character, that a roast turkey formed part of it.

I once went with Lyons to pass a Sunday afternoon with a Catholic Priest who kept a school, I think at Rathfarnham,[24] where the Lyons boys were boarders. At dinner, among the other guests was a Protestant Dean, who got very tipsy without exciting much scandal. This was a trait of manners. I was deeply shocked and offended. My opinion of the established Church, never very high, sank in consequence even below its former level.

I have mentioned most of my youthful loves, but have not until now, mentioned one lady, whom as a youth I greatly admired. This lady was Miss Lucy Leblanc,[25] sister to our neighbour Mrs Cobb,[26] to two Colonels and to

[23] [Henry Sneyd, timber merchant, of 48-49 Sir John Rogerson Quay, Dublin.]

[24] [A suburb of Dublin on the south side. It contains historic buildings including Rathfarnham Castle and Loreto Abbey.]

[25] [The Le Blanc family was descended from Thomas Le Blanc, 1704-65, a wealthy merchant of Huguenot origin. The family seat was at Northaw in Hertfordshire. One of the colonels mentioned was Henry Le Blanc, 1776-1855, Lieutenant Colonel 1807-14, Major of Chelsea Hospital 1814 to death. According to Le Blanc family records in the Huguenot Library at University College, London, he married Elizabeth McClintock, sister of Admiral Sir Leopold McClintock, was Colonel of the 71st Regiment, and Colonel Commandant of the 5th Battalion of the Guernsey Regiment, and lost a leg at Buenos Aires in action against the Spanish, under General Whitelock. The Le Blanc family records show the other Colonel to have been Francis Le Blanc, born in 1790, who married Harriet Porter. He joined the 4th King's Own Regiment, and served under Sir Thomas Moore in the Walcheren Campaign. He is reported to have taken part in the Peninsula campaign, being involved in the defence of the line of Torres Vedras, the battles of Fuentes de Oñoro, Salamanca and Vitoria, and the sieges of Badajos and St Sebastián (where he was wounded in the right arm during storming of the town), and was a Captain in the Rifle Brigade at Waterloo. He was Commander of the 37th and 53rd Regiments, and died in 1880 at the age of 90. We are indebted to Lucy Gwynn of the Huguenot Library for the information from the Le Blanc family records.]

[26] [According to the manuscript account of the Le Blanc family in the Huguenot Library at University College, London, Mary Le Blanc was the daughter of Henry Le Blanc, later Major of the Royal Hospital, Chelsea. She married John Cobb, of Doctors Commons, Hawkhurst, Kent, had three daughters, and died and was

Mr Thomas Leblanc, Master of Trinity Hall.[27] She was older than me and of course with her marriage was out of the question, but her nice figure, pretty features and attractive manners greatly pleased me, and she was besides, in a high degree amiable and agreeable.[28]

It was a scandal on the male sex, that she died a Miss. It need hardly be said that I made no attempt to gain her affections, but I have some reason to believe that I was not altogether indifferent to her. Women are sharpsighted in detecting an admirer.

Almost all my Irish male acquaintances had been engaged in duels and I recollect having pointed out to me on one occasion at dinner at Mr L. Bolton's a very mild and agreeable gentleman (Captain Hoey I think) who I was informed was the best second in Ireland, and had shown his superiority in that capacity when acting for O'Connell in the fatal affair with D'Esterre.[29] Indeed the death of the Orange champion was attributed to his skill in having placed him on a slight elevation, with a tree behind him, which guided his antagonist's aim. It may be noted as a trait of manners, that some thousands of people were present on that occasion.

Before I leave Dublin and its lawyers I must mention that I was present

buried at Hawkhurst. She was thus the niece of Lucy Le Blanc, not her sister. We are indebted to Lucy Gwynn for a copy of the Le Blanc manuscript.]

[27][Thomas Le Blanc, DCL, died 1843 aged 70. Master of the Court of Queen's Bench and Master of Trinity Hall, Cambridge, 1815-43. Fellow of Trinity Hall, 1800, called to the Bar in 1803. He was the nephew of Sir Simon Le Blanc, 1748/9-1816, who was a Fellow of Trinity Hall 1779-99.]

[28][Thomas Le Blanc (born in Threadneedle Street about 1745) married 3 April 1771 Felicia Pelham (born at Northaw, near Hatfield, Herts, about 1750). Lucy Le Blanc was born 13 April 1786 in Suffolk. She was thus seven years older than Norman. She was the niece of Sir Simon Le Blanc, 1748/9-1816. She died in 1855.]

[29][John D'Esterre was a merchant who chose to challenge O'Connell to a duel after a remark by the latter concerning Dublin Corporation. On 1 February they faced each other with pistols at Lord Ponsonby's seat, Bishop's Court Demesne in County Kildare, 13 miles from Dublin. D'Esterre was fatally wounded. O'Connell, though his standing was enhanced at the time, is said to have later regretted the death of D'Esterre. O'Connell's seconds are reported to have been a Major M'Namara, Nicholas Purcell O'Gorman, and Richard Nugent Bennett. O'Connell was accompanied by his brother James O'Connell. Also present was the brother of Nicholas Purcell O'Gorman, Richard O'Gorman.]

for several days at one of the jury trials in the great Trimlestone case.[30] A disputed will, said to have been made under the undue influence of a second wife, sister to General Eustace, by which the children of a former marriage had been disinherited. I never heard any thing like the surpassing eloquence of Bushe afterwards Chief Justice, of Burton, Wallace and so of the many other counsel employed. After a trial which lasted many days, the verdict (a just one) was given against the will to the enormous delight of the worthy Dubliners.

During the latter portion of my stay in Ireland Mr Lyons took me a little tour through the County of Wicklow, with which I was greatly delighted. We visited Bray, the Vale of Avoca, the meeting of the Waters, the Vale of Arklow, Luggilan[31] and Glendalough. Some portions of this district are as beautiful in their way as anything that can be imagined but on a very small scale. The Picts towers and the seven churches are the only buildings of the sort I ever examined. Mr Petrie has shown their ecclesiastical character.[32]

[30] [*Times* 12 March 1819 (3d) reported from the *Dublin Journal* of 8 March, 'This very important case which had for 12 days occupied so large a share of legal argument and investigation, in the Court of Common Pleas, was decided at 11 o'clock last night, by the jury, which had been engaged in the deliberation on it from Saturday evening, giving in their verdict in favour of Lord Trimlestone'. The jury had decided that a will of December 1812 was not the last will and testament of his father, the late Lord Trimlestone. Nicholas Barnewall, 14th Baron Trimlestone, born 1726, married, secondly, in 1797, Alicia (born 1773, died 1860), second daughter of Lieutenant General Charles Eustace of Robertstown, Co. Kildare. The 14th Baron died in 1813, aged 86. A will dated 8 December 1812 left a considerable estate to his second wife, by whom he had no children, to the exclusion of his son. At the time of the second marriage the bride was about 24 years old, and the groom about 71 years old. The widow subsequently, and rapidly (in 1814/15), married Lieutenant General Sir Evan Lloyd, KCH, of Farney Hill, Salop. He died 1846 aged 78. The disinherited son was John Thomas Barnewall, 15th Baron Trimlestone, 1773-1839. However Norman's rejoicing was premature. After the remarriage of the widow, the Dublin verdict was the subject of appeal. The House of Lords, which recorded that Alicia Eustace had been, in 1797, a young lady of considerable beauty, directed in 1829 that the case should be re-heard. In the end the will of 1812 was 'proved'. Though Norman was writing in 1857, and subsequently, it is not clear that he was aware of this outcome.]

[31] [Correctly Lugnaquilla, the highest mountain (3,039 feet) in Leinster, near to Aghavannagh, Co. Wicklow.]

[32] [George Petrie, 1790-1866, artist. He published *The Ecclesiastical Antiquities*

They were probably receptacles for objects of value belonging to churches and also places of refuge and protection, in troublous times.

It must have been about March 1819 that I quitted Ireland, returning to Bromley alone by the way of Holyhead Chester and Shrewsbury. I had greatly gained in point of health and was deeply grateful to Mr Lyons for his attention and hospitality to me. He is a man of considerable ability, a thorough gentleman in all respects, and this I can say, after an acquaintance of at least forty-five years. From 1819, we have always corresponded. I have frequently seen him in England, and once again in Ireland *vizt.* in 1829, as will appear hereafter.[33]

My general uselessness in the world, and especially the little aid which I had been able to render to my father had long preyed upon my spirits, and now feeling myself better, I urged my father to send me to Norway with a view to save from the wreck a portion of the debts owing him in that country, which exceeded in the aggregate £70,000.[34] To this plan he consented.

It must be remarked that I had long pressed upon him the propriety of employing an agent to look after his foreign debtors, as had been previously done by Wolffs and Dorville,[35] Sewell and Necks,[36] and Boultons and Baker,[37]

---

*of Ireland* in 1845.]

[33][See p. 336. On Lyons, see p. 197. Norman and Lyons kept in touch, as the Autobiography indicates, despite Norman's aversion to Catholics. There are some letters of 1850-3 from Lyons to Norman in the Norman papers at U310/C127.]

[34][This would be £4,356,100 in 2009 prices.]

[35][Wolffs and Dorville, described as 'merchants', were at 24 New Bridge Street, Blackfriars.]

[36][Sewell and Necks, 'merchants', were at 1, Chatham Place. They were neighbours to Boulton and Baker, also described as 'merchants' at 14, Chatham Place.]

[37][As noted on p. 323, the connection between Norman and Charles Boulton was initially through the timber trade. The *London Gazette* contained a notice of 31 May 1821 dissolving a partnership between Henry Boulton, Charles Boulton, and John Henry Pelly, and replacing it with one between Charles Boulton and John Henry Pelly. Sir (as he became) John Henry Pelly, 1772-1852, 1st Bt, was Charles Boulton's brother in law, being married to Emma, the 6th daughter of Henry Boulton. She died in 1856. He was also a Director of the Bank of England, 1822-52 (Deputy Governor 1839-41, Governor 1841-2) and a Director of the Hudson's Bay Company from 1806. Another *London Gazette* notice, dated 27 February

the other Houses in the Trade. But he was slow to move from his accustomed habits of business. He said that he had[38] nobody to send and in short, up to that time, nothing had been done by personal application and arrangements.

In offering to go to Norway with so much heavy responsibility on my shoulders and still in very feeble health, I was certainly actuated by a feeling of duty. I had strong apprehensions that I should break down under the task and never see England again. The truth however being that what I required was the being driven to an effort, forced into something quite new. Thus then the Norwegian expedition was really the very thing that I wanted. Marriage alone would have been a fitting, possibly a superior substitute for it.

It so happened that Mr Marcus Ploen, an important correspondent of my father's, was at this time in London. It was settled that I should accompany him and Mr Lange, a Dane settled at St Martin, Isle de Rhé.[39] I also invited Howard Galton[40] youngest son of old Mr Galton to join the Party, which he agreed to do.

My dear and fond mother fitted me out with leather sheets to guard against damp beds. A medicine chest, now in my wife's room, which contained physic enough to cure a regiment, and every thing else she could think of likely to be useful to me.

The party proceeded to Harwich and embarked April 17th 1819, on board

1829, recorded the dissolution of a partnership between Charles Boulton and John Henry Pelly, described as Norway merchants and thus in the timber trade, and its replacement with a partnership of Charles Boulton and Thomas Baker. The presence of Henry Boulton in the partnership dissolved in 1821 shows that the elder Boulton was a contemporary of Norman's father in the timber trade. Norman's father died in 1830, and Henry Boulton in 1836. That the partnership was in the timber trade is also confirmed by entries of 1815 and 1816 in the records of the Sun Fire Office. Given the need of the timber trade for fire insurance, it is perhaps not surprising that, as will be seen on p. 324, both Henry Boulton and Charles Boulton appear in the lists of Sun Fire Office managers.]

[38] [Norman wrote 'have' here.]

[39] [The Isle de Rhé is a small island 9 miles by 3, with a capital St Martin which is 6 miles from La Rochelle.]

[40] [John Howard Galton of Hadzor House, 1794-1862, the father of Douglas Strutt Galton; see p. 190.]

the Thetis,[41] Gothenburg Packet, Captain W. Living. She was a small cutter of about sixty or seventy tons. Our voyage was prosperous. On the morning of the third day after our departure we sighted the rockbound coast of Norway, and in the middle of the day took the pilot on board, who steered us into Tromoesund near Avendah, where we disembarked leaving the Thetis to pursue her voyage. We had much reason to be obliged to Captain Living, who had thus spared us a long and uncomfortable land journey with some risque to himself in deviating from his instructions.[42]

From Avendahl we went to Chistiansand, and thence returning back, paid successive visits to Krageroe, Risoer, Brevig, Schien, Lanroey, Drammen and Christiania, staying a day or more at each place as the exigencies of my business required. I made Christiania my head quarters for several months, visiting from it Moss, Frederickstadt, Frederickshald and Hafslund, and going into the interior as far as the Mjösen to look at the estates belonging to the Ankerske Fidei Commis, which were widely scattered and also that of Carsten Anker at Ejdsvold. To Drammen I made frequent excursions staying there sometimes three or four days at a time.

As I have in my possession a journal kept during this expedition to Nor-

[41][The name *Thetis* is a common one for ships. There have been 12 ships of the Royal Navy named HMS Thetis. A 38 gun frigate of that name, built at Rotherhithe and launched in 1782 was sold, after taking part in a number of naval operations, 9 June 1814. Thetis was one of the Nereides in Greek legend, and the mother of Achilles. A square stern smack, a kind of sloop, is recorded at being registered at Harwich in 1817. This, it appears from other evidence, was the ship commanded by Captain Living.]

[42][Captain William Living by 1835 was operating a Post Office packet called *The Flamer* from Weymouth to the Channel Islands. In this role he delivered a statement (dated 29 September 1835) to the Commission of Inquiry into the Management of the Post Office, which is reproduced in Appendix C to the Report of the Commission. In this he recorded that he had been 26 years in the service of the Post Office, and formerly commanded a vessel of his own in the Post Office service (the Weymouth packet was owned by the Post Office) on the Harwich station. This was a sailing vessel, unlike the steam powered office operated by the Post Office. *6th Report of Commissioners appointed to inquire into the Management of the Post Office Department, Parliamentary Papers* 1836 vol. XXVIII pp. 145ff, App. C pp. 209-10. It is clear that the vessel concerned was the *Thetis*, to which Norman refers.]

way, I am spared the necessity of any details as to my adventure in that country referring to the above document for all necessary information.[43] There are a few general remarks, however which I think it proper to make.

My first Norwegian journal is the worst specimen of its class which has proceeded from my pen. It is marked in many places by ignorance and expresses opinions as to individuals, some of which, I am now persuaded, were erroneous. I have often been tempted to burn it and have abstained. Firstly because it can do no harm, secondly because I purpose sometime or other to look over and to erase the obnoxious passages and thirdly because after all, it contains memoranda of persons and events of which I desire to retain some more stable and reliable record than the memory of a man, now aged sixty-four, who feels a steady decay in all his vital powers.

On the whole I was much pleased with Norway and its inhabitants. The former abounds in picturesque beauty of a very high order. Mountains and forests, lakes and rivers, dark ravines and sunny vallies are mingled together in most of the forms which delight the painter's eye. To be sure you have not the splendid cities, the cathedrals, the palaces, the ruined castles and temples of the south, with all the recollections belonging to them. Nor have you mountains elevated to the towering height of the Alps. Still I must say, that no scenery seen in my subsequent travels has ever afforded me so much delight as that of Norway.

The people too, their social and political relations seemed to me full of interest. They were in a state of financial distress of the severest kind. Prosperous from their neutral character during the early part of the revolutionary war, their merchant fleet had been in great measure captured by the English after the attack on Copenhagen. The utter break down of the Danish paper had destroyed the fortunes of most persons possessing monied capitals.[44] The

[43] [Notes on Norway and Norwegian affairs are in the Norman papers at Maidstone, at U310/F59/10.]

[44] [On the breakdown of the Danish currency, see p. 313.]

licence trade had indeed somewhat alleviated their condition, but the heavy fall in the price of timber and of iron, subsequently to the peace, the pressure of the enormous duty on foreign wood in England,[45] which amounted to nearly £3 a load on deals and the very low freights, had obliterated this slight flicker of returning prosperity, and on my arrival in Norway, I found bankruptcy and ruin the order of the day.[46]

It cannot be supposed that my mission, as respected its main object of getting in old debts, was very successful. In truth, I recovered very little. Yet I cannot reproach myself with any want of diligence. I worked early and late, spared no pains and exerted myself to the best of my strength, mental and bodily. Nor did I waste time in pursuit of amusement. I went into society indeed a great deal, but I hardly made even a short journey with a merely pleasurable purpose.

In 1819 Norway had only been united to Sweden for four years. The feelings of animosity engendered by centuries of conflict were still in full vigour and were embittered by a forced submission to a new state of things, which appeared to place a proud, vain and gallant people under a sort of dominion to a neighbouring people whom they hated and despised. Nor had the new order of things which had made Charles XIII of Sweden,[47] King of

---

[45] [According to McCulloch's table in *A Dictionary of Commerce and Commercial Navigation*, London: Longman, 1832, p. 1041, the duty on Baltic deals of up to 10 feet in length was £8.2s.6d per 120, on deals 6 to 16 feet was £19 per 120, for 16 to 21 feet it was £22 per 120, and for 21 to 45 feet it was no less than £44 per 120. The corresponding duties for 6-16 feet were £2 and, for 16-21 feet, £2.10s, for Canadian timber. McCulloch (1832, p. 1040) quoted a House of Lords report on the decline of British exports to both Sweden and Norway as a direct result of the discriminatory duties. (Lords Report on the Foreign Trade of the Country, 3 July 1820, p. 34.) See *Report by the Lords' Committees appointed Select Committee to Inquire into the Means of Extending and Securing the Foreign Trade of the Country and to whom were referred the Petition of Certain Shipowners of Sunderland respecting the Duties on Wood &c. Parliamentary Papers* 1820 (269) III, 381.]

[46] [On timber duties see Norman's *Essay on Taxation*, pp. 61, 78, 86-7, 189-90, 192, 194.]

[47] [Charles XIII, 1748-1818, elected King of Sweden in 1809 in place of the deposed Gustavus IV. Bernadotte was elected Crown Prince in 1810, and assumed effective power; see p. 160. Charles XIII was by this time senile, though he was

Norway,[48] nor even the Ejdsvold constitution guaranteed by the Convention of Moss, brought with them any material advantages, apparently indeed the very reverse.

Even at this early day however the Grundlov[49] was silently working its way into the popular heart. Free Institutions were extending their beneficent influences and on all sides the seed was sown, which was soon to produce a rich harvest of good.

There existed in Norway, among the great mass of political ignorance, a few able, honest and enlightened men who had long seen the advantages likely to accrue from an union with Sweden rather than with Denmark. These men were selected by the new ruler as his chief agents, and with infinite zeal and sagacity did they fight the battle of their country. On one side they had to deal with an empty exchequer and the cause of a state newly erected with every thing to be created, when money was to be raised from a community at the verge of ruin and where the value of property had reached the lowest point of depression. They were stigmatized by their country men as the chiefs of the Swedish faction, and suffered under all the unpopularity arising from this circumstance, as well as from the necessity they were under of upholding the finances of Norway and of enforcing the payment of taxes then felt to be very burdensome.

As true lovers of the freedom and independence of their country, they were obliged to show that she was in a condition to pay her way and to support the burdens of an independent existence, and hence aroze another source of danger and of difficulty for them. The legal sovereign Charles XIII was in his dotage. The real ruler was the Crown Prince Carl Johan, (Bernadotte) who indeed succeeded to the Crown I think, in 1818. He was kind and benevolent, of engaging manner and willing to do all the good he could, consistently with

nominally King of Norway and Sweden in the years 1814-18.]

[48] [The manuscript has 'Army' in ink, corrected in pencil to 'Norway'.]

[49] [Constitution.]

the attainment of his personal ends. On the other side, with great ability, he was false and unscrupulous, knowing little about free institutions and feeling painfully the restrictions imposed upon the royal authority by the Norwegian Grundlov. He would have been most happy to have got rid of these, either by force or fraud, as he showed in 1821, had he found ministers to second his views. But the men he was compelled to employ were not made of the stuff he required, and held on the even tenor of their way, as duty called, unseduced by the temptations held out to them and the difficulties thrown in their path, by the Crown on one hand and by the Nation on the other.

Of these distinguished men, Statzraad Collett,[50] Falsen,[51] Papuher Wedel Jarlsbergh,[52] the last named was by far the most distinguished.

Johan Casper Herman Count of Wedel-Jarlsberg descended from an ancient Pomeranian family. An ancestor had entered the Danish service in the

[50][Johan Collett, 1775-1827, Norwegian politician, Governor of Buskerud and elected to the Storthing (Parliament), he was a member of the constituent assembly at Ejdsvold in 1814 (see p. 171) which produced the Norwegian constitution. He remained in Parliament, being re-elected in 1818, 1824 and 1827, until his death.]

[51][Christian Magnus Falsen, 1782-1830, Norwegian statesman, lawyer and historian. In 1808 he became a circuit judge at Follo, and from 1814, and the union with Sweden, he played an important part in Norwegian politics. He was a supporter of the attempt by Prince Christian Frederik to become King of Norway, and was one of those involved in the drafting of the Ejdsvold constitution, modelled on that of the United States. In 1822-5 he was Attorney General, and in 1827 he became President of the Supreme Court. He also produced a major work on the history of Norway to 1319, *Norges Historie* (1823-4).]

[52][Johan Caspar Herman Wedel-Jarlsberg, 1779-1840, Norwegian aristocrat and politician who played an active role in the constituent assembly at Ejdsvold (see p. 171) in 1814. He exercised the important function of Governor, who represented the absent King in the Norwegian Cabinet, during the union with Sweden. He was born in Montpelier in France, studied law in Copenhagen, and became in 1806 the Danish King's representative in Buskerud in Norway. He was a strong supporter of the union of Norway with Sweden, and opposed the attempt of Prince Christian Frederik to establish himself as an independent Norwegian monarch. He became Minister of Finance in 1814, and remained in this position until 1822, restoring Norwegian monetary stability. Despite difficulties in dealing with Bernadotte, he undoubtedly helped to maintain relations between the Storthing (Parliament) and the King. He was married to Karen Anker, the only child of the Prime Minister Peder Anker, and she brought him huge wealth, in the form of forestry land around Christiania (now Oslo).]

reign of Christian V, had rizen to the rank of Field Marshal and obtained large possessions, and among these the County of Jarlsberg. The previous possessor of the Tittet Estates had been minister at Naples where his distinguished son was born, and subsequently in London, where the latter learned our language perfectly and obtained a deep insight into our laws and institutions. He had married the only daughter of Peder Anker of Bogstad,[53] the head of the most wealthy Norwegian family, whose estates however although immense, were very heavily encumbered.

A man naturally of great ability he possessed also extensive knowledge, vast power of application, and an utter contempt for what is called pleasure. He was animated by the most earnest desire to do right, and despised[54] alike the clamours of the crowd, the secret libels, and open attacks of rivals and of enemies, and the seducing influence of Royal flattery. Few men could be more able, none could be more honest.

I feel it a high honor, when I am enabled to say, that of this distinguished person, on whose character and conduct I should like to dilate for many pages I became the intimate friend, and that I retained his friendship and confidence, until worn out with ceaseless toil, and wasting cares he died while Statholder of Norway on a visit to the German Baths in [blank in original]. I had, if I mistake not, seen Count Wedel in England previously to 1819. I saw a good deal of him during that year, both in Christiania and at Bogstad, but our intimacy greatly increased subsequently.

[53] [Peder Anker, 1749-1824, Norwegian businessman and politician, a son of the wealthy merchant Christian Anker, 1711-65, who owned extensive forests around Christiania and whose wealth was built upon timber export. Peder Anker bought the Bogstad estate with additional forests, and constructed a substantial mansion there. He also invested in iron mines and foundries. He was a delegate to the constitutional convention in 1814, and supported the union with Sweden. After the union came into effect he was appointed Prime Minister of Norway, and remained Prime Minister until 1822. He was the brother of the wealthy ship owner, merchant and industrialist Bernt Anker, 1746-1805.]

[54] [Norman wrote 'dispised' here.]

Another friend whom I acquired in 1819 was Myer Myers,[55] son of a merchant at Norfolk Virginia who had come to Norway to recover the value of a large cargo of tobacco and was pursuing a weary lawsuit through the several Courts. We were introduced to each other, I think by Marcus Ploën, lodged in the same house Skipper Skoeyen at length, always messed together and became very intimate. I lived a great deal with Myers during the following year, and have kept up an epistolary correspondence with him ever since. He was good-looking, with the Jewish descent strongly marked in his features, clever, and most kind and accommodating. I shall ever retain a pleasing recollection of our long intercourse, and the most earnest desire for his well-being. I have never seen him since 1820, excepting about 1832, when he was in England.

My other chief male associates in Norway during my first visit were Peder Cappelen of Drammen,[56] Pavel Lined, Dr Professor Keyser,[57] M. Ploën and

[55] [Myer Myers was probably of the family of Myer Myers, 1723-95, successful silversmith and businessman. He was the most prolific silversmith working in New York, in the late 18th century. His talents and productivity as a silversmith were augmented by an advantageous marriage to Elkaleh Myers-Cohen, the daughter of a wealthy merchant in the transatlantic trade. He also went into partnership with Benjamin Halsted which expanded his business further.]

[56] [Peder Juel von Cappelen, 1763-1837. He had extensive forestry interests, and was active in politics.]

[57] [Jens Jacob Keyser, 1780-1847, Professor of Physics and Chemistry. He was born 1 October 1780 at Tangen Stromso and died 18 January 1847 at Sorgenfri, Aker. He was born Krum, but he was only nine when his mother died, and was brought up by his uncle, a clergyman, Johan Michael Keyser, 1749-1810, in Christiania, and he took the name Keyser. He attended the Cathedral School in Christiania, and Copenhagen University. In 1806 he was employed as a teacher of mathematics and physics at Frue School, now Metropolitan School, in Copenhagen. The school was destroyed in 1807, and he took a job in the university library and acquired a legal degree. However he returned to teaching maths and physics when the school re-opened. He was appointed Professor of Chemistry at the University of Christiania, now Oslo, in the summer of 1814. He taught physics and chemistry to medical and other students. He built up science teaching and equipment. He was a traveller, visiting Italy, Denmark, and Britain, and also undertook other travel at the request of Jens Esmark; see p. 235. In 1837 he gave up trying to teach both physics and chemistry, abandoning chemistry, as it was no longer possible to cover both subjects, given the extent of scientific progress. His wife, to whom Norman refers, was Maria Frances Fredericia, whom he married in Edinburgh in 1824.

Ludvig Mandoe in Christiania but I knew all the world.

But I must now say a few words upon a certain female, who excited in my heart a deeper emotion and maintained her sway there for a longer period than any other woman I have ever known, with the sole exception of my wife. This charming person was Frohen Louise von Haxthausen, the third daughter and fourth child of Lieutenant General von Haxthausen,[58] who had been Statzrad under the ephemeral sway of Prince Christian Frederick and had undergone an impeachment (Riksrett)[59] along with General Staffeldt[60] in connection with the warlike operations, which preceded the Convention of Moss.[61]

---

She was born in Barbados in 1802, and died in Norway in 1829. Her father was Jurriaan François de Frederici, 1751-1812, who was the Dutch Governor General of Surinam, 1790-1802, and her mother was Mary Anne Stuart.]

58[Frederik Gottschalck von Haxthausen, 1750-1825, was born at Copenhagen. He came to Norway in 1779 when Denmark still ruled Norway. In 1786 he was appointed Major General, and given command of the Fredriksten fortress. During the years 1803-10 Haxthausen was in Denmark, though retaining his Norwegian appointments, and in 1806 he was appointed commander of the Akershus fortress. As a Dane he was close to Prince Christian Frederik, who attempted to become the first King of an independent Norway in May-October 1814. During the Swedish campaign against Norway in 1814, his military leadership was felt to lack resolution and he was accused of treachery. Five days after the Convention of Moss, 14 August 1814, which brought an end to the war, his house was attacked by a mob and Haxthausen had to flee from Christiania (Oslo). He was impeached in 1815, but was found not guilty. His reputation was subsequently restored and in 1879 a street of Oslo, in the Frogner area, close to the home which Norman mentions, was named after him.]

59[Impeachment was a judicial process with the power to convict members of the Storthing (Parliament), government ministers, and Supreme Court judges for criminal acts, and was based on the 1814 constitution of Norway. The grounds for the impeachment of Haxthausen (see fn 58) were that he was regarded as having given incorrect information about the state of the army during the war. He was not convicted. Wedel-Jarlsberg was impeached in 1821-2 on a charge of causing the Ministry of Finance to do business with two British houses which subsequently failed. He was not convicted. Staffeldt does not appear to have been impeached, and Norman's account is thus incorrect.]

60[Staffeldt, then a Colonel, commanded a brigade of the Norwegian army during the Swedish invasion of Norway in 1808. With inferior forces, he managed to make life very difficult for the Swedish commander Gahn. He subsequently defeated a larger Swedish force and conducted a skilful guerrilla operation, despite the inferiority of the Norwegian weaponry.]

61[In response to Prince Christian Frederik's attempt to become King of an

General von Haxthausen was a well informed gentleman, possessed of ability. He descended from an old Hanoverian family, some scion of which had entered the Danish Service.

He was the officer who during the short campaign of the Prince of Hesse in Sweden in 1788[62], was sent into Gothenburg to [be] summon[ed to] the P[a]lace,[63] and being admitted blindfold into the W[?][64] and conducted into a room, on his eyes being unbandaged, he found himself in the presence of Gustavus III who had hurried from Stockholm and thrown himself into the beleaguered town. I ought perhaps to add that I never heard this story from the general himself, and that others may have misinformed me.

independent Norway, and the popular Norwegian endorsement of this, Sweden invaded and met with little effective resistance. By 4 August 1814 the fortified city of Fredrikstadt had fallen and on 7 August a delegation arrived from Bernadotte, then Crown Prince of Sweden but its effective ruler, offering a cease-fire, based upon acceptance of the Norwegian constitution of May 1814, but with Norway joined to Sweden under a joint monarchy. Peace negotiations began on 10 August, and on 14 August they were concluded with the Convention of Moss, resulting in a general cease-fire.]

62 [This is a reference to the so called 'Theatre War' of 1788-9 between Sweden and Norway. Gustavus III of Sweden had attacked Russia in 1788, thereby inaugurating the Russo-Swedish war of 1788-90, and Denmark was bound by a treaty of 1733 to assist Russia. Denmark controlled Norway at that time; and thus Norway was also at war with Sweden. The majority of the troops employed by Denmark were probably Norwegian. The first nominally Danish force was under the command of Prince Karl of Hesse. It attacked Bohuslan, from Norway, on 24 September 1788, and met with feeble resistance. In addition 700 Swedish troops under the command of Colonel Johan Werner Tranefelt were defeated by a much larger Danish force commanded by Major General Mansbach. The Danish force continued to encounter little resistance, and was not stopped until it reached Gothenberg. Gustavus III arrived to take command of the city, and the defences were quickly strengthened. A British diplomat, Sir Huges Elliot, arranged an armistice in October, and this was prolonged until the following May. By that time Holstein was threatened by both Britain and Prussia, and the Danish forces were withdrawn. The name of the war reflects the fact that military casualties were very light; but the hardship of the conditions led to the deaths of several thousand men in the Danish led force. Gustavus III, 1746-92, was King of Sweden 1771-92. His attack on Russia was an attempt to revive his popular fortunes, but this failed. He was assassinated at a masked ball in 1792 by conspirators amongst the nobility which he had crushed.]

63 [In the manuscript, Norman appears to have written, 'to summon the Place'.]

64 [The manuscript is illegible here.]

Frau Generalnidett whose maiden name I forget, was sister to Mrs General Mansbach, widow of another German-Danish officer and mother of Colonel Johan Mansbach and of Ulrike Mansbach whom we met at Carlsbad in 1850.

The Haxthausens were wealthy according to the measure of Norwegian wealth in those days, kept a carriage and had a house in town and (a Lekke) villa about a mile from the town on the right of the road to Drammen. It was approached by a drive through large gates. There was a garden and a sort of wilderness on a rocky ridge planted with firs in which a colony of hooded crows built their nests. Its name was Lille Frogner.

The household consisted of the two old people and the two younger daughters, Frederikke and Louise. The eldest daughter and son being married.

The young ladies were accomplished, good musicians, good dancers, spoke German and French well and made some progress in English under my instructions. Our intercourse was always carried on in French, as at that time, I had not learnt Norwegian.

My acquaintance with this amiable family commenced soon after my establishment at Christiania and during the remainder of my stay there in 1819, and again in 1820. I passed two or three evenings a week with them, either at Lille Frasner or in town. I used to go about six o'clock to tea and remain till after supper say till ten o'clock. Here was plenty of opportunity for falling in love and into love I did fall, and that to a very considerable extent.

I must here describe the pretty creature who so long held me captive. She was seventeen when I first saw her, rather tall than short, than small. Rather plump than thin. Her figure was by [no] means perfect, although fine figures are common in Norway. Some of the envious indeed were cruel enough she was not quite strait, but this I could never perceive.[65] Her features were very

[65]In looking over old letters I found one from Count Wedel, dated about 1833 or 4, in which he told, on a recent journey of the Queen's she had stopped at Sanne Herregaard, then belonging to me for refreshments, Louise being with [her], as Hoff Frue. And the latter had mentioned my ownership, talked of me, as an old

pleasing without possessing classic beauty. Her mouth was perfect, with coral lips and the whitest teeth, nose well formed, chin round and dimpled, hair a very light brown, darker however than what is called flaxen, of a colour indeed which I hardly know how to describe, as it is so seldom seen in this country. It was very long and abundant and of exquisite fineness. But how shall I give an idea of her skin and complexion. The first of a delicacy of texture and of a pure whiteness, such as poet may imagine, but can hardly describe, while the colour which suffused her cheeks could not be exceeded in purity of tint, by the choicest rose. She had good teeth, which shewed admirably when she smiled, and her eyes were of a perfect cerulean blue. Much of the same colour as the sky during the intervals between the showers of a May day. In truth she was as bright and fresh as May herself and formed a charming specimen of the best style of Norwegian beauty. She was the prettiest girl in Christiania and universally admired. But the homage paid her did not spoil her. She was perfectly unaffected modest, simple and good-tempered, and an agreeable companion, although not what is called very clever.

As marriage never entered into my contemplation at that time the object of my journey being to save my father money and not to add to his burthens, I never strove to gain Louise's affections, but merely her friendship. I attained my object. She had a sincere regard for me, but nothing more. We each knew the real position of the other. My connection with her, cost me not a few of the lover's pains, such as occasional fits of jealousy, but on the whole, my intercourse with the von Haxthansen family was a source of great pleasure and helped to divert my mind from the mass of disagreeable business which occupied the greater part of my time and attention. It must be recollected that in 1819 and 1820 hardly a Norwegian lady spoke English and not many French. For female society I was thus mainly confined to

---

and esteemed friend, and proposed my health, which the Queen had drunk calling me the 'Cher Inconnu'. [Note added by Norman in January 1866.]

the Haxthausens, Mansbachs, Wedel-Jarlsberg and Kaltenborns,[66] by whom French was spoken.[67] In other families, I was compelled to trouble the ladies with my miserable Danish, worse then, even, than it is now.

My intercourse with Louise continued as warm as ever in 1820, and was kept up by correspondence for 25 years, In 1826 when in Norway with Henry, I found her a married woman. She had espoused Baron von Stedingk,[68] son to Field Marshal Count Stedingk, one of the Swedish Senate and a person of the first rank in Sweden. Count Stedingk lived to a great age. He had, I think, served in the French Regiment 'Royal Suedois' before the great revolution, and against Russia in the War of 1788-9. In 1813 he filled a high place in the Army under Bernadotte in Germany.

Louise and Fredenkke, who is still unmarried, were in my time 'Hof Froekenen', Maids of Honor, to the Queen.

Perhaps I have devoted too much time to this love passage in my history, but I cannot have hardly passed it over with less attention, for it exerted a powerful influence over my mind and character, and that for many years.

Finding that I could do little in Norway during the winter, and that it

---

66[A family which had migrated to Norway from Germany. Other branches of the family went to the United States.]

67[The Norman papers at Maidstone contain at U310 C35 letters from various Norwegian friends of Norman, written in French.]

68[Kurt Bogislaus Ludvig Kristoffer von Stedingk, 1746-1837, successful Swedish army officer and diplomat. He was born in Pomerania, the son of an army officer; his mother was Countess Kristina Charlotta von Schwerin. At 13 he was an Ensign in the personal regiment of the Crown Prince of Sweden. In 1763 he began his military career in the Royal Suédois Regiment in pre-Revolutionary France. He served in America, in the French forces supporting the American Revolution. During the Swedish war with Russia started by Gustavus III in 1788 (see p. 217) von Stedingk commanded the defence of Savolax. In this he was very successful, and was promoted to Major General. He was subsequently appointed by Sweden to be Ambassador to Russia with which he forged close links. Recalled from Russia in 1811 he was made Field Marshall, and Supreme Commander of the Swedish army in Germany, commanding it in the battles of Grossbeeren, Dennewitz and Leipzig; see pp. 150-1. After the war he went to Sweden to claim compensation for damage done to his family's estates in Pomerania. In this he was unsuccessful. He was head of the Swedish War Academy 1818-26 and died in Stockholm at the age of 90.]

would be necessary for me to return thither in the spring for the purpose of overlooking the arrangements I had made with various debtors, and desirous of seeing my father and mother and of helping the former in his business, I determined to return home for a few months and took the route of Gothenburg. Myers accompanied me. We started in a sledge, but the snow deserted us near the Glomnen and I was forced to buy a carriage at Hafslund. Just beyond Srinesund Myers left me and returned to Christiania. I embarked once more on board the Thetis on the 23rd November, at Gothenburg and reached home in about ten days after a very disagreeable voyage. My health was greatly improved by this expedition and I had acquired great muscular power.

I am not sure whether I have mentioned that Howard Galton[69] left me very early in my Norwegian tour. He proceeded to Stockholm and thus commenced a course of travel, which has I fancy gone on, almost to the present time.

The year 1819 was I think that of the insurrection of the Army at Cadiz against the tyranny of Ferdinand VII.[70] This event excited the warmest interest in my mind. I have always deeply sympathised with Spain since its gallant efforts against Napoleon, and that interest continued most warm down to the

---

69 [John Howard Galton, the youngest son of old Mr Galton; see p. 187. Norman seems to have confused him with his nephew (Sir) Francis Galton 1822-1911, who was an inveterate traveller in his early years.]

70 [There was an army rising in Madrid, which was followed by Riego's coup d'état in 1820. There were a number of Carlist wars, in which pretenders fought to establish their claims to the Spanish throne. They occurred between 1833 and 1876. The Carlists were the followers of Infante Carlos, later Carlos V, and his descendants. They represented the monarchist and Catholic side, against the liberalism and republicanism of the Spanish governments. When Ferdinand VII died in 1833, his fourth wife Maria Christina became Queen Regent on behalf of their daughter Isabella II. War then followed between the supporters of Isabella and the Carlists who supported Carlos V, who was the brother of the late Ferdinand VII. The first Carlist war, to which Norman is referring, lasted more than seven years and ranged widely, though the main conflict centred on the Basque region. But there was a second Carlist war, 1846-9, and a third when Queen Isabella, as she had become, was removed by a conspiracy of liberal generals in 1868, although the main conflict was in 1872-6.]

close of the Carlist War. Alas! How have I been disappointed since. Agustin Arguelles[71] became an acquaintance of mine in England, and used to drive with me in Berkeley Square. He was an honest man and great orator, but had little statesmanship or common sense. In short a real Spaniard.

I have said some way back that I had kept journals of all my travels since that with Grote, but this I believe was a mistake. At least I can find nothing but a few notes as to my three last Norwegian expeditions.

It was during my visit to Norway in 1819, that I first acquired the habit of smoking, then uncommon in England. Cigars were almost unknown. I ordinarily used a long merschaum pipe and puffed away when I was reading, writing or travelling and that for hours in the day, when opportunity served. I never however smoked in the house at Bromley. In 1830 after my marriage, I ceased to use pipes, of which I had a large and rather valuable collection, and confined myself to cigars. Of these, I usually consumed two or at most three a day, after breakfast, luncheon and dinner. I never liked smoking with an empty stomach. This went on till 1850 when Headland, a sworn enemy to tobacco in all shapes, persuaded me to abandon my small modicum even of cigars. For the last 8 years I have never consumed anything larger than a cigarette, and for the last two years, I have abandoned even this small indulgence.

I cannot say that I have ever felt any mischief to arise from smoking in my case, but it must be recollected that I did not begin till I was twenty-six and I am very desirous that my sons should not smoke at all, or if absolute abstinence with the present habits of young men can hardly be expected,

[71] [Agustin Arguelles, 1776-1844, Spanish liberal politician and notable orator, who worked for free market reforms, the abolition of torture, and the prosecution of the slave trade. When in 1814 Napoleon was defeated for the first time, and Ferdinand VII returned to Spain as absolute monarch, Arguelles was imprisoned. But after the coup d'état of 1820 he was appointed Minister of the Interior. When the Bourbons regained control in 1823 he fled to Britain, returning to Spain in 1834. After the Revolution of 1836 he pressed forward radical policies, including confiscation of Church property. He was a Freemason.]

then that they should use moderation. I cannot doubt but that a very large number of young in this country injure themselves by smoking, and still more in Germany.

My love of snuff taking has been more inveterate and has lasted longer than that of smoking. It began when I was almost a boy, from my seeing on the chimney piece in East Street some cephalic snuff which had been recommended to my father for a defluxion in his eyes, and after a few years became a habit which continued down to 1851, when at Headland's earnest advice I broke the spell, alas! only for a time. For the last two or three years I have again taken snuff, and now in 1858, am resolved to make a vigorous effort to release[72] myself from its thraldom.[73] God knows if the effort will succeed and how much it will cost me. Happy are those who have never yielded to the allurements of tobacco in any shape.

Before I proceed further with my narrative, I will say a few words upon a matter of great importance which has had much influence on my conduct and happiness during a large portion of my life, and has also affected my treatment of my children.

I lived during all my youth and early manhood in an atmosphere of theological controversy. My grandfather was an Unitarian, my grandmother likewise.[74] They were personal friends of Lindsey[75] and Disney,[76] clergymen

[72] [Norman wrote 'reliese' here.]

[73] [Norman does not seem to have been successful in his aim to give up snuff. Mrs Grote wrote to her sister Mme F. von Koch 6 June 1876: 'I fancy my mind is still unimpaired. Old Snuffy, as we call G.W. Norman, declares that I beat him hollow at brain work; but the villain can travel 100 miles on the railroad and still be fresh, and ready for his dinner at the end of the journey. I gave him a petit diner here on May 27th, and we talked over old times.' *The Lewin Letters*, vol. 2 p. 336. The party included Gladstone, the Duke of Bedford, Thomas Henry Farrer of the Board of Trade, and others.]

[74] [James Norman, 1713-87; see p. 1. He married in 1751 Henrietta Wroughton.]

[75] [Theophilus Lindsey, 1723-1808, Unitarian Minister, arrived in London in 1774. With the help of Joseph Priestley, Richard Price, and other prominent Unitarians, he established the famous Essex Street Chapel. This was originally a rented room, though a chapel was built and opened in 1778.]

[76] [John Disney, 1746-1816, had married Lindsey's step sister, and joined Lindsey

who seceded from the church and established the chapel in Essex Street. Priestley[77] also was friend of theirs and I through my grandmother and father was well acquainted with Belsham,[78] who preceded Madge[79] in Essex Street and had a great respect for him.

My father was sent for three years to the Reverend George Walker, an Unitarian minister at Nottingham.[80] It is not to be wondered at then that he had strongly imbibed the opinions in which he had been bred, nor did he keep them to himself. Far from this, he was always bringing them prominently forward, with the firmest conviction that they most nearly represented genuine, unadulterated Christianity, such as it was, in the early days of the Church, among the immediate successors of our Lord.

In his days the Bishops and Ministers of the establishment were a very different set of persons, from their successors in the present day, and my father did not spare their shortcomings but enlarged upon them often and severely.

It must not however be imagined that he was insensible even to episcopal merit. He was a great admirer of the Butler,[81] used to speak with high

at Essex Street in 1783.]

77 [Joseph Priestley, 1733-1804, theologian and scientist. He supported Lindsey in establishing the Essex Street Chapel, which was the first openly Unitarian place of worship.]

78 [Thomas Belsham, 1750-1829, Unitarian Minister, adopted Unitarian theological beliefs by 1789 and succeeded Joseph Priestley at Gravel Pit Chapel in 1794. In 1805 he succeeded John Disney at Essex Street.]

79 [Thomas Madge, 1786-1870, Belsham's assistant at Essex Street after 1825. Had originally been Pastor of the Octagon Chapel, Norwich, 1811-25. He was at Essex Street 1825-60.]

80 [George Walker was the Minister of High Pavement Presbyterian Chapel at Nottingham. This later became the Unitarian Chapel. In 1774 he was appointed Assistant Minister at the Chapel, and for the next 25 years he enjoyed a dominant position in Nottingham's religious and intellectual life. A mathematician, he was a friend of Price (the Unitarian mathematician famous for fallacious calculations of the National Debt through the power of compound interest), and of Priestley, and a Fellow of the Royal Society.]

81 [Joseph Butler, 1692-1752. Originally a Presbyterian, he joined the Church of England, entered Oriel College, Oxford, and graduated in 1718. He was appointed to the lucrative living of Stanhope in Weardale by the Bishop of Durham, and as

respect of Pearce,[82] whom he recollected in his boyhood. Thought much of Horsley's[83] pulpit eloquence and lived on the most neighbourly terms with him, with Dampier[84] and with King.[85] Dampier used to pass hours and indeed days in looking over our engravings.

My father was a man of strong religious feelings, read the Bible, and I have known him cry over the sufferings of our Lord, for whose character, he had the most pious and profound admiration.

Circumstanced as I was, having one set of opinions daily impressed upon my mind with nothing to counteract them, it cannot be a matter of wonder that they obtained a mastery over me and that I became firmly convinced of their truth.

In subsequent times, I was thrown among men of great ability[86] whose views on the subject of religion, enforced with all the power of learning and of logic, were directed at revelation itself, and in some instances even at the great truths of natural religion. I did my best to overthrow the arguments thus brought to bear against opinions, the maintenance of which appears to me to be essential to the well-being, virtue and the happiness of our race.

Preacher at the Rolls Chapel. This he resigned in 1726. But in the same year he published 15 sermons delivered in that position, for which he was to become famous. He retired for the next seven years to Stanhope, but in 1733 he was made Chaplain to the Lord Chancellor, and in 1738 he was appointed Bishop of Bristol. In 1740 he became Dean of St Paul's. In 1750 he became Bishop of Durham. His *Analogy of Religion* (1736), a defence of revealed religion against the Deism so despised by Norman, is regarded as a major work of English theology.]

82 [Zachary Pearce, 1690-1774, Bishop of Rochester and Dean of Westminster.]

83 [Samuel Horsley, 1733-1806. His father was a Dissenter, but conformed to the Church of England in 1727. An opponent of Joseph Priestley, he was also a scientist – FRS 1767. Rector of Newington Butts, he was a High Churchman, but tolerant of Catholics.]

84 [Thomas Dampier, baptised 1749, died 1812, Bishop of Ely from 1808, book collector and half brother of Sir Henry Dampier, 1758-1816, Judge of the King's Bench 1813-16. Dampier was Bishop of Rochester 1802-8. The bishop's palace was at Bromley, which explains the freedom to visit the Norman family. He is regarded as having been a great scholar.]

85 [John Glen King, 1731/2-87, Rector of Wormley, Herts from 1783.]

86 [This is a reference to James Mill and George Grote; see p. 64.]

I never flinched from a firm avowal of belief in Christianity, which with its ennobling precepts and consolatory hopes is so admirably felt to satisfy the feelings and supply the moral wants and yearnings of mankind. No form of infidelity can do this. If a man is driven by the constitution of his mind, unfortunately for him, to reject the arguments and evidences adduced in favor of Revelation, he is to me an object of the sincerest pity. No man can derive pleasure from scepticism. No person enveloped in its mighty shadows can lead so happy an existence as he, who sees through the mystery of our being and future destiny by the clear light of revealed truth.

As for dogmatic infidelity, that which goes beyond simple scepticism and thinks it can reach positive results, I can hardly believe in the existence of a rational being holding that dreary opinion. Perhaps pantheism,[87] or Hegelism[88] may somewhat represent what I have alluded to, but as I have never studied them, or mean to do so, I cannot pretend to criticize them.

At the time which is now employing my pen, the form of infidelity which prevailed in Europe was deistical, of the kind which may best be described by calling it Voltairian.[89] It was to be found to a considerable extent in England,

[87] [The doctrine that God is identified with everything natural.]

[88] [Georg Wilhelm Friedrich Hegel, 1770-1831, German philosopher. In religion he was a follower of Fichte 1762-1814, who was highly critical of the idea of Revelation as the basis for religious belief. Hegel was influenced by Fichte's concept of 'subjective idealism' which involves not scepticism, however, but the idea that the individual has no existence independent of divine purpose. All phenomena have no separate existence, but are the product of divinely inspired human perception.]

[89] [Voltaire, pseudonym of Jean François Marie Arouet, 1694-1778, French philosopher, playwright, and historical writer. *Candide* (1759) is a novel in the form of a political and social satire. *La Pucelle*, to which Norman refers on p. 227, is Voltaire's ribald satirical poem about St. Jeanne d'Arc. He also published a *Dictionnaire Philosphique* (1764), which was highly sceptical in tone. He was a sworn enemy of the Catholic Church, as is apparent from the 1764 work. He was a Deist who, like humanists, believed that social morality was simply a human characteristic. Deism can be briefly defined as the belief in a God as merely a sort of divine clockmaker, with no further influence upon the world. It was however very much associated with opposition to Christianity and Revelation, notably in the work of Voltaire, but also in 18th century England. Voltaire's own Deism, however, evolved to include a theory of conscience implanted by God, and thence to a belief in a God, the essence of goodness with some direct relationship to mankind.]

in Norway and other teutonic countries. In Roman Catholic countries, it was still more widely and deeply spread, comprehending a large proportion of educated, and half educated men, fewer women. Its dogmatic teaching was of the most slender kind. Its positive arguments consisted mainly in attempts to shew the improbability of particular miracles as related in the Bible. The impossibility of miracles altogether. The faults of David, in spite of his having been called the man after God's own heart &c. Its favorite weapon was ridicule, which it employed not merely in attacking the truths of revelation but also against the holiness of marriage, chastity and other things which ought to be held most sacred among men. Candide and La Pucelle are living exponents of this school of philosophy with which it attempted to overthrow existing forms of belief and systems of morals, but substituted really nothing in their room. It made a great pretence of kindness and charity, but as its precepts in this respect were loose and ill-defined and without any sufficient warrant or sanction, and as they included the wildest licence for the free play of our selfish appetites and passions, they produced practically no beneficial influence.

To Voltairianism, I was ever most strongly opposed. It always excited my disgust and abhorrence, and I never heard its doctrines mentioned without striving to impugn them. Nothing can in my view be more base and crude than to attack by ridicule the religious opinions of others, especially when one has nothing to substitute in their room. Of course I do not mean to maintain that under no possible circumstances it is proper to use ridicule as an argument even in serious matters, but that this should be done sparingly, and never as the chief weapon. I would not even use it against a Mohametan.

Thank God Voltaireism has had its day, and may be considered in its most offensive shape, as almost extinct. It has been replaced by infidelity of perhaps a more dangerous character, but at any rate it is now felt by all that religion is a matter of the deepest import, that it concerns the holiest feelings of mankind, the happiness and safety of society and that these are not things to be disposed of by a laugh or a sneer.

I have often thought upon the possibility of a large civilised nation existing in peace and order without any religion at all. I think that this, perhaps some centuries hence, may be attempted, but of its speedy and entire failure, I have no doubt. If all existing forms of belief were to vanish from the minds of men, some new forms of belief would infallibly spring up to replace them. Even Comte,[90] the positivist, was compelled at least to swerve from his principles and construct a sort of religion for himself.

When I was in Norway, few of the educated classes in the towns ever went to church.[91] The believers in that class were idle and indifferent. I hardly ever went to a place of worship in that country, nor subsequently during my journeys on the continent, or made much difference between Sundays and other days. I never however ceased to be a Christian, nor neglected daily prayer, in my bedroom.

But although my faith was not overthrown by the attacks made upon it, yet it occasionally received some severe and painful shocks, and during a great many years, I suffered greatly from the difficulty of making up my mind upon several important points. This difficulty has been increased by a tendency in my mind to give the greatest weight to arguments leading to results which I most strongly deprecate. For many years, I have striven to

[90] [Auguste Comte, 1798-1857, regarded as the founder of positivism. He became a disciple of Saint-Simon in 1824. After a period of mental illness, 1826-7, he became a teacher of mathematics. One of his most famous works is his *Cours de Philosophie Positive* (1830-42, 6 vols.). He maintained that every science passed through three successive stages, beginning with the theological, followed by the metaphysical, and finally the positive. The fundamental principle of positivism was that sense experience is the only subject of human knowledge and its only criterion, and all theology and metaphysical speculation are without value. This fundamental assertion is not proved. Comte was however much admired by his contemporaries amongst English intellectuals, and he was in particular supported financially by George Grote, J.S. Mill and other friends, for which support he showed little gratitude.]

[91] [Norway had fallen under Danish control in 1536, and was then forced to accept the Lutheran faith. Catholicism did not again enjoy religious liberty until the mid-19th century.]

content myself with something less than absolute certainty, and have learned to tolerate the opinions of those who differ from me far more than I should have done forty years ago.

I desire specially to know what were the doctrines of St Paul, St Peter [and] other immediate Disciples of our Saviour? I cannot discover this, but am persuaded that they more nearly resembled those of the Unitarians than of any other sect. They certainly were not Athanasian.[92]

Looking back upon my own experience, I have avoided the discussion of polemical divinity with my children, leaving them to form their own opinions. There are more ways to heaven than one. I cannot teach them with any claim to infallibility, I might shake, without settling them. Of course, if I saw them likely to become infidels or even Romanists, I should strive to enlighten them to the best of my power. In short I have abstained from the enforcement of my peculiar views in religion on my children, not because I think them unimportant, but the very reverse. I am overwhelmed by a sense of their supreme importance, and fear to pull down, where I am not sure that I could build up.

It appears certain to my mind, that had not the Supreme Being designed to leave some latitude of belief among his feeble creatures, he would have revealed the truth more clearly to them. It must be further recollected that the faith of instructed, cannot be exactly that of the ignorant man. Happy is the man who without violence to his reason and feelings, can heartily adopt the religious opinions in the midst of which he has been brought up, and that, without mingling in the strife of controversy. But happier still, thrice happy indeed is he, whose faith has been rendered purer and firmer,

[92] [St Athanasius, c.296-373, Archbishop of Alexandria in the reign of the Emperor Constantine. He emphasised the doctrines of the Incarnation and the Trinity in Christian theology. It is remarkable that Norman, writing in 1857, should have maintained this view while at the same time being responsible for the establishment of a Church of England church on Bromley Common, from 1838, which was called unambiguously Holy Trinity Church.]

by having passed through the furnace of hostile discussion and whose armour has come out of the conflict still bright and unstained. He indeed may well thank a kind Providence for the misery he has escaped, and for the mental tranquillity he enjoys.

But to return to my narrative. Having determined to return to Norway in the Spring of 1820, I resolved to look out for a companion, having always had the greatest objection to either living or travelling alone. It struck me that Mr John Welsford Cowell,[93] a schoolfellow at Eton,[94] but with whom, I had perhaps never exchanged a word there, might like to accompany me. I had recently become acquainted with him as a great friend of my intimate friend C.H. Cameron. Mr Cowell readily accepted my proposal and from this time a friendship commenced between us of the most intimate kind, which continued unimpaired for more than ten years, and with some slight diminution afterwards, until about 1835 when, as will be related in its place, Cowell took offence at some part of my conduct, and ceased his intercourse with me. Since that time, we have met as acquaintances and have occasionally interchanged letters. The intimacy which once existed between us can never, however, be restored.

As will be seen hereafter, I owe to Mr Cowell a very heavy debt of gratitude. He in a manner devoted himself to me for years. He watched over me in sickness. He bore with the infirmities of my temper, and if with others

[93][John Welsford Cowell, 1796-1867, one of the founding members of the Political Economy Club, and its Hon. Sec. 1821-54, Treasurer 1831-4. He was in turn an Assistant Poor Law Commissioner 1832-4, member of the 1833 investigation into the employment of children in factories, an emissary from the Bank of England sent to investigate the state of the American banks (1837-9), and a government official in New Zealand, from which post he was dismissed by Lord Grey (O'Brien, *The Correspondence of Lord Overstone*, 1971 vol. 3 pp. 1077-8). In a pamphlet published in French in 1865 Cowell called for France to support the Southern States in the American Civil War. He had earlier published pamphlets in English calling for Britain to support the South. This appears to reflect a deep dislike of 'Yankees', probably stemming from his experience in America in the 1830s.]

[94][Cowell is recorded as being in the Upper School, Fifth Form, Lower Division, in H.E.C. Stapylton, *The Eton School Lists, from 1791-1850* (2nd edition, London: Williams, 1864) p. 68.]

irritable and captious, to me his forbearance and spirits of conciliation were most exemplary. I felt deeply my obligation to him and strove to evince the intensity of my feelings by my acts.

And here I ought not to omit to mention that I became a friend of Lord Overstone[95] mainly through Mr Cowell's introduction.[96]

Cowell's character: Mr Cowell is a man endowed with high mental gifts, eminently acute and subtle, with considerable power of acquiring knowledge and capable of great application in case of need. Certain defects of temper, which have become more apparent as he has advanced in age, have in a great degree marred his prospects in life, have greatly diminished his usefulness and have generally estranged from him almost all his early friends. These faults were for long time hidden from me.

Cowell and I travelled to Harwich and after staying a day there, embarked in the Thetis, Captain Living, and on I think the 30th April 1820, sailed for Gothenburg, where we arrived after a journey of seven or eight days.

My residence in Norway during the year 1820 much resembled that during the year 1819. I lodged with Cowell at Conditör Werner's but we dined at Schon's with Myers, was much employed in my business, made many excursions to Drammen and one to Schien, both to look after debtors. I also accompanied Cowell to Kongsberg to see the town and silver mines. This was an affair of pleasure. I went to the Court of the Akershusiske ridende[97] Jagercorps commanded by Baron F. Wedel-Jarlsberg at Gardermöen and thence accompanied Statzraad, afterwards Stadholder Løvenskiold,[98] to Statzraad

[95][See p. 251.]

[96][In 1821 Cowell had travelled in France with Overstone; see O'Brien, *The Correspondence of Lord Overstone*, 1971 vol. I, pp. 157, 160-1, 165, 167, 169, 174, 179, letters 8-15).]

[97][Aggershuske ridende or Akershusiske ridende is the cavalry of Akershus, a Norwegian county. The camp seems to have been at Gardermöen. Norman was moving from Kongsberg towards Ejdsvold, and this military area is on the route between the two places.]

[98][Severin Løvenskiold, 1777-1856, educated in Germany from the age of nine to that of seventeen. Subsequently he obtained a law degree at Copenhagen. Elected

Anker's at Ejdsvold.

Cowell did not always remain with me. On one occasion he went with Professor Keyser into the interior on a scientific trip, was upset in a kerriol[99] and confined in a bonde's[100] house for many days with a sprained ancle, where he was greatly captivated by the pretty daughter of his host.

During the whole of the summer and autumn, I was constant in my visits at Lille Fragner and drank in large drafts of love from the pretty eyes I saw there, but upon this matter, I must refer to my details as to last year.

I used very frequently to pass the Sunday at Bogstad, Count H. Wedel-Jarlsburg's and enjoyed the benefit of my kind host and friend's most interesting conversation. He used always to keep open house on Sunday. Sometimes there would be forty people at dinner, but if the weather was bad, hardly more than the family. There was always however enough to eat. How this was managed I could never exactly understand, for there never appeared any great superfluity, the number of dishes was nearly the same with a small as with a large party.

1820 was a year of great political excitement. I recollect on one occasion at Bogstad Count Wedel came to me with a newspaper in his hand, told me there had been another revolution and asked me to guess where. I guessed wrong, it was at Naples.[101] At that time, and for long afterwards, I rejoiced at any thing in the shape of a revolution and could hardly imagine how

to the constitutional assembly at Ejdsvold in 1814, and was an enthusiastic member of the group advocating union with Sweden. He was Governor General of Norway under the Swedish Crown, 1841-56, and encouraged the development of railways, telegraph, and postage.]

[99] [A cariole (or carriole) was a type of carriage used in the nineteenth century, a light two or four wheeled vehicle drawn by a single horse. The name can also be used for a dog-drawn toboggan.]

[100] [A bonde is a Norwegian free landowner and farmer.]

[101] [In 1815 Ferdinand, the Bourbon King was restored to Naples. His rule was severe, and in 1820 revolution broke out in Naples. Ferdinand then swore to accept a democratic constitution. However the Austrian army soon suppressed the revolution, and the Bourbon dynasty lasted until the entry of Garibaldi into Naples in 1860.]

any attempt to overthrow an established government could be other than meritorious. In that respect experience has changed my views greatly and has probably rendered me wiser. It must be recollected however that the old despotisms of forty or fifty years ago were far worse than any thing of the kind that now exists, excepting perhaps in Turkey or Persia, and that mankind had not been then enlightened by the conduct of Mazzini and such like firebrands.

Both in 1819 and 1820, I had an opportunity of seeing the King Carl Johan[102] and also the Crown Prince Oscar now the reigning sovereign.[103] My first presentation to the King took place in company with Myers. We were told that we should be received as foreigners, privately after the general Levée. I wore a white Kovseymen, breeches, made for the occasion by Skredder Abel and now kept in my clothes press as a relic, white silk stockings, white waistcoat and a blue coat. This was a recognised Court costume. We were introduced into an anteroom at the door of which stood as sentinel, my friend Hans Faye,[104] in the yellow uniform of the Horse Burgher guard, sword in hand and looking very worldly. I peered down a passage and saw the King with his coat off washing his hands. On being told of our arrival he put on a dress coat with many orders, came out and talked to us in French very graciously for a few minutes. He asked me how much I was owed in Norway, and on being told £60,000 or £70,000,[105] mentioned the amount to

[102] [Charles XIV, Bernadotte; see p. 160.]

[103] [Oscar I, born Joseph François Oscar Bernadotte, 1799-59, was King of Sweden and Norway 1844-59. Unlike his father, he quickly acquired the Swedish language, and became popular. He advocated liberal measures, including education and prison reform. Indeed his father became suspicious of his close ties with the liberal opposition.]

[104] [The Faye family, thought to be of French origin, came from Orkney to Norway, and Marckus Faye was sworn in as a citizen of Bergen in 1642. The two main branches of the family were in Bergen and Tønsberg. There is also a branch of the family called the Christiania Fredrikshald branch, and two branches in Dramen. It is not known with which branch Hans Faye was associated, though that in Christiania (Oslo) seems the most likely.]

[105] [Equivalent to £4,566,100 in 2009 prices.]

his son, remarking that it was a very large sum. He asked us to dinner more than once and gave us a real good feed. I often saw him afterwards both at Christiania and Bogstad, and also at balls given at Ullevold and Fragover and at Etterstad.

He lodged at what had been Bernt Anker's house,[106] a miserable substitute for a palace. The new palace near the Drammen Road was not commenced until some time afterwards.

The King's expenditure must have been very large, far exceeding his allowance, if I recollect aright 64,000 shillings, or at the then exchange about £8000[107] per annum but he had a large private fortune, which I believe that he mainly dissipated in loans and gifts and in purchases of estates intended to relieve embarrassed owners and finally in abortive speculations.

Bernadotte, although a little disfigured by a nose of extravagant dimensions was a very handsome man, tall, dark with black hair, and features expressive of ability. His talents were evinced by his keeping possession of two thrones,[108] under most difficult circumstances. He was I believe of a kind and humane disposition talked much and well and was very profuse of promises, which were not always performed. He was a true Gascon.[109] In his manner, nothing appeared, which betrayed his humble origin.

The Crown Prince was tall and thin with regular features and a mild and expressive countenance. In an hussar uniform, well-padded he looked very handsome, I recollect cutting ducks and drakes with him on the lake at Bogstad.

---

[106] [Bernt Anker, 1746-1805, was reputed to be the richest man in Norway. On the Anker family see p. 214. Bernt Anker was the owner of a mansion called Paléet. It has been described as a palace. It was built by his father Christian Anker in the years 1744-55, with a garden stretching to the sea. He left his house for public use, and his garden to the cathedral school.]

[107] [This would be £521,840 in 2009 prices.]

[108] [See pp. 171, 211 concerning the union of Norway and Sweden in 1814.]

[109] [Gascony is a province in the south west of France, containing the départements of Landes, Gers, Hautes Pyrénées, and Basse Pyrénées. Pau, where Bernadotte was born, was the capital of French Navarre, which was united to France in 1598.]

The year 1820 was remarkable in my career because I then first commenced the study of geology from which I subsequently and for a long period derived both health and pleasure.[110] Cowell and I began by working together but he soon gave the matter up, having no real taste for it. This was unlucky for me as it deprived me of a companion who could assist me and sympathise in my enthusiasm.

Professors Keyser and Esmark[111] were very kind to me. The latter had been a disciple of Werner and was a believer in the Neptunian theory, until his dying day.[112]

The dirtiest man I ever saw, unable to speak any language intelligibly, but learned, simple, benevolent and on the whole an excellent person. To me

[110] [Norman continued his interest in geology for many years, and references to the geology of Norway, Wales, and the Cotswolds, in particular, will be found in the Autobiography. Though Norman makes no mention of this, he was elected a Fellow of the Geological Society, 3 February 1836. However, though his death was reported to a meeting of the Council of the Society, 1 November 1882, no obituary appeared in the Society's *Quarterly Journal.*]

[111] [Jens Esmark, 1763-1839, was an expert mountain climber and Professor of Mineralogy who is recognised to have contributed to many of the initial discoveries and analyses of glaciers. He was the first person to climb many of Norway's highest mountains. He believed that glaciers had been larger and thicker, and had covered much of Norway and the sea floor surrounding it, recognising glaciers as powerful agents of erosion that had carved the Norwegian fjords. In conjunction with his son, Hans Morten Thrane Esmark, he made important mineral discoveries.]

[112] [The rival geological theories of the time were Hutton's theory, called the Plutonian Theory, and the Wernerian or Neptunian Theory. The rival geological theories were associated with Abraham Werner, 1749-1817, who believed that all rocks originated in the ocean, and James Hutton, 1729-97, who showed that this was incorrect as certain rocks were igneous and had cooled from a melt. These were volcanic rocks, such as basalt, and plutonic igneous rocks notably granite. Hutton emphasised the continuity of geological processes. The Plutonian theory involved the idea that the causes at present working on the surface of the globe were those which had been entirely responsible for the form of its surface, having been in operation for many millennia. The Wernerian theory distinguished between causes still in operation, and others which had ceased to act as the earth cooled and granite was formed. As strata were formed they were again fractured and other strata deposited. In the process of these changes, the continents rose above the level of the waters. In Werner's theory all rocks are thus of marine origin. Werner is now regarded as a founder of mineralogy and petrology. Esmark had been a disciple of Werner and was a believer in the Neptunian theory, as Norman correctly recalled.]

he usually spoke a mixture of English, French, Danish and German. He used to roam about the country in a Kerriol, making observations and collecting specimens and has been known to throw into the middle of the road in front of a post station the few clean clothes, which his daughter had put into a portmanteau for him, and replace them with stones. Such behaviour, joined to his uncouth manners and appearance, created a strong opinion among the peasants, that he was mad. I must add that in those days and in all countries, the popular views as to the sanity of geologists were[113] not favorable.

I will cite one of Esmark's replies made to myself in answer to the question, 'Mr Professor, do you ever find granite stratified?' Mange manger you find de granit en couches, and mange manger you not find it.

It was remarkable that a man so well-informed and intelligent as Esmark should remain a convert to the Wernerian system.

Jacob Keyser Professor of Chemistry[114] at Christiania, was a very different person. He had married an English woman, was intelligent, a good linguist and man of the world. I liked his society greatly and enjoyed it for many years, both in Norway and in England. Towards the end of his life he got into pecuniary difficulties and borrowed £100 of me,[115] which I lost.

Before I went to Norway in 1820 I bought at Knights[116] two hammers, both steel,[117] the one large and heavy, with a convex extremity designed to break off specimens, the other small for the purpose of shaping them. I had also an instrument intended to measure the inclination of strata, with a compass attached to it. All these are still in my possession, after having travelled with me full 10,000 miles, and of this distance, many 100 miles in my pockets or slung over my back.

My fondness for geology was long very great and had I now to choose one

---

[113] [Norman wrote 'was' here.]

[114] [Norman wrote 'chymistry' here. On Keyser, see p. 215.]

[115] [This would be worth £8,674 in 2009 prices.]

[116] [R. and G. Knight, Ironmongers, 41 Foster Lane, Cheapside.]

[117] [Norman wrote 'stealed' here.]

favorite study with which to begin life anew, I should hesitate between it and archaeology.[118] For many years it furnished me a vast deal of pleasure, and when in a new country it occupied a great deal of my time and attention.

I was unfortunate in never having a friend possessed of similar taste, from whom I could derive sympathy or instruction. Almost all I ever knew was drawn from books or from my own observation. After having studied the primary and transition (now silurian[119]), formations in Norway, the volcanic systems of Auvergne, and of Italy and the tertiaries of various countries, I became a passable geologist for those days. The vast extention of the science in later times, especially as regards organic remains, has left me almost an ignoramus, the more so as I have had little opportunity of keeping up my knowledge or power of observation. I have never however ceased to take an interest in geological matters.

I very early perceived the nonsense of Wernerianism and acknowledged the great truths that the crystalline rocks had resulted from igneous fluidity and that the land had been elegated above the waters. Many geological memoranda will be found among my papers and some of my collections are interesting.[120] There is also an article of geology which I wrote for a magazine called [blank in original], written by Miss Fry, subsequently Mrs Wilson, a friend of ours.[121]

---

[118] [Norman seems to have been particularly interested in the Saxons. In the Norman papers at U310/Z50 there is a pamphlet *Remarks on the Saxon Invasion*, dated 1879.]

[119] [This is a geological term for the third paleozoic system of strata. The Silurian began between 435 and 460 million years ago, and ended about 405 million years ago. Rocks of Silurian age are also to be found in Wales, southern Scotland, the Lake District and western Ireland.]

[120] [In one of the four boxes catalogued under the single number of U310/F37 in the Norman papers at Maidstone, there are geological papers.]

[121] [Caroline Fry, 1787-1846, was born in Tunbridge Wells, the daughter of John Fry, a gentleman farmer. She was educated at home until the age of 17. After spells as a companion/governess, and a conversion to evangelical Protestantism from the High Anglicanism of her upbringing, she wrote poems and hymns, but after illness she turned to writing as a source of income, and over the years 1823-8 she published 10 volumes of *The Assistant of Education, Religious and Literary*,

I have often lamented that I did not publish a work on Norway after my return from it in 1820.[122] I knew the country, its laws, history, social state &c at that time better than any other Englishman, better than any Englishman, Laing included,[123] who has ever written upon it and I am persuaded that I could have produced an interesting and instructive work. I think upon the whole that no class of writers come up so little to the beau ideal as those who undertake to describe foreign countries. They are usually in a high degree ignorant, inaccurate and superficial. De Tocqueville,[124] Kohl[125] and

---

which enjoyed widespread patronage. Norman's curious phrasing here, using 'written' rather than 'edited' reflects the particular format of *The Assistant.* No other authors were acknowledged, though the enormous range of subjects in volumes of 400 pages makes it clear that Miss Fry employed other hands extensively. The failure to acknowledge the primary contributors means that Norman's own contribution, probably rewritten in any case by Miss Fry, since the style of the volumes is uniform, cannot be identified. It does seem that she must have obtained contributions from a number of people with expertise in geology, for volumes V, VI, VII, VIII and IX each contain six articles in the form of 'Conversations on Geology', a total of thirty articles. Her later religious writings also enjoyed success. In 1831 she did indeed become Mrs Wilson, marrying William Wilson, a merchant. They settled firstly at Blackheath, and then moved to Woolwich. She died at Tunbridge Wells, 17 September 1846.]

122[Though Norman did not publish a work on Norway in his lifetime, there exists a posthumous publication. It appeared in Norway as *Mine Erindringer fra Norge* Af G. Norman (*My Memories of Norway* by G. Norman) translated by T.H. Aschehoug. Oslo: Groendahl and Sons, 1898.]

123[Samuel Laing, 1780-1868, was not an Englishman but a Scotsman. He came from Kirkwall on Orkney, originally a Norwegian possession. After travels in Germany, and service in the Peninsula, followed by working as a mine manager in southern Scotland, he returned in 1818 to Orkney. Facing business ruin, he left Orkney in 1834 and lived in Norway 1834-6. In *Journal of a Residence in Norway*, 1836, he idealised the Norwegian peasantry. Sympathetic to the Norwegians, he was subsequently very critical of Sweden (*Tour in Sweden*, 1839). Laing was to influence John Stuart Mill, who expressed great enthusiasm for peasant cultivation. With the exception of his enthusiasm for the Norwegian peasantry, Laing as a travel writer was bitterly critical of countries he visited.]

124[Alexis Charles Henri Maurice Clérel de Tocqueville, 1805-59, French historian. He went to America in 1831 and subsequently produced *De la Démocratie en Amérique*, 1835-40, now regarded as a classic account of popular government.]

125[Johann Georg Kohl, 1808-78, German travel writer, historian and geographer. After studying law at Goettingen, Heidelberg and Munich, he published *Der Verkeher und die Ansiedlungen der Menschen in ihrer Abhängigkeit von der Gestalt der Erdoberfläche* (*The Transport and the Settlements of People in their Dependence on the Shape of the Earth's Surface*), 1841 and 1850. He formulated

Humbolt[126] are among the rare exceptions who now strike me.

Having completed my business in Norway so far as circumstances allowed, I started with Cowell from Christiania early in December, having taken a somewhat tender leave of Louise v H and travelled to Gothenburgh. There we found the inevitable Captain Living with the Thetis. Two or three days elapsed before our embarkation, during which we enjoyed the hospitality of Mr James Dickson[127] who had a pretty Swedish wife[128] and subsequently acquired a very large fortune, of Mr Alexander Barclay and of M. La Chaumette des Fossés the French Consulate,[129] a learned man of high accomplishments but of epicurean habits, who strove to make the most of all the good which life presents, taking a special care of health first of all. He had previously been employed at Constantinople and Bucharest and subsequently went to Lima in Peru.

James Dickson was uncle to the Dickson whom we met at Carlsbad,

a mathematical theory of the development of spherical cities. In 1854 he travelled to the United States, where he published a book on travels in Canada and the states of New York and Pennsylvania (1856), and he was commissioned by the US Congress to compile a history of the discoveries of the western, southern and eastern coasts of the country, resulting in a collection of nearly 1,000 drawings.]

126 [Friedrich Wilhelm Karl Heinrich Alexander, Baron von Humboldt, 1769-1859. His early publications were in geology. In 1799 he went to South America and spent five years exploring Venezuela, Columbia, Ecuador, Peru, Cuba and Mexico. He subsequently published 30 volumes, *Voyages aux Régions Equinoxiales du Nouveau Continent*, 1807. In 1829 he journeyed through central Asia, on which he subsequently published a work primarily concerned with geology and climate.]

127 [The son of James Dickson, 1748-1826. There was a large Scottish colony at Gothenburg, attracted by the fact that it was outside the Continental blockade of 1806-12. It thus became an important transit port. Given the difficulties faced by Norway because of the British blockade, Norway's ruler Denmark being in alliance with Napoleon, Swedish timber operations developed and the leading figures in this were Robert and James Dickson from Kelso or Montrose. The firm James Dickson and Company became one of the largest commercial operations in Gothenburg, and in addition to the timber business the firm operated a significant merchant fleet which also exported iron ore.]

128 [James Dickson married Christian Murie, 1755-1813. They had ten children. However Norman must have been referring to the younger James Dickson, 1784-1855, who married Margaretha Eleonora Bagge, 1795-1857. They had six children.]

129 [Jean Baptiste Gabrielle Amedée Chaumette des Fossés, 1782-1841, book collector and diplomat, who was eventually Consul General in Peru.]

labouring under a liver complaint, of which he has since died.

Just at this time the Queen Caroline trial was going on in England.[130] While stopping to change horses at a post-station near Uddewalla, we observed a number of people carousing, and on asking what was the occasion of the festival, were told Dronningen av England er frikjendt. The Queen of England is acquitted. Thus the cruelty and perfidy and baseness of George IV had awakened sympathy for his ill-used and profligate wife even in the distant North.

Two or three days after leaving Gothenburg, the wind became contrary and weather bad; and we put into Arendal subsequently removing to Grimstad. At both places I was well known, and we were most hospitably received. Dinners and suppers were given to us daily, at one of which Captain Living got very drunk.[131] At another I was asked whether I had any objection to drink the Queen of England's health the remark being added that it was always drunk at Grimstad. Of course I said 'no', so we had the toast with many hurraahs and hobbynobbing.

The Thetis had finally a very bad passage across the North Sea of eight days, in which we narrowly escaped shipwreck among the sands on the Norfolk coast. We landed, I forget whether at Lowestoft or Harwich and I reached home the day before Christmas day. I was rapturously received.

These two trips to Norway had been of the greatest benefit to my health. I had become, in spite of labour, anxiety and love, plump and very strong

[130] [Caroline Amelia Elizabeth, 1768-1821, Queen of Great Britain, wife of George IV, daughter of Charles William Ferdinand, Duke of Brunswick, and of Princess Augusta of England, the sister of George III. She married the Prince of Wales, as George IV then was, in 1795. After the birth of a daughter in 1796 a formal separation took place, and in 1814 Princess Caroline moved abroad to escape her husband. When she became Queen six years later she returned to England, and a bill to divorce her was introduced into the House of Lords. She was defended with great eloquence by Lord Brougham, and the bill was not proceeded with. She was subsequently excluded from her husband's coronation and died a few days later.]

[131] I saw Captain Living some months ago. He called upon me at the Bank. He is now a landsman, and Chairman of some Metropolitan Board of Guardians. [Note added by Norman in July 1864.]

and active. This improvement in some respects was permanent, not so in all as will subsequently appear.

My endeavours to recover the Norwegian debts had in a great degree failed. Great losses had also been incurred among the yardkeepers and my father's business had almost ceased to yield a profit. Under these circumstances, with a noble disregard of self, my father determined to let our house at Bromley for three years and to remove to Hastings, where he hired a house belonging to old Wenham the Smuggler on the East hill.[132] Mr H. Meux the brewer, subsequently Sir Henry,[133] became his tenant agreeing to pay £500 per annum rent, free of all taxes, rates and repairs. He subsequently hired Baston farm at £150 per annum in addition. Our wine-cellar was locked up and sealed. The outer cellar being used by Mr Meux. The prints were all sent to Frognall where the late Lord Sydney[134] allowed them to remain, much I believe to his own inconvenience, a strong proof of his neighbourlike and friendly feeling.

132 [As noted on p. 44, the tenancy of Norman's father, described as 'George Norman, the Blackfriars merchant of the same family as Montagu Norman of the Bank of England', was recorded in the remarkable book by M.A.N. Marshall (*Hastings Saga*, 1953, p. 12) long before the discovery of Norman's Autobiography.]

133 [Sir Henry Meux, 1st Bt, 1770-1841, of the Horseshoe Brewery, Tottenham Court Road, London.]

134 [John Thomas Townshend, 2nd Viscount Sydney, 1764-1831, died at Frognall. Under Home Secretary 1783-9, a Lord of the Admiralty 1789-93, Lord of the Treasury 1793-1800. The 2nd Viscount was succeeded by John Robert Townshend, 1805-90. Frognal House, Foot's Cray near Sidcup was the birthplace of the 1st Viscount Sydney. It was bought by the father of the 1st Viscount Sydney, the Hon. Thomas Townshend, who died in 1752. It later became famous as Queen's Hospital, Sidcup.]

# Chapter 8

# The Bank and Economic Studies

Just before we left Bromley an event happened, which had a most important influence upon my subsequent career. I was calling on George Grote, when his father[1] remarked to me, 'Why do you not strive to get into the Bank Direction?' I told him that such a thing had never entered my mind. He enlarged upon the advantage and honor that attended it and advised me to consult my father and if he approved then to speak to Mr Manning.[2] My father, to whom in his younger day the same thing had been suggested, had no objection and I drove over to Combank where Mr Manning then resided and consulted him. He strongly advised me to persevere, indeed he took me under his patronage, telling me however that I must not expect to get into the Bank Court for some time to come, if at all. This was in February 1821. Judge then of my astonishment when in a few weeks afterwards, I received a note from him to say that I was in the house lists and would be recommended to the proprietors at the April election.

Accordingly at the day of the election I appeared in what was then consid-

[1] [George Grote, 1762-1830, a London banker.]

[2] [William Manning, 1763-1835 (see pp. 8, 11), a Director of the Bank of England 1792-1831, Deputy Governor 1810-12, Governor 1812-14, had purchased in 1813 the Coombe Bank estate at Sundridge, near Sevenoaks, for £40,000. In 1831 he became bankrupt.]

ered full dress. Colored coat, white waistcoat, tight pantaloons, silk stockings and pumps. The Governors used in those days to exercise a very strict surveillance over the costume of directors especially of the juniors and I have known a Director ordered to go home and to change his habilliments.

The suddenness of my elevation to the honor of a Seat in the Bank aroze from the unexpected retirement of two or three gentlemen of whom I recollect Holford[3] and S. Thornton[4] as two who declined to take the Chairs which then was a matter of obligation, unless in the case of age or infirmity. Directors excused on this account become a sort of retired admirals and took their Seats in Court, just below the committee of Treasury. I found two of these milites inveteri, Langley[5] and Smith.[6]

I entered the Bank with three colleagues, D. Barclay,[7] Cockerell[8] and Porcher,[9] and it is remarkable that we have not furnished a Governor among us. Barclay retired early in consequence of the events of 1825, Cockerell and Porcher remained longer.

The Governor and Deputy Governor in 1821 were C. Pole[10] and J. Bow-

---

[3][John Josiah Holford, born 1765, date of death unknown, a Director of the Bank 1805-20.]

[4][Samuel Thornton, 1754-1838, MP Hull 1784-1806, Surrey 1807-18, a cousin of William Wilberforce, a Director of the Bank 1780-1836, Deputy Governor 1797-9, Governor 1799-1801.]

[5][Thomas Langley, 1755-1829, a Director of the Bank 1798-1825, London merchant.]

[6][Henry Smith, 1760-1826, a Director of the Bank 1802-26, a merchant in Laurence Pountney Place, London.]

[7][David Barclay, 1784-1861, second son of Robert Barclay of Bury Hill, Surrey, a Director of the Bank 1821-6. He was MP for Sunderland 1841-7.]

[8][John Cockerell, 1787-1869, a Director of the Bank 1821-37.]

[9][Henry Porcher, a Director of the Bank 1821-39. No further details available.]

[10][Charles Pole, 1772-1864, partner in the firm of Pole, Thornton and Company, a Director of the Bank 1796-1843, Deputy Governor 1818-20, Governor 1820-2. Pole, Thornton and Company failed in the crisis of 1825, and Sir Peter Pole was connected by marriage with the Governor of the Bank, Cornelius Buller, forcing the Deputy Governor John Baker Richards to take the lead in handling the crisis. See J.H. Clapham, *The Bank of England*, Cambridge: Cambridge University Press, 1944 vol. II p. 99.]

den,[11] neither of them deficient in ability, although utterly without the scientific knowledge which a Director of the present day would be expected to possess. The other members of the Committee of Treasury were persons of still humbler grade of intellect. Jeremiah Harman who had long ruled the Bank with almost despotic sway, was ignorant, pompous, prejudiced, and overbearing.[12] The opinion of a junior, if opposed to his, he hardly thought of answering, excepting by an exhibition of scorn and contempt. Manning and Mellish,[13] amiable but feeble, Dorrien feeble but less apparently amiable, in fact a nobody.[14] Pearse a man of some sense, but little knowledge.[15]

The most powerful man among the Dir[ector]s was old Samuel Thornton, the senior, elected in 1780. He was a man of strong mind and general ability. His courage was displayed in the equanimity he shewed in the almost utter wreck of his fortune, brought about by the absurd speculations of his partner Bailey about 1810, and in his undergoing an operation for the stone at the age of 75.[16] His ability was conspicuous in all he said. Unfortunately he was

[11] [John Bowden, 1770-1844, a Director of the Bank 1803-41, Deputy Governor 1820-2, Governor 1822-4, wine merchant.]

[12] [Jeremiah Harman, 1763-1844, partner in the firm of Harman and Company, a Director of the Bank 1794-1827, Deputy Governor 1814-16, Governor 1816-18. Norman's dislike of Harman was such that, despite his own interest in painting, he fails to mention that Harman was a notable collector of paintings and, when his collection was auctioned at Christie's in the May following his death, the sale, which attracted great attention and included works by Reynolds, Van Dyke, Rembrandt, Poussin and other notable artists, realised nearly £27,000. According to a contemporary report of the sale, 'His pictures attracted the admiration of all who were capable of judging of their merit, and were hardly surpassed by any private collection in Europe.' The Harman home at which this magnificent collection was kept was Higham Bensted, Essex, a substantial area of 477 acres.]

[13] [William Mellish, 1764-1838, MP Grimsby 1796-1807, Middlesex 1807-38, a Director of the Bank 1792-1838, Deputy Governor 1812-14, Governor 1814-16.]

[14] [George Dorrien, 1769-1835, partner in a banking firm in Finch Lane, a Director of the Bank 1794-1835, Deputy Governor 1816-18, Governor 1818-20.]

[15] [John Pearse, baptised 1759, died 1836, clothier and financier, MP Devizes 1818-32, a Director of the Bank 1790-1828, Deputy Governor 1808-10, Governor 1810-12.]

[16] [Samuel Thornton was the elder brother of Henry Thornton, 1760-1815, one of the most famous of economic writers. Samuel succeeded his father as head of the family business in Hull in 1790, trading with the Baltic. By about 1810

by nature sly and a thorough intriguer. He liked secret paths and crooked ways and it was with the utmost difficulty one ever arrived at a knowledge of his real wishes and opinions. He has more than once encouraged me to make a suggestion or bring forward a motion in Court and then opposed me. These peculiarities in the character of old Sam deprived him of that influence, which were otherwise due to his talents and experience.

At the time I entered the Bank Direction the power of the old aristocracy, embodied in the Committee of Treasury, which had previously been omnipotent, began to wane, not but that it still governed the proceedings of the Court. The voice of opposition was however heard from time to time on the right hand of the Governor and the leaders of the malcontents were W. Haldimand[17] and W. Ward,[18] who ventured to assert that it was not

the business had got into difficulties and temporarily halted trading. He sold his estate at Albury, Surrey in 1811 for £72,000. He eventually recovered much of his wealth, and at his death in 1838 he was worth close to £45,000, a very large sum for probate in those days.]

[17] [William Haldimand, 1784-1862, son of Anthony Francis Haldimand, a London merchant, MP for Ipswich, 1820-6, a Director of the Bank 1809-24, died at Denantou near Lausanne where he had settled in 1826.]

[18] [William Ward, 1787-1849, was a Director of the Bank 1817-36. He was the second son of George Ward (died 1829) a London merchant and Hampshire landowner, of Northwood Park, Isle of Wight, by Mary, daughter of Henry Sampson Woodfall, and a partner in business with his father in 1810. He was the youngest Director in 1819, at the time of the Resumption of Cash Payments (that is, of convertibility of the note issue into gold), and dissented from the views of the senior Directors. MP for the City of London, 1826-31. He was also a great cricketer who saved Lords from speculative building, and father of William George Ward, a celebrated Roman Catholic theologian. There is a serious error in the *Dictionary of National Biography* entry on Ward, apparently based upon a misreading of Clapham's *History of the Bank of England.* The entry refers to Ward's evidence before the 1831-2 *Committee on the Renewal of the Bank Charter* (*Parliamentary Papers* 1831-2 vol. VI). Ward gave evidence on 19 June (qq. 1822-1927, pp. 126-30) and 21 June (qq. 1928-2149, pp. 130-49). The relevant passage is qq. 2073-5. Contrary to the impression given in the *Dictionary of National Biography*, vol. 57, pp. 361-2, it is not correct that 'on 6th December 1827 he moved and carried a measure rescinding its [the Bank's] policy of reducing its issues so as to obtain a favourable turn in the exchanges'. On the contrary, examination of Ward's evidence shows that the resolution that Ward caused to be rescinded in 1827 was one stating that the Bank itself did NOT agree with regulating the circulation of its notes by the exchanges. Ward was opposed to the Bank establishment, which believed that the money supply should respond to demand for Bank accommodation, and he told

always safe to discount all the bills that might be tendered at a fixed rate of interest. That it was wise in managing the Bank to advert to the state of the exchanges and finally, oh scandalous heresy, that the notes had been depreciated by over-issue. I gradually joined this small minority, taking care however and especially as I was the youngest member of the Court not to give any just offence to the seniors by a peremptoriness of tone, or offensiveness of manner.

Just as I entered the Bank, the resumption of cash payments took place and at every meeting of the Court, the proportion between the sovereigns issued and the £1 and £2 notes paid off, used to be announced from the Chair. For some time the amounts were nearly equal.

I forgot previously to mention that during my visits of form to the members of the Committee of Treasury Mr Thornton asked if I was in partnership with my father. Upon my saying 'No', he remarked that he never knew an instance of a Director being chosen who was not actually a merchant. Mr Manning who was present remarked to him that Mr Bosanquet never was a merchant.[19] Upon mentioning this to my father he at once proposed to alter his firm to G. Norman and Son.[20] This was done at once and circulars issued accordingly, but no articles of partnership were ever drawn up. I drew what money I required for my private expenses and my father never questioned me about them.

On the removal of the family from Bromley to Hastings, I took up my residence at number 21 Earl Street, Blackfriars where the business had been carried on since 1810 and continued to live there until July 1822, when I was

the Committee in his evidence that he was embarrassed to find himself in this position as early as 1819 (q. 2078). Ward was thus a natural ally for Norman, as Norman relates here.]

[19][Samuel Bosanquet, 1744-1806, a Director of the Bank 1771-1806, Deputy Governor 1789-91, Governor 1791-3.]

[20][In the Norman papers at U310/B12 there is Assignment by George Norman of London, merchant, to his sons George Warde Norman and Richard Norman of his business, carried on in Earl Street, Blackfriars, London, dated 1822. There is also the notice of this as published in the *London Gazette*.]

compelled by bad health to go abroad. There were no clubs in those days, and Richard[21] and I kept house with an establishment of two servants. I kept a horse, and took long rides for the sake of exercise when I could find a leisure afternoon. Even then I found it difficult to get out of London. On Sunday, I attended the chapel in Essex Street, where I had a regular sitting. Belsham was the minister and my private friend. I recollect his delivering a course of lectures on the Epistles of St Paul, which seemed to me the most powerful defences of revelation I had ever heard. I remember on one occasion, a Mr Fox of Norwich preached.[22] I believe the present member for Oldham to be the man.

I used now and then to go to Hastings for two or three days at a time, but this happened rarely, certainly not more than once a quarter, for it took a whole day to go there, unless one travelled at night by the mail, which I hardly ever did, on account of the disagreeables attending that mode of conveyance.

I also visited the Rohdes at Oakley,[23] the Wells at Bickley,[24] the Cum-

[21] [Norman's brother, born 20 October 1800, died 7 March 1860.]

[22] [The Reverend William Johnson Fox, 1786-1864, Unitarian Minister at Chichester, 1812-17, leading orator of the Anti-Corn-Law League, MP Oldham 1847-62. He was Minister of a chapel built for him at South Place, Finsbury, London, 1824-52. Though Fox was born in Suffolk, the family had moved to Norwich when he was a child, and it was there that he grew up.]

[23] [Major (a name not a title) Samuel Rohde of Oakley Farm, Kent was in the sugar refining business but also became an entrepreneur in the coal trade. As a sugar refiner he is listed in the 1812 Post Office London Directory at 28 Wellclose Square and 86 Leman Street. He was the son of Peter Rohde, who was a sugar refiner. The family, Norman notes in his Bromley Memoir, was of German origin. Norman's father bought Oakley House from the Rohde family in 1825 for £20,000, on Norman's advice. There are papers of 1827 relating to the purchase of Oakley Farm in the Norman papers at U310/A168A. According to Norman's account in his Bromley Memoir, Oakley was originally a farmhouse, as he discovered, as its later owner, when repairs were being carried out in 1850-1. Between 1760 and 1770 it was possessed by a West India merchant named Lewis Brotherson who was said, by Norman's father, to have had black servants whom 'he governed with a whip and treated like slaves'. He was succeeded by a member of the Mitford family, and then by Admiral Cornwallis, from whom Rohde purchased the property about 1795.]

[24] [William Wells of Bickley, shipbuilder of Deptford, 1729-1805, father of

mings at Trent Park,[25] H.C. White at Two Waters[26] and Sir S. Scott at Sundridge.[27] An invitation to the latter place was a great compliment and implied as I thought a tacit permission to pay my addresses to Anna Maria, who was then a pretty and agreeable person. I might perhaps have availed myself of this opportunity, had it not been that I had no idea of marriage and that the image of Louise was still fresh in my memory. Perhaps I was wrong in my supposition.

The visits above alluded to involved the sleeping from home, but I also dined out occasionally, and often went on a Sunday evening to Octagon House

---

Thomas Wells, Vice Admiral, 1759-1811, sold Bickley Hall to his brother John Wells, who was a partner in the Blackwall shipyard and the banking firm of Whitmore Wells; see p. 112.]

[25][Trent Park was at that time the home of John Cumming (died 1832, aged 75), a Russia merchant, who married Eleanor (Nellie) Hunter, who, as Norman relates, had been the companion of Norman's mother, and was the sister of the second Mrs William Manning. It was part of Enfield Chase. In 1777 George III gave the site to Richard Jebb, as a reward for saving the life of the King's younger brother, the then Duke of Gloucester, at Trento in the Tyrol. Richard Jebb was the King's doctor. A deer park was laid out, and Sir Richard Jebb converted one of the old Enfield Chase hunting lodges into a villa known as Trent Place, in honour of Trento. The architect of the house was Sir William Chambers, and the grounds were landscaped, reputedly by Humphrey Repton.]

[26][Henry Campbell White owned a number of properties in Hertfordshire, notably the Corner Hall estate. Two Waters was a hamlet in the parish of Hemel Hempstead. The nature of Norman's connection with Henry Campbell White is at first puzzling. There is no other mention of H.C. White in the Autobiography, and none in the Bromley Memoir. However the connection is to be found, as with Charles Boulton, through the timber trade. Henry Campbell White was a partner in the timber firm of John White and Sons, together with John White and William White. The firm was sold to Benjamin Sewell, in which Richard Norman, Norman's brother, was a partner, in 1833.]

[27][There were two estates bearing this name. One was about 3 miles south west of Sevenoaks in Kent. The other however, the home of the Scott family, was on the north east side of Bromley. It is now the location for the Sundridge Park Management Centre.]

at Wimbledon, the residence of Mr Tooke,[28] where I met Grote, Ricardo,[29] Malthus,[30] Mill,[31] McCulloch[32] and other men of mark.

It must have been in 1821 that I was first introduced by Cowell to S.J. Loyd, now Lord Overstone, who has been for many years one of my most

---

[28] [Thomas Tooke, 1774-1858, born at Kronstadt, Russia, eldest son of the chaplain to the British 'factory' at Kronstadt. He began working, in Russia, at the age of 15. He subsequently moved to London, becoming a partner in Stephen Thornton and Company, and Astell, Tooke and Thornton. FRS 1821. He was an important economic writer, and a major figure in 19th century currency debates. His main addresses seem to have been in London, at 12 Russell Square, Richmond Terrace, and at 31 Spring Gardens, where he died in 1858. Norman reports Tooke as living in Wimbledon in 1821, but it is not clear how long he stayed there.]

[29] [David Ricardo, 1772-1823, stockbroker and economic writer, made a fortune dealing in government stock and retired 1814. MP Portarlington 1819-23.]

[30] [Thomas Robert Malthus, 1766-1834, economic writer, Professor of History and Political Economy at the East India College at Haileybury 1805, FRS 1819.]

[31] [James Mill, 1773-1836, author of a history of British India and of works on economics. One of the leading Utilitarian propagandists of his day, and the father of John Stuart Mill.]

[32] [John Ramsay McCulloch, 1789-1864, pioneer writer on economics and of economic journalism, editor of the *Scotsman* 1817-21, prolific author, Professor of Political Economy at University of London 1828-37, Comptroller of the Stationery Office 1838-64.]

intimate friends.[33] We had been at Eton together but he being my Senior,[34] had perhaps never exchanged a word there.

S.J. Loyd then resided with his father[35] in Norfolk Street, Park Lane. I was speedily struck by his great abilities and the many admirable points in his moral character. He is, I think, the most acute man I ever met with. The readiness and logical power with which he can decompose, as it were, the most complicated question, resolving it into its most simple elements and arranging them in proper order and applying to each the full force of his admirable judgment, have often excited my wonder and delight.

---

33 [Samuel Jones Loyd, 1796-1883, was a close friend and advisor of Norman, and their relationship forms the backbone of the three volumes of *The Correspondence of Lord Overstone*, edited by D.P. O'Brien (Cambridge: Cambridge University Press, 1971). He was the son of a former Unitarian preacher called Lewis Loyd, born in 1769, who had married Sarah Jones, the daughter of a Manchester banker, and transformed an obscure country bank into one of the leading private banks. In the process he made a fortune from the gilt edged market during the Napoleonic wars and, although precise figures are not available, a reasonable estimate, based upon subsequent wealth, would suggest that Lewis Loyd may have made even more money out of the market than the celebrated market operator David Ricardo. Overstone was born in September 1796, and was thus three years younger than Norman. Like Norman he attended Eton, but unlike Norman he went on to Cambridge. After Cambridge he joined the bank of Jones Loyd, and was also an MP (for Hythe) in the unreformed Parliament, from 1819 to 1826. He was never again an MP, and after an unsuccessful attempt to be elected to the reformed Parliament he seems to have been banned by his father from further political involvement. Overstone ran the bank of Jones Loyd, working with two of his cousins, with considerable success, although his remarkable father, who did not die until 1858, was in the background and was a widely respected City figure, as was his son. But in 1850 Samuel Jones Loyd was raised to the peerage as Lord Overstone, through the agency of Lord John Russell, and retired from the bank, being replaced as a partner by Norman's brother Henry. Throughout the 1830s, 1840s, and 1850s, he exercised a powerful voice on questions of monetary reform, working with Norman and Robert Torrens.]

34 [Norman presumably meant to write 'Junior' as Overstone was born in 1796. Like J.W. Cowell (see p. 230), Overstone, then Samuel Jones Loyd, is recorded by H.E.C. Stapylton as being in the Upper School, Fifth Form, Lower Division, in 1811.]

35 [Lewis Loyd, 1769-1858, Overstone's formidable father. Originally a Unitarian Minister, he had married Sarah Jones, 1759-1821, the daughter of a Manchester banker, in 1793. He left the Unitarian ministry, and joined the bank. He rapidly became the driving force behind the firm, which he transformed from an obscure country bank into onc of the leading private banks. Like Ricardo, he made a huge fortune and became one of the City's most powerful figures; see pp. 297, 341, 364.]

He is not a man of very extensive knowledge, but whatever he desires to learn, he learns well.

His talent of exposition is unrivalled. Nothing can equal his powers of language, both written and spoken. He is a most eloquent speaker and had he begun sufficiently early, so as to overcome his natural nervousness, would I think have become the first orator of the day. Highly as he is looked up to by the public its estimate of him is far too low.

It was most unfortunate that he was defeated in a contest for Manchester about 1834, as success there would have compelled him to speak.[36] He had been a silent member of the old House for many years.

As a man of business he was most distinguished for application, thorough knowledge and sound judgment, and was proportionately successful.

He is a thoroughly truthful and honourable man, kind too, considerate and ready to help those less favoured by fortune. Some peculiarities of temper, added to the envy excited by his enormous wealth, have tended to diminish his popularity.

I regard the steady friendship which he has shown me for nearly forty years, as a high honour, and hope to retain it till my dying day. Of all my friends he is the person to whose advice I have ever resorted with the greatest confidence in all cases of difficulty.

I have always considered that the State has incurred a heavy loss, from the fact that Lord Overstone has never been called upon to fill important offices.

I must now advert to a circumstance, which has had a very important

[36] [On this electoral episode, see D.P. O'Brien (ed.), *The Correspondence of Lord Overstone*, Cambridge: Cambridge University Press, 1971 vol. I pp. 20-1. There were later approaches to Overstone to stand for Parliament (O'Brien, 1971, p. 231) in 1837 (Oxford) and 1841 (South Lancashire) but, faced with his father's opposition, Overstone declined to go forward as a candidate. On his silent membership of the unreformed (pre-1832) Parliament, see O'Brien (1971, p. 16). He was MP for Hythe, 1819-26. If *Hansard* is to be believed he did not speak, although he is said to have been active in committees.]

influence on my career and enabled me perhaps to do some good in my generation, I mean the direction of my studies towards political economy.

As early as 1817 I had begun to pay some attention to this subject, one of the most important as respects the happiness and prosperity of nations. In 1817 and the succeeding years, I read with attention the works of J.B. Say,[37] Adam Smith[38] and Malthus, and formed to myself sufficiently clear ideas upon the leading doctrines of the science as they were then known. The most important practical result to which I arrived was a thorough conversion as to the advantages of free trade, from which, among many other changes of opinion, I have never in the slightest degree swerved. It may have been that the heavy losses, which had been brought upon Norway and upon my father, by the enormous duty imposed on foreign timber in 1811, somewhat sharpened my views upon this subject.[39] Still the line of reasoning applicable to it seems to me so thoroughly convincing that had I been disinterested, I could never have come to a different result.

Early in 1821 some question was raised by the ministry of the day as to a modification of the timber duties and I wrote in consequence for distribution a short pamphlet, which was begun and completed in about four days of hard work.[40] I have not seen it for many years, but suppose that a copy may exist among my papers. I gave a copy to Mr Samuel Thornton, who after reading

---

[37] [Jean Baptiste Say, 1766-1832, French economic writer and businessman. His *Traité d'Economie Politique* appeared first in 1803, and went through a number of editions. He is particularly famous for having stressed the circularity of the economic system, with aggregate demand generated by incomes received in return for productive activity.]

[38] [Adam Smith, 1723-90, the most famous author in the entire history of economics, and author of *The Wealth of Nations*, 1776. Professor of Moral Philosophy at Glasgow 1752, Vice Rector 1762, Lord Rector 1787.]

[39] [Discrimination against Baltic timber began in 1809, and was intensified up to 1814. In 1809, 428,000 tons of British shipping returned from the Baltic with imports; in 1814 the figure was 242,000 tons. By 1816 the figure had fallen to 181,000 tons. Of course not all of that shipping carried timber, as Danzig was a major port for grain. See J.R. McCulloch, *A Dictionary of Commerce and Commercial Navigation*, London: Longman, 1832 pp. 1039-40.]

[40] [*Hints on the Timber Trade* is amongst the Norman papers at U310 Z4.]

it, told me that I was the sort of person required in the Bank Direction.

Sometime afterwards I wrote a mock petition from the market gardeners to the legislature asking for protecting duties against foreign fruit. It was inserted in 'The Traveller' then edited by the present distinguished lawyer, Walter Coulson.[41]

I was told that it attracted the attention of Jeremy Bentham and was highly praised by him.[42]

I was one of those who signed the petition from the merchants of London in favor of free trade.[43] This document was drawn up by the late Mr Tooke and is probably the best piece of writing which he ever put upon paper. It told the whole truth, was plain, lucid and convincing and acquired many adherents for the cause, so far as to induce them to give their signatures, although some so little appreciated its doctrines as steadily to resist their practical application, especially if this application in any way appeared to touch the private interest of the signers.

The Political Economy Club was instituted in 1821[44] and I was among

[41][This is reprinted in Norman's *Papers on Various Subjects* (London: T. and W. Boone, 1869) pp. 3-7.]

[42][Jeremy Bentham, 1748-1832, British writer on law and economics, regarded as the great patriarchal figure of British Utilitarianism. Bentham campaigned for causes close to Norman's heart, especially reform of representative government, and reform of the Poor Laws, and for other issues on which Norman remained silent, such as prison reform, criminal law reform, and reform of the legal system. But the ideological framework involved in all of these was Utilitarianism, and this Norman embraced enthusiastically.]

[43][Tooke was prominent amongst those calling for freedom of trade after the end of the Napoleonic wars, and was responsible for the Petition of the Merchants of the City of London, which was presented to the House of Commons by Alexander Baring, later Lord Ashburton, 8 May 1820. It is discussed in vol. VI of the great book by Tooke and William Newmarch, *A History of Prices and the State of the Circulation*, a six volume work appearing over the years 1838-56. It may well be that the Merchants' Petition was the springboard from which the Political Economy Club was founded in the following year, 1821. On the foundation of the Club see *Political Economy Club, Centenary Volume*, London: Macmillan, 1921.]

[44][The Club was founded 18 April 1821, at 13 Russell Square, the home of Swinton Holland, a partner in Baring and Company, and those present were Tooke, Robert Torrens, Norman, James Mill, Cowell, Holland himself, George Larpent, Robert Mushet the statistician, and J.L. Mallet, whose diaries were later to provide

the original members, of whom I think that Cowell and perhaps Coulson,[45] are the only other persons who survive and still belong to it, Torrens[46] and McCulloch[47] and Grote having retired. I have certainly derived great advantages from my association with the many distinguished men, who have at different times, belonged to the Political Economy Club and from listening to their arguments and opinions.

At the commencement, our meetings were peculiarly interesting and instructive. Ricardo used to propound and explain with inimitable clearness and precision the fundamental truths and doctrines of the science, such matters then formed the ordinary subjects of discussion. We now employ ourselves, less usefully, as I think, upon the practical influences from these primary doctrines, and upon mixed questions, in which politics and morals are involved, as well as the science which treats of the production of wealth.

I may here remark that I have rarely if ever met with Ricardo's equal in logical power and that when at Munich in 1823, I heard of his untimely death, I regarded the event as a national calamity. I doubt if his close intercourse with Mr James Mill was not injurious to the quality of his mind in later years. I say this however, without meaning the least disrespect for the latter, who in

an important account of proceedings at the Club. Coulson was not among those present. The first meeting at which his presence was recorded was that of 3 December 1821. Grote appears only shortly after the foundation, in the meeting of 30 April 1821. Tooke is certainly regarded as the prime mover in the foundation of the Club, and Norman, one of the founder members himself, remained in the Club, and spoke at the banquet in 1876 which the Club held to honour the 100th anniversary of Adam Smith's *Wealth of Nations.* Norman was, particularly in the early years of the Club, an assiduous participant in its proceedings.]

45 [Walter Coulson, 1794-1860, lawyer, member of the Political Economy Club, and one time editor of the *Traveller* and of the *Globe and Traveller.*]

46 [Robert Torrens, 1780-1864, Royal Marine officer, Lieutenant Colonel 1819, FRS 1818, a founder member of the Political Economy Club, MP Ipswich 1826-7, Ashburton 1831, Bolton 1833-5. He was, with Overstone and Norman himself, centrally involved in developing the theory that lay behind the 1844 Bank Charter Act, and in particular with the replacement of a discretionary system with a rules-based system of monetary control. He was, after 1844, in the forefront of defending the operation of the Act.]

47 [Norman wrote 'Maculloch' here.]

his way was a great man, although one sided, from the want of imagination and anything like poetry in his composition. These defects led to his gigantic errors in politics and religion.

I have taken a fair share in the discussions at the Political Economy Club, but seldom in the way of opening questions, indeed I do not think that I have ever opened half a dozen.[48] My abstinence from doing so has mainly arizen from my being shy and nervous and not liking it to be obliged to express my views upon a difficult and complicated subject with the risque of breaking down. It is the same feeling which has gone far to keep me out of Parliament, and in fact has rendered me unfit for public life. I have before now laid awake all night in terror and bathed in perspiration at the idea of making a speech at a public meeting the next day. Yet strange to say, when the moment of trial has arrived, the giant, which so affrighted me, has turned out to be a dwarf.

Towards the end of 1821, I commenced an essay on taxation, redolent of Bentham and Mill, the object being to shew, how all the revenue of a country might be levied with least pressure on the taxpayers.[49] The conclusion to which I came was that a single property tax and that only was the scheme which offered the greatest advantages, as taking least from individuals and imposing the fewest sacrifices on them. I was so far I believe right, if people could only be found to agree with me in feeling, but that they never will do

[48] [Norman participated in the Proceedings of the Political Economy Club rather more than this comment might suggest. His questions included the connection between the rate of profit and interest (1822), three questions (connected with his work on his *Essay on Taxation*) on the best mode of taxation (1822), direct versus indirect taxation (1828), a single property tax (1829). All of these reflect the continuation of his work on the *Essay*. Then, after a long gap, when Norman was working on the first edition of his *Essay on the Pressure of Taxation*, there are two questions; whether British prosperity was checked by taxation (1849) and whether taxation was heavier in Britain than in other countries (1850). Norman's final question was on the impact of the gold discoveries on the value of gold (1857).]

[49] [Norman's *Essay on Taxation* has now been published as *Taxation and the Promotion of Human Happiness. An Essay by George Warde Norman.* Edited by D.P. O'Brien with John Creedy, Cheltenham: Edward Elgar, 2009.]

and it is probable that an attempt to establish one sole tax in England or France, would infallibly fail, and if persisted in, would occasion commotions and civil war. Upon another important matter, I was decidedly wrong. I proposed to capitalize all incomes not in their nature perpetual and to tax them in proportion to their capitalized value. The discussions upon the income tax during the last few years have led me to reconsider at this point and I now feel thoroughly convinced that justice demands an equal tax upon all incomes, whatever may be their probable duration. The arguments adduced by Warburton[50] and others are quite irresistible, and I came to this result in a discussion with Hubbard sometime ago.[51] The tax on a terminable annuity appears at first sight to be the heaviest, but this is only apparent. It ceases with the annuity, while that on a perpetuity lasts for ever.

It must be remarked however that to make an equal tax on terminable annuities just, the tax must be perpetual. If temporary, it is unjust.

My essay on taxation was never printed but still exists in manuscript. It cost me a vast deal of thought and labour. I may here remark that I have ever found composition to involve a severe strain on my whole organism, one reason why I have written comparatively so little. Perhaps if I had tried narrative or description instead of subjects involving so much of argumentation, I should have been able to write more and better.

---

[50] [Henry Warburton, 1784-1858, politician. He ran the timber business of his father, John Warburton, in the years 1808-31. FRS 1809. Member of the Political Economy Club. MP Bridport 1826-41, Kendal 1843-7. On the influence of Warburton see the introduction to Norman's *Essay on Taxation*, p. xxvii.]

[51] [John Gellibrand Hubbard, 1st Baron Addington (1887), 1805-89. From 1821 he worked in his father's business which had branches in both London and St Petersburg, the former involving banking, and the latter involving textiles. He married Margaret, daughter of the 9th Lord Napier. Hubbard was a Director of the Bank 1838-89. He was Deputy Governor 1851-3, Governor 1853-5. He was Chairman of the Public Works Loan Commission from 1853 until his death. MP Buckingham 1859-68, City of London 1874-87. Hubbard fought continuously for a reform of the income tax, through the introduction of differential rates of tax on income from activity on the part of the taxpayer and income from investments. See D.P. O'Brien (ed.), *The History of Taxation* (London: Pickering and Chatto, 1999) vol. VI. See also the introduction to Norman's *Essay on Taxation*, p. xxvii.]

# Chapter 9

# More Illness and Travels

I had returned from Norway, fat, strong and vigorous, and continued in fair health during the whole of 1821, but early in the following year the scene changed. My stomach became deranged and very distressing nervous symptoms supervened. Disgusting and morbid thoughts and sensations plagued me, almost day and night. Medicine gave me no relief, and it was at length determined that I should make an excursion of a few weeks on the continent and I selected Auvergne and its volcanoes as the district to be visited.

My kind friend Cowell who had no profession offered to accompany me, and we embarked at Brighton for Dieppe on the 6th July 1822.

At this time my father had a house at Brighton in addition to that at Hastings, in consequence of an opinion of the doctors, that the climate of the latter place did not suit my sister Charlotte.

My absence from London necessarily recalled my father to East Street, which he had hardly seen for one-and-a-half years. This fact caused me the sincerest sorrow for I could not bear to think that so fond a parent at his advanced age should be obliged to sacrifice his tastes, and ease and domestic enjoyments in consequence of my infirmities.

Among the passengers who accompanied Cowell and myself from Brighton were General Buller[1] and Colonel now Sir J.M. Wilson[2] of Chelsea Hospital whom I saw afterwards at Paris, and with whom I have kept up an acquaintance ever since. He is a distinguished soldier, having been in the navy, and wounded before he entered the army. His blood has been repeatedly shed in his country's service, but his last wound was inflicted in a duel, by a person, even whose name he did not know after a quarrel in a coffee house. The conduct of George IV being the matter in dispute. Wilson had been hit at the first fire, in the leg. At the second fire he hit his antagonist in the breast, and is even now ignorant of what became of him, or of the result of the wound.[3] I have thought this story worth recording.

We travelled from Dieppe to Paris by Yvetot, Rouen, Pont de l'Arche, Mantes and St Germain. I was much pleased with the country, as appears by the notes I made of this tour to which I refer for further information.

After staying a short time at Paris we left it on the 14th July, passed through Fontainbleau and admired the forest which on a very small scale put me in mind of Norway, slept at La Bussierre, and on the 16th July reached Riom,[4] from which we visited the Lava Quarries of Volvic and also the Puy de la Nugère and Chavoudiat.[5] From the crater of the former a lava stream has flowed and is even now in appearance almost as fresh as that produced

---

[1] [General Sir Frederick William Buller, died November 1855 aged 83. He was the father of General Sir George Buller, 1802-84.]

[2] [Sir John Morillyon Wilson, 1783-1868, distinguished professional soldier. Wilson's challenger has not been identified, but he acted with little regard for the danger, for Wilson was a much decorated veteran and a soldier with a remarkable record. After wartime service in the navy, in the course of which he displayed conspicuous bravery, Wilson was invalided out in 1803. But he recovered sufficiently to enter the army, served in the Walcheren expedition, in which he was wounded, and later served in the Peninsula, taking part in major engagements. He subsequently served in Canada in the war with the United States, was wounded seven times, and left for dead on the battlefield, recovering as a prisoner of war in American hands. Although on half pay from 1822, he rose through the ranks and reached the rank of Colonel in 1837. He was Major of the Royal Hospital Chelsea from 1855 until his death in 1868.]

[3] Sir J.M. W[ilson] rece'd message to say he was dead.

[4] [This is quite a large town north of Clermont Ferrand.]

[5] [Norman did not make clear that this was another Puy.]

by a recent eruption of Vesuvius.[6]

On the 18th July we went on to Clermont where we remained several days, making excursions to all the places in that neighbourhood, possessing either picturesque or scientific interest and these are numerous. Our companions were an old soldier named Rougeot,[7] who supported himself chiefly by keeping a school but also by acting as guide and selling minerals, and an honest peasant named Bonnieu who had fought in the levée en masse,[8] which had taken and plundered Lyons in 1793. This man furnished and drove our patache[9] and formed such an attachment to us, as to beg us earnestly to take him to England.

Rougeot affected to be a Royalist, Bonnieu a Republican, and their friendly disputes and arguments used to furnish us the greatest amusement as did Rougeot's campaigning stories. For details as to our expedition, I must once more refer to my notes written at the time.

On the 24th July we left Clermont, slept at Rochefort,[10] and on the following day arrived at the Baths of the Mont d'Or.[11] There we took up our quarters, at one of the two lodging houses which the place contained,

---

[6] [In the 18th century a French geologist, Jean Etienne Guettard, 1715-86, first noticed the resemblance to Vesuvius. The Puy overlooks Volvic, and the pumice stone and areas of lava confirm the theory that these were volcanic mountains. In 1752 Guettard announced his findings before the Académie des Sciences but his theory was not accepted for more than a quarter of a century.]

[7] [There is some correspondence from Rougeot amongst the Norman papers at U310/C37.]

[8] [Literally mass uprising, a French term for mass conscription during the French Revolutionary wars. It was applied particularly to the form of mass conscription from 23 August 1793. Despite the rhetoric of the revolutionaries, the Levée en Masse was not popular, and there were widespread attempts to evade it. Though it produced enough manpower to turn the tide in favour of France in the war with European states, regular organised conscription was introduced in 1797.]

[9] [Literally, travel at a very low price. This seems to have been a basic horse-drawn carriage.]

[10] [This was probably Rochefort Montagne, north of Mont Dore (or d'Or, as Norman spells it) near Orçival. There is however also Rochefort north west of Clermont.]

[11] [Mont Dore is the conventional spelling.]

breakfasting and dining every day at a table d'Hôte, with from forty to fifty, ladies and gentlemen, many of them belonging to the first families of France, both Royalist and Imperialist. There were no Republicans in those days. Among them were many interesting and agreeable people, who treated us, the only English present, with the utmost kindness and attention. We used to ride and walk daily to all the most remarkable places in the neighbourhood, to which I need not now refer as details of these expeditions with the names &c of our companions are contained in my journal.

This was the only time in my life that I ever had an opportunity of seeing much of French society and I thoroughly enjoyed it. Our friends comprehending people of all parties, amused us greatly by confiding to us their several grievances and their accusations against their opponents.

I may here remark as respects the ladies, without as I hope incurring any charge of ingratitude for the amiability they always evinced to us strangers, that I was greatly struck by their general want of personal charms and with the vivacity of their attacks on the good things, fish flesh and fowl, with wine, fruit &c, which were set before us twice a day.

It has always appeared to me, as very remarkable, that the English should be regarded by all foreigners as great eaters. So far as my observation goes the very reverse is the truth, and the English consume less food than the French, Germans or Scandinavians.

During the latter part of our residence at the Mont d'Or, Cowell was attacked by influenza and was attended by Dr Bertrand,[12] the official physician of the place, upon the P'tisan system,[13] the great advantage of which in com-

[12][Alexandre Jacques François Bertrand, 1795-1831, a French physician and physicist, and native of Rennes. He was the father of the mathematician Joseph Bertrand. He was associated with the Saint-Simonians, and is remembered for scientific investigations concerning animal magnetism, somnambulism, and hypnosis.]

[13][This involved a nourishing decoction (boiling down so as to extract the essence) especially of barley water.]

parison with the strong cathartics[14] and sudoforics[15] of English practitioners, I have from that time thoroughly appreciated.

My visit to Auvergne greatly augmented my geological knowledge, as I had there an opportunity of studying the phenomena of volcanoes and their products in almost endless variety. The study gave me intense pleasure and my little cabinets still contain numerous specimens, the result of my explorations in 1822.

On 9th August we left Mont d'Or, returned to Clermont and thence to Paris by our former route intending to proceed to England, but at Paris circumstances happened which altered all our plans and have influenced my whole existence from that time to this.

My foreign trip had done me good, had salved over the mischief by soothing to a certain extent the extreme excitability of my nervous system, but the evil still existed and it was soon brought into fearful activity.

We reached Paris on the 15th August and I felt the utmost dread at the prospect of returning to my past avocations, to which a few weeks before I had proved so unequal. At this time there occurred the unhappy death of either Lord Londonderry or Sir S. Romilly I forget which,[16] and I who felt many sensations, which I deemed quite irrational, was seized with the notion that I was no longer master of my own actions and that their fate would be mine. No words can describe the horror I felt. Cowell was afraid to leave me even for a moment and was placed in a condition of the greatest difficulty.

[14] [Purgatives.]

[15] [Drugs causing perspiration.]

[16] [Sir Samuel Romilly, lawyer, law reformer and politician, 1757-1818. He is reported to have experienced symptoms not unlike those described by Norman himself. After the death of his wife, 29 October 1818, he suffered a mental collapse, and cut his throat on 2 November. This is thus almost four years before the time that Norman was in France. The death to which he meant to refer was that of Robert Stewart, Viscount Castlereagh, 2nd Marquess of Londonderry, 1769-1822, who cut his throat with a penknife 12 August 1822. He had been Foreign Secretary and Leader of the House of Commons, 1812-22, but he suffered a mental breakdown in the spring of 1822.]

Nothing could exceed his kindness. Had I been his brother, it could not have been greater.

He determined to consult Dupuytren, then the most celebrated practitioner at Paris, who was making £200,000 per annum[17] and Dupuytren[18] gave me advice, which I am convinced was on the whole most injudicious. A course of munatic acid[19] medicine and marriage, would I doubt not have cured me. But I recollect Dupuytren's expression. He said 'Je pourrais bien vous draguer mais cela ne menerait a rien. Ne retournez pas chez vous, allez, courez partout, amusez vous. Abandonnez la café, le thè, la viande et le vin. Ne mangez que le poisson, les legumes, des oeufs, de temps en temps, des puddings.'[20]

The recommendation as to diet, I consider to have been specially ill-timed and as having greatly tended to keep up that morbid condition of the digestive organs, upon which doubtless my suffering mainly depended. I persisted however in abstinence till I reached England in the Spring.

Thus, then it was resolved that we should direct our course to the South instead of the North, a carriage and a courier, one Vincenzo Cantrivi[21] who had served Lady Oxford[22] were hired, and in order to lighten Cowell's respon-

[17] [This would be worth £12,748,000 in 2009 prices.]

[18] [Guillaume Dupuytren, 1777-1835, regarded by medical historians as a dazzling technician and eloquent lecturer. He studied medicine in Paris, and his early studies were directed chiefly to anatomy. In 1811 he was appointed professor of surgery, and in 1816 he became head surgeon at the Hôtel-Dieu. Active there both in operating and in lecturing, as well as in advising out-patients like Norman, he amassed a fortune. A medical pioneer, he was one of the first surgeons successfully to drain a brain abscess, using trepanation. He is said to have gained much esteem for treating Napoleon Bonaparte's haemorrhoids. He is best known for Dupuytren's contracture, in which the fingers bend towards the palm and cannot be fully straightened, which he described in 1831. He developed an operation to correct it.]

[19] [Or muriatic acid; both are old terms for hydrochloric acid, though muriatic can simply mean relating to brine or salt.]

[20] ['I could well purge you but that would achieve nothing. Do not go home. Go, travel around, enjoy yourself, give up coffee, tea, meat and wine. Eat only fish, vegetables, eggs and, from time to time, [plum] puddings.']

[21] [Probably – manuscript not clear.]

[22] [Jane Elizabeth née Scott, the sister of Norman's friend Hobbes Scott. She

sibilities, a medical attendant was engaged under Dupuytren's advice whose name was Sanson, and he proved an intelligent and amusing companion, and travelled with us for several weeks, leaving us at Florence.

My family was of course informed of what had occurred and my brother Henry who had just taken his degree at Oxford was forthwith dispatched to join us.[23] He proceeded to Geneva where we found him on our return from Chamouny.

I will now say something more as to the symptoms of my malady. I sometimes suffered from a fearful nervous agitation, during which violent perspiration would break out. Sometimes from a feeling of concentration in which my whole being appeared to be fixed in that part of the forehead, just above the brows. When in this state I found it almost impossible to direct my attention to any thing external or indeed to abstract my thoughts from a painful perusal of my own condition and prospects. I suffered much from sleeplessness and found the only remedy to be fatigue produced from bodily exercise pushed to excess.

---

married in 1794, Edward Harley, 5th Earl of Oxford; see p. 143.]

[23][Henry Norman matriculated at Oxford 13 March 1819 aged 17, BA 1822. Henry later became a partner in Jones Loyds, the family bank in which Overstone was a partner and which he left on receiving a peerage. The intention was that Henry Norman should replace Overstone. See the letter from Overstone to his father Lewis Loyd, 22 January 1850, in O'Brien, *The Correspondence of Lord Overstone*, 1971, vol. 2 p. 475. According to Overstone's letter, it was Overstone's retirement which was the occasion for the invitation to Henry Norman to join Jones Loyds. Henry had previously been a partner in Bouverie, Norman and Murdoch of 11 Haymarket, from 1831. See *London Gazette* 18 January 1850 p. 196 for the dissolution of this partnership between Philip Pleydell Bouverie, Henry Norman and James Gordon Murdoch, dated 22 January 1850. However problems later arose. In a letter to Norman of 26 February 1864, *ibid.* vol. 3 pp. 1029-30, Overstone refers to his cousins Lewis Loyd Junior and William Jones Loyd, and told Norman that, 'The incapacity of your Brother to render efficient assistance in directing and controlling the general management of the business, and thus relieve his partners occasionally from the necessity of their personal attendance, is a great embarrassment'. Henry Norman died 28 December 1867, and according to a letter from Overstone to Norman of 30 December 1867 (O'Brien, 1971, vol. 3 p. 1135), he had suffered from a prolonged illness such that 'life had ceased to be a field of enjoyment or usefulness'.]

As for my mental condition, besides the horrible fear to which I have before alluded and which constantly haunted me, there was an indescribable feeling of self-disgust at the vague notion that I was not what I ought to be. General depression of the most painful kind was either superadded to or grew out of these separate annoyances.

I could not bear to be alone even for a few minutes. Society was most painful and the sight of an old friend induced me to avoid him.

Every place which I visited however interesting in itself caused me painful sensations in a short time, and I was driven from it in order to seek in vain repose somewhere else.

The dread of insanity which so long pursued me, was unaccompanied so far as I know and believe by the slightest approach to its reality. My memory was as retentive, my judgment as sure, and the reasoning faculty as powerful, as they had ever been. I was conscious of all this and well aware also of the fortunate social position in which I was placed. Some additional suffering aroze from this very circumstance. It was so difficult to explain the coexistence of all these things with the dark cloud of despondency, which constantly overshadowed my very being upon any idea that my intellect was entire. Yet there can be no doubt, but that my malady was purely physical.

In one important respect, my illness differed altogether from that under which I had suffered 1816, 1817 and 1818. I was then unable to bear exercise, now on the contrary, I was particularly strong and active, equalled by few men of my weight in the short application of muscular power and by still fewer in endurance. I have often striven to fatigue myself with a view to obtain sleep, and that in vain. I should remark however that the change of diet consequent upon Dupuytren's advice did at first, and for some time, produce a feeling of weakness, but this gradually passed away.

The first outbreak of the malady, if such it can be called, was the most painful. In the course of a few days, under the influence of constant change of scene, an improvement took place and in the course of a few weeks this improvement became very perceptible. I was always able to derive relief to a certain extent from reading, geological and archeological observation &c and here I may remark that few men can be found, who owing to a restless curiosity and interest in a variety of different objects, derive more pleasure from travel than myself.

The effects of this malady of 1822 have[24] never disappeared from my system. Some thing like it has repeatedly appeared at intervals, while the recollection of its horrors has never left me. Its consequences, or that constitution and temperament which led to it have kept me out of the Chair of the Bank, out of Parliament and crushed most other opportunities of doing good and obtaining illustration and have prevented me from engaging in literary labours of any considerable extent, or requiring much research. Thus then I have always felt within me, intellectual powers, and an amount of knowledge far greater than I have been able to exert and have been condemned to see men, whom in my vanity perhaps, I deemed only equal or perhaps inferior to myself acquire a much higher reputation.

The fidgety dread of fire, or of having written an improper letter, or directed it wrongly, or of having made a mistake in a cheque or the endorsement of a bill. All these several things, the every day annoyances of my life, take their origin from the malady of 1822 and have long become so habitual that I cannot hope to shake them off. Those who know not what such things are, ought to thank God for it.

I must now however turn to my journey and of this I need give here but a very slight sketch, having kept a journal, to which reference can be made.

We left Paris on Tuesday the 20th August 1822, travelled by Nogent Sur Seine, Dôle, Bourg, Nantua and reached Geneva on the 27th. On the 30th we proceeded to the Valley of Chamouni and employed ourselves for a few days in visiting some of its most remarkable objects, on Thursday the 3rd

[24] [Norman wrote 'has' here.]

September we set off from Chamouni, in order to go round Mont Blanc. We went by the Valleys of Bien Assez and Mont Joye, slept in a Chalet, walked or climbed over the Col de Clarver, or rather I did, for Cowell went round by the Col de Bonhomme, crossed the Col de la Seigne[25] into Italy, and slept at St Didier. From thence we proceeded down the Val d'Aoste to the town of that name, crossed the Great St. Bernard where I was laid up by a feverish cold for a couple of days at the hospital. Descended to Martigny and thence proceeded to Geneva, where we arrived on the 13th September and found Henry waiting for us. On the 16th September we again left Geneva for Martigny. Thence we again visited Chamouni, by the Tête Noire[26] returning by the Col de Balme. We afterwards visited the Valley of Bagne and saw the effects of the recent debâcle.[27]

On the 25 September we started on our journey into Italy crossed the Simplon and proceeded on to Milan and Genoa. Thence by the Riviera di Levante, to Lucca and Pisa, and so to Florence. On several occasions we made excursions out of the direct road as for instance to the Lakes of Como and Lugano often going on foot for long distances. By this time, my muscular power and endurance of fatigue had been pretty well restored. We reached Florence on the 29th October, and after passing a few days there, made two expeditions into the Maremma for the purpose of sporting. In our way stopped for a day or two at Volterra and paid a visit to a Tuscan gentleman named the Cavaliere Guarnacci at his Villa where he was residing with his wife and family.[28] This was a very interesting epoch in my life as I have

25 [This is in the area of Mont Blanc.]

26 [Norman seems to have been referring to Aiguille Noir. The 'noir' comes from quartz crystals.]

27 [Valley of the Bagnes. No disaster precisely in this area has been identified. Some sixteen years ealier, there had been a serious accident in which the summit of Mount Rosenburg collapsed, falling into Lake Lauwertz, with more than 1,000 killed; and ten years before Norman's visit, an avalanche near Villeneuve had killed about 12 people and buried 30 cottages.]

28 [Volterra is a major centre for anyone interested in the Etruscans, and is surrounded by the remnants of Etruscan walls. It contains the Guarnacci Museum,

always had a great desire to observe the domestic habits and customs of foreigners, comparing them with our own.

Our head quarters during the Maremma expeditions were at Piombino, whence Cowell and I visited the Fumaechie or smoking springs containing boracic acid of Monte Serboli and Monte Rotondo and the alum works of Montione and to the iron works at Follonica, as also the Isle of Elba.

Our sport was not great, with Italian guns and ammunition, it was difficult to do much execution and we were none of us great performers. The quantity of acquatic birds, including snipes, was very remarkable.

I got on pretty well with my gun for some time, but an excess[29] of nervous apprehension respecting it at length came on, and I was compelled after a sharp struggle to abandon an amusement, of which I was very fond, and which as a means of distraction it was difficult to replace.

It was, I think in 1821 or 22, that the two portraits of me by Francis Wilkin,[30] M. Marshall's[31] brother in law, one in crayons, the other in oils were produced. They are very poor things as works of art, but were very like when done, and give a good idea of my appearance when about thirty. They may thus be interesting to those who come after me.

We left Piombino on Christmas day and proceeded to Sienna by the Valley of the Cecina, Volterra and Colle. During this journey made almost wholly on foot, I walked one day over forty miles, and that without feeling even tired.

At Sienna, we found our carriage and a new courier named Paolo Ciona-

---

which houses a major display of Etruscan antiquities. The museum was founded in 1761 by Abbot Mario Guarnacci, 1701-85. The Cavaliere was no doubt a member of this family.]

[29] [Norman wrote 'access' here.]

[30] [Francis William Wilkin, society portrait painter, 1791-1842. This picture is now owned by the Bank of England, is reproduced on the cover of the present book, and forms the frontispiece of volume 2, *1797-1914*, of Sir J.H. Clapham's *The Bank of England, 1694-1914* (Cambridge: Cambridge University Press, 1970).]

[31] [Matthew Marshall, First Assistant Cashier of the Bank of England, 1829-35, Cashier 1835-64. Died 30 June 1873.]

soni (Cantrivi having broken down in health) and proceeded on to Rome by Radicefani,[32] Acquapente and Bolsena. From Rome we proceeded to Naples, and finally started on our way home on the 6th February, our return having been hastened by the approaching departure of Dr Abel (Lord Amherst's Chinese Abel) for India,[33] my family being eager that I should consult him.

We travelled very rapidly by Rome, Civita Castellana, Perugia, Florence, Bologna, Modena, Parma, Turin, the Mont Cenis, Lyons, Mâcon, Autun, Auxerre, Paris and reached London on the 8th March, only stopping a day or two now and then.

I found my father and mother residing in Green Street, Grosvenor Square, where they had taken a house, I know not exactly why. We had thus three, if not four establishments going at once, *vizt* in Earl Street, Hastings and Green St, perhaps too at Brighton, yet altogether they did not cost half as much as that at Bromley.

The effects of the foreign travel on my health had been very beneficial. I had become very robust and my spirits had improved. Still I felt unable to face my ordinary occupations and could afford little or no assistance to my father in Earl Street. He had however the help of my brother Richard, who was a very efficient second when acting under orders, although thoroughly unfit to manage a mercantile concern himself, from his sanguine temper and eagerness for gain, which made him wholly disregard risques, and obstacles.

I omitted some pages back to mention that in 1821 or 1822 my father

[32] [This is a town in Tuscany.]

[33] [William Pitt Amherst, 1st Earl Amherst of Arakan, 1773-1857, led an embassy to the court of the Chinese Emperor in 1816. This failed due to his refusal to 'kow tow' (kneeling three times on the floor, touching the head on the floor nine times) to the Emperor. In 1823 he was appointed Governor General of India. He had Kentish estates, and died at his home, Knole House, near Sevenoaks, in March 1857. Dr Abel was Clarke Abel, 1780-1826, naturalist and surgeon. He was educated for the medical profession, and served as a surgeon in Norwich. It is not clear if he qualified as a doctor. He was chief medical officer to Lord Amherst's embassy to China in 1816. FRS 1819. He was appointed surgeon to Lord Amherst when the latter became Governor General of India. He died in India in 1826.]

handed over the business to Richard and to me, allowing however the firm to remain G. Norman and Son in order to give us the more credit.[34] It was stipulated that we should be allowed to draw £1,000 per annum each.[35] The business at that time was small and far from profitable. When I was unable to retain the management, my father returned to his former post.

I went out of the Bank direction by rotation in April 1823, and thus had a year's furlough, which I could devote to the recovery of my health.

At this time, I consulted Dr Holland now Sir Henry[36] for the first time, and he continued my regular attendant for twenty-seven years. He is doubtless a very eminent person, but I cannot say that he ever clearly hit off the nature of my complaint, so far as it was accessible to medical treatment. At a subsequent period he counselled marriage, and by pressing the propriety of this upon me, he no doubt greatly influenced my conduct and most essentially contributed to my health and happiness. His usual prescriptions included blue pill[37] occasionally, and more especially 'Baume de Vie', compound decoction of aloes,[38] from which I have often derived great advantage.[39] Tonics, such as bark, were often tried but I never could bear

[34] [See p. 247.]

[35] [This would be worth £81,690 in 2009 prices.]

[36] [Sir Henry Holland, 1st Bt, 1788-1873, physician and traveller, fashionable doctor in London, with a well-developed bedside manner, and a particular interest in the relationship between physical illness and mental states, as explored in his *Medical Notes and Reflections* (1839) and *Chapters on Mental Physiology* (1851).]

[37] [Calomel (mercurious chloride) appeared in every physician's bag throughout the 19th century. It was an active ingredient in the Blue Pill, and acted as a violent purgative. See R. Porter, *The Greatest Benefit to Mankind*, London: Harper Collins, 1997 pp. 266-7, 674.]

[38] [For decoction, see p. 262. There seems to have been some connection between this remedy and Baume de Vie, through the use of aloes. In the former the bitterness of the aloes was concealed by the other ingredients. It is a purgative, but an early 19th century manual of pharmacy makes the observation, which may not be irrelevant to Norman, that 'This is a mild and commendable remedy where a warm and stomachic aperient [laxative] is required, which is often the case in hysterical and hypochondriacal affections, and in certain spasmodic disorders where the bowels have become torpid from the use of opiates'.]

[39] [Baume de Vie was a tincture prepared from 4 parts aloes, 1 each of agaric, rhubarb, zedoary, gentian, myrrh, and theriac, with 100 to 120 parts dilute alcohol.

them.

Treatment such as that employed in 1850 by Headland would, I doubt not, have thoroughly answered at an earlier period and afforded me a lengthened period of increased usefulness, and pleasurable existence.

As I was, or at any rate thought I was, unable to face business as travel had been beneficial to me, and as moreover the continent is neither healthy or agreeable in Summer it was determined that I should employ a month or two in a visit to Wales. Of this tour I kept no regular journal, although I have a good many notes chiefly geological relating to it. This being so, I will shortly describe it.

We went to Cheltenham and on a coach between that and Gloucester[40] were much amused by the zeal of a groom who challenged Cowell to fight because the latter ventured to impugn the conduct and character of Colonel Berkeley (the late Lord Fitzharding).[41] The defence of that personage was also taken up by a decent man of middle age, who affirmed that Berkeley Castle was an excellent school of manners and morals for a young man entering on life. To illustrate his meaning he described the way in which a day was passed under the Colonel's auspices. They had a good breakfast, hunted all day, dined, got drunk and went to bed. This en passant, as an instance of correct moral judgment.[42]

I had seen the Colonel act at the Leamington Theatre, then belonging to R.W. Elliston in 1818, a coarse, vulgar looking man by no means I should

There were variants in this recipe, including saffron and liquorice. It is also known as Swedish Essence of Life. It became available in an over-the-counter form, and was advertised in the late 18th century as a panacea for an enormously long list of illnesses. As advertised in the *Oxford Gazette* for 26 May 1788 it was priced at three shillings (fifteen decimal pence) per bottle.]

[40][Norman wrote 'Gloster' here and below.]

[41][The 5th Earl of Berkeley had a tangled marital history, and his claimed earlier marriage to the daughter of a publican and butcher was not recognised by the House of Lords. But his son William Fitzhardinge Berkeley, 1786-1857, was created 1st and last Earl Fitzhardinge in 1841.]

[42]He especially insisted upon the discouragement held out to gaming at Berkeley Castle.

have said likely to please woman, which was his chief aim in assuming the bear skin.[43]

From Gloucester we visited Berkeley at which I was disappointed. We then went to Bristol, Ross and Monmouth, walked to Ragland and then by Tintern to Chepstow, and here I may observe that Tintern Abbey is the most beautiful ruin of an ecclesiastical character I ever saw, as is Heidelberg of a civil character.

From Chepstow we went to Merthyr passing by the ruins of Caerphilly Castle, one of the Royal Fortresses built by the Plantagenet Kings to restrain the Welsh, and exhibiting by its size and strength a proof of the great efforts which it cost, to keep the stubborn, brave and cunning Cymri[44] in a state of subjection to the Sassenach whom even now, six centuries after the conquest, they thoroughly hate.

At Merthyr we remained two or three days, during which I passed my time in the coal mines and at the iron works. The immense extent to which the industrial operations were even then carried on. The hills of Sarnau[45] &c excited my astonishment. What should I think now.

---

[43] [Leamington's first theatre opened in 1813. It was initially owned by a Mr Simms, but passed in 1818 to Robert William Elliston, 1774-1831. It subsequently passed to an owner called Chamberlin, and then to one called Bennett, and closed in 1856. Elliston was educated at St Paul's School, but ran away from home, and made his first appearance on the stage in *Richard III* at Bath, in 1791. He was a very successful actor, and appeared at Drury Lane 1804-9. From 1819 he was the lessee of the theatre, presenting amongst others Edmund Kean. He had a successful career in theatre management, but a combination of ill-health and commercial misfortune led to his bankruptcy in 1826. He seems to have been a heavy drinker, like many of his theatrical contemporaries.]

[44] [Norman wrote Kymri here. There is no letter K in the Welsh language. Cymri means Welshmen. However, it does seem that Kymry was an English term used for the Welsh. See R.W. Morgan, *The British Kymry, or Britons of Cambria. Outlines of their History and Institutions from the Earliest Times*, Ruthin: Clarke; London: Hardwicke, 1857.]

[45] [It is not clear what Norman meant by Sarnau. Given his frequent resort to capitalisation, which has been modified by the editors of the present edition, the capital 'S' has no particular significance. But he was probably referring to spoil heaps of some kind. There is a Welsh word 'sarnu' meaning spoil.]

Our next points of interest were Pont Neath Vaughan,[46] Neath, Swansea and Caermarthen. At the first I remarked the largest vein of carbonate of barytes I ever saw, and at the two next last we saw the copper works, the largest by far I suppose in the world.

We had walked a great deal up to this point, but after reaching Aberavon on the sea coast, Cowell and I walked exclusively until we reached St Asaph, sending our luggage as best we could.[47] Robert less robust, usually contrived to find a conveyance. On one occasion we struck up an acquaintance with a Huckster who had a cart loaded with 30,000 eggs bought of the farmers, which he was conveying to Manchester.

I will now mention from memory our sleeping places after quitting, Aberavon, Aberystwyth,[48] Machynlleth,[49] Tal–y–llyn,[50] Dolgellau,[51] Tremadog,[52] Tan y Bwich,[53] Beddgellert,[54] Carnarvon, Bangor, St Asaph, Chester. It is probable that I may not have placed all those names in proper order. We returned home by Manchester, Shrewsbury and I think Birmingham.

I was very much pleased by this tour. The mountain scenery of Wales, although on a very small scale, as even Snowdon is only 3,600 ft above the level of the sea, is extremely beautiful and the people, although not amiable, are an interesting relic of a race, who having been swept away from the fertile

[46] [There has been some difficulty in reconstructing the Welsh place names to which, writing from memory thirty years later, Norman refers. The road from Merthyr to Neath would have passed through Penywaun, Hirwaun, Glyn-Neath and Resolven.]

[47] [Perhaps for those unfamiliar with Wales, it should be made clear that Norman, despite his concerns about his health, managed to walk the entire length of Wales, a mountainous country, from south to north, starting on the coast of South Wales. It was an astonishing feat of stamina, particularly given the terrain. For Cowell, who was bronchitic, it must have been very taxing indeed.]

[48] [Norman wrote 'Aberystwith' here.]

[49] [Norman wrote 'Mackynleth'.]

[50] [Norman wrote 'Tuloyn'.]

[51] [Norman wrote 'Dolgetly'.]

[52] [Norman wrote 'Tremadoe'.]

[53] [Norman wrote 'Tan y Bwlch'.]

[54] [Norman wrote 'Bedgellert'.]

plains of England, probably also from Germany and Belgium, by a superior race, when they found nothing but the sea behind them, made a fierce stand, and during 700 years kept the foe at bay. Subjected at length by the military skill and statesmanship of Edward I[55] to the dominion of the stranger, they have still resisted anything like amalgamation and retain to this day their language, their feelings, including first and foremost hatred of the Saxon and their nationality.

It is a curious proof of the tenacity of life in this branch of the Celts, that along the Cheshire frontier which I have examined, the Welsh and Saxon names of places, still indicate the languages prevailing in them, or at least did so twenty years ago. Thus Wrexham must have been Saxon ever since, perhaps even before the conquest, and English is spoken there while on the other side of the bridge, in a sort of suburb Welsh is current. This I learned from a shopkeeper there.

The Highlanders and Irish more easily care less with the stranger, learn his language and forget their own. Does this fact belong to a radical distinction in character, between the Gaelic and Cymri Branches of the Celts?[56]

During our Welsh tour, Robert chiefly employed himself in fishing. He had occasionally great sport in a small way, I geologized and looked for the picturesque. Cowell had no special occupation.

I will now mention an anecdote or two relating to our adventures in Wales. We had gone to a place called Tal–y–llyn[57] meaning to take up our night quarters and to cross Cader Idris to Dolgellau[58] the next day. The landlord told us that he could not house us as he expected the members of a

---

[55] [Edward I, 1239-1307, King of England, eldest son of Henry III. He distinguished himself as a soldier early in life, and he set about unifying the outlying parts of his kingdom. After the second Welsh war, which ended in the overthrow and death of the last Llewellyn (1282), he was able to annex Wales. The Statute of Rhuddlan made Wales an English possession.]

[56] [Norman wrote 'Kymrie' here.]

[57] [Norman wrote 'Tallyn'.]

[58] [Norman wrote 'Dolgelly'.]

club, whose object it was to fish the neighbouring lake. In the meantime the weather became dreadful, the rain poured down in torrents and it became almost impossible for us to proceed. The gentlemen, perhaps ten in number had arrived, while we were deliberating and most kindly pressed us to remain and share their sport and fare. We did so, dined with them, saw part of the lake dragged and many trout caught and passed a very jolly evening when full justice was done to the crw[59] and grog. Among the party were Colonel Vaughan and Mr Thomas a Clergyman, who, if I recollect aright did the honours.[60] We packed very close at night.

We afterwards ascended Cader Idris and I had an opportunity, which pleased me greatly, of observing the effect produced on the texture of the sedimentary rocks by the juxtaposition of prismatic porphyry.[61] The view also delighted me.

We stopped at Bedgellert two or three days, waiting for clear weather to enable us to enjoy the view from the summit of Snowdon and at last failed. Being pressed for time, we started in a mizzling rain, which grew worse as we ascended. We reached the top, drenched to the skin and having narrowly escaped from the danger of being blown off a ridge along which we had to pass, by a hurricane of wind. We were unable during any part of our ascent

[59][It is possible that Norman meant to write Cwrw which is the Welsh word for beer. Crwst, the Welsh word for crust, is another possibility. Food would be bwyd.]

[60][The owner of Tal-y-llyn Lake at that time was Colonel Vaughan of Hengwrt, Llanelltyd, near Dolgellau, about seven miles from Tal-y-llyn, He later built an inn on the shore of the lake called Tynycomel. He provided boats for the use of visitors and anglers. He was Colonel Griffith Howel Vaughan, 1770-1848, Colonel Commandant of the Royal Merioneth Militia. Mr Thomas has not been identified. He was not the Vicar of Llanelltyd, nor was he the Rector of Dolgellau. Roger Clough was the Vicar of Corwen, where Colonel Vaughan had his other home. We are indebted for this information to Merfyn Wyn Tomos of Dolgellau Record Office.]

[61][Prismatic refers to crystalline form. In the case of prismatic sulphur this form is obtained by melting the ordinary form and allowing the liquid to crystallise. Porphyry is an ancient term denoting a decorative rock composed of crystals, often of feldspar or quartz. It is not now used as a geological term.]

or descent to see more than fifty yards from us, being in the clouds all the time.

This, in short was an 'operation manqué', as had been the ascent of Vesuvius in the preceding year from a similar cause.

From Bangor we went to the Penrhyn slate quarries, by which I was greatly delighted both as a geologist and an admirer of an industrial establishment, skilfully worked.

I returned to London in improved health, but still unable to face business and as travel seemed to suit me better than any other remedy, and as the Bank would have no claim upon me until April 1824, it was determined that I should once more go to Italy and my kind friend Cowell again agreed to accompany me.

I have omitted previously to remark that by the advice of Mr Scott, I had abandoned after my return to England Dupuytren's ascetic dietary, and lived like other people, eating meat and drinking wine, the latter however in moderation.

As there exists among my papers the journal of my second Italian tour, I shall here merely give a short resumé of our proceedings, referring to the above document for fuller information.

We left London on the 9th August 1823 by the packet for Ostend,[62] having hired as travelling servant a native of Lodi named Ferdinando Peverada who in all respects, was about the best of his class, excepting that he could not ride. From Ostend we went to Bruges, Ghent, Antwerp, down the Scheld to Rotterdam, Leydon, Haarlem, Amsterdam, Utrecht, Breda, again Antwerp and Brussels.

[62][Mrs Grote wrote to her sister Frances Lewin 8 April 1823: 'We [she and George Grote] are both concerned about poor George Norman's malady, which has returned, and he is preparing to set forth to the Continent again with his dear friend Cowell. His mind is, I fear, partially alienated, and his poor mother must be miserable. I would I were able to attend and minister to him. The doctors have prescribed travel as the only remedy.' *The Lewin Letters*, vol. 1 pp. 200-1.]

I may here remark that Holland had pleased me very much, as it did during a subsequent tour in 1851. The Dutch have always struck me, as having been the first people in Europe during the last 300 years, taking their numbers into account. Look at their commerce, wealth and political power. Their eminence in literature and the arts. The great men they have produced in every branch of greatness, soldiers, sailors, lawyers divines, scholars, physicians, naturalists, painters and statesmen. Look at their oriental Empire and at their own country itself a miraculous result, of science industry and wealth, and compare them since the union of Utrecht with Spain. Surely the 2,000,000 of Dutch (there were hardly more in the time of their greatness) have done more, and can exhibit more and greater men than 10 millions of Spaniards or 20 of Italians. It may be said that the superiority of the former arose in a great degree from the difference of religion and government, be it so, but then do not men usually choose for themselves in such matters?

But to proceed. From Brussels we went to Spa, Aix la Chapelle and Cologne, ascended thence by the left Bank of the Rhine to Mainz,[63] where we crossed the river and proceeded to Frankfurt, where we stopped for three or four days during the fair. Thence to Darmstadt and Heidelberg, Stuttgart and Carlsruhe, Ulm and Augsburg to Munich, where we stopped for several days and enjoyed the society of my Cousin C.T. Barnard, who at that time was acting as secretary to Sir Brook Taylor the English Minister.[64]

C.T. Barnard still remains in Germany, having gone there in 1814.[65] He is now resident in a diplomatic capacity at Coburg, and having married a German wife has become thoroughly Teutonized.

---

[63] [Norman wrote 'Mentz'.]

[64] [Sir Brook Taylor, 1776-1846, joined the Diplomatic Service under the patronage of Lord Granville, and was British Minister to Cologne and Hesse-Cassel 1801-6, Denmark 1807, Würtemburg 1814-20, Bavaria 1820-8, Minister at Berlin 1828-31, GCH 1822.]

[65] [Norman's cousin Charles Townsend Barnard, born 1790 at Chislehurst, educated at Eton, admitted pensioner at St John's College, Cambridge, 1808, Chargée d'Affaires at Coburg 1842. He married Emily Unges. He died in 1878.]

Our route from Munich took us to that lovely place Saltzburg, and thence to Innsbruck, over the Brenner to Bolzano, and then down the valley of the Adige by Trent and Rovereto to Verona.

We reached Verona on the 6th October and remained there some days, having the advantage of an introduction from old Mrs Lefevre and John[66] to an Italian family who were extremely civil to us, received us at their houses, and gave us letters to their friends at Venice. We also formed at Verona an acquaintance in Count Mosti[67] who was very kind to us and invited us to his villa near Ferrara.

From Verona we went to Vicenza, Padua and Venice, remaining at the latter place several days and crossing from it to Trieste, whence we went, chiefly on foot, across Istria to Pola, returning by the same route.

Leaving Venice again we went to Ferrara and thence to la Missola an old hunting seat of the Dukes of Ferrara, where we aired our guns obtaining however but little sport, it was there however that I shot at stags and roe for the only time in my life.

From Ferrara we went to Bologna where we again received civility from the Marchese Lampiere and were present at a concert given by Cardinal Spina, the Papal Legate.[68] We also saw the Abbate Mezzofanti, the celebrated

[66] [Sir John George Shaw Lefevre, 1797-1879, the second of four sons of Charles Shaw, 1758-1823, and his wife Helena, 1767-1834, daughter and heiress of John Lefevre of Heckfield Place, Hampshire. Charles Shaw assumed the extra name Lefevre on marrying into the Huguenot family; see p. 52. 'Old Mrs Lefevre' was thus Helena née Lefevre. Her son, John George Shaw Lefevre was a mathematician, elected Fellow of Trinity College, Cambridge in 1819, FRS 1820. In 1821 he was one of the founder members of the Political Economy Club, and remained a member until 1831. He later had a successful career as a lawyer and civil servant. Like Norman and Overstone, he was educated at Eton. He was knighted in 1857. He married Rachel Emily Wright, 1801-85, the sister of Harriet Loyd, who became, with her husband's elevation to the peerage, Lady Overstone. The sisters were the daughters of the Nottingham banker Ichabod Wright. Mrs Shaw Lefevre was thus the sister in law of Norman's close friend Overstone.]

[67] [The Mosti family was one of the ancient families of Ferrara. Count Mosti to whom Norman refers was a friend of Byron, and is mentioned in Byron's correspondence.]

[68] [Guiseppe Spina was Archbishop of Genoa 1802-16. He had not at that time

Linguist.[69]

Our next move was along the Emilian Way[70] to Riverini. Thence we took a walk to San Marino and proceeded through the Romagna and La Marca to Ancona and here it may be observed that hardly any tract of similar extent in Europe can produce more fertility, more powerful cultivation and more numerous and interesting towns than the Northern part of the Ecclesiastical States, which border the Adriatic.

From Ancona, we struck into the interior, visited Roretto crossed the Appenines at Serravalle and then went by Foligno, Perugia, Assissi and the Val de Chiana to Florence, which we reached on the 6th December and remained till the 22nd when we set out on return home. We found at Florence Lord Rendlesham (John[71]), Frederick the late Peer,[72] the G.R. Smiths[73] and other friends.

We now once more took the Road to Bologna, where we remained for two or three days. Some of the events referred to a page or two back had reference to this visit. From Bologna we went to Mantua, Cremona and Milan Pavia, Asti, Alessandia, Coni across the Col de Tendi[74] to Nice which we reached on the 9th January.

In the South of France we saw Frejus, Toulon, Arles, Marseilles, Nimes,

---

received his Cardinal's hat.]

[69][Giuseppe Mezzofanti, 1774-1849, Professor of Arabic at Bologna. In 1833 he became Vatican librarian. In 1838 he was made a Cardinal. He spoke 58 languages.]

[70][The Aemilian Way was constructed by Marcus Aemilius Lepidus in 187 BC. Emilia Romagna is a region of northern Italy comprising the provinces of Bologna, Ferrara, Forli, Modena, Parma, Piacenza, Ravenna and Reggio nell' Emilia. It is bounded by the watershed of the Apennines to the south and the river Po to the north. The Aemilian Way runs north west to south east through most of the region's main towns from Rimini to Piacenza and divides the hill from the plain.]

[71][John Thellusson, 2nd Baron Rendlesham, 1785-1832; see p. 114.]

[72][Frederick Thellusson, 4th Baron Rendlesham, 1798-1852, succeeded his twin brother William as 4th Baron, 13 September 1839. He lived in Italy for some years. William Thellusson, 3rd Baron, 1798-1839 was Vicar of Aldenham, Herts.]

[73][George Robert Smith, 1793-1869; see p. 62. He married in May 1818 Jane, eldest daughter of John Maberley. She died in October 1879.]

[74][Col de Tende on the French Italian border.]

Vienne, Lyons. As I felt very unwell, dreading a return to England as likely to bring back my old sufferings, Cowell advised that we should once more visit Clermont, which we did. At Clermont Cowell was taken ill with acute rheumatism and confined to his bed so long, that I almost doubted if we could reach home in time for the Bank election. However he recovered sufficiently to enable us to set out on the 17th February 1824 and on the 25th we reached home and found my family in a house in George St Portman Square where they only remained however a few weeks longer and then removed to Bromley, Sir H. Meux's tenancy having expired.

Before I pursue a detail of my career, I may pause for a moment and look back upon my two years wanderings, especially as regards that portion of them devoted to Italy.

The extent of ground travelled over hardly fell short of 10,000 miles. The expense was full £2,000, which my dear father furnished without the least repining.

I always travelled with a servant and private carriage hired at either Paris or Brussels. This carriage was a single headed Barouche, a most comfortable and convenient vehicle with dickey behind, platform in front, well, and in short every contrivance for holding luggage, of which including books and minerals, the latter accumulating as we went on, Cowell and I had no small quantity.

In the Alps on excursions we hired mules and guides and through the Maremma a Vettura, at so much a day.

We were not extravagant, but always lived well. The pay for post horses in France was thirty sous a post for two horses, or forty sous when we ought to have had three horses, and in the provinces we gave the postillion thirty sous a post or forty sous near Paris, fifteen being the legal payment. We ordinarily gave three francs for bed, three francs for dinner and two for breakfast. In all eight francs a day for living. This was cheap enough, I forget how we managed for the third meal, or if we had any.

I enjoyed my tours as much as a person could whose health was bad and spirits at times depressed to the lowest point of wretchedness. Geology, archaeology, agriculture, scenery, the arts, manners &c all engaged my attention and my curiosity was never satiated, although always employed.

Italy afforded me especial enjoyment. Previously to going there, I had made myself a fair scholar in the language, had read most of its classics and was well acquainted with its history as told by Sismondi[75] or by its original chroniclers and historians. Thus, then I was ever surrounded by souvenirs which carried me back to the past, during the two eras of glory, which that country alone has enjoyed and which have been separated and followed by such innumerable woes.

I was soon able to converse in Italian, so as to enjoy society and to obtain information. This fact and the gratitude we evinced for any attention enabled Cowell and I, with a little luck, to obtain many friends, and had our journey been prolonged, we might have obtained introductions of the most valuable kind everywhere. I have always striven when abroad to obtain the acquaintance of the natives by every proper means, and have been amply repaid for my pains. I must pronounce the Italians judging from my own experience to be a very hospitable people.

Previously to my Italian tour I had gained a great fondness for pictures at Mr Wells's of Redleaf.[76] This I carried much farther in Italy. A large portion

[75][Jean Charles Léonard Simonde de Sismondi, 1773-1842. The work referred to is his *Histoire des Républiques Italiennes du Moyen Age*, which Norman recounts (p. 180) that he bought at Ramsgate in 1816. Given the publishing history of this work, Norman's date of purchase suggests that he bought part of the first edition. Volumes 1-4 were published by H. Gessner in Zurich; volumes 5-8 by Nicholls in Paris, and volumes 9-15 by Treuttel and Würtz in Paris, extending over the years 1807-15. Given Norman's imprecision about how many volumes he initially purchased, and the fact that he later completed the set to include the later volumes, to which he refers, it seems possible that he purchased the final volumes from a later edition, such as the Paris 1809-18 or Paris 1826 editions, both published by Treuttel and Würtz.]

[76][William Wells (see p. 99) was a patron of Landseer, but infuriated John Constable by his lack of interest in his own paintings.]

of my time, when in the cities, was devoted to art and I gained enough knowledge of painting to be able to point out works of the chief masters in galleries before I was told their names. This knowledge I have not altogether lost, although it has become rather rusty. My fondness for pictures, provided they are good, remains unabated. The proviso, I must allow, will cover my dislike of a Royal Academy exhibition.

But to proceed with my biography, I had returned home, with a strong and active body, able to bear any fatigue and with a mind strengthened and enriched with fresh stores of knowledge. My nervous system however although somewhat invigorated, was still in a shattered state and on my arrival in England I looked forward with horror to the Bank and a return to my Earl St occupations. However Mr Scott urged strongly that I should not give way and I determined at all hazard to follow his advice. The struggle was dreadful, especially at the Bank. My dear mother more than once has gone there with me and waited in a carriage till my business was over. A friend, Cameron, for instance, has performed the same kind office. After a few weeks however my nervous feelings became less acute. The dread of myself and of every body else diminished and I could execute my duties with but little sufferings.

After my father's return to Bromley I used to pass the end and beginning of each week there, usually going there on Friday evening and returning to London on Tuesday morning. But as Earl Street abounded with painful associations, my kind friend Cowell proposed that I should take a lodging westward with him. This suited me exactly and we continued to live together until my marriage in 1830.

The places at which we lodged were Green Street, Davis Street, Berkeley Square, Regent Street, and then Berkeley Square again for two or three years. We had there the whole of a small house, close to Hay Hill and to Gunter the pastry cook's.[77] A married couple named Sutton did for us. There were no clubs until about 1825 when we joined the Athenaeum. Previously when not engaged out we dined at home on beef steak or mutton chops or a leg of mutton, which lasted always two days, being hashed the second. I was never much of a gourmand although I like my food to be good of its kind and palatably dressed. Now and then we had a friend or two to dine with us, I recollect among others Dumont and Arguelles.[78]

I never went out much to evening parties or was in any sense a man of the town, but I used not infrequently to go to a ball, being deeply sensible to the pleasures of female society. Among the houses, which I most frequented at this time, were those of Mr George Smith, Mr John Smith, Mr Ord and Mr Loyd.

In 1824, I resumed after long disuse my gun and cricket bat. With the former, copper caps, being now common, I soon became a very tolerable performer and I may say the same thing as to the latter, although of course I never quite recovered the effects of eight or nine years disuse of my tool, the more so, because a change in the style of bowling had taken place in the interval.

[77] [Gunter's tea shop was at 7-8 Berkeley Square. The shop had been established in 1757 by Domenico Negri who took James Gunter into partnership in 1777. By 1799 Gunter was the sole proprietor. He died in 1819. The business continued to be run by his family for several generations. It was an extremely fashionable place for light refreshments.]

[78] [Pierre Etienne Louis Dumont, 1759-1829, Swiss/French political writer born at Geneva. He was initially intended to be a clergyman, and on finding it necessary to leave Geneva he went to St Petersburg where he was, for 18 months, Pastor of the French church. In 1785 he moved to London. Under the patronage of Lord Shelburne, he became acquainted with many of the Whigs. While on visits to Paris he associated with the younger Mirabeau, spending the years 1789-91 as a speech writer and editor for the revolutionary. But on his return from Paris in 1791 he attached himself to Jeremy Bentham, of whom he became a great admirer. He devoted much of the rest of his life to collecting and editing Bentham's scattered and prolix writings. He worked with Bentham as editor of his works, which appeared initially in French. He returned to Geneva in 1814, while maintaining his links with the English Benthamites, as his visits to Norman indicate, and became leader of the Supreme Council in Geneva. He died at Milan. For Arguelles, see p. 222.]

My chief place of cricket was at Chislehurst, on the then new ground but I used also to play club matches in the neighbourhood, almost always declining them however, if they were to last more than a day.

My father finally quitted business in 1824, handing over to my brother and self as a gift the entire capital then actively employed, which deducting all visible bad debts, amounted to above £60,000, a noble gift,[79] but he was a noble man and I regard his memory with the deepest respect and affection.

In 1824 our business had somewhat recovered. Young and venturous, Richard and I, who thought our father over-cautious, resolved to extend it and made advances to Ernst Rohde[80] and others, which bore the appropriate fruits of loss in subsequent years.

No important change took place in my habits of life, during the years 1825 and 1826. I continued to reside in London with Cowell and at the end of each week went to Bromley, and obtained air and exercise with my gun and cricket bat.[81]

In 1825 I began to attend a gymnastic school regularly. My master was named Hamon[82] and his rooms were in Regent Street on the West side, just

[79] [This would be worth £4,901,000 in 2009 prices.]

[80] [Ernest Rohde has not been traced in any Post Office London Directory of the period. It is likely that he was working in a commercial centre other than London.]

[81] [Cricket had a long history in Bromley. The earliest recorded match dates back to 1735. Bromley Common was subsequently the scene of a number of major cricket matches and also for single wicket matches. In 1812, a new ground was established on a field owned by the Norman family called Prince's Plain, as Norman relates; see p. 100. The Princes Plain Cricket Club was then formed. Norman was its first Treasurer. After the enclosure of Bromley Common in 1821, the club moved to Chislehurst and changed its name to West Kent Cricket Club. According to Norman's Bromley Memoir, the name Prince's Plain was given to the south eastern portion of the Common because races patronised by Frederick, Prince of Wales, father of George III, were held there. Norman played first class cricket. He played for Kent 1832-8, having resumed his cricket after his absences in Norway in the 1820s. He is recorded as having played in 9 matches, to have had 11 innings, to have been not out 3 times, with total runs of 81, an average of 10.12 and his highest score was 37 not out. One catch is recorded and, consistently with remarks in the Autobiography, he did not bowl at all. These scores should be seen in the context of those typically recorded at the time; see the note on p. 90 concerning Beldham.]

[82] [It seems likely that the name Hamon was a pseudonym. It is the name of

beyond the quadrant. I followed him thence to other places. He was a man of Herculean strength in the arms, although his right arm had been seriously damaged by shot and sabre, and was a capital fencer. He was a very civil well-conducted man and continued to give lessons until quite recently in a little street leading out of the Haymarket and close to Bouverie's old Banking house, where I used to see him from time to time. He is probably still alive.

I used to go to Hamon's rooms every day after breakfast on my way to the City, go through a regular form of exercise for the arms and legs, in which the horizontal bar and the ropes played a principal part, and finish with an Assaut d'Armes either with Hamon or some of his pupils. I derived great advantage from gymnastics, and continued to practise them, until I quitted London at the time of my marriage, indeed partially long afterwards. The increase of muscular power which they produce is so good, as hardly to be credible without experience. I was a very distinguished athlete, although I did not begin my studies until past thirty. My greatest exploit was to place myself on the ground in a sitting posture with legs extended before me, then taking a rope in each hand, I ascended by the ropes, with the legs still extended, until I could touch with my head a cross bar, fifteen to twenty foot high, to which the ropes were attached, descending in the same manner. This was a 'tour de force' of which very few were capable. It required particular strength in the loins and thighs.

When going to Norway in 1826 by the Fortuna, Captain Ries, I was able to beat all the sailors in exercises upon the ropes, when a prize had been offered by the captain to the best performer.[83] I did not however ascend great heights. My head was never strong enough for this. It may be supposed that

the visual effect created on the blade of a sword by the hardening process applied to the blade edge. However M.P.G. Hamon established a gymnasium at 26 St James's Street in 1824. In 1827 he published *Manuel ou Cours d'Exercises de Gymnastique*. The work, which is very rare, has a folding frontispiece showing the interior of the gymnasium in St James's Street.]

[83] [See also p. 301.]

the sailors did not understand being beaten by a landsman. What astonished them most was that I could mount with a rope in each hand, my head down and legs in the air. I never required any help from the use of my legs in ascending by a rope.

I was tolerable, but not a good fencer, having begun too late in life. I was however often successful against Angelo's pupils,[84] who had a superior command of their weapons to mine, owing to the system taught me by Hamon. This system consisted in always thrusting either high or low in tierce, and in always using the circle as a parry. Angelo's system was more shewy and complicated but less effective. He parried or thrust in second, tierce or quart and his pupils invariably failed both in attack and defence when opposed to the élèves of our school, of equal experience.

As an example, I may mention that Charles Cameron who was decidedly a better fencer than myself, having studied under Angelo for many years before I ever touched a foil, could gain no advantage over me in an Assaut. If any thing I think I was the superior.

On the whole, I look back with satisfaction to my exertions as a gymnast and a fencer. They strengthened my muscular power in a very remarkable degree, to an extent indeed which can hardly be imagined by a person who has not experienced their effects. They gave me also courage self-possession and confidence in myself. When walking away from the fencing room, it seemed to me, that there was nothing within the scope of personal prowess

[84] [There were three generations of this family teaching fencing in London. Dominico Angelo Malevolti Tremamondo, 1716-1802, known as Angelo, came to London in the company of the celebrated actress Peg Woffington. He was from Leghorn in Italy, and was originally a riding instructor, but had studied fencing in Paris. After a number of successful public matches, he rapidly gained wealthy patrons including the royal princes, being an instructor to both George III and George IV. His son Henry, 1760-1839, was trained by his father and then sent to Paris for further instruction in fencing. The third generation was represented by Henry Charles, 1780-1852, who held the position of fencing master and superintendent of sword exercises in the British army from 1833 until his death. He moved the academy to St James's Street in London from Haymarket where it had been since 1770, having previously been adjacent to Soho Square.]

beyond my powers, and this feeling was accompanied by an incomparable sensation of lightness and elasticity.

Even now, when from want of opportunity, I have abandoned almost entirely scientific exercise for nearly thirty years, I still feel some advantage from it. At any rate, I attribute to it the possession of an amount of bodily activity and command over his limbs, not common in a man over whose head more than sixty-four years have passed.

I have endeavoured to inculcate on my children the advantage of gymnastics, but as respects Charlie with little success. His occupations are chiefly sedentary, and apart from the advantages above described which proceed from scientific exercise, he would find the additional advantage, of being able to throw much muscular exertion into a very small portion of time. An hour a day well-employed would balance clerkly labour for the rest of the day.

I must now mention a circumstance which in its consequences has had the most important effect upon my subsequent life.

Mr George Stone the Banker of Lombard Street resided at Chislehurst.[85] His family had long been good friends of ours. He had several daughters. The eldest Emma was a very pretty and amiable person. With her my brother Richard fell in love and was accepted.[86] They were married in 1825, Emma brought him two children and died of consumption in the house belonging to Mr Newell[87] at Southborough[88] in 1828 or 29.

The loss of his wife was an inestimable misfortune to my brother. Had Emma lived, she might have restrained his folly and disposition to evil, and

[85][George Stone was a partner 1793-1843 in the bank of Martin and Company, 68 Lombard Street, and senior partner 1831-43. He died 20 February 1844, aged 72.]

[86][Norman's brother, 1800-60; see p. 11. He married Emma Stone in 1826. This was before the death of his father, and is likely to have incurred the disapproval of Norman himself, as will be clear from the subsequent account of the marriage of his siblings.]

[87][Mr Newell was possibly Robert Newell, 1778-1852, Rector of Great Hornmead, Herts, 1813-52, and amateur artist. Not otherwise identified.]

[88][A parish two miles north of Tunbridge Wells.]

he might now have been a virtuous, happy and prosperous man.

The two last paragraphs must be considered a parenthesis and I will now proceed to the pith of my story.

I think it was in the winter of 1824 that the Chislehurst Stones gave a ball. I was asked, while there if I had seen the Stones' handsome cousin, and upon my saying no, I was shewn a tall graceful girl then about eighteen, slender rather than fat, with a dark ruddy complexion, very regular features, dark brown eyes and a profusion of dark hair. She was extremely graceful and appeared quite unconscious of her extreme beauty and of the admiration she excited. This charming creature was Sibella third daughter of Mr Henry Stone,[89] a retired Bengal civil servant, but who had been for some time a partner in the Bank and resided at a villa called St Leonards at Stanmore. She is now my wife, the mother of my children and for more than twenty-seven years has been the charm of my existence, the choicest gift that the Almighty in his goodness has ever bestowed on me. At our first interview however, I only regarded her with that admiration for female charms, which naturally belongs to me. I do not recollect having spoken to her.

[89] [The official history of Martin's bank notes that two of Henry Stone's grandsons, Sibella's sons, were two of the last four partners of the bank as a private bank. Frederick Henry Norman became a partner in 1880, and Edward Norman became a partner in 1884. Henry Stone was a partner 1824-45. See G. Chandler, *Four Centuries of Banking* (London: Batsford, 1964) vol. 1 pp. 302, 319-20.]

# Chapter 10

# Monetary Problems

The year 1825 was that of the great monetary crisis, the first I had ever seen, although I have had plenty of experience in similar occurrences subsequently. That which distinguished the crisis of 1825, was first, the enormous number of bubble companies which preceded it, such companies evincing for the most part the utmost ignorance, as to the sort of business which is[1] likely to be carried out successfully on the joint stock principle, and indeed as to the objects calculated to yield a profitable return to the expenditure of capital. Secondly, the great amount of insolvency among Bankers, both in London and the country, but especially the latter. There was the usual speculative excitement and absurd rize of prices.

A large class of companies was formed to work mines in Mexico and South America. The revolted colonies of Spain had recently been opened to the rest of the world. It was known that many of their silver mines, the working of which had been interrupted by the civil war, had yielded vast and profitable returns almost up to the breaking out of hostilities. It was known too that the mode of working had been most unscientific and it seemed highly probable, indeed all but certain, that greatly increased profits would follow an extensive application of the theoretic knowledge and practical skill of Europe to the production of the precious metals in Mexico and Peru.

[1] [Norman wrote 'are' here.]

Considering the above circumstances, and that the working of mines is but little suited to individuals, from its uncertainty, the regular rules upon which its success depends, and the vast amount of capital often required, and that it is specially fitted, and is usually carried on by joint stock companies, I am unable to blame those who in 1824 and 1825 took shares in the various Anglo-American mining companies. It seems to me that they acted on principles a priori sound, which had also been supported by a wide experience.

I myself acted in conformity to the above opinions. I took shares and became a director of a company formed under the auspices of the late Mr John Smith, for work in the mines of Tlalpuxahua in Mexico.[2] Mr Smith was Chairman. Sir H. Cooke, Mr Deacon, Mr Sampson &c &c my co-directors. A remarkable venturer who called himself the Chevalier Don Vincent de Rivafinoli was the promoter and chief agent.[3] My friend Cowell, secretary,

[2] [The mine workings were at a place variously named Tlalpujahua, Tlalpuxatua or Tlalpuxahua. The town is located in north east Mexico. Silver mines had been opened during Spanish rule in 1558. The company that Norman joined was called the Tlalpuxahua Company. It was formed in November 1824 to work the mines on a 30 year lease. The company published a statement about its plans on 22 December 1824. The London directors were John Smith, MP, who was Chairman, William Sampson, who was Deputy Chairman and also a director of the Royal Exchange Assurance Office, Colonel Henry Cooke, Norman's friends John Welsford Cowell and George Robert Smith, George Green, William Hartley, and Norman himself. (John Murray, *American Mining Companies*, 3rd edition, London 1825 pp. 47-8.) The company proposed to raise a capital of £409,000, chiefly by selling 1,000 shares of £400 each, though this seems later to have been reduced to £400,000. However only £320,000 was invested. The company was involved in 19 mines, and acquired additional mines in Santa Cruz, Valenciana and Socabon. At Tlalpuxahua the company possessed 86 shafts, but not all were working. As late as January 1827, up to 23,000 labourers are reported to have been employed.]

[3] [This was the director of the company in Mexico, known as the Chevalier de Rivafinoli. Captain Beaufoy (see p. 293) was also in Mexico, as Norman mentions. The Chevalier spent impressively on infrastructure, but failed to produce silver. Norman's friend Cameron was sent by the company to Tlalpuxahua and, when he arrived in December 1827, Rivafinoli felt it appropriate to resign. Cameron's report was damning. Rivafinoli's expenditure had contributed nothing to the company's success, and further heavy investment would be required. It was subsequently argued that, had the directors kept their nerve, the project could have been highly profitable; see H.G. Ward, *Mexico* (London: Henry Colburn, 1829, vol. 1 p. 428). As it was, in August 1828, the directors decided to wind up the company. It is apparent that the investment in silver mining companies was in the nature

Colonel W. Wylde,[4] and Captain Beaufoy[5] were dispatched to Mexico to cooperate with and in case of need to control the chief agents. There were also several English and German miners, the latter men of high scientific reputation.

On the whole the speculation was conducted with great ability and I may add also with sterling honesty. As an instance of this, I may mention, that although the shares were for a long time at a high premium, not more than one or two directors sold a share until full reports had been received of the state of things in America, and these reports had been laid with the most

---

of a bubble. 624 joint stock companies were started in 1825, and by far the largest category, 74 companies, was that of mining companies. (Henry English, *A General Guide to the Companies Formed for Foreign Mines*, London: Boosey and Sons, 1825). See also Benjamin Disraeli, *An Inquiry into the Plans, Progress and Policy of the American Mining Companies*, 3rd edition, John Murray, 1835. Count Chevalier Vincente de Rivafinoli subsequently surfaced in North America. He went to the United States in 1829-30, and was involved in the exploitation of mines in Charlotte, North Carolina. In this he seems to have had some success though, as in Mexico, living in great style, and accounts of the outcome also vary. Sir Henry George Ward, 1797-1860, was an important source of information especially for investors already committed to investment in Mexico. The full title of the work referred to above is *Mexico. By H.G. Ward, His Majesty's Chargé d'Affaires in that Country during the years 1825, 1826 and part of 1827, second edition enlarged, with an account of the mining companies, and of political elements in that republic, to the present day.* London: Colburn, 1829.]

4 [Colonel William Wylde, RA, 1788-1877. From February 1840 he was Equerry and Groom in Waiting to Prince Albert, who employed him on confidential missions to Spain, and he was a strong supporter of Queen Isabella (see p. 221). In 1863 he became Colonel Commandant of the Royal Artillery.]

5 [Captain Mark Beaufoy, 1793-1854. He was the second son of Mark Beaufoy FRS and Margaretta Beaufoy. He was educated at Eton, where he was a contemporary of Norman, joined the Coldstream Guards, and was present at Waterloo. He retired from the army in 1825. He became Adjutant of the Coldstream Guards 17 April 1823, but after two years was offered an appointment with the Tlalpuxahua Mining Company, at £800 per annum. He paid £4,860 on his shares, which ultimately proved a loss when the company was wound up, and resigned from his job in dissatisfaction at an impossible task. According to the family historian, 'The Mexican appointment proved to be a great disappointment also a pecuniary loss, and for which he had given up his military career'. Gwendolyn Beaufoy, *Leaves from a Beech Tree*, Oxford: Blackwell, 1930 pp. 199, 231-40. Captain Mark Beaufoy wrote *Mexican Illustrations, Founded on Facts* (1828), and travelled extensively subsequently. He was, according to Gwendolyn Beaufoy, an unhappy man. He retired to Bowness where he died.]

perfect fairness before the shareholders.

Notwithstanding all this, however the speculation completely failed and at the end of two or three years the company was dissolved and the assets divided, after a loss had been incurred of over £200,000.[6] C.H. Cameron, with J.G. Graham now Official Assignee,[7] as his secretary were sent to Mexico when affairs looked black and we began to distrust the management of Rivafinoli and it was to the judgment and firmness of the former we owed the final abandonment of the mines and the consequent avoidance of further loss.

It may be remarked that the mines of Tlalpuxahua, although very pro-

[6] [£13,908,000 in 2009 values.]

[7] [George John Graham, 1801-88, Official Assignee of 25 Coleman Street, London, and close friend of John Stuart Mill. When, in the winter of 1822-3, John Stuart Mill set up the Utilitarian Society, one of the members was 'George Graham, afterwards an official assignee of the Bankruptcy Court, a thinker of originality and power on almost all abstract subjects', as Mill described him. See John Stuart Mill, *Autobiography*, 8th ed., London: Longman, 1886 p. 81. Elsewhere Mill referred to Graham as 'a friend of whom it is to be regretted, that his great capacity for abstract metaphysics has never exercised itself in the composition of any work on the subject'. See *The Collected Works of John Stuart Mill*, vol. VIII ed. J.M. Robson, Toronto: University of Toronto Press, 1974 p. 816n. In addition to his intellectual qualities, Graham was also a traveller who went to Mexico in 1827-9, as Norman reports in connection with the Mexican mining venture, and while there collected 400 specimens of Mexican plants. A group of Utilitarians also met for two or three years at Grote's house in Threadneedle Street. See J.S. Mill, *Autobiography*, 8th edition, London: Longman, 1886 pp. 119-20. The members were Grote, J.S. Mill, Roebuck, William Ellis, W.H. Prescott, two brothers Whitmore (probably, given the banking connection with Grote, Edward and Frederick), and G.J. Graham. The meetings were presided over by James Mill. Graham also joined J.S. Mill in a tour of Sussex in 1827. As an Official Assignee, Graham appeared in hearings which made clear the precarious legal position of an Official Assignee, if goods seized in a bankruptcy case, even by an agent of the Assignee without his knowledge, proved to have a prior claim attached to them. Liability for legal costs in such a case also rested with the Assignee. Indeed one such case involved William Whitmore, Norman's brother in law. Graham argued that Assignees should be protected, and that they should receive part of their income by way of retainer. Their existing income was modest. Graham put it at £500 per year net. See *Parliamentary Papers* 1840 (274) XVI, 1, *Report of the Commissioners for Enquiring into Bankruptcy and Insolvency*, qq. 2274, 2278, 2283. From this we learn that Graham had been an Official Assignee since the post was created by the English Bankruptcy Act of 1831.]

ductive of silver in times long past, had not yielded abundantly for a long period before the time when we undertook to work them. Those companies like the Real de Monte,[8] and Anglo-Mexican[9] &c, which obtained the possession of mines whose yield had been abundant up to the moment of their abandonment fared much worse than ourselves. Their hopes were higher and lasted longer. They expended more capital and have finally broken down. One or two may still drag on a rickety existence but I do not believe a single company has proved to be other than a most losing concern.

I have said that the great mass of the joint stock companies of 1825 were founded on most erroneous views. Many of course were bubbles, merely intended for the stock exchange. A few, chiefly insurance companies such as the Alliance, have survived and thriven, and I may add the Continental Gas Company which for some time was vastly profitable.

I took no shares in any of the miscellaneous companies, excepting the Australian Land Company and a Silk Company both chartered. Of the former I became a director and continued to act for several years.

I will not enlarge further upon the panic of 1825, but refer to the full relations respecting it, to be found in well-known publications, confining myself to what relates personally to myself.

By the year 1825, I had obtained a certain standing in the Bank Court, and was listened to. I of course opposed the old regime, thus acting in union with W. Ward and a few others, but in doing this, I tried to give as little

---

8 [The Real de Monte was formed in 1825. Its board of directors contained Henry Cooke, who was also involved in the company of which Norman was a director. It continued to trade unprofitably for years. It is reported that, by 1846, 10 million pesos in silver had been coined at a net loss of 5 million pesos. It was wound up in 1848. Its total loss was around £1.5 million.]

9 [The Anglo-Mexican Mining Association was formed in January 1824. Like those involved in other companies, the projectors believed that the introduction of English capital and skill would make the mines productive. This company was centred at Guanajuato, which had been the most productive mining district in Mexico. But the mines were in a very bad state, and the company seriously underestimated what was involved. None the less its output of silver is reported to have been $573,000 by 1828.]

offence to the seniors as possible.[10]

When the troubles came to their acme and the probability that the Bank must stop became imminent, not owing absolutely to the want of gold, for the exchanges had turned and gold was sure to come from abroad,[11] but to the difficulty of getting it coined fast enough, a general cry on the part of the directors was that an order in council ought to be issued, that we were ill-treated, abandoned and left in the lurch. I ventured most strongly to oppose these views, maintaining that the government was right, that we ought to pay to the last sovereign and then publicly explain our position and resume payment at the earliest period, which would probably be in a few days.

It is rather a remarkable fact that some years afterwards when I became slightly acquainted with Sir W. Napier the historian,[12] he told me on one occasion that he had long felt a great respect for me on account of the part I had thus taken in the Court of Directors when a suspension of specie payments was imminent. I allowed of course his remarks to pass unnoticed, without agreeing to their truth or denying it.

Considering the profound secrecy which was then enjoined on Bank Directors as to their proceedings, and even opinions, I never could understand how this little piece of intelligence had oozed out. I had certainly never divulged it to a human being.

The opinions of the great historian and myself on matters of currency were as strongly opposed as they well could be. He was a Cobbettite, a believer in the then renowned William Cobbett, who told so many fibs and

[10] [It is worth emphasising, in view of the mistake in the authoritative *Dictionary of National Biography* noted on p. 246, that Ward, like Norman, believed strongly in regulating the note issue of the Bank with respect to the exchanges.]

[11] [Silver had been shipped to France and gold was due in exchange, thanks to Rothschild's negotiations, and the French bimetallic system. See Clapham, *The Bank of England*, vol. 2, p. 101.]

[12] [Sir William Francis Patrick Napier, 1785-1860, army officer, Peninsula war veteran, author of a history of the Peninsula war. Major General 1841, General 1859. For some months in 1824 he was in close contact with Wellington, who may have passed on to him gossip concerning the Bank.]

wrote such capital English.[13]

One evening about ten o'clock, when I was sitting before the fire at the joint lodging of Cowell and myself in Berkeley Square during the height of the crisis, Cowell came in and told me that he had just come from old Mr Loyd's in New Norfolk Street and that as he left the house, he had heard Mr Buller the Governor[14] and Deputy Governor[15] of the Bank announced. I was greatly moved by this intelligence but concealed my feelings, made an excuse for going out, called on James Pattison in the Albany,[16] told him what I had heard, found him as ignorant as myself and as anxious to be informed, and went with him to old John Pearse,[17] a leading member of the Committee of Treasury, who lived at the Sun Company's house in Craig's Court.

Pearse was out when we got there, but about twelve o'clock he came home and we then learned that the object of the Governor's visit to Mr Loyd, had been to sound him on the propriety of a contemplated issue of £1 and £2 notes to supply the want of sovereigns. That measure, subsequently adapted, was a good measure and answered particularly well.

[13][William Cobbett, 1762-1835, political writer and ally of the Birmingham inflationist Thomas Attwood. He is estimated to have written some 30 million words over the course of 40 years. In the 1820s he caused trouble at local meetings held to discuss agricultural distress, by advocating universal manhood suffrage.]

[14][The Governor was Cornelius Buller, a Director 1803-31, Deputy Governor 1822-4, Governor 1824-6.]

[15][The Deputy Governor was John Baker Richards, died 1833, a Director 1805-33, Deputy Governor 1824-6, Governor 1826-8. According to Clapham (*The Bank of England*, vol. 2 p. 99), Richards had to handle the crisis because amongst the 1825 commercial failures was Pole, Thornton, Free, Down and Scott, Henry Thornton's firm, and Sir Peter Pole was connected by marriage with the Governor, Cornelius Buller. Richards did not see his children for a week (Clapham, p. 101).]

[16][James Pattison, 1786-1849, the son of Nathaniel Pattison of Congleton, Cheshire, and the nephew of another James Pattison, a director of the East India Company 1805-30 when he was apparently disqualified. The family home was Plumstead, Kent. He is described as a spectacle maker. MP City of London 1835-41, 1843-9. He was a Director of the Bank 1813-49, Deputy Governor 1833-4, Governor 1834-7. As an MP he was a radical, favouring triennial Parliaments, vote by ballot and church reform. It was at Norman's suggestion that he was invited to stand as MP for the City of London; but, as Norman relates, relations became very strained during the crisis of October 1847 (see p. 418).]

[17][John Pearse, Governor 1810-12; see p. 245.]

Not so the measure of buying gold at a high price or paying a commission to Rothschild, I forget which, which was continued long after the changes had turned in favor of England when consequently the gold would have flowed into the Coffers of the Bank, without any direct action on our part, especially as the contraction and discredit were most severe. The cost of this operation if I recollect aright was over £100,000,[18] how the Jew must have laughed at the Christians?

The great fall of prices in 1825 and the numerous bankruptcies operated most prejudicially to the interest of our house. Like most other people we had extended our operations in 1824 and had made large advances to foreign correspondents, one alone of £10,000,[19] to Ernst Rohde[20] the purchaser of Hafslund from Mr G. Rozencrantz. Our losses abroad were heavy. They were also heavy among the yard-keepers at home and on the whole, after deducting very considerable apparent profits, I conceive the net diminution in our capital during 1824 and 1825 could not have been less than from £15,000 to £20,000.[21]

My brother and I were saved from want of money by my father's generosity. He placed at our disposition a large amount of French stock, which we sold to supply our wants at very low prices.

For many weeks during the height of the crisis, my time and attention was absorbed at the Bank and I could not attend to my private affairs. Previously I had allowed far too much rein to Richard, whose inexperience, sanguine temper and eagerness for gain, rendered him a most dangerous Lieutenant. The truth was, that although not disliking mercantile business en gros, and especially the general direction and correspondence, he hated many of the details and above all the buying and selling.

One important measure was undertaken at the Bank in the early part of

[18] [Worth £6,954,000 in 2009 prices.]
[19] [Worth £816,900 in 2009 prices.]
[20] [See p. 285.]
[21] [From £1,043,100 to £1,390,900 in 2009 prices.]

1826, in which I bore an important part, I mean the establishment of the Branches.[22] This measure had been suggested by the Government some time previously and was then rejected by the Bank Court.

During the storm of 1825, representations came from several towns, which had suffered from the failure of private banks and from want of Banking accommodation, inviting such establishments. I brought the matter before the Court and carried my point in spite of the opposition of most of the seniors and of the Committee of Treasury.

My opinion was that the branches would give increased stability to the currency generally. That they would augment the necessity for, and the importance of, the Bank of England, which was then at a low ebb, and that they would furnish large profits to the proprietors.

I must confess that like my colleagues and the public at large, I by no means foresaw distinctly what would be the effect and operation of the branches and as to one important object, that of profit, I formed an exaggerated view. Still I have ever regarded them as highly useful both to the Bank and the public and look back with pleasure to the part I took in their original formation. The country issues have been far more sound since 1825, than previously.

---

[22] [The establishment of the country branches is recounted in Acres, *The Bank of England from Within, 1694-1900* (London: Oxford University Press for the Bank of England, 1931) vol. 2 pp. 426-37. See also Clapham, *The Bank of England*, vol. 2 pp. 91-2, 103-6, 110-16. Neither Clapham nor Acres mentions Norman's role in this development.]

# Chapter 11

# More Travels

In April 1826 I left the Bank Court by rotation and took advantage of my holiday to run over to Norway and look after the business of the house. My brother Henry was my companion. We sailed in the Fortuna, Captain F. Ries, belonging to agent Jacob Nielsen[1] of Christiania and had a long but agreeable voyage to that town. On our way we were stopped for a week off Sheerness.

So far as regarded the recovery of bad debts, my expedition did but little good, but I put a few things in order and made one or two good connections.

The Louise von Haxthausen of 1819-1820 had become two or three years previously Baronisse von Stedingke[2] and was sojourning with her family at the Lokke (a country house) called Lille Frogner on the Drammen Road.

I paid two or three visits there along with Henry to whom I had told, though not in much detail, the story of my love. I cannot describe with how much emotion, I entered by the gate leading from the road, walked through the pleasure ground, and knocked at the door, all which I knew so well. Er herskapet hjemme (Is the family at home?) Yes. I entered with a beating heart and was most kindly received as an old acquaintance. Louise looked very pretty, but time and childbearing had somewhat changed the brilliant

[1] [Possibly Jacob Nielsen, 1754-1826, a member of a family that originated in Denmark, and moved to Norway in the 13th century.]

[2] [See p. 218 for information about the family.]

hue of 18 and after half an hour, I had somewhat recovered my composure and cheerfulness. I paid many subsequent visits and the result of all this was that I finally regarded the woman of whom I had been so passionately fond, as little more than an old friend.

I used to correspond with her for many years. Now and then sent her a present, but at length our topics of common interest gradually died away and the interchange of letters ceased. I know not who allowed it to drop.

In 1850, when at Carlsbad, I met Marie Mansbach and Colonel Mansbach,[3] first cousins to Louise, and heard a great deal about her. It afforded me much pleasure to talk over old times with them.

I may here remark as somewhat of a peculiarity in me, that with all my admiration of women I never, so far as I recollect, ever fell in love with a wife. Why this was I really cannot say, but it is certainly, that she who had become the property of another ceased to possess any overwhelming charm for me.

I was never a man of intrigue. Any attempt upon the virtue of a married woman never occupied my thoughts. I ever thought adultery a wicked and a base act.

During my visits to Norway in 1826 I saw a great deal of my dear friend Count Wedel, and was several times at Bogstad. An extraordinary Storthing was sitting either then or in 1828, the only time when I witnessed the debates in that assembly. They pleased me much. The system of double election makes the representatives the very elite of the nation.[4]

I think that Henry and I went as far West as Schien, for I recollect visiting with him the beautiful beech woods of Laurvig. Our whole visit however did not exceed six or seven weeks. We returned home by the way of Wenersburg, Gothenburg, Uddewalla, Halmstad and Helsingburg, so far travelling by land,

---

[3] [Major General Mansbach had commanded the Danish troops (Norway then being a province of Denmark) in opposing the Swedish invasion of 1788-9; see pp. 217-8, 220.]

[4] [On double election, see p. 172.]

and a very severe journey it was. We had stayed a day at that most beautiful place Röd near Frederickshald, then belonging to Statzraad Tank. The first night we slept at Wenersburg. On the second day we overtook our forebud, or avant-courier near Trolhatta, and from thence to the sound had to wait for horses at every station, just long enough to fidget us and not long enough to procure us rest, excepting at Karby where we lay down in our clothes for two or three hours. We crossed from Helsingborg to Helsingoer, hired a carriage and proceeded to Copenhagen which we reached at three in the morning on the third night after a journey from Wenersborg of about sixty-seven hours.

I need not dwell longer upon our journey home in 1826, because since I wrote the preceding paragraph, I have discovered some notes of this tour. Suffice it to say, that we staid a few days at Copenhagen, went in an open boat to Kiel in four days, crossed Holstein to Hamburg and had a very bad voyage home, so bad indeed that we were insured at ten per cent.

I recollect nothing particular as having occurred during the remainder of 1826 or 1827. I went on as usual, passing about four days in the week in London and the remainder at Bromley, where I amused myself at shooting and cricket. When in London, I practiced fencing and gymnastics assiduously.[5]

Every year I used to go to Stoneham, to Purley Hall, the residence of my uncle Mr Wilder[6] and to Chicksands near Shefford[7] which had been hired

[5] [See pp. 285-6.]

[6] [Frederick Beadon, Norman's maternal uncle, the third son of Norman's grandfather, Edwards Beadon, Rector of North Stoneham, who himself became Rector of North Stoneham, married Mary Anne, eldest daughter of the Reverend Henry Wilder, LLD, 1744-1814, of Purley Hall, Berks, Rector of Sulham. The Wilder uncle referred to seems to have been John Wilder, of Sulham. He matriculated at Oxford in 1787 aged 18. He was married to Harriet Beadon, Norman's maternal aunt. He died in 1834.]

[7] [The Chicksands Estate was originally a Gilbertine priory, and it passed into private hands following the Dissolution of the Monasteries, organised by Thomas Cromwell, in 1537. It became the home of the Osborne family until 1935. It subsequently passed into the hands of the Ministry of Defence. It is not clear when Norman started going to Chicksands, but it was the property of Sir George Osborne, 4th Bt, 1742-1818, and then of Sir John Osborne, 5th Bt, 1772-1848, a Lord of the Admiralty 1812-24.]

by our friend Mr C. Dixon afterwards of Stansted park, who had married a Wilder.[8]

In London, my acquaintance was not very numerous, it comprehended the Ords, Blakes, John and G. Smiths, Lord Lansdowne and many miscellaneous people.

I continued to employ all my spare time in reading and made somewhat a study of political economy, towards which the [Political Economy] Club and my position at the Bank naturally impelled me.

My political feelings at this time were very strong and what would now be called radical, and especially did I entertain the most earnest desire for the emancipation of the Catholics.

On the 12 April 1828, I made my last visit to Norway, again accompanied by my brother Henry. The immediate occasion of it was large advances, which had been made to Ernest Rohde[9] by the houses of Sillem[10] and Grantoff and our own, exceeding in each case £10,000.[11] Herman Sillem, a highly respectable man who died a few years ago, was our companion and we took the route by Hamburg and Copenhagen, stopping a day or two at both places.

At Hamburg, we were most hospitably received by old Senator Sillem, H.S.'s half brother. He invited us to dinner telling us that we must only expect pot luck. However the banquet, which took place at about two or three o'clock in the afternoon, as the Hamburg merchants in those days always went to their counting houses after dinner, was of a most varied and sumptuous kind. There was turtle, fish of several kind, venison, woodcocks

[8] [Charles Dixon married Harriet, daughter of the Reverend Henry Wilder of Purley Hall, Berks.]

[9] [See p. 285.]

[10] [See D. Morier Evans, *The History of the Commercial Crisis, 1857-8* (London: Groombridge, 1859) pp. clviii-clix. The firm of Herman Sillem, Son and Company, in the Hamburg and German trade, ran into difficulties in December 1857, due to commercial problems in Hamburg and elsewhere in Germany, rather than in London. Though insolvent, the anticipated loss was only £22,000 (£1,779,800 at 2009 prices .]

[11] [Worth £809,000 in 2009 prices.]

&c profusion of costly wine, and to close all, the strongest coffee I ever drank. For all this I paid dearly, for after going to the opera in the evening, where was performed Don Giovanni in German with Heizinger as first tenor, I returned to my hotel in a state of the most pitiable nervous suffering. Not a moment during the night did I lose the most painful consciousness, and I doubt if during any part of my life I ever passed more miserable hours. I was very ill too the next day, when I walked with Henry to look at Klopstok's monument in the cemetery at Altona.[12] It took me several days to recover my ordinary condition.

I fancy that at the time in question the Hamburg merchants were great gourmands and lived altogether a very dissipated life, taking little or no exercise. The results were visible in their physical condition. They were a bad-looking set of men and I made a similar remark as to the whole population. The number of deformed people in the streets struck me as being very large.

Either on this visit to Hamburg or that in 1826 or probably the former, I was invited by Mr C.H. Donner a Merchant at Altona[13] to dine with him at his country seat.[14] Henry and I went together and found a pretty residence on the banks of the river with fine trees gardens and a very sumptuous repast. It so happened, that I mentioned having been in Italy a few years previously. Donner then asked me if I knew Thorvaldsen,[15] I replied in the

[12][A monument to the poet Friedrich Gottlieb Klopstock, 1724-1803.]

[13][Conrad Hinrich Donner, 1774-1854. Businesses in banking and shipbuilding, such as the Conrad Hinrich Donner Bank AG, which was founded by Donner in 1798, still bear his name. He was an art collector and, with the assistance of Gottfried Semper, he combined sculpture and gardens in 1834.]

[14][Donner's Park is situated on the bank of the river Elbe. Donner was not the original owner. The property was created in 1676 by Barthold Jencquel, nephew of a Hamburg senator. In 1793 it became the property of Sieveking, Poel and Mathiessen. One of the guests there included Klopstock. In 1820 Donner bought the property.]

[15][Albert Bertel Thorvaldsen, 1770-1844, a Danish/Icelandic sculptor. After winning the gold medal at Copenhagen's Royal Danish Academy of Art, he received a royal grant to enable him to complete his studies in Rome, where he arrived in

negative adding that Thorvaldsen was not in Rome when I was there but that I had examined his studio. I was then asked which of his works I most admired. I mentioned the Triumph of Alexander in Basso Relievo at the Villa Sommarina on the Lake of Como and others of his best productions. I concluded by saying that I had seen nothing which pleased me more than the sitting figure of a youth, with I think a staff in his hand and a dog by his side, usually called the Shepherd Boy. This indeed is a beautiful work from its simplicity, truthfulness and perfect execution. No sooner had I finished my story than Donner drew aside a green curtain on one side of the room and behind it was the veritable Shepherd boy in all its loveliness, one of the most perfect products of modern-art. Donner then told me a long story of his having given a commission to Thorwaldsen, when the latter was poor and struggling for subsistence, at a price I think of 100 crowns, of the choice of a subject, of the long time which elapsed bcfore the completion of the work was announced. Of the unwillingness which Thorwaldsen showed to part with it, although offered repeated augmentations in the price, and finally that Donner was forced in order to obtain his due, to direct his agent to claim the statue by legal means, tendering, if I recollect aright 2000 crowns in payment. At any rate Donner in this way gained his object.

While naming C.H. Donner, who was reckoned a very sharp, not to say unscrupulous man of business, I may mention that he like Sillem and ourselves, was a large creditor of Ernest Rohde[16] and had obtained security from him, contrary to the understanding which existed between us and Rohde. This I learned in London from a casual expression which dropped from Johan Donner, C.H. Donner's brother. I immediately went to Rohde, who was then in London, and insisted upon his also giving us security, which after much resistance, he did, on his stock of timber and deals. I agreed however

March 1797. Such was his success that he did not leave Italy for 16 years. His 'Shepherd Boy with Dog' is regarded as very much Classical in style, as is his bas-relief of Hylas and the Nymphs.]

[16] [See p. 285.]

that I would not have the document registered (tinglyst) unless Donner did this with his. We soon heard that Donner had directed his documents to be tinglyst and gave similar directions as to ours. It so happened that owing to the superior activity of our agent, or the neglect of his, our security, although latest in date was placed first on the registry and thus obtained a priority, after a good deal of litigation in the Norwegian Courts.

The above was about the only sharp thing I ever did as a man of business, and although Donner was extremely angry, he perhaps in his heart gave me the credit of having tricked him. The truth was that I had done nothing of the kind. He had extorted the security from Rohde, meaning to obtain an advantage over the other creditors. Owing to the mistake of his agent, he failed in this and the tables were turned upon him.

I may add that the security turned out good for little, owing to the expence we were put to in Norway and the low price of deals in England.

Rohde had been Banker to Carl Johan[17] and had much interest with him. I therefore insured his life at the Crown thinking that if he lived, he might through the royal favour, be placed in improved pecuniary circumstances and be enabled to pay the whole or at any rate a portion of his debt. This was done while Rohde was in London. At the dissolution of partnership, I took this policy at a valuation, in order to save Richard from the annual drain of the premium. Rohde only lived for two or three years afterwards and the transaction thus became very profitable for me.

I had subsequently some painful scruples as to this whole affair, arizing upon the question whether Rohde's was a good life at the time the insurance was made, and also, as to whether I was justified in acting as non-medical reference for Sillem, when Rohde's life was insured in some other office, while he was non-medical referee in [my] application at the 'Crown'. The fact was that Rohde had no other friends in London who could testify as to his

[17] [Bernadotte, Charles XIV of Sweden; see p. 160.]

constitution and habits. That I fully believed him to be a healthy although not a strong man. That he presented himself to the directors and medical officers of the companies, and that I had no idea his life would be so short. He died within five or six years after the issue of the policies.

I sometimes thought of repaying the money to the Crown, but after mature and somewhat painful reflection, made up my mind that I should not be justified in doing this and that I had no good ground for reproaching myself in the transaction.

I paid Richard no more than the regular value of the policy, tolerable proof that he at any rate had no idea that the purchase would turn out a bargain.

I believe the truth to have been that Rohde, although little dyspeptic now and then, was a strong man who would probably have lived to the calculated age, but that the ruin of his fortune acted on his health and shortened his days, he may indeed have died of some accidental illness.

I have referred at some length to the aforesaid transaction because for some years it gave me pain from a doubt if my conduct in it had been irrepproachable. I can now, after mature reflection, look back upon it without remorse.

Henry and I and Sillem proceeded from Hamburg to Lubeck, one of the most quaint and curious old towns I ever saw, and thence to Copenhagen where Sillem was detained by a fit of indigestion and we left him.

I was always much pleased with Copenhagen, a fine city, beautifully situated and containing many objects of interest. We went to Noravacs in a steam boat, landed at Fredericksvarn and had a most severe and painful journey of twenty-four hours to Christiania, just as the frost was breaking up.

I forgot to mention that we found Henry H. Berens at Hamburg and saw him constantly.[18] He was learning business in the house of Merke and Co.

I have no notes of my visit to Norway in 1828, I was busily employed in looking after my affairs especially as respected the claims on E. Rohde and Pavel Thrane of Borregaard[19] both of whom had failed by this time. I passed some days in consequence at Borregaard and Hafsland[20] and had an opportunity of watching the management of an insolvent estate in Norway. I also in company with Henry and my agent Seml,[21] visited the property of Sanne and Soerli which had come into our possession owing to the failure of Carsten Tank.[22]

This was a very fine estate on the Glommen and had been mortgaged to us by the Bernt Ankerske Fidei Commis,[23] before its sale to Tank. We did not claim the regular payment of the instalments and this allowed the second mortgagee Benjamin Sewell[24] to slip in before us. He had a claim for

[18][Henry Hulse Berens, 1804-83, second son of Joseph Berens of Kevington, St Mary Cray by Charlotte, daughter of Richard Benyon of Englefield House, Berks, Deputy Chairman of Public Works Loan Office 1849-52, a Director of the Bank of England 1849-80, Governor of the Hudson Bay Company 1858-63. The Berens were a Kent family with whom Norman was well acquainted.]

[19][Borregaard is now the site of a chemical works.]

[20][Hafslund Manor has used since the 17th century the waterfall Sarpsfossen in Glomma to work a mill, a grist mill and a saw mill. At the end of the 19th century Hafslund became a pioneer source of hydroelectric power generation. This was the first large scale power plant in Norway.]

[21][Probably – not identified.]

[22][Carsten Tank, 1766-1832, was the Norwegian Counsellor of Government to the first Ministry of Finance in March to November 1814, during the short lived Norwegian monarchy of that year. He was later in the same position for the Ministry, under Swedish rule.]

[23][A number of big landed holdings in Sweden were possessed by noble families. When these were categorised as Fidei Commis, the aristocrats maintained a feudal retinue, with some tenants paying their rent in kind, through labour or through output, but rarely in money.]

[24][The firm of Sewell and Neck in the Norwegian trade was one of those which failed in December 1857. Its failure was, however, only temporary; the firm requested time to pay 20 shillings in the pound, due to the difficulty of realising assets in Norway. This sum was to be paid over 6, 12, 18, and 24 months with interest at 5 per cent. This plan seems to have been carried out successfully, as in 1873 Benjamin Sewell is recorded as having bought a water-powered pulp paper mill beside the waterfall at Damfossen in Skien, Norway.]

nearly £5,000. Just before I quitted business, I paid him £4,500, in full of his claim.[25] The estate then became ours and I took it in the settlement with Richard, leaving him the active capital. The result was very advantageous to me as I sold Sanne and Soerli in 1838, I think to a company for no less than 90,000 silver dollars or £20,000,[26] all of which was regularly paid in ten years by instalments of ten per cent with interest at four per cent. The estate was put up to auction on lease, at the same time as for an absolute sale, of £1,300 per annum, which was bid for it by Christie of Moss. Sales in Norway by auction are usually made on approbation by the seller. Time was thus given me to make up my mind and I preferred the absolute sale and wisely too, inasmuch as the dams and mills required a large outlay and constant attention to prevent damage during high water, which would not have suited a foreigner.

I have sometimes lamented however, that I had not retained an estate which would have furnished a profitable maintenance and occupation for a son or two, and that in a country beautiful, healthy and with an excellent government.

It was in 1826 or 1828, I think the latter, that the King[27] came to Christiania and Lord Bloomfield, the English minister, with Lady Bloomfield and her daughters accompanied him.[28] We met the latter at Bogstad and accom-

[25][See p. 339. Norman merged the family timber business with that of Benjamin Sewell on his retirement.]

[26][Worth £1,649,800 in 2009 prices.]

[27][Bernadotte, Charles XIV of Sweden; see p. 160.]

[28][Lieutenant General Benjamin Bloomfield, 1768-1846, 1st Baron Bloomfield. Major General 1814, Lieutenant General 1830. Bloomfield was a courtier who was made Gentleman in Waiting to the Prince of Wales 1808, Aide de Camp to the King 1811-14, Clerk Marshall and Chief Equerry to the Prince of Wales 1812-17, Auditor and Secretary to the Duchy of Cornwall 1816-17, Keeper of the Privy Purse and Secretary, 1817-22. He became Commander of the Garrison at Woolwich. MP (Tory) Plymouth 1812-17. Knighted 1815, created Baron Bloomfield of Oakhampton and Redwood, County Tipperary, 1825. He married Harriott Douglas (c.1776-1868), daughter of John Douglas of Grantham, Lincs, September 1797. He held the office of Envoy to Sweden 1822-32, having been relieved of his Court duties; while there was some suggestion of financial impropriety, he may just have

panied them to the Krokkleiva and Ringerike, which afford snow[29] landscapes of exquisite beauty. We often saw the King. I perfectly recollect him at a review at Ettersted, galloping along the lines of troops with an immense staff, on this occasion the artillery fired grape at a barricade of palings six foot high and I was struck with the little effect produced by these projectiles at a distance of 200 to 300 yards.

I forgot to mention that while at Sanne we saw caught in nets and subsequently ate the gjoers[30], (jack perch of Lagd[31]) one of the best of freshwater fish, which ought to be introduced into England.

During this visit to Norway one or two other circumstances occurred worth recording. The King had written some long and elaborate instructions for the Crown Prince, now King Oscar,[32] and had placed them in the hands of Count Wedel. The Count, as there were no State secrets in them and as they did his Majesty credit rather than the reverse, was so good as to permit me to peruse them. I set speedily to work upon them and had been so employed for an hour or two when the Count burst into my room in a great hurry and begged for the manuscript which the King had just demanded from him. It was lucky that he found me at my lodgings. After so many years, and a partial and hurried perusal, I have but slight recollection of this royal effort of paternal care. At any rate it did not strike me as displaying any very remarkable depth of information or acuteness of intellect, but abundance of fatherly love and good feeling.

Another anecdote worth preservation is the following. While I was in

---

been the victim of Court intrigue. While in Sweden he joined the Wesleyan sect. His daughters were Georgina Mary Amelia (died 1893), and Harriott Mary Anne, 1806-1901.]

[29] [Probably, manuscript is not clear.]

[30] [Norman wrote 'gjirfs' here. The fish is Gjørs or Gjoers; the English term is Pike-Perch or Jack-Perch. Norman says that these should be introduced into England. It seems that they were, and have become a huge nuisance, like other imported species.]

[31] [Probably – manuscript unclear.]

[32] [Bernadotte's son; see p. 233.]

Norway, or just before, news had arrived of the downfall of the Ripon[33] Ministry in England. This Ministry was the first check and interruption which the Tory rule had received, with the single exception of the 'Talents' for few months,[34] in more than forty years. It produced a great commotion on the continent, excited many hopes and fears and in taking the measures which led to the Battle of Navarino,[35] produced the permanent good of freeing Greece from the Ottoman Yolk.

Carl Johan was well aware that the holy alliance and its adherents did not like Parvenu Kings, and suspected that its members would see with pleasure a restoration of the House of Holstein to the Swedish throne.[36] He thought that a Liberal ministry in England would not fail to take his part and was therefore considerably alarmed at learning that a Peel and Wellington cabinet had replaced the Riponites. This being the state of things, I was one day told that Count Wetterstedt,[37] the Minister for foreign affairs who had accompanied the King to Christiania, wished to see me. We met and he began by talking to me about the timber duties[38] and about the mission

[33][Frederick John Robinson, Viscount Goderich and 1st Earl of Ripon, 1782-1859.]

[34][The coalition ministry of 1806-7, known as the Ministry of All the Talents, and headed by Lord Grenville, 1759-1834.]

[35][Canning, the British Prime Minister, died 12 August 1827, four months after taking office. He had tried to avoid open conflict. Ripon succeeded Canning, and did not resign until the following year. Greece became subject to the power of the Ottoman Empire in 1460 and, apart from a brief episode of Venetian control of Athens in the early 18th century, it remained under Turkish sway until the 19th century. Attempts at overthrowing the Turks in 1821 were ruthlessly crushed. But, after further unrest, the British, French and Russian fleets destroyed the Turkish and Egyptian fleets at the battle of Navarino in October 1827. In 1830 Greece was declared an independent kingdom. After the assassination of a Greek President, the Crown was offered to Otto I, son of King Ludwig I of Bavaria, in 1833. He was deposed in 1862, and Prince George of Denmark was chosen as King.]

[36][The Danish king, Frederick VI, was also Duke of Holstein, in which capacity he joined the German confederation in 1815, but refused to allow Schleswig to become part of it.]

[37][Count Gustaf af Wetterstedt, 1776-1837, Swedish Foreign Minister 1824-37. He was a member of the Swedish Academy, and of the Royal Swedish Academies of Agriculture, Music and Sciences.]

[38][See pp. 167, 211, and Norman's *Essay on Taxation*, pp. 61, 78, 86-7, 189-90,

of Count Wedel to London, with a view to obtain some change in them. He then questioned me closely upon the probable policy of the new ministry. I knew that what I said would go to the King and expressed a strong opinion that no important change in the foreign policy of England need be feared. I found Count Wettersted a very agreeable and sensible man, speaking fair English, in which language we conversed. This was the first and last time in which I was ever taken into the councils of a Sovereign.

Either on this visit to Norway or in that in 1826, Henry and I visited Ejdsvold, which we had purchased on the death of Carsten Anker,[39] paying off the prior mortgages due to the Government. We lodged with the Forvalter (agent) house, but inspected the Hovedgaard in which the Diet of 1814 was held. The Hall was by no means an imposing apartment. This purchase of Ejdsvold, which was worked for our joint, or Richard's sole account, was a very unfortunate operation. We paid I think Sh 50,000 to Sh 60,000 in money.[40] The deals were unprofitable and I should think that from first to last the connection with Carsten Anker,[41] who was a great rogue, impoverished our family nearly £20,000. Richard sold all of the property, the Hovedgaard

---

192, 194.]

[39][When Prince Christian Frederik attempted to become King of Norway, it was at the estate of Carsten Anker in Ejdsvold that he convened a constitutional assembly in April 1814. The Norman family were subsequently involved in providing bail surety for Anker; see p. 173.]

[40][Shillings. The Danish currency system established in 1625 consisted of 16 skillings (shillings) to one mark. From 1713 two separate systems existed; a debased currency used for bank note issue, and a silver shilling. In 1813 a new currency system based upon the Rigsbankdaler was introduced. This was divided into 96 skillings. Norway itself had a currency denominated in two different Rigsdaler, the Rigsdaler Courant, and the Rigsdaler Specie. The latter in 1816 was renamed the Speciedaler, which explains Norman's reference to silver dollars elsewhere in the Autobiography. Norman's statement about paying 50,000 to 60,000 in money indicates that the transaction was in specie rather than in the debased paper currency.]

[41][See p. 173. He was the envoy sent to London to negotiate on behalf of Christian Frederik's short lived Norwegian monarchy of May to October 1814, and had been imprisoned for debt. It is possible that he skipped bail, the Normans having put up the bail surety, and that this is the source of the loss to which Norman refers.]

to a patriotic association. It now, I think belongs to the State.

We returned home in the middle of June, this I know by perceiving in my cricketing records that I played at Chislehurst on the 23rd. Our route was by steam from Christiania. On arriving at Gothenburg we found my old friend, the Thetis Captain Living, ready to sail. We embarked in her and landed at Yarmouth after a prosperous voyage.

In the Autumn, I think of 1828 I attended a celebrated county meeting at Penenden Heath.[42] It was called by the Tories to denounce any concession to the Romanists and its exciting cause was a growing dread that Peel and the Duke of Wellington were meditating concession, or what was then called treachery.[43]

I went to Maidstone with Count Wedel, John Abel Smith[44] and one or two other people whom I now forget, in a carriage and four joining them at Footscray.

The Meeting was extremely numerous. In fact the Heath was covered, the feeling enthusiastic and highly anti-Catholic. Lord Camden[45] the Lord

---

42[As the *Times* of 23 October 1828 (2d) reported, Penenden was a famous meeting place on the edge of Maidstone, scene of the trial in 1076 to determine the truth of allegations by Archbishop Lanfranc against the rapacious Odo, Bishop of Bayeux, who was forced to return much of his spoils. The meeting to which Norman refers was on the day following that *Times* report, 24 October, and was itself reported in the paper on 27 October (3b). According to the report, the meeting would have been in favour of Catholic Emancipation but for the import of servants and working people by those who opposed it. The issue of 30 October (2e) had another account of the meeting, reporting that 20-25,000 were present.]

43[Ripon (see p. 311) resigned 8 January 1828, and the following day Wellington became Prime Minister. Peel became Leader of the Commons, and Home Secretary. On Catholic emancipation, see p. 320.]

44[John Abel Smith, 1802-71, member of Smith, Payne and Smith, bankers, MP Midhurst 1830-1, Chichester 1831-59, 1863-8. He took an active part in the agitation for the 1832 Reform Bill. He gave up his partnership in the bank in 1845, because other partners were uncomfortable with his other commercial interests, many of which were not very successful. He was also a friend and patron of Edward Gibbon Wakefield.]

45[John Jeffreys Pratt, 1st Marquess Camden, 1759-1840, Lord Lieutenant of Ireland 1795-8, friend of the younger Pitt, cabinet minister 1798-1812, supporter of Catholic Emancipation. His personal residence was at Bayham Abbey on the Kent-Sussex border. He was Colonel of West Kent Militia 1827-32.]

Lieutenant presided. The Chief Speaker, who I think moved a petition, was the late Lord Winchilsea,[46] who was fluent, very loud and used the most vehement action. I thought him admirably fitted for a demagogue. Lord Darnley[47] spoke on the other side, but was little listened to. In the small band of Whigs, I saw and for the first time, Mr Hodges of Hemsted,[48] who subsequently became my intimate friend and died full of years and honour in 1857.

Among other notorieties who were present and spoke, were Shiel and Cobbett, I was in a wagon very near both of them and could not hear a word they said.[49] Shiel I had frequently met at Dublin in 1818, Cobbett I never saw either before or afterwards. He was a redfaced, burly man, exactly in appearance what one would have expected him to be.

In a Register published after the meeting and in which he described it,[50]

[46][George William Finch Hatton, 5th Earl of Winchilsea, 1791-1858, succeeded 1826. He opposed the Catholic Relief Bill of 1829, and fought a duel with the Duke of Wellington (in which however he declined to fire, the Duke following suit) in 1829. Lieutenant Colonel Commandant of East Kent Yeomanry 1830. For an account of the duel see Elizabeth Longford, *Wellington vol. 2, Pillar of State* (Frogmore: Panther Books, 1975) pp. 237-41.]

[47][Edward Bligh, 5th Earl Darnley, 1796-1835; see p. 89. He was MP for Canterbury 1818-30. The family owned extensive estates in Kent and Co. Meath.]

[48][Thomas Law Hodges, 1776-1857, MP Kent 1830-2, West Kent 1832-41, 1847-52.]

[49][See *The Speech of Mr Shiel, as it was Intended to have been Delivered, at the County of Kent Meeting... 24th October 1828*, pp. 8, London, 1828. There is a copy in the British Library.]

[50][The reference is to Cobbett's *Weekly Register* vol. LXVI, 5 July to 27 December 1828, cols. 545-77, 1 November 1828. Writing about the Penenden meeting, Cobbett recounted his difficulties in being heard (cols. 546-56) and attacked Catholic Emancipation. He also denounced the way in which the previously printed speech of Shiel had been distributed to the *Morning Herald*, the *Times*, the *Chronicle* and the *Morning Advertizer*, prior to the meeting. In a second article, 8 November 1828, cols. 578-602, Cobbett continued his attack on Catholic Emancipation, and he conveyed the impression that the Penenden meeting had been strongly opposed to it. On the meeting itself, see also R.L. Shiel and R.S. MacKenzie, *Sketches of the Irish Bar by The Rt. Hon. Richard Lalor Shiel... with Memoir and Notes by R. Shelton Mackenzie,* 2 vols., New York: W.J. Widdleton, 1851. From this it appears that, although there was a small group of supporters of Cobbett, a much larger number of those present ridiculed him.]

he said that great attention was paid to him and that he carried the majority with him. More impudent mendacity could not be imagined for there were thousands present, every one of whom could have borne evidence to the falsehood of this statement. In truth, Cobbett had no regard for veracity. He said and wrote whatever suited his purpose at the moment. In this he resembled O'Connell in his later years. The exigencies of demagogy press heavily on the moral character of a man. A multitude is inclined to be tyrannical and like other despots, requires that its servants should set aside every consideration, excepting the necessity of pleasing its fancies.

This meeting at Penenden Heath was the first I ever attended there, or indeed any where else, of a political character. Count Wedel was quite delighted with it. The vast assemblage, the enthusiasm of all, the disorderly order, the perfect security which every body seemed to feel in such a sea of excited passions and that without the existence of any repressive means, for neither police nor soldiers were visible or indeed near. In this point of view it was certainly an interesting spectacle for a foreigner.

I was of course most enthusiastic for the Catholics and I will now tell an anecdote which has some bearing on the question of Peel's honesty before 1829, and which to a certain degree bears out an opinion, which I often expressed then and which I still entertain *vizt* that Peel's conversion to sound opinions on the Catholic question long preceded his assertion of them.

I was led to take this view, partly because I thought it impossible that a young man of Peel's calibre could honestly think it either right or politic to keep up the disabilities and partly because it seemed to me that his arguments bore every mark of insincerity. He had long abandoned the good old bigoted grounds, which might be honest and were intelligible, however little convincing and taken up with a set of sophisms and platitudes, which never could have convinced his reason.

I was not singular in taking this view of Peel's conduct. At the time in question Michael Bruce, (Lavalette Bruce as he was called from having aided in the escape of Lavelette[51]), lived with his wife Lady Parker at Plaistow.[52] He had been introduced to me by J. A. Smith and I saw him not unfrequently. I was telling him what I thought of Peel's sincerity. He expressed strongly a similar opinion and added that a few days before he had met G.R. Dawson[53]

[51][Antoine Marie Chamans, Comte de Lavalette, 1769-1830, Napoleonic General. Lavalette was close to Napoleon who left him 100,000 francs in his will. After the first Bourbon Restoration, in 1814, Lavalette declined to go into exile with Napoleon, because he had a pregnant wife (though she subsequently miscarried) and a 13 year old daughter. After the second Bourbon Restoration, in 1815, he was condemned to death, on 21 November 1815, but escaped by changing clothes with his wife, Emilie de Beauharnais, 1781-1855, a niece of the Empress Josephine. She had, in a plea for clemency on 20 December, thrown herself at the feet of the King, who refused to intervene. That same evening the escape took place. Those who secured his escape were, in addition to his wife: Sir Robert Thomas Wilson, 1774-1849, Major General 1813, and MP Southwark 1818-31; Michael Bruce (see next fn); and Captain John Hely Hutchison, later 3rd Earl of Donoughmore. Lavalette, having escaped in his wife's clothes, then changed into those of a British officer and was conveyed by Wilson safely to Mons. Unfortunately Wilson's letter to Earl Grey recounting the adventure was intercepted and all three were sentenced to 3 months' imprisonment. Lavalette's wife herself remained in prison until 23 January 1816.]

[52][Michael Bruce, 1787-1861, married in 1818 Marianne Parker, the widow of Captain Sir Peter Parker, 2nd Bt, 1785-1814. He was an English naval officer, the son of Vice Admiral Christopher Parker, and Augusta Byron. He died of wounds in Maryland in 1814. Lord Byron was his first cousin. He married Marianne Dallas, daughter of Sir George Dallas, 1st Bt, and they had three sons. Michael Bruce was called to the Bar in 1826, and was MP for Ilchester 1830-1. English readers would have been familiar with the story of Lavalette's escape, leading to the nickname 'Lavalette Bruce', as both the trial and the escape were reported in the *Times* newspaper between 16 November 1815 and 2 January 1816. The trial was reported in considerable detail, and the paper also carried an account of Comtesse Lavalette's plea for clemency for her husband.]

[53][George Robert Dawson, 1790-1856, MP County Londonderry 1815-30, Harwich 1830-2, Home Secretary 1822-7. Peel was married to Julia Floyd, 1795-1859, daughter of General Sir John Floyd, whom he met in Dublin during his time (1812-18) as Secretary for Ireland in the Liverpool government. Dawson was his brother in law not through this connection but because he married, in 1816, Mary, daughter of Sir Robert Peel, 1st Bt, 1750-1830, Peel's father. Peel was Home Secretary under Wellington 1828-32, MP Tamworth 1830-52. He had delivered an outspoken expression of the case against Catholic Emancipation in 1817. He was elected as an avowedly anti-Emancipation candidate to one of the two Oxford University seats, which he occupied 1818-29. He resigned from office in 1827 when George Canning became Prime Minister, because Canning proposed to introduce a bill for Catholic Emancipation before Parliament. Wellington on the other hand had been convinced of the need for such a measure from 1826. Having formed his administration in 1828, he led the repeal of the Test and Corporation Acts

Peel's brother in law in Bond Street and had said to him, 'Dawson I cannot imagine how you and Peel can talk such nonsense about the Catholics, when every body knows that your real opinions are quite different', the reply was, 'We cannot help it. What are we to do with our constituents at Oxford and Londonderry?'. I do not pretend at the end of thirty years to give Bruce's words with perfect correctness, but their meaning is contained in what precedes.

It is remarkable that in Peel's posthumous defence of his conduct as respects Catholics and corn, he only addresses himself to the vulgar accusation of the Tory party, that with a sort of malice prepense he set himself to trick and deceive his political friends. He says nothing about what I and many others accuse him of, *vizt* that in both cases his reason was convinced before he acknowledged it and that for a long period, perhaps many years, he continued to make use of arguments of the futility of which he was thoroughly convinced.

In short, Peel appears to me to be an over-estimated man, morally at least, perhaps intellectually. The popular oration lavished on him would have been more worthily bestowed on those who for long and dreary years, undeterred by reproach and obloquy, had fought the battles of toleration and of free trade and who would finally have gained the victory, at the worst although not so soon, or so easily as after Peel's defection.

---

which imposed disabilities on Catholics, and prevented all who were not Anglicans from holding public office whether in Britain or Ireland. Having refused to serve under Canning, Peel became Home Secretary under Wellington in a government from which Wellington, as Prime Minister, had otherwise excluded those opposed to Catholic Emancipation. Since Wellington, as a peer, could not sit in the Commons, Peel had to represent the government, and suffered a campaign of ridicule for his change of position. In February 1829 he presented the Catholic Emancipation Bill to an astonished House of Commons, and it became law in April of that year. As a result Peel had to resign his Oxford seat. In the ensuing bye-election he was defeated. Under the Catholic Emancipation Act, Catholics were eligible for most public offices, though the posts of Lord Chancellor and Lord Lieutenant of Ireland and Monarch were excluded.]

# Chapter 12

# Some Family Matters

However I must return to matters more nearly connected with myself. My dear and honored father continued throughout 1828 in a very feeble and declining state. He grew very thin and unable to walk much. I used to drive him about the country in a pony chaise, and to draw him in the grounds in a garden chair. However I need say nothing more upon this subject having written a separate memoir of him, whom I so dearly loved.[1]

During the course of 1828 and the preceding year, I had seen a good deal of Sibella Stone. We used to meet at her uncle's, Mr Martin's,[2] at Camden Place, where under the palings while cricket was in progress a good deal of quiet flirtation might be carried on, and also now and then at her father's house in Montague Square. A ball there I especially recollect as at it, I drank large draughts of love. In short I became a devoted admirer, although having no idea of marriage, I adhered to my usual maxim and made no attempt to

[1] [This has not been traced. Like other missing items, it was presumably a victim of the fire which destroyed the Norman family home at Bromley Common.]

[2] [John Martin III, who was senior partner in Martin's Bank until 1831 and the brother in law of George Stone I, himself the brother of Sibella's father Henry Stone. John Martin became MP for Tewkesbury in 1813, and represented the borough in six successive Parliaments up to 1832, dying just before the Reform Act of that year. He was one of the signatories, together with Norman himself, and Norman's brother Richard, of the petition to the Lord Mayor of London to call a meeting of the City figures to express their dismay at the rejection of the Reform Bill by the House of Lords. It was this petition which led to the meeting at the Mansion House which is referred to later in the Autobiography on p. 341.]

gain her affections.

I well recollect on one occasion that Count Wedel accompanied me to Chislehurst to see the cricket and I then pointed out to him Miss Sibella Stone as the person whom I most admired. He was much struck with her.

My health was by no means first-rate at this time, I was often nervous and depressed and used to consult Scott,[3] Pennington[4] and Dr Holland,[5] who from that time for twenty years became my regular medical attendant. Blue Pill[6] occasionally and alternatives were the remedies used. Tonics were tried in vain. The amendment when it took place was never durable.

During the year 1829, no event happened materially affecting my condition; I was however deeply excited by politics and took the most enthusiastic interest in Catholic emancipation.[7]

---

[3][James Scott MRCS of Beckenham; see p. 41.]

[4][Robert Rainey Pennington, 1766-1849, Diploma Membership of the Corporation of Surgeons, 1787, FRCS 1843, one of the original 300 Fellows of the Royal College of Surgeons. He was trained under Percivall Pott at St Bartholomew's Hospital, and practised in London. He was President of the National Institute of Medicine, Surgery and Midwifery. According to an article signed J.F.C. in the *Medical Times and Gazette* 1869, Pennington was a man of astonishing stamina who, in addition to seeing patients in London would travel to the country at night, see patients, sleep in the coach on the way there and back, and attend to patients in London the next day. Like many fashionable practitioners, he earned a great deal of money by this hard work – in his case his income is said to have been £10,000 per annum (in excess of £760,000 at 2009 prices). He is said to have been an excellent diagnostician, with a great deal of common sense. In addition to surgery, he manufactured and dispensed large quantities of medicines which must have been of doubtful value. He was himself the nephew of a leading apothecary. This medical practitioner has proved very hard to trace, and we are grateful to Geraldine O'Driscoll of the Royal College of Surgeons for locating crucial material leading to his identification.]

[5][Sir Henry Holland; see p. 271.]

[6][See p. 271.]

[7][Catholics were prevented, under the penal laws, from acquiring property, until 1780. There was further relaxation in 1791, but Catholics were still barred from being Members of Parliament. However Daniel O'Connell was elected to Parliament in 1828, standing in the County Clare election against Wellington's nominee, and the issue became acute in the context of maintaining civil order in Ireland, because the law did not allow him to take up his seat. Wellington and Peel supported the Catholic Emancipation Act of 1829 which removed most of the remaining restrictions, and enabled Catholics to become MPs. The Emancipation

My affection for Sibella Stone continued to increase. She became the established empress of my heart, reigning there without a rival. Yet I was as nearly as possible losing her, for she had a bevy of admirers and I did not at that time contemplate marriage and ran much risque of sinking into the condition of an old batchelor. My want of purpose to become a Benedick[8] aroze partly from a nervous dread of change, partly from peculiarities of health and partly from unwillingness to press upon my father's resources. The last-named apprehension was however very absurd, for I drew £1,000[9] per annum from the business and the Bank salary was £300.[10]

Looking back, I wonder how living so much at Bromley and with such inexpensive habits, I continued to get rid of this large income. I certainly gave away occasionally considerable sums. Thus, I paid £100 to a person named Cameron for an attempt to cure Robert's stammering. I also paid the expence of Henrietta's[11] tour to Switzerland with my uncle Frederick Beadon,[12] and shares in the London University cost me £200.[13] I also bought of Cadwell three cottages close to Barnet Wood, and a piece of land for which I paid him £400.[14] The cottages have since been pulled down. Their site forms part of one of the fields, let to Letts.[15] I also bought of James Gould the lease of several cottages at the top of Barnet, for which I paid, I think £800,[16]

---

Act was followed the same year by the Catholic Relief Act.]

[8] [A newly married man, especially a confirmed bachelor who marries. The reference is to Shakespeare *Much Ado About Nothing*.]

[9] [Worth £81,690 in 2009 prices.]

[10] [Worth £24,507 in 2009 prices.]

[11] [Henrietta was Norman's sister, born 21 July 1799. She was at that time unmarried.]

[12] [See p. 303. He succeeded his father as Rector of North Stoneham, Hants in 1811 and remained Rector for the rest of his life. He was a centenarian, born in 1777 and dying in 1879. On his death he was aged 101 years and 6 months. He was a Canon of Wells Cathedral 1812-75, Chancellor 1823-79.]

[13] [Worth £16,338 in 2009 prices.]

[14] [Worth £32,676 in 2009 prices.]

[15] [The Six Home Counties Directory for 1845 lists, under Bromley, Thomas Letts, a farmer of Bromley Common.]

[16] [Worth £65,352 in 2009 prices.]

far more than the value. The Freehold was subsequently purchased from the ecclesiastical commissioners.

Even after making allowances for these gifts and purchases it must be allowed, that proved I myself but a poor economist and such has been my character through life. I never understood the art of making money go far, although my strictly personal habits have been inexpensive. I often reproach myself for my laches[17] on this point. They arize mainly from idleness. It is a luxury to me, not to watch my expenditure narrowly and my extreme dislike of bargaining and haggling leads to a similar result. Knowing my own fault, I have always felt much admiration for those of my acquaintance who possess the art of making their money go a great way.

I suffered much sorrow and anxiety during the course of 1829 from the declining health of my beloved and honored father. He had gradually become very feeble and it was clear that although he was not suffering under a mortal malady he was hardly in a condition to resist any accidental disease.

My health was far from good during any part of this year, and towards the Autumn became very bad. Having tried medicine in vain, it was resolved that I should have recourse to my usual remedy a trip abroad. It may be remarked that I had quitted the Bank Direction in April. The symptoms of my malady were as usual nervous agitation, deep depression and want of self-reliance.

Henry had then no employment. Robert had formed the unfortunate connection with N. Winter & Co,[18] but liked a holiday and could be spared. These two brothers then agreed to accompany me. We left London on 15th December, crossed the next day and travelled in the diligence and reached Paris after a journey without stopping of forty-six hours on the 18th, the distance 165 miles. The winter of 1829 was very severe, the country covered

---

[17] [Negligence. Norman's personal accounts for 1831-82 are in the Norman papers at U310/A172, A173.]

[18] [Nathaniel Winter and Co., of 12 Copthall Court, Throgmorton Street.]

with snow and the cold so intense that every thing metallic in the coupée which we occupied was coated with ice. The cold at Paris too was almost unbearable. I recollect that at our lodgings, there was no stove in Robert's sleeping room and that the water in his jug froze almost solid. At that period the means of warming a house were miserably deficient in France.

I need say little about this residence in France because I can refer to a journal kept at the time.[19] I only note therefore a few particulars. In 1829 for the second time, the first having occurred during my visit to Piombino in 1822, I was obliged to leave off shooting. I had become so nervous that I could not trust myself with a gun. I felt at every moment as if I should injure either myself or others, as if indeed something within impelled me to do so. The feeling in short was like to that species of vertigo, which seizes many persons, myself among them, on looking down from a lofty building.

I suffered in a similar way about 1845, but then only for short time. At the end of a week or two however I contrived to break the spell by a violent effort. The important illness of 1850 brought back this plague with more than usual intensity, and for all the latter part of the season I laid aside my gun. At present September 1858, I am suffering great annoyance from the insidious attacks of my old foe, and much doubt if I shall not be obliged to succumb. It is possible that snuff may have something to do with my nervous condition. Headland says so and I mean to make a desperate effort to leave it off, but what a sacrifice this will be I dread to think of it.

On the 1st of January I heard from C. Boulton that I had been nominated a manager of the Sun Fire Office and a director of the Life Office;[20] and that

---

[19][Norman's journal of his time in France in 1829 is in the Norman papers at Maidstone, at U310 F13.]

[20][It would appear that Norman's invitation to join the Sun Fire Office was connected with his friendship with Charles Boulton (who died in 1850). The Boulton family owned substantial properties around Leatherhead. Charles Boulton seems to have lived at Aldenham in Hertfordshire. Norman was connected with the Boulton family through the timber trade, as Charles Boulton was a partner in the firm of Boulton and Baker, and subsequently the firm of Boulton and Pelly (see p. 208). (Sir John Henry Pelly, Boulton's partner in the latter case, was married

I must return to London in order to take my Seat at the Board. I set off accordingly on the 3rd January by the Malle Poste,[21] was introduced to my new colleagues, sitting in full conclave on the 7th. On the 14th I again left London to return to Paris and reached that city on the 18th having been 48 hours en route from Boulogne. My association with the Sun board has been a source of much satisfaction and very considerable emolument to me.[22] The salaries, or attendance money as we euphemistically call them, for the two offices reach full £400 per annum,[23] and my shares have been very profitable. The fire shares cost one 157 for 35, and I think 193 for 15, and successive bonuses must have brought their cost price to me much below par. The Life shares cost me I think 27 for about half and 36 for the remainder, and successive bonuses at each valuation must have far more than paid off all the cost. They stand me in, less than nothing. The Fire shares are now worth about 250. The Life shares over 50.

I have always felt great interest in the Sun business and have devoted much time and attention to it.[24] My endeavours have been constantly di-

to Charles Boulton's sister, the daughter of Henry Boulton.) Charles Boulton is listed as one of the managers of the Sun Fire Office at various times, including 1826, 1833 and 1844. There was a social connection between the Norman family and Charles Boulton, as Charles Boulton was married to Caroline Thellusson (died 1862), daughter of Peter Isaac Thellusson, 1st Lord Rendlesham. They married 15 July 1822. Not only were Norman and his father visitors to the family seat, Rendlesham in Suffolk, as the Autobiography relates, but Norman's father was a trustee of the 2nd Lord Rendlesham.]

[21] [Mail coach.]

[22] [Norman was a director of the Sun 1830-64.]

[23] [Worth £33,996 in 2009 prices.]

[24] [The Sun Fire Office originated in a business established by Charles Povey in 1708 and known as the Exchange House Fire Office, which used the Sun symbol as its fire mark. In 1710 it became the Sun Fire Office. In 1824 a rival was founded by Nathan Mayer Rothschild and Moses Montefiore, as the Alliance Insurance Company. The Treasurer of the Sun in 1808-9 was Henry Boulton, the father of Charles Boulton, though, by the time that Norman joined, the Treasurer was Charles Pole. Henry Boulton owned substantial properties. He is listed as one of the managers of the Sun Fire Office from 1794, giving his business address at that date as the Jerusalem Coffee House, to 1833. He died in 1836. Much later on Norman's son, Frederick Henry Norman, was to be the Treasurer for 31 years, 1880-1911, by which time the post was also that of Chairman. (He had

rected to enforce a cautious mode of transacting business and the maintenance of a sufficient capital to meet all liabilities. These efforts, which have not been unsuccessful, have not added to my popularity with some of my colleagues. Among them, I never numbered many intimate friends, C. Boulton, poor Joseph Cockrell,[25] brother to the architect,[26] who fell with his house in the hurricane of 1847, Raikes Currie,[27] a nominee of my own, and P.P. Bouverie,[28] brother to that excellent person Lord Radnor[29] and afterwards the partner of my brother and my banker were however cronies of mine.[30]

I have always regarded C.B. Ford[31] the managing director, still alive but

---

been Secretary of the company 1878-80.) The records of the company show that Norman's friends Charles Hay Cameron and John Welsford Cowell were insured by the company, and that they shared accommodation at 19 Chester Street, Belgrave Square, in 1832.]

[25] [Cockerell, Larpent and Company, in the East India trade, failed for £619, 333, one of the largest failures of 1847-8. D. Morier Evans, *The Commercial Crisis 1847-8*, 2nd edition (London: Letts, Son and Steer, 1849) pp 5-21, has the financial details.]

[26] [Samuel Pepys Cockerell, architect, 1754-1827.]

[27] [Raikes Currie, 1801-81, banker, partner in the firm of Glyn and Company, MP Northampton 1837-57. His uncle Thomas Raikes was a Director of the Bank 1776-1810, Deputy Governor 1795-7, Governor 1797-9. Like Norman, Currie was a committed Benthamite throughout his career.]

[28] [The Hon. Philip Pleydell Bouverie, 1788-1872. He was the youngest son of Jacob Bouverie, 2nd Earl Radnor. He was for many years a partner in the London bank of Ransome, Bouverie and Company. MP Cockermouth 1830-1. In the next Parliament he sat for the borough of Downton, which was subsequently disenfranchised. MP for Berkshire 1847-65. His second daughter Janet married, as his second wife, Sir Frederick Peel, 1823-1906, the second son of Sir Robert Peel the statesman.]

[29] [William Pleydell Bouverie, 3rd Earl Radnor, 1779-1869. MP radical Whig, Downton 1801-2 and 1818-19, Salisbury 1802-18, 1820-8. Succeeded to the title 1828.]

[30] [The firm appears to have been started in 1813 at 33 Craven Street, Strand, by the Hon. F. Pleydell Bouverie who had been a clerk in the bank of Messrs Bosanquet, and E. Antrobus. In 1827 it became Bouverie and Lefevre, and in 1830 it moved to 11 Haymarket. Two years later the partners were the Hon P.P. Bouverie, Henry Norman (Norman's brother), and James Gordon Murdock (see p. 265). It later became Ransome Bouverie and Company, merging with an older partnership dating from 1786.]

[31] [Charles Bell Ford, 1784-1860, became Secretary of the Sun Fire Office in 1840 at the age of 30. He took over as the position of the company was weakening. He ruthlessly pursued market share, both through price competition and through no

verging into decrepitude, as a man of great ability, although with many faults of temper. I consider that the office owes him a deep debt of gratitude.

The visits to Paris had been of considerable service to me, but had by no means restored me to my ordinary state of health, a poor one after all. I therefore planned a tour in Spain. A carriage was hired, passports, letters of credit and of introduction procured, and a day fixed for our departure from the French metropolis, when at twelve o'clock at night on the 27th January my kind friend Cowell arrived from England to tell us that our father had died of bronchitis after an illness of two days on the 24th. We instantly countermanded all our Spanish preparations, got new passports, and were enabled to set off for England on the following day, and travelling without stopping reached Bromley on Saturday the 30th January.

I felt on my father's death, that which an affectionate son must feel at the loss of a parent, who had ever showered upon him every proof of the tenderest and most self-sacrificing love, and my grief was more acute because I was conscious that my strong desire to give effect in deed, to the ardentcy of my filial sentiments, had been marred by the repeated occurrence of illness which had incapacitated me for active exertion.

I need not however enlarge upon this topic, having in a written memoir of my father, given utterance to what I thought of, and towards him.[32]

I have already said that a journal of our French expedition renders any details as to it, unnecessary here. I may however remark that to a casual observer the throne of Charles X at the beginning of 1830, exhibited every outward mark of stability.[33] I well recollect being in the gallery of the Louvre

fewer than 17 take-overs. He paid keen attention to possible weaknesses in likely targets for this activity. He was appointed Deputy Chairman in 1845, and held this, together with Chairmanship of the Sun Life Office, until death. For much of this period he was also the Secretary of the company. He retired as Secretary in 1856, on an annual pension of £1,000 per annum (£80,380 at 2009 prices).]

[32] [This has not been traced; see p. 319.]

[33] [Louis Philippe, 1773-1850, became the 'Citizen King' after the overthrow in 1830 of the last of the senior branch of the Bourbons, Charles X, Comte d'Artois, who had succeeded his brother Louis XVIII in 1824.]

on the jour de l'an,[34] and seeing the immense assemblage of distinguished persons civil and military, who had collected to compliment the sovereign. They comprehended men of all political parties, and I am persuaded, that apart from the folly of the King, and of the Polignac ministry,[35] there was then a fair chance in favor of the stability of the dynasty of the elder Bourbons.

That this chance was thrown away and that the revolution of July took place, I have long regarded as a most unfortunate event for France, although I did not think so at the time. A revolution in itself is always a calamity, indeed a great calamity. It usually involves bloodshed, and thus carries desolation into families. It interrupts all industrial occupations, and thus occasions a destruction of capital. It often produces foreign war, and almost always a large increase of expenditure, being usually the expression of new wants and wishes the gratification of which demands such increase. It is sometimes merely a struggle for place, the object being to eject the ins from power and to replace them by the outs, who consider the public revenue as the spoil of conquest and fasten on it, like the tiger on its prey.

So strong is my opinion as to the evil of a revolution that I am inclined to doubt if at this time (1858) there is any European Government (always excepting that of Turkey), the overthrow of which would not be dearly purchased at the cost of a violent and sudden revolution. It must be recollected that almost all Governments are far better than they were a few years ago, and that the seeds of improvement are every where thickly sown.

It must also be recollected that a violent revolution does not necessarily lead to something better, it is often followed by some thing worse, witness

[34] [New Year's Day.]

[35] [Auguste Jules Armand Marie, Prince de Polignac, 1780-1847, who was given the title of Prince in 1820 for his Ultramontaine emphasis on Papal authority. He became the head of the last Bourbon ministry in 1829. This decreed the authoritarian St Cloud Ordinances that cost Charles X his throne. He was imprisoned until 1836, and then in exile in England until 1845.]

that of 1848.

There is one consequence of my opinion as to the effect of violent revolutions to which I will here just advert. I consider it to be bounden duty of every established Government, whatever be its nature or origin, to resist by force any violent attempt to overthrow it. Such a line of conduct can alone protect society against the efforts of a small knot of conspirators and prevent them from trampling down the rights and feelings of an enormous majority of their country men. This fault disgraced Louis Philippe in his final catastrophe and deeply has France had cause to rue it.[36]

It may appear remarkable to some that I did not at once erect some monument to my father, as in addition to all I personally owed him, he was a man of mark in his generation both in town and country. The truth is, I often thought of doing so, composed Latin Epitaphs &c but could never satisfy myself. In the mean time, months and years stole on, the fitting opportunity passed bye, and I finally thought it best to commemorate both my parents together in the tablet now standing on the North side of Bromley Church.[37]

The immediate consequences of the altered circumstances in which I found myself at my father's death were beneficial to me. I had become the head

[36] [Louis Philippe, having succeeded Charles X as the 'Citizen King' in 1830, became more and more authoritarian himself, and more than a decade of unrest culminated in the revolution of 1848 and the accession of Louis Napoleon (later Napoleon III). Louis Philippe, 1773-1850, was the eldest son of the Duc d'Orléans. After the revolution of 1830 he was appointed Lieutenant General, and then King. There were numerous rebellions and assassination attempts, though the country prospered. After his overthrow in 1848 he fled to England.]

[37] [This is puzzling. Norman's mother did not die until 1853. Accordingly the tablet would naturally have been in the Bromley Common Church. This was actually Holy Trinity Church, Bromley Common, built on Norman's initiative, despite his Unitarianism, in 1838. It was built on land owned by the Norman family who sold it for £50. The building was completed in 1841. It is a large church, with seating for 480, and it cost £2,643. It is this church which contains memorials to members of the Norman family. Indeed the apse was added in 1884 in memory of Norman himself. However, the tablet is not there. Bromley Church proper was destroyed by bombing on the night of 16 April 1941, and it is possible that the tablet was in that church.]

of the family with new duties, new employments, new responsibilities. All these proved a powerful means of distraction to me, and my health became apparently better.

My father had made me an elder son, leaving me a fortune of about £200,000[38] in money, houses and land; while to the two younger boys he only left £20,000[39] consuls each, and to the four girls £10,000[40] each, with an annuity of £1,500 to my mother. Richard was already provided for. In this sum of £200,000 I put the London property at £40,000.[41] Country ditto £60,000.[42] This is perhaps a low valuation. On the other hand the personal hardly reached £100,000[43] and was subsequently diminished by American repudiation and some loss by debtors. There was the value too of my mother's annuity say from £15,000 to £20,000.[44]

At my father's death I was entitled to one half the capital of the business, but this had been so greatly reduced by losses from 1825 downwards that in settling with Richard, when I subsequently dissolved the partnership I thought it right to hand over to him £100,000 of my half share thus leaving him £260,000[45] and myself only £60,000 of the joint capital. It so happened however, that among the assets which I took then, or in later arrangements were a policy on E. Rohde's[46] life and the estate of Sanne and Soerli in Norway, both of which proved very profitable, so that I probably took out of business fully as much as my brother. In after years, I lost by him a very considerable sum, but this need not be alluded to now.

On the whole, upon a fair balance of property, losses and profits, I con-

38 [£16,998,000 at 2009 prices.]
39 [£1,699,800 at 2009 prices.]
40 [£849,900 at 2009 prices.]
41 [£3,399,600 at 2009 prices.]
42 [£5,099,400 at 2009 prices.]
43 [£8,499,000 at 2009 prices.]
44 [£1,274,850 to £1,699,800 at 2009 prices.]
45 [£22,097,400 at 2009 prices.]
46 [On Rohde see p. 285, and on the insurance policy see p. 307.]

ceive that at my father's death, I was fairly worth in meal and malt £200,000, as before assumed.

And here I will make a few remarks on the subject of primogeniture, and am the more tempted to do so because my own will is based upon that principle and I must therefore be considered as regarding it to be wise and just, at least in my own case. I do not think it applicable to all families or to all scales of fortune and it may often happen that the character and disposition of an eldest son render him an unfit depository of the bulk of the family fortune.

I of course abjure the notion that the younger children ought ever to be left without due provision and perhaps exposed to want, while the elder is rolling in wealth. This is indeed the height of injustice and cruelty.

But supposing the eldest son to be a person of an intellectual and moral character which render him fit for his position, and that the father's fortune is large enough to furnish a competency to the younger children and still to furnish provision for an elder son, then I see many advantages in primogeniture.

I regard in such a case the elder son as the chief and representative of the family, who is bound to consider that he holds his elevated position under a sort of trust and obligation to afford aid and support to those of his kith and kin who may require it, and should he neglect this great duty I consider him a delinquent.

Even the younger children are, I think, better off in this case than they would be under an enforced system of equal division. With enough to keep them above want, they have not enough to leave them without a strong motive to apply themselves vigorously to some profession, which may enable them to marry without imprudence and to bring up a family. Their struggles in a profession are often greatly facilitated by their belonging to a distinguished family while in case of misfortune, they ought to be able to turn to their elder brother with a certainty of obtaining help from him.

A considerable fortune divided equally among a number of children will probably furnish just about enough to each, to weaken if not to destroy, the motive to strive for fortune and advancement in the world through active exertion.

There was much concealed truth in the reason given by Johnson for his liking primogeniture, *vizt.* that it made only one fool in a family. Not indeed, that I regard the eldest son as necessarily a fool, far from it. On the contrary, if he properly discharge his duties he will find quite enough of occupation to employ his time and to sharpen his intellect.

What I have said in the last few paragraphs mainly applies to younger sons. I am of opinion that daughters derive little if any advantage from anything that goes beyond a moderate fortune, say £10,000 to £20,000.[47] In the event of their not marrying this will afford them sufficient means to live a respectable spinster life, (a most respectable life too) especially if two or three sisters club together, while the sum is quite as much as any English gentleman, even the first nobleman in the land, has a right to expect with his wife. Women of very large fortunes are often sought for in marriage mainly on that account and for the prey of fortune-hunters.

It is the custom of England that the husband and not the wife should bring the fortune. Equity therefore prescribes, that among the younger children the portions of sons should be greater than that of daughters, or in marriage it is probable that two large portions will be brought together in their case, and one smaller and one only equal portion in the marriage of sons. In my own will I have fixed two to three as the relation in amount of the portions of daughters and sons and am of opinion that I have thus obeyed the dictates of reason and justice.

It must be observed that the results to which I have thus come, do not in my view justify a law of primogeniture in the event of intestacy. If a father

[47][£849,900 to £1,699,800 in 2009 values.]

is unable or unwilling to make a will I would have his real property divided by the same rules which now regulate the distribution of his personalty.[48]

I am of opinion that a forced law of equal division like that of France is highly inexpedient. Among other inconveniences it has the effect of grinding down and finally extinguishing all families, or of leading to the habit of confining the number of children in each distinguished household to two or three, which I believe to have a pernicious effect on domestic happiness and morality.

I am far from considering the making an elder son any hardship to the younger children, provided the matter be regarded and treated from my point of view. On the contrary, I am inclined to believe that it produces a balance of advantage even to them. In my particular case, at any rate it did no harm. My brothers Richard and Robert would have been equally ruined, had they inherited £18,000 or £30,000,[49] while I should not have been in the condition of being able to assist them, as I have done.[50] My sisters might have made more advantageous marriages with larger fortunes, or been rather more comfortable had they possessed larger incomes, but Henrietta[51] is the only one who has really suffered from poverty and with what I have allowed her, her income has been nearly as great as it would have been, had she inherited a full share of our father's fortune (say £20,000 to £25,000[52] – 2/3rds). Having married a man, who however honorable and amiable, possesses absolutely nothing she could never have been comfortable with a family of children.

[48] [Personalty is that part of property which passes to executors, and is distinguished from 'realty' which goes to the heirs at law.]

[49] [Worth £1,529,820 or £2,549,700 in 2009 prices.]

[50] [The Norman papers at U310 C52 contain material concerning Robert and Richard Norman. At U310/F49* there are accounts and papers concerning financial arrangements between Norman and his brother Richard, covering 1835-47.]

[51] [Henrietta, born 1799, married 26 October 1830 Captain Thomas Spark Thompson, RN. She died in 1866.]

[52] [Worth £2,124,750 in 2009 prices.]

At the time of poor Charlotte's marriage, her husband William Whitmore was without fortune, but his office of Official Assignee has since afforded him a sufficient income.[53]

I am now led to say a word on the subject of entails because I have

[53][Charlotte, Norman's sister and the sibling closest to him in age, born in 1795, married 18 May 1830 William Whitmore. Although Norman had known the Whitmore family for many years, as indicated by his remark below that he had long known William Whitmore to be a man of honour, he is remarkably reticent about him, and his Bromley Memoir provides no more help. However St George's Church, Beckenham, records William Whitmore 24 March 1791-17 June 1869. That this is Norman's brother in law is confirmed by the dates given for his wife Charlotte, 30 June 1795-15 February 1855. The Whitmore family were involved in the bank of Whitmore, Wells and Whitmore. In 1799 this had been Fuller and Chatteris, but in 1821 it became Whitmore, Wells and Whitmore. The two family members in that, together with John Wells the younger, were Edward and Frederick Whitmore. This bank failed and was declared bankrupt in 1841. However a William Whitmore was recorded as being a director of the Crown Life Assurance Company in 1831, the bank of which was Whitmore, Wells and Whitmore. It is possible that Norman's influence in the insurance industry may have played a part in this appointment, assuming that the individual was his brother in law. William Whitmore did, as Norman recounts, become an Official Assignee, like George John Graham to whom Norman also refers in this role. He operated under the overall control of the Commissioners in Bankruptcy, giving his address as 2 Basinghall Street, which was the Bankruptcy Court itself, unlike G.J. Graham who had an independent address. The Official Assignee was responsible for the collection of moneys from bankrupt estates, such moneys to be paid into the Bank of England, under the English Bankruptcy Act of 1831. This Act created the position of Official Assignee. The work of an Official Assignee was quite demanding and, as the evidence of George John Graham (see p. 294) makes clear, precarious and not particularly remunerative. For instance Graham himself dealt with no fewer than fifty bankruptcies, many if not all of which would have been complex and time consuming, between January 1832 and July 1833 (*Parliamentary Papers* 1833, vi, p. 723). The Official Assignees were subject to constant suspicion as liable to retain sums in their hands, and their expenses were large. Whitmore reported his expenses as being between £400 and £500 (*Parliamentary Papers* 1833, xxxi, p. 161) and said that his remuneration was £611 11s 2d. Graham gave his expenses as £529 17s 2d (*Parliamentary Papers* 1835, xlvi, p. 28). In addition it must have been necessary to keep a prudential reserve, because of the constant threat of legal action by a creditor of the bankrupt party, and the liability for legal costs. The Official Assignees were not paid salaries (*Parliamentary Papers* 1843, vol. xli, p. 1ff), and there was significant competition between them. There were twelve such individuals for London alone, with others in such centres as Birmingham, Bristol and Newcastle (*Parliamentary Papers* 1844, vol. xxxviii, p. 479). It is not surprising that Norman expressed concern about the financial position of his married sister Charlotte.]

thought it right to create an entail in my own testamentary dispositions.[54]

The old Scotch entail and continental substitution which locked up land permanently and left the younger children to want or a convent, I consider in the highest degree unjust and impolitic, but an English entail is quite a different affair, rarely enduring more than thirty years. Still I doubt if even an English entail should be allowed on grounds of public policy. At the worst however it does little harm, and is often very convenient.

Such it appeared to be in my particular case. I have made an elder son not as any special favor to him, but because I think that on the whole, I thus best consult the general interest of all my children who equally deserve and possess my love. Charles being in business and liable to all its risks, I have deemed it fitting, in the interest of the whole family, to protect the estate against the risque of his mercantile insolvency. Had Charles been out of business, I should probably have left the estate at his complete disposal. I had done this in the case of dear Herman.

I will conclude these remarks by stating that the dispositions of my will have occupied a great deal of my most serious thoughts and that in making up my mind upon them. I have been influenced by a sincere desire to do my duty and have prayed to God for a blessing on my determination.

I have not however altogether relied upon any own view of what is right and expedient in my position but have had recourse to the advice of Lord Overstone, one of the wisest of men, as to the primogeniture and entail, the only difficult points, and have acted in conformity to his opinion.

May my beloved children, whose filial affections are so strong and their merits to their parents so great, approve of what I have done for them and be prepared to shed the tears of unalloyed affection and respect over my tomb.

The making of a will has always appeared to me to be one of the most solemn and important duties which man can be called upon to perform.

[54] [An entailed estate is a settlement of inheritance in land on a succession of heirs.]

But now once more to my narrative.

The effect of my father's death imposing upon me, as it did, new duties, employments and obligations was beneficial to my health, by affording me incessant distraction, and for some time I felt better.

Several of the family having ascertained their pecuniary position, married within a few months: Robert to Miss Emily Martin,[55] Charlotte to William Whitmore and Henrietta to Captain T. Sparke Thompson, then only a Lieutenant in the Navy. I opposed the two last marriages, by pointing out their imprudence, but when I found that my advice was of no avail, I was persuaded that Captain Thompson was a gentleman and man of honor, (Whitmore I had long known to be so), I made up my mind to avoid anything like a quarrel and welcomed my new relatives with as much cordiality as I could muster.

The unmarried sisters, Maria[56] and Emma,[57] continued to reside with me at Bromley, making an allowance if I mistake not of £200 per annum each for their maintenance.

My own feelings, and the advice of Dr Holland, led me seriously to turn my thoughts on matrimony, and Sibella Stone. She was the only woman on earth whom I regarded with love, yet I could not at once make up my mind to strive to gain her affections, or to propose to her. Still in the first half of 1830, I saw her several times and my sentiment for her waxed stronger with every interview.

I tremble even now to think, how nearly my doubts and hesitations caused me to lose her. Had she become the wife of any body else, at thirty-six, I could have hardly have loved another woman and then the remainder of my life must have been miserable.

[55] [Robert Norman, born 30 April 1805, Norman's brother, married in 1830 Emily Martin. He died in 1875.]

[56] [Maria, born in 1803, married in 1835 Herbert Jenner-Fust of Hill Court, Glos; see p. 352. She died in 1891.]

[57] [Emma, born in 1807, married in 1832 Captain Henry Boden of the Fusilier Guards, and died in 1836.]

So soon as the novelty of my new position had lost its effects, the symptoms of my complaint returned with much severity, and I determined once more to have recourse to travel, and accordingly with Henry as my companion, and George Clarke who had been servant to Cowell and myself in Half Moon Street when we had a house in common, I quitted London on 7th July for Cambridge, visited Ely, Peterborough, Lincoln and York crossed Blackstone Edge[58] to Manchester and Liverpool, and while at this last-named place, took part in a trial trip on the Manchester and Liverpool railway, on which Huskisson received his mortal injury a day or two afterwards.[59] On the 17th July we sailed from Liverpool for Ireland and landed at Dunleary,[60] now Kingstown, and soon afterwards saw my old friend Lyons who as usual overwhelmed us with hospitality, and who is now my guest at Bromley, while I am writing this.

I need not further enlarge upon this Irish tour, inasmuch as among my papers, will be found a journal of it. Suffice it to say, that leaving out the extreme South, we made almost an entire circuit of the Island, visiting Drogheda, Dundalk, Antrim, Belfast, Coleraine and the Giant's Causeway, Londonderry, Ballyshannon, Castlebar, Sligo, Tuam, Galway, Ennis, Limerick, Cork, Waterford, Wexford, Wicklow and again Dublin.

On the 15th August I left Howth for Holyhead and reached home a few days afterwards by the way of Chester Shrewsbury &c.

While staying at Moriarty's hotel at Limerick we heard the news of the French Revolution. I was extravagantly elated by them and recollect writing

58 [Blackstone Edge is an area of moorland 1,323 feet high along what is now the Greater Manchester and West Yorkshire county boundary, then the Lancashire and Yorkshire county boundary. It is now known as a landmark on the Pennine Way.]

59 [William Huskisson, 1770-1830, politician and writer on economics, member of the Bullion Committee of 1810. He fell on 15 September 1830 into the path of the Rocket engine at the opening of the Liverpool and Manchester Railway. He died the same evening.]

60 [This is the conventional pronunciation of Dun Laoghaire.]

a letter to Mrs Grote, in which I gave full utterance to my enthusiasm.[61] In those days, I could hardly imagine a revolution in which I should not rejoice, be it understood if the popular cause was triumphant.

Age, experience, and reflexion have now sobered me down and I am inclined to think that the 'trois Jours' were unhappy for France, and for Europe.

On my return home arrived the crisis of my fate. My mother and sisters were well aware of my feelings for Sibella Stone. One of my sisters had written to me while in Ireland 'La bella ha perduta qualche cosa della sua beltâ'.[62] This I told my mother, who immediately remarked I do not know what they mean. She is almost the finest young woman I ever saw.

A day or two afterwards the Stone girls were invited to pass a day or two with us. They came, and during a walk round the grounds, just to the East of the penstock, I proposed and was accepted. I wish that I could recollect the exact day which has since been productive to me of so much felicity. God be thanked for it.

A day or two afterwards, I saw Mr Henry Stone in Lombard Street explained my pretensions and obtained his approbation of the match.

I have a great objection to long engagements, thinking them particularly undesirable for the woman, who is often kept dangling to a man who finally does not marry her, and thus prevented from forming a better connection, or perhaps any at all. There are other objections to these affiances, which are customary in Norway where I have known them to produce very bad results.

At any rate there was no long engagement in our case. We were married at St George's Hanover Square, that grand temple of Hymen on the 12th October by my uncle the Reverend F. Beadon, Rector of North Stoneham, Hants.

My wife came from Stanmore and after the ceremony, we adjourned to

[61] [Mrs Grote does not mention this letter in her remarks relating to the revolution (*The Personal Life of George Grote*, London: John Murray, 1873 pp. 61-5).]

[62] [The phrase means 'The beauty has lost something of her beauty'.]

the house occupied by Cowell, and myself number [blank in original] Half Moon Street, where we had a breakfast and then drove off to St Leonards, at which place, and subsequently at East Bourn and Brighton, (our honeymoon, it was not four weeks long) was passed.

Sibella was twenty-two on the 15 October, three days after the marriage, and certainly a handsomer woman than she then was could hardly be seen or imagined. Tall, with an elegant figure, good features of a classical turn, bright eyes an abundance of dark brown hair and a clear brunette complexion, she was moreover in the full bloom of youth and health.

Her fortune was small, but she brought me what was still better than wealth or beauty, an abundance of good sound sense, a temper which if not perfectly even, is most kindly, and an affection, warm and constant. In short she has ever been to me the choicest gift, which a kind providence has ever bestowed upon me. She has also been an excellent mother to our nine children, all of whom she has nursed.

I was thirty-seven on the 20th September 1830, rather too old for my wife, and older than the best age for marriage, which I consider to be from twenty-five to thirty. However better late than never, I should have been a miserable batchelor and only escaped that melancholy fate by a hair's brea[d]th.

A sad circumstance greatly damped the pleasure of our honeymoon. Sibella had taken with her a faithful old servant named Charity Kearns. This excellent person was unwell while we were at St Leonards became worse during the journey to Brighton and died there, of internal inflammation, in spite of the best medical aid which we could procure for her. We strove to shew her kindness, but it was difficult in our circumstances to convince ourselves that we shewed her kindness enough.

I now carried into effect a scheme I had long entertained that of quitting business. My father had been aware of my purpose and had not disapproved of it. Twenty years had elapsed since I entered the counting house. These had been almost all years of anxiety and loss. The effects of the double duty and the gradual fall in the price of wood amounting on such deals to 60 to 70 per cent, and £30 and £80 per cent was ruinous to exporters and yardkeeper[s] who failed in great numbers, throwing upon us a vast amount of bad debts. These losses might have been less had not my father received a mercantile education in very different times. Had I been more attentive to details, and Richard less sanguine and reckless. But under no circumstances could our business have been made lucrative.

I waited for some time[63] and until I could make a satisfactory arrangement for Richard by uniting our house with that of Benjamin Sewell, thus saving expence and doing away with the danger of competition in Norway.[64]

It may be remarked that the Norway business had never employed more than three or four houses, besides the scrapings which devolved on a few interlopers. Of these Wolffs and Dorville had failed in 1812. Boultons and Bakers, afterwards Bakers and Pelly had ceased to do business excepting on their own account.[65] There remained only Sewell and ourselves.[66]

The new establishment commenced with every promise of prosperity. The worst had been reached. A reaction took place and had it not been for my brother's folly,[67] he might by 1850 have been at the head of one of the most

[63] [The partnership of George Warde Norman and Richard Norman, trading as George Norman and Son, was dissolved 31 December 1830, as recorded in the *London Gazette*. Benjamin Sewell was an expanding firm, and in 1833 it also acquired the timber firm of John White and Sons.]

[64] [In the Norman papers at Maidstone at U310/B13 there is a Deed of Dissolution of Partnership of George Warde Norman of Bromley and Richard Norman of Tokenhouse Yard, London, merchant, and assignment of George Warde Norman's share to Richard Norman, with the corresponding *London Gazette* notice, dated 1831.]

[65] [By 1857 this had become Albert Pelly and Company. It also failed temporarily in 1857 (D. Morier Evans, *The History of the Commercial Crisis, 1857-8* (London: Groombridge, 1859 pp. clxxxv-clxxxvi), but was able to pay 20 shillings in the pound subsequently.]

[66] [On the timber firms see also p. 207.]

[67] [The Norman papers at Maidstone contain, at U310 B31/9, documents concerning the dissolution of the Sewell partnership with Richard Norman. There is an agreement between George Warde Norman, Richard Norman, Benjamin Sewell and Benjamin Sewell the younger, concerning financial arrangements on the dis-

flourishing houses in London of the second class, making profits at the rate of £15,000 per annum.[68] It is true that this house fell under the storm of 1857, but only I hope for a time, and with every prospect of future success.[69]

On looking backwards, I cannot disapprove of my having quitted business in 1830. My fortune was ample to meet my wants. Although not above business, I had no great love for it or desire to accumulate vast wealth. With several sons, I might have found it convenient to put them into a house of my own, but according to what I can now see, they are likely to do as well or better than they would have done as partners in Norman and Sons.

My health revived wonderfully after my marriage. I became as it were a new being. My spirits greatly improved and for several years I had no relapse and was able to enjoy the many blessings with which I was surrounded and which were so much greater than I deserved.

One consequence of the change in my condition was that my existence no longer presented such landmarks, as foreign tours, but flowed on under my own vine in a calm untroubled stream. This circumstance will shorten these memoirs. It will probably also produce the effect of introducing some errors of date into my narrative. I have no longer journals to refer to and do not recollect the exact sequence of events, or the precise time when some of them occurred. Note must be taken of this by those who may read these lines, but they may be assured that they will not be betrayed into important error.

solution of the partnership of Richard Norman and Benjamin Sewell senior and junior, 1843. There are also letters and receipts relating to the matter.]

68 [The *London Gazette* contains a notice, dated 3 May 1843, that the partnership between Richard Norman, Benjamin Sewell, and Benjamin Sewell junior was dissolved. There is some indication of bad blood. Whereas such notices of dissolution of partnership normally contained the phrase 'by mutual consent', this notice contained the phrase 'by mutual consent, so far as regards the said Richard Norman'.]

69 [For the temporary failure of Sewell in 1857, see D. Morier Evans, *The History of the Commercial Crisis, 1857-8* (London: Groombridge, 1859) pp. 47, 53. He mentions that though Sewell and Neck initially failed for £500,000, it was subsequently enabled, through the realisation of assets, to pay 20 shillings in the pound. The estate of Messrs Sewell and Neck is on pp. clxxx-clxxxiii of Evans (1859).]

# Chapter 13

# Public Life

The leisure arizing from my quitting business, my new position in Kent, my strong political feelings and other circumstances impelled me at this time to take a part in public business, which I had never done previously.

The agitation in favour of the Reform Bill awaked in me the strongest enthusiasm. I was called upon to move or second a resolution at a great meeting at the Mansion House where old Mr Loyd made his appearance as an Orator and spoke remarkably well.[1]

I also became very active in the election movements of Kent and did my best to organise that opposition to Sir Edward Knatchbul,[2] before which he

[1] [Following the resolution signed by Norman, and by John Martin (see p. 319), amongst others, the *Times*, 19 September 1831 (5d) reported City support for the Reform Bill. Lewis Loyd's speech, on Friday 23 September, was reported in the *Times*, 24 September (5e). He was followed as a speaker by Thomas Tooke and by Pascoe Grenfell. Both Norman and George Grote took part in the meeting. Grote moved one of the resolutions, and he was seconded by Norman (*Times*, 6a). The platform at the meeting contained many City dignitaries, and associates of Norman, including John Smith MP, John Wells, John Martin MP, John Abel Smith MP, Charles Grenfell, W.G. Prescott, and George Stone II. Norman was again on the platform at another Reform meeting the following month – *Times*, 14 October 1831 (3c). On this occasion Norman and Grote both spoke again. Norman might have been less surprised by the eloquence of Lewis Loyd on the earlier occasion, had he remembered that the latter had been originally a Unitarian preacher.]

[2] [Sir Edward Knatchbull, 9th Bt, 1781-1849, of Mersham Hatch, Kent, succeeded his father as MP for Kent, 1819-30. He was a strong opponent of Corn Law reform, and of Catholic Emancipation. He upset Peel in the House of Commons, 12 February 1829, by taunts of inconsistency on the Catholic question. He was elected MP for East Kent in 1832, and retired in 1845. In November 1830, with

quailed in 1831.[3]

From that time to this, I have taken great part in public business and have attained, by practice, a certain facility in managing men and affairs. But I began too late in life to be a good speaker and my nervous temperament would have required much and early practice to enable me to preserve self-possession when making a set speech. On such occasions I never say what previously I intended, and never produce much effect, although giving utterance to reason in not very inappropriate terms.

The best maxim I could give to a young man anxious to become an orator would be to speak loud and slow. I always strive to follow it.

Besides the attention I paid to politics, I took great interest at this time in the discussions and inquiries as to the Poor Laws.[4] I was led to this partly

---

Sir Richard Vyvyan, he engineered the fall of Wellington's government.]

[3][*Times* 30 April 1831, 3f-4a, reported that Knatchbull was alarmed at the prospect of opposition from Hodges and Rider. *Times* 12 May, 4f-5b, reported that Knatchbull had resigned, and Hodges and Rider were elected unopposed at an assembly at Penenden Heath. *Times* 28 May, 4e, reported that there had been a widespread public subscription to support Hodges and Rider.]

[4][The Poor Law Amendment Act, 1834, was passed by the Whig government of Earl Grey, to reform poor relief on Utilitarian lines, replacing the Elizabethan Poor Law of 1601 and practices developed from it. In 1832 a Royal Commission had been set up to investigate the operation of poor relief. The original Commissioners were the Bishops of London and Chester, W. Sturges Bourne, Nassau William Senior, H. Bishop, H. Gawler, Walter Coulson and J. Traill. Edwin Chadwick was added to the Commission in April 1833. The findings of the Commission – and contemporary critics such as the economist J.R. McCulloch noted that the Assistance Commissioners deputed to investigate the system knew what they were supposed to report – was that the old system was a bad one. The Utilitarian principle underlying the New Poor Law, which resulted from the enquiry, was that poor relief should act as a deterrent. The Act required parishes to be put into Poor Law Unions, each of which had to establish a workhouse, and the Commissioners had considerable powers of supervision over the operation of the workhouses. Under the new regime, relief should only be available within a 'workhouse', and conditions in the workhouse should be worse than any conditions available outside. The latter was the principle of 'less eligibility'. Amongst the unintended consequences, the rural poor migrated to the towns in search of work, since poor relief in the countryside was now restricted, and urban rate payers were faced with a significant increase in their Poor Rate as the hopes of employment were disappointed. In practice, implementation of the legislation was less rigorous than intended by Senior and his Commissioners, but conditions were certainly harsher. However an outdoor 'labour test' order was introduced, something in which Norman became

by their connection with political economy, to which I devoted much time and attention, partly by my old acquaintance with N.W. Senior, the moving spirit in the movement, partly from my constant association with Cameron and Cowell both of whom were employed as assistant commissioners.[5]

I repeatedly saw Senior's draft report, or portions of it, in manuscript and ventured to suggest some changes in it. I may here remark that, as it finally appeared, it was nearly the most beautiful public document I ever read and one that has produced the most important and beneficial effects.

At this time Cameron and Cowell had a house in Chester Street, in which I had some share and used to go there occasionally for a night.

John Black, sometime editor of the Morning Chronicle, was an acquaintance of mine and came to Bromley occasionally.[6] He had been a literary

---

involved and, on the basis of this, 'outdoor relief', that is outside the workhouse, could be given. Nonetheless the system involved much greater State control than under the Elizabethan Poor Law, despite the fact that Bentham and his followers believed that it would cause the labour market to function more efficiently. There was considerable resistance to the system, and most of the workhouses were not built for more than two decades after 1834. The Act ran into particular problems in the North of England, where cyclical unemployment could be dealt with much more easily and cheaply through outdoor relief. The whole Utilitarian system was in any case based upon a fundamental misunderstanding – that the Elizabethan Poor Law, and in particular the Speenhamland system (which subsidised the price of bread), encouraged the development of pauperism and the growth of a pauper population. In truth the Speenhamland system only operated in the southern counties, and subsequent research has shown that there was no difference with regard to the 'breeding of paupers' in the southern counties and those in which the Speenhamland system did not operate; see M. Blaug (1964) 'The myth of the Old Poor Law and the making of the new', *Jurnal of Economic History*, vol. 23 pp. 151-84.]

[5] [There were 25 Assistant Commissioners. Chadwick had originally been an Assistant Commissioner, appointed 9 July 1832. Cowell was the first Assistant Commissioner appointed, 2 June 1832. They were not salaried, but had a subsistence allowance of £1 per day, plus travelling expenses. Cameron's name does not appear on the list of Assistant Commissioners in *Lists of Commissions and Officials; 1830-39* (nos. 12-28), *Office Holders in Modern Britain: Volume 9: Officials of Royal Commissions of Inquiry 1815-1870* (1984) pp. 16-28. However Norman's recollection is supported by other sources, and Cameron does seem to have been appointed as an Assistant Commissioner in 1833.]

[6] [John Black, 1783-1855, journalist and newspaper editor. He was born in a farm cottage four miles north of Duns in Berwickshire. From the parish school at Duns, Black gained a knowledge of English, Latin and Greek. Like his friend J.R.

hack and in this capacity I fancy translated the lectures of A.W. Schlegel on dramatic literature.[7]

He was very good-tempered, I believe honest, but in a high degree gauche both in manners and appearance. Few men had read and knew more, but his multifarious knowledge was ill-digested and ill-arranged. He was a great collector of books. The Morning Chronicle was an excellent newspaper in his hands but his writing was too deep for the public, too honest for a party.

He finally retired to a Kentish village and lived, I fancy on a small annuity furnished by Sir John Easthope.[8] He was not an old man at his death.

---

McCulloch, he became, at an early age, a book collector. As well as occupying various positions as a clerk, and attending Edinburgh University part time, he also pursued a literary career, and was clearly a very difficult and fractious employee of the various people who offered him employment. He left Edinburgh, where he had been well paid, for London, in 1810. Within three months he found employment translating German works, a task he had also performed in Edinburgh, for the proprietor of the *Morning Chronicle*. By 1817 the health of the editor of the paper was failing, and the editorial duties were taken over by Black. The paper maintained a critical and radical position, and Black reinforced this, attracting the praise of J.S. Mill and of Bentham. In 1821 the newspaper changed ownership, though Black retained his post as editor. Under its new owner, circulation declined, and it was sold in 1834 to Sir John Easthope (see fn 8 below). The paper prospered, and supported the Melbourne administration, while the *Times* switched its own support to the Tories. In 1843 when Black reached 60 his services were no longer required by the paper. He had no money, and had to part with his library of 30,000 volumes, some of which, it appears, had not been acquired in a straightforward manner as Black was liable to retain any book that he borrowed. This may explain the comment of his friend McCulloch that it was better to have a book stolen than borrowed, as there was a better chance of getting it back. After the auction of his library, friends contributed to purchase an annuity of £150 per annum, and Walter Coulson (see p. 255) lent him a cottage near Maidstone. Norman's account is thus not entirely accurate, though Easthope may well have contributed to the purchase of the annuity, and it is surprising that he found Black good tempered, given what is known of his early career.]

[7] [August Wilhelm von Schlegel, 1767-1845, the German translator of Shakespeare's plays. His *Lectures on Dramatic Art and Literature*, which were delivered in Vienna in 1808, were published in 1809-11, and are considered a fine achievement.]

[8] [Sir John Easthope, 1784-1865, politician and journalist. In 1818 he became a member of the Stock Exchange, and realised a substantial fortune. He was Chairman of the London and South Western Railway Company, and also Chairman of the Mexican Mining Company (see p. 292). MP St Albans, 1826-30, Banbury 1831, Leicester 1837-47. In 1834 he purchased the *Morning Chronicle* for £16,500, selling his interest in the paper in 1847. He was created a baronet by

On the 26th July our eldest son was born. We named him George after his father, and Herman after my intimate friend Count Wedel-Jarlsberg. He was a beautiful infant, far more beautiful than those who knew him as a youth or a man can easily imagine. He was not a person of distinguished abilities but possessed a good head, the power of application and a strong sense of duty, and excepting in the case of one or two trifling escapades at Sandhurst, never gave me pain, until the war with Russia broke out, and his regiment was ordered from Malta[9] to the Crimea. Then indeed I passed a year of intense anxiety, which ended with his death June 30th 1855, from a wound in the head received during the attack on the Redan at Sebastopol on the 18th June.

I need say the less about dear Herman, as he will be frequently mentioned hereafter and as I have annexed a short memoir of him to those of my father and mother.[10] I may here however observe that no other event in my life gave me half the pain, which I felt at his death. Indeed it still continues a constant source of bitter feeling. Had I been aware that I was to have so many children, I should have named them all George Warde with some name preceding. This among so many Normans would have marked the line.

In 1831 took place the second act of Robert's melancholy drama, the connection with N. Winter & Co by his retirement from the firm.[11] What were his motives for so retiring I now forget. Probably they were not well-considered, as he was always apt to make up his mind and act in a great

Lord Melbourne in 1841.]

[9] [This was replaced by Corfu but in a pencilled hand which may not be Norman's.]

[10] [This has not been traced. It does not appear to be in the Norman papers at Maidstone.]

[11] [The *London Gazette* recorded the dissolution, 16 May 1831, of the partnership between John Innes and Robert C. Norman in the firm of Nathaniel Winter and Co., West India merchants. However the remaining partner, John Innes, was declared bankrupt in 1835. Nathaniel Winter himself had died in November 1824. Despite Norman's disappointment with his brother, Robert safeguarded himself against personal bankruptcy by leaving the partnership.]

hurry. He left in the house the sum of £22,000.[12] At any rate this step protected him from the subsequent bankruptcy and prevented his being at all mixed up with John Innes's rascalities,[13] in which he certainly never took part, for with all his peculiarities, he is a man of honor. Still to relieve himself from suspicion however unfounded, much and difficult explanation might have been required.

About two or three years ago, Robert, who had long ceased to hold any intercourse with us, charged me with having ill-used him in the matter of N. Winter & Co and demanded first in manuscript then in print that as residuary legatee of my father, I should assume his claim on that firm and deducting what I had subsequently given him, and charging interest on both sides, that I should pay him over the balance.

This demand struck me with astonishment, for although willing enough to question my conscience and to find in it grounds of self-reproach for transactions long past, I must say, that I never felt any remorse arising from my treatment of Robert and am at this moment thoroughly persuaded of my innocence as respects him.

I might enlarge on this matter but have done this already in a separate paper, which I leave to my children, as affording a valid defence against Robert's charges should they find it necessary to protect their father's memory from unjust reproach.[14]

[12] [Worth £1,698,180 in 2009 prices.]

[13] [Not definitely identified. Possibly John Innes, 1786-1869, a West Indies merchant of Mincing Lane and Moorgate Street, City of London. In the Norman papers at U310 C42 there are letters from one John Innes. The Norman family was involved in a legal action against John Innes; Norman v. Innes and others. King's Bench. Concerning the assurance policy of the ship, cargo, passengers and crew of the ship Gantzen. Brief for the Plaintiff and letters. Norman papers U/310 L5, dated 1822-3. The dating suggests that the action was priory to the involvement of Robert Norman.]

[14] [The Norman papers at Maidstone contain, at U31/F34, papers relating to Norman's brother Robert, including, at U310/F42, a promissory note for £2,000 left to Robert by Norman in his will. At U310/F51 there are papers and letters concerning Robert's estrangement from other members of the family covering the years 1854-75.]

I deeply lament that Robert should suffer from poverty, and should be most ready to afford him help if he would permit me so to do, by renewing our intercourse and withdrawing all charges of pecuniary misconduct. Unless this be done, any assistance I might yield him would appear to be a sort of compromise of a claim, which I hold to be essentially unfounded.

I shall have hereafter more to say, as to my conduct towards Robert.

Nothing of importance to me took place so far as I now recollect, in purely domestic matters in 1832. I continued to derive from my marriage the greatest comfort. The arrangement by which my ever dear and honored mother was made a permanent resident in my house afforded me the utmost pleasure. My health continued good in consequence no doubt of the tranquil happiness which I enjoyed.

I forgot to mention that in 1830 for the first time, at the persuasion of Henry and Uncle Frederick, I took up fly fishing. I had never previously been an angler except as a boy, and in ponds.

I commenced this new occupation at Stoneham in the above year, and was present as a visitor at Stockbridge during the Mayfly, and in the following year 1831 was admitted a member of the Houghton Club, which has afforded me ever since an abundant source of health and recreation. I have passed some years of my life at the Grosvenor Arms.

Fond as I have been of cricket, shooting and athletic amusements of all kinds, there is nothing of the kind which charms me so much as fly fishing.

To wander in the months of May or June through heads, gemmed with flowers, along the banks of a stream now forming a cascade at some weir, now bubbling over a shallow and now slowly winding its way through deeps, fringed with flags[15] or willows, while the birds are singing from every bush and all nature seems to rejoice, is in itself delightful, and then comes the additional gratification of the attempt to inveigle the pearl of the river, the

[15] [Leafed plant growing on moist ground, especially iris.]

beautiful, agile and wary trout.

In the use of the artificial fly the minimum of suffering is inflicted. If the captive trout is drawn from his native element, a blow on the head speedily puts an end to his pain. Should the hook break its hold or the tackle give way, the animal suffers but little, as I have had several opportunities of ascertaining, having known fish who have been caught twice within a short time, in one instance within ten minutes, although the first struggle had been very severe.

Besides fishing two or three times a year at Stockbridge, I have been enabled through the kindness of friends to try my luck in the Cray, the Darent and the Wandle. I hired for several years a share in the Lock at Mapledurham, where I caught a Trout weighing 10 lb 12 oz, my greatest piscatory triumph. I have also fished in the Lamburn and Kennett, at Littlecott, Amesbury as also at Whitchurch &c.

As a fly fisher, notwithstanding my fondness for the gentle art and that I have not been deficient in either strength of arm or manual dexterity, I certainly have not been successful. My returns of sport, kept for many years, have been very meagre, and it must therefore be pronounced that I am greatly deficient in skill; and this is decidedly the case in my use of the blowing rod, a branch of the art in which I have taken far less delight than in whipping. I do not throw the artificial fly amiss. My management of a hooked fish is not first-rate. Perhaps I began too late. At any rate I feel grateful to my rod for the pleasure it has afforded me and hope it may still yield distraction and amusement to my declining years.

The year 1832 was a period of great political excitement to me, and enthusiastically did I rejoice when the House of Lords gave way and the Reform Bill became the law of the land.[16] I look back with satisfaction to my strenuous effort within my little sphere to forward that great measure.

[16] [The Reform Bill received the Royal Assent 7 June 1832.]

At any rate, I was a disinterested combatant. I neither asked for or desired any special advantage for myself, nor had I any envy or dislike for those above me in the social scale. So far as I know and believe, I passed many and many [sic] toil-some days and some sleepless nights in the discharge of what I considered a public duty.

I shall have a great deal more to say on this subject and will now only remark that although the consequences of the Reform Bill have been in some respects very disappointing, although constituencies and representatives have shown far less intelligence and honesty than in my sanguine hopes I had anticipated, yet still it must be allowed that the great measure of 1832 has been followed by enormous improvements which may fairly be traced to it, and by twenty-eight years of the best government the world has ever seen. We owe to it also an escape from the convulsion of 1848 which, had it overthrown the constitution, would probably have led[17] in England, as it has in other countries, through anarchy to a military despotism.

In the year 1832, I was examined for the first time before a 'Bank Committee'.[18] Lord Althorp was the Chairman. I advocated with less distinctness than subsequently, those ideas, as to the perfect identity in their effects on prices &c of paper and metallic money, excepting as respects foreign payments, which I and others, Lord Overstone especially, have subsequently adopted and developed more completely. I also propounded, although I did not originate it, Palmer's plan, that in the management of the Bank, the securities, during an oscillation of the currency, ought to be kept at a fixed amount so that the increase or diminution of the treasure might act on the circulation (out of the house) and the deposits. The above although far from being a perfect rule, was more scientific than any, which had been previously

[17] [Norman wrote 'lead' here.]

[18] [*Parliamentary Papers* 1831-2, vol. 6, *Report from the Committee of Secrecy on the Bank of England Charter.* Norman gave evidence on 26 and 29 June, pp. 176-205; qq. 2388-2825. On Norman's theory of monetary control see D.P. O'Brien *The Development of Monetary Economics*, Cheltenham: Edward Elgar, 2007.]

suggested for the management of an issuing Bank.

It is many years since I have looked over my evidence of 1832, and I dare say that it would now strike me as being very imperfect. Further experience and reflection has doubtless modified my views upon many points. Still on the whole, I am persuaded that this evidence did good and yielded me personally some credit. I had many sharp[19] encounters of wit with the coryphans of the Birmingham school, Mathias Attwood, who with all his nonsense was a very subtle and ingenious person.[20]

It may be further remarked that the general effect of this committee of 1832 was to enlighten the public as to the importance and public utility of a great central issue, and of the Bank of England as the regulator of the currency.

The absurdities of the Harmans[21] &c of former days as to the uselessness of adverting to the state of the exchanges in managing the Bank of England, and the impossibility of overissue when we only discounted good bills not having more than sixty days to run,[22] and at five per cent, had disgusted

[19] [Norman wrote 'a sharp' here.]

[20] [Matthias Attwood, 1779-1851, Birmingham banker, MP Callington, 1820, Boroughbridge, 1830, and Whitehaven, 1832-47, brother of the more famous Thomas Attwood. With Joseph Hume he was the main critic, in Parliamentary enquiries, of the developing orthodoxy of monetary control on the part of the Bank of England, and was to play a significant part in committee hearings in 1840 in which Norman was also a witness.]

[21] [As noted on p. 296, Ward was Norman's ally in arguing that the Bank should regulate its note issues with regard to the exchanges, and the resolution that Ward had caused to be nullified in 1827 was one that the Bank did not agree with regulating the circulation in this way. This is clear from Ward's evidence before the same committee. He gave evidence on 19 and 21 June, *Parliamentary Papers* 1831-2, vol. 6, pp. 126-49, qq. 1882-2149. The relevant exchange is qq. 2073-5. Indeed Ward testified (q. 2078) that, in the Committee hearings on the Resumption of Cash Payments in 1819, he had been embarrassed by his opposition to then establishment in the Bank.]

[22] [Jeremiah Harman told the Committee considering the renewal of the Charter of the Bank that the Directors always took notice of the exchanges, but that it was impossible to regulate the issues of Bank notes with reference to them (*Parliamentary Papers* 1831-2, vol. vi, q. 2155). He said (q. 2151) that instead issues were regulated by considerations of 'the security of the Bank', an answer which was a reflection of the adherence of the Directors, especially during the

sensible men and made them regard the Bank as a great overgrown job, deserving of being consigned to the Limbo of things that were, so soon as the public should be alive to its own rights and interest.[23]

Since that time how great a change has taken place in this respect. How fully is the necessity of a great central issuer recognised, and how much personal respect has the Court of Directors inspired. And here I must readily bear testimony to the fact that this change of opinion, so beneficial both to the Bank and the country, had its origin during the three years when J. Horsley Palmer occupied the Chair. He first abandoned the rule of thumb system of management, or rather the absence of all rule. He devised a principle which although not quite sound, had at any rate some reference to sense and reason, and he thus won for us many and powerful adhesions.[24]

---

'Restriction' era (when convertibility of the notes into gold was suspended), to the Real Bills doctrine. Under this doctrine, the quality of the bill issuer determined the Bank's willingness to discount a bill in exchange for its notes, irrespective of the macroeconomic circumstances. See *Report from the Committee of Secrecy on the Bank of England Charter, Parliamentary Papers* 1831-2 , vol. vi, p. 1. Harman's evidence is 23 June, pp. 150-66, qq. 2150-2387. It cannot have helped his position that he was preceded as a witness before the Committee by Norman's ally William Ward (pp. 126-49, qq. 1882-2149, 19 and 21 June), and that he was followed by Norman himself (pp. 167-205, qq. 2388-2825, 26, 29 and 30 June).]

[23] [5 per cent was the maximum allowed by the Usury Laws. Underlying Harman's position, and that of others classified as Anti-Bullionists, was the so-called Real Bills Doctrine. Under this there was no necessary limit on the issue of Bank of England notes, as long as this took place in discounting bills of the kind Norman describes. There was thus no reference to the state of the balance of payments, or any pretence of monetary control. For the theoretical problems of the Real Bills doctrine see D.P. O'Brien, *The Classical Economists Revisited* (Princeton: Princeton University Press, 2004) and D.P. O'Brien, *The Development of Monetary Economics* (Cheltenham: Edward Elgar, 2007).]

[24] [The Palmer Rule was essentially a balance sheet rule that brought the note issues of the Bank into some correspondence with the exchanges. According to the Rule, assets on the balance sheet should be made up of gold and securities, the former constituting one third of the assets when the exchanges were 'full', that is just on the point of becoming unfavourable. When gold subsequently flowed out, due to a balance of payments deficit, the rule required that the liabilities side of the balance sheet – notes and deposits – should be correspondingly contracted. However the Rule made no distinction between notes issued by the Bank and its deposits, so that a drain of gold could simply leave the note circulation untouched while deposits fell in line with the outflow of gold. Indeed this was the normal course of events under the Rule.]

J.H. Palmer was in some respects a remarkable man. He had been educated very imperfectly but he had much sound sense, a clear vision in his own way.[25] Love of business and ability to bear any quantity of it, and finally, and above all a force of will, which I never saw exceeded in any man. When he had made up his mind it was all but impossible to turn him and his resolute advocacy of his opinions bore down all opposition. I have discovered this more than once to my cost, having had to give way, although my reason remained unconvinced because it was necessary that one or other of us should give way and Palmer would not. I may allude to the compromise with the State of Indiana in [blank in original], as one instance that now rises to my memory.[26]

The events of 1832 increased considerably my influence in the Bank. This however subsequently declined, with the increased knowledge of other directors and in consequence of my inability to take the Chair.

It must have been about this time that my third sister Maria married Herbert Jenner, eldest son of Sir H. Jenner Foot, who died [a] Judge in the Ecclesiastical Courts.[27] This marriage has been altogether happy. Herbert

[25] [John Horsley Palmer, 1779-1858, a Director of the Bank 1811-57, Deputy Governor 1828-30, Governor 1830-3. Palmer was one of the most, probably the most, influential Directors. He was the fourth son of the nine children of William Palmer, 1737-1821, merchant of Nazeing Park, Essex. He was a partner with his brother George Palmer, and a Captain Wilson, as an East India merchant 1802-57. Norman refers to Palmer's education. He was educated at Charterhouse, like Norman's friend George Grote, so Norman's remark about his lack of education is puzzling.]

[26] [The default of the State of Indiana was part of the debt crisis in the United States over the years 1839-43. Eight States, and the Territory of Florida, defaulted in 1841 and 1842. It was the States with the highest per capita debt which defaulted. Indiana had expected to pay the interest on its debts through taxes and the interest on bank investments, but the value of land fell and with it the income from property tax. By 1842 it was clear that the State could not service its debts. Indiana defaulted. Borrowing had been undertaken in order to construct roads, canals and railways. Interest payments did not resume until 1848. Indiana was also affected by the default of the Morris Bank which acted as agents for its bonds.]

[27] [Maria Eleanora Norman, born 20 July 1803, married 20 October 1835 Herbert Jenner Fust, JP, LLD, of Hill Court, Glos, eldest son of the Right Hon. Sir Herbert Jenner Fust, PC, LLD, of Chislehurst, Kent. She died 2 March 1891. He died 30

Jenner worked hard at his profession as advocate during his father's lifetime and after his father's death inherited the estate called Hill Court in Gloucestershire, which makes him quite comfortable although not affluent.

In April 1832, I was returned to the magistrates as a person liable to act as overseer of the poor and was selected by them to serve. I determined to serve to the very best of my power, and was glad of an opportunity to do the parish good service, and to test the truth of my Poor Law opinions by actual practice.[28] I continued in office for four successive years, always attending the vestries where relief was then dispensed, and also attending at the workhouse when bills were audited and paid. My colleagues were Cocks[29] and Innous.[30] The assistant overseer was Abraham Nettlefold,[31] a man of great ability who thoroughly fell into my views, or rather had anticipated them. The result of our management was a severe check to pauperism and a large diminution to expenditure. We met of course with much opposition and obloquy from ignorance and dishonesty and spurious benevolence.

We used a labour test on the field now belonging to Cooper and opposite Bencewell and, when the magistrates threatened interference with us, always offered to take applicants for relief into the workhouse. I could mention absurd instances of the mode in which things had been managed before our

---

July 1904. Sir Herbert Jenner Fust, 1778-1852, son of Robert Jenner, 1743-1810, assumed the additional name of Fust in 1842 on the death of his cousin Sir John Fust. Sir Herbert was knighted in 1828. He was a judge of the Prerogative Court of Canterbury, 1834-52.]

[28] [On the Poor Law, and the 'labour test', see p. 342. The test was to permit outdoor relief – this is the sense of the threat to take applicants for relief into the workhouse. However the saving of expenditure to which Norman refers was probably due not to the discouragement of voluntary idleness, as the Utilitarians believed, but to the migration of the rural poor to the towns, Bromley being at that time a rural area, and the consequent transfer of much of the burden of the poor rate from rural properties to urban ones.]

[29] [Not traced. The Six Home Counties Post Office Directory for 1845 does however list a Mrs Mary Ann Cocks, grocer at Bromley.]

[30] [John Innous is listed in the Six Home Counties Post Office Directory as a tailor at Bromley.]

[31] [Abraham Nettlefold has not been traced. The Six Home Counties Post Office Directory for 1845 lists only a John Nettlefold in Bromley, a cabinet maker.]

time, but must forbear or I should never finish these memoranda.

We introduced the custom of printing and distributing a short sketch of our accounts every year.

Among all the laws that have passed the legislature in my time, excepting the Reform Bill, of which it was the eldest child, and perhaps the laws introducing free trade, I know of none which can compare as to beneficial results with the new Poor Law. To be sure the effect of the latter depended greatly upon the labours of the able and honest men, by whom it was worked in the first few years after its enactment, and when it had to struggle with party spirit, ignorance and dishonesty.

The old Poor Law had become a moral plague; as administered it struck at the root of virtue. Prudence, honesty, industry, filial and parental love fell before its deadly assault, and the public mind was poisoned by the doubt and confusion it introduced as to the proper relation of the capitalist and labourer.

A few more years under the old system would probably have produced something like a civil war. The owners of property would hardly have submitted to beggary without a struggle, while the claims of pauperism with their constant tendency to increase would hardly have stopped short until they had exhausted all their 'pabulum', and reached the impossible.

There was this special danger in the old system, that in most cases, through the rural districts the largest employers of labour *viz* the farmers, were strongly opposed to improvement. They felt that rates were only a portion of rent, that what they paid to the overseer they would otherwise have to pay to the landlord and they usually preferred the former channel of payment. They liked the sort of command which they obtained over the labourer, in being able to discharge him at the moment they did not want him, even for half a day, as in the case of rain or snow. They felt too that they could saddle through means of the rates, a portion of their wages on the parson, or the shopkeepers of the village or town, if there was one.

In short, the old Poor Law, in its worst form, involved an aggra[vated][32] specimen of socialism, a division of property, in which the worst got the most, the better less and in inverse relation to their merits, and the best of all nothing.

I apprehend that in all old and populous countries, a system of laws for the relief of destitution is either absolutely necessary or is at least less pernicious than that wide-spread mendicancy, which we see in Catholic countries. It is a fair subject of boast to England that while, in accordance with the humane spirit of the age, she has placed the condition of the pauper as to food, clothing and lodging, far higher than is to be found in any other country, she has effected this object at the same time, that she has so arranged her Poor Laws as to deprive them in great part of their degrading and demoralising features.

I must conclude this digression by stating that, after all, I can only regard Poor Laws as a necessary evil. That I am quite aware of their mischievous tendencies and fully expect that future generations will have to deal with them under perhaps far more difficult circumstances than those in which we were placed forty years ago. Poor Laws may afford the field of battle in the great conflict between have and get, or at any rate, become complicated and mixed up with it.

About the year 1832, took place my quarrel with my oldest and all but dearest friend George Grote, an event which I cannot look back to even now without severe regret and which at the time caused me more pain and annoyance than any other event in my life, excepting the death of relatives.[33]

I have papers, which explain the facts and dates of this most distressing affair.[34] But even now, I cannot bear to look at them and will content myself

[32] [Manuscript torn here.]

[33] [There is no mention of this in the book by Harriet Grote, *The Personal Life of George Grote* (London: John Murray, 1973). Norman's sister Mrs Whitmore was his closest sibling, his sister Charlotte.]

[34] [The Norman papers at Maidstone contain, at U310 C122/2, a copy of a letter

here with giving from recollection a short statement of the case.

Cowell had been for many years the friend with whom I had most closely associated. I had lived with him. I had the highest idea of his ability and honor, a lower opinion of his temper and discretion. I felt the deepest obligation to him for the kindness and attention he had shewn me during years of illness and depression. I was therefore on the most intimate terms with him.

On several occasions Cowell told me that Mrs Grote conversed with him in a way little accordant with feminine delicacy, in a way in short, which would have thrown deep suspicion on the character of any other lady, than such a sort of privil[eged][35] person as Mrs Grote was. I considered these communications as strictly confidential and never mentioned them to any human being. I fully imagined that Cowell had told the story to me, and to me only. It never struck me that I ought to communicate to George Grote what I had heard. I well knew that he and his wife held opinions differing from those commonly received, and imagined that he might allow her a latitude of conversation, which other husbands would have objected to.

This being the state of things, I heard one day something from my sister Mrs Whitmore, which convinced me that she was aware of what had taken place between Cowell and Mrs Grote and told him of it. He seemed to imagine that Mrs Grote had spread unfavourable reports of him and an angry correspondence ensued between him and William Whitmore, the object being so far as I recollect, to elicit information respecting the truth of these suspicions. This correspondence at length assumed a character, which threatened ulterior consequences, and I was obliged to interfere with both parties in order to put an end to the dispute. To effect this caused me much labour and great anxiety and placed me of course in a most painful position to my sister and her husband. The result of my interference was finally to

from Norman to George Grote about the quarrel, showing how Norman attempted to end the estrangement.]

[35] [Manuscript is torn here.]

bring about a surrender of the hostile correspondence on both sides and a restoration of tranquillity so far. Very angry feelings continued however to be entertained by the several disputants.

While this imbroglio existed I learned to my astonishment that Cowell himself had communicated to Mrs Whitmore what had occurred between himself and Mrs Grote, or at least so much of it as was suitable for a lady's ear, and that the apparent discrepancy between what he said and something which has [sic] fallen accidentally from Mrs Grote but which did not involve a complete narration, had led to the remarks, which I had heard which again led me to say what I did to Cowell.

During the progress of the correspondence between Cowell and the Whitmores, the latter being severely pressed and thinking they perceived a great discrepancy between the statements of the two parties, thought it right to inform George Grote of what they had heard from Cowell of the conduct of Mrs Grote. In doing this, I cannot think that they were to blame although the result to me was most disastrous. George Grote, naturally perhaps, thought that I had committed a breach of friendship in not having communicated to him what I had heard from Cowell so soon as it reached my ears. A verbal explanation and some epistolary correspondence failed to change his views, and severely as I felt the loss of his friendship, and the cessation of that intimate intercourse which had subsisted between us since infancy, I cannot blame him for the course he took, I should probably have acted like him under similar circumstances. Yet I can lay my hand upon my heart and say that I acted with the utmost purity of intention and in the way which I thought most likely to prevent mischief. I have since this time only met Grote as a common acquaintance. My estrangement from Mrs Grote has been more complete. I can only recollect having met her in company once.[36]

[36] [There is no reference to the Cowell affair in *The Lewin Letters* (see p. 140). However there does seem to have been a partial reconciliation between Norman and Mrs Grote, in the 1870s, after Norman had completed the Autobiography. He does not seem to have considered it worthwhile returning to it to record the

That was at Senior's, when she would not speak to me. For this, under the circumstances, I can hardly find fault with her.

The position in which Cowell and Grote were placed to each other was of course of a most painful and hostile character. Mutual friends stepped in, and a sort of reference was made to Mr James Mill and Lord Overstone who examined into all the circumstances of the case and drew up a paper containing explanations,[37] which was accepted by both parties as a finale to the whole affair.

Among the most remarkable men whom I have known, was James Mill, the historian of British India, father of the now living philosopher John Stuart Mill.[38]

I used to meet him frequently at S.C. Holland's,[39] T. Tooke's, Grote's and at the Political Economy Club. I once dined with him at his residence in Queen Square Westminster and once he passed a day or two here when his companion was C.H. Cameron.

He was a person of great learning and acuteness, and energy. The latter quality was evinced by his successful struggles against poverty, which landed him, to the immortal honor of the India directors, in the examiner's office in Leadenhall Street.

---

reconciliation. Mrs Grote wrote to her sister Mme F. von Koch, 20 June 1872, referring to the printing of some of George Grote's poems: 'I have just printed a selection of G.G.'s early poetry, 100 copies only. ... George Norman it was who prevailed on me to print these poems'. See *The Lewin Letters*, vol. 2 pp. 308-9. See also Mrs Grote to her sister, 6 June 1876, on giving a dinner party for Norman and talking 'over old times'. *The Lewin Letters*, vol. 2 p. 336. George Grote had died 18 June 1871.]

37 [The matter is alluded to in a letter of 5 November 1832 from Norman to Overstone. See D.P. O'Brien (ed.), *The Correspondence of Lord Overstone*, Cambridge: Cambridge University Press, 1971, vol. 1 pp. 204-5.]

38 [John Stuart Mill, 1806-73, philosopher, economist, employee (like his father) of the East India Company 1823-58, regarded as the most prominent intellectual of his day, educated intensively by his father James Mill and by Jeremy Bentham, and subsequently suffered a nervous breakdown.]

39 [Swinton Holland was a partner in Barings bank and, as recounted on p. 254, had a key role in the foundation of the Political Economy Club.]

Mill was a favourite disciple of Jeremy Bentham and pushed the principles of his master to their furthest point. I apprehend that nobody made more converts (inter alios Grote and Ricardo) to the peculiar doctrines of the sect in religion, politics and morals.

About the year 1825, I was a thorough convert to Benthamism in politics, although not on the still more important subjects mentioned above, and subscribed to a reprint of two or three articles, originally contributed to an encyclopaedia by Mill, which contained a thorough exegesis of the true faith, according to Queen Square.[40]

I believe that Mill was a very honest man, desirous of doing all the good in his power. He was also benevolent in his way, although a strong hater and not what is called a good-humoured man. I have heard him say that he and his son could not agree because they once stood in the relation of master and slave.

The defect in his mental constitution appears to me to have been its one-sidedness. What he saw he saw clearly, but he did not see all, and more especially what he did not wish to see. To those who differed from him he gave no quarter and had a difficulty even in thinking them honest. He had not a spark of fancy or poetry in his composition and this is a great defect.

Mill was a little fair man, with bright blue eyes and a long sharp nose. He was particularly attentive to his dress. He was I fancy, son of a Scotch clergyman.[41] I know nothing of his early life.

---

[40] [Mill had several of his articles from the Supplement to the 4th-6th editions of *Encyclopaedia Britannica* reprinted separately. However the collection to which Norman refers here was probably *Essays on 1. Government 2. Jurisprudence 3. Liberty of the Press 4. Prisons and Prison Discipline 5. Colonies 6. Law of Nations 7. Education. Reprinted from the Supplement to the Encyclopaedia Britannica.* London: J. Innes, 1828. It was marked 'Not for Sale' and it was clearly supported by people like Norman who were enthusiastic about Utilitarianism.]

[41] [James Mill was born in Forfarshire, Scotland. He was the son of James Mill, died 1808, formerly Milne, a shoemaker and his wife Isabel Fenton, 1755-1801, daughter of a farmer from Kirriemuir. It was she who, socially ambitious, changed the Scots Milne to the more English sounding Mill. Like his son John Stuart Mill, James Mill experienced a childhood directed to study. After Montrose Academy,

I have said that my part in the business involved more pain and anxiety to me than any other event of my life, excepting the loss of relatives. It produced a breach between myself and my oldest and almost my dearest friend, which has never been repaired. It placed me in a most painful position to my sister and her husband and involved a coldness and awkwardness between us, which continued for many years. The ladies of my family who heard of course something of what had happened, naturally took part against Cowell. Finally it shook my confidence in Cowell. It exhibited him as animated by an overweening vanity and a large stock of vindictive feeling. I also felt that in his endeavors, as he professed to vindicate himself, an attempt which in his case usually involved the utter abasement of his opponent, he had shewn little or no consideration for me and had ridden rough shod over my dearest sentiments and sympathies, without hesitation or compunction.

The change of my views as to Cowell, his character and conduct, as evinced in this affair, came on me gradually. At first I assumed that he was decidedly in the right. His many high qualities which I knew so well, and gratitude for his past kindness to me, led me to take up his cause with enthusiasm. I gradually perceived that his conduct had not been irreproachable, and looking back upon it by the light of subsequent experience I should probably form a judgment still more severe upon it. But I have never attempted of late years to reopen the case, a perusal of the letters still in my possession would inflict great pain upon me and lead to no good result. I have written what has preceded, not with any intention to preserve a knowledge of matters which had better be buried in oblivion, but simply to give a notion of the causes which in the first place produced to me the loss of Grote's friendship, which I have always considered a heavy calamity and which subsequently led to my rupture with Cowell, as will hereafter appear. My biography would

he enrolled at Edinburgh University, destined for the Presbyterian Ministry. He graduated in 1794. He was licensed to preach – reportedly incomprehensibly – in 1798, but was unsuccessful and left for London in 1809, where he became a journalist.]

have been incomplete without some account of these transactions, but I have only given such a general notion of them as was necessary for my purpose, without descending into details, which it is unnecessary to rake up.

I have often reviewed my own conduct during these distressing transactions, and on the whole am acquitted by my conscience of any intentional misconduct. I acted for the best. Had I known everything, I should certainly have acted in many respects differently, but I could only use the lights I then possessed.

My early post-nuptial life possessed few of the landmarks, which my journeys and maladies had established for my younger years and it may happen not infrequently, that I shall hereafter assign some anecdote, even relating to public events, to a wrong year. but mistakes of this kind will not affect the substantial truth of my narrative and may be corrected as to the date of public events by the reader, when necessary, from extraneous evidence.

I shall never forget the delight with which I regarded the passing of the Reform Bill. The election which succeeded it was the first county business in which I took an active part and resulted in the return of Mr Hodges[42] and Mr Rider[43] for West Kent.[44]

From that time to the present I have had much to do with our county politics, having always been behind the scene in the deliberations of the Liberal party and from time to time with encreasing influence.

[42] [Thomas Law Hodges, 1776-1857; see p. 315.]

[43] [Thomas Rider lived at Boughton Monchelsea Place, near Maidstone. The Riders had owned the seat since 1685. In 1830 the area had seen serious disturbances, due to agricultural distress. Rider, and another local magistrate called Best, attempted to control this. The combination of threatening to read the Riot Act, conciliatory behaviour by Rider, and the appearance of cavalry in the background seems to have been sufficient to calm the immediate situation. However machine breaking and incendiarism continued in Kent for two more years.]

[44] [*Times* 30 August 1832, 3e, reported that Sir William Geary described his Whig opponents as 'rebels'. *Times* 22 September, 3b, reported the likely return of Hodges and Rider. *Times* 18 December, 4d, reported that Thomas Law Hodges and Thomas Rider were nominated. *Times* 21 December, 1d, reported the votes as Hodges 3,380, Rider 3,107, Geary 2,488. Hodges and Rider were duly elected.]

For many years, I managed personally with a little assistance from Mr Latter,[45] the registration of the Bromley district, filling up claims and signing notices of objection myself. I made great efforts to establish a local committee, so as to secure a voluntary[46] agency in the different parishes. This scheme however utterly failed in our case, as in fact it always will. Paid and organized agency is alone to be relied upon, in such a matter as the registration.

My expenditure on matters connected with elections has been very considerable. I have never subscribed less than £100 to the central fund and in Mr Hodges's contests, always held him harmless from any claims from our district. Sometimes I had a little help from others, but a contest has more than once cost me in the district an additional £100. To this must be added the expence of the registration. To the registration I have subscribed since 1852, £25 per annum. There are other pecuniary claims growing out of county politics, to which I need not allude, but on the whole it must not be thought that such matters can be carried on without heavy calls on the purses of those who bleed freely.

I must here bear evidence to the disinterested zeal of Mr Latter who freely devoted to what he considered a righteous cause his time and legal knowledge during many a long year, and that without asking for any remuneration. There were times too, when his conduct drew upon him the ill will of Tory magistrates.

Previously to, and many years after, the Reform Bill, party spirit ran very high and it was difficult to keep on good, at any rate on cordial, terms with one's neighbours.

[45] [The Latters were a Bromley legal practice, and it is likely that Norman was referring to a member of this. According to Norman's Bromley Memoir, the first Latter worked for a lawyer called Greenwood 'in a very humble capacity', subsequently became his articled clerk, and finally his successor. Those members of the family mentioned in the Memoir are Robert Booth Latter and Robinson Latter. There is no indication of the family member to which Norman was referring.]

[46] [Norman wrote 'voluntarily' here.]

For myself I can say that I never carried politics into private life, but then it must be recollected that among persons of my own sphere I belonged to a small minority and it was therefore my interest to profess, and thence to feel, the merits of toleration. At any rate, I had the good luck never to quarrel with anybody and here I cannot but do justice to the kindness shewn to me by my neighbours on this and all other occasions.

In the height of the Reform Bill struggle, a report somehow or other reached the Bishop,[47] that the Palace at Bromley was to be attacked by the mob. He (Dr Murray) was a good deal frightened and determined to send his wife, Lady Sarah, and numerous children to this house being persuaded that I had the will and more than any other person the power to protect them. I need hardly say that the report was a 'canard', and that the Plebs, of this district at least, was good-humoured and well-intentioned. At any rate the Bishop never fulfilled his intentions.

It was about this time however that incendiary fires began in this district and indeed over the whole Kingdom. Their first occurrence was in pauperized parishes and they have always been most rife in such, but the example has been contagious and has extended to others.

Since about the year 1830, incendiary fires have never wholly ceased. They afford a singular instance of the blindness of revenge and illwill, as the loss is inflicted not on the farmer or landowner but on the insurance office. To be sure the final result is a rise in premiums, but this is a consequence too distant and refined for the comprehension of the ignorant incendiary.[48]

As I have felt so warmly on political subjects and have taken so active a part in local party contests, it may appear remarkable that I never entered Parliament, nor became a candidate, nor even seriously thought of doing

[47] [George Murray, 1784-1860, Bishop of Rochester 1827-60. He married in 1811 Lady Sarah Hay Drummond, second daughter of the Earl of Kinnoull. They had five sons and six daughters.]

[48] [On the incendiary fires see p. 361 in connection with Mr Rider. On Norman's connection with the Sun Fire Office, see p. 323.]

either one or the other.

The wonder will appear still greater when I declare that to represent his county in the House of Commons seems to me, one of the most attractive objects of ambition for an English gentleman. The truth is, that the idea of Parliament was often present to my mind. I regarded it with longing eyes, and weighed and pondered it in every point of view, finally making up my mind that my extreme nervousness and excitable temperament would render the canvass and contest, setting aside the duties of the House, far more than I could bear. My ordinary occupations have always tried my strength to the utmost and I felt persuaded that a very slight additional weight would altogether break me down.

It has frequently been proposed to me to stand for West Kent, but in addition to the objections alluded to in the last paragraph, my fixed convictions in favor of free trade, would until the repeal of the corn laws have rendered me unpalatable to an agricultural constituency.

A few years later than that under review, either in 1835 or 1837, the late Mr Travers[49] and some other gentlemen proposed that I should stand for London. We had a long conference. I finally declined and suggested James Pattison then Governor of the Bank.[50] He was brought forward and succeeded, I do not however pretend to say that I was the first person who thought of him.[51]

---

[49] [Not positively identified. Possibly a relative of Benjamin Travers, 1783-1858, surgeon at the London Infirmary for Diseases of the Eye 1810-16, FRS 1813, Surgeon Extraordinary to the Queen 1837, and to the Prince Consort 1840. However he was one of a large family. He was the son of a London sugar baker, and the second of ten children. He began work in his father's business before taking up medicine. The initial of the person active in the City election is J; see p. 365.]

[50] [See p. 297. He was Governor 1834-7, in succession to Horsley Palmer (and was Deputy Governor 1833-4). On a refusal by Norman to stand for election to Parliament, see letter 23, vol. 1, p. 203, of D.P. O'Brien (ed.), *The Correspondence of Lord Overstone*, Cambridge: Cambridge University Press, 1971.]

[51] [*Times* 2 January 1835, 2d, 3 January, 3a, 6 January, 3e-4c. A Mr J. Travers nominated a Mr Crawford. Pattison was proposed by Lewis Loyd, and seconded by Samuel Gurney. According to *Times* 8 January 3a, Pattison came second in the poll, behind Alderman Wood, with 6,141 votes. George Grote came fourth in the

Some of the matters alluded to in the preceding paragraphs would more properly belong to succeeding years and have been mentioned here in the order of topics rather than of time. I now return to my narrative.

The following year, 1833, produced few events that need occupy me long. In March, my present eldest son, Charles Loyd,[52] was born and named after my most intimate friends Charles H. Cameron and Samuel Jones Loyd, now Baron Overstone. He has always been dutiful and affectionate and has never by any important fault either of commission or omission caused me grief. He will, I hope and believe, when I am gone prove a kind and sensible head of the family, duly alive to the important duties that will be devolved upon him, and especially to his obligation of watching over and counselling the younger members to whom he will stand 'in loco parentis', and of protecting and aiding those less endowed with fortune than himself.

In the Autumn of 1833, my wife, self and the two children took a journey into the North. We first passed two or three days at Overstone and in our way to Berwickshire slept at Derby, Barnsley, Leeming Bar[53] and Durham; we went a little out of our way to see Richmond Castle.

At Lees near Coldstream we passed two or three weeks with Sir William Marjoribanks[54] who had married my wife's elder sister, Mary Stone. He had

poll with 6,104 votes. The voting figures reported in *Times* 9 January, 2d, differ slightly but are significant in placing Pattison at the head of the poll with 6,656 votes. It seems possible that the Mr J. Travers featuring in the *Times* election report, and referred to by Norman as 'the late Mr Travers', was Joseph Travers of Joseph Travers and Sons, wholesale grocers, 19 St Swithin's Lane.]

52 [Charles Loyd Norman, Norman's second son, was born 10 March 1833, and died 17 February 1889.]

53 [Norman wrote Lemming Lane.]

54 [Sir William Marjoribanks, 2nd Bt, 1792-1834. He was succeeded by Sir John Marjoribanks, 3rd Bt, 1830-84, who in turn was succeeded by his brother Sir William Marjoribanks, 4th Bt, 1832-88. The name derives from the lands of Ratho-marjorie in Renfrewshire, which came into the possession of a family called Johnston who assumed the name Marjoribanks. A younger branch of the family had succeeded in the 18th century to the estate of Lees in Berwickshire, and this is the one that Norman visited. Sir William Marjoribanks was the eldest surviving son of the 1st Bt, Sir John Marjoribanks, died 1833, a partner in a banking house in Edinburgh, MP for Buteshire (1811) and Berwickshire (1818), and Lord Provost of

been at one time I think a wine merchant, then commanded an East Indiaman, and finally held an office at Madras. He succeeded to the Baronetcy in consequence of the death of his father and elder brother. He was not a man of much education but was kind and generous and to us most hospitable. I used to go shooting from Lees but with moderate success and also tried my luck with the rod in the tweed, caught one salmon and lost another.

A more melancholy household than at Lees when we were there cannot be imagined. Old Lady Marjoribanks was manifestly failing.[55] Sir William was diseased and so was Charles Marjoribanks, the youngest son, M.P for Berwickshire and a man of some mark. In short, it must have been anticipated as actually occurred that none of the party would be alive in a twelve month.

From Lees we made an excursion to Edinburgh, where I was introduced to various Boswells, friends and connections of my wife by whom in her youthful days she had been treated with great kindness, having lived some time under the care of old Mrs Boswell while her father was in India and her mother dead. At Edinburgh, Charlie, then an infant at the breast, was seized with a sort of croup which frightened me greatly.

I was much struck with the improvement, which had taken place at Edinburgh since I was there with the Ords in 1812.

On finally quitting Lees we went across country, sleeping at Cambo and Whitfield, where also I had not been since 1812. I need hardly say that we were received by our kind friends the Ords with the utmost cordiality and admired greatly their beautiful residence, the equal of which England can hardly shew. I went out shooting two or three times but with no great success. Poor W. Ord was my companion.

---

Edinburgh in 1825. Sir William Marjoribanks, on whose demise Norman remarks, died 22 September 1834.]

[55] [Sir John Marjoribanks, 1st Bt, married in 1790 Alison, eldest daughter of William Ramsay of Barnton.]

From Whitfield we posted to Aldstone[56] and over to Cross Fell to Carlisle.[57] Then by Penrith to Manchester and Liverpool and crossed into Cheshire where we established ourselves at Gresford Lodge, the residence of Mrs William Egerton.[58]

In our way home, we visited Mrs Pochin at Backley in Leicestershire[59] and my uncle Richard Norman at Melton Mowbray. The result of this tour was thus to introduce my wife to many of my friends and connections, and me to hers.

My uncle drove us over to Belvoir which I saw with interest, not having previously seen it since the great fair. The Duke[60] was away but we were introduced to Lady Adeliza who has since married her cousin and mine Frederick H. Norman, the Rector of Bottesford.[61]

It was, I think in 1833, that sitting in the library, I heard some disturbance in the passage, and going out to inquire into its cause, found a man in hot dispute with Waghorn the butler.[62] The former declaring that he must give a letter of which he was the bearer into my own hands. The latter insisting

56 [Norman meant Alston.]

57 [Norman could not have gone to Carlisle from Whitfield over Cross Fell. He meant Glendue Fell.]

58 [William Grey Egerton of Gresford Lodge, Denbighshire, born 1770, married 1807 Sibella (died 1883), daughter of Robert Boswell, and died in 1827. Norman mentions the kindness of the Boswell family of Edinburgh to Sibella Stone, who later became his wife.]

59 [As noted on p. 123, Elizabeth Pochin, née Norman, was Norman's cousin. George Pochin had died either in 1829 or in 1831.]

60 [John Henry Manners, 1778-1857. His sister, Elizabeth Isabella Manners had married, as his second wife, Norman's uncle Richard Norman, 21 August 1798; see p. 123.]

61 [Lady Adeliza Elizabeth Gertrude Manners, 1810-77, daughter of John Henry Manners, 5th Duke of Rutland, married in 1853 the Reverend Frederick John Norman (died 1888), who was her first cousin, as he was the son of the 5th Duke's sister Lady Elizabeth Isabella Manners, and Richard Norman, Norman's paternal uncle. Her husband was Rector of Bottesford, Leics, a living in the gift of the Duke.]

62 [According to Norman's Bromley Memoir, 'The first butler I remember was named Waghorn. He was succeeded by Woodhouse who came from Mr Jones Loyd (Lord Overstone).']

upon taking it from him.

I stopt the fray and learned that the stranger was a Government messenger, and the missive, a communication from Lord Althorp[63] proposing to me to join Mr Hyde Villiers at Paris for the purpose of meeting certain French commissioners, in order to lay the basis of a commercial treaty.[64]

The proposal was very flattering to me, I was however frightened at its suddenness, wanted time to make up my mind and arrange business at home, which could not be granted, and finally the whole thing slipped through my fingers, and Bowring,[65] a much fitter person, doubtless, took the place, which had been destined for me.

Thus was lost one of my opportunities of becoming a public man, probably with no injury to my reputation. I might have turned out like Galba in

[63] [John Charles Spencer, 1782-1845, 3rd Earl Spencer, Chancellor of the Exchequer as Lord Althorp, 1830-4.]

[64] [It seems that the recollection by Norman is inaccurate. Thomas Hyde Villiers, 1801-32, died in December 1832. He was the brother of Charles Pelham Villiers, 1802-98. In the House of Commons he had made a long speech on the Methuen Treaty with Portugal, and clearly had an interest in trade negotiations. But it appears that Norman may have had the date wrong, and also that he had the wrong member of the Villiers family. For George William Frederick Villiers, 1800-70, 4th Earl of Clarendon, was appointed in 1831, with Sir John Bowring (see next fn), as commissioner to investigate commercial relations with France. Correspondence concerning this episode, dated 1831-2, and containing a draft of Norman's reply to Lord Althorp, is in the Norman papers at U310 C38A.]

[65] [Sir John Bowring, 1792-1872, linguist, writer and traveller. LLD Groningen, 1829, MP Kilmarnock 1835-7, Bolton 1841-9. He was also a supporter of decimal currency, and was responsible for the introduction of the florin (2 shillings, ten per cent of one pound) as a step towards this. Like Norman, he was a Unitarian, and he was active in Unitarian circles. He became a disciple of Bentham, who made him his literary heir. He was the son of a wool trader in Exeter, and in working for his father he learned several European languages. He travelled on business in Spain and France during the Peninsula war, and travelled extensively in the years after the war. However he ran into commercial difficulties, and by 1827 his firm, Bowring & Co., had collapsed. He sought public employment, and in 1830 was appointed to Sir Henry Parnell's commission on public accounts, which involved Bowring in investigating public accounting procedures in France and the Netherlands, a task for which his previous experience made him well suited. In 1831 he was appointed, with George Villiers, later Lord Clarendon, to investigate commercial relations between England and France. In 1832-4 he was sent on three long coach journeys through the centre and south of France.]

Tacitus,[66] Major privato visus &c.

It may be remarked that the negotiations at Paris altogether failed. The French, I believe, would make no concessions in their restrictive system. At least we said so.

In 1833 was written and printed, but only for distribution, my first currency pamphlet. It contained in substance the chief doctrines which I have since maintained and formed the foundation of another pamphlet published in 1838. In the original pamphlet was contained the first declaration of the doctrine that a perfect paper currency, in addition to being strictly convertible and little liable to discredit, should 'at every moment be of precisely the same value as the metallic medium which might supply its place, being increased and diminished under the same circumstances, at similar periods, and to a like extent'. So far as I know, this opinion was original and it may have had something to do with the act of 1844, in which it was embodied. I followed it out on all subsequent occasions.[67]

[66] [Tacitus characterised Galba as weak and old, a man equal to the imperial office if he had never held it. Publius or Gaius Cornelius Tacitus, c.56-c.117 was a Senator and historian of the Roman Empire. His two major works, which have survived in incomplete form, are the *Annals* and the *Histories*, spanning the history of the Roman Empire from the death of Augustus, 14 AD, to the death of Domitian in 96 AD. Galba was Galba Servius Sulpicius 5 BC to AD 69, Roman Emperor. He commanded with success in Gaul, Germany, Africa and Spain. In AD 61 he was living in retirement when Nero (AD 37-68, Emperor AD 54-68) appointed him Governor of Hispania Tarraconensis. On Nero's death he was proclaimed Emperor, and marched to Rome. But a conspiracy was organised, and he was murdered. The classic phrase of Tacitus is 'Capax Imperii Nisi Imperasset' or, worthy of empire had he never been Emperor. The phrase quoted by Norman is from Book 1 of Tacitus's *Histories*, paragraph 49. Major privato visus dum privatus fuit et omnium consensu capax imperii nisi imperassat. 'He seemed greater than a subject while he was a subject, and would have been commonly regarded as equal to empire had he never been emperor.']

[67] [Norman's 1838 pamphlet was *Remarks upon Some Prevalent Errors, with Respect to Currency and Banking and Suggestions to the Legislature and the Public as to the Improvement of the Monetary System.* Norman was incorrect in believing that he invented the principle that a mixed currency of notes and coins should fluctuate in amount in exactly the same way as a similarly circumstanced purely metallic currency would have done. It is to be found in a number of authors from around 1823, priority belonging to Thomas Joplin. See, O'Brien, *Thomas Joplin and Classical Macroeconomics* (Aldershot: Edward Elgar, 1993) pp. 22-3; O'Brien,

During the year 1833, I made a purchase of Burr's Oak farm in the two parishes of East Peckham and Nettlefold for £8,650, the largest single investment which I ever made in land.[68] It was bought of a Yeoman named Welfear, who had bought it and another farm of Sir William Twisden of Roydon Hall about 1792, owing part of the purchase money.[69] When low prices came, he found it desirable to sell. The farm has been occupied by one or other of his sons ever since. The purchase was not a bad one as it paid full three and a half per cent. Old John Fuller of Croydon[70] was my agent in the transaction, I subsequently bought seventeen acres of wood adjoining Burr's Oak farm from Lord Gainsborough[71] and was compelled to sell about four acres to the South Eastern railway for £280, a very inadequate price.[72]

I may here observe that of all property land is that which I like the best, it certainly pays but a moderate return. On the other hand the security is perfect and a steady increase of rent and value may always be anticipated, if the purchase is made with discretion.[73]

---

*The Classical Economists Revisited* (Princeton: Princeton University Press, 2004) p. 182; O'Brien, *The Development of Monetary Economics* (Cheltenham: Edward Elgar, 2007) pp. 170-1.]

[68] [Material relating to these two properties is in the Norman papers at U310/T32, T33, T44, P23, P24, P25, A50.]

[69] [There is some difficulty in identification due to variant spellings of the name. Sir Thomas Twisden, 1st Bt, 1602-83 had his seat at Royden Hall, East Peckham. The most likely candidate for the person referred to by Norman is Sir William Jervis Twysden, 7th Bt, 1760-1834, who succeeded to the baronetcy in 1767, though he may possibly have meant Sir William Twysden, 8th Bt, 1788-1879. The name seems to have been spelt Twisden and Twysden at various times in the history of the family. It was originally Twysden, but the 1st Bt changed it to Twisden.]

[70] [Fuller and Marsh, Auctioneers, High Street, Croydon are listed in the Six Home Counties Directory for 1845.]

[71] [Charles Noel Gainsborough, 1781-1866, 1st Earl Gainsborough 1841, MP Rutland 1802-14.]

[72] [See Overstone to Norman 18 May 1856 in D.P. O'Brien, ed., *The Correspondence of Lord Overstone* (1971) vol. 2 pp. 647-8. If the sale was 1856, the 2009 equivalent value would be £22,434. Material concerning Norman's dealings with the railway companies, which procured the passage of private acts of Parliament to enable them to make compulsory purchases, are in the Norman papers at U310/E33.]

[73] [At the end of the Bromley Memoir, Norman comments that 'The landed prop-

I like land too, as a sportsman and agriculturist, and on the whole I heartily wish that I had bought more freely and that my father had done so too. I abstained chiefly because I thought that with my numerous children, money was more convenient and desirable than land.

It must have been I think about 1834, that my youngest sister Emma married Captin Henry Bowden of the Fusilier Guards,[74] second son of Mr John Bowden then of Homewood, Chislehurst, a retired Portuguese merchant, and my colleague at the Bank of England.[75] This marriage to a man of sense, honor and sufficient fortune, was thoroughly happy while it lasted and promised a long continuance of happiness when it was terminated by my sister's death from puerperal fever after the birth of an only son and second child. The children were Emma, wife of Richard Mills, and Henry, now an officer in the guards.

Emma was a very pretty and amiable young woman, beloved by all and especially by her husband. Had she lived he would have remained in the Army, and would have escaped from that absorption of his mental energies in the boundless sea of theological controversy which has ended in landing him at Rome. Henry Bowden was an excellent officer, senior I believe to Sir W. Codrington[76] and might have had a high command in the Crimea.

---

erty which has cost say £100,000 is hardly worth more than £150,000.' He regarded this, it would seem, as a reproach and as casting a slur upon his investment policy. 'Much landed property in a similar time has increased in value more than 200 or 300 per ct.' However in the Memoir he regretted that his grandfather, James Norman, had not invested more in land. Charles Loyd Norman, his eldest surviving son, subsequently commented in the margin of the Memoir: 'Perhaps if my Father were alive now he would see reason to modify his opinion as to the advisability of buying land.' This was written some time before Charles Norman's death on 17 February 1889. The manuscript was copied from the original by Eleanora Norman, and the copy is dated February 1891.]

[74] [Emma Norman, born 3 July 1807, married in June 1832 Captain Henry Bowden, Fusilier Guards, and died 22 February 1836.]

[75] [John Bowden, a Director of the Bank of England 1803-41, Deputy Governor 1820-2, Governor 1822-4.]

[76] [Sir William John Codrington, 1804-84, army officer, second son of Admiral Sir Edward Codrington, 1770-1851, commander of the British fleet at the Battle of Navarino in 1827; see p. 312. Mainly by purchase, he rose from Ensign in the 88th

The year 1834, was very uneventful to me. My days glided away happily in the society of my dear wife, with whom I enjoyed a degree of comfort that had never fallen to my lot, in my batchelor days. I was occasionally however unwell with a touch of my old dyspeptic complaint, and in that case had recourse to the advice of my kind friend Sir H. Holland.

I continued to take the warmest interest in politics and well recollect the anger and dismay I felt at the downfall of the Grey Ministry, after the accession of Lord Althorp to the Peerage.[77] I was staying at Overstone and knew that Lord Spencer was most dangerously ill,[78] having learnt it

---

Foot (1821) to Lieutenant Colonel in the Coldstreams (1836). He was promoted Major General at the time of the Crimean War, and fought with courage and distinction at the battle of Alma and at Inkerman. He was subsequently promoted to Lieutenant General. By November 1855 he had become Commander in Chief. In 1857 he became Liberal MP for Greenwich.]

[77] [Lord Grey had become Prime Minister on 16 November 1830, after the Duke of Wellington's government was defeated on the vote on the Civil List the previous day. In 1834 the Grey government fell, over the Irish question, having to its credit the Reform Bill of 1832. The Cabinet was at odds on the question of Ireland. In particular, Edward Stanley, the Chief Secretary for Ireland, was opposed to lay appropriation of the surplus revenues of the Church of Ireland. Stanley, Graham, Ripon and Richmond all resigned, and Lord John Russell opposed the government on this, being strongly in favour of the transfer of such Church of Ireland revenues to lay purposes. Lord Althorp, the Leader of the House of Commons (as the bearer of a courtesy title he could sit in the House of Commons), who was also Grey's strongest supporter in the Cabinet, refused to continue in office, and resigned on 8 July 1834. The following day, Grey delivered his resignation speech in the House of Lords. Following Grey's resignation, Lord Melbourne became Prime Minister, but on 14-15 November William IV dismissed the Whig government, and summoned Wellington. Wellington declined to become Prime Minister, but acted as caretaker for Peel and on 9 December became Foreign Secretary, with Peel as Prime Minister. However the administration lasted only until 7 April 1835. But from 15 November until 9 December, Wellington more or less ran the government single handedly. Althorp did not become Earl Spencer until November 1834; while this deprived Melbourne of both the Leader of the House of Commons and of the Chancellor of the Exchequer, the Whigs were in serious disarray long before that.]

[78] [The 2nd Earl Spencer was George John Spencer, 1758-1834, who died 10 November 1834 at Althorp. He had withdrawn long before from involvement in the political life of Northamptonshire, though he was MP (Whig) for Northampton 1780-2, Surrey 1782-3. He was First Lord of the Admiralty 1794-1801, Home Secretary 1806-7. He formed a magnificent library at Althorp which was however sold by his grandson to form the Rylands Library in Manchester. John Charles Spencer, 1782-1845, styled Viscount Althorp 1783-1834, thus succeeded his father as 3rd Earl in November 1834 and was forced to leave the House of Commons. He

at Althorp, where we had made a call to see the library &c. One day at breakfast my friend Loyd who had just opened the paper (an evening one) read aloud with an unmoved voice the great news that the King had sent for the Duke of Wellington and Peel. I broke out with a cry of indignation and did not recover my equanimity for several days. My resolution was instantly formed to struggle against a restoration of old Tory sway to the utmost of my power, and this resolution I kept.

I went from Overstone to Melton and later to Stoneham, the residence of my uncle the Reverend F. Beadon, and to Stansted park the Seat of Mr Charles Dixon, who had married a Wilder.[79]

We had no child born in 1834 owing to a mishap of my wife's, her only one, and which, thank God, produced no bad consequence.

In 1835, C. H. Cameron went to India to take his place in the Law Commission at Calcutta and remained there till 1848.[80] We corresponded regu-

was Whig MP for Okehampton 1804-6, for Northants in 7 Parliaments 1806-32, and for South Northants 1832-4, as Lord Althorp. He was a Lord of the Treasury 1806-7, FRS 1820, Chancellor of the Exchequer 1830-4.]

[79] [Charles Dixon of Stansted, Sussex, married Harriet, the daughter of Henry Wilder of Purley Hall, Berks, Rector of Sulham (1744-1814). Stansted House was in the parish of Stoughton, seven miles north west of Chichester. The mansion and park were regarded as outstanding. The park itself covered an area of more than 1,000 acres. The house had been owned by a wealthy India merchant called Richard Barwell, who died in 1805. It was subsequently bought by Lewis Way and his executors sold it to Charles Dixon. Dixon seems to have been extremely wealthy. At one stage he owned the Titian painting St Catherine of Alexandria at Prayer, now in the Museum of Fine Arts, Boston, which he bought at Christies in 1826.]

[80] [Thomas Babbington Macaulay, who had Benthamite sympathies, was law member of the Governor General of India's Council, 1834-8. From 1835 he was in charge of a new law commission designed to reform India's laws. Cameron, who had previously worked on the reform of the law of Ceylon, was appointed a member of the commission, and worked under Macaulay. Cameron, with others, also produced a Benthamite report on prison discipline, and agreed with Macaulay's policy of anglicising Indian education. In 1836 Cameron fell ill, and went to the Cape of Good Hope to recuperate. On returning to India he replaced Macaulay as Chairman of the law commission, and in 1843 he became a member of the Governor General's Council, where he represented what could be described as a Benthamite interest. He continued with his work on Indian law reform, and on education. He did not return to England until 1848, and subsequently made visits to estates

larly every month, retained each other's letters and finally exchanged them. Mine form a large packet and I propose some time or other to read them over. Should I not do so, they will I think afford some interest to the person into whose hands they may fall, as proceeding from a man who narrowly watched passing events and wrote in full confidence to a friend, with a wish to convey a true and complete picture of their nature and character. Lord Overstone and I accompanied Cameron to Portsmouth and remained there with him for a day or two before his embarkation.

In 1835 commenced my first appearance as a Politician on Pennenden Heath. I seconded, if I recollect aright, the nomination of Mr T. Rider of Boughton and let me here remark as a tribute of truth to that gentleman, that a more honest and consistent Liberal never lived. He was neither very able, nor very eloquent, but he was thoroughly high-principled and had followed the Banner of Freedom in the worst of times when it led to social ostracism.

In this election of 1835 we were thoroughly beaten.[81] The reaction had set in, the Tories had recovered their spirits and energies. Moderate men were alarmed by the O'Connellites, and English radicals. The Peelites had many and influential canvassers in every parish of the county. We had little of either.

---

which he had acquired in Ceylon. In later years his health seems to have declined and he is reported to have taken 'opiates' for relief from kidney trouble. In 1875 he returned to Ceylon where he died in 1880.]

[81] [This was the West Kent election. See *Times* 15 January 1835 (5e), 16 January (1e), 20 January (2e), 5 February (3b). Norman's friend William Wells proposed Thomas Law Hodges; a Mr Rice proposed Thomas Rider, and Norman seconded this. The Tory opposition also involved Norman's friends. The candidate Sir William Geary was proposed by Sir Percival Hart Dyke (see p. 406), and seconded by Joseph Berens (see p. 112). The final figures were: Geary 2,553, Hodges 2,093, and Rider 2,000. Geary and Hodges were elected. The Tories were said to have spent £3,000 on the election (*Times* 20 January, 2e), and Mr Hodges was to accuse them of intimidation – *Times* 23 January (1d). Norman mentions that Rider resigned at the end of the first day's polling; the figures reported at that stage were: Geary 2,567, Hodges 2,074, Rider 1,937. It seems likely that such early figures were subject to revision, but the reporting of a final figure for Rider, when he had withdrawn, is puzzling.]

Mr Rider resigned at the end of the first day's poll and an express signifying this was sent to me in the middle of the night. The object of this resignation was to prevent the Tories from giving the second of their unpolled votes to Mr Rider and thus throwing out Mr Hodges whom they considered their most dangerous foe.

I may remark that from this time, my personal friendship with Mr Hodges commenced and gradually ripened into a close intimacy. When in Parliament he used frequently to pass his Sundays at Bromley and my wife and I paid a yearly visit to Hemsted.

I have met with few men, whom to know was more certainly to love, than Mr Hodges. A gentleman in the best sense of the word, steadfast, kind, truthful, honest. I said no more than what I really felt of him when delivering to him the portrait painted by subscription in the Autumn of 1856.

I exerted myself to the utmost of my power at the election of 1835 and from that time have always taken part in all the deliberations of the Liberal party in West Kent up to the present time. Nothing important has in fact been done, without my opinion having been heard in the matter and generally followed.

At this time, it may be observed that flags and music always appeared in every polling district, and of course caused great expense. I do not believe however that without taking into account the local efforts of individuals in the several districts, we ever spent more than £1,500 or £2,000[82] at an election before those of 1857. The Tories usually spent three or four times as much.

I may here mention that two or three events out of England, since the great war of the revolution have awakened, in a special degree, my feelings and sympathy.

One of these was the Greek insurrection and the ensuing struggle. I followed this with intense interest in all its changes, until it finally ceased

[82] [Worth £141,810 to £189,080 in 2009 prices.]

with the Battle of Navarino. Surely a more holy and noble cause never called men to arms than that for which the Greeks fought. They were oppressed, religiously, politically, socially. A race with high aspirations were bowed down under the most stupid, intolerant, cruel and corrupt despotism in Europe. Under other forms of misgovernment there is hope of improvement. Under the Turkish none. The sword then is the only resource.

It is the fashion to abuse the Greeks, I think most unjustly. They had of course the defects of slaves, but from these, in their new position they are gradually recovering. The slight progress which the Hellenic Kingdom has made is owing, I think to the pedantic bureaucracy, which the Bavarians imposed upon them. The national idiosyncracy leads to individualization, and municipal freedom strongly developed.

Please God that a Greek Emperor may yet be crowned in Saint Sophia.

The Carlist War in Spain also excited my strongest sympathies. My feeling in favor of the Spaniards had arisen in my boyish days, when I read of the 800 years conflict against the Moors and was confirmed by the struggle against Napoleon. The idea that the nation should once more be subjected to the Inquisition filled me with disgust. In short, I took part with the Liberals as the Tories all took part with the Serviles. I hardly recollect ever feeling more anxious, when an important political event was hanging in the balance, than I did during the seige of Bilbao. That was the turning point of the struggle. The success of Espartero in relieving the place and driving off the insurgent Army was a decisive event.[83] From that time the cause of Isabella

[83] [Baldomero Espartero, Count of Luchana, Duke de la Victoria, Prince of Vergara, 1793-1879, Spanish General associated with the radical part of Spanish politics. He was granted a dukedom and the title of Prince by Isabella II. Espartero became one of the strongest defenders of the right of Isabella, a child on the death of her father Ferdinand VII in 1833, to the throne, though legally she was debarred by the salic law which restricted the throne to males. In the first Carlist war, when the supporters of Ferdinand's brother Don Carlos, 1788-1855, claimed the throne, he was very successful, defeating the Carlist forces on a number of occasions, and twice forcing the Carlists to raise the siege of Bilbao. In 1836 he was appointed Commander in Chief of the Northern army. He inflicted a major defeat on the

gradually gained ground, until the war was terminated by the Convention of Bergara.

It must be allowed that Spain has not gained by the defeat of Don Carlos as much as my fond fancy anticipated. Still the success of the Liberals was a great event and gave her a chance of improvement, and of this to a certain degree she has availed herself. She has at any rate done better than she would have done had the stupid old despotism been restored.

The great fault of the few honest people, who have managed the affairs of Spain since the termination of the great civil war, has been somewhat analagous to that of the Germans in Greece. Instead of striving to improve the existing national institutions, the municipalities especially, which were strong and deeply connected with the national feelings and habits, they have done their best to weaken and overthrow these and to introduce everywhere an uniform centralized administration upon the model of France. A model bad in itself, as tending inevitably to a despotism and to constant revolutions and moreover quite unsuitable to the Transpyrenean people, who like the Italians are strongly inclined to group themselves into small political integers which they are tolerably fitted to manage, although far from that degree of social developement, which enables them to combine into one great whole, for the general management of state affairs.

The wisest mode of governing such a country as Spain would be to strengthen the municipalities, to leave as much power as possible in their hands and to form at least one out of the two chambers of deputies elected

---

Carlists at the battle of Ramales, 12 May 1839, and opened negotiations with the Carlists. The end result was the Convention of Vergara (or Bergara), which was essentially a Carlist surrender. It was signed by Espartero and Rafael Maroto, the Carlist leader. Colonel Wylde (see p. 293) was present as an observer. The negotiations were tense and, while they were taking place, both armies remained in position and prepared for battle. At the end of the war Espartero was elected Regent for Isabella, after the resignation of Queen Christina from the position, defeating Norman's friend Arguelles; see p. 222. But he became ruthless in power and, although he crushed early uprisings, he was forced to flee to England in July 1843 and was not able to return to Spain until the end of the decade.]

in some way by them.

I have not time or space at present to explain any further this idea, which is applicable to many other countries besides Spain.

While speaking of civil wars and insurgents, I may observe that I never felt so strongly for the Polish cause as many of my friends. I can hardly explain why. I will however give some reasons good or bad. An union with Russia, a country inhabited by the same race, seemed to me quite a natural event for the Poles. I further thought that the old Polish Government had been the worst Christian Government upon record and I saw no chance of any thing much better, in the case of a resuscitation of Poland,[84] a large portion of the inhabitants of the annexed provinces were real Russians, and of the Greek Church, and had been cruelly oppressed by their Roman Catholic and Polish Masters. That the existence of Russia as a great power was essential for the well-being of Europe, both as a continental equipoize to France, and as the grand centre of civilization and advancement for the eighty millions of Slavons who inhabit the centre and East of our quarter of the globe, and who are destined to play so important a part in its future history.

I fancy that the resistance in Poland to Russia has been chiefly that of the

[84][Poland had been repeatedly partitioned by neighbouring states. The first partition was in 1772, the second in 1793, and the third in 1795. In 1804 the Poles sought salvation from their Prussian, Austrian and Russian oppressors in alliance with Napoleon who faced the same enemies as they did, and who in 1807 created a Grand Duchy of Warsaw from territory then held by Prussia but which was part of the old Poland and inhabited by Poles. In 1809 forces of the Duchy reclaimed some of the territory taken by Austria in the 1795 partition. The forces were led by Jozef Pontiatowski; see p. 380. But the Russians re-occupied the Duchy in 1813, as Napoleon was forced back across Europe, and after the Congress of Vienna, set up at the conclusion of the war in 1815, the 1795 partition of Poland was largely reinstated. The re-imposition of Russian rule over Eastern Poland was initially quite liberal, but from the 1820s it became oppressive and pressures for an insurrection began to build up. In 1830 the Polish troops in Warsaw rebelled against the Russians, but by late 1831 the Russians had overcome the resistance and imposed harsh repression. There was another, and unsuccessful, rising in 1846 which was undermined by divisions within the Polish ranks. There was a major uprising in 1863 against a Russia weakened by defeat in the Crimean War. It had been crushed by 1864, and a large part of Poland became a Western Region of the Tsarist Empire.]

nobility, lawyers &c, and that oppressive, and cruel, as may have been the Russian rule, it has done more for the country and has better promoted its prosperity than a national Government would have done. There is a strong resemblance between the Poles and Irish.

I hope that my readers, if any, may not after this avowal, consider me an enemy of freedom or unable to sympathise with a Kosciuszko,[85] a Ponia-

[85][Andrzej Tadeusz Bonawentura Kosciuszko, 1746-1817. He led the 1794 uprising against the Russians, following on the partition, with the acquiescence of the Polish King Stanislaw August Poniatowski, of Poland in 1793. Prior to that he had fought in the American Revolutionary War, in which he was raised to the rank of Brigadier General by the United States Congress and became a naturalised American citizen. Although trained as a soldier, he had initially found it difficult to obtain military employment in Europe, but was recruited in France by Silas Deane and Benjamin Franklin, and in 1776 went to America where he rapidly rose to the position of Colonel of Engineers in the Continental Army. He was extremely active in the construction of fortifications against the British. In 1784 he returned to Poland. With the creation of an enlarged army he became, in 1789, a Major General. When the Russians, at the invitation of Polish landowners opposed to a new, liberal, constitution of 1791, invaded Poland in 1792, he was appointed Second in Command to Poniatowski (see next fn). He defeated much superior Russian forces at Raclawice but was overpowered at the Battle of Maciejowice. With the surrender to the Russians by the King, under pressure from the landowners, and the partition of Poland in January 1793, Kosciuszko was imprisoned by the Russians. He was freed in 1796 and emigrated to France. He did not return to Poland when the Duchy of Warsaw was created by Napoleon in 1807, and he died finally in Switzerland.]

towski,[86] a Skrzynecki[87] &c. It is quite true that I have little sympathy for simply national hatred or for what are called oppressed nationalities, when little more than antisocial feeling is involved. The sufferings of Italy from French, Spaniards or Germans, of Greeks from Turks or of Ireland in former days from the English were a very different matter.[88]

About this time, and for many years both before and afterwards, I was

[86][Prince Jozef Antoni Poniatowski, 1762/3-1813, Polish General who went on to become a Marshall of France. He was the nephew of the last King of Poland, Stanislaw August Poniatowski. His father, Andrzej Poniatowksi, was an Austrian Field Marshall. His father died when he was ten, but under the influence of the King he regarded himself as Polish rather than Austrian, and eventually transferred to the Polish army in 1789 at the age of 26. He had originally joined the Austrian army and fought in the Austrian war against Turkey in 1788. Together with Kosciuszko he received the rank of Major General. In 1792 he led his troops successfully against the Russians but King Stanislaw August Poniatowski, under pressure from the large landowners who had put him on the throne, effectively surrendered Poland to the Russians and Poniatowski resigned. He was drawn back to Poland in 1794 and fought against the Prussians, but left Poland again, moving to Vienna in 1795 when the third partition of Poland took place. Later, after Napoleon's creation of the Duchy of Warsaw, he became Minister of War and head of the army of Warsaw, leading his men successfully against the Austrians. Subsequently he led his troops in support of Napoleon's invasion of Russia. He fought at the battles of Smolensk, Borodino and, with particular distinction, at the Battle of Leipzig (see p. 150), and was made a Marshall of France. But after the battle he was entrusted with covering the French retreat, and was left marooned on the enemy side of the Weisse Elster River because the retreating French blew up the bridge. He was killed at the river, either by drowning or by 'friendly fire' from the French on the far side.]

[87][Jan Zygmund Skrzynecki, 1787-1860, Polish General who organised the Polish army in the revolution of 1830. After Napoleon's creation of the Grand Duchy of Warsaw, Skrzynecki fought in the Polish Legion from the Duchy, with particular distinction at the Battle of Leipzig in 1813; see p. 150.]

[88][See G.W. Norman, *Papers on Various Subjects*, London: T and W Boone, 1869. This contains two essays on the question; pp. 141-7 'On the doctrine of nationalities' and pp. 161-7 'Austria with reference to the doctrine of nationalities'. Both essays had appeared in the *Economist*, in 1866 and 1867 respectively. Norman was cynical about the doctrine of nationalities, according to which nations had a right to self-determination, which he believed to have flourished since 1848. He held that it led to bloodshed. He deplored nationalism, which he believed was inimical to the welfare of the citizens of the Austrian Empire. The diverse peoples living under the rule of the Austrians would be wise not to seek self-determination. Norman emphasised that the English and the French, who were strong supporters of nationalities in the abstract, themselves controlled considerable empires. All this represents a significant change, as Norman himself was well aware, from his youthful enthusiasm for revolutions.]

often troubled by sleeplessness and under the direction of Scott[89] and Sir H. Holland tried the usual remedies: infusion of hop and a hop pillow; extract of lettuce; hyoscymus;[90] and now and then a little opium.[91] None however of these things answered their object and several disordered me greatly, doing harm rather than good.

At length Sir H. Holland advised me to keep some bottled ale, Edinburgh or Burton in my room,[92] and if I could not sleep to warm a glass in an Aetna[93] and drink it, eating at the same time a piece of hard biscuit. I

---

89 [James Scott, MRCS, 1770-1849, a general practitioner living at Clay Hill, Beckenham, Kent; see p. 41. He was the father of John Scott, 1799-1846, who was to become one of the original 300 Fellows of the Royal College of Surgeons, in 1843.]

90 [This is used to treat conditions such as irritable bowel syndrome and enterocolitis. It is essentially an anti-spasmodic drug within the group Belladonna Alkaloids. If used for long periods or in high doses it may cause dependence. Withdrawal may result in a wide range of side effects including anxiety, shakiness, dizziness, nausea and weakness. The width of the range of side effects makes it hardly surprising that Norman should have commented that some of the medicaments did him harm rather than good.]

91 [From the 18th century, opium was freely available over the counter and widely used. Often it was taken in the liquid form of laudanum. In this form it was used for pain killing, fever, sedation, and even to counter diarrhoea. Some doctors recognised the dangers. Even in the 18th century a doctor called Samuel Crump, 1766-96, recorded withdrawal symptoms with patients becoming 'languid, dejected and uneasy'. R. Porter, *The Greatest Benefit to Mankind*, London: Harper, 1997 pp. 269-70. Given that the other standby of 19th century medicine was purgatives, as Norman's account confirms, it is not surprising that opium was employed to treat diarrhoea.]

92 [This was the famous Burton Pale Ale, which was a dark, rather sweet, beer, that the brewers of Burton on Trent exported to Russia. Confusingly it is known as Pale Ale. A Scottish version of this was Edinburgh Ale. This was also dark and sweet. It was this kind of beer that Sir Henry Holland was recommending to Norman; the beer is said to be warming to the drinker, which may have helped with Norman's insomnia. This may also explain why Norman was advised to warm the glass.]

93 [This device, advertised in *The Athenaeum* 9 June 1832 p. 375, as 'Jones's Aetnas for boiling half a pint of water in three minutes', continued to be sold up to the early part of the 20th century. Harrod's Stores Price List 265 of 1895 lists them as Etnas, after the volcano. Prices ranged from 11d for a half pint one to 2s 3d for a two pint version, in polished tin. A small measured cup of methylated spirit was poured into a base surrounding the container and ignited. A handle enabled the container to be lifted when warm. The device was recommended for nursery, sick room or bedroom where there was no fire lit. We are indebted to the

adopted his advice and with very good success. The glass of ale usually produced drowsiness and sleep, which if not as refreshing as natural sleep was at any rate far preferable to perfect wakefulness, and never, so far as I know, did me any harm.

Headland[94] however objected to the ale and biscuit, and since 1850, I have given them up.

It must be remarked that I have often laid awake for a whole night and in a miserable state of nervous agitation, especially when I have had a heavy day of business before me, when all my powers at their very best were sure to be taxed. In my opinion, ability to sleep well under the pressure of trouble and anxiety is one of the surest marks of a great man. I know not how anybody can occupy a distinguished place in active life without it.

In the year 1836 an event took place, which has furnished me much thought and occupation from that time to this. The measures of the Poor Law commissioners were in full progress. Mr E.C. Tufnell, the assistant commissioner, formed the Bromley Union.[95] A meeting of Guardians took place, I think in the month of May, and I, who was known to have paid much attention to the subject, was chosen Chairman on the motion of Mr Josph Berens of Kevington. Mr S.N. Ward[96] of Baston was vice Chairman.

The work for some time was very severe. We had to root out immense abuses in many parishes. The working classes, the farmers, clergy and magis-

---

remarkable expertise of Peter Brears for all this information about the warming device.]

94[Edward Headland, 1803-69, the leading general practitioner of his time, one of the first doctors to charge for his services rather than for medicines. He was also the medical advisor of Norman's close friend and confidant Lord Overstone. In the Norman papers at U310/C125/4 there are letters to Norman from Headland, about the former's health.]

95[Edward Carleton Tufnell, 1806-86, Assistant Poor Law Commissioner 1835, retired on a pension of £400 per annum in 1874. With Sir James Kay Shuttleworth, he founded Battersea College. He was a member of the Royal Commission on child labour 1862-7, and of the Royal Commission on the employment of women and children in agriculture 1867-71.]

96[Samuel Nevil Ward, of Baston, Hayes, Kent born 13 August 1773.]

trates were almost all more or less imbued with the errors of the old system. With all this, I and a few staunch coadjutors had to struggle. I also met with not a little opposition connected with political feeling and on the whole I found my task laborious and ungrateful. My old friend Mr Wells and Mr Scott, Chaplain of Bromley College,[97] were most strenuous opponents. The leading motives of the former, I believe to have been an ignorant humanity. The latter was a very foolish person and a bitter Tory.

We retained at first three workhouses out of the fourteen which existed in our sixteen parishes before the formation of the Union, and it cost several years struggle and repeated motions and discussions before we could make up our minds to build at Lock's Bottom.[98] This in fact, was not I think accomplished until the years 1841 or 1842.

In the latter part of 1836, I fell into bad health. My digestion became much impaired. The nervous system gave way and I was at length compelled to resign the Chair of the Board of Guardians leaving however the business well-arranged, and the new system slowly making its way. Lord Sydney who had always given me a liberal support was chosen as my successor.[99] At the new election in April, he was I think for the first time placed in the Chair. I, whose health was by that time tolerably restored, agreed to become vice Chairman, and we two have occupied these respective offices from that time to this, with close union of opinion and without any disputes or difficulties,

---

97 [The Chaplain of Bromley College was Thomas Scott, BD, 1765-1846. There is a memorial tablet in St Mary Cray Church to the parents and wife of Thomas Scott. Bromley College had been founded in 1666 by John Warner, Bishop of Rochester, for twenty widows of clergymen. It had been intended to build it in Rochester, but it was built in Bromley, where a site near the Bishop of Rochester's Bromley Palace was available, in 1672. It was extended in the 18th century.]

98 [In the Norman papers at U310 Z42 there is a 'Letter' to the rate payers of Bromley from Norman about 'the propriety of building a central workhouse for the Bromley Union'.]

99 [John Thomas Townshend, 2nd Viscount Sydney 1764-1831, died at Frognal near Foot's Cray and was succeeded by his only son John Robert Townshend, 3rd Viscount and 1st Earl (1874) Sydney, 1805-90, Captain of the West Kent Yeomanry 1830, MP Whitchurch 1826-31, Colonel Kent Artillery Militia 1853-90, Lord Lieutenant of Kent 1856-90.]

and as I hope much to the public advantage. I firmly believe, that as respects expence alone, more than £100,000 has been saved to the sixteen parishes of the Union by the new system.

At the beginning of 1837, being very unwell and engaged to go to Stansted, I thought it best to consult Dr Holland previously and for that purpose to go to Mivart's Hotel in Brook Street where he resided.[100] It was at once pronounced that the Essex journey must be given up, in fact I was unable to face society at any rate on a large scale. So we remained in the Ostelrie. While we were there, the great influenza broke out and never shall I forget it. I was attacked in the shape of feverish cold with alternate fits of burning and shivering. My wife had this also and in addition a cough so violent, that it almost shook her to pieces and made me fear that she would break a bloodvessel or miscarry, being then pregnant. However she escaped both these misfortunes and at length recovered.

We remained at Mivart's for ten days or a fortnight. Dr Holland used to see us every morning to supply us with books and again to visit us in the evening and tell the remarkable anecdotes of the epidemic which fell under his observation. He mentioned that scraggs of mutton for making broth were not to be had. That the stock of phials was exhausted and the whole class of medical men either prostrated by disease or by over-work. Business at the Bank and other public establishments could hardly be carried on for lack of hands. At Mivart's in one day, 120 basins of gruel were made and no dinner dressed. The mortality was very considerable especially among old people,

[100][Mivart's Hotel was at 51 Brook Street. It is now Claridges Hotel, at the corner of Brook Street and Davies Street. Mivart's Hotel had been founded in 1812 in a normal London terraced house, and expanded into neighbouring houses. It was sold in 1854 by the founders to a Mr and Mrs Claridge, the owners of a smaller hotel next door. The son of Mr and Mrs Mivart was St George Jackson Mivart, PhD, MD, FRS, 1827-1900, a famous opponent of Norman's friend Charles Darwin. His parents were Evangelicals but Dr Mivart became a Roman Catholic. A distinguished medical biologist, he was appointed to the Chair in Zoology at St Mary's Hospital Medical School in 1862. As a critic Mivart was somebody whom Darwin was forced to take seriously.]

much greater it was said than from cholera four or five years before.

In March was born our eldest daughter, christened Sibella Charlotte[101] after her mother and grandmother. She was a pretty infant, with very dark eyes and has always proved by her intelligence, industry and affectionate disposition, one of the dearest blessings that providence could have bestowed on me. God grant that her future career may be fortunate. My strong desire at this time is to see her well married, but I know not how to provide her with a suitable helpmate.[102] She is endowed with an excellent understanding, great love of knowledge and much power of application. Perhaps in these points taken together she stands at the head of the family. Of her filial devotion, I cannot speak too highly. Nor of the pleasure I have ever derived from her society.

In July of this year took place a general election at which the Tories animated by their success in 1835, when they succeeded in replacing Mr

[101] [Norman's daughter Sibella Charlotte was born 27 March 1837.]

[102] Sibella Charlotte married 1862 to Henry Bonham Carter. [Two of Norman's daughters married Bonham Carters. Mary Henrietta Norman (born 5 March 1845) married, 27 May 1872, Alfred Bonham Carter (1825-1910). She died 24 November 1893. Henry ('Harry') Bonham Carter (died 22 March 1921) married 10 June 1862, Sibella Charlotte Norman (died 7 October 1916) the eldest daughter of Norman. In 1853 Harry's widowed mother moved to a large Victorian house, standing in 30 acres, called Ravensbourne, at Keston, which she was persuaded to buy by Norman himself. Sibella and Harry had eleven sons. Interestingly, despite a strong Unitarian background in both families, which had prevented Harry from receiving his degree at Cambridge, their eleven sons were brought up as Anglicans. The eldest, born in 1863, was named Herman, no doubt in memory of Sibella's eldest brother who had lost his life in the Crimea. Sibella had had more eligible admirers, and Norman was unhappy about a match with Harry Bonham Carter, whose talents lay in mathematics and who was a struggling and unsuccessful barrister. However, due no doubt to Norman's own influence, Harry became Managing Director of the Guardian Fire and Life Assurance Company in 1861, in which position he remained for the next forty years. See Victor Bonham Carter, *In a Liberal Tradition*, London: Constable, 1960 pp. 107-8, 121. Apparently unaware of Norman's position in the insurance world, Victor Bonham Carter attributed the rescue of Harry from his unsuccessful legal career to 'other Normans'.]

Rider by Sir W. Geary,[103] attempted to eject Mr Hodges also.[104] Sir E. Filmer was their new candidate.[105] I worked like a dray horse, spent my money and my energies and proposed Mr Hodges at the nomination. We succeeded at the election by a majority of 105.

I recollect nothing particular as having happened to me during the remainder of the year. I paid several visits during the shooting season, as usual, going to Stoneham, Stansted and Ditcham near Petersfield,[106] then rented by my kind friend Mr J. Bonham Carter[107] who had married a daughter of the well-known William Smith, member for Norwich and for many years the recognised leader of the Protestant Dissenters in the House of Commons.[108]

His tenets were Unitarian. He took greatly to me and was one of the most truthful and conscientious men whom I have known. He was a barrister, rizing so rapidly in his profession that a judgeship was fairly in his view when, having a large fortune by inheritance, he gave up the law and dedicated himself to politics. At parliamentary business and at the registration he worked with untiring energy, until at length his constitution, naturally not

[103] [The Geary family had a long history of involvement in Kent politics. Sir William Richard Powlett Geary, 3rd Bt, 1810-77, to whom Norman is referring, was the son of Sir William Geary, 2nd Bt, baptised 1756, who succeeded as 2nd Bt in 1796, MP Kent 1796-1806, 1812-18. He died in 1825.]

[104] [See O'Brien, *The Correspondence of Lord Overstone*, 1971, vol. 1 p. 232. The figures were Geary (Tory) 3,578; Hodges (Whig) 3,329; Filmer (Tory) 3,227.]

[105] [Sir Edmund Filmer, 8th Bt, 1809-57, succeeded to the baronetcy in 1834. He was MP for West Kent, 1838-57.]

[106] [The Bonham Carters had taken a ten year lease of Ditcham, near Petersfield, Hants, then called Ditcham Grove, in 1832. Harry Bonham Carter (see p. 385) had spent his childhood at Ditcham.]

[107] [John Bonham Carter died of diabetes in February 1838, aged 49. See Victor Bonham Carter, *In a Liberal Tradition*, p. 70. He was the son of John Carter of Portsmouth, 1741-1808, a brewer who was Mayor of Portsmouth nine times and was knighted by George III in 1773. The family were Unitarian. John Bonham Carter was Whig MP for Portsmouth 1816-38. It was on inheriting the estate of his cousin Thomas Bonham of Petersfield in March 1827 that John Carter assumed the additional name of Bonham.]

[108] [William Smith, 1756-1835, MP Norwich 1784-1826. He was another Unitarian, and worked with Wilberforce to abolish slavery. But his support for good causes led to the loss of his fortune, and he had to sell Parndon Hall, his seat, and live with his son.]

very strong, gave way under the effort. His complaint was diabetes from which he died I should guess about 1840.

At this time and for many years before and afterwards and indeed up to the present time, I had ordinarily gone to Stockbridge three times a year, *vizt*, in April, at the Mayfly and late in October for the grayling.[109] On the first and last excursions my wife has been usually kind enough to accompany me and thus add greatly to my pleasure.

On the 3rd July this year took place the great event of my piscatorial career at Mapledurham in Oxfordshire. I there caught a trout, spinning a gudgeon,[110] which weighed 10 lb 12 oz. It was taken in the flush of the lock and was dressed on the following day at the great house belonging to the Blunts[111] and then rented by Mrs Charles Smith, mother of Sir Charles Smith of Suttons in Essex, with whom I was staying.[112] For a fuller account of this fish, I refer to my sporting memoranda. I recollect positively nothing as having occurred in 1838. I continued to play at cricket and occasionally

[109][See also p. 347.]

[110][A small freshwater fish used as bait.]

[111][The Blunt family had two branches, one with a seat at Wallop House, Hants, and the other with a seat at Kempshott Park, Hants. They were descended from Sir John Blunt, 1st Bt (1720) who died in 1732/3, fourth son of Thomas Blunt a Baptist cobbler of Rochester, Kent, and Sir John's son Sir Henry Blunt, 2nd Bt who died in 1759. The 3rd Bt was Sir Charles William Blunt, 1731-1802, the 4th was Charles Richard Blunt, 1775-1840, and the 5th Bt was Sir Walter Blunt 1826-47.]

[112][Charles Smith, 1757-1814, of Suttons, married Augusta Smith, daughter of Joshua Smith of Erlestoke (see p. 70) in 1798. They had five children, the last of whom was born a few days after her father's death. Suttons was an estate at Stapleford Tawney near Romford, Essex. Charles Smith, MP for Westbury and Saltash, was the son of Charles Smith of Stratford, East London, 1713-77. His own son was Sir Charles Joshua Smith, 2nd Bt, 1800-31. The baronetcy was created in 1804 for Drummond Smith, 1740-1816, the brother of Joshua Smith. It was created with remainder to the heirs male of Sir Drummond Smith's niece Augusta, the daughter of Sir Joshua Smith. Thus it was that Sir Charles Joshua Smith was the 2nd Bt. He married Mary Gosling. On his marriage, his mother Augusta moved to the estate of her late uncle Sir Drummond Smith, Tring Park in Hertfordshire. This was sold in 1823 by his trustees. She then moved to her last house, Mapledurham near Pangbourne. Charles Smith, 2nd Bt, was succeeded by Sir Charles Cunliffe Smith, 3rd Bt, 1827-1905.]

with some success, and my last match is of a date some years subsequent, as will be mentioned in its proper place.

My political enthusiasm about this time began to become less vehement. Many of its objects had been attained. Others appeared unattainable and I was disgusted by the conduct of O'Connell and of his adherents. I never however leant to the Tories. My feelings were those of disappointment, especially as regarded the virtue and intelligence of the electors generally.

In 1838 I published a pamphlet entitled 'Remarks upon some Prevalent Errors in Currency and Bank &c'.[113] It was a refaccimento of that printed, but not published five years before, with such additions and changes as my subsequent experience had afforded. It had no great sale but still produced a certain effect on the public mind and seemed to give weight to my evidence before parliamentary committees. A year or two ago I read it over and found little to object to in its doctrines. The chief change that has since taken place in my opinions has been as to the extent to which a well-managed currency operates to the public advantage. I then thought that it would prevent more surely abuses of credit than subsequent experience has justified.

The year 1839 produced no important event in my biography that I now recollect. I see by my game book that I paid the usual visits to Stansted and Stoneham, but that I made no distant journeys.

I may here allude to the commercial difficulties of this year, as well as to those of 1837, the last named particularly. Every monetary crisis that I have seen has exhibited some peculiar features belonging to itself. Thus that now in question was mainly connected with the American trade. Its most

[113] [*Remarks upon Some Prevalent Errors, with respect to Currency and Banking, and Suggestions to the Legislature and the Public as to the Improvement of the Monetary System*, London: P. Richardson, 1838. See the letter of Overstone to Norman 16 December 1837, O'Brien, *The Correspondence of Lord Overstone*, 1971, vol.1 p. 236. The earlier version to which Norman refers was *Remarks upon Some Prevalent Errors, with respect to Currency and Banking, and Suggestions to the Legislature with Respect to the Renewal of the Bank Charter*, London: R. Hunter, 1833.]

important feature consisted in the stoppage of four houses, Wilson, Wild, Wiggin[114] and [blank in original], for about ten millions. At the instigation of J.H. Palmer the Bank upheld them to an extent indefensible on any sound view of Banking. This conduct however if it did no good to the Houses in question, or to the public, produced less loss to the establishment than its imprudence merited. I was out of the Court by rotation when Palmer carried his motion, or I should have certainly opposed it. During all the previous turmoil I had urged upon the Court strong measures, the sale of securities, increase in the rate of discount &c and to a certain extent with success.

I inherited from my father a considerable amount of American stock and of shares in the Bank of the United States.[115] Some Pensylvania stock I handed over to my brother Henry in part payment of his legacy and by that, I regret to say, he lost money.

My democratic tendencies made me place implicit trust in the honesty of the Republicans of the West, while I knew that their means of gain and power of payment were abundant. I therefore made new purchases of American securities as money came in from different sources, until my venture in them

[114][See J.H. Clapham, *The Bank of England*, vol. II, 1797-1914 (Cambridge: Cambridge University Press, 1944) pp. 157-61. Known as the three W's, Wiggin, the first to ask the Bank for assistance, Wilde and Wilson were each granted £200,000 of abnormal discounts. Clapham commented that 'This proved only the beginning of a long dreary tale of debt. Fourteen years later Timothy Wiggin's heir was writing about his "unfortunate position" during all that time, and offering some settlement' (Clapham, p. 157). The fourth house was Brown's (later Brown Shipley) and the Bank backed the firm to the extent of nearly £2,000,000, and saved it. According to Clapham (p. 158) 'Brown's were loaded up with bills on exports to America that had not been paid for'.]

[115][See Clapham *The Bank of England* vol. 2 pp. 150-1, 159-61. In 1836 this bank had lost its federal charter, after a conflict with President Andrew Jackson. This significantly weakened its commercial position. The US bank then arranged a loan in London in the same year. The Bank of England had co-operated with it over realising assets for the 'three W's' (see fn 110), though relations were strained. Matters were not improved by an attempt by the US bank to persuade the Bank of England to provide it with capital. The Governor was not amused. It approached the Bank again in 1839 and was again refused. However it did raise £800,000 in the London market. In 1841 the United States Bank failed, and none of its capital of $28 million was returned.]

reached if I mistake not, £40,000.[116] At this time I considered the European states little trustworthy. In truth with the exception of French, I never purchased any of their stock.

At length the crash came and I found myself deceived. By an amount of $36,000 in Bank of the United States shares, $10,000 in Florida, $10,000 in Mississipi Bonds and sundry other investments which fell greatly in value, without being altogether repudiated, I was a loser of from £15,000 to £20,000.[117] In alluding to these events here I somewhat anticipate, for they did not all occur until some years afterwards.

I bore my losses with very tolerable equanimity. In truth, I was never very fond of money and knew that I had enough left for my wants. I felt however rather keenly my want of prudence and knowledge of mankind, and have never since placed any special confidence in Democrats, as more honest than other people.

It was unfortunate for me, that previously to this time a final rupture had taken place between me and Cowell, for he had been sent to America by the Bank of England to look after its claims and to his credit, be it said, had formed a strong opinion as to the rotten state of financial matters there and especially as to the unsound position of the United States Bank.[118] This

[116] [Documents relating to Norman's purchases of American securities are in the Norman papers at U310/B25, for the years 1825-37.]

[117] [Worth £1,157,850 to £1,543,800 in 2009 prices.]

[118] [Cowell was sent to the United States by the Bank of England in September 1837, with the aim of recovering sums of money owed on American bills of exchange. He remained there until the spring of 1839, staying in Philadelphia because he was dealing with the United States Bank (which had become the United States Bank of Pennsylvania). His experiences seem to have given him an extremely unfavourable view of the business community of the northern United States. He later made several attempts to get England to intervene on behalf of the southern states after the outbreak of the civil war and, when these failed, he published a pamphlet in French attempting to persuade France to intervene. According to the researches of Charles Priestley, who discovered this work, Cowell had a number of meetings with southern spokesmen, during his time in the United States, and these seem to have impressed him a great deal more favourably than the 'Yankees' whose character had, according to Cowell's French pamphlet, 'degenerated into a mixture of hypocrisy, cruelty, falsity, total lack of self-respect, gross presumption,

opinion had our intimacy continued, I should have known as a matter of course and probably acted upon it, and I should have had plenty of time and opportunity to get out of my transatlantic entanglements.

I must here say a word as to my separation from Cowell. I forget the exact year when it occurred, but should say that it was about 1836. That is however a matter of small importance. I could hunt up the correspondence relating to it, but do not think perfect exactness would pay for the trouble.

Ever since the quarrel with the Whitmores in 1832, I had remarked a change in Cowell's conduct. He had become more impracticable and tracassier than before and I had more difficulty in soothing his irritability. On reflection too, it seemed to me that in the whole imbroglio with the Whitmores and Grotes, he had shewn but little regard for my feelings and had been ready to sacrifice them on all occasions to the gratification of his own passions. I also considered that his conduct had been less irreproachable in that affair than at first I thought it.

Such being the state of things, and my intercourse with Cowell having ceased to afford one the same pleasure as before, he demanded of me that I should write a letter wholly condemnatory of the Whitmores, which he might exhibit to a third person. This I firmly refused to do, although with all the conciliatory expressions I could command. I thought that I had done and suffered enough, indeed too much for him as respected the quarrel of 1832, and that it ought to be buried in utter oblivion. I at least was determined to have nothing more to do with it.

My refusal gave mortal offence to Cowell and our intercourse ceased. Some years afterwards his irritation diminished. We shook hands when we met. More recently he has treated me like an old friend, we correspond and I think that now in 1858 he would not be sorry to renew our intimacy. But this can no longer be. I am grateful for his many acts of kindness. I acknowledge

---

indifference to the opinions of others, absolute ignorance of good, savage delight in doing evil and total moral depravity'.]

his great ability and respect parts of his character, but on the other hand, I fear his irritability and think on the whole we had better remain as we are. His failings have increased with age. My mind has been made up deliberately on this point.

In January 1839 was born our fourth son, Frederick Henry, who having always been blessed[119] with excellent health, has never given any cause for anxiety on that score, while his conduct has ever been such as to merit the deepest affection and respect on the part of his parents.[120]

While recovering from this confinement my wife was siezed with rheumatic fever, owing as was supposed to imprudent exposure. She suffered dreadfully, for some time indeed could hardly turn in bed. Even now she retains in the hands and feet the marks of this attack and as a consequence, the occasional recurrence of rheumatic pains. I think too that a change in her previously gay and cheerful temper may be traced to this unfortunate accident, unless indeed, as she sometimes says, she has imbibed this from me.

When she got better, it was recommended that she could go to Dover, where she remained with the children for three months, I joining her for a fortnight at a time. We posted the journey through Maidstone and Ashford, sleeping at the latter place.

While at Dover I saw a good deal of my friend E.C. Tufnell, the assistant Poor Law commissioner, and visited with him Canterbury, [and] Barfrestone.[121]

A great dinner took place at Dover while we were there. It was 'cense'[122]

---

[119] [Norman wrote blest here.]

[120] [Frederick Henry Norman, fourth son of George Warde Norman, was born 23 January 1839. He was educated at Eton and Trinity College, Cambridge, BA 1861. He died in 1916. His eldest son was Montagu Collet Norman, Governor of the Bank of England 1920-44, and a very famous figure in 20th century finance. His second son was Ronald Collet Norman, Chairman of the BBC Governors 1935-9, and Vice Chairman of the National Trust 1924-48.]

[121] [Barfrestone has one of the most sumptuously decorated 12th century churches in England. It is about 6 miles from Dover.]

[122] ['Worship with burning incense', Norman's ironical term.]

to be given to the Duke of Wellington as their warden by the Cinq Ports, but was in truth a Tory device to catch as much as they could of the popular gale by the help of his great name.[123] I attended, as did S.J. Loyd, now Lord Overstone, who had kindly paid us a visit. We both thought that the great man shewed physical weakness and even a falling off in mental power. This might have been owing to special causes and I believe was so, and that he altered his habits and rallied afterwards.

At this time too, we found it desirable to place our eldest boy Herman at school. He was a difficult child to teach and quite beyond his mother's power of control and management in this respect. As for myself I have never attempted to teach my children anything systematically, partly from want of time, knowledge and strength, and partly because I have observed that in some instances evil results have followed up on the union of the two characters of parent and professional instructor. The father has been regarded as a stern disciplinarian, who interfered with all pleasurable pursuits, and the children on the other hand, as a heavy clog and burthen. Of course, although persuaded that I did right in my own case and that my course was wise as a general rule, I do not mean to assert that many men may not be found, so eminently qualified, as to enable them to act as instructor to their sons with advantage.

The school we chose for Herman was kept by a Lady named Hart[124] and situated at Lee. A year afterwards we sent both him and Charlie to a school kept by a Dr Mayo at Cheam, which at the time enjoyed the highest credit and was specially recommended to me by Raikes Currie. Never was reputation less deserved. Dr Mayo was a narrow-minded low churchman, conscientious I believe, but of no considerable ability. He paid his assistants

[123]I was once examined before a committee of the Lords. Of this committee the Duke of Wellington was a member. He sat next to me and put several questions to me. [This must have been the 1848 Lords Committee on the commercial crisis of 1847; see p. 400.]

[124][Inserted in pencil.]

badly and of course got on the whole a bad set. He professed to adopt the Pestalozzian system. What this amounted to, in his hands, I could never understand.[125] The boys did not like nor, I believe, respect him.

I may here remark that I looked back with so much regret, at the years, which I had thrown away at Eltham and Eton, that I was led to think any thing which differed from them, must be an improvement. I have since somewhat changed my opinion. The variety of bad schools is almost infinite, of good, surprizingly small, and until a new system of education has been discovered and tested by experience, I believe the wise course is to adhere to the old forms of badness.

I believe that the best schools, which now exist in England are some of the district and training schools, and I have often been surprized that their mechanism has not been adopted in some of those designed for the upper and middle classes. The matter of instruction would of course, not be the same. Languages should be taught by rote, as in the Hamiltonian system, and not through the medium of a grammar, which ought to be the crowning stone of the edifice and not the foundation.

My wife recovered from her attack of rheumatism, but slowly and imperfectly. Her feet and hands still bear traces of it and her general health has never become what it was previously. She has nevertheless continued to discharge all her duties with a conscientious devotion which I cannot too

[125][Johann Heinrich Pestalozzi, 1746-1827, a Swiss educator who believed in 'child-centred learning through discovery'. He attracted disciples, including Dr C. Mayo, who was a personal friend of Pestalozzi. Another disciple was Herman Krusi (born 1817). Krusi obtained a position teaching at the school at Cheam, Surrey, run by Mayo, to which Norman sent his son Herman as he relates. Krusi however stayed only one year in the school before moving to the United States where he spread the Pestalozzi gospel. The Pestalozzian system places special emphasis on spontaneity, self-directed activity on the part of the child, and discovery. Children, it is held, should discover answers themselves through observation and then subsequent exploration of the background to the observation. See [C. Mayo], *Lessons on Objects: As Given to Children Between the Ages of Six and Eight. In a Pestalozzian School at Cheam*, Surrey, 12th edition, London: Seeleys, 1851. In the 1960s this approach received some support from the Council of Europe, which set up a Pestalozzi programme.]

highly prize, and has been the great source of comfort to me in all the trials which I have had to undergo.

I do not recollect any thing very particular as having occurred to me in domestic matters during the following year 1840, unless it was the birth of our fifth son, Richard James, in the month of July.[126] He was at his birth and for some time afterwards a fine and promising infant. Nothing remarkable appeared in him, until he was two or three years old excepting that he was backward. His peculiarity became gradually more marked and we took him to Mr Watson[127] at the deaf and dumb institution, who pronounced at once that he was suffering from pressure on the brain, which he had probably brought with him into the world. He grew a stout boy, but his intellect did not improve, on the contrary it grew weaker, while his bodily powers at length gave way. For several years, we hired a female attendant specially to wait upon him. He became unable to walk, was drawn about in a little chair. He sunk gradually and died in the Spring of 1853, under circumstances which compelled us to think that his death was not a misfortune.

We have reason to thank God that with nine children, we have as yet only lost one from disease. The death of dear Herman, although glorious was a stunning blow, which I have not, and never shall get over. Not an hour passes without my thinking of it.

In the session of 1840, a committee of the House of Commons was appointed to inquire into matters connected with the circulation. Of this committee Mr Charles Wood, now Sir Charles,[128] was chosen Chairman and

[126] [Richard James Norman was born 26 July 1840, died 25 March 1852.]

[127] [Joseph Watson, 1765-1829, Principal of the 'Deaf and Dumb Asylum' Old Kent Road, London, 1792-1829, was succeeded by one of his sons, Thomas James Watson, who was Principal until 1857.]

[128] [Sir Charles Wood, 1800-85, 1st Viscount Halifax (1866), MP Great Grimsby 1826-31, Wareham 1831, Halifax 1832-65, Rippon 1865-6, Secretary to the Treasury 1832-4, Secretary to the Admiralty 1835-9, Chancellor of the Exchequer 1846-52, President of the Board of Control 1852-5, First Lord of the Admiralty 1855-8, Secretary of State for India and President of the Council 1859-66. Wood had been appointed Chairman of the Committee, but was taken ill on 14 July, and did

discharged his duties with eminent ability and impartiality, displaying at the same time a thorough acquaintance with the subject of inquiry. Before this committee I was examined for six days, with more credit to myself and advantage to the public than on any previous or subsequent occasion.[129] In all essential points, I maintained the opinions which I still entertain and which I firmly believe to be based in truth and reason.

From this time, dates the commencement of an acquaintance with Sir Charles Wood, which has been renewed from time to time. I may here say that of all the public men whom I have known, he is the most thoroughly candid and honest, while his mental qualifications are of a high order. His want of power as a speaker and a certain superciliousness of demeanour in the presence of ignorance and jobbery, have lessened his influence and usefulness.

Among the Members of the Houghton Fishing Club, one of the most remarkable was Sir Francis Chantrey,[130] the eminent sculptor, upon whom I will make a few remarks, not touching his biography, as that is too generally known. He never appeared to me a person of much genius, on the other hand he always exhibited a large amount of practical good sense. For instance he never mingled in conversation upon points which he did not understand. When such topics were broached, he was silent.

He had little poetry in his composition, refused what he called fancy designs and even laughed at them. Had no due appreciation of the great

---

not resume his place until 28 July. He was replaced during his illness by Henry Warburton.]

[129][See *Parliamentary Papers 1840, vol. iv, Reports from the Select Committee on Banks of Issue.* Norman was examined 23, 24, 26, 30 June, 3, 7, 8 and 10 July, pp. 141-211, qq. 1666-2650. He was examined again on 30 July, pp. 300-16, qq. 3307-3464. With Horsley Palmer, he was the main witness on behalf of the Bank of England. It was remarkable testimony, in which he was subject to sustained attack by Matthias Attwood and Joseph Hume, and he seems to have stood up to it rather better than Overstone, despite his nervous problems. Overstone attempted to withdraw from his examination by the Committee (O'Brien, *The Correspondence of Lord Overstone* 1971 vol. 1 pp. 280-92). He was persuaded to continue by Wood and by Warburton.]

[130][See p. 189.]

masters of his art, especially of the ancients, and when a beautiful group was placed before him, I have heard him ask ironically, 'Is it like ?' as if imitation in its lowest grade or portraiture was all that sculpture could effect.

Chantrey was a great sports man and proud of his fame as a good shot and angler. As an angler, he was apt to enhance his reputation by trying as his friends believed to shine in borrowed colours. He was a great eater and drinker and owed probably his early death to his extravagant appetite. After making all necessary defalcations it cannot be denied that Chantrey was a very remarkable man. In a very few years, he attained high reputation acquired a large fortune, and a ready admission into the best society of England, and I am not aware that he ever made use of any unworthy arts to rize. He doubtless sold his labours as dearly as he could, but surely this was not reprehensible. I believe him to have been charitable and benevolent.

In the following year 1841, my political feelings having considerably cooled, as will hereafter be explained, a general election took place and the chiefs of our party held a meeting at Maidstone to determine what we should do. We had already tried the pulse of the electors and spent some money in preparations, but at the eleventh hour, discovered that a contest held out no reasonable prospects of success and Mr Hodges consequently retired.[131] Thus vanished for the Western division the electoral triumph of the Reform Bill. We lost one Seat in 1835, when Sir W. Geary defeated Mr Rider, and now our cherished member, a man universally popular, was gone from the rolls of Parliament only however for a time.

The feeble course of the Melbourne Government had long cast a slur on

[131] [*Times* 7 March 1841, 6b, reported that Hodges would not stand, and that Sir William Geary and Sir Edmund Filmer would be unopposed. *Times* 8 March 3c carried a denial by Hodges of the report. However *Times* 3 July, 3d, reported that Hodges had withdrawn, and Sir Edmund Filmer and Viscount Marsham, both Tory candidates, were unopposed. Filmer was proposed by Norman's friend Behrens, with a Mr Hoare seconding him. Lord Marsham was proposed by another of Norman's friends, Colonel Austen, seconded by Sir William Geary. Mr Hodges was however persuaded by Norman to stand at a later election, and was MP for West Kent 1847-52.]

Whiggism. They could carry none of their measures and had only been kept in office by a trifling majority, the casting weight in the balance being found by O'Connell and his tail.[132] Their retirement resulted from the appeal to the country on the general election.

But now then for the state of my political feelings. My hopes had been raized too highly at the passing of the Reform Bill, and excellent as its effects were, they fell short of my expectations. Public men proved less able and honest than I anticipated and what was worse, the electors appeared to be animated by far other motions, than a desire to choose the wise and good. They aspired to govern rather than to reign. Sycophancy and imprudence seemed in many instances the best passports to their favor and ignorance and even dishonesty no bar.

Thus then was cut from under me some of the best reasons for extending

[132][William Lamb, 2nd Viscount Melbourne, 1779-1848, Prime Minister 1834-41. Melbourne was a remarkably relaxed politician, while the major forces affecting the Whig government were Lord John Russell and Lord Palmerston. Melbourne seems to have acted as chairman and arbitrator. The Whig majority had been reduced by the election of 1837, and there were complicated negotiations, conducted for the most part by Russell, to retain the support of the radicals. The years 1837-41 were dominated by Melbourne's tutelage of the young Queen Victoria, while the government was at the mercy of fluctuating radical support. In 1841 Peel won when the sugar duties were made the occasion for a vote of confidence, and the Whigs lost power. O'Connell and his followers had supported the Whigs, but the association was fraught with difficulties, and tied O'Connell's hands with respect to agitation in Ireland. From 1828 onwards O'Connell was identified with popular and radical reform. He pressed for House of Lords reform, after two bills, relating to Irish tithes and Irish municipal reform, that he had steered through the Commons were then rejected by the Lords. When Melbourne replaced Grey (see p. 372) as Prime Minister, O'Connell was encouraged to convey views concerning the suitability of candidates for Irish appointments, and he became associated with the Whigs, whom he strongly supported in the general election of 1835. He was subsequently at the head of the radicals and Whigs in the Commons, and held the balance of power there. The price of this was silence on his part concerning the Act of Union. His dealings with the government effectively prevented him from agitating in Ireland. In 1840, when it became clear that the days of the Melbourne government were numbered, he founded an organisation to repeal the Act of Union called the Loyal National Repeal Association. At the general election of 1841, however, his dealings with the Whigs cost him dear, and he lost a number of seats.]

the suffrage, which in a great degree I ceased to desire. For the Ballot I was still an advocate, as in a certain shape, I still am, short Parliaments I never desired.

Another reason was derived from my confidence that the victory was really won. That Toryism in its rank and offensive shape could never again sway the destinies of the empire.

There was however one question that of free trade, on which I still felt enthusiastically, and few persons could be found who admired Cobden more than I did.[133] He seemed to be able, honest and free from the faults of the vulgar democrat. For the sake of his fame he ought to have retired from public life on the repeal of the Corn Laws. His subsequent career has been purely mischievous, less so however than that of Bright,[134] of which more hereafter.

In 1841 I published my last currency pamphlet, 'A Letter to Sir Charles Wood'.[135] It had no considerable sale, but excited as much attention as I could expect. On reading it over last year, after so much subsequent experi-

---

[133] [Richard Cobden, 1804-65, calico printer, MP Stockport 1841-7, West Riding of Yorkshire 1847-57, Rochdale 1859-65. He was a pillar of the Anti-Corn-Law-League and its most active member, 1838-46. He negotiated the commercial treaty with France in 1860. It is likely that Norman objected to the wholesale repeal of duties in the treaty, and that this explains his reservations about Cobden.]

[134] [John Bright, 1811-88, MP Durham 1843-7, Manchester 1847-57, Birmingham 1857-85, Birmingham Central 1885-8. President of the Board of Trade 1868-70, Chancellor of the Duchy of Lancaster 1873-4 and 1880-2. He worked with Cobden in pressing for financial and Parliamentary reform and for free trade, and was active with him in the Anti-Corn-Law-League. He opposed the Crimean War.]

[135] [Norman's work was *A Letter to Sir Charles Wood, Esq., MP, on Money and the Means of Economizing the Use of It* (London: Pelham Richardson, 1841). In an appendix to the work (pp. 101-6, Appendix D), Norman also published the main points of his evidence in his examination before the 1840 Committee on Banks of Issue (see p. 396). The proofs of the first version of the work, as distinct from the final published version, are amongst the Norman papers at Maidstone. It was subject to considerable changes, largely of phraseology, following criticism by Overstone, whose comments are written on the proofs. Overstone also supplied lengthy manuscript comments with detailed suggestions for replacement of Norman's text by insertions, usually to the same effect but in a more ornate style. See O'Brien, *The Correspondence of Lord Overstone*, 1971 pp. 300-1, 316-17.]

ence, I find little to object to in it. Were I to publish another edition I should have little to alter. My task would be chiefly confined to the applications of its doctrines to the great facts of 1847 and 1857.[136]

About this time, I cannot tell in what precise year, I was induced by the advice of some friends to read Comte's 'Philosophie Positive'.[137] Few circumstances in my life ever gave me so much pain. To find that a man of so much knowledge and mental power dogmatized against the being of a God, of itself distressed me greatly. Could he be right? Could I answer all his arguments? Was I indeed obliged to give up a belief which forms the greatest comforts of humanity? I neither did, or could. Still the struggle and tumult in my bosom, were for a long time most distressing. The more so, because I suffered alone. I had no comforter, nobody to whom I could apply, to settle my doubts and remove my difficulties.

It may here be remarked that one symptom of my nervous complaints have always been a distrust of my self and of my own reasoning powers and

[136] [Under the Bank Charter Act of 1844, the Bank was no longer able freely to issue its own notes in order to act as Lender of Last Resort. It was constrained by the state of its gold reserves. In both 1847 and 1857 a liquidity panic, arising from market awareness of the limits on the Bank, took place. On both occasions the Chancellor of the Exchequer issued a Letter of Indemnity, permitting the Bank to exceed the limits laid down in the 1844 Act. The Letters of Indemnity were, on both occasions, subsequently ratified retrospectively by the House of Commons. On the first occasion the mere issue of the letter was sufficient to quell the panic without it being necessary for the Bank to breach the limits laid down in the Act; on the second occasion, in 1857, however, it did prove necessary for the Bank to exceed such limits, though the crisis subsided fairly quickly after that. See D.P. O'Brien, *The Development of Monetary Economics*, Cheltenham: Edward Elgar, 2007 pp. 171-5.]

[137] [See pp. 64, 228. The identity of Norman's 'friends' is not clear. Comte was much admired by George Grote and J.S. Mill, as noted above, but by that date Norman's breach with Grote was complete, and he was never close to J.S. Mill. Indeed there is amongst the Norman papers a letter from Mill, declining an invitation from Norman in terms which could really only be interpreted as a snub, and given Norman's acute sensitivity this is particularly unlikely to have escaped him. The letter, dated 19 August 1852 is at U310 C128/7. Mill wrote: 'We find it impossible to give up the time required by general society and therefore are obliged to decline many invitations which would otherwise be very agreeable and to limit ourselves to a small circle of the same opinions and pursuits with our own.']

logical conclusions. In short, a tendency to believe or to disbelieve what I desire to disbelieve or to believe. Before his career was closed by death, Comte had abandoned his original opinions and imagined for himself some sort of a divinity as necessary I presume to explain the phenomena of the universe. I never even perused his later publications, although I believe that on the subject of government he has some good notions.

In the year 1842 took place the great fire at Hamburg, by which the Sun Office lost £118,000,[138] and this was soon followed by a fire at Liverpool costing £47,000[139] and other large conflagrations.

I had always taken great interest in the insurance business, but these great calls upon the funds of the office affected me painfully from their bearing on the amount of capital and the liability of the shareholders to the whole amount of their fortunes.

The scheme of management for some time previously so far as I could understand it, had been to get business at all hazards, and at any rate, and to keep down the amount of capital by dividing profits.

---

[138] [See *Times* 12 May (5d), 13 May (7c), 14 May (7a), 17 May (5a), 19 May (3d), 21 May (7b), 23 May (5d), 1 June (9b), 6 June (8f), 26 June 1842 (6f). The involvement of the Sun, Royal Exchange, and Phoenix insurance companies was public knowledge, and the *Times* reported that the total liabilities for the three amounted to £1 million. There was public interest in the fire, and the *Times* reported the role played by English engineers in checking its spread. A large part of the city of Hamburg was destroyed, including nearly 2,000 houses. The insurance cover proved incomplete, and a system of mutual insurance, relying on a levy on households, proved quite inadequate to deal with the problem. Ultimately the city decided upon incurring a large debt. But donations came from all over Northern Europe, including Britain. Hamburg had been destroyed before, and there had been a great fire in 1284. In the fire of 1842 about a quarter of the inner city was destroyed. The fire killed 51 people, and left an estimated 20,000 homeless. Reconstruction took more than 40 years. £118,000 at 2009 prices would be £9,933,588.]

[139] [There had earlier been a fire in Liverpool (*Times* 14 September 1842, 6a), but it was localised and contained by the 'fire police'. Even so the loss was in the region of £20,000. Later in September there was another, and very much larger, Liverpool fire (*Times* 24 September 1842, 4e, 26 September, 5a, 27 September, 5e-f). Buildings worth up to £350,000 were destroyed, as well as cotton bales. The insurance liabilities were estimated at £350,900, of which the Sun, Norman's firm, was thought to be liable for £47,000 (or £3,954,580 in 2009 prices).]

I urged a different course of management, *vizt* a more careful selection of risques and a gradual increase of capital. The advice was not popular. Still I met with supporters, our system was gradually modified and we have now a much larger capital and a business altogether more carefully conducted. Could I act as I please, the capital should be still further increased.

It is very remarkable, how small is the profit, upon the whole mass of inland fire insurances compared with the trouble and risque incurred. It hardly compensates the shareholders. The truth is that secretaries, directors and other officials find their account in it, and the body of shareholders are passive.

For a long time I was very nervous about my connection with the Sun and in consequence paid great attention to its concerns.

On 7th July 1842, my sixth son Philip was born. He has, thank God, always enjoyed good health and now (1858) being a slender, loose made lad, growing fast promises to be the tallest of the family. I named him after my kind and excellent friend the Honourable P.P. Bouverie,[140] who was his godfather. He has not had a first fault.

About this time, I forget the exact year, I was appointed a member of the Committee of Treasury at the Bank, in which I have ever since continued.[141] I am the only member of the Court of Directors so far as I know, who have ever occupied that situation without having filled the Chair or purposed to do so, and here I must say that it has always been a source of much regret to me that the state of my health has rendered it imprudent for me to become Deputy Governor and Governor of the Bank. I have declined the first with great reluctance and have relied in doing so, not merely on my own connections, but on the deliberate advice of Sir Henry Holland, then my medical adviser.

In the natural course of things I was senior to Sir J.H. Pelly[142] and Mr

[140] [See p. 325.]

[141] [Norman was elected to the Committee of Treasury in April 1840. We are indebted to Professor Forrest Capie for this information.]

[142] [Sir John Henry Pelly, 1st Bt (1840), 1772-1852, Deputy Governor Hudson's

Cotton.[143] I have always felt a certain sense of inferiority in my self to those of my brethren, who have undertaken to bear the burthen, which I declined. My influence in the Court has no doubt suffered from this cause.

I continued about this time to partake of my usual amusements as heretofore. My ability to play efficiently at cricket gradually diminished and I did not play regularly in the matches of the West Kent club after the year of 1840. However for several subsequent years, I was a pretty constant attendant on club days, taking a hand[144] in a match occasionally. My last match was played on the 17th August 1847, when I got twenty each hands, not being out in the last. I felt this a fitting conclusion to my cricketing career as I was then fifty-four years old and had played as a man, during thirty-seven years after leaving Eton. I may remark that on this occasion, Charlie was in with me.

I have always considered cricket to be the finest game ever invented by man, requiring in order to succeed thoroughly in it an union of uncommon qualifications mental and bodily. It possesses the inestimable advantage of bringing together, and with a common object, men of the most different classes and thus breaking up those distinctions of rank, wealth and station, which are the bane of English society.

Feeling how great are the merits of cricket, in this and other points of view, I have always done my best to encourage it and have been pleased to see my sons excel in it. The game has greatly improved in my time and

---

Bay Company 1812-23, Governor 1823-52. He commissioned important exploration work on behalf of the Company. He was a Director of the Bank of England 1822-52, Deputy Governor 1839-41, Governor 1841-2, FRS 1835.]

[143][William Cotton, 1786-1866, a Director of the Bank of England 1822-66. He was a merchant and philanthropist, a social reformer, and an inventor (FRS 1821). Cotton's maternal grandfather John Harrison had also been a Director of the Bank. Cotton was Governor in the years 1842-5, after Pelly (see fn 136) had served only one year as Governor, and he helped to pilot through the 1844 Bank Charter Act which he then defended in the hearings of Select Committees set up by both Houses of Parliament to investigate the commercial crisis of 1847.]

[144][Obsolete term for Innings. For Norman's cricketing record, see p. 285.]

has now I think reached its acme both in bowling and batting. The only improvement which I could suggest would be an increase in the size of the wickets, so as to shorten matches, which have become decidedly too long.

As respects the civilizing tendencies of cricket, I may mention, that playing as I have with labourers and mechanics in all sorts of matches, I hardly recollect an expression falling from any of them which could annoy the most fastidious. I have always so behaved as if I considered all equal, excepting in point of skill.

I continued to use my gun as usual both at home, at various places where we visited, the chief of which at this time, were Stoneham and Stansted. In the year 1843, after a considerable intermission, we went to Whitfield in the month of August and continued to do so most years until the death of our dear friend Mr Ord in 1855.[145]

At this time an event took place which in its consequences has been productive of intense anxiety and grief to my self and wife. I have mentioned already that Herman was difficult to teach. I may now add that he shewed no such disposition, as held out the prospect that he would succeed in the law, the profession to which I had destined him. He was a strong and bold boy. Under these circumstances we turned our attention to the army, I considered that he never could be wealthy as a country gentleman, but that he would probably inherit enough from me to make him comfortable as a soldier, one of the advantages of whose profession it is, their small income goes a great way and that if after my death, or even before, he should think fit to retire, the experience he had acquired might be most useful to him in his subsequent life. Besides, I had observed among my acquaintances that old soldiers formed a most amiable, useful and respectable class. Having made up our minds on these grounds and consulted Herman's wishes, so far as a boy of twelve has any wishes on the subject, I applied to Lord Raglan[146] then Lord F. Somerset

[145] [William Henry Ord (see p. 133), born 2 January 1781, died 28 July 1855.]

[146] [Fitzroy James Henry Somerset, 1st Baron Raglan, 1788-1855, Major General

and Master General for a nomination to Woolwich, which I readily obtained. This was subsequently changed for a cadetship at Sandhurst.

On dear Herman's career in the Army I need say nothing more, as among my papers will be found a short memoir of him.[147] I will only remark here that my bitter sorrow at his death was not further embittered by self-reproach.[148] In dedicating a son however beloved, to the service of the fatherland, I have never felt that I had done an act unworthy of the tenderest parent, and the fact that the Almighty in his wisdom should have claimed his precious life on the field of battle, has not inspired me with [con]scious[ness][149] that I had acted unkindly and improperly. Hardly a waking hour passes over my head that I do not think of him. Time has done little in bringing me comfort, but I am sometimes consoled by a reflection similar to that of the Duke of Ormond,[150] respecting the Earl of Arran,[151] but in a mitigated form, that

---

1825, Master General of the Ordinance 1819-27, Military Secretary 1827-52.]

[147] [As noted above, this has not been traced.]

[148] [George Herman Norman, born 26 July 1831, Captain in the 57th (Middlesex) Regiment, died of a head wound received in the attack on the Redan Fort at Sebastopol, 18 June 1855. Norman himself had been seriously concerned about the fate of his son in the Crimea (O'Brien, *The Correspondence of Lord Overstone* 1971 vol. 2 pp. 596-8). Herman was reported in the *Times*, 26 June 1855 (10b), as severely wounded. He died of wounds on 30 June. Even on 9 July, Norman was unaware of the outcome (O'Brien, 1971, vol 2, p. 614). Norman's grief never left him. In his journal for 1881 he recorded that he dreamt of Herman on the night of 18-19 June and was deeply distressed. In the Norman papers, at U310/123/1 there are letters from Herman in the Crimea, including a report of the charge of the Light Brigade, making in particular the point that 'By some mistake' the charge had been ordered before there was infantry support. In U310/F33, there are papers of 1855-7 relating to the death of Herman. At U310/C132/2 there is a letter of 1856 from the War Department sending the medals awarded to Herman for service in the Crimea.]

[149] [Manuscript is torn here.]

[150] [James Butler, 1610-88, 1st Duke of Ormond. Ormond was an Anglo-Irish statesman and soldier, best known for his involvement in the wars in Ireland in the 1640s when he commanded the English royalist forces. His son was Richard Butler, Earl of Arran, 1639-86. He served as his father's deputy as Lord Lieutenant of Ireland in the years 1682-4.]

[151] [This reference has not been traced. In Thomas Carte, *A History of the Life of James, Duke of Ormonde from his birth in 1610 to his death in 1688* (London: Knapton, 1736, vol. 2, appendix pp. 125, 128) there is a touching letter of 9 August 1680 on the death of another son, the Earl of Ossory, and a prayer written

my dead son is to be preferred to the live sons of many other fathers.

Death on the battle field is a glorious death, may no son or descendant of mine be unwilling to give his life at duty's call and in his country's cause.

I will now advert to a very difficult circumstance. Many years before this time, a little vein on the right side of my nose had burst and obstinately refused to heal permanently although repeatedly cauterized. At length I went to Travers about it.[152] He endeavoured to ease it by washes and plaisters and ultimately treated it by internal remedies such as sarsaparilla. All failed, it grew worse, I then went to Brodie[153] who told my wife that it must be cured or that the final result would be very bad, and further that cauterization was the best means to use. To this then, I again had recourse and finally with success. Nothing now remains of the wound which was never so large as the smallest pin but a scar. I consider that I ought to be very thankful for this cure.

At this time I renewed my acquaintance with Frederick Lord Rendlesham,[154] who had been my father's ward, but had long resided in Italy. He came to Bromley and we went to Rendlesham in this and several subsequent years, and I enjoyed there first-rate shooting.

In the Autumn of this year, I had the most serious acute illness, which I have ever had since the internal inflammation which seized me at Eltham. I had been shooting over Orpington Court Lodge with Henry on the invitation of the present Sir P.H. Dyke,[155] and in riding home felt greatly fatigued and unwell. I was obliged to go to bed and was soon attacked by what was called

by the Duke of Ormond on that death. To judge from the extensive secondary literature, including the diary of John Evelyn, it was Ossory who was regarded as the heroic figure amongst the sons.]

152 [See p. 364.]

153 [Sir Benjamin Collins Brodie, 1st Bt, 1783-1862, Assistant Surgeon and Surgeon at St George's Hospital 1808-40, Surgeon to George IV, 1828, to William IV, 1832.]

154 [4th Baron Rendlesham; see p. 280.]

155 [Sir Percival Hart Dyke, 6th Bt, 1799-1875, succeeded his father the 5th Bt in 1846.]

inflammation of the mucous membrane of the stomach. I had much pain and subsequent weakness, and as is usual with me great depression. Thinking myself in danger, I sent for Amory to make some alteration in my will.[156] This was done, Moores came down and with Barnes the gardener, witnessed my signature. Scott[157] attended me with the greatest kindness. In ten or twelve days, under the blessing of providence I was able to leave my bed, and then gradually recovered.

I recollect nothing particular as having occurred in 1844. We went to Whitfield and Rendlesham, besides our usual visits to Stansted, Stockbridge &c, and on returning from Whitfield, I think we took the route by Carlisle and Lancaster, and then crossing the Mersey, visited Lady Marjoribanks at Gresford.[158]

The conduct of Sir Robert Peel respecting free trade and the Corn Laws, excited of course my deepest attention and I looked forward enthusiastically to the final triumph of those great principles to which I had always adhered and which alone can emancipate industry, and allow the capital and labour of a country to be employed most advantageously.

My respect for Peel however fell a good short of that felt by the public in general. I considered that he had acted by free trade, and the Corn Laws, just as he had done in the case of Catholic emancipation. That he had professed and made use for party purposes, of protectionist opinions, which his reason had long rejected, and of arguments of which he knew the invalidity, and that his apparent conversion had been merely the result of a conviction that protection could no longer be maintained and that internal peace and security of the country absolutely depended on a change of measures. For his having made a great sacrifice of position, as the Chief of a great party, under this conviction, I give him credit, but much more than this is claimed for him, by

[156] [The legal firm was Amory, Sewell and Moores of 25 Throgmorton Street, London. The partners were Samuel Amory, Isaac Sewell, and Samuel Moores.]

[157] [On Dr Scott, see p. 41.]

[158] [See p. 366.]

those who have erected statues in his memory.

I have before observed that my party feelings and desire for further organic changes had gradually cooled down. The conduct of the lowest strata of democracy upon the question of free tradc, contributed some thing to this result. The repeal of the Corn Laws was never a democratic question in its proper sense. It was supported by most men of intelligence in the country, and also by the manufacturers under the erroneous opinion that their direct pecuniary interest was specially involved in it, but it was opposed by all farmers, and often by the workmen in towns, under the supposition that it would lower wages. With a Parliament chosen by low suffrage, I believe that the measure would have been rejected.

The spread of Chartist opinion, based as they were on communistic views, also acted in my change of opinion and impressed me with some apprehension as to the tranquillity of the country.

The state of things on the continent where the most ardent Liberals, usually professed socialistic doctrines could hardly fail to react on the English Chartists.

The differences of rank, wealth, social position and apparent happiness and enjoyment, are striking facts, and nothing is more natural than that the toiling many should regard those above them with envy and dislike, should overestimate their relative advantages, should attribute these advantages mainly, not to the necessary conditions of humanity, but to unjust and one-sided legislation, and should desire and strive to attain political power with a view of bettering their condition through the medium of direct legislation.

Of course I well knew that these views were erroneous, that the poor could not be made and kept rich by Act of Parliament. But I also thought the Chartists could never be taught this truth but by experience, or by the result of a bloody conflict. This conflict, this war of classes I always looked forward to. It was adjourned by the revolution of 1848, but I fear that it is still in prospect.

On the 5th March 1845 was born our second daughter, Mary Henrietta.[159]

At this time and for many preceding and succeeding years, I used to devote my leisure in summer to fishing. Besides my visits to Stockbridge, usually three in a year and of a week each, *vizt* in April, at the Mayfly and in October, I now and then went to other places at a distance, for instance to Mr Smith's at Ramsbury,[160] General Popham's at Littlecot,[161] Lord Portsmouth's[162] and Mr Portal's at or near Whitchurch.[163] These visits were usually in the company of my friend Richard Penn.[164]

With Richard Penn and my Brother Henry,[165] I hired the fishing at Mapledurham Lock, which contained many large Trout and there some years before this time, I caught the Trout 10 lbs 12 oz, my greatest exploit as a fisherman.

My neighbours in Kent were always very kind to me, and I had free licence to go whenever I liked to Mr Chapman's[166] and Snelling's[167] at North Cray

---

[159][Mary Henrietta was born 5 March 1845, married in 1879 Alfred Bonham Carter. She died in 1893.]

[160][Ramsbury is a village in Wiltshire on the River Kennet, 5 miles from Hungerford. The manor house belonged to a family called Jones. It is not clear which member of the extensive Smith banking clan was at Ramsbury at that time, though the most likely candidate is Norman's friend from his Eton days, George Robert Smith, 1793-1869.]

[161][Lieutenant General Edward William Popham of Littlecote, Wilts, 1764-1843.]

[162][Newton Wallop, later Fellowes, 1772-1854, MP Andover 1802-20, North Devon 1832-7, 4th Earl of Portsmouth, succeeded 1853. He was the brother of the 3rd Earl, John Charles Wallop, 1767-1853.]

[163][John Portal of Whitchurch, Hants, 1764-1848.]

[164][Richard Penn, 1784-1863, served in the Colonial Office. FRS 1824. Author of *Maxims and Hints for an Angler and Miseries of Fishing. Illustrated by Sir Francis Chantrey*, 1833. He was thus, like Chantrey, part of Norman's circle of cronies in the Houghton Club. He produced similar volumes on chess and shooting.]

[165][Norman's younger brother, born in 1801.]

[166][Possibly Edward Henry Chapman, born 1803, one of Norman's colleagues at the Bank of England, but probably James Chapman of St Paul's Cray, died 1845, or his son, also James Chapman, 1797-1878, lawyer and Major, West Kent Yeomanry, 1848. St Paul's Cray is four and a half miles east of Bromley. James Chapman of Paulscray Hill, St Mary Cray is listed in the Six Home Counties Directory for 1845.]

[167][Joseph Snelling, a miller, lived at Chislehurst, two and a half miles from Bromley, according to the Six Home Counties Directory for 1845. It is possible

on the Cray,[168] to Sir P.H. Dyke's[169] and Mr Mildmay's on the Darent,[170] and to Sir J. Lubbock's on the Wandle as long as he resided at Mitcham.[171]

Of all sporting amusements, fly fishing has been always that which pleased me best. To walk by a beautiful stream in the month of May or June with birds singing and flowers blowing around, and then to listen to the rippling sound of the clear water is in itself delightful, and when to this is added the excitement of the sport, the beauty of the prey when captured, the exertion or skill on the part of the angler and the small amount of pain inflicted, especially with the artificial fly, there seems to me nothing wanted, excepting danger, to make trout fishing the most attractive of the sports of the field.

I have not confined myself quite exclusively to the taking of trout and grayling. I also, when these fail me, fish for perch and jack, and I once at Stockbridge caught in the large peat pits a jack which weighed lbs 23. I always however thought these fish a very poor capture.

With all my fondness for the gentle art and my extensive practice in it I have never been a really good fisherman, and this is the more remarkable, as

---

that, by the later dates at which the Autobiography was written, he had acquired property at North Cray.]

168 [There were several seats in the parish of North Cray, North Cray Place, Vale Mascall, Mount Mascall, and Woollet Hall, at one time the home of Lord Castlereagh.]

169 [Sir Percival Hart Dyke; see p. 406. The River Cray rises at Orpington and runs 8 miles NNE through Crayford marshes to the River Darenth, between Dartford and the Thames.]

170 [Humphrey St John Mildmay, 1794-1853, a Director of the Bank 1828-49, MP Southampton 1842-7. There was a social as well as a professional connection, as the second wife of Norman's friend Lord Radnor, 3rd Earl, 1769-1869, was Ann Judith née Mildmay, sister of the Bank Director.]

171 [Sir John William Lubbock, 2nd Bt, 1774-1840, and John William Lubbock, 3rd Bt, 1803-65, London banker, partner in Lubbock and Company 1825, sole working partner 1840-60, FRS 1829, astronomer and joint author of a book on probability erroneously attributed to Augustus de Morgan. The 3rd Bt lived 1834-40 at 29 Eaton Place, London, and at Mitcham Grove, Surrey. But upon succeeding to the baronetcy on the death of his father in 1840, he moved his country home to High Elms, Farnborough, Kent. It was the second Bt who settled at Mitcham initially, finding the distance from Farnborough to London too great. When the 3rd Bt moved to Farnborough he pulled down the house and built a new one, as well as greatly enlarging the park.]

I have succeeded in most things, which require muscular skill and exertion. Something may be attributed to the advanced age, about 36, at which I commenced my apprenticeship and something to my inability of late years to work.[172] Hearing other people talk of their great sport, I have often thought that there must be some grand error in my mode of throwing a fly, yet on comparing my performance in this way with that of others, I cannot perceive my inferiority. I am conscious however, that I manage a fish ill, when hooked, more especially with the long blowing rod. I am also lazy in changing tackle, and thus doubtless throw away a good many chances.

On the [blank in original] 1845 died at Leamington my father in law, Mr Henry Stone.[173] He had been a civil servant of East India company in Bengal, and returned home with a competency in 1818, having previously lost his first wife, daughter of Dr Roxburgh a distinguished naturalist.[174]

In England he took a second wife, *vizt* Margaret daughter of Colonel Beaufoy the mathematician and astronomer.[175] This turned out a most un-

---

172 [Probably 'work', but manuscript not clear. ]

173 [Henry Stone was a partner in Martins Bank. He was one of four brothers, George, Henry, Richard and Andrew. George Chandler in his book *Four Centuries of Banking* (London: Batsford, 1964) gives two different dates for Henry Stone's time as a partner in Martin and Stone. On p. 99 the dates given are 1821-49. On p. 302 the dates given are 1821-52. However on this page he gives the year of death as 1845, and indeed the correct date was 7 September 1845 (O'Brien, *The Correspondence of Lord Overstone*, 1971 vol. 1 p. 366, n. 3). Interestingly, in view of Norman's comment about the over-fondness for wine on the part of the deceased, the cause of death was given as a diseased liver.]

174 [William Roxburgh, 1751-1815, botanist and medical doctor. He married three times. By the first wife he had one daughter; by the second wife, five sons and three daughters; and, by the third wife, two daughters and one son. There was also at least one illegitimate son.]

175 [Mark Beaufoy, 1764-1827, astronomer and physicist. At age 20, in 1784, he eloped with his cousin Margaretta (died 1800), who was an excellent mathematician, and he was expelled from the Quaker community. FRS 1790. Despite being from a Quaker family, his brother was an army Major, his own two sons became officers in Guards regiments, and he himself was gazetted Colonel in the 1st Royal Tower Hamlets Militia in 1799. In 1814, after scandals of maladministration, he was relieved of his command. He was also a mountaineer, and only the fourth person to climb Mont Blanc. His daughter was Henriette Beaufoy. She was taken by her mother to watch her father ascend Mont Blanc.]

fortunate connection. The lady had an unfortunate temper the result perhaps of disease, which after shewing itself in various forms of insanity, ended in hopeless idiocy and death. She died in 1840, having had four children of whom three sons died in India, and only one daughter, wife of Mr Edward Salter[176] now survives. Mrs Stone was a very bad stepmother, especially in her later years.

Mr Stone was a man of amiable disposition, honest and well-disposed, but with little mental cultivation. From a love of ease, and facility of disposition, he allowed his wife to illtreat his daughters of the first marriage, and a similar origin may be assigned to the careless negligence with which he allowed his fortune, once not inconsiderable, to melt away, until besides the small settled property, only a trifle was left, and this notwithstanding he had for many years a share in the business in Lombard street, which must have brought him in a fair income. It may be added, that like his brother Richard and nephew, Mr H. Stone was overfond of wine and that this failing probably shortened his life by many years. I attended the funeral with my brother Henry and G. Stone at a small church yard, near Leamington.

And here I cannot refrain from saying a few words about the subject of the Stone family, now on the point of extinction in the male line.[177] The

[176] [Norman's writing is not clear, though a possible reading is Salter. There was an Edward Salter in the Post Office London Directory for 1857 at 1 Elm Terrace, Cambridge Heath, in north east London.]

[177] [Andrew Stone, died 1711, born probably in Winchester, son of jailer and property owner, obtained in the early 1690s an apprenticeship to Richard Smith, senior partner in the Grasshopper Bank in London. In 1697 he married Smith's niece Anne Holbrooke. When Smith died in 1699, Andrew Stone became senior partner in the firm. In 1703 Thomas Martin was made a partner. Sibella Stone, Norman's wife, was Andrew Stone's great great granddaughter, and two of her sons, Frederick Henry (partner from 1880) and Edward (partner from 1884) joined the bank. The eldest son of Andrew Stone, himself Andrew Stone, 1703-73, became Commissioner of Trade and Customs. He worked for the Duke of Newcastle for twenty years, 1732-52, but was accused of Jacobite sympathies. He was MP for the Treasury borough of Hastings, 1741-61, and tutor to George III, when Prince of Wales, from 1751 and, from 1756, secretary to the Prince. His brother, George Stone, 1708-64, enjoyed a meteoric rise in the Church of Ireland, going to Ireland after the appointment of the Duke of Dorset as Lord Lieutenant of Ireland in

house in Lombard street is one of the oldest banking houses in London. It was founded in the 17th century and fell to the Stones soon afterwards. The Martins entered subsequently. In the reign of George II, the Stones reached their zenith. One of them, Andrew, was Secretary of the Treasury and I believe tutor to George III. His brother was archbishop of Armagh and Primate of Ireland. Both were very important political personages. A Stone afterwards married a daughter or granddaughter of archbishop Herring and thus the Stones became relative to the Barings and many other families of mark.[178]

When I was a young man, the head of the family, and of the house, was Mr Stone of Chislehurst, grandfather to my wife.[179] He was a short, fat man, and I have a faint recollection of him. He had a very large family, among whom I recollect four sons, George, Henry, Richard and Andrew who reached manhood, and of these the two first had both sons. There were also collateral males. Nevertheless, extraordinary to say, G. Stone is the only male of the family and he is separated from his wife and has only a daughter Mrs Claudet.[180] The full diminution in point of numbers, G. Stone living

1830, as one of the Duke's chaplains. By 1740 he was Bishop of Ferns. In 1747 he became Archbishop of Armagh, and Primate of all Ireland. He was a contentious and highly political, rather than religious, figure.]

[178][Richard Stone, c.1738-1802, who was a partner in the bank, 1760-1802, married in 1766 Mary Herring. Her sister married Sir Francis Baring, thus providing the family connection to which Norman alludes. The Barings had already opened an account with the Stone bank in 1764. Thomas Herring, 1693-1757, was Archbishop of Canterbury 1747-57. He never married. He had been Archbishop of York, 1743-7. Sir Francis Baring, 1740-1810, founder of Baring Brothers bank, MP Grampound, Wickham and Calne, 1784-1806, married, 12 May 1767, Harriet (died 3 December 1804), daughter and co-heir of William Herring of Croydon, who was the cousin and co-heir of Thomas Herring, Archbishop of Canterbury. This was a very profitable connection for the Barings. Over the years Harriet née Herring contributed about £20,000 to the family coffers, money received from her merchant father William Herring.]

[179][George Stone, partner 1793-1843, Senior Partner 1831-43. The estate at Chislehurst was known as Coopers and George Stone had succeeded to it on the death of his father Richard Stone.]

[180][At first sight, given the way in which Norman refers to Mrs Claudet, implying that she was the wife of someone well known, this should be the wife of Antoine

on charity. There is no longer a Stone in the bank,[181] which has passed altogether to the Martins, and the fortune of the race is confined to the portions of daughters, which were mainly derived from life insurances on the late Mr G. Stone. All this forms a melancholy recital.

In this year 1845, if I do not mistake, dear Herman went to the military college[182] at Sandhurst[183] where I often visited him, and made the acquaintance of Sir G. Scovell the Governor who two or three times went to Stock-

François Jean Claudet, born Lyon 1797, inventor and photographic pioneer, FRS 1853, Chevalier of the Legion of Honour, 1863, who died in London in 1867. But he had married in Paris one Julie Bourdelain, who did not die until 1881. He was well known in London society, and a pioneer of the use of the process for producing pictures invented by Louis Daguerre. He also invented the red dark room light, and suggested the idea of using a series of still photographs to create the impression of movement. From 1841 to 1851 he operated a studio on the roof of the Adelaide Gallery behind St Martin's in the Fields Church in London. In 1853 he was appointed Royal Photographer. However there was another Mrs Claudet. Apart from Antoine Francois Jean Claudet, FRS, there was another member of the family, F. Claudet, who lived at 5 Rochester Terrace, Camden Road, and who worked as an assayer at 6 Canon Street, City, according to the Post Office London Directory for 1857. His presence in the City would explain Norman's assumption of familiarity with the name Claudet on the part of the reader.]

181 [After the death of Henry Stone, George Stone II, 1808-61, was a partner 1830-52. He was the last family representative. However, as noted on p. 412, two of Sibella's sons became partners in the bank. George Chandler, *Four Centuries of Banking*, London: Batsford, 1964, vol. I pp. 98-9, 232. The life insurances presumably relate to the elder George Stone, as the younger George Stone is referred to as still alive and 'living on charity'. The observation predates his demise in 1861.]

182 [George Herman Norman was admitted to the Royal Military College, Sandhurst, 8 July 1845 aged 13. His height was recorded as 5 feet 2 inches. Three years later, 24 November 1848, he was commissioned into the 57th Regiment of Foot, and on 31 December 1848 he left Sandhurst. He had three decorations of merit, and was 'College Recommended'. This meant that he was given his first commission, the rank of Ensign (later known as Second Lieutenant) free of charge, as opposed to having to purchase it himself.]

183 [Major General Sir George Scovell, KCB (see p. 415) was Lieutenant Governor of the Royal Military College, Sandhurst, 1829-37 and Governor, 1837-56. The Governor was in reality a figurehead; the College was run by the Lieutenant Governor, and there was a Commandant responsible for the Gentlemen Cadets. In 1888 the Post of Lieutenant Governor was abolished, and in 1902 that of Governor was also abolished, so that the responsibilities of all three posts were assumed by the Commandant.]

bridge to fish on my invitation.[184] He was a good-humoured old gentleman, and in his military service had displayed considerable ability. He was not however well calculated to preside over an educational establishment.

The spirit existing among the cadets when I knew them was far from good. The best strove to gain their commissions, but did not aim at any thing higher and there was a pretty general conviction among them, that what they learned at the college would be of little use in their future career as soldiers. Discipline was maintained upon a bad system, *vizt*, a constant superintendence and espionage by the sergeants. There was but little appeal to the sentiments of duty and honor. The dietary was indifferent and the means of healthy amusement provided insufficient.

The following year 1846 produced really no event which I can now call to mind. I see however by my game book, that I went to Rendlesham, Stansted &c. It was not so however with 1847. In that year, we had a general election and although my hope of great improvement in the public happiness from large measures of legislation had greatly diminished, I still retained my party attachments, especially in what regarded the western division [of Kent].

At a meeting held at Maidstone it was considered that we might have a fair chance of returning Mr Hodges. He was unwilling to stand, mainly from pecuniary considerations, his financial position being very bad. I was deputed to endeavor to overcome his scruples and did so.[185] A severe contest

[184][Major General Sir George Scovell, 1774-1861, had a distinguished military career. He played a significant role in the Peninsula war. A gifted linguist, he broke the French military codes, in the spring of 1811. At the end of that year, the French army was given a much more complex code, but by July 1812 Scovell had made significant progress in breaking the code. This no doubt assisted in Wellington's crushing victory over Marmont at Salamanca 22 July 1812, and by the end of 1812, when a letter from Joseph Bonaparte to Napoleon had been intercepted, Scovell was able to complete the breaking of the code, and the information proved vital in Wellington's victory over the French at Vitoria, 21 June 1813, in which, as noted on p. 115, George Thellusson lost his life. Scovell is not mentioned in Elizabeth Longford's magisterial account of Wellington as a military commander in *Wellington. The Years of the Sword* (Frogmore: Panther Books, 1971).]

[185][See *Times* 4 August 1847 (3b-c). The candidates proposed were Sir E. Filmer, proposed by T.F. Best and seconded by Sir W. Riddell, Colonel Austen, proposed

was the result, and we succeeded in ejecting my kind and old friend colonel Austen by a bare majority of forty-five.[186]

I was to have proposed Mr Hodges but it so happened that at the very moment of the election, my wife was brought to bed. I was very nervous about her, and could not leave her, and Francis Dashwood[187] officiated in my room. The child born on the 31st July was our youngest son Edward.

This year was also rendered important to me by the occurrence of the commercial crisis. I did not neglect my duty at the Bank during its continuance. Throughout the month of October, I do not think that I was absent from London more than a day or two. I used to go early in the morning, first call at the Bank in order to learn how things were going on there and how the accounts had closed on the preceding evening. I then proceeded to Downing Street, reported to Sir Charles Wood, then Chancellor of the Exchequer, and consulted with him and carried back his views to the City, or remained in the West End, as the case might require. I usually dined at the Athenaeum and went to Bromley afterwards. After two or three weeks of this work, I found it too hard for me and then went with my wife to Mivart's Hotel, where we remained for more than a week.

I was of course deeply mortified by the apparent failure of the Act of

by Sir P.H. Dyke and seconded by Mr Chapman, and Mr T.L. Hodges, proposed by Colonel Dashwood and seconded by J. Whatman. Norman's friend Hodges made it clear that he had not intended to stand, as Norman reports. The *Times* 15 July 1847 (8e) had reported that there was no likely opposition to the re-election of Sir Edward Filmer and Colonel Austen. The outcome of the election was reported in the *Times* 7 August 1847 (3b) and 9 August (3b). It is clear that Mr Hodges did not enjoy strong support either in Bromley or Tonbridge. However he topped the poll. The figures at close of poll on 8 August were: Hodges 2,462, Austen 2,200, Filmer 2,191. It is not clear where Norman's figure of 45 comes from though earlier (State of Poll at 6 August, reported in the *Times* 7 August) the results were given as: Filmer 2,483, Hodges 2,384 and Austen 2,369, giving Hodges a majority over Austen at that stage of 15. However the press report may well be inaccurate.]

[186] [Thomas Austen, Lieutenant Colonel, 60th Regiment of Foot, 1805-17, MP West Kent 1845-7. Died 23 July 1859 aged 84.]

[187] [This was Francis Dashwood of Halcot, Bexley, according to the Post Office Directory of the Six Home Counties for 1845.]

1844,[188] and with many of its ardent friends was inclined to attribute this in a great degree to mismanagement on the part of the Bank Court.[189] That their conduct was open to severe criticism cannot be doubted, still especially after the experience of 1857, I am inclined to think that nothing within the power of the Directors could have averted the catastrophe.[190]

During the course of the year I did not fail to impress upon the Court my views of the propriety of acting earlier, and more efficiently by raising the rate of discount. I did this especially by a formal motion in March of this year,[191] by which and my subsequent conduct, I acquired no little obloquy

[188] [Norman's stake in the crisis was personal. With Overstone and Robert Torrens, he was the architect of the intellectual framework of the Bank Charter Act of 1844 and, with Torrens, shares the paternity of the idea of splitting the Bank into Departments of Issue and Banking, the former to be subject to stringent controls over the issue of Bank of England notes. As noted below, he was called upon to defend the Act before the Lords Committee in 1848, following the crisis of 1847.]

[189] [Norman is referring to the policy of seeking market share through low rates of discount in the separated Banking Department of the Bank, and to the prevailing orthodoxy that the Banking Department could be conducted like any other bank, even though Norman himself had expressed such a view.]

[190] [See Clapham, *The Bank of England*, vol. 2 pp. 200-1. The discount rate charged by the Bank was 3 per cent, from August 1846 to January 1847, when it was raised to 3.5 per cent. Clapham reports that a section of the Court had wished to raise it the previous November. Such rates were extremely competitive in the London market, for the market rate varied between 5 and 3.75 per cent. Later in January 1847 the rate was raised to 4 per cent, at which level it was held until April, though the market rate in April was no less than 7 per cent. In April the Committee of Treasury, of which Norman was a member, despite having refused to become Governor (see p. 402 and Clapham, vol. 2 pp. 212-13), advised the Court to raise the rate to 5 per cent.]

[191] [The Court Minutes for 11 March 1847 contain the following entry: 'A motion was made and seconded "That the Minimum Rate of Discount on Bills of Exchange not having more than 95 days to run, be advanced to $4\frac{1}{2}$ per cent per annum". And the question having been put thereon and the same was negatived'. Though the proposer and seconder are not recorded, it seems reasonable to assume that this was Norman's motion. Norman was certainly present at the meeting of the Court. He was probably behind subsequent attempts to rein in the reckless behaviour of the Banking Department of the Bank. At the meeting of the Court on 1 April 1847 it was proposed that the interest rate should be raised to $4\frac{1}{2}$ per cent on bills of 30 to 60 days, and 5 per cent on bills of 60 to 95 days, but these proposals were also 'negatived', and the discussion adjourned until the meeting of the Court on 8 April when, at last, the minimum rate of discount was increased to 5 per cent. We are indebted for this information to staff of the Bank of England. The Bank

and unpopularity on the part of certain members of the court, some of whom had overtraded and regarded an easy state of the money market as vitally important to them. The fact that I was out of business, and could thus look without alarm as to my private interest upon the storm raging around, did not tend to make my counsels more acceptable. Among my fiercest objurgators was James Pattison, with whom I had one regular shindy, having put up with a great deal, before I thought it right to stand upon my defence.[192]

Any little hostile feeling however on the part of any members of the Court speedily passed away, and I am happy to bear testimony to the great kindness and consideration I have all but uniformly experienced at the hands of my colleagues. I am also happy to record my opinion that the attention to sound principle, the courage and devotion to duty evinced by the Governor and Deputy Governor of that day, Morris[193] and Prescott,[194] could not be exceeded.

archive reference for these minutes is G8/34.]

[192][As a former Governor of the Bank, Pattison would have enjoyed particular standing within the Court of Directors. Norman was a member of the Committee of Treasury, as noted in fn. 190, and in August 1844, shortly after the passing of the 1844 Act, the Bank had rescinded a vote forbidding discount of bills endorsed by banks of issue (that is, rival issuers of bank notes). The Bank was pursuing market share. In September the Bank reduced its discount rate to 2.5 per cent for bills and 3.0 for notes. It had never previously discounted at less than 4 per cent since 1699.]

[193][James Morris 1795-1882, a Director of the Bank 1827-80, Deputy Governor 1847, Governor 1847-9. He was the head of Morris, Prévost and Company, merchants. Morris had replaced W.R. Robinson who had become Governor in 1846. Robinson was the senior partner of Robinson and Company, which was in the corn trade. It failed, though it ultimately paid 20 shillings in the pound (Evans, *The Commercial Crisis*, 1847-1848 pp. lxxiv-lxxv). William Robinson was disqualified as Governor, 21 August 1847. The mother of James Morris was the sister of William Haldimand, an earlier Director, and ally of Norman; see p. 246.]

[194][Henry James Prescott, 1802-56, a Director of the Bank 1835-56, Deputy Governor 1847-9, Governor 1849-51. He was a merchant, with premises in Old Broad Street in London. His brother William George Prescott was a friend and correspondent of Overstone, and a partner in the banking firm of Prescott, Grote and Company, and took his own life in 1865. See O'Brien, *The Correspondence of Lord Overstone*, 1971 vol. 2 p. 651, vol. 3 p. 1,073.]

# Chapter 14

# The Storms of 1848

The year 1848 was one of the most interesting to me in my whole career. The commercial storm had been succeeded by a calm, but the dream of public tranquillity was broken up by such a political tornado as had not been seen in Europe since the years 1790-94. Like the rest of the world I was quite unprepared for the immediate outbreak at Paris, but had long expected a contest between 'have and get', to which I knew that St Simonianism[1] and Communism and Chartism, and all the 'isms' of the day directly pointed, and had often discussed these matters with my friends. Thus then when the first fighting took place in Paris, I at once walked over to Loyd in Lothbury, and told him that the battle, which we had foreseen, had at length arrived.

I was greatly alarmed at the consequences, I was aware of the state of feeling in the working classes in all countries, in whose minds the doctrine that their sufferings resulted from unjust legislation had been sedulously inculcated. I knew that this doctrine was most congenial to their feelings, and that had I been one of them, I might perhaps have felt like them. I knew that the attempt to make all people happy by infringing the rights

[1] [Claude Henri de Rouvroy, Comte de Saint Simon, 1760-1825, who put forward projects for a restructuring of society on a socialistic basis, in which industrial organisers would provide the aristocracy and the management of society. He was associated with Comte (see p. 228), and the scientism which Comte promoted. See F.A. Hayek (1942-4), 'Scientism and the Study of Society', *Economica*, vol. 9 pp. 267-91; vol. 10 pp. 34-63; vol. 11 pp. 27-39.]

of property must fail, but I did not foresee how soon this point might be ascertained by undeniable experience, how wide the contest might spread, how long it might last, how much bloodshed and confusion might take place before the problem was solved.

I foresaw however at once that the attempt to establish a republic in France could only end in a military despotism, and expressed this opinion most strongly to John Mill at and after a Political Economy club dinner, when he was led to take a very cheerful view of the political and social prospects of France.[2]

I should extend this biography to a most inconvenient length were[3] I to introduce long reflections on the various phenomena exhibited by Europe in the Spring and Summer of 1848, but for one or two, I will find room.

Louis Philippe and his advisers neglected a most solemn duty,[4] in allowing the throne to be overturned without any serious efforts to protect it. It seems to me that a most serious obligation rests upon every established government, whatever may have been its origin, of repelling force by force. Unless this obligation be recognised and acted upon, it may often happen that a daring

---

[2] [Norman was probably referring to the meeting of the Political Economy Club 2 March 1848 when Mill proposed the question 'What are the essential differences between Bank Notes and other forms of credit?' According to the diary of J.L. Prévost, Norman insisted on separating notes, which were money, from bills of exchange. Overstone, who was also present, stressed that only metallic money or bank notes could close a transaction. *Political Economy Club Proceedings*, vol. 6 pp. 61, 295-6.]

[3] [Norman wrote 'was' here.]

[4] [Louis Philippe, 1773-1850 (see p. 326), who was overthrown after ten or more years of unrest and of increasingly authoritarian rule. After his overthrow he fled to England. He was succeeded by Louis Napoleon, 1808-73, who later became Emperor of France as Napoleon III. Originally Charles Louis Napoléon Bonaparte, the son of Napoleon's brother Louis, he was enabled by the revolution of February 1848 to return from England where he had fled after a failed coup d'etât against Louis Philippe. He was elected Deputy for Paris in 1848 and took his seat in the Constituent Assembly in June 1848. Two days later he resigned and left France, but in September he won a huge victory over General Louis Cavaignac, his genuinely republican competitor, and in December 1848 he became President. At the end of 1851 he dissolved the constitution and suppressed opposition. He was re-elected as President, and assumed the title of Emperor in 1852.]

minority, even if inconsiderable in itself, may overthrow the government, convulse the state and introduce innumerable evils.

This happened in France in 1848, so soon as the people acquired the means of expressing their opinions they at once pronounced by an overwhelming majority against the republic. For such was the real meaning of those who chose Louis Napoleon President in opposition to Cavaignac[5] in December 1848.

Louis Philippe ought to have resisted the mob and used the military unsparingly when attacked. He would probably have succeeded, for his assailants were few and ill-provided. At the worst he and his sons could have died like brave men, with swords in their hands, and posterity would have done justice to their memory.

But if we blame the king and his ministers, what shall we say of the 40,000 national guards of Paris, the bodily incarnation of the Juste Milieu, the worthy epiciers, who of all things upon earth love peace and order, who with muskets in their hands allowed a few thousands of ragamuffins to revolutionise France. What shall we say? Why that a national guard is a very useless institution – indeed worse than useless. It never did and never can resist a foreign enemy, and is far less efficacious in maintaining internal peace than a well-organised police, such as that of London. It really means an armament of the middle class, against the lower, but in this, it usually fails and why should we array one class against another?

Well did the reforms of the preceding twenty years in England do justice to the wisdom of their supporters. They had cut the very ground from beneath the feet of the agitators. There was really no important grievance to complain of and at a Bromley bench in the Spring of this year, I could say to my colleagues, well my good Tory friends what do you think of the Reform

[5][Louis Eugene Cavaignac, 1802-57, French soldier and politician. He was recalled to Paris from Algeria in 1848, and became Minister of War. He quelled the formidable insurrection of June 1848.]

Bill and of the abolition of the Corn Laws now?[6] They of course began to make excuses for their past mistakes but could not deny that these measures had been a great source of present security.

Just at the time when Europe was most convulsed, Committees of the Two Houses were appointed to examine into the effect of the existing currency laws.[7] I was examined by that of the Lords, over which Lord Lansdowne presided,[8] and gave a very poor evidence, so poor indeed that I am ashamed to look at it, and in fact have never perused it since it was published.[9] The great events going on in the world occupied all my attention, and I could not command my thoughts and direct them on a subject, which had lost almost all its importance in my eyes.

I recollect that when I first appeared before the committee Lord Lansdowne read aloud a newspaper, or dispatch which had just arrived and which announced the outbreak at Vienna,[10] and this piece of news seemed to divert

[6] [With the fall of the Melbourne government in 1841 (see p. 372), Peel had become Prime Minister, and embarked upon financial reform. He re-introduced the income tax, and reduced the duties on 750 out of 12,000 items. In 1846, at the cost of his political career, he abolished the duties on imported grain, principally wheat – the 'Corn Laws'.]

[7] [*Parliamentary Papers* 1847-8, vol. viii, parts i, ii and iii. The Commons Committee report is in parts i and ii.]

[8] [Henry Petty Fitzmaurice, 3rd Marquess of Lansdowne, 1780-1863, MP Calne 1802-6, Cambridge 1806-7, Camelford 1807-9, Chancellor of the Exchequer February 1806-March 1807, Home Secretary 1827-8, Leader of the Opposition in the Lords 1841-6, FRS 1811. He refused the office of Prime Minister in 1852, and was in the Cabinet without office, 1852-8.]

[9] [Norman gave evidence to the Lords Committee, vol. viii, part iii, pp. 298-313, qq. 2679-803. However, though Norman had taken a central role in the dealings between the Bank and the Chancellor of the Exchequer, Sir Charles Wood, the main spokesmen for the Bank were Morris and Prescott, the Governor and Deputy Governor (see p. 418), as well as Horsley Palmer, still a major force within the Bank.]

[10] [In April 1848 a liberal constitution was published in Vienna, and in May more concessions were forced upon the Emperor by a mob of students with whom the National Guard did not interfere. He fled secretly to Innsbruck. There were demonstrations in Vienna, culminating in riots, in the autumn. But the Austrian government was saved by its Generals, Windischgrätz and Jellăcić, a Croat who supported the Emperor against the Hungarians.]

much the minds of all present from the business on hand.

I was to have been examined before the Committee of the Commons, but asked to be excused upon the pleas that I had nothing new to say and was not very well, and these pleas availed me. In truth I was not well. The turmoil that existed on all sides disgusted and alarmed me. The views of the agitators in all countries, either avowedly or concealedly socialistic, could never, I was aware, be permanently realized, but the attempt to realize them might involve an enormous loss of property and the spilling of oceans of blood, might throw back civilisation for years, and perhaps give rize to long and desolating wars.

These distressing thoughts deeply affected me. I could not sleep, and at length consulted Sir H. Holland who recommended me to take a light supper, such as a sandwich or Macaroni and negus[11] just before I went to bed. I did this, for some time, and derived advantage from it. Sir Henry told me that I was by no means a solitary sufferer in this way. That he had many patients with symptoms similar to mine.

Instructions had been sent to all magistrates to swear in special constables, if they thought such a step necessary. The bench at Bromley debated this matter and as we had only one avowed Chartist[12] in the place *vizt* a man named Bob Sutton,[13] who was the very reverse of a hero, we contented

[11] [Hot sweetened wine and water.]

[12] [The Chartists had been formed in England about 1838, mainly as an outcome of poor economic conditions, and disappointment over the achievements of Grey's Reform Bill of 1832 which still confined the vote to men of the property owning classes. The Chartists petitioned for universal male suffrage, abolition of the property qualification for a seat in Parliament, annual Parliaments, payment of MPs and vote by ballot. Amongst their leaders was Thomas Attwood, the Birmingham critic of the Bank of England and advocate of inflation. They distanced themselves from the Anti-Corn-Law-League, which they regarded as a middle class organisation. After petitions presenting Chartist demands were presented to Parliament in 1838, 1839 (followed by rioting), and 1842, a monster demonstration at Kennington Common in South London was organised in April 1848. There was a real fear of revolution, as Norman shows. But Wellington posted troops to guard London, and the movement ended in failure.]

[13] [The Six Home Counties Directory for 1845 lists Robert Sutton 'officer of court

ourselves with enquiring of each respectful tradesman and labourer, if he was willing to be sworn in when called upon and all answered in the affirmative, we drawing up a list of these persons, to be used in case of need.

I was considerably puzzled to decide how I should pass the notorious 10th April. I might have gone to the Bank, which was protected by sandbags and armed to stand a seige, but I knew that there would be plenty of Directors there and I determined that my place of duty as a magistrate was at home, where I should be ready at any call.[14]

The day seemed very long and as I was walking in Brook Wood then partly a coppice, I listened attentively to the sound of any gun coming in the direction of Kennington Common, in fear lest it should be in reality the sound of a volley of musketry, or of a discharge of artillery. However I heard

---

of requests' as living at Bromley.]

[14][See W. Marston Acres, *The Bank of England from Within, 1694-1900* (London: Oxford University Press for the Bank of England, 1931) pp. 508-11. In contrast to the defeatism of the government of Louis Philippe, to which Norman refers, the British government responded with firmness in the face of civil disorder. The Duke of Wellington deployed troops to defend the capital. At a Chartist convention held in London on 3 April 1848, it was decided to present a monster petition to Parliament in favour of the Charter (on which see p. 423) on 10 April. Supporters were invited to assemble on Kennington Common in South London and to march to Westminster with the petition. The meeting at Kennington was organised by Feargus O'Connor. The Bank of England was one of the principal public buildings to the defence of which particular attention was paid. Royal Engineers arrived at the Bank the day before, to place sandbags on the roof, with loopholes for firing. On 10 April itself, the Bank was defended by 200 soldiers and had available 600 Special Constables, 80 of whom were available to bear arms. (For the capital as a whole there were 150,000 Special Constables.) The demonstration, though huge (estimates of those attending vary but it may have been as high as 50,000, while O'Connor claimed 300,000), petered out because the Duke of Wellington had massed 8,000 troops, particularly to defend the bridges over the Thames, and the demonstrators, who were on the Surrey (south) side of the river were told firmly that there would be no permission for the procession to cross the Thames. Instead the petition, containing 1,957,496 signatures (O'Connor had claimed more than 5.5 million), was sent to Parliament in three cabs. (Many of the signatures were later discovered to be forgeries.) So complete was the failure of the demonstration in the face of such resolute defence that by 12 April the Bank defences were removed. But there was no complacency. Cockerell (see p. 325), the architect employed by the Bank, was consulted subsequently about the installation of permanent fortifications at the Bank. The work was put in hand and the fortifications remained in place until rebuilding work at the Bank in 1924.]

nothing but an occasional shot at a rabbit, and at length about 5 o'clock, Sir John Lubbock passed by and left a message to say that every thing had passed off peaceably. It is certain that had the Chartists been under the control of skilful leaders, they might have greatly puzzled the authorities. The game should have been to execute alarms night after night in different quarters before they attempted anything like a decisive blow. This would have worn out the troops and police, the latter as it was, being greatly exhausted. Instead of this the[y][15] risqued their all in one great effort and both they and their followers were cowed and paralyzed when they perceived the unanimous loyalty of the middle and of a large proportion of the working class. To be sure, the specials even with Louis Napoleon in their ranks would not have done much in the fighting line, but their appearance was invaluable.

[15] [The manuscript is torn here.]

# Index